IMPACT OF MASS MEDIA

CURRENT ISSUES

SECOND EDITION

Edited by

Ray Eldon Hiebert

University of Maryland

Carol Reuss

University of North Carolina at Chapel Hill

Longman

New York & London

Impact of Mass Media, Second Edition

Longman Inc., 95 Church Street, White Plains, N.Y. 10601

Associated companies:
Longman Group Ltd., London
Longman Cheshire Pty., Melbourne
Longman Paul Pty., Auckland
Copp Clark Pitman, Toronto
Pitman Publishing Inc., New York

Longman Series in Public Communication
Series Editor: **Ray Eldon Hiebert**

Executive editor: Gordon T. R. Anderson
Production editor: Halley Gatenby
Production supervisor: Judith Stern

Text design: Joseph DePinho
Cover design: Jill Francis Wood
Cover Art: Bas-relief sculpture by Karin Goodlive. It is a Multimedia construction of wood, copper, fired enamel, computer components, electronic circuits, and oil paints. This sculpture, done in the mid 1960s, is an early image of the impact of mass media as a function of "social intelligence."

Library of Congress Cataloging-in-Publication Data

Impact of mass media.
   (Longman series in public communication)
   Inclues index.
   1. Mass media—United States.   2. Mass media—
Influence.   3. Mass media—Social aspects.
I. Hiebert, Ray Eldon.   II. Reuss, Carol.
III. Series.
P92.U5I46   1987   302.2'34'0973   87-16743
ISBN 0-8013-0040-1 (pbk.)

Compositor: Best-set Typesetter Limited

88   89   90   91   9   8   7   6   5   4   3   2

Copyright Acknowledgments

Contents

Introduction   1

I. Impact of Mass Media   7

1. Media and a Changing America, by Leo Bogart   9
2. The Rise of the Newsocracy, by Louis Banks   20
3. Are We Better Informed Now—or Worse?
   by John Weisman   28
   For Further Reading   35

II. Freedom versus Responsibility   37

4. How the Press Is Copping Out, by Harrison
   Schmitt   39
5. Media Power: On Closer Inspection, It's Not
   That Threatening, by Albert E. Gollin   41
6. Objectivity Precludes Responsibility, by
   Theodore L. Glasser   44
7. The Might of the Media: Media Self-
   Censorship, by Robert G. Picard   52
   For Further Reading   57

III. Mass Media and Ethics   59

8. An Epidemic of Arrogance, by Clark
   R. Mollenhoff   61
9. Media Ethics in Perspective, by Claude-Jean
   Bertrand   66
10. Those Newsroom Ethics Codes, by Karen
    Schneider and Marc Gunther   73

11. AIDS: Reporting the Tragedy, by Margaret
    Genovese   78
12. When a Public Figure's Private Life Is News, by
    Carl Sessions Stepp   83
    For Further Reading   89

IV. **Mass Media, Access, and Pressure Groups**   **91**

13. The Citizens Movement Takes a Turn, by Susan
    Witty   93
14. The Charge of the Right Brigade, by Robert
    Becker, Judy Kantrowitz, Conrad MacKerron,
    Nick Ravo, and Susie Smith   102
15. Who's Watching the Watchdog? by Neil
    D. Swan   109
    For Further Reading   122

V. **Crime, Violence, and the Mass Media**   **123**

16. Crime Doesn't Pay Except on the Newsstands,
    by Mitchell Stephens   125
17. Go Get Some Milk and Cookies and Watch the
    Murders on Television, by Daniel Schorr   132
18. Terrorism, by Margaret Genovese   143
19. What Did Mr. Dwyer Do, Daddy? by David
    B. Dick   155
    For Further Reading   160

VI. **Sex and Sensationalism in the Mass Media**   **161**

20. Censor Entertainment? Teens, Parents Speak
    Up, by *U.S. News & World Report*   163
21. Sex in the Media, by Jane D. Brown   167
22. Dirty Words and Blushing Editors. *Warning:
    This Article Is Rated X*, by Linda Lotridge
    Levin   171
    For Further Reading   176

VII. **Mass Media and Politics**   **177**

23. The Decline of the Boys on the Bus, by Joel
    Swerdlow   179

24. Presidential Timber: Grooming the Candidates, by Daniel Burstein 190
25. Trust Me: How TV Changed the Politics of America, by Charles McDowell 196
    For Further Reading 210

VIII. Mass Media and Government **211**

26. The Media as Shadow Government, by William L. Rivers 213
27. Dealing with the Media, by Griffin B. Bell with Ronald J. Ostrow 223
28. The Fourth Branch of Government, by Walter H. Annenberg 235
29. The Press and the President. *There They Go Again*, by George E. Reedy 237
30. Always on Saturday? by Ron Nessen 241
    For Further Reading 244

IX. War, the Military, and the Media **245**

31. War Isn't War without TV, by Amnon Rubinstein 247
32. Beirut—and the Press—Under Seige, by Roger Morris 250
33. How Britain Managed the News, by Leonard Downie, Jr. 267
34. Too Bad for Our Side: War Is a Video Game, by Ben J. Wattenberg 271
35. War Coverage in a TV Age, by Nick Thimmesch 273
36. In Defense of Casualty Pictures on TV, by Ellen Goodman 276
    For Further Reading 278

X. Mass Media and Nationalism **279**

37. Eyeball-to-Eyeball with the Big Red PR Machine, by David M. Rubin 281
38. The Television Pharaoh, by Doreen Kays 288
39. Islands in the Swirl of the Storm, by Tom Shales 297
40. Separating Fact from Fantasy. *Letter from Managua*, by June Carolyn Erlick 300
    For Further Reading 310

XI. Mass Media and Minorities   311

41. American Indians and the Media: Neglect and
     Stereotype, by James E. Murphy and Sharon
     M. Murphy   312
42. The Navajos, the Hopis, and the U.S. Press, by
     Jerry Kammer   324
43. The Emergence of Blacks on Television, by
     Regina G. Sherard   328
44. The Black Press: Down but Not Out, by Phyl
     Garland   337
45. Minority Press, by Marcia Ruth   349
     For Further Reading   357

XII. Mass Media and Women   359

46. Getting There: Women in the Newsroom, by
     Terri Schultz-Brooks   361
47. Mythogyny, by Caryl Rivers   371
48. Women's Magazines, by Sheila J. Gibbons   379
49. Bringing the Moving Picture into Focus, by
     Lori Kesler   383
     For Further Reading   388

XIII. Mass Media and Religion   389

50. Media View Religion in a News Light, by David
     Shaw   390
51. Not Ready for Prime-Time Prayers, by Cal
     Thomas   399
52. The New Awakening: Getting Religion in the
     Video Age, by Margaret O'Brien Steinfels and
     Peter Steinfels   406
53. Exploring the Role of the Ethnic Press, by
     Robert Israel   416
     For Further Reading   420

XIV. Business and Mass Media   421

54. Business and the Media: Stereotyping Each
     Other, by Jim Hoge   422
55. The Corporate Complaint Against the Media,
     by Peter Dreier   425
56. Business and the Media: Sometimes Partners,
     Sometimes Adversaries, by Ward Smith   444

57. Media and Business Elites, by S. Robert Lichter
    and Stanley Rothman   448
    For Further Reading   462

XV. Mass Media and Culture   **463**

58. The Guilt Edge, by Clark Whelton   465
59. Archie Bunker and the Liberal Mind, by
    Christopher Lasch   470
60. Showdown at Culture Gulch, by Brian Winston   475
    For Further Reading   483

XVI. Mass Media, the New Technology, and the Future   **485**

61. Pass the Sugar and the Video Tube, Dear, by
    Jerome Aumente   486
62. Condominiums in the Global Village, by
    Richard A. Blake   492
63. The Second American Revolution, by Benjamin
    Barber   500
    For Further Reading   509

Index   510

Introduction

In the preface to the first edition of this book, we pointed out that, because of his communication abilities, Ronald Reagan is uniquely qualified to exercise political power as the president of the United States for most of the decade of the eighties. The 1980s, we said, are the age of mass communication, and President Reagan's background and experience have trained him not for law or statesmanship or management but, rather, for dealing with reporters and editors and producers, the gatekeepers of the mass media. He knows how to play to the masses through the cameras of the media.

Toward the end of his two terms in office, however, even President Reagan couldn't control the news media when the White House blundered in trading arms for hostages held in Iran and let that ransom be sent to aid the Contras in Nicaragua, in contradiction to American foreign policy and congressional legislation.

By focusing their efforts on this scandal, the news media put the issue on the public agenda. And the public reacted by losing some faith in the president who until then could hardly seem to do any wrong.

The story of the Reagan administration is important to any study of the impact of mass communication in the 1980s because it illustrates so many facets of the problem. On the one hand, there are people who would give the press credit for exercising ultimate power. "The press giveth and the press taketh away," they would say. On the other hand, some would say that the press was the victim—first of the president, who used the media for his own gain, and then of the president's supporters, who blamed the media for crippling an innocent man.

These are the kinds of argument that the subject of mass media impact has launched. But what are the answers? What is the truth? Is it possible to arrive at a satisfactory conclusion? We cannot argue with the fact that the mass media have played an important role in shaping politics in America, perhaps even in shaping America. The dominant medium today—television—has changed much in America in its ascendancy starting in the early 1950s.

1

Questions about the precise impact of mass media remain unanswered. We know that the mass media have an impact, but just how and why and what remain elusive. Behavioral scientists are examining the effects of mass media; we know that we can predict certain outcomes in certain situations. But the variables are numerous. Two social scientists, Bernard Berelson and Morris Janowitz, summarized knowledge about the effects of mass media in their book *Reader in Public Opinion and Communication* (Free Press, 1966):

> The effects of communication are many and diverse. They may be short-range or long-run. They may be manifest or latent. They may be strong or weak. They may derive from any number of aspects of the communication content. They may be considered as psychological or political or economic or sociological. They may operate upon opinions, values, information levels, skills, taste, or overt behavior. (p. 379)

In other words, it would be difficult to make any sweeping generalizations about the impact of the mass media, even though we know they have impact. And social scientists in the 1980s have not moved much beyond Berelson and Janowitz's statement. The effects of the mass media must be measured and predicted on a case-by-case basis, taking into consideration all the variables in each situation.

This book is not a scientific examination of the specifics of mass media impact. Instead, it presents current arguments about the impact of the mass media by some of the media's leading thinkers, experienced observers, and thoughtful critics.

Questions of mass media impact usually bring about heated debate. The answers are still not agreed to universally, even with increased scientific analysis. This book is about those debates. The arguments raised here may be among the most important questions of our age, because we are all affected by the mass media. And we have all debated these questions ourselves, ever since we emerged from behind the dark glasses of childhood to realize that the TV tube and the silver screen and the printed word may not, after all, represent reality.

When we realize that the illusions we have received from the mass media are exactly that—illusions, not real or accurate or perfectly matched to our perceptions—we become disillusioned. The first time we read a story in the newspaper that describes an event in which we participated or a person we knew, we are likely to say, "Hey, that's not the way it was; I saw it myself and it didn't happen at all like that." The first time we visit a television studio and see the painted sets for the local news show, we say, "I thought that was the real city skyline behind the anchorperson." The first time we go to Washington, D.C., and see the White House, we remark, "How small it is! It seemed so much bigger on TV."

This book is about the illusions we get from the mass media and our disillusionment when we find out that everything isn't the way we thought it was. Dispelling these illusions may be one of the most important responsibilities of education. In America today young people spend more time in front of the television set than they do in classes. By the time the average American graduates from high school, he or she will have spent about 12,000 hours in class and about 15,000 hours in front of the TV. The illusions and disillusionments of young people in our society are greater than they have ever been in any society before.

What can we believe? What is true, and what is not? Education must provide a way of answering these questions. We have to be educated about mass media if we want to steer a clear course between illusions, on one side, and disillusionment, on the other.

This book takes up some of the basic issues of the impact of the mass media, issues that are hotly debated; and it examines these issues from several different perspectives. Some of the authors presented here are vigorously in favor of the mass media as they are and set about to defend the media. Others are vigorously opposed to the mass media and criticize their operation. And some try to take a balanced approach. Sixteen different issues are presented here—those that are the most important, and those that are the most often argued.

What are the effects of the mass media on our society? To what extent are we molded and shaped by the media? Are we informed? Or are we manipulated? Are we in control? Or are we merely dancing at the end of strings pulled by mass communicators?

Should the mass media be as free as they are in our society? What rights should they have? And what limits should be placed on them? Should they be responsible to the government? To society? To their listeners and viewers and readers? To themselves?

Are the mass media ethical institutions? What role should ethics play in mass media operations? Where do the mass media overstep ethical boundaries? And what should be done about it when they do?

What about those of us who are not part of the mass media? What rights do we have to communicate to the masses? How can we get access to the media? Or how can we bring pressure on the media to get them to perform in a manner acceptable to us? How can we exercise some control over the process?

And what about crime and violence in the mass media? Have we become a violent society because we read about crime in our newspapers and watch violence on television? Do news stories about rape inspire rapists to action? Do stories about terrorism inspire terrorists? Do stories about airplane hijacking inspire hijackers? Do the mass media create violence in our society by reporting it, or do they merely reflect the violence that is already out there?

Have we become more sexually free because of sexual explicitness in the mass media? Or are we becoming jaded about sex because of its over-exposure in the mass media?

What have the mass media done to us politically? Can anyone be elected to political office without the endorsement of the mass media? And are the media giving us an accurate picture of our politicians? When we go to the voting booth, can we rely on the information we have received from the mass media?

To what extent does our government control the mass media? And to what extent do the media control our government? To what extent do the media control business, and to what extent does business control the mass media?

Has the nature of war been changed by mass communication? Television certainly was a factor in the war in Vietnam; what role will TV play in future wars?

What about the role of the media in building nationalism and inspiring patriotism? Do the mass media have an obligation to further the cause of the state? In many societies they do, by law. In the United States, freedom of the press has always restricted the legal obligations of the press to support the government, and in fact the press is sometime seen as the enemy; the adversary of government. But the mass media are bigger than America. Their influence and reach are international. What obligations do the media have—in our country and in other countries—to diplomacy, international relations, and cultural imperialism?

Do the mass media present a fair and accurate picture of minorities and women in our society? And are minorities and women adequately represented in the mass media? What are the results of the media's distortions of minority cultures and viewpoints?

How have the mass media affected religion in our culture? And how are religious groups changing in order to use the mass media?

How have the mass media affected our culture as a whole? Are we becoming a classless society as the result of mass media? Are we becoming a tasteless society? Have the mass media brought about a leveling of our culture to the lowest common denominator?

And finally, as the media are changing because of new technologies, what impact will this have on our culture and our society? What will satellites and cable television and laser beams and computers do to us? And what can we do about it, if anything?

There are no clear-cut, final answers to most of these questions. Each individual must ultimately answer these questions for himself or herself. This book does provide a variety of viewpoints on these questions, and it presents facts and ideas that readers can use in reaching their own conclusions.

The age of mass communication has made it possible for us to gain access to far more information than any society ever had. Information is indispensable to a complex and advanced civilization. We are an information-hungry society; we need an ever-increasing amount of facts in order to maintain and increase our standard of living. Information today is a commodity we are willing to pay for. And the mass media today are not only entertaining the masses; they are selling information as well.

We have often been told that information is power. The question is, what do we have to do to ensure that the information we receive from the mass media will serve our needs, not the purposes of someone else?

This last question too must be answered by each of us individually. This book is designed to help readers formulate their own conclusions about the role of mass media in their lives. Conflicting arguments are often presented here, deliberately. These arguments should be aired and discussed, and new facts and perspectives should be brought to that discussion. Only in this manner will truth emerge from this vast marketplace of facts and ideas—truth for each individual.

Today, the mass media are too important for us not to know where we stand on the issues affected by communication. The mass media are too essential to be ignored. And the issues raised by mass media will no doubt continue to grow in importance in the foreseeable future.

I

Impact of Mass Media

If you feel comfortable when information is presented in neat packages, when discussions are definitive and irrefutable, when conclusions are summarized before you move on to a new topic, you're heading for trouble in your study of mass media.

The mass media of communication operate in and for and with mass society, and both are alive and constantly changing. Sometimes the changes seem to be revolutionary. Most times, though, the changes in the mass media and in society start slowly and are linked. Early communication researchers believed there was a direct cause–effect relationship between media messages and their audiences—a person who read a credible article would do what the article said to do. We're wiser now and admit that the situation is much more complex. People do use mass media for information to help make decisions important to their lives, but not in a vacuum free of "impurities"—what some researchers call noise or static.

By the same token, the media—the people who make them tick, really—have to realize that their relationships or associations with their audiences and potential audiences can be tenuous. They have to know those for whom they're reporting, writing, editing, and producing. They have to be willing to recognize changes in society or their usefulness will cease and so will their publications and programs.

The articles in this section should help explain those relationships. Consider them and you'll realize that the mass media have numerous impacts on society—and vice versa. Sometimes we can be comforted by such thoughts because the media can help us in our daily lives, can entertain us, can draw us together as a society. Sometimes we can and should be disturbed about media–society relationships—the impacts of mass media on society and society on the mass media.

Although only the articles in this section are linked under the title "Impact of Mass Media," actually, all the articles in the book address this topic. You are being forewarned: There are no neat packages when it comes to the study of the mass media.

1 Media and a Changing America

by Leo Bogart

"Changes in society, not changes in American beliefs or values, will change our communication needs," says Leo Bogart, executive vice president and general manager of the Newspaper Advertising Bureau. He explains many of the changes taking place. This article is from *Advertising Age*, March 19, 1982.

Revolutionary changes in technology are transforming mass communications, and will be changing the advertising business. Consider the following:

1. As of March, 1982, an estimated 55% of the 83,531,900 households in the U.S. are "passed" by cable systems, and approximately half of these passed households—23,219,200—are already cable subscribers.
2. Fifty percent of cable households also subscribe (for an additional fee) to some form of pay television. Moreover, among new cable subscribers a much higher percentage are choosing a pay tv option.
3. Videocassette and videodisc players are being heavily promoted, with the suggestion that "any time can be prime time." At present there are 3,157,000 videocassette recorder/players in U.S. homes and 238,000 disc players, and the sales curve slopes sharply upward.
4. The Federal Communications Commission is in the process of considering more than 6,000 applications for tv stations, which will provide highly localized coverage of small communities and neighborhoods. It is moving to authorize direct satellite-to-home broadcasting (DBS) that would cover the entire nation.
5. Fiber optics promise to lower the cost of data transmission and to expand the choices available to include a wide range of auxilliary services like security, financial and retailing.
6. Personal computers, some of them already selling for less than $1,000, can be used for a rapidly growing number of information and news services. Approximately 1,500,000 are now in U.S. homes, with 450,000 of them being purchased in 1981.
7. The line between data processing and communication is blurring,

and the process will be accelerated by the recent Justice Department settlement with AT&T.

Even if no revolution in technology were taking place, mass communications would still undergo important changes in the next 10 years both because of predictable factors like demographic changes and unpredictable ones like inflation.

What marketers want to know is: Which changes are truly important, and which are ephemeral? How can we distinguish between the real long-term trends and the short-run cyclical fluctuations? Here are some reflections on what the guideposts ought to be. They restate the obvious about the changes already under way, but perhaps they add up to some conclusions that are not so obvious.

The conventional wisdom knows all about the generation gap, the "age of me," the demise of the family, the new era of mass transit; about the greening of America, the graying of America, the return to the land, the downtown revival, the "gentrification" of urban slums, the decline of literacy, the rejection of higher education, the return of career women to hearth and home. Some of this shorthand fits the evidence. Most does not. A dramatic journalistic buzzword can give a small ripple in the statistics the appearance of a great new wave.

Actually, in the last two decades there has been very little change in people's over-all sense of personal well-being, their hopefulness about the future or their trust in others.

Values change slowly. Even nations overwhelmed by the upheaval of revolution or the catastrophes of war do not change their national characters overnight, nor their established ways of doing things.

The classic study of American values was made in Muncie, Ind., disguised as "Middletown." In a 1977 survey the religious and patriotic feelings of Muncie high school students were almost the same as those of their grandparents in 1924. Parental discipline turned out to be no less effective than it was half a century ago. There was actually a slight narrowing of the generation gap. That gap is narrower than the gaps within either generation.

People do bend to the pressures of the time. Their sense of optimism and well-being goes up and down with the business cycle. In general, the idea of progress is far less taken for granted today than it was by earlier generations. In national opinion polls 20 years ago, individuals in their 20s were happier than older ones. That is no longer true. The world's bad news is something that more and more people, especially young people, show a tendency to avoid. But who accepts the view that humanity is doomed to get progressively more pessimistic? There are similar ups and downs in the tendency toward egotism or altruism, in political participation or apathy.

Such cycles of mood generate attention and even alarm, but we would be more interested in the trends that are deep-seated and not likely to be reversed. Several such trends are worth singling out and elaborating later: Tolerance of diversity, changing sex roles and concern with the quality of life. All have consequences for mass communications. But none suggest any dramatic rearrangement of the demands for information or entertainment.

This means that new communications technology must carve out a place for itself by better serving a society whose needs and interests are not going to be fundamentally different, even though it is undergoing changes in population, social structure and life styles. Yet the new technology requires major capital investments and substantial continuing expenditures both by advertisers and consumers. Can the economy afford it?

The economic appraisal must begin with a global perspective. The health of the American economy depends less and less on what businesses decide or on the actions of our government.

We live in a world of nuclear stalemate where there can be no final victory in war, where madmen rule nations and where good guys don't necessarily win.

It's a world with a steadily expanding population and steadily increasing demands on its resources, with a growing gap between haves and have nots that brings political instability to more and more places.

Thus, national security will take ever more of our gross national product and put new pressures on the federal budget and, when the draft comes back, on our political system. Inflation, the major concern of the American people and the major ailment of our economy, will be hard to control as long as our wealth keeps flowing to the oil cartel. (Rising costs of raw materials and energy affect print media, especially newspapers, more than broadcasting and thus shift competitive advantages among the media.)

Economies are interdependent, caught in a vulnerable chain of imbalances in international trade, currency values and debt. Today, no successful business can remain provincial. In the age of the cheap dollar, more and more of our leading advertisers are non-American: Saks Fifth Avenue, Toyota, Nestle.

In communications, international exchange has accelerated the rate of technical change. The three leading contenders for American home communications systems are the Canadian Telidon, the British Viewdata and the French Antiope. As more channels provide the tv viewer with more choice, more overseas programing will fill the tube to satisfy its insatiable demands. Before too long, direct satellite-to-home television (fiercely opposed by the Soviets) will cross national boundaries.

If our domestic economy will be more dependent on world-wide forces and thus more precarious than in the past, does this mean that it will stagnate or decay?

Between 1973 and 1979, our annual growth in productivity per worker was 0.1%, the lowest of any major non-communist country. (By contrast, Japan's average was 3.4%.) In 1979, 1980 and 1981, productivity actually went down. That doesn't mean that people are working less hard; it means the total economy is less efficient. In the last few years, real family income has failed to show the gains that Americans have come to take for granted. From the trough of the current recession, these conditions may appear to mark the beginnings of a continuing decline. There are at least three reasons, however, to believe that this country is entering a period of renewed economic growth:

- The first is new technology, which whets the national appetite for information. Innovation is the key to greater productivity. It arises from the density of potential linkages among existing ways of doing things, which means that it is likely to proliferate rapidly in our complex industrial society. Of course, the rate of growth would be quickened if we stepped up our much too limited investment in research and development and if we could learn to save more and spend less. (Only one-third of American families save at all.)
- A second reason for optimism is the growth of the labor force and especially of its most productive elements. The postwar baby boom generation has reached maturity and begun to raise families of their own. The over-75s are the fastest growing age group. But more significantly, by 1990 there will be 15,000,000 more people in the "age of acquisition," 35 to 54, than in 1970—or 33% more.
- A third factor promoting economic growth over the long haul is the increased level of education, which is closely linked to productivity. Between 1959 and 1978, the work force increased by about 30,000,000. More than half the increase was in professional, technical and managerial types of jobs.

An important stimulus to marketing demand is the fact that there are more consumption units relative to people. Though households have become smaller, they still require basic furnishings and equipment. In the 1970s, the number of households grew by 25%, population by 8.5%. And this trend will keep going, with an expected growth of more than one-fifth in the 1980s, over 17,000,000 homes.

In the past half-century, U.S. Gross National Product grew 24 times in current dollars and five-fold in real terms. The momentum of that growth is not about to grind to a halt in the next 10 years. Personal consumption expenditures, in real terms, will expand by 22%.

There is an important byproduct of the affluence that permits most Americans to take the necessities for granted: A rising interest in the intangible quality of life. It is demonstrated by a concern with the preservation of the environment, by more involvement with the arts, by new kinds of self-expression and by a new conception of work as a source of satisfaction in itself rather than as a means of survival. This trend is already reflected in the new sections of newspapers and in the experimental cultural aspects of cable tv. It should lead to a general upgrading of media content as time goes on.

The growth of consumer purchasing power will make it possible for both consumers and advertisers to spend more money on mass media, existing and new.

In the 1970s, advertising investments grew 170% in current dollars. Rate increases accounted for 121%, leaving a real growth of 49%—greater than that of the consumer economy. The ratio of advertising to sales was raised in the 1950s by the advent of television, which created advertising budgets where none had existed before. In the 1980s, new forms of tele-communications may very well stimulate a similar spurt in advertising investments at a faster rate than growth in the consumer economy. Total investments in advertising will reach $150 billion in inflated dollars by 1990. Newspapers will be a $44 billion advertising medium, 18% bigger in real terms than today.

The ratio of advertising to sales may be set back by the striking shift from goods to services, which now represent two-thirds of GNP and 46% of consumer spending. (McDonald's employs more people than U.S. Steel.) Over-all, services advertise less, and they generally require more informative advertising—texts rather than demonstrations and images.

Media are affected also by the social consequences of another important economic trend, the trend toward concentration. The big retail chains have steadily increased their share of the market. Twenty-five years ago, the top 100 national advertisers accounted for 35% of the total. Today, they account for 43%. The top 10 agencies had 17% of the billings and have 27% today.

Concentration and conglomeration lead to more formalized and more bureaucratic decision-making and to an insatiable appetite for data. The growth of the computer industry has provided management with the means to realize the efficiencies of size, and in turn that growth has been stimulated by increased business concentration. This feeds the flood of information already loosed by the demands of a steadily more intricate and specialized economy. The fact that people are drowning in paper on their jobs will have an effect on the use of reading matter in their leisure time.

More and more, advertising decisions tend to be directed from a central source. They are more often reduced to formula, more impersonal, more quantitative, less sentimental, less flexible and less imaginative. Media salesmen must contact and confront a larger and more complex hierarchy of corporate "influentials." By the popular criterion of "cost per thousand," the ability of media to maintain their share of advertising will depend on their ability to hold their audiences.

The concept of marketing suggests a national market. We have become a culturally more homogeneous nation, entwined in an intimate web of transportation and communication. This makes it possible to think of market segments made up of drinkers of imported liqueurs, compulsive cleaners of pots and pans, one-time users of razor blades—people scattered across the continent but linked together by common attributes. In a society of greater complexity, affluence and education the citizen-consumer's avocational interests multiply, as well as the means to indulge them.

People have always defined themselves by their media preferences and habits. The more restrictive the medium, the greater the sense of kindred spirit among those who share it. There are half a dozen magazines for joggers alone, and over 10,000 magazines altogether. Radio has become a medium of specialized audiences.

The spread of cable television has been hailed by advertisers as a means of permitting them to zero in more efficiently and selectively on particular interest groups. In Dallas today, Warner Amex offers 100 different channels on its cable system. New applicants for cable franchises are promising to double that choice. Does this mean trouble for media that try to speak to everyone, at least in a definable geographic area? I think not.

Inevitably, the cost efficiency of reaching tiny slivers of the population has to be less than the cost efficiency of placing messages before vast audiences. In addition, serious problems of measurement and evaluation occur when audiences are fractionated as they are in radio today and as they may be for television tomorrow. The advertiser can't be really sure of what he's getting.

One advantage of specialized media for the advertiser is that the audience has already defined itself as interested in the kind of information he wants to give them. And when people are willing to search actively for information, they may be ready to pay to get it in a way that saves their time and adds to its value. This suggests that the public will be required to bear more of the financial burden of mass communication. In 1981, advertisers spent $61 billion on the media, and the public $52 billion, including what they spent to purchase, repair and operate radio and tv sets, to buy books and records, and to go to the movies. With the growth of the new media, the public's contribution of 46% in 1981 should go up substantially and might well reach 55% by 1990.

By 1990, consumer spending (at current dollars worth half what they are today) could be $30 billion for cable, pay tv and satellite-to-home services, including View data; $20 billion for videodiscs and cassettes and players and $10 billion for interactive home computer services and hardware. Although the consumer aspect of the British Prestel experiment seems to have failed, 100,000 American households already have computer terminals. There could be 7,000,000 by 1990.

As for entertainment, even in 1990 when at least half the homes are on the cable (mostly pay cable) and a fifth have disc or cassette players, network television will continue to have the lion's share of prime time viewing, though less than the present 85%. (They get most of the prime time audience in cable homes.) Most people seem to want formula, main line, Broadway-Hollywood entertainment. The networks are uniquely equipped to provide it. Pay television can siphon off substantial audiences for first run movies, major sports attractions and soft pornography. It can't capture a majority every night of the year. But pay tv doesn't need most of the audience to change the economics of present-day commercial television. Home communications systems could similarly shift the delicate economic balance of the current media, both broadcast and print.

The media get about the same percentage of consumer expenditures today as they did 20 years ago. Telecommunications can raise this proportion, not as a substitute for the media we know but by delivering new utilities and functions that now don't exist.

Even in the era of market segmentation, the most significant links among people remain those that connect them to a particular place.

Local markets are changing shape under the pressures of urban change. Forty-four percent of all advertising now is local rather than national, up from 39% in 1960. Although Americans everywhere share the same network television programs and the same brands of soap, soup and corn flakes, their communities continue to be different in character and in shape and volume of consumer perferences.

Among the local media, newspapers are the peculiar embodiment of these differences, and the health of newspapers can be no better than that of the communities whose names they carry. The new 1980 Census documents with statistics what the eye can see: The continuing cancerous destruction of our urban centers. Beyond the glitter of the new malls and civic centers, the grim realities still face us. While the old industrial cities of the Northeast and North Central states have drawn most attention, the same blight has hit cities in the Sunbelt, too. And newspaper readership there is lower than in the rest of the country.

Between 1970 and 1980, cities of 250,000 and over lost 5% of their population. This tells only part of the story. Blacks and Hispanics have become a majority in a number of cities and over 49% of the central city population in all metropolitan areas of over 1,000,000. So here we are, facing the urgent warnings of the 1968 Kerner Commission Report, whose message has receded further and further into the national unconscious.

Social disorganization in America's ghettoes, as measured by family disintegration, illegitimacy, crime and drug use is unmatched anywhere in the world.

How will the bright new possibilities of advanced telecommunication jibe with the unemployment, dependency, incapacity, despair and rage of the black underclass?

Changes in the cities have important consequences for local media. The vitality of downtown shopping areas is essential to maintain their retail advertising base. As the big stores have followed their best customers to the suburbs, some of their daily newspaper budgets have been deflected to shoppers, mail, "doorknobbers," and other pinpointed forms of advertising. Cable and low-powered tv will provide additional opportunity for this kind of concentrated coverage.

Sixty-eight percent of Americans live in the metropolitan areas, and a growing majority of these live in the suburbs. In some parts of the country nonmetropolitan areas have grown more than metropolitan ones, and this trend may well continue in the 1980s. This does not represent a return to the farm or, in today's terminology, the rural commune. It instead reflects the further decentralization of new industry and the expansion of metropolitan regions to farther-reaching exurbia. Since people measure commuting distance in time and not in miles, the interstate highway system allows them to enjoy rural amenities without feeling isolated. The development of more sophisticated communications systems may accelerate this trend.

To what degree can communication substitute for personal movement? Not many Americans can just walk down the village street to their jobs, their shopping, their bank, their dentist and their friends. The result is a vastly increased volume of communications to sustain these widely scattered relationships. In 1980, there were 200 billion telephone calls made in the U.S. and 100 billion pieces of mail handled by the Postal Service.

We think of ourselves as a mobile population, though about the same proportion of us (one in five) move every year as did 20 or 30 years ago. But among young people in their 20s, 68% move in a four-year period, over half to a different locality. All this is making us less provincial in outlook, less rooted in regional customs and parochial loyalties. It has changed the meaning of local news and thus changed the public's expectations of the media.

We are mobile not only over our lifetimes, but day by day. Our reliance on the automobile is as great as it ever was. In the past 30 years, the number of cars has grown 2½ times faster than the number of people, and the car today is typically a personal rather than a family utility. Thus shopping goes on over a wide orbit, affecting the retailer's advertising requirements. Out-of-store shopping of all kinds—by catalog, mail and phone—has shown a steady increase, and the Sears catalog is already on videodisc. (As for business travel, only one-fourth of it is to see customers; most of it is for company and industry meeting.)

But per capita local auto trips went down only 6% during the years of the oil crisis. We have a long way to go before rising fuel costs force Americans to stay at home, relying on telecommunications to do their shopping and their work. We won't go that route completely because shopping and work are social experiences, and a computer keyboard is not a substitute for human contact. But even a minor shift of, say, 10% of general merchandise purchased from the store to the communications systems can have a dramatic impact on retailing and on advertising.

And home itself is a different place than it used to be. That picture book family of a working father, a mother at home and two school age children now accounts for only 7% of all U.S. households. More families have a handicapped child than have two children with a mother at home. Marriage takes place later; the divorce rate has doubled since 1970 and there are fewer children per average household. We all know that there are more singles, up 16% since 1970; more female-headed households, up 49%; more households of two or more unrelated individuals living together. Yet to keep this in perspective, 97,000,000 Americans live as married couples, only 2,700,000 as unmarried ones.

For the time being, we've seen the last of the so-called "youth culture." In 1970, four out of ten Americans were under the age of 21. In 1990, it will be three in ten. The actual numbers of those under 21 dropped from 81,000,000 in 1970 to 75,000,000 today, and that number will not change in the next decade. A lot of radio stations will be looking for new music formulas.

Changes in family structure affect communications media and vice versa. Television intrudes into the time that previous generations spent in conversation, play or common projects. This has weakened the mutual allegiance of family members and the emotional bonds that are the basis of trust and understanding. The impersonal communication of the media substitutes, to a degree, for the close, interpersonal family communication of the past. Members of a household are less likely to share the same reading matter and the same broadcast programing.

Since media activity has become more individual, there is a growing discrepancy between household exposure to a medium and the individual's exposure to it. Television sets have been on for more hours in the '70s, but individual viewing hours have not changed.

Increased education moves people away from broadcasting and toward print. They also move in the direction of more sophisticated and cosmopolitan content and specialized media that meet broader interests. They become information seekers. The rise in the average level of schooling has been phenomenal. In 1957, 45% of the civilian labor force were high school graduates. By 1978, the proportion was 73%.

There are ample causes to complain about the deficiencies of the

American school system. In New York, half of the students drop out from the ninth grade on. Our complaints about the schools seem to reflect our higher levels of aspiration for our children. But what is commonly regarded as a decline in reading skills may actually represent a decline of reading interest. The average reading and writing abilities of American students didn't change significantly during the '70s.

The rising level of education and the functional demands of a complex industrial society have fostered secularism and a weakening of the traditional moral code. In spite of the continuing strength of religious institutions and the high visibility of certain right wing political groups masquerading with religious labels, there will be more Sunday store openings, not less.

A related consequence of more education is the increased level of public tolerance for racial minorities, for nonconformity, for idiosyncracy in belief and in personal habits. In an incredibly hetergeneous and urbanized country, there is more room for variety than on Sinclair Lewis' "Main Street."

The shift in attitude is most dramatic when young people are compared with older ones. Tolerance for homosexuals, unmarried couples, people with beards and long hair and employes who wear sneakers to work goes with more tolerance in the realm of ideas and of politics. This augurs well for freedom of the press and for the further spread and public support of diversity in communication.

What used to be a substantial educational gap between men and women has been reduced almost to the vanishing point. This helps explain why so many more women have entered the work force: Sixty percent of those between 18 and 64. By 1990, the figure will be 71%. This represents a truly revolutionary change in the attitude of women toward work and in the way men and women relate to each other.

Today, most young women accept work and a career as the norm and feel that fulltime housework is unsatisfying. As time passes, we will no doubt see some mellowing of today's militant feminism, but there will be no reversal of the moves toward equality of the sexes at work, the redefinition of responsibilities in the home and toward children. Since a substantial part of media content, including advertising, is directed at one sex, much of it may require overhauling.

Changes in sex roles might bring about long-term changes in attitudes toward sex itself. But history shows these have always gone through cycles of conservatism and permissiveness.

Both the psychological and economic consequences of women's work will become even more significant as more move up to higher skilled and better paid jobs. There is a second wage earner in a majority of families of working age, two-thirds of all married couples under 35. The median income of two-earner households will rise 50% faster in the '80s than it will for all households.

The effects of new technology can best be understood in the context of the social changes with which they must interact. Out of this interplay come predictions like these:

- Changes in society, not changes in American beliefs or values, will change our communications needs.
- International communication will become more common.
- There will be no letup in the rising demand for information.
- More information will be sought out actively, not randomly delivered.
- Both consumers and advertisers will spend more on the media, in real dollars.
- Consumers will pay a larger share of the cost of communications, advertisers less.
- Economic growth can sustain both the consumer market for media and greater advertising support.
- New communications technology will boost advertising investments, offsetting the shift of consumption from goods to less well advertised services.
- More advertising decisions will follow formulas.
- Advertisers will seek more efficient concentration on key market segments, but...
- Advertisers will continue to want mass coverage of local markets at low cost.
- Urban blight will continue to change the media mix for local advertising.
- Geographic dispersion adds to the demand for communication.
- Shopping at home may change the economics of retailing and thus of local media.
- Working women need more information to save time and motion.
- Media experience will be more individual, less based on the household.
- More education builds demand for better and more specialized media content.
- Media content will no longer be dominated by the "youth culture" as it was in the 1970s.
- The networks will continue to dominate prime time tv.
- The leisure time available for media will not soon be increasing.
- More entertainment choices will not add significantly to viewing time.
- Time spent on new forms of communication will have to come from existing media.

The existing media organizations will inevitably find new electronic channels to transmit the vast quantities of information and to use the vast entertainment talents that are their resource. People will make use of broadcast channels that aim at their own special nerve, but they will still want to be part of the popular mainstream of mass entertainment.

As for print, it won't succumb easily to electronic competition. There are limits on the time that the public at large will be willing to give to alphanumeric information served up on a cathode ray tube. Conveying data line by line, screenful by screenful, will never be a substitute for the satisfying package of paper and print that carries its own unique character and that generates ideas, discussion and action.

2 The Rise of the Newsocracy

by Louis Banks

The press is increasingly becoming the arbiter of American life, but the values of the news media aren't always the values of the society they serve, says Louis Banks, formerly senior editor of *Time* and managing editor of *Fortune*, now adjunct professor of management at the Alfred P. Sloan School of Management, Massachusetts Institute of Technology. This article is from *Atlantic Monthly*, January 1981.

Viewers who chanced to switch to Washington's channel 4 (WRC-TV) on the evening of March 28, 1979, found themselves looking down the barrel of an ordinary hand-held hair dryer. "This is not a gun, and it doesn't shoot bullets," said the voice-over. "But what comes out can be just as deadly." The program was the result of nine months' investigation by WRC's "Consumer Action" team, and for the extraordinary span of nearly twenty minutes ("without commercial interruption"), it developed a case that Americans were in considerable peril because many hand-held hair dryers were spewing fibers from asbestos insulation. Making the connection between the ingestion of asbestos fibers and the death rates from various forms of lung cancer, investigator Lea Thompson said gravely, "How many of those [deaths] can be attributed to hair dryers...no one knows."

By consumerist standards, the program was a stunning success. Such companies as Hamilton Beach, General Electric, Norelco, Sears, Penney's, and Montgomery Ward, all named as culprits, were besieged by angry customers. Gillette and American Electric, which had long used mica instead of asbestos for insulation, were exonerated on the program, but besieged nonetheless. The Consumer Products Safety Commission, a federal agency, was stung into confusion and open hearings, subsequently forcing a voluntary recall of asbestos-insulated dryers. A Senate consumer subcommittee opened hearings and called Ms. Thompson as a star witness.

By media standards as well, the program scored high. Reversing the usual practice, print media "picked up" the exposé from a local television station and gave it wide coverage. The UPI accounts were reprinted in hundreds of newspapers. Channel 4 being an NBC affiliate, the story made the NBC evening news. It was subsequently featured on both NBC's *Today* show and ABC's *Good Morning America*. (One manufacturer feared that his business would be destroyed just by David Hartman's silent scowl of disapproval as he looked at a hand-held dryer; it wasn't.) The WRC investigation team won the George Polk Award for Distinguished Journalism. And the "genuine coup" was eulogized in a two-page essay in *People*, which revealed what the TV camera had not: that Lea Thompson, the daughter of a journalist and a University of Wisconsin graduate in journalism and marketing, was eight and a half months pregnant at the time of the story.

The strong combination of action pictures, whirring motors, stern interviews, and authoritative explanations certainly alerted millions of Americans in record time to the asbestos fiber problem. But the consumerist consequences, as important as they were, can be seen as part of a much larger societal point. We are rapidly approaching a situation in which reporting is the arbiter of other institutions in American life; in this microcosmic case we see and hear it imposing its own values, standards, and priorities with irresistible impact on agencies of both government and business.

The point is made more broadly when we review the principal categories of news coverage over the past decade. The media—and particularly television—take credit for turning the public against the Vietnam War ("the living room war") and forcing its termination. "Watergate was the greatest journalistic triumph of the twentieth century," wrote one correspondent for Columbia University's "Survey of Broadcast Journalism," and unrelenting media attention certainly prompted the politics that forced President Nixon's resignation. Journalistic coverage was a prime mover in forcing government agencies and boards of directors to ventilate a series of corporate scandals in the mid-1970s, the most notable investigations of which led to the dismissal of top management at the 3M Corporation and the Gulf Oil Company, and eventually to antibribery legislation. The emergence of President Sadat of Egypt as a folk hero and the constant television posturing of the principals in the Iranian hostage crisis suggest that we have, through media coverage, carried foreign policy into a period of "mass diplomacy," as Flora Lewis of the *New York Times* describes it.

One can pursue the point through the agenda of quality-of-life issues: consumerism, dating back to the elevation of Ralph Nader to national prominence; ecology and environmentalism, ranging from the effect of supersonic transports on the ionosphere to the greenhouse effect to acid rain; energy concerns, from off-shore oil spills to the hazards of coal and nuclear power; safety in the workplace, with latter-day attention to potential carcinogens; toxicity, from Kepone to Love Canal.

Such is merely the stuff of news, one might argue. And to a degree this is true. But to another degree these areas represent coverage by selection, which suggests an imposition of media values and standards in contrast, perhaps, to the values and standards of other institutions. In writing *The Brethren*, their gossipy best seller on the disrobed U.S. Supreme Court, Bob Woodward and Scott Armstrong noted proudly in a preface that they had breached "the authority, traditions and protocols" of the Court to subject it to journalistic inspection for the first time. Some critics doubted that this inspection did much for the set of values involved in the American system of justice.

It is becoming clear that the increasingly pervasive power of the media is central to the development of most other American institutions. We are, in fact, becoming what might be called a "newsocracy." The technology and substance of today's newscasting combine for an impact greater than that of any other informational force in the history of democratic societies—redirecting even the traditional processes of politics. This is a matter of social consequence, because some aspects of media value judgment might be perceived as being at odds with the general welfare. Accordingly, I would argue that affected "others" (e.g. government agencies, educational institutions, and publicly held corporations) have both a right and a duty to enter the informational competition. This contention should not be interpreted as a challenge to press freedom; rather it is an acceptance of today's news coverage for what it is, and an attempt to broaden its intellectual vision in the interests of the society that the First Amendment serves.

In my view, media dominance has been powerfully abetted by two major trends of the past decade. One is a widening perception of the interaction of one kind of endeavor upon another in the post-industrial society. To a certain extent this integrative process has always been manifested in political reform movements, but it gained a kind of personal relevance in the so-called youth movement of the late sixties and early seventies. It has, loosely, been called "holism." The second is a spreading of public awareness, the sense of direct participation in events, which has loosely been described as "populism." These two trends, combined with video technology, have stepped up the power of journalistic influence.

Recently MIT's *Technology Review* gathered a group of the nation's top science writers from print and television to talk about "Science, Technology and the Press." Science is their beat, but as they contrasted the simpler days of "happy talk" reporting with the multidimensional demands of today's assignments, they could be speaking for almost any group of earnest journalistic specialists. David Perlman of the San Francisco *Chronicle* saw science reporting broadening into "the politics of science or public affairs emerging from science." Mark Dowie of *Mother Jones* spoke of the reader's desire to know about "the interface between science and technology and even more, about the interface between technology and the corporate world because...that's where science ceases to be apolitical." Cristine Russell of the Washington *Star* confessed that "coverage of recombinant DNA, for example, was always 'biased' toward its possible impact on the public and not toward special interests—be they science or the government, or whatever." This group, gathered soon after Three Mile Island, was properly humble about the responsibilities involved in the widening media function, yet, by implication, quite confident that nobody else could perform it as well. (As a reflection of this attitude, the cover of *Technology Review* pictured a youthful reporter opening his shirt to show a Superman emblem across his chest.)

But if interrelatedness has inspired complex reportorial judgments, populism inspires a broad simplicity—or a low common denominator. Network news not only has usurped the role of the newspaper as the principal source of information, but has constantly increased the number of people who make news-watching part of their lives. For example, ABC-TV, proud of its recent high news ratings, believes that its audience is drawn mostly from people who never before watched TV news regularly. "I don't think there's any doubt that we've created a heightened consciousness of the news," says a vice president of research. Also, there is no doubt that of the three networks, ABC has the most kinetic and visually stimulating and the least mentally taxing news format.

Nobody is more aware than the network professionals of the lowest-common-denominator aspect of their work. Four years ago, Walter Cronkite expressed concern to the Radio and Television News Directors' Association: "We fall far short of presenting all, or even a goodly part, of the news each day that a citizen would need to intelligently exercise his franchise in this democracy. So as he depends more and more on us, presumably the depth of knowledge of the average man diminishes. This clearly can lead to a disaster in a democracy."

"Disaster" may be too strong a word, but TV news does seem to be changing some meanings of democracy by offering a simplistic kind of inter-relatedness. For example, one consequence has been the translation of hitherto abstract or impersonal subjects into people, places, and crises. The administration of justice becomes the judge, the lawyer, or the criminal (and his family). The presidency is words, facial expressions, today's necktie, and Amy and Rosalynn [Carter] in the background. The political convention is almost a plaything of television personalities. A plant closing is people wondering aloud what they will do next—and a congressman sympathizing. A gasoline shortage is angry customers and angry service station operators damning the oil companies—and a congressman sympathizing. A nuclear power accident is pregnant women in tears—and nervous officials trying to cope with a backwash of emotion as well as with unknowns of physics.

In their embrace of holism the media—already under pressure to produce specialists in such areas as science, finance, energy, and business—play an interdisciplinary role. To do so, the "supermen" who take this role seriously apply themselves to continuous learning. Yet we see some television journalism that could lead a long way toward Cronkite's "disaster."

Electronic journalism can claim antecedents in the rich history of radio reporting during and after World War II, and many of the leading figures of television news, including Cronkite, have struggled to keep alive that heritage. But TV news is also the bastard child of the entertainment industry. All commercial media contract in one way or another to deliver a certain audience to advertisers, but in the case of the three major networks, variations in audience size, as measured by the ratings, represent millions of dollars in advertising revenue. That fact is reflected in news selectivity, and leads to an image of the world projected daily, competitively, and with striking homogeneity on the evening news.

Since network news was, by definition, confined to national news (so as not to transgress the domain of a network's local TV affiliates), cameras focused on a minimal number of recognizable characters from Washington and New York; the more they could be translated into villains or heroes, the easier the journalistic assignment and the higher the audience attention. The visual nature of the medium put a premium on color, movement, excitement, sensation, novelty. There has always lurked in modern journalism the knowledge that bad news sells better than good. Witness the proliferation of the "question mark" headline, which suggests a threat to mankind on a speculative basis. Under competitive pressures, this stress on anxiety and negativism came to prominence in television.

Attitudinal researchers have wondered for some time about survey results that showed a discrepancy between the average citizen's dim view of government, business, education, etc., and his/her relative satisfaction with the company that he/she works for, the way local government functions, the schools the kids go to. Assessing the data for the 1970s, Everett Carll Ladd Jr. and Seymour Martin Lipset concluded: "To some considerable degree this contradiction may reflect the difference between the steady dose of disasters which people get from television, and their personal experiences."

It is not difficult to project such rogue trends into a gloomy prospect.

"Disaster" would not be far if the nation came to see itself primarily through the lenses of critics with an addiction to novelty or blood and guts, and no responsibility for consequences. Not only would the democratic process suffer from a diminished "depth of knowledge," as Cronkite has it, but something vital could be lost if responsible leaders of other institutions were regularly consumed by the "bite 'em off, chew 'em up, spit 'em out" habits of television news.

Some critics think they see this approach already manifest in the techniques of *60 Minutes*, designed to provide the controversy which keeps that weekly "newsmagazine" at the top of the Nielsen ratings. In 1979 the Illinois Power Company of Decatur allowed *60 Minutes* access to the construction site of its nuclear power plant at Clinton to film a segment on escalating nuclear construction costs. Illinois Power's one condition was that it be allowed to put its own cameras alongside those of *60 Minutes* to film everything seen and said in the interviews. The broadcast *60 Minutes* segment, in fact, found Illinois Power guilty of mismanagement of the power project. But by playing its version of what was said and explained, spliced with excerpts from the *60 Minutes* telecast, Illinois Power made a persuasive case for having been the victim of dramatic and serious distortion.

This and similar examples raise the question of whether, in TV's stress on "populism," corporations exist primarily to provide a ready source of "heavies" in the manufactured dramas that hold those customers and those Nielsen ratings.

Media judgments, of course, do not occur in a vacuum. As Illinois Power found out, the media's stories powerfully affect the "others" who are the objects of their attention, and their composite story defines the society for millions of people. The principal problem in a newsocracy is that there is, at the moment, no force to offset the net range and impact of today's informational technology. Since the constructive and the exploitative forces of journalism are constantly in tension, with no certainty about the outcome, it behooves other affected institutions to recognize the problem and accept the fact that they, too, have a stake in the battle.

The beginning of such counterstrategy is the realization that the "others" have allies within the media. Professional journalists can recognize the short-term, audience-grabbing excesses and know that the long-term test is credibility. One catches the essence of embattled professionalism in a credo voiced by David Perlman during that *Technology Review* forum on science-related reporting.

"There are some things," he said, "that we can properly do.... We can look for self-serving statements. We can expose biases that exist. We can expose lies; scientists lie occasionally, like everybody else, and they're going to lie publicly at times. So that's our job. It's not to say whether nuclear power is bad or good. Present the debate and be very careful about ascribing expertise to those who are experts."

Professionalism is at work in the development of such thoughtful interpreters of science as Perlman and his colleagues, and in the training of specialists in business and economic affairs as well. As generations change, more and more business and economic news is being handled by editors and reporters who are educated in business practice, rather than by "general assignment" people. This new sophistication is evident in many regional newspapers, whose healthy intellectual diversity is thinning out the New York- and Washington-centered judgments of the national media. Even the TV networks are learning to give more discretion to their economics editors, who, while constrained to simplisms by time limitations on camera, can sometimes moderate the more sensationalist anti-business onslaughts of their general-assignment colleagues.

The first step for "others," then, is to support and encourage media professionals by providing them with information that makes them better able to report factually and to perform the demanding integrative function. But there is more to it than that. All affected institutions must realize that a newsocracy is a different kind of environment, and that they must engage with that environment in a different way. Perhaps the media's concern with interrelatedness provides a clue. If a firm can come to think of itself not only in economic terms but as a unit in a network of social and political values, then it need have no unreasonable fears about explaining itself to media that seek to understand just those relationships. This requires, first, that a company learn to see and feel itself in the consciousness of its particular publics and infuse that sense of public-relatedness into every level of its operations.

For example, the Mobil Corporation's controversial "op-ed" advocacy campaign, which has been a fixture on the editorial pages of influential newspapers, was developed as a result of Mobil's analysis of the political and social prospects for the company and the oil industry. "We decided more than ten years ago that our problem was literally one of survival in a hostile external climate; it was more political than economic," says Herbert Schmertz, Mobil's vice president for corporate affairs and the principal architect of the campaign. "We decided to enter the argument through the media and thus put our case before people whose opinions count." Not everybody likes Mobil's abrasive style—which on occasion has drawn the wrath of the President of the United States—but critics would be hard put to deny that Mobil's editorial insistence has brought new facts to the public debate on energy, and in the process has influenced editorial thought and political action.

Exxon and Shell, affronted by charges of duplicity in an NBC-TV series in late 1979, eschewed flamboyant counterpunches and took their respective cases to the National News Council. In both situations the council examined the facts and came down hard against NBC, agreeing in the Exxon case that the telecast contained "factual error, the selective use of information, lack of perspective, and the building of effect through innuendo."

The reaction of the Gillette Company in the hand-held hair dryer exposé reflects a more positive, and perhaps more internal, kind of operational public-relatedness. Out of its tradition of precise quality control of razor blades, Gillette long ago gave consumer concern high priority and set up a medical test laboratory for all its products. In 1964, the company named Robert Giovacchini, a Ph.D. in medical science, head of the lab; ten years later, he was made vice president for product integrity and given final review of the medical safety of new products and of marketing and advertising claims relating to medical safety. In addition, his group performs a quality review of new and existing products. In 1973 he directed a redesign for the hand-held hair dryers that substituted mica for asbestos as an insulator, even though asbestos particle emissions from Gillette dryers averaged only 5 percent of the maximum allowable under OSHA standards.

Of all the major hair dryer companies, only Gillette offered to help the producers of the WRC-TV program. David Fausch, vice president of corporate public relations and a former *Business Week* editor, argued internally that the story would be told more accurately if Gillette supplied accurate data. It helped, of course, that Gillette was "clean." It helped, too, that in return the program's producers warned in advance of the screening so that Gillette could alert its sales force and its merchandisers to possible trouble. In the fallout, Gillette did not escape damage—and did not really expect to. The relevant point is that the company's operations had long since been sensitive to public concerns, and it could move smoothly into a media spotlight with a clear understanding of its own objectives, and without fear that the world would end if it did not win all the points in the telecast.

Such an approach, in my view, is far more sophisticated than conventional public relations. It is corporate acceptance of the same long-term values that concern the responsible media, and it reflects the First Amendment premise that everybody benefits when the terms of the debate are broadened. The media, after all, live on information, and "others" can influence the outcome by providing accurate material. It is a corollary, of course, that "others" have a right to keep at arm's length media agents who have a record of distorting facts to fit preconceived notions of high drama. Journalists and their organizations have unforgiving memories for those who put out misleading or dishonest information, and corporate public relations departments practice a similar form of "redlining." One of the favorite topics when people from those departments gather for a friendly drink is "what to do when Mike Wallace calls."

Should corporations and the "others" resort to end runs around the media to get their stories out? Mobil and Illinois Power suggest varieties of end runs: one through advocacy advertising, and the other through counter-video. In 1978 the Supreme Court, in a 5–4 decision, validated the right of the First National Bank of Boston to advertise in opposition to an income tax referendum in Massachusetts (*First National Bank* v. *Belotti*). In some quarters this and other related court decisions were perceived as unleashing the mighty economic power of big corporations to influence public opinion unfairly. In fact, in writing for the minority, Justice Byron White saw the majority opinion as opening the door to corporate domination of "not only the economy, but also the very heart of our democracy, the electoral process." But Justice Lewis Powell, Jr., for the majority, said, "The inherent worth of the speech in terms of its capacity for informing the public does not depend upon the identity of its source, whether corporation, association, union or individual." And Chief Justice Warren Burger, in a separate opinion, added that "media conglomerates" pose "a much more realistic threat to valid [political] interests" than other corporations.

In the context of my argument, the issue is one not of unleashing corporate power but rather of prodding media power to think in broader social terms. In a newsocracy, the media's implicit role is to translate the values of our conventional morality—what we really want for ourselves and our world—to the institutions that make it operate. Those institutions, in turn, must be heard and understood before judgment is passed. Conceivably, such media power could lead toward "disaster" if it adheres to a Nielsen-rating value system. Conceivably, though—and I prefer this view—it could prompt a higher order of intellectual performance from all components of the society, and especially from the professionals who tell us every day in every way what our world means. Ultimately it might even help a confused society to define its values more clearly.

3 Are We Better Informed Now—Or Worse?

by John Weisman

The Washington bureau chief for *TV Guide* asks about TV news now that the networks' evening news programs are shifting from headline services to picture magazines. John Weisman's article is from *TV Guide*, August 23, 1986.

Friday, March 5, 1976. The Dow Jones Industrial average closed at 972.92. Former California governor Ronald Reagan challenged President Gerald R. Ford in the Florida primary, while a virtual political unknown named Jimmy Carter stumped for votes there, too. Newspaper heiress Partricia Hearst was on trial in California. There was heavy street fighting in Beirut. And the British pound dropped below $2 for the first time in history.

Walter Cronkite was the anchor of the *CBS Evening News*, John Chancellor anchored *NBC Nightly News*, and Harry Reasoner sat at the helm of *ABC News*. That night, ABC and CBS broadcast 20 stories; NBC, 15.

Wednesday, March 5, 1986. The Dow closed above 1686. President Ronald Reagan pressed for aid to anti-Sandinista Nicaraguan rebels. Experts investigated the midair explosion of the space shuttle Challenger. There was still street fighting in Beirut, where Islamic fundamentalists reportedly killed one of their four French hostages.

Dan Rather was the anchor of the *CBS Evening News*, Tom Brokaw anchored *NBC Nightly News*, and Peter Jennings sat at the helm of *ABC World News Tonight*. That night ABC and CBS broadcast 15 stories; NBC, 16.

But there was more: On CBS, Dan Rather, sounding like a headline writer for the New York Post, described two stories, neither of them exclusive or investigative, as "extraordinary reports...that strike to the heart of America." ABC included four anchor-read promos (including one for the network's late-night newscast *Nightline*). On NBC, viewers listened to majestic theme music by John Williams (who composed the score for "Jaws"), watched Tom Brokaw promote the show's upcoming stories twice and chat with White House correspondent Chris Wallace, and heard a John Chancellor commentary. (In 1976, ABC and NBC each ran one promo.)

How radically has nightly news changed in the past decade? Are viewers seeing more, or less news than they watched in 1976? Is there less so-called "hard" news on the networks' evening news shows these days? To find out, TV Guide selected at random a week of 1976's nightly newscasts from the Vanderbilt University Television News Archive, then studied the same week this year. The time frame was March 1–7. Our examination was subjective, not scientific (and it includes only weekdays, not Saturday and Sunday broadcasts).

The nutshell results: nightly newscasts have changed. In 1976 they were, as Walter Cronkite once described them, 23-minute headline services. They were ahead of the daily newspapers—most of the stories broadcast March 5, 1976, for example, appeared in the March 6 New York Times. But stories were still, in some instances, shot on film, not videotape. Satellite feeds were expensive; computer-generated, animated graphics were rare.

In retrospect, the 1976 broadcasts had a raw, unsophisticated look about them; a no-nonsense, wire-service approach to news. The anchors were basically news readers who told viewers what had happened. Except for occasional end-pieces, there was no cute writing and virtually no inter-action between anchors and correspondents, the kind of chatter common in the late '70s to local newscasts. Viewers still heard the clatter of wire-machines on CBS and NBC. News operations were not so profit-oriented, and anchor salaries hadn't yet reached the $1-million threshold.

Quantitatively, viewers got more news stories in 1976—at least on two networks. A decade ago, ABC broadcast 98 stories in five days, while CBS did 92, and NBC had 75. From March 3–7, 1986, ABC broadcast 67 stories—32 percent less. CBS broadcast 66–28 percent less. NBC was up by five percent to 79 stories.

The shows themselves were also longer: in 1979 there were five minutes of commercials. Now there are six or more. Other elements also shorten today's broadcasts. These days, for example, NBC spends roughly 80 seconds a night showing viewers its Statue of Liberty graphics or pro-moting upcoming stories.

But numbers alone don't mean much. The very quality of news has changed, evolved, even been revolutionized in the past decade. One of the main reasons for this change is an information explosion that's taken place over the last 10 years, facilitated by technological improvements such as microwave transmissions and satellite feeds. A decade ago it took weeks to set up live coverage. Today, live pictures from Beirut, Moscow or Tokyo are commonplace. Viewers have come to expect up-to-the-minute reports by satellite from all over the world.

As Tom Brokaw puts it, "The information cycle has become intense. You've got CNN; you've got longer local newscasts; you've got all-news radio. You've got national newspapers: The New York Times reaches parts of the country that it didn't. USA Today is out there, for better or worse. And The Wall Street Journal's national now. The general level of awareness in the country, I think, is slowly going up all the time. So we have to figure out where we fit in that cycle."

On all three networks, Cronkite's concept of TV news as headline service has been replaced by a kaleidoscopic picture-magazine. Burton Benjamin, who produced the Cronkite *Evening News* in 1976, remembers that his show was "very hard news oriented. . . . We were much more Washington-conscious then."

Today's viewers get an eclectic, electric combination of front page, feature section, Op-Ed, magazine, tabloid and gossip column. In 1976, for example, ABC, CBS and NBC broadcast 15 feature stories the first week in March—feature stories being segments that had no direct news peg to the day's events. ABC did seven, CBS five and NBC three. During March 3–7, 1986, there were 29 such pieces on the evening news, almost double the earlier number; ABC did 10, CBS 10 and NBC nine. And on today's news shows, features are often run during the first half of the program, which 10 years ago generally was reserved for headlines and hard news.

More features mean less headline news. This is a conscious decision on the part of those who put today's shows together. Lane Venardos, the former executive producer of the *CBS Evening News*, says that the most significant change in the past decade "was the conscious decision to move the news out of the hearing rooms and briefing rooms of Washington and into the towns and cities where one could assess the impact of Washington developments." In 1976 Venardos was one of CBS's Washington producers. He says the Washington orientation Cronkite demanded "fulfilled the mandate of telling the viewer that something had happened today, but frequently didn't fulfill what we now see as our larger mandate to explain the whys, and what it means to you."

But Mark Levy, a broadcast-journalism professor at the University of Maryland who has worked as a consultant for ABC and NBC, says the networks' claim of taking the news out of a New York-Washington axis is simply "a conscious decision to try *a shtick* that may or may not work." Levy studies what audiences learn from the news. And he says that despite what people like Venardos say, news is still Washington-oriented: "I'm constantly impressed by the high levels of bureaucratic jargon." He cites the anchor's use of acronyms such as COLAs (cost of living adjustments) and CPI (Consumer Price Index) without accompanying explanation. "And by concepts that are just not in the vocabulary of the average viewer." Levy adds that, like a decade ago, network news is "still dominated by news of public officials and official spokesmen."

ABC anchor Peter Jennings argues that, unlike 10 years ago, "we are consciously saying to ourselves. 'If you have the lead story, it must be supported by a background story'." Sometimes, adds Jennings, there is also "a third piece, and fourth piece, and sometimes a fifth piece."

When the networks cover a crisis like the reactor disaster at Chernobyl, for example, they may devote more than 50 percent of their 22 minutes to one story. This, says Jennings, causes problems: "I get up the next morning and see stories we left out in the newspapers and, you know, it hurts. It's a hard intellectual hurdle for us—to say that we're going to leave out more news, because we leave out a lot of news already."

In 1976, the networks were the acme of television news: the best local news operations strove to emulate their seriousness and professionalism. Today, that has changed. The networks now copy personality oriented local newscasts and morning "infotainment" formulas. Anchor interviews and cross talk with correspondents, for example, have become commonplace. In the past few months ABC, NBC and CBS have all increased the use of live reports by correspondents, another local-news staple.

The value of anchor interviews and cross talk with correspondents is debatable. It is defended by those currently doing the nightly news. But former Cronkite producer Burton Benjamin says that when anchors question their correspondents, "there is an implication there that his report was not complete." Benjamin feels that often such two-ways are simply "muscle-flexing" by the anchor.

But interviews, after all, are one way to spotlight news anchors. And at the going rates—Rather makes an estimated $48,000 a week, Brokaw somewhere around $34,000 a week and Jennings in the area of $17,000—the more an anchor is perceived as the keystone of network news coverage, the better. Not necessarily better for the viewer, but for the ratings. And today's ratings are much closer than they were 10 years ago. The week of March 3, 1986, just over 1.5 ratings points separated top-ranking CBS from third-place ABC—and by midsummer they were less than a point apart. A decade earlier, CBS had a clear lead of more than five points over ABC. (Each ratings point represents 859,000 households. A single ratings point can mean roughly $15 million in nightly-news revenue on an annual basis, according to CBS estimates.)

The news segments you see today are also vastly different from those you saw a decade ago. The editing is more sophisticated, and there are more separate visual elements to each story. A March 4, 1976 report by ABC correspondent Dick Shoemaker that ran one minute 40 seconds, for example, contained 13 shots, three static graphics and one interview of 18 seconds.

A March 5, 1986 report of about the same length by ABC correspondent Greg Dobbs, for example, contained 20 different shots, three computer-generated graphics that spun on and off the TV screen, five "bumpers" (identifications) and four interviews, one six seconds long and three that were four seconds each. A one minute 48-second report by NBC's Lisa Myers on March 6, 1986, contained 22 different shots, five interviews and one animated graphic. Today's evening-news reports often move with the razzle-dazzle speed and kinetic energy of an MTV video.

The dizzying pace at which audio and visual "factoids" and "info-bits" blitz the audience these days concerns both those who do the news and those who study it. Say CBS's Venardos: "All too often what looks understandable in a script goes by so fast on the air that you barely have a chance to put up the 'super' identifying who's talking." NBC's Brokaw adds: "There's too much shorthand involved. There was then, and there still is."

According to Prof. Mark Levy, something he calls meltdown occurs when audiences are presented with an information blitz. It means that stories, or elements of stories, blend into one another, leaving the audience confused. Therefore, the fact that the nightly news does fewer stories than 10 years ago is something of which Levy approves: "The research shows that, as a general rule, fewer and longer is better in terms of comprehension." But as to whether complicated issues are being explained any better than they were 10 years ago, Levy is uncertain: "I'm not at all sure that television is any better today in telling complicated stories."

"Context is very difficult for television news in general, and particularly on the evening newscasts," says CBS's Rather. "That's where we get in trouble: on the short sound bites and not long enough setups as to who the person is who's speaking. There's an increasing tendency just to put on a super. I don't think a super always works, to tell the truth—that you can sum it all up in two words. You know—'Dan Rather, Anchorperson,' or 'Mrs. Jones, Housewife.'"

While context remains difficult, other elements of the nightly news have become easier in the last decade. New technologies now allow shows, as *NBC Nightly News* executive producer William Wheatley puts it, to "pack your gear in seven suitcases" and do the show from anywhere in the world. Only a decade ago, says CBS's Venardos, "when the *Evening News* wanted to go someplace, at least a couple of weeks in advance the trucks would start rolling out of New York—these big semitrailers, not unlike the ones that do sports stuff today."

Now anchors can pick up and go on a moment's notice, and they have. Although the phrase "floating anchor" is oxymoronic, today's anchors float. In all, Jennings, Rather and Brokaw anchored the nightly news from on the road more than 80 times between May '85 and May '86. Some critics believe that such moves are made to spotlight the anchors and bolster ratings.

"I think," says Rather, "although I'm not finally convinced, that we at *CBS Evening News* may have overdone it some. I am not in favor of motion of motion's sake."

Sometimes, however, there *is* motion for motion's sake. Rather broadcast the *Evening News* from Los Angeles and San Francisco because CBS's affiliates were meeting there. He did the show from Seattle when CBS News's new bureau opened. And the *Evening News* came out of Salt Lake City not because of the news there, but because he'd been invited by the local CBS affiliate.

All three network anchors say that the nightly news has changed radically in the past decade; that the news you see these days is better and more informational than it was in 1976. In one respect they are right: the way the nightly news is packaged today has changed radically. The Cronkite-styled headline service has been replaced by nightly news magazines that feature longer, more interpretational pieces. There are more features and fewer anchor-read "tell" stories. Satellite feeds, live interviews and on-air promotion of news shows are commonplace.

Do these changes help? Mark Levy doesn't think so. His research shows that TV-news audiences fail to understand about two-thirds of the stories they see on the nightly news. That figure, he adds, hasn't changed in the last 10 years. So despite the cosmetic changes, the razzle-dazzle, the glitz, the floating anchors and all those factoids and info-bits blitzing the audience night after night, viewers aren't comprehending any more of the news they see today than they did a decade ago. The bottom line, says Levy, is that although "it's possible to make the news more understandable...by and large, I don't see broadcast journalists picking up on that challenge." And *that*, perhaps, is the way it really is.

Impact of Mass Media: For Further Reading

Elie Abel (ed.). *What's News: The Media in American Society*. San Francisco: Institute for Contemporary Studies, 1981.

Pearl D. Aldrich. The Impact of Mass Media. Rochelle Park, N.J.: Hayden, 1975.

J. Herbert Altschull. *Agents of Power: The News Media in Human Affairs*. White Plains, N.Y.: Longman, 1984.

John Chancellor and Walter R. Means. *The News Business*. New York: Harper & Row, 1983.

Herbert Gans. *Deciding What's News*. New York: Pantheon Books, 1979.

Michael Gurevitch, Tony Bennett, James Curran, and Janet Woollacott (eds.). *Culture, Society and the Media*. New York: Methuen, 1982.

Elihu Katz and Tamas Szecksko (eds.). *Mass Media and Social Change*. Beverly Hills, Calif.: Sage, 1981.

James B. Lemert. *Does Mass Communication Change Public Opinion After All? A New Approach to Effects Analysis*. Chicago: Nelson-Hall, 1981.

Shearon Lowery and Melvin L. DeFleur. *Milestones in Mass Communication Research: Media Effects*. White Plains, N.Y.: Longman, 1983.

Joshua Meyrowitz. *No Sense of Place: The Impact of Electronic Media on Social Behavior*. New York: Oxford University Press, 1984.

Neil Postman. *Amusing Ourselves to Death: Public Discourse in the Age of Show Business*. New York: Viking Penguin, 1985.

Neil Postman. *The Disappearance of Childhood*. New York: Dell, Delacorte Press, 1982.

II

Freedom versus Responsibility

In no other society do the mass media have as much freedom as they have in the United States. Journalists have frequently argued that the constitutional guarantee of freedom of speech and of the press should be absolute. Truth, this argument poses, can only emerge from an open marketplace of ideas. Throughout the last half of the nineteenth century and the first half of the twentieth, American journalism was guided by the notion of objectivity, the objective search for and communication of facts, without regard for feelings or beliefs. Any attempt—on the part of government or any other institution—to object to objective reporting was an infringement on constitutional rights.

In the name of objective reporting and searching for the truth, American news media have brought us sex, crime, violence, gossip about the private lives of our public figures, rumors about the graft and corruption of our public officials, revelations of government secrets that affect our diplomatic relations and our national security, and even information on how we can build our own nuclear bombs in our basements. The public, according to the theory, will sort out the truth from the falsehoods and thus be informed so that they can fulfill their responsibilities as citizens at the polling booths.

Some resent the media's freedom to present anything they want. And yet, if the press did not search out all the information that the public will pay for, whether or not some like that information, how would the people know all that is going on, both good and bad? Who should tell the news media what they can and cannot disseminate? Where should the line be drawn between freedom and responsibility? Who should draw the line? And who should enforce it? These questions have plagued democracies as long as they have been in existence. For the most part, we have left it to the courts to determine when and how the press has been irresponsible in individual cases. And most of the time in American history, the courts have ruled in favor of freedom, even when that freedom has resulted in articles about how to build your own nuclear bombs.

As the media have become more powerful, the arguments have increased. After World War II, the Commission on Freedom of the Press was established to deal with these questions. Leading philosophers and statesmen were named to the commission. Ultimately, the commission produced a document that expressed a new theory about the press in democracy—the "social-responsibility" theory. This theory suggests that in a society with the potential for total self-destruction and with mass media that have become such powerful institutions in that society, the press has an obligation larger than a simple search for the truth. In such a society, the commission suggested, if the search for truth should threaten the welfare of the society as a whole, some apparatus must be established to step in and protect society from such a threat.

To some extent, the social-responsibility theory operates in the broadcast media in our society: The Federal Communication Commission can, within limits, protect society from threatening broadcasts. It does not operate on the print media. And as a result, the arguments on both sides of the freedom-versus-responsibility debate continue to grow.

4 How the Press Is Copping Out

by Harrison Schmitt

Harrison Schmitt, the first scientist to walk on the moon, chaired a special Twentieth Century Fund task force to investigate coverage of technological risk. Task force members agreed that the press was doing a reasonably good job. Not Schmitt. In this article from *Discover*, October 1984, he tells why.

In recent years the press has shown a distressing indifference to the consequences of what it publishes. Information, whether it is known to be true or is merely speculation, is rushed into print or onto the air so long as it is considered "newsworthy." Only in the most extreme cases of possible slander or imminent danger to specific individuals—say, in the event of a kidnapping—is the press likely to delay or withhold information. Nor are seemingly responsible members of the fourth estate disturbed by this trend. As Bob Woodward of the Washington *Post*, winner of a Pulitzer Prize for his Watergate reporting, has put it, "Our job, simply and happily, is to find out what's going on and publish it." Michael Gartner, president of the highly regarded Des Moines *Register*, is even more succinct. He recently told me, "We are not the public's mother." I cannot agree with the abrogation of responsibility implicit in such statements.

This attitude is of special concern to me when it affects reporting about certain apparent risks created by technology, like the disposal of toxic wastes. To be sure, the question of handling these substances properly has been neglected for too long. Still, I wonder how much needless mental trauma and economic hardship were caused by the media's emphasis on possible, rather than real, risks of chemical pollution in the accounts of the discovery of contaminants at Love Canal and Times Beach. Few reports of these incidents made the critical point that a particular chemical might be toxic and still not constitute a risk to human beings. Nor did most news reports explain that predictions about the long-term effects on human beings of exposure to low concentrations of chemicals are based on very brief exposure of laboratory animals to high concentrations of the substances. There is nothing in science or common sense to support the conclusion that short-term animal experiments are somehow relevant to the long-term health of people.

Other instances of sloppy scientific journalism include the reporting of the swine flu scare during the Ford administration and outbreaks of German measles. By sensationalizing the few times that vaccines caused unfortunate reactions in a few people, the press gave short shrift to the very real benefits of the mass inoculation effort to the public as a whole. Obscured in the reporting was a key point: any risk to an individual getting a shot is far less than the risk to the total population if many do not receive the vaccine.

The press also seems unable, or unwilling, to make subtle but essential distinctions—for example, between a commercial *nuclear* accident and a commercial nuclear *plant* accident. The first involves a major release of radioactivity from a reactor and has occurred only once in the history of nuclear power (at Three Mile Island, and with little risk to the people living near by). The second, relatively common at all power plants, usually involves nothing more than a problem with valves, pipes, wires, and human operators. There is little or no release of radioactivity. Yet by blurring this important distinction, the press has encouraged the public to prefer coal power to nuclear power for generating electricity. That choice is exacting a terrible price not only in dollars but also in the quality of our environment for generations to come. By any objective measure of air and water pollution, land destruction, risk to miners or to plant operators, and global habitability, the choice of coal over nuclear power is, to put it bluntly, dumb.

In these cases and others, the press cannot escape its responsibility. It has tended to be a strong polarizing force that emphasizes the negative aspects of an issue over the positive. Editors and reporters I have talked to say their approach is forced on them by the rapid flow of events, competitive journalistic pressures, and the public's appetite for bad news.

To them I say: you are copping out. Good research and good writing, even under deadline conditions, can make a positive story interesting. In addition, ever since Watergate, there has been a zealousness on the part of the press to look for a cover-up of facts rather than admit the possibility that officials or even scientists may not know the answers to all reporters' questions or that there may be some understandable uncertainty. The stress on bad news over good, on the dramatic rather than the humdrum, tends to create, in scientific language, an "unstable amplifier": an issue of relatively limited and local importance that suddenly gets national attention, as during the dioxin scare at Times Beach.

I admit that the science journalist's job is not always easy. Sources of information are too often reluctant to cooperate or have only an incomplete command of the facts. Still, if I could make major recommendations to editors and publishers, as well as to radio and television news directors, they would be: First, instill in your people a willingness to learn enough about the basics of technology, science, and nature so that they can communicate objectively with their sources and their public. Second, encourage them to show the same sense of responsibility and compassion for the public and for future generations that they have already demonstrated for specific individuals, like kidnap victims, for whom untimely publicity can be dangerous.

The press plays a key role in establishing much of today's political agenda, but along with this power comes responsibility. Most of us would agree that a free press is important to our constitutional system and should not be subject to artificial or imposed checks and balances. Yet in the absence of such restraints, the press is obliged to exercise voluntarily at least as much caution as is required of the government. Unless the press recognizes this obligation to our democracy, the public will continue to be ill informed on issues of risks, not understand what information should be sought, and, either passively or actively, support unwise national policies. Eventually, this could endanger all our institutions, including our free press.

5 Media Power: On Closer Inspection, It's Not That Threatening

by Albert E. Gollin

Albert E. Gollin argues that the very diversity of our mass media today reduces their power. Even though they are at times irresponsible, it doesn't really matter because they are not so powerful as their critics claim, and the public is not stupid or gullible enough to believe the media's excesses. Gollin is vice president/associate director of research of the Newspaper Advertising Bureau. This article is excerpted from a presentation he made at a public forum in Washington, D.C., "Can the Mass Media Control Our Thoughts?" The forum was part of the Smithsonian Institution's eighth international symposium, "The Road after 1984: High Technology and Human Freedom." This article is reprinted from *presstime*, February 1984.

There are several key assumptions underlying prevailing beliefs about media power. It is useful to recall that concern about the effects of the mass media is rooted in the seeming success of propaganda efforts conducted during World War I, and by Nazi and Soviet regimes subsequently, to mobilize, coerce or control their own citizens. More recently, the agenda of concerns has broadened, without wholly losing the edge of anxiety that characterized discussions in that earlier era. Here are just a few examples of questions that have been raised.

- Has the graphic treatment of sex and violence by the media contributed to a decline of morality and trivialized or vulgarized significant aspects of human experience?
- Has the aggressive handling and criticism of political and economic elites by the media eroded their leadership mandates and led to a general decline in the perceived legitimacy of soical institutions?
- Are the media persistently exploited for political and commercial purposes, selling us candidates and products we otherwise would not buy?
- Have the media created a popular culture that has steadily cheapened public taste—"sitcoms" and soap operas instead of Shakespeare and Verdi, Harlequin romances instead of Hemingway?
- Did the news media drive Richard Nixon from office, and did they cost us victory in Vietnam?

The list goes on and on. It might be noted in this regard that the criticisms and questions raised are far from consistent internally or devoid of special-interest motives.

Evidence from mass communication research provides a basis for commenting on several mistaken assumptions made by media critics and others who believe in the media's power to affect our thoughts and actions and to shape our society in various ways, good and bad.

The first of these assumptions is the equating of media content with media effects. In this view, what people see, read or hear—especially when they are repeatedly exposed to the content—actually has the effects one hopes for, or fears, depending upon one's own assessment of a particular message. Based on this simplified stimulus-response conception, for example, are the following convictions:

- Violence in children's TV programming leads to violence on the playground.
- Sexually permissive norms highlighted in films, on television, or in books and magazines are echoed in the behavior of those exposed to such erotic content.
- Sympathetic portrayals of minorities generate compassion and tolerance.
- Media-based campaigns to reduce energy consumption or to get people to lead healthier lives will yield socially desirable results.

Linked with the equating of content with effects is another assumption: that the *intent* of the communicator is faithfully captured in the responses of those exposed to the message. Thus, according to this view, "M*A*S*H" not only entertains, it also successfully conveys the anti-war intent of its producers. Or Archie Bunker's bigotry, rather than giving sanction to prejudiced attitudes, is perceived as misguided, out of date, and morally reprehensible.

The evidence from communications research, while admittedly uneven and less than conclusive, nevertheless portrays a set of relationships between the content or intent of media messages and their effects that are far more complex and variable in nature. People bring to their encounters with the mass media a formidable array of established habits, motives, social values and perceptual defenses that screen out, derail the intent or limit the force of media messages. The media certainly do affect people in obvious and subtle ways. But no simple 1:1 relationship exists between content or intent and effects.

Moreover, while media audiences are massive in size—a precondition for mass persuasion—they are socially differentiated, self-selective, often inattentive, and in general—to use a term once employed by Raymond Bauer of Harvard University—"obstinate." As targets they are elusive and hard to please or to convince. People actively use the media for a wide variety of shared and individual purposes. People are not readily used by the media. Why is it, then, that we believe that others in the viewing or reading public are more gullible or passive than we ourselves?

Another assumption often held is that the mass media now operate in an unrestrained fashion, and that their autonomy is a prime source of their power. But media publics not only are individually resistant to the content offered them, in free societies they also significantly affect content through the operation of various feedback mechanisms. In this connection, one has only to recall the decisive role of broadcast ratings, film box-office receipts, subscription and circulation revenues, and the like as market forces that constrain the predilections of media operators and producers. To these "bottom-line" influences one must add the constant stream of criticism, letters and phone calls, self-criticism based on professional values that include service to the public, legal restraints, and the results of marketing studies that seek to discover public tastes, preferences and needs.

Thus, in various direct and indirect ways, the public acts upon the mass media rather than simply being influenced by them. And with the variety of content choices and exposure opportunities expanding steadily, thanks to new communications technologies, the likelihood of successful mass persuasion by the media diminishes still further.

This last point bears upon the initial reception of new technologies, including each of the mass media. As a new type of technology emerges, it is often met by either or both of two sharply contrasting reactions. The first of these is aptly symbolized by the image of the cornucopia—the horn of plenty. The new technology is hailed for its potential benefits—enriching people's lives, removing burdens and contributing to human progress. The contrasting perspective is symbolized by the image of the juggernaut—the machine that is unstoppable, crippling or constraining human freedom.

Most technologies, the mass media included, rarely fulfill either set of extravagant hopes or fears. As they diffuse and become integrated into societies, they change things in the process of extending human capacities. But so too do new forms of art, law, scientific knowledge, war and modes of social organization. Only with hindsight, and often with great difficulty, does it become possible to assess which of these has affected society more broadly and decisively, especially when it comes to human freedom.

To sum up, while at times unquestionably guilty of harmful excess and error, the mass media are less powerful or autonomous than their critics fear—or than their own agents sometimes like to believe. Media publics are far from compliant or passive, and they are becoming increasingly less so as media choices multiply.

Finally, to contradict Ralph Waldo Emerson, things are not in the saddle, riding humankind. Given the existence of media diversity and continuing feedback from the public, the risks of media-fostered political or cultural hegemony remain small.

In any case, such risks are inseparable from those intrinsic to the functioning of free societies, in which the media now play a variety of indispensable roles.

6 Objectivity Precludes Responsibility

by Theodore L. Glasser

Theodore L. Glasser argues that objectivity is not the best basis on which to make responsible journalistic decisions. Glasser teaches journalism at the University of Minnesota. This article is adapted from a lecture prepared for the Second Annual Seminar in Applied Ethics, sponsored by the Minnesota Journalism Center, Augsberg College, and the Minnesota Humanities Commission. It is reprinted from *The Quill*, February 1984.

By objectivity I mean a particular view of journalism and the press, a frame of reference used by journalists to orient themselves in the newsroom and in the community. By objectivity I mean, to a degree, ideology; where ideology is defined as a set of beliefs that function as the journalist's "claim to action."

As a set of beliefs, objectivity appears to be rooted in a positivist view of the world, an enduring commitment to the supremacy of observable and retrievable facts. This commitment, in turn, impinges on news organizations' principal commodity—the day's news. Thus my argument, in part, is this: Today's news is indeed biased—as it must inevitably be—and this bias can be best understood by understanding the concept, the conventions, and the ethic of objectivity.

Specifically, objectivity in journalism accounts for—or at least helps us understand—three principal developments in American journalism; each of these developments contributes to the bias or ideology of news. First, objective reporting is biased against what the press typically defines as its role in a democracy—that of a Fourth Estate, the watchdog role, an adversary press. Indeed, objectivity in journalism is biased in favor of the status quo; it is inherently conservative to the extent that it encourages reporters to rely on what sociologist Alvin Gouldner so appropriately describes as the "managers of the status quo"—the prominent and the élite. Second, objective reporting is biased against independent thinking; it emasculates the intellect by treating it as a disinterested spectator. Finally, objective reporting is biased against the very idea of responsibility; the day's news is viewed as something journalists are compelled to report, not something they are responsible for creating.

This last point, I think, is most important. Despite a renewed interest in professional ethics, the discussion continues to evade questions of morality and responsibility. Of course, this doesn't mean that journalists are immoral. Rather, it means that journalists today are largely amoral. Objectivity in journalism effectively erodes the very foundation on which rests a responsible press.

By most any of the many accounts of the history of objectivity in journalism, objective reporting began more as a commercial imperative than as a standard of responsible reporting. With the emergence of a truly popular press in the mid-1800s—the penny press—a press tied neither to the political parties nor the business élite, objectivity provided a presumably disinterested view of the world.

But the penny press was only one of many social, economic, political, and technological forces that converged in the mid- and late-1800s to bring about fundamental and lasting changes in American journalism. There was the advent of the telegraph, which for the first time separated communication from transportation. There were radical changes in printing technology, including the steam-powered press and later the rotary press. There was the formation of the Associated Press, an early effort by publishers to monopolize a new technology—in this case the telegraph. There was, finally, the demise of community and the rise of society; there were now cities, "human settlements" where "strangers are likely to meet."

These are some of the many conditions that created the climate for objective reporting, a climate best understood in terms of the emergence of a new mass medium and the need for that medium to operate efficiently in the marketplace.

Efficiency is the key term here, for efficiency is the central meaning of objective reporting. It was efficient for the Associated Press to distribute only the "bare facts," and leave the opportunity for interpretation to individual members of the cooperative. It was efficient for newspapers not to offend readers and advertisers with partisan prose. It was efficient— perhaps expedient—for reporters to distance themselves from the sense and substance of what they reported.

To survive in the marketplace, and to enhance their status as a new and more democratic press, journalists—principally publishers, who were becoming more and more removed from the editing and writing process— began to transform efficiency into a standard of professional competence, a standard later—several decades later—described as objectivity. This transformation was aided by two important developments in the early twentieth century: first, Oliver Wendell Holmes' effort to employ a marketplace metaphor to define the meaning of the First Amendment; and second, the growing popularity of the scientific method as the proper tool with which to discover and understand an increasingly alien reality.

In a dissenting opinion in 1919, Holmes popularized "the marketplace of ideas," a metaphor introduced by John Milton several centuries earlier. Metaphor or not, publishers took it quite literally. They argued—and continue with essentially the same argument today—that their opportunity to compete and ultimately survive in the marketplace is their First Amendment right, a Constitutional privilege. The American Newspaper Publishers Association, organized in 1887, led the cause of a free press. In the name of freedom of the press, the ANPA fought the Pure Food and Drug Act of 1906 on behalf of its advertisers; it fought the Post Office Act of 1912, which compelled sworn statements of ownership and circulation and thus threatened to reveal too much to advertisers; it fought efforts to regulate child labor, which would interfere with the control and exploitation of paper boys; it fought the collective bargaining provisions of the National Recovery Act in the mid-1930s; for similar reasons, it stood opposed to the American Newspaper Guild, the reporters' union; it tried—unsuccessfully—to prevent wire services from selling news to radio stations until after publication in the nearby newspaper.

Beyond using the First Amendment to shield and protect their economic interests in the marketplace, publishers were also able to use the canons of science to justify—indeed, legitimize—the canons of objective reporting. Here publishers were comforted by Walter Lippmann's writings in the early 1920s, particularly his plea for a new scientific journalism, a new realism; a call for journalists to remain "clear and free" of their irrational, their unexamined, their unacknowledged prejudgments.

By the early 1900s objectively had become the acceptable way of doing reporting—or at least the respectable way. It was respectable because it was reliable, and it was reliable because it was standardized. In practice, this meant a preoccupation with *how* the news was presented, whether its *form* was reliable. And this concern for reliability quickly overshadowed any concern for the validity of the realities the journalists presented.

Thus emerged the conventions of objective reporting, a set of routine procedures journalists use to objectify their news stories. These are the conventions sociologist Gaye Tuchman describes as a kind of strategy journalists use to deflect criticism, the same kind of strategy social scientists use to defend the quality of their work. For the journalist, this means interviews with sources; and it ordinarily means official sources with impeccable credentials. It means juxtaposing conflicting truth-claims, where truth-claims are reported as "fact" regardless of their validity. It means making a judgment about the news value of a truth-claim even if that judgment serves only to lend authority to what is known to be false or misleading.

As early as 1924 objectivity appeared as an ethic, an ideal subordinate only to truth itself. In his study of the *Ethics of Journalism*, Nelson Crawford devoted three full chapters to the principles of objectivity. Thirty years later, in 1954, Louis Lyons, then curator for the Nieman Fellowship program at Harvard, was describing objectivity as a "rock-bottom" imperative. Apparently unfazed by Wisconsin's Senator Joseph McCarthy, Lyons portrayed objectivity as the ultimate discipline of journalism. "It is at the bottom of all sound reporting—indispensable as the core of the writer's capacity." More recently, in 1973, the Society of Professional Journalists, Sigma Delta Chi formally enshrined the idea of objectivity when it adopted as part of its Code of Ethics a paragraph characterizing objective reporting as an attainable goal and a standard of performance toward which journalists should strive. "We honor those who achieve it," the Society proclaimed.

So well ingrained are the principles of objective reporting that the judiciary is beginning to acknowledge them. In a 1977 federal appellate decision, *Edwards v. National Audubon Society*, a case described by media attorney Floyd Abrams as a landmark decision in that it may prove to be the next evolutionary stage in the development of the public law of libel, a new and novel privilege emerged. It was the first time the courts explicitly recognized objective reporting as a standard of journalism worthy of First Amendment protection.

In what appeared to be an inconsequential story published in *The New York Times* in 1972—on page 33—five scientists were accused of being paid liars, men paid by the pesticide industry to lie about the use of DDT and its effect on bird life. True to the form of objective reporting, the accusation was fully attributed—to a fully identified official of the National Audubon Society. The scientists, of course, were given an opportunity to deny the accusation. Only one of the scientists, however, was quoted by name and he described the accusation as "almost libelous." What was newsworthy about the story, obviously, was the accusation; and with the exception of one short paragraph, the reporter more or less provided a forum for the National Audubon Society.

Three of the five scientists filed suit. While denying punitive damages, a jury awarded compensatory damages against the *Times* and one of the Society's officials. The *Times*, in turn, asked a federal District Court to overturn the verdict. The *Times* argued that the "actual malice" standard had not been met; since the scientists were "public figures," they were required to show that the *Times* knowingly published a falsehood or there was, on the part of the *Times*, a reckless disregard for whether the accusation was true or false. The evidence before the court clearly indicated the latter— there was indeed a reckless disregard for whether the accusation was true or false. The reporter made virtually no effort to confirm the validity of the National Audubon Society's accusations. Also the story wasn't the kind of "hot news" (a technical term used by the courts) that required immediate dissemination; in fact ten days before the story was published the *Times* learned that two of the five scientists were not employed by the pesticide industry and thus could not have been "paid liars."

The *Times* appealed to the Second Circuit Court of Appeals, where the lower court's decision was overturned. In reversing the District Court, the Court of Appeals created a new First Amendment right, a new Constitutional defense in libel law—the privilege of "neutral reportage." "We do not believe," the Court of Appeals ruled, "that the press may be required to suppress newsworthy statements merely because it has serious doubts regarding their truth." The First Amendment, the Court said, "protects the accurate and disinterested reporting" of newsworthy accusations "regardless of the reporter's private views regarding their validity."

I mention the details of the *Edwards* case only because it illustrates so well the consequences of the ethic of objectivity. First, it illustrates a very basic tension between objectivity and responsibility. Objective reporting virtually precludes responsible reporting, if by responsible reporting we mean a willingness on the part of the reporter to be accountable for what is reported. Objectivity requires only that reporters be accountable for *how* they report, not what they report. The *Edwards* Court made this very clear: "The public interest in being fully informed," the Court said, demands that the press be afforded the freedom to report newsworthy accusations "without assuming responsibility for them."

Second, the *Edwards* case illustrates the unfortunate bias of objective reporting—a bias in favor of leaders and officials, the prominent and the élite. It is an unfortunate bias because it runs counter to the important democratic assumption that statements made by ordinary citizens are as valuable as statements made by the prominent and the élite. In a democracy, public debate depends on separating individuals from their powers and privileges in the larger society; otherwise debate itself becomes a source of domination. But *Edwards* reinforces prominence as a news value; it reinforces the use of official sources, official records, official channels. Tom Wicker underscored the bias of the *Edwards* case when he observed recently that "objective journalism almost always favors Establishment positions and exists not least to avoid offense to them."

Objectivity also has unfortunate consequences for the reporter, the individual journalist. Objective reporting has stripped reporters of their creativity and their imagination; it has robbed journalists of their passion and their perspective. Objective reporting has transformed journalism into something more technical than intellectual; it has turned the art of story-telling into the technique of report writing. And most unfortunate of all, objective reporting has denied journalists their citizenship; as disinterested observers, as impartial reporters, journalists are expected to be morally disengaged and politically inactive.

Journalists have become—to borrow James Carey's terminology— "professional communicators," a relatively passive link between sources and audiences. With neither the need nor the opportunity to develop a critical perspective from which to assess the events, the issues, and the personalities he or she is assigned to cover, the objective reporter tends to function as a translator—translating the specialized language of sources into a language intelligible to a lay audience.

In his frequently cited study of Washington correspondents—a study published nearly fifty years ago—Leo Rosten found that a "pronounced majority" of the journalists he interviewed considered themselves inadequate to cope with the bewildering complexities of our nation's policies and politics. As Rosten described it, the Washington press corps was a frustrated and exasperated group of prominent journalists more or less resigned to their role as mediators, translators. "To do the job," one reporter told Rosten, "what you know or understand isn't important. You've got to know whom to ask." Even if you don't understand what's being said, Rosten was told, you just take careful notes and write it up verbatim: "Let my readers figure it out. I'm their reporter, not their teacher."

That was fifty years ago. Today, the story is pretty much the same. Two years ago another study of Washington correspondents was published, a book by Stephen Hess called *The Washington Reporters.* For the most part, Hess found, stories coming out of Washington were little more than a "mosaic of facts and quotations from sources" who were participants in an event or who had knowledge of the event. Incredibly, Hess found that for nearly three-quarters of the stories he studied, reporters relied on no documents—only interviews. And when reporters did use documents, those documents were typically press clippings—stories they had written or stories written by their colleagues.

And so what does objectivity mean? It means that sources supply the sense and substance of the day's news. Sources provide the arguments, the rebuttals, the explanations, the criticism. Sources put forth the ideas while other sources challenge those ideas. Journalists, in their role as professional communicators, merely provide a vehicle for these exchanges.

But if objectivity means that reporters must maintain a healthy distance from the world they report, the same standard does not apply to publishers. According to the SPJ, SDX Code of Ethics, "Journalists and their employers should conduct their personal lives in a manner which protects them from conflict of interest, real or apparent." Many journalists do just that—they avoid even an appearance of a conflict of interest. But certainly not their employers.

If it would be a conflict of interest for a reporter to accept, say, an expensive piano from a source at the Steinway Piano Company, it apparently wasn't a conflict of interest when CBS purchased the Steinway Piano Company.

Publishers and broadcasters today are part of a large and growing and increasingly diversified industry. Not only are many newspapers owned by corporations that own a variety of non-media properties, but their boards of directors read like a *Who's Who* of the powerful and the élite. A recent study of the twenty-five largest newspaper companies found that the directors of these companies tend to be linked with "powerful business organizations, not with public interest groups; with management, not with labor; with well established think tanks and charities, not their grassroots counterparts."

But publishers and broadcasters contend that these connections have no bearing on how the day's news is reported—as though the ownership of a newspaper had no bearing on the newspaper's content; as though business decisions have no effect on editorial decisions; as though it wasn't economic considerations in the first place that brought about the incentives for many of the conventions of contemporary journalism.

No doubt the press has responded to many of the more serious consequences of objective reporting. But what is significant is that the response has been to amend the conventions of objectivity, not to abandon them. The press has merely refined the canons of objective reporting; it has not dislodged them.

What remains fundamentally unchanged is the journalist's naïvely empirical view of the world, a belief in the separation of facts and values, a belief in the existence of *a* reality—the reality of empirical facts. Nowhere is this belief more evident than when news is defined as something external to—and independent of—the journalist. The very vocabulary used by journalists when they talk about news underscores their belief that news is "out there," presumably waiting to be *exposed* or *uncovered* or at least *gathered*.

This is the essence of objectivity, and this is precisely why it is so very difficult for journalism to consider questions of ethics and morality. Since news exists "out there"—apparently independent of the reporter—journalists can't be held responsible for it. And since they are not responsible for the news being there, how can we expect journalists to be accountable for the consequences of merely reporting it?

What objectivity has brought about, in short, is a disregard for the consequences of newsmaking. A few years ago Walter Cronkite offered this interpretation of journalism: "I don't think it is any of our business what the moral, political, social, or economic effect of our reporting is. I say let's go with the job of reporting—and let the chips fall where they may."

Contrast that to John Dewey's advice: that "our chief moral business is to become acquainted with consequences."

I am inclined to side with Dewey. Only to the extent that journalists are held accountable for the consequences of their actions can there be said to be a responsible press. But we are not going to be able to hold journalists accountable for the consequences of their actions until they acknowledge that news is their creation, a creation for which they are fully responsible. And we are not going to have much success convincing journalists that news is created, not reported, until we can successfully challenge the conventions of objectivity.

The task, then, is to liberate journalism from the burden of objectivity by demonstrating—as convincingly as we can—that objective reporting is more of a custom than a principle, more a habit of mind than a standard of performance. And by showing that objectivity is largely a matter of efficiency—efficiency that serves, as far as I can tell, only the needs and interest of the owners of the press, not the needs and interests of talented writers and certainly not the needs and interests of the larger society.

7 The Might of the Media: Media Self-Censorship
"The public will never know"
by Robert G. Picard

> In an effort to avoid an increasing number of lawsuits
> caused by irresponsible actions, the media may actually be
> causing greater damage to the public by being more
> cautious, less investigative, blander and weaker. So sug-
> gests Robert G. Picard, a former newspaper reporter and
> editor and, when this was written, a doctoral candidate in
> journalism at the University of Missouri. He has written on
> media topics for a variety of journalism publications,
> including *The Quill, Editor and Publisher*, and *Grassroots
> Editor*. This article is reprinted from *The Press*, March
> 1981.

American publishers and broadcasters are increasingly exercising self-
censorship to avoid costly litigation and the result is a decline in press
freedom, say journalists and legal experts.

The self-censorship is denying the public a wide range of information
because journalists fear libel and privacy suits, and confrontations with
government attorneys, which can result in legal fees of up to $200 an hour.

The cost of lawyers for the media has spiraled upward in recent years,
as the number of suits filed against the media has increased. The media
themselves have also increased their legal costs because a large number of
papers and broadcasting enterprises have chosen to hire permanent legal
staffs.

The attorneys on media staffs are not only handling legal defenses for
their employers—they have also moved into the editorial decision-making
process and are encouraging self-censorship and making decisions on
whether articles will be printed or broadcast, say industry observers.

"There's a lot of self-censorship by editors unwilling to rock the boat.
They fear the heavy court costs that could come from a tough investigative
article," says Bruce Sanford, a former *Wall Street Journal* reporter who is
now an attorney for United Press International and the Society of Professional Journalists.

His analysis is echoed by Dan Paul, attorney for the *Miami Herald*.
"Costs of trying libel suits...quashing subpoenas, fending off privacy

actions and obtaining news under freedom of information laws are already substantial, and the burden is growing," he says. "Because of this burden the hometown newspaper or small radio station may decide to steer clear of news prone to generate litigation costs or search warrants. That is chilling."

Floyd Abrams, an attorney who has represented *The New York Times* and other major media clients, believes such censorship may increase. "If things develop to the point where large jury verdicts or large counsel fees on a yearly basis are the norm and not the exception, then I don't have any doubt that publications will be obliged to trim their sails.... The real danger is that the public would never know," he warns.

Many journalists and attorneys believe that libel victories by plaintiffs may be increasing the number of suits in recent years because high damages awarded by juries could be an incentive for many individuals to pursue a case even if it is unwarranted.

"The country is in a litigious mood—everybody sues these days, and even if there are no real grounds, suits are expensive to defend," says Art Spikol, a columnist for *Writer's Digest*.

The cost of defending any suit, with attorney fees averaging $1,000 a day, is enough to scare most media managers, and many news organizations have begun settling even unwarranted suits with out of court payments in order to avoid more costly defense costs and the possibility of large jury verdicts.

In a celebrated case, the *San Francisco Examiner* recently sought to reduce its liability in a libel suit brought against it by two policemen and a prosecuting attorney. The case involved stories in the paper that alleged a police frame-up against a member of a youth gang.

The story was written by a free-lance reporter and a member of the *Examiner* staff. When the suit was filed, the paper chose to cut its litigation costs and attempted to reduce its liability by refusing to defend the free-lance writer and blaming the alleged libel on him. As a result both reporters sought separate counsel because they felt the paper did not have their interests at heart.

A defense committee, composed of horrified colleagues, raised $20,000 to pay the reporters' legal bills for the trial. A finding against the reporters in the trial is now being appealed and their defense costs are expected to double, as will the costs for the *Examiner*, which also lost its case.

Defense costs in libel suits involving other parties have also resulted in high expenditures. Litigation costs of nearly $100,000 were recently encountered by Palm Beach, Florida, and Baton Rouge, Louisiana, newspapers when they lost and appealed sizable libel cases. Although both won their cases on appeal, they still had to bear the costs of their defenses.

John Zollinger, publisher of the *New Mexico Independent*, laments, "It's no joke anymore.... You win and you still pay."

In addition to litigation costs posed by libel and other suits, the media in America are confronted with significant costs when they attempt to defend press rights and privileges. The high cost of such First Amendment defenses is reportedly keeping many publishers and broadcasters from pursuing such cases and leading some to censor material which might bring them into conflict with the government.

The Progressive magazine recently chose to challenge the government's attempt to restrain publication of an article about the H-bomb, and the litigation costs nearly forced the journal out of business.

The magazine, which had already been losing about $100,000 a year, spent nearly $250,000 pressing its case before the government dropped its efforts.

"Our lawyers said at the outset this was likely to be a protracted and horrendously expensive case that could jeopardize the survival of the magazine," says Editor Erwin Knoll. But he reports supporters have raised much of the money needed to cover the defense costs and that only $60,000 remains unpaid.

"As legal costs go up and legal complications grow ever more ramiferous and Byzantine, publishers may increasingly try to avoid these types of difficulties," warns Knoll. 'If we were still bearing the $60,000 debt from the last go around. . .and knowing fully the burdens of pursuing such a case, we would do it again. But we would do it with the knowledge that the magazine would not be likely to survive."

Knoll believes few publishers or publications with circulations the size of his 40,000 circulation magazine would elect to pursue such an expensive and potentially harmful course. "I think the cost has a chilling effect to say the least," he says.

The 1980 U.S. Supreme Court ruling limiting the closure of trial to press and public was also an expensive victory for the press. The costs were borne solely by Richmond Newspapers, Inc., which pursued the case after a Virginia judge closed a murder trial in which the defendant was acquitted.

According to Publisher J. Steward Bryan III, the final costs of the case are not tallied yet, but he expects them to be between $75,000 and $100,000. "I don't think there are many newspaper companies who could afford this kind of case. Even daily newspapers between 20,000 and 25,000 circulation couldn't possibly afford it," he says.

Challenges to broadcast licenses are also proving expensive, and pressure groups are increasingly challenging the licenses in order to force changes by broadcasters. It is estimated that even the simplest challenge requiring legal representation before the Federal Communication Commission can cost a broadcaster between $50,000 and $100,000.

Few broadcast license challenges have proved successful, but many challenges are being made only to force changes in station policy or programming content rather than to take the license away from the broadcaster. Owners, who must pay large fees to defend against the license challenges, are often saddled with the challengers' legal costs as well when they come to an agreement that halts the proceedings.

Such costs have the apparent result of encouraging many broadcasters to avoid controversial subjects which may bring about the need for legal representation.

In the mid 1970s, Richard Schmidt, general legal counsel for the American Society of Newspaper Editors, noted "a subtle but pervasive attitude of self-censorship motivated by fear of libel suits." Today, he still believes the litigious climate is making publishers exercise self-censorship.

"Self-censorship is rather prevalent," he says, "but it can't be proved with empirical evidence. It's something publishers don't like to talk about, but I hear about it in conversations at conferences all the time."

Avoiding litigation by self-censorship adds a raw economic factor to an industry that has claimed to be guided by the interests of society and ethical principles. It is an unfortunate reality that there can be no appeal of this kind of censorship because it is instituted by the media themselves and is usually unseen and undetected by their audiences.

"Self-censorship has always been the most pervasive form of censorship," notes Erwin Knoll, editor of *The Progressive*. "Keeping out of trouble has always been publishers' main interest."

The rising popularity of libel and First Amendment insurance policies may help some media, however.

About half of the 1,750 daily newspaper and 425 weeklies now carry libel insurance, but deductibles of up to $25,000 can pose problems because some cases are settled or ended at costs below that level. The interest in libel insurance has brought about the establishment of First Amendment insurance, which aid[s] media in pursuing or defending cases involving First Amendment issues. About 300 companies, mostly daily newspapers, have purchased policies ranging from $100,000 to $1 million in coverage.

Critics of such policies, however, argue that the insurance will not be effective against self-censorship because they actually encourage more litigation which will only increase the cost of insurance policies. They also point out that the smaller news organizations, which are most prone to self-censorship, often cannot afford the policies.

The litigious spirit in the nation has been heightened by some journalists becoming "First Amendment junkies," who seek legal relief whenever they feel any privileges have been infringed, charges Don Reubens, an attorney who has represented *The Chicago Tribune, The New York Daily News* and Time, Inc.

Reubens recently warned journalists attending an Illinois newspaper association meeting that such a "knee jerk reaction" allows bad cases to be brought to court and that such cases can bring unfavorable rulings that cost fellow journalists existing freedoms. It is ridiculous to see, confrontation and test cases that have no real importance or that could be counterproductive, he said.

Whether the media in the United States will be able to break loose of the bonds of litigation costs, self-imposed censorship and the continued growth of the litigious spirit remains to be seen. But many observers in America believe few efforts by the media seem directed toward those goals.

Freedom vs. Responsibility: For Further Reading

Daniel L. Brenner and William L. Rivers, *Free But Regulated: Conflicting Traditions in Media Law*. Ames, Iowa: Iowa State University Press, 1982.

Bill F. Chamberlin and Charlene J. Brown (eds.), *The First Amendment Reconsidered: New Perspectives on the Meaning of Freedom of Speech and Press*. White Plains, N.Y.: Longman, 1982.

John Lofton, *The Press as Guardian of the First Amendment*. Columbia, S.C.: University of South Carolina Press, 1980.

Abraham H. Miller, *Terrorism: The Media and the Law*. Dobbs Ferry, N.Y.: Transnational Publishers, Inc., 1982.

Hugh A. Rundell and Thomas H. Heuterman, *The First Amendment and Broadcasting: Press Freedoms and Broadcast Journalism*. Pullman, Wash.: Washington State University, 1978.

III

Mass Media and Ethics

Whether we describe ethics as the study of moral values and duties or simply as the "oughtness" of one's actions—what one *ought* to do—there's no shortage of discussions of media ethics. Reporters, editors, publishers, producers—everyone involved in gathering, evaluating, publishing, or broadcasting information and entertainment—make decisions about who *ought* to be believed and what *ought* to be included in news reports. Everyone else—their sources, their readers and listeners—on the other hand, makes decisions about what's included and what's not included, and few days pass without questions as to the adequacy or inadequacy of the work done by the mass media. Admittedly, these public discussions are usually after-the-fact reactions to something recently published or aired. The instances that stay on the public agenda tend to be the negative criticisms. What often remain unreported are the discussions held in newsrooms and other media offices as reporters, editors, and others attempt to prepare accurate, fair, and complete reports of complex issues.

The study of media ethics has remained a popular topic. Public figures and private citizens have voiced their opinions about the ethics of the news media and individuals on their staffs, about the entertainment media and their work. The media have developed codes and sponsored conferences and will continue to do so. Books about media ethics continue to be published, and people still pay to see movies that dramatically portray media gone astray. There is continuing interest in the topic even though there is no unanimity in evaluating potential or real problems. The *National Observer* was right a decade ago, when it headlined a discussion of journalistic ethics, "Not Black, Not White, But a Rainbow of Gray."

The articles in this chapter cover some contemporary topics relating to media ethics, from the codes of ethics developed by media organizations to media treatment of some timely topics. The specific topics and situations change from year to year, but the basic questions continue. Right now, questions include, How much should the public be told about AIDS and the persons afflicted with this disease—and how much have they been told? How much should media tell about the private lives of public figures? About anyone? Accuracy, fairness and thoroughness, potential personal and professional conflicts of interest, social responsibility and personal responsibility should be considered as you ponder the selections in this section and as you evaluate other topics and other situations that either do or don't receive media attention in the future.

8 An Epidemic of Arrogance

by Clark R. Mollenhoff

"Preserve rights; don't trample them," says veteran Pulitzer Prize–winning reporter, columnist, and author Mollenhoff to arrogant journalists in this article from the November 1986 issue of *The Quill*. Mollenhoff now teaches journalism at Washington and Lee University.

The public image of the press as "arrogant" is the biggest problem the press has in retaining its First Amendment rights. The men and women whose actions are responsible for that arrogant image do more damage to the cause of the press than all of those in government who are hostile to the idea of a free press.

The greatest responsibility of the nation's media is to preserve the First Amendment, and that responsibility rests equally upon print and broadcast journalism. In accepting that responsibility, journalists must engage in more than clever rhetoric. Professional actions must represent more than a rallying around every reporter or editor who gets into trouble of any kind, while whining about the need for more legal protection.

To preserve the First Amendment, the press must engage in the kind of self-criticism suggested by the Code of Ethics of The Society of Professional Journalists, Sigma Delta Chi when print or broadcast performance fails to meet acceptable ethical or legal standards.

The press frequently chastises lawyers and judges for defending lawyers engaged in unethical conduct and occasionally criticizes bar associations and prominent members of the bar for remaining silent, thereby seeming to condone improper conduct.

And yet, journalists and journalistic organizations often defend, or by their silence seem to condone, the performance of colleagues even when they violate ethics codes that stress accuracy, balance and fair play. If ethics codes were more often practiced than ignored, the media would be held in higher regard by the public today.

All that we need to do to understand the low standing of the media in recent opinion polls is to review press performance of the last 10 or 15 years. It is a record littered with arrogance. Ten common journalistic sins:

- Disregard of privacy rights of public and private figures under highly distorted interpretations of the "people's right to know."
- Betrayal of confidential news sources through irresponsible use of

the confidential information in news stories in a manner that makes indentification inevitable.

- Ignoring basic journalistic procedures designed to ensure accuracy, balance and fair play.
- Disregard of the traditional secrecy of grand juries, when there are no sound reasons for ignoring the secrecy.
- Disregard of free press-fair trial standards, when there is no overriding public need to know.
- Disregard of national security classifications, under circumstances where it could cost lives or jeopardize military missions.
- Arguments that justify the publication of false or fictitious news stories or articles.
- Refusal to acknowledge the errors of blatantly false stories or to correct those stories.
- Self-righteousness in blaming government officials and others for the low stature of the press in public opinion polls.
- Demands for changes in federal and state laws designed to provide near-total immunity from criminal prosecution or civil liability.

In listing these sins of arrogance, I am not accusing all—or even a large majority—of journalists of these practices. Most journalists are honest and conscientious in carrying out the responsibility to be accurate, balanced and fair.

But, as in any profession, the majority is tarred by the actions of the few, and this is particularly true when the worst examples of arrogance involve the conduct of journalists who work for the nation's most prestigious newspapers or for the television networks.

Unfortunately, some of those with the highest public profiles have the poorest judgment. The conscientious work of hundreds of reasonable and talented editors and reporters is compromised when one well-known anchorman with a kingly income goes on a nationally televised panel show and declares that if he should come into possession of highly classified documents "that are news," he would broadcast that information, without regard for national security.

I suggest that his explanation that national security is not his business and that the public has a "right to know" the classified information is likely to strike viewers as needlessly macho, callously arrogant, and just plain destructive. It's no wonder that respondents in public opinion polls tend to lump journalists with used car salesmen, insofar as honesty and ethical standards are concerned.

The 1985–86 report of the SPJ, SDX national Ethics Committee contained more than a dozen articles that were largely critical of broadcast and print media for ignoring a wide range of ethical problems. Ethics

Committee Chairman Casey Bukro, a reporter for the *Chicago Tribune*, wrote a stinging column raking SPJ, SDX members for being "wimpish toward its code of ethical standards."

Another group, Investigative Reporters and Editors, has emerged as a strong voice for sound research and careful analysis before publishing or broadcasting as the best way to build credibility and to avoid costly libel hassles.

Despite these strong voices that argue for sound and responsible practices in reporting and editing, there are prominent journalists who pay little attention to correcting mistakes of the past. And they demand even more freedom from liability for the damage they may inflict on public and private persons by false or seriously misleading stories.

Recent libel verdicts against newspapers, magazines and broadcasting corporations have resulted in caterwaulings that freedom of the press is in danger of being lost, and that various court decisions have so chilled news sources that it's becoming increasingly difficult to prove corruption and mismanagement in government. There are even some who suggest that laws should be passed that would bar public officials from filing libel or defamation actions against the media.

Nonsense. If we examine the libel cases in detail, we see that truth is still a rather complete defense. Why should anyone argue, in effect, that the press should have a license to broadcast or publish false information about public officials or public figures without concern for damage to reputation?

Those who push for the most expansive definition of a free press often quote Thomas Jefferson's comment, "The basis of our government being the opinion of the people, the very first objective should be to keep that right; and were it left to me to decide whether we should have a government without newspapers, or newspapers without a government, I should not hesitate a moment to prefer the latter."

Jefferson made that statement before he became president. It is usually forgotten that he expressed some sharply different views on June 11, 1807, in a letter to John Norvell in which he wrote:

"It is a melancholy truth, that a suppression of the press could not more completely deprive the nation of its benefits, than is done by its abandoned prostitution to falsehood. Nothing can now be believed which is seen in a newspaper. Truth itself becomes suspicious by being put into that polluted vehicle. The real extent of this state of misinformation is known only to those who are in situations to confront facts within their knowledge with the lies of the day...that man who never looks into a newspaper is better informed than he who reads them; inasmuch as he who knows nothing is nearer the truth than he whose mind is filled with falsehoods and errors."

A cartoon by Steve Benson of *The Arizona Republic* shows three executives in the penthouse tower of Time Inc. raising a toast and smiling, while one of them quips:

"We defamed Sharon. We printed false information. We were careless and negligent, but, hey, it was all an honest mistake. Cheers, Gentlemen. Another triumph for the First Amendment."

To be sure, in early 1985, Ariel Sharon, the former Israeli defense minister, and General William Westmoreland, former commander of U.S. forces in Vietnam, failed to win their celebrated libel suits against Time Inc. and CBS, respectively. But the trials revealed error and arrogance aplenty on the part of these news organizations, as well as a near-fanatical reluctance on the part of the people involved to concede that anything had been amiss.

One of the issues the Sharon jury struggled with was whether or not *Time* had falsely suggested in a 1983 story that Sharon had somehow encouraged Christian Phalangists to massacre hundreds of unarmed men, women and children in two Palestinian refugee camps in West Beirut, during the 1982 Israeli invasion of Lebanon.

Only one paragraph in the story was in dispute, and testimony regarding that paragraph was alarming to anyone who values the concept of press responsibility. In effect, the *Time* correspondent in the field had merely guessed as to the contents of a secret appendix in an Israeli government report that had probed events leading to the massacre. The correspondent guessed wrong.

Furthermore, the New York–based *Time* writer who actually wrote the piece had dressed up the correspondent's somewhat ambiguous report to make the information seem more solid than the correspondent had intended. An inept guess in the field had been alchemized into a *Time* scoop in New York. It was shoddy, even sleazy journalism.

In his instructions to the jury, the federal trial judge, Abraham D. Sofaer, required the jury to come to conclusions regarding different elements of the trial. The jury found that *Time* had, indeed, defamed Sharon.

However, added the jury, the magazine had not acted in "knowing or reckless disregard" of the truth, though "certain employees" had been negligent and careless.

Giving the jury the leeway to find defamation even if the defamation did not technically add up to libel was important. Too often, when a jury brings in a verdict for a news organization, the fact that false and defamatory information was actually published or broadcast is lost in the legal shuffle. That's because a public figure must prove that those who published or broadcast the false and defamatory information knew or had reason to believe the information was false at the time it was published or broadcast.

In cases such as the Sharon/*Time* fiasco, we see the executives for newspapers, magazines or networks gleefully congratulating each other and proclaiming that the jury has rendered "a victory for truth." Alas, such "victories" may in fact be victories for well-paid lawyers who use Supreme Court rulings and widely varying trial court interpretations of those rulings to avoid liability for negligence and falsehood.

In a less publicized suit, Carl Galloway, a physician in Los Angeles, lost a case against CBS despite the fact that false and distorted information was broadcast about him. That trial convinced jurors that Galloway's signature had been forged on a document that *60 Minutes* used to link him with medical insurance frauds.

While there was no evidence that demonstrated that Galloway participated in or had any knowledge of the frauds, the trial judge instructed the jury that it could not hold for Galloway unless it believed Galloway had proved that CBS knew the document was forged at the time of the broadcast.

On the witness stand, CBS anchorman Dan Rather said he was not aware that Galloway's signature had been forged on the false medical report, and he asserted that he still believed it might be Galloway's signature, despite the testimony of handwriting experts to the contrary.

CBS heralded the jury's verdict as "a victory for truth," and hardly anyone in the business disagreed, at least publicly.

Admittedly, any of us can make mistakes that will make us legally or at least ethically vulnerable if we become too confident and fail to do the skeptical checking, double-checking and triple-checking of sources and documents that was Standard Operating Procedure 20, 30 or 40 years ago. The need for double-checking and triple-checking of sources and documents is particularly important when it involves investigative reporting, in which the stories raise questions about the propriety or legality of the actions of public officials or private citizens.

I don't suggest less aggressiveness in pursuing evidence of wrongdoing either in the private or public sector. But I do suggest that we employ more hard-nosed professionalism in analyses of sources and independent evidence, including witnesses and documents. That will give us the maximum amount of knowledge before—not after—we print or air a story that accuses a person of impropriety or unlawful acts.

And, unless we are merely reporting the formal charges of law enforcement officials or allegations included in an official report, fairness requires that we face the accused with the specific charges and give him an opportunity to respond before the story is published or broadcast.

It is wrong to use "the people's right to know" as a reason for failing to confront the subject of a derogatory story with the charges and giving him an opportunity to deny them or to explain them in full. People do *not* have a right to know a charge that is false or unsubstantiated.

9 Media Ethics in Perspective

by Claude-Jean Bertrand

Taking quite a different approach from Clark Mollenhoff, Claude-Jean Bertrand argues that American media, in the face of the Grenada invasion "lockout" and the Westmoreland/Sharon libel actions, seem to be running scared. No longer are there accusations of "imperial media," as newspaper, radio, and television news consumption declines. The media response should be to look to ethics and to learn that corporate consciousness is less important in guiding the medium than is service to public or audience, says Bertrand.

It is sometimes useful to get a perspective from abroad, like the one Bertrand brings to this assessment. He is a French scholar and professor the the Université de Paris. This article is from the *Journal of Mass Media Ethics*, Fall/Winter 1986–87.

One impression a European observer gets of the American media in the mid-1980s is that they are running scared. They seem terribly concerned about their credibility, about the hostility which the public is claimed to feel towards them. No longer is much heard about the U.S. having become a "newsocracy," a nation run by "imperial media." The Pentagon Papers victory and the Watergate triumph have faded deep into the fogs of history. Among headline-grabbing events of recent years: the Janet Cooke affair which still looms in the not too distant past, together with a few other scandals at the *New York Times*, the New York *Daily News*, *The New Yorker* and *The Wall Street Journal*; the exclusion by the U.S. Armed Forces of the media from its clumsy intervention on the little island of Grenada and the approval of that exclusion by public opinion; the exceptionally thorough and entirely successful manipulation of the media by the White House before, during, and after the 1984 presidential campaign; the huge libel suits which generals Sharon and Westmoreland lost but which the media certainly did not win. Behind the events, an unpublicized, sinister trend: In the 1980s the consumption of daily newspapers has gone down, that of radio has gone down, that of network television has gone down.

In the late 1940s, when the famous Hutchins Commission report came out, to a large extent, it was arrogantly ignored in press circles. Such is not their reaction nowadays toward opinion surveys which document the relatively low esteem in which the public holds the media. Nor is the reaction to criticism now to bark back furiously—as was done against the Agnew diatribes in the 1960s. The response is an ever-growing interest in ethics: books, special issues of reviews, editorials and articles, conferences and workshops, task forces and surveys, even a journal exclusively devoted to media ethics.

This is not entirely new, of course. The first renowned code of ethics dates back to 1923. Actually, the interest in ethics had surged at the turn of the century, not long after the media turned into an industry and a big business. This, I wish to stress, was no accidental coincidence. When a highly diversified, often militant, press grew more and more commercial and started concentrating, the more enlightened citizens were bound to worry. The interest in ethics, however, remained largely academic, until the late 1960s. Then a threshold was passed, with symbolic occurrences such as the experiments in local press councils launched in 1967 by the Lowell Mellett Fund (entrusted to The Newspaper Guild) and the flowering of dozens of reporter-generated journalism reviews, beginning in Chicago in 1968. The councils, especially the Minnesota News Council and the National News Council (both born in the early 1970s), implied that some media owners acknowledged that media workers were entitled to a "voice in the product." They also implied that some journalists acknowledged the public too was entitled to a say. That was made even clearer by the appointment, starting in 1967, of over 30 ombudsmen by daily newspapers to field complaints by readers. What councils and ombudsmen have manifested was that mass communications was a very special, unique sector of the economy where making a profit could not be the sole motivation. Serving the public well was at least as important. What journalism reviews showed was that some journalists were willing (as they said) "to bite the hand that fed them." They were no longer obedient and dumb wage-earners; they wanted journalism to resemble a profession as much as possible.

They are *not licensed*. For the U.S. at least, this is held to be incompatible with freedom of speech. Is information so unimportant that, contrary to medicine, it can be left to incompetents and quacks? Are Italian reporters shackled who are required to be members of an Order of Journalists? Be that as it may, unless journalists are free-lancers (and not many are), they are *not independent*. News people are keenly aware that their employment and promotion are not in their control. In most cases, they are not even protected by a union. Such facts are too often left aside when ethics is discussed. Nevertheless, informally, American journalists have come quite close, closer than any other group of journalists, to fulfilling several requirements for a profession, such as specialized higher education, guild-like associations, and codified ethical standards.

Because journalists are now better educated, they are more aware of their duties in society and of the fundamental importance of those duties in the post-industrial era. More of them wish to fulfill their function properly. More are eager to deserve and obtain social prestige. In that quest, many may suffer from the sins of a few. Black and female journalists certainly did not appreciate the Janet Cooke caper. Obviously it would be safer and better for every newsperson to be educated, encouraged, pressured into behaving as ethically as possible. A further, and essential, benefit would be more total support by the public for freedom of the press against constant governmental threats—hence a better chance for democracy to be preserved.

Well, not quite. A first point I wish to make is that (a) ethics is largely irrelevant in the American media world and (b) journalistic ethics, or rather violations of it, are being used, perhaps unwittingly, as a cover-up for what is most seriously wrong about American media. Practical ethics consist of rules of behavior. These normally derive from a set of moral principles. A given individual subscribes to those principles because they correspond to a satisfying vision of man and the universe he or she has. Hence it is his/her conscience, not immediately the fear of being punished, that will compel him/her to comply with the rules. Because some people's consciences are less forceful than is desirable, reinforcement by external moral pressure is sometimes needed. This works through peers, because of the individual's need to be accepted and respected.

Now I have two questions:

1. In a corporation, whether it be a media company or any other, are major policy decisions made at the top or at rank-and-file level?
2. For making those decisions, is the major criterion economics or ethics?

Rhetorical questions, of course. One does not need to be a very close analyst of the business world to know the answers. In a corporation (especially a public one whose thousands of shareholders have only a financial stake in it) a top executive, himself an employee, usually does not, cannot, *should not* consider anything but the survival, profitability, and expansion of the firm he manages. That is the corporate rule. As was made clear during the Gilded Age, in the absence of governmental regulation ethics is basically irrelevant to business. Some firms, I hasten to add, have discovered that, on a long-term basis, ethical behavior was profitable, just as quality in the product, or rather as part of that very quality. It is often, though not always, under external pressure that they make the discovery.

An ethical behavior? The usual definition of this seems not at all the same for a reporter and for a media company. A journalist who can be bribed into killing a story is certainly unethical. But what of a radio station that opts to increase its revenues by not hiring the extra journalist it needs to give a full report of local affairs? It is indisputably ethical to ban freebies and junkets for reporters, but what of media which omit to report information affecting big advertisers negatively, e.g. (since the 1930s) medical evidence of the dangers of tobacco? It is considered unethical in the U.S. for a journalist to let his political (often progressive) persuasion show in his stories, but why is it perfectly acceptable for a large majority of newspapers actively to support the more conservative candidate in just about every presidential election?

Janet Cooke passed off as authentic a character she had invented so as to symbolize a real situation. That is unethical. She wanted her byline on the front-page, a prize, a promotion, whatever. She knew what would please: real-life, personal, extra-ordinary drama—and what would not please: another data-laden report about ghetto squalor and misery. I agree, a lie is a lie, even though what you seek to express, deep down, is the truth. Now, on the other hand, consider the hundreds of media companies which for years ignored disease and famine in Africa because they would not spend the money to maintain correspondents in that part of the world and because their only purpose, as that of any whore, is not to serve but to please customers, who happen not to be interested in the Third World. *Whore* may be judged too strong a word. The author of *The Brass Check* (1919) being an unquotable radical, let me turn to Britain for an authority. It was Prime Minister Stanley Baldwin who accused the popular press of enjoying power without responsibility, the prerogative of the harlot throughout the ages. Ignorance of the Third World might be what the public desires, but is it moral? Is it humanly responsible? More important, maybe, is it good for the American people? Vietnam and Iran seem to have proved it is not.

The commercial media's hooking of audiences to be sold to advertisers, using various means, from "happy talk" TV news to Life Style sections in dailies, is better, after all, than the earlier enslavement of the press to the powers-that-be, as denounced by Will Irwin in the first decade of this century. And it pays. The media make enormous profits. (See B.H. Bagdikian, *The Media Monopoly*, Boston: Beacon, 1983). That embarrassing wealth was a well-kept secret for a long time. How could it be now, when (in 1985) a daily newspaper, with a circulation of 240,000, is bought for $165 million and a television station is bought for over $500 million and when media corporations have become the object of multi-billion dollar takeover bids? The profitability of almost all media in the U.S. is a unique phenomenon in the world. The fact has to be underlined. It is, I believe, central to any discussion of media ethics. The customer orientation of media, on the other hand, judging from surveys made over the past few years, has not made American readers, listeners, and viewers extremely pleased with the media. They do not feel they are served as they should be. To sum up, media make a lot of money *without* serving their customers adequately.

What is ethical is what serves the public, be it news, entertainment, or even educational material (though commercial media rarely provide any)—as opposed to what merely keeps the public quiet and happy. Of course, those who do the serving, public servants in the noblest sense of the term, are the journalists and television producers as a whole. But they can do little properly unless they are trained for it, authorized to do it, inspired to do it, and decently funded. All that will, or will not, be provided, depending on the policy of the media firms.

As I said before, corporations cannot be ethical or unethical: They can keep within the law or step beyond it. But a corporation can decide whether to make it possible for its employees to be ethical. A journalist had better not use a free seat at a play he has been assigned to review, but will his publisher pay for the ticket? A journalist had better not reveal his sources, but will the station cover his legal expense? Even without perfectionist ambitions, being ethical can be very expensive. Maybe only the exceptionally wealthy American media could be strictly ethical and remain wealthy, though much less than they are now. Elsewhere? In Mexico, most journalists cannot survive without taking a second (sometimes a third) job, often with an advertiser or a news source.

Certainly there are sins that belong to journalists alone. If they are ignorant, naive, lazy, sloppy, cowardly, vain, over-ambitious, prejudiced, dishonest, greedy—whatever professional faults derive from such failings are their own. Some of those people will soon be fired by a watchful editor. Certainly lack of ethical education and awareness, lack of ethical guidelines and reinforcement by peers in the newsroom and within professional association can lead to very poor journalism, of the kind practiced by the weekly tabloids.

But whatever the hundreds or thousands of sins that individual journalists may commit, do they compare sins, mainly sins of omission? To a European observer, it seems incredible that American newspeople spend so much time and energy discussing ethics, i.e. the failings of the individual journalist—as if the poor wretch was truly in charge. It is certainly bad:

- to misspell somebody's name and get a person's age wrong,
- to invade the privacy of a grief-stricken family,
- to publish the name of the victim of a rape,
- to distort the meaning of a speech, by misquoting it.

But as violations of ethics, meaning "disservice to the public," can anyone, even for a second, dream of comparing them with corporate behavior of the two following kinds:

1. When media corporations for many years block the development of new means of communication to protect their vested interests, as

was the case with FM radio, the UHF television band and, later cable television;

2. When media do not provide coverage of news that will not interest their richer customers, or might upset them or advertisers or fellow corporations. Examples: the coverage of Blacks before the 1960s and of prisons now. Or again, the coverage of the arms industry or of corporate crime.

The discrepancy between the anti-social behavior of journalists and that of corporations is such that the talk about ethics can sometimes sound totally vacuous. Worse, such talk may be dangerous. Is it not a ploy to steer public dissatisfaction onto scapegoats, the media (semi-) professionals? Reds, traitors, nabobs of negativism, trespassers, libelers—the carriers of unpleasant news always get it in the neck. The apparent strategy is to make them feel like true professionals (which they are not allowed to be).

That, however, is not the whole story. Ethics is also a soft, slow yet very efficient weapon in the hands of media people. I believe that, coupled with expertise in social communications, it is their best weapon. To assume as fully as possible their responsibilities as professionals, media workers need autonomy. Their No. 1 goal is not to increase corporate revenues but to serve the various groups that make up the public. But, being employees, they cannot oppose their employers openly, except (for some of them) as members of The Newspaper Guild. But that labor union has not often struggled for anything beyond better wages and working conditions. The best way to obtain autonomy is to work as first-class craftsmen. Thus can they provide profits to their profit-obsessed employers and keep them off their backs. The commercialism of U.S. media provides journalists with a paradoxical advantage: Most owners have invested in media for the money, not to assist a political career, preach an ideology, or obtain personal fame. The situation is quite different in Europe.

By providing unexceptionable journalistic service, media people win the support of the public for the media as a business, of course, but also for the Fourth Estate as an institution—and for themselves as independent experts. If undue pressure is ever exerted on them by the media corporation, they must be in a position to resist it by standing on their professionalism. They must certainly excel at observing events, interviewing people, orchestrating data, explaining facts, writing stories. But they must also be ethically impeccable. One Janet Cooke, one negligent *Time* reporter in Beirut (Sharon case), and one CBS producer who ignores standards of fairness (Westmoreland case), and the whole profession hurts: Irresponsible behavior translates into loss of autonomy.

Even now, American interest in media ethics makes for better service to the public both directly and indirectly. This becomes obvious if you contrast the U.S. media to those of countries in which ethics is irrelevant, such as communist or Third World nations, where all media are government-related agencies run by civil servants to propagate the instructions of the central government to all party members. The quality of U.S. media also appears high by comparison with media in nations where ethics is not much of an issue yet, for partisan or mercantile reasons. The American daily press, for instance, is free of gutter sheets like the London *Sun* (circ. 4 million) or the West German *Bild Zeitung* (circ. 5 million). And the (money-losing) *New York Post* stands as an example not to follow.

Together with better training, to which it is closely related anyway, interest in ethics seems to me to have been a major cause of the clear improvement of American media over the past 20 years. The U.S. system is now by far the "least worse" in the world. It is not very good, assuredly, considering the resources available, but it is better than it used to be and it is better (on the whole) than all the others. It must be noted that during that period, few, if any, national media systems on earth have improved, except in some countries that have turned from fascist dictatorships into democracies, such as Spain or Argentina.

Ethics, however, must be considered in context and perspective. While the commercialism of U.S. media partly accounts for their wealth and their wealth partly accounts for their quality (including ethical quality), the quasi-total commercialism is also the major source of imperfection for U.S. media. Neither the public nor the media people should forget or ignore it. Certainly one unthinkable alternative, i.e. media entirely owned and operated by government, would be infinitely worse. But another alternative is true competition between noncommercial media and commercial media. Broadcasting in Japan and Britain provides an excellent illustration of it. Actually more commercial media are now appearing in European democracies, as technology and public opinion force governments to relinquish the traditional State monopoly on broadcasting. Thus competition can play its very positive function, within a mixed system. And Europeans, far more than Americans, still trust to legislation and regulation to keep commercial media from the most serious sins. Apparently, they have a less optimistic concept of man and are more skeptical about any natural inclination of business towards public service.

What this whole essay points to is that in the U.S., interest in media ethics should not be looked upon as short-lived counter-offensive in reaction to a surge of public distrust—as previously it was a response to radical criticism. It must not be left to degenerate into a public relations gambit. It must be more and more widely acknowledged as a sign that communication professionals are gradually taking over, people motivated by a fierce appetite, not for money or power, but for the prestige, the authority, the satisfaction that come from high quality public service. If their slow, glacier-like progress continues, not only will American media be the first to become excellent, meaning truly democratic—but they will have opened an original and great way for other nations.

10 Those Newsroom Ethics Codes

by Karen Schneider, Marc Gunther

> Codes alone won't guarantee ethical performance, the
> authors write. "What is required is fair and thorough re-
> porting and vigilant editing...professionalism on the job."
> Karen Schneider is a copy editor and reporter at the *Detroit
> Free Press*. Marc Gunter is television critic of *The Detroit
> News*. Their article is from *Columbia Journalism Review*,
> July/August 1985.

Want to run for public office? March in an antinuke rally? Sign a petition? If
you work for the *Los Angeles Times*, and the answer is yes, you'd "be in big
trouble," editor William F. Thomas says. Thomas warned against such
activism in a code of ethics he wrote for the *Times* in 1982. "It's bad for a
Times person to be involved on one side of a very emotional issue," he says.
"All you've got is your reputation. You're selling your reputation every
day."

It's a long way from L.A. to Burlington, Wisconsin, where William E.
Branen, publisher and former editor of the *Burlington Standard Press*,
worked last fall for Friends of Reagan-Bush, a national organization of
newspaper executives. Branen calls it a "terrible mistake" when journalists
refuse to get involved in their communities. "That's why many large newspapers are going down the drain," he says. "They've lost contact with their
readers."

But Branen would seem to be in a minority. A growing number of
newspapers and television stations have recently been promulgating
written codes governing newsroom conduct and specifying what reporters
and editors (and, in some instances, their spouses) are permitted to do on
their own time. In 1974, an Associated Press Managing Editors survey
found that fewer than one in ten newspapers had such codes. Nine years
later, by contrast, three out of four news organizations replying to a questionnaire by Ohio University journalism professor Ralph Izard said they had
written policies governing newsroom standards and practices.

The obvious purpose of such codes is to prevent conflicts of interest.
"They serve as a reminder, a constant flag within the newsroom, that ethical conduct is a primary concern here every day," *Chicago Tribune* editor
James D. Squires says. But Squires acknowledges that ethics codes also are
good public relations. "The codes are symbols," he says. "They are signals

to the public that we are concerned about our own behavior." Managing editor Pete Weitzel of *The Miami Herald*, who recently wrote his paper's first code of ethics, agrees. "Newspapers have a credibility problem," he says. "If people trust and respect your paper, believe in your paper, they are more likely to buy your newspaper."

Writing a code is a fairly simple—and noncontroversial—job when it comes to such questions as whether journalists should accept gifts, favors, free tickets, or travel from news sources. At big papers, at least, most editors and reporters oppose such practices. And few would argue with the lofty sentiments expressed in introductions to the codes. This one from ABC News is typical: employees "must refrain from doing any act or following any course of conduct which would permit their objectivity in the performance of their duties to be either challenged or impaired."

Disagreement surfaces, however, when the codes reach into areas that some reporters believe are nobody's business but their own. Most codes cover part-time employment, free-lance writing, and participation in political and community affairs, reflecting the belief of many editors that readers view a reporter as an extension of his or her newspaper—even when the reporter is acting as a private citizen.

Observance of ethics codes often requires the sacrifice of some personal freedoms. But Charles W. Bailey, former editor of the *Minneapolis Star and Tribune*, argues that it is quite legitimate for a news organization to require such sacrifices. "Pay no attention," he wrote in a report on ethics codes commissioned by the National News Council, "to those who argue that rules restricting political involvement, community activism, or questionable outside employment are somehow a deprivation of individual rights. [Reporters] are not forfeiting their rights; they are temporarily suspending the exercise of some of them."

That strict view is reflected in many codes. At the *Chicago Tribune*, journalists who run for office risk losing their newsroom assignments. NBC News says it will discipline employees who speak publicly on a controversial issue, while at *The Philadelphia Inquirer* staff members are warned against "wearing an antiwar button at a rally."

Some journalists have strenuously resisted such restrictions, arguing, among other things, that getting involved in their communities rounds them out as journalists. Humor columnist John Hinterberger of *The Seattle Times* decided in 1981 to run for the obscure post of water commissioner, figuring he could perform a little public service and also get some new material for his column. "I believe firmly that journalists should be involved in their communities at all levels except to where that involvement clearly compromises their integrity," Hinterberger says. "I think people should run for the school board, the library board, parks commission.... We're better journalists to the extent that we are participating in society."

Besides, the nonpaid, nonpartisan job of water commissioner was unlikely to generate controversy. "All you do is sit and watch the pipes rust," says Hinterberger, a twenty-year veteran at the *Times*.

His editors disagreed. "When you run for office, we feel you are choosing another vocation," says *Times* executive editor James B. King. "We can't see that you can be an unbiased journalist and also a city councilperson."

It was too late to drop out of the race, so Hinterberger, in one of his columns, begged his readers, "Please don't vote for me!" Fortunately, they obliged. (A year later, Hinterberger was vindicated when an arbitrator ruled that the newspaper's prohibition against running for office violated its contract with The Newspaper Guild.)

Knoxville News-Sentinel reporter Jacquelyn McClary also won a grievance against her paper—and won back her job—in 1984 after she was fired for winning election to the Alcoa, Tennessee, school board. McClary, who didn't cover education or the town of Alcoa but who has three children in Alcoa schools, was told by her editor that he wouldn't give permission for her to run for office. "I regarded that statement in the same way as I would regard my father's statement that he couldn't give me permission to marry," she says. "If I wanted to do it, I would."

Television reporters with a yen for public office may run into trouble too, as Bill Branch, a reporter for KOVR-TV in Sacramento, learned when he tried to run for the Loomis village council last year. Branch was halted, not by his bosses, but by a Federal Communications Commission rule that would have required the station to grant equal time to his opponents every time he appeared on the air.

Branch has petitioned the FCC to drop the rule. "Once in a lifetime there comes that one moment when you say my duty as a citizen outweighs my duty as a journalist," he says.

Some news organizations with codes of ethics, it should be noted, are relatively permissive about community and political involvement. Employees at *The Boston Globe* need written permission to run for office but "are generally free to engage in political activities." *The New York Times* says it "wants to leave room for staff members to do creative, community, or personal work and to earn additional income in ways that are separate and distinguishable from their work at the paper."

Newsroom codes are silent on the subject of religion. But Garry Moes, a born-again Christian now on leave from The Associated Press, for which he covered the Montana state government, was reassigned to a desk job last fall after an interview in which he outlined his religious views was published in a Christian newspaper.

"I don't believe it is appropriate for a reporter to proselytize or serve as a missionary, no matter how admirable the cause," AP executive editor

Walter R. Mears said. The AP returned Moes to the capitol beat, however, after he threatened to file a $1 million lawsuit claiming that his religious freedom had been curbed. (Earlier, Moes had been barred from writing about abortion after his wife and father became identified with anti-abortion activities.)

Moes's case is unusual, but journalists are grappling every day with a more common problem—namely, what kinds of after-hours jobs and assignments reporters can properly take on.

Both ABC News and *The New York Times* bar their editorial employees from accepting paid speaking engagements from groups they cover. But, as George Watson, vice president of ABC News, says, "If you're a correspondent covering the Supreme Court, the speaking invitations tend to come from legal groups. Does that constitute a conflict?"

The *Times*, for its part, objected when national security correspondent Leslie H. Gelb was listed as a "foreign relations consultant" by Paine Webber Inc. But the paper permits Gelb, who no longer has the title, to be paid for speaking at six to eight meetings a year sponsored by the brokerage firm.

"Reporters ought to be able to speak to whatever groups they choose," Gelb says. "It's up to them and the editors to see that no conflicts are produced in stories." But, he adds, "If you're about to do a series of articles on the aircraft industry, I would hardly accept a fee to go speak to the aircraft association. If you did, you're either a damn fool or worse."

The existence of a conflict of interest is not always as easy to establish as in the case outlined by Gelb. Frank O'Brien, a photographer at *The Boston Globe* and a self-described baseball nut, filed a grievance when the paper told him he couldn't take pictures for the Boston Red Sox, whom he rarely covers. An arbitrator ruled against him.

O'Brien says he accepts the ruling, but he is puzzled at the vigor with which the *Globe* pursued the case: "They had lawyers crawling all over this building for a week prior to the hearing," he says. "You'd think I was the worst criminal that had come down the pike."

"He would [have been] on the payroll of the Red Sox and we felt there would be an appearance of a conflict of interest," S.J. Micciche, *Globe* associate editor, says. Typically, ethics codes prohibit apparent conflicts as well as direct ones.

Many codes extend their rules to journalists' spouses. Their provisions vary widely. While *The Washington Post* code says that relatives "cannot fairly be subject to Post rules," CBS News holds all employees responsible for ensuring that no family members come into conflict with its policy.

At *The Seattle Times*, managing editor Michael R. Fancher was told he would be transferred out of the newsroom if his wife accepted a job as press secretary to the city's mayor. She resigned from the job after one day. On the other hand, John Corry continues to review TV shows—including programs carried on public television—for *The New York Times* while his wife, Sonia Landau, serves as chairman of the Corporation for Public Broad-casting, which funds some public-television programming. And Charles Bailey, as editor for the *Minneapolis Star and Tribune*, told his staff that it was none of his business when his wife made a large contribution to a U.S. Senate candidate.

Neither ABC nor correspondent Bettina Gregory had a problem when her husband, John Flannery, declared his candidacy for a Virginia congressional seat in December 1983. Gregory, who usually covers regulatory agencies, was even assigned for a while to Gary Hart's presidential campaign. "A con-gressional primary in Virginia is a far cry from covering the national political scene," she says.

When Flannery won the Democratic primary, Gregory says she couldn't help getting involved. She took a leave of absence from Labor Day through mid-November to manage her husband's unsuccessful campaign. Now, she says, "I've come back to the network, and I don't have any problems."

While many working journalists accept the need for written codes of ethics, their promulgation reflects a double standard, since publishers—and often top editors as well—are free to do as they please. Hundreds of publishers serve on local boards of directors, lead charity drives, and support arts groups. "The pressure is very intense to serve in the com-munity," says Russell G. D'Oench, Jr., editor and co-owner of the Middle-town, Connecticut, *Press*, a 21,000-circulation daily.

D'Oench sits on the boards of, among other organizations, a local insurance company, a hospital, and United Way. He also is chairman of a powerful commission that governs the state's colleges. "I'm into so many things my conflicts are self-cancelling," D'Oench says with a laugh. But he also believes that "you don't resign from the human race when you join a newspaper."

While D'Oench, whose paper has only a sketchy written code, says he hasn't sought the limelight, other news executives have intentionally thrust themselves into controversial stories. The *St. Petersburg Times*, which says it will fire any journalist with a conflict of interest, helped finance a 1978 campaign to keep casino gambling out of Florida. (*Times* chairman Eugene C. Patterson, while continuing to insist that community involvement is a good thing, says that the paper won't contribute money to causes again because of the controversy that was stirred up in the newsroom.)

Many newspapers also have corporate ties. The *Chicago Tribune*, for example, is owned by the same company that owns the Chicago Cubs. And while *Tribune* editor Squires insists that, if anything, this has worked to the detriment of the ball club—"The Cubs have a hard time getting a fair break in the *Tribune*," he says—this view has not gone unchallenged. The *Los Angeles Times*'s Thomas says of the *Tribune*-Cubs connection, "That's the worst of all. My God, how does anybody believe your sports section?"

Publishers argue that they must get involved in their communities to protect their investment in their newspapers. But reporters and editors have stakes in their communities, too, and should be permitted to exercise their rights as citizens—as long as that doesn't pose a direct conflict. Since publishers are unlikely to submit themselves to codes barring outside business, civic, or political interests, and since a double standard for employees will thus persist, is there any point in having codes at all? The answer is probably a qualified yes.

For no matter what a publisher does outside the office, readers are clearly being shortchanged if, for example, a reporter is on the payroll of a real estate developer whose projects he is covering, as was the case not long ago at *The Jersey Journal*. . . . Similarly, it is a bad idea for a reporter to cover city hall if his or her spouse is the mayor's press secretary. And news organizations ought to let their staff members know what is acceptable and what is not from the outset—not after a conflict has occurred.

The danger is that news organizations, in their zeal to demonstrate their purity, will reach too far into the personal lives of their employees by regulating outside activities that pose no real conflict. Reshuffling newsroom assignments in the face of a possible conflict might be a fairer solution than prohibiting political or civic activities.

As for the industry's concerns about its image problems, codes of ethics alone will not restore the public's trust. What is required is fair and thorough reporting and vigilant editing—in short, professionalism on the job. Putting out a good newspaper or newscast, of course, is a lot harder than drafting an ethics code. But improving the performance of reporters and editors will pay more dividends than worrying about what they do once they've left the office.

11 AIDS: Reporting the Tragedy

by Margaret Genovese

The age-old question of privacy versus the need to know gets a new test almost every time the news media consider covering stories about Acquired Immune Deficiency Syndrome (AIDS) patients. Margaret Genovese describes early news coverage and poses anew what the media might do. The article is from *presstime*, December 1986.

A prominent public figure in Anytown, USA, is rumored as having acquired immune deficiency syndrome, better known as AIDS. Does the local newspaper publish the story?

A private citizen dies of complications from AIDS. Should the obituary mention AIDS?

Some people with the disease have made a point of publicizing the fact, including one daily newspaper editor. And there appears to be an emerging trend for survivors to acknowledge AIDS as the cause of death. But other AIDS victims and their families prefer to keep it secret, in large measure because so far in the United States the killer disease has predominantly struck homosexual and bisexual men and intravenous drug users.

This much is certain: The toll for AIDS victims will increase, and as it does, so will the ethical dilemma for editors on whether, how and when to identify them.

So far, there does not seem to be any consensus on this issue. Even individual editors are not sure what their newspaper's policy should be.

For example, following the death of a prominent Bostonian, reporters for *The Boston Globe* talked to the man's family, close friends and doctors but were unable to confirm widespread rumors that he had AIDS. "Therefore, we never knew it" for certain, says City Editor Kirk Scharfenberg, "and, therefore, never had to confront the next question"—whether to publish the information.

In the case of private citizens, the *Globe* would abide by survivors' wishes and not publish such information if they so requested, according to Scharfenberg. However, the *Globe* has no policy on prominent people, and Scharfenberg admits, "I don't know what is the right policy." On one hand, he says, it is important to get word out that "real people" have AIDS. On the other hand, it is important to respect a person's privacy.

The potential magnitude of this growing problem for editors comes into better focus when the statistics and projections for AIDS victims are examined. According to the federal Centers for Disease Control in Atlanta, 26,875 cases of AIDS has been reported as of late October—and 56 percent of these had resulted in death. In the next five years, the number of AIDS cases is expected to increase tenfold—including a greater number as a result of heterosexual contact. The CDC estimates that by the end of 1991, about 270,000 people will have contracted the disease and about 179,000 of them will have died.

Among the Living

The AIDS story is "just fraught with extraordinary issues" both within and outside of the newsroom, says Bob Mong, assistant city editor of *The Dallas Morning News*. According to the CDC, the Dallas metropolitan area currently has the 10th highest number of reported cases of AIDS in the United States, 460.

"We have vigorously covered individual cases. We've covered the phenomenon. We've tried to stay up-to-date on the medical situation," says Mong.

However, the newspaper has yet to encounter a situation where it ascertained that a prominent resident had contracted the disease but declined to acknowledge so publicly. If that did happen, says Mong, someone from the *Morning News* staff would probably talk to the victim and to his or her family. "It's such an explosive, sensitive topic, we would want to be compassionate about it and try to get some sense about how they feel about it."

Other editors say the question of whether to print such a story would depend on the prominence of the person and whether the information could be verified.

"It depends on who it is," says Richard Harwood, deputy managing editor of *The Washington Post*. "If we knew that President Reagan had AIDS, I'm sure we would report it." But, he adds, "there are a great many people who have terminal diseases that we don't customarily publicize."

"It all depends on degree of prominence," agrees Kent D. Bernhard, executive editor of the *Detroit Free Press*. "If it is a person who is known among a real small circle of people, but very well known, likely not. If it were a person who would be a major, major political figure who was ill, probably so. *If* I knew it.

"The thing is," he continues, "on the condition of anyone's health— whatever the illness would be—I would need to make certain we absolutely knew it, and I am a tough person to convince on a lot of scores."

Like Mong, Bernhard says he would approach the person and invite him or her to discuss the illness. "If we are talking about an extraordinarily prominent person—among the most visible people in a state, let's say, or a region—I think it would beg credulity to feel that that person would not at some point...acknowledge the illness. If you are a governor or mayor or president of a major corporation, that is just not the type of thing that will stay out of the public prints because you are too prominent."

But what if the person denies having the disease? "It's tough to report that they have it when they are denying it," says Larry W. Tarleton, executive editor of the *Dallas Times Herald*. "I don't think we'd do that."

However, if the person died and a knowledgeable person came forward and said the victim had suffered from AIDS, Tarleton says he would report that, along with the victim's previous denial.

Recent Examples

One of the very few cases in which a prominent living person was reported to have had AIDS was that of Perry Ellis, a New York fashion designer who died last May at the age of 46. The *Daily News* in New York reported on Ellis' hospitalization and said a hospital spokeswoman would not comment on reports by friends that the designer was suffering from AIDS.

In its obituary on Ellis, *Newsday* also mentioned speculation in the fashion industry that he was suffering from AIDS. "It had become such a widely rumored thing that his company had put out a disclaimer saying he didn't have AIDS," says *Newsday* Executive Editor Anthony Marro.

On the other hand, neither the *New York Post* nor *The New York Times* mentioned AIDS in the coverage of Ellis' death. Both cited the cause of death as "viral encephelitis" [*sic*].

"We, in no case, will report AIDS on the basis of a rumor or public speculation, no matter how rife that speculation might be," says Leonard Harris, a spokesman for the *Times*.

There are three situations in which the *Times* will report AIDS as the cause of death, Harris says: If a hospital spokesman says so, if the family says so, or if the decreased person has made the request in advance of death that the disease be identified.

One of those situations existed in August when Roy M. Cohn, a widely known New York lawyer, died at the age of 59. The *Times'* obituary quoted a spokesperson for the National Institutes of Health, where Cohn was being treated, as saying that the immediate cause of his death was cardiopulmonary arrest and that the death certificate also listed two secondary causes, dementia and "underlying HTLV-3 infections."

The next paragraph explained that most scientists "believe the HTLV-3 virus is the cause of AIDS." Finally, the *Times* obit reported that in newspaper and television interviews Cohn had repeatedly denied widespread rumors that his treatment at the federal hospital was the result of AIDS; he said he had liver cancer.

The Cohn case raised another issue, the use of medical records to confirm AIDS. About a week before Cohn's death, syndicated columnists Jack Anderson and Dale Van Atta reported that Cohn was suffering from AIDS, quoting from confidential medical records obtained by Van Atta.

William Cox, a former managing editor of the *Honolulu Star-Bulletin* who disclosed last summer in a front-page column in the newspaper that he was suffering from AIDS, worries that if the press begins trying aggressively to identify who has AIDS, state governments will enact tougher privacy laws making it harder for the press to do its job.

"I don't think we ought to be snooping into hospital records, laboratory records and doctors' records. I think we are asking for big trouble with the public if we start doing that," he said in an Oct. 24 presentation to the Associated Press Managing Editors convention in Cincinnati.

Cox said he came forward about his illness because he is a journalist "who just couldn't live with saying 'no comment' to my friends and colleagues and others in the media" and because he wanted to "fight the stigma that comes from this damned disease." But, he added, "not everyone can be as open as I was.... There are people who don't want to be denied their livelihood or the support that usually is given by friends or family to people who are sick. I hope that we in the press aren't going to try to make that decision for them, that we're going to reveal that somebody has AIDS."

Cause of Death

At some newspapers, the question of whether to list AIDS as the cause of death in the case of an ordinary citizen is moot. The *Kansas City Star*, for example, does not usually list the cause in its obituaries, according to City Editor Darryl W. Levings. That policy would not change in the case of AIDS, he says, "If I knew somebody died of cancer and I don't traditionally put that in, why would I go out of my way to put the person died of AIDS if I knew that?"

At the *San Francisco Chronicle*, the cause of death is always asked, says Edwin Epstein, deputy city editor. But if the family does not want it in the obituary, the newspaper abides by those wishes, whether the cause of death is "cancer or cirrhosis or AIDS."

The *Atlanta Journal* and *The Atlanta Constitution* include the cause of death in obituaries when it can be obtained. But it is his understanding, says Managing Editor Glenn McCutchen, that AIDS "is seldom, if ever listed as the cause of death." That is so because AIDS is caused by a virus that weakens the body's immune system and leaves it vulnerable to infection and disease, particularly pneumonia and cancer, which may then be given as the cause of death.

In the case of private citizens, few newspapers go beyond what is supplied by the family or funeral home to discover whether the underlying cause of death was AIDS.

The *Washington Post* is one newspaper that has assumed an aggressive policy in giving AIDS as cause of death in obituaries. Unlike some other big-city newspapers that run news obituaries only on prominent people, the *Post* will publish a news obit of "any private person who's lived in this community, in the way of being a permanent resident, for a substantial part of a lifetime regardless of rank, status or achievement," says obituary editor Joe Smith....

However, the paper's policy is to publish the cause of death in all cases, including that of AIDS victims. "We are not in a position of treating people differently," Smith says. If survivors request that the cause of death not be published, the Post gives them the option of canceling the obit request.

When the newspaper suspects the cause of death is AIDS, it will raise the question. "If we get an obituary of say, a 36-year-old man, and we are told he died of pneumonia and he's never been married, I'd be suspicious," says Smith. "I think any reasonable person would be suspicious because 36-year-old people don't normally die of pneumonia."

If the person requesting the obituary denies that AIDS is the cause of death and the obituary writer is still suspicious, the Post will check further. Smith declines to say by what means. He emphasizes, however, that the Post never publishes a news obit for a private person saying he or she died of AIDS without telling survivors first and permitting them the option of withdrawing the obit.

An attorney working with AIDS victims in Washington strongly opposes the *Post*'s policy. Mauro A. Montoya Jr., legal services coordinator for the Whitman-Walker Clinic, thinks obituaries of AIDS victims should be run, without cause of death, if that is survivors' preference.

Lori Behrman, public information director for the Gay Men's Health Crisis Inc. in New York City, believes obits should list AIDS as the cause of death. While it's "very important to respect families' wishes," she also says that covering up the cause of death "makes this disease shameful to people, and it makes people think that there's something to hide when you have AIDS, and that's not the case."

Burr Van Atta, obituary writer for *The Philadelphia Inquirer*, says he has seen "a great deal" of change in the past year in the willingness of survivors to publicize AIDS as the cause of death.

"That's not an unusual position in many cases, whether you are talking about AIDS or cancer or brain tumors," he says. "The family will hope by making a point of announcing the cause to get support for research in the field—in other words, turn the death into a positive thing."

12 When a Public Figure's Private Life Is News

by Carl Sessions Stepp

This article and the one that follows were published under the heading "Tough Calls" in *Washington Journalism Review*, December 1986. Carl Sessions Stepp, a former reporter and editor who teaches journalism at the University of Maryland, probes news coverage of public figures and asks how private a public person can be.

Psst: Want to hear some juicy news the press has not reported? For example:

- The story about the Michigan politician who showed up at a campaign rally the night after his son had committed suicide.
- The story about the presidential candidate's reputation as a womanizer and the evidence to support it.
- The details about the prominent figure in an Oklahoma criminal case who cavorted nude at a hotel swimming-pool party.

Why haven't you read these stories in your papers or heard them on the air? Because they all concern the personal lives of prominent people, and editors and producers did not consider them relevant to public issues.

The *Detroit Free Press* did not write about the Michigan politician who attended a campaign rally after his son's suicide because an editor vetoed publication, arguing, "People deal with their grief in different ways," according to then-assistant managing editor Stephen Seplow. (Seplow, incidentally, now disagrees: he thinks the incident *should* have been reported because it showed "a guy that was out of touch with reality.")

The *Washington Post* did not pursue a story about a reputed womanizer running for president because "what we had, had absolutely nothing to do with fitness for office," says Managing Editor Leonard Downie, Jr.

The *Tulsa Tribune* did not report on the nude revels of a prominent figure in an Oklahoma criminal case because "it wasn't relevant," says Mary Hargrove, the paper's special-projects editor.

Some private incidents in the lives of public people *do*, of course, make it to the printed page or to the airwaves. For example:

- In July and August this year, Jack Anderson wrote columns about the illness of the late Roy Cohn, including reports that he was suffering from AIDS. (Mike Wallace had reported a related story in March on "60 Minutes.")
- Chicago's WMAQ-TV in August broadcast allegations that a Chicago-area U.S. marshal had taken home confiscated pornographic materials for his personal use. The Chicago newspapers, the *Tribune* and *Sun-Times*, covered it later.
- In March, the *Birmingham* (Alabama) *News* reported allegations that state cars had been used to transport a female reporter to Lieutenant Governor Bill Baxley's apartment, and later referred to an "apparent close personal relationship" between the reporter and the married politician.

Even when producers and editors decide to go forward with such stories about public people, they usually do so only after intense discussions among themselves and with their lawyers. Peter Karl, investigative reporter for WMAQ-TV, remembers long discussions with reporter Paul Hogan and producer Marsha Bartel, who reported the U.S. marshal story, before his station aired it. "We sat down for hours before and during this story," Karl says, "and talked about, 'Is this fair? Is this right? Should we do this?'"

John R. Finnegan, editor of the *St. Paul Pioneer Press* and *Dispatch*, describes the dilemma his paper faced in April this year when a well-known local high-school athlete hanged himself in a school building. Although newspapers often do not write about or identify the young people involved in such personal tragedies, this one involved a prominent young man and drew wide attention. So the *Pioneer Press* and *Dispatch* wrote about the boy's suicide on April 22, but withheld his name. "This was a private act. I could not see any major public value to be served," he says. Across town, the *Minneapolis Star and Tribune* the next day *did* name the boy because, says Managing Editor Tim J. McGuire, "It was the second very visible student athlete in a local high school who had killed himself within three or four months." The paper also decided to go forward with the story because of "the extremely public nature of what he had done and where he had done it," says McGuire.

Although journalists interviewed by *WJR* disagreed over particular public-figure/private-life cases, they all believe the press has become increasingly aggressive in poking into the lives of public figures.

"Where you draw the line is getting more and more difficult," says St. Paul's Finnegan, who also chairs the ethics committee of the American Society of Newspaper Editors. "But in the last few years there has been greater willingness to use this kind of information. Editors are more willing to cross the line."

"Fifteen or 20 years ago, there was more a sense that these issues weren't going to be put in the paper," says Heath Meriwether, executive editor of the *Miami Herald*. "There's less sanctity now. There's more public discussion of heretofore taboo subjects."

Leonard Downie says that not too long ago the press ignored "people stone-cold drunk on the floor of Congress." And other private excesses of politicians went unreported. "John F. Kennedy's womanizing when he was in the White House, which now clearly had national-security implications, was not pursued by reporters contemporaneously," Downie says.

"I'm very sympathetic to what it means to be thrust into the public eye," says Downie. "It changes your life and it's difficult to live with, and we must be sensitive to that. At the same time, I'm impatient with people who thrust themselves aggressively into public positions—and that includes senior executives in private corporations who have sway over people's lives. It is quite unreasonable for these people to not be held publicly accountable."

A turning point in the debate may have been the 1974 Tidal Basin escapade of House Ways and Means Committee chairman Wilbur Mills and strip-tease dancer Fanne Foxe, which was widely reported and caused Mills to admit he was an alcoholic and seek treatment. After the Mills story, Downie and other editors say, the press has been less willing to overlook such conduct.

On what grounds do editors decide when to publish private material about public figures? Almost uniformly, editors say they do so when the material can be verified and can be shown to affect the individual's public performance.

For his part, veteran *Washington Post* investigative reporter Howard Kurtz says, "I like to stick to job-related criteria." Stephen Seplow, now metropolitan editor at the *Philadelphia Inquirer*, puts it less delicately: "I don't care if a judge is going out and getting laid. I do care if he's getting laid with a defense attorney or prosecutor."

Publishing almost any story or photograph can be rationalized by the argument that it tells something about an individual's character, according to Finnegan. For example, Marion Goldin, a producer for "60 Minutes," says seemingly private matters often relate to public behavior. "Drinking? I think I can make an argument, at least for people in the public eye, that it affects their performance. Womanizing? If affects the way a person thinks about all kinds of ideas and decisions involving women," she says.

Downie also believes press coverage is justified "when the private conduct of a public figure is symptomatic of a large societal problem." In such cases, "personification in people that the public knows is a good way to discuss it." He cites as examples recent stories linking public figures to AIDS and wife abuse.

The *Wall Street Journal* used similar reasoning in a February 25, 1985 article titled "John Fedders of SEC Is Pummeled by Legal And Personal Problems," The article noted that Fedders, the Securities and Exchange Commission director of enforcement, faced financial troubles and had "confessed to periodically beating" his wife, who was suing for divorce. It quoted Charlotte Fedders as saying her husband broke her eardrum, beat her while she was pregnant and tried to throw her over a bannister. The article said that while Fedders called some of the charges overblown, he admitted to physically abusing his wife.

In the article, reporter Brooks Jackson explained the paper's "compelling reasons" for publishing: "Family violence, whether tied to pressures of the job or other root causes, is becoming a matter of increased national concern. So, too, in a different way, are the financial problems incurred by successful people when they leave the private sector for positions in government."

Albert Hunt, the *Journal*'s Washington bureau chief, says it was "an easy decision to publish" the Fedders story. Hunt says Fedders stood accused of wrongdoing in beating his wife, was government enforcement officer with financial troubles and was under review by the White House. "What the story did was raise a number of questions about Fedders that were relevant to his job," Hunt says.

Should press coverage extend to the private lives of *relatives* of public figures?

Janet Sanford, publisher of the 20,500-circulation *Visalia* (California) *Times-Delta*, says her paper printed an article about a county supervisor's son who was charged with drunken driving after an automobile accident. Because there had been an accident, with injuries and charges, the decision to print was not difficult, she says. Later, the same supervisor's husband was arrested for drunken driving and, although this time there had been no accident, the paper published the second story, also.

"We felt," Sanford says, "that because he was so often seen with her, because the family was so well known, we printed [it]." She admits she felt less comfortable about printing the second story than the first.

Last February, the *Tulsa Tribune* published a series of articles about evangelist Oral Roberts that included reporting the suicide of Roberts's older son in 1982. The *Tribune* quoted a court document describing the son's feelings of "alienation and rejection from the family" because he did not adhere to their religious convictions.

"What we were doing," says the *Tribune*'s Mary Hargrove, "was showing how you can't separate anything Oral Roberts has achieved from his personality." But, she says, the paper chose to omit other material that was "sort of brutal" and sweated over the exact wording of the item because "we were tuned in to what might be offensive."

Some editors and reporters acknowledge that public or competitive pressure can affect their decisions to go forward with a story.

"Part of your business is selling papers and providing information people want to know," says Hargrove.

Janet Sanford says, "If I'm walking down the street and I know everybody in town is talking about something, I think they should be reading about it too."

When one news organization publishes, others usually follow. "Everyone else follows because at that point the cat is out of the bag," says Kurtz. Peter Karl of WMAQ-TV says that in 1983, his station withheld for several weeks information about psychiatric tests taken by Chicago mayoral candidate Bernard Epton on the ground that not doing so would invade Epton's privacy. But as soon as the story turned up elsewhere, or, as Karl says, "as soon as the ice had a crack in it, we jumped on it."

Deciding how to handle rumors about prominent people is a separate kind of dilemma for editors. Last year, many of them struggled with the problem of whether to report rumors that actor Burt Reynolds was afflicted with AIDS.

The *Washington Post*, in an August 15, 1985 story headlined,

"Rampant Rumors and Alarm on the Set," referred to the subject only as "one star" and quoted the star's manager as saying. "He has no disease and no illness!" Downie says the *Post* decided not to name the actor "because there was absolutely no evidence whatsoever that he had AIDS."

At the *Miami Herald,* on the other hand, columnist Bill Cosford hit the rumor head on. His August 8, 1985 column began, "Does Burt Reynolds have AIDS?" It noted the absence of any evidence Reynolds was ill with AIDS and concluded, "There are things, we were all told while growing up, that are none of our business. And that's the story on Burt Reynolds and AIDS." Executive Editor Meriwether says the column was published because Reynolds was being "maligned" by the rumor.

Both "60 Minutes" and columnist Jack Anderson carried stories about reports that the late Roy Cohn had AIDS. Anderson and Dale Van Atta wrote a July column quoting National Institutes of Health records that Cohn was being treated for AIDS. Then, they felt compelled to defend their action in an August column after receiving "a blizzard of mail... questioning our journalistic ethics," according to the column. It also stated that they decided Cohn, the former aide to Senator Joseph McCarthy, had "engaged in a public fraud" by denying he had AIDS and that "the truth needed to be told." Marion Goldin, who produced the "60 Minutes" segment on Cohn, says CBS reported the story because "we felt there was such a discrepancy between what the man had practiced all his life and what he preached."

John Ullmann, assistant managing editor for projects at the *Minneapolis Star and Tribune,* points out that ethical considerations surface only "when you're trying to do the right thing. It's not an issue if you aren't worried about what's fair. It becomes an issue only when you're sensitive to it and worry about things other than, 'I know it so let's print it.'"

Printing such stories also can make it clear the press will not protect a public figure from exposure for wrongdoing.

The *Times-Delta's* Janet Sanford recalls printing an article about a local candidate's drunken-driving record. The candidate subsequently lost the election.

"The town...took me apart," she says, "because they felt I was doing this person wrong. But what it did do was establish a set of rules in the community. It told them that this newspaper was going to make the tough decisions."

Mass Media and Ethics: For Further Reading

Clifford G. Christians, Kim B. Rotzoll, and Mark Fackler, *Media Ethics: Cases and Moral Reasoning*, 2nd ed. White Plains, N.Y.: Longman, 1987.

Tom Goldstein, *The News at Any Cost: How Journalists Compromise Their Ethics to Shape the News.* New York: Simon & Schuster, 1985.

H. Eugene Goodwin, *Groping for Ethics in Journalism.* Ames, Iowa: Iowa State University Press, 1983.

John L. Hulteng, *Playing It Straight: A Practical Discussion of the Ethical Principles of the American Society of Newspaper Editors.* Chester, Conn.: Globe Pequot Press. 1981.

Stephen Klaidman and Tom L. Beauchamp, *The Virtuous Journalist.* New York: Oxford University Press, 1987.

Edmund B. Lambeth, *Committed Journalism: An Ethic for the Profession.* Bloomington: Indiana University Press, 1987.

John C. Merrill and S. Jack Odell, *Philosophy and Journalism.* White Plains, N.Y.: Longman, 1983.

Philip Meyer, *Ethical Journalism: A Guide for Students, Practitioners and Consumers.* White Plains, N.Y.: Longman, 1987.

Lee Thayer (ed.), *Ethics, Morality, and the Media: Reflections on American Culture.* New York: Hastings House, 1980.

IV

Mass Media, Access, and Pressure Groups

Who has a right to communicate with the masses? Only those who are wealthy enough to own newspaper and magazine publishing companies, radio and television stations, and national broadcasting networks? Or does the principle of freedom of speech in a democracy imply the rights of all individuals, wealthy or not, to access to mass communication?

When our Founding Fathers conceived a free press as a bulwark for democracy, times were different. It was not beyond imagination that an average citizen could acquire the means to have his opinions printed, or to have her voice heard in the village square or town meeting. But in our modern society, the average citizen's voice, without the megaphone of mass media, has been reduced to a puny whimper that few will ever hear.

With the skyrocketing costs of mass media since World War II, questions about who should have access to mass communication have caused heated debate. An increasing number of citizens and citizens' groups have insisted that laws be passed permitting them to use the media whether they own or are employed by the media or not. Movements have even been started by reporters' groups to demand a say in the final editorial decision making of editors and publishers and owners.

The most powerful of these groups have sought more than access. They have fought for the right to influence the direction and the content of the media and to "reform" those media they regard as irresponsible. But media reform has often turned into politics, especially liberal versus conservative politics rather than Democratic versus Republican party politics.

A great variety of media reform and media watchdog groups has come into existence, so many that they tend to cancel each other out and lose their effectiveness. And yet they are probably needed in some ways to keep watch over the watchdog.

13 The Citizens Movement Takes a Turn

by Susan Witty

The deregulation of broadcasting that has occurred in the 1980s has significantly altered the media reform movement. The movement is not dead, but it has changed. "The electronic media are awesome tools of power," writes Susan Witty. "Whoever can dominate them can determine not only how people spend their money, but also what ideas people are exposed to, the decisions they make based on those ideas, and ultimately the political process." Witty is a writer who has served as an editorial consultant to WNET, New York. Her article is reprinted from *Channels of Communications*, June/July 1981.

The way Howard Symons of *Congress Watch* remembers it, the mark-up of HR3333, Congressman Lionel Van Deerlin's widely publicized rewrite of the Federal Communications Act, was like the madcap stateroom scene in *A Night at the Opera*. Squeezed into a very small room were the fifteen members of the House communications subcommittee, their staffs, and as many lobbyists as could push themselves through the doorway—common-carrier people, church people, labor people, public interest people. The bill, purportedly attempting to bring communications law up to date with technology, had upset nearly everyone.

It dealt with the entire telecommunications industry, but its most controversial feature was the elimination of the public interest standard, which has stood since 1934—the requirement that broadcasters, acting as public trustees, serve "the public interest, convenience, and necessity." Chairman Van Deerlin's rewrite trusted that the public interest would be served by market forces.

Van Deerlin had devoted his last two terms in office to creating the bill, then laying the groundwork for its acceptance, promoting it in the House and in the industry. But the mark-up session went badly. Several days later, the whole project was quietly scrapped. Some mighty industries contributed to its collapse—the American Telephone and Telegraph Company and the broadcast industry had fought certain segments—but a major contributing force was a nationwide coalition of citizens groups determined to preserve the established avenues of public access to radio and television. Each member of the subcommittee had been heavily lobbied in his district and, when it came time for mark-up, Van Deerlin could not enlist the support of his own colleagues. Mobilized as a national lobbying force, the citizen-action groups carried the day.

These groups, which sprouted in the sixties and early seventies, and came to be known collectively as the media-reform movement, had become in the last decade a full-time component of the American broadcasting system. They pressured for minority ownership and employment, for greater sensitivity to the needs of children, and for fair treatment in the licensed media for women, gays, Hispanics, and other segments of society that broadcasters seemed to ignore. They lobbied against discrimination, violence, and excessive commercialism in television programming; they were for localism and against monopoly. Generally, they worked to assure a communications system that would respond and contribute to a pluralistic society. Now they saw Van Deerlin's proposals undermining much of what they had striven for.

"When we heard the House wasn't going to hold local hearings on the bill," said Janice Engsberg, field director for Telecommunications Consumer Coalition (TCC), "we came up with something pretty creative. We decided to hold our own hearings in all the subcommittee members' districts." TCC and its parent, the Office of Communication of the United Church of Christ (OC/UCC), in a joint effort with the National Organization for Women's Media Project, got on the phone to affiliates, sent out mailings, and held workshops to prepare local people for effective action. Meanwhile, the National Citizens Committee for Broadcasting (NCCB) kept interested parties around the country alerted to updates in the bill through articles in its magazine, *access*. Other national groups, like the Media Access Project (MAP), the public interest communications law firm, delivered testimony against the bill in Washington.

When HR3333 breathed its last, media reformers heaved a sigh of relief, but they didn't celebrate. "The bill was like Act Two of a five-act play that may not conclude in this century," comments Kathy Bonk, director of NOW's Media Project. Still, TCC's Engsberg concedes, "we were able to hold our turf." The media-reform movement had managed to preserve the mechanisms for guaranteeing public access to broadcasting and affirming public ownership of the airwaves.

This happened in July 1979. Since then, technology has opened new media frontiers, and the scramble for markets by giant corporations has raised important public interest issues. But just when they might be most active, the media-reform groups appear severely weakened. Some observers claim that on the eve of a communications revolution, the groups are fighting a losing battle with the changing times.

The media-reform movement had flourished in the era of social consciousness bracketed by *Brown v. Board of Education* and the beginning of the end of the Vietnam War. Though occasionally capable of wielding a

Mighty-Mouse kind of clout, the media-reform groups were relatively low-budget organizations. They operated with small staffs and meager resources. Like many other holdovers from that not-so-distant past, they aren't faring too well.

"Media reform is not dead per se, but it's a far cry from the movement it once was," says Timothy Haight, assistant professor of communications arts at the University of Wisconsin in Madison. According to Haight, the reform effort was an outgrowth of the civil rights movement, and was ultimately liberal and progressive. But then, "the citizen-action groups got pulled into going to Washington and depending more and more on government, which has become increasingly conservative. Media reform is continuing," Haight explains, "but it's being continued by the right instead of the left. The right wing have become much better grass-roots organizers. In the sixties the liberal churches were very active—now the fundamentalist churches are. The left is still trying but they're not in power."

Being out of fashion makes it difficult to attract money. "We are feeling the same fund-raising pressures other public interest groups are feeling," states Peggy Charren, president of Action for Children's Television (ACT), who admits her 1981 budget of $350,000 is "somewhat less than last year's."

"The funding is following the political climate," observes Engsberg. "In the last year and a half, the Ford Foundation has withdrawn its support for every program working for social change."

When Ford, estimated to have provided 57 percent of all public interest funding, got out of the public interest business, a seismic shock traveled through the media-reform movement. One of the most serious repercussions was the decline of the Citizens Communications Center (CCC), a Washington-based public interest law firm representing media-reform groups before the Federal Communications Commission and the federal courts. For ten years, Ford had sustained CCC at the cost of $220,000 a year, which constituted 99 percent of CCC's annual budget. Early this year, its professional staff down to two, CCC was forced to merge with the Institute for Public Interest Representation, itself affiliated with the Georgetown University Law Center.

While other foundations, such as Rockefeller, Veatch, Markle, Stern, and Carnegie, contribute to public interest activities in communications, they are not rushing to fill the hole left by Ford's exodus. NOW's Kathy Bonk suggests their caution may be because very few media-reform groups have become self-sustaining. Others feel the foundations may be readjusting their priorities to align with the perceived rightward drift of the national mood; perhaps they too have been bitten by the "new" conservatism.

"We were largely responsible for Henry Ford's blast at the Ford Foundation for the way it was using its money for social upheaval," says Dr.

Everett Parker, director of OC/UCC. In 1964, the OC/UCC and two black citizens of Jackson, Mississippi, challenged WLBT's license renewal on grounds that the NBC affiliate's programming and hiring practices discriminated against blacks in its community. Ford supported OC/UCC in this legal battle for ten years, but discontinued its grants three years ago. The foundation's retreat happened in part, Dr. Parker speculates, because some powerful broadcast figure said to Henry Ford, "What the hell are you doing giving out money for people to put me out of business? I don't give out money for people to put you out of business."

A decidedly less personal view of the situation is offered by Sandy Jaffe, a program officer at the Ford Foundation: "Foundations like to give seed money. We had been there for about ten to twelve years. That's long enough for a foundation to stay in." In addition, Jaffe believes some goals were achieved. "What you do," he says, "is open up a process and let a lot of people in that hadn't gotten into it, you improve decision-making, make a society a little more responsive. And that's been accomplished. Public interest law is pretty well recognized today," he says. "I think in some form it will persist."

"I'm sorry to say the prognosis for these groups is not good," says Henry Geller, former director of the National Telecommunications and Information Administration (NTIA). "In the Carter Administration we tried to get bills through to provide some funding for those groups that make a useful contribution to the regulatory hearing process, because their participation served the public interest. But Congress did not want to enact such bills.

"It was hoped," says Geller, who had been CCC's board chairman in the mid-seventies, "that Ford's support [of the movement's legal arm] would be replaced by tithing the bar, by more contributions from settlements, by Congress—and none of these have been forthcoming."

Most groups are currently squeaking by on budgets at the low end of six figures. The exception is Accuracy in Media (AIM). This organization, working to counteract what it views as the frequently left-leaning bias of the media establishment, is riding high on the right-leaning financial tide. AIM's present budget of more than $1 million, far more lavish than that of any other group, is double what it was in 1980. AIM's chairman, Reed Irvine, a former Federal Reserve Board official, sees "nothing but growing support for our activities."

"Money is power," says ACT's Charren, referring to the combined force of advertisers and broadcasters who often band together to oppose her organization's proposals concerning children's television. "Those industry groups all have lots of lawyers, and one of their salaries is practically our whole budget."

Money *is* power. But in a nation of laws, those who don't have recourse to vast wealth still believe they have recourse to justice. In 1966, Judge

Warren E. Burger handed down a precedent-setting U.S. Court of Appeals decision in *OC/UCC v. FCC*, which said listeners and viewers of radio and television have a right to participate in FCC proceedings even though they may have no economic interest in the matter. Since Judge Burger's ruling, media-reform groups have worked mainly within the legal and regulatory system. But now that system is threatened by the swelling ranks of "market forces" advocates.

The cry for deregulation is reverberating through Congress more loudly than ever. And the expectation is that the salient features of the defeated Van Deerlin bill—which sought to abolish the license-renewal process, eliminate all forms of program regulation, including the Fairness Doctrine, and strike down such structural means of achieving diversity as limitations on the number of radio stations individual broadcasters could own—will be reintroduced in other bills over the next few years.

The FCC, perhaps in anticipation of a Congressional slashing, has already begun to slit its own throat. Its January decision to release radio broadcasters from some of their legal obligations—such as keeping detailed program records—also stripped the agency of some of its own oversight responsibilities.

The loss of these records, useful to citizens groups, broadcasters, and the FCC when a station's license renewal is being challenged, is a serious one.

Most of the media-reform groups are gamely attempting to make the best of deregulation, but that doesn't mean they have to like it. "When you take the rules away," warns Andrew Schwartzman, executive director of Media Access Project, "you may create a situation in which responses have to be more free-form and perhaps more threatening to the First Amendment."

At the moment, the conventional wisdom among media reformers is that radio deregulation is a stalking horse for what's to come. "There will be changes in TV regulation in the next three years legislatively," predicts Samuel Simon, executive director of the National Citizens Committee for Broadcasting (NCCB). "Our objective," he says, "would be to see that when these rules come out, they significantly increase access opportunities, and do not result in excessive concentration of the media. Teleprompter-Westinghouse is an example of this kind of concentration," Simon explains. "*The New York Times* buying into cable is another. There are going to be information monopolies in this country, and that's very serious for democracy. The stakes are higher than most people are willing to admit, especially the regulators."

A painful irony is that a number of the regulators advocating deregulation were people drafted into government from, of all places, the media-reform movement. In the late seventies the Carter Administration co-opted some of the movement's most articulate and charismatic leaders—lawyers who had hitherto argued persuasively on behalf of the public interest. By 1980 a number had taken jobs with the government agencies before which they used to plead their cases, including the FCC, the FTC, the National Telecommunications and Information Administration, and the Corporation for Public Broadcasting.

The hope among their former clients was that they would further the cause of diversity by working from the inside to strengthen the regulatory process and make it more effective. But in several key instances exactly the opposite happened.

Frank Lloyd, for example, was a former executive director of Citizens Communications Center. But as administrative assistant to the chairman of the FCC during the Carter Administration, he supported the commission's *laissez-faire* deregulatory philosophy.

"The public interest groups have to be very concerned about protecting the First Amendment rights of broadcasters. I'm more and more convinced of the importance of that," Lloyd said, shortly after the commission announced its radio-deregulation decision. "Some groups have thought the FCC should decide what is not good programming, and that's folly. When you see the potentially whimsical or political nature of those decisions, giving the government power over program content is very dangerous."

What is government's proper role? According to Lloyd, it is to define the rules of the game so the largest number of people can play, to create as many outlets as possible, to fashion structural rules that assure a fairly open-entry marketplace—in other words, more business opportunities for more people and less government intervention in business.

"Deregulation will not go away," asserts Henry Geller, another former bulwark of the public interest law community, after having been general counsel at the FCC for close to twenty years. He claims that the public-trustee scheme, under which the broadcaster is considered only a temporary trustee for what is essentially a public property, has been a failure. "The FCC never came to grips with what they meant by the public interest," he says. "They never defined what they meant by being 'an effective local outlet.' Licenses were renewed 99 percent of the time."

An NTIA report issued while Geller was the department's chief calls upon Congress to "drastically" change the 1934 Communications Act and eliminate the public-trustee programming regulation of radio broadcasting. "The broadcaster should be given a long-term license (e.g., twenty-five years . . .)," the NTIA report recommends, "with no renewal of license within that period and no need to obtain prior approval for an assignment."

"Henry Geller and I are very good friends," says Everett Parker of the OC/UCC, "but he's inconsistent. He didn't have a good experience at the FCC. He was there at a time when nobody would do anything so he thinks that because they didn't make the law work, the law should be repealed."

Whether they are simply putting up a brave front or are indulging in a self-protective act of psychological denial, the surviving media-reform groups refuse to be disheartened by their co-opted confreres, their depleted ranks, their disappearing legal options, and their uncertain financial future. "Nothing could completely handcuff us, short of giving the broadcasters licenses in perpetuity, with no accountability to the public," says National Black Media Coalition (NBMC) chairman Pluria Marshall.

This kind of outsized determination will carry the wounded media-reform movement forward. It may not be riding the wave of the moment, but one of the things that should buoy the movement in difficult times is the record of its past achievements.

The gains the media-reform groups have made may seem minimal to some, but they cannot be called inconsequential. They cracked open a closed legal system. "The media-reform movement has had a tremendous impact in the FCC," says former commissioner Tyrone Brown. "If it weren't for them the commission would not have included the public in any way in its deliberations."

As he pointed out in a 1979 speech to the NBMC, "The general public needs to be reminded of the major role public interest groups have played. For example, a public interest group (OC/UCC) won the right of listener and viewer groups to petition for denial of broadcast licenses at renewal time, and initiated the proceeding that led to the commission's policy and rules on affirmative-action employment in the broadcast industry."

Pluria Marshall's NBMC spearheaded the drive that led to FCC's adopting tax-certificate and distress-sales policies, which facilitate minority ownership. He believes blacks have made "some progress" in employment in the industry. An increase of about 8 to 9 percent since 1973, he estimates. But "the behind-the-scenes jobs are where we're getting our butts kicked," he says. "In management the least progress has been made in news: news directors, executive producers, assignment editors."

Black progress in employment in the broadcast industry is currently being "somewhat stymied," says Marshall, because white women are being hired instead of blacks. "The women's movement is not helping black folks," he says. "If anything, it's hurting them—in broadcasting that's for sure."

"I can name you a dozen or so women news directors and maybe fifty or so women program managers and a few women owners and a couple of station managers, but it's token," says Kathy Bonk, who doesn't think women have come such a long way since NOW got the FCC to amend its Equal Employment Opportunity rules to include women in 1971. It can't be denied, however, that the gains for women in on-air representation over the past decade have been dramatic.

"When we started this," Bonk says, "there were no women on-air as network reporters, no women in sports anywhere, no news about women.

After we filed against NBC, they put on *Police Woman*, the first major prime-time network program that had a woman in a leading, dominant role."

Increased broadcaster sensitivity to stereotyping women and other minority groups can be counted a victory for media reformers. So can a number of improvements in children's television, such as the reduction of advertising on children's weekend television by 40 percent.

For the thirty-three million school-age television viewers in the U.S. many of whom spend more hours in front of the set than in the classroom, Action for Children's Television has been a force for eliminating commercial abuse and encouraging diverse programming. "The genius of Peggy Charren," according to Frank Lloyd, "is that she has evolved a carrot-and-stick strategy. She goes to great lengths to give positive feedback. It has become a source of pride for a broadcaster or cable company to win one of ACT's annual 'Achievement in Children's Television Awards.'"

"People give public television credit for changing children's programming for the better," comments Charren, "but public television only released other broadcasters from the responsibility. If it hadn't been for public pressure nothing would have been done."

Most likely, neither would anything have been done about increasing news and public affairs programming, initiating government funding of public television, opening up public television's board meetings to the public, televising Presidential debates—all of which can be credited to the public interest movement in broadcasting, as can efforts to block mergers that would lead to monopoly.

One such effort, a recent legal action by the National Citizens Committee for Broadcasting to foil a General Electric-Cox merger, precipitated a quarrel within the movement. Because GE and Cox had agreed to spin off some stations into black ownership, National Black Media Coalition was willing to have them merge. In this instance, the goals of NCCB and NBMC were different, but that is not so unusual. From time to time the groups will get together in loose coalitions, but basically, as Media Access Projects's Schwartzman phrased it, "we cherish our diversity."

Another NCCB initiative that did not have unanimous support among the disparate groups, due to concerns about censorship, was an attempt to reduce violence on television by monitoring shows, identifying the ten with the most acts of violence, and then putting pressure on the companies whose commercials accompanied these shows. NCCB's strategy, which won the cooperation of national organizations like the Parent-Teachers Association and the American Medical Association, and resulted in the disappearance of some targeted programs, was the brainchild of Nicholas Johnson, chairman of NCCB before it moved under the umbrella of Ralph Nader's organization.

Johnson, a maverick FCC commissioner in the sixties and now head of a group called National Citizens Communications Lobby, is the most unreservedly enthusiastic member of the media-reform movement when it comes to rating the movement's achievements. "In the fifteen years from 1965 to 1980," he says, "we accomplished what we set out to accomplish in that we now have media reform firmly ensconsed right in the center of middle America. We expanded from groups specifically interested in media reform into major organizations like AFL-CIO, the Roman Catholic Church, PTA. You can go all across the country now and find innovative things that have been done in terms of improving children's programming, reducing commercials, or increasing public-affairs programming. People's consciousness has been raised."

Johnson's brand of euphoria is not the dominant mood, however. For most of the groups it is not a time of exuberant self-congratulation. It is, instead, a time of reassessment. It could also be called a time of floundering.

Kathy Bonk categorizes the media-reform groups' current discussions as "positive." "We're trying to get some vision in this movement again," she says. Many veterans would agree with Wisconsin's Timothy Haight that "the movement is on the defensive," struggling to preserve former gains in a hostile environment. They would also agree with Engsberg of the Telecommunications Consumer Coalition that, though the first job of the public interest groups may still be to make sure *all* the rules don't get taken away, the next job is to get into more creative roles.

With its focus on a new technology and grass-roots work in local communities, the National Federation of Local Cable Programmers (NFLCP), formed in 1976 to promote and protect public access to cable around the country, seems to be on the right track. "Fortunately, we did a better propaganda job than we knew," says George Stoney, one of the group's founders and co-director of New York University's Alternate Media Center. "There isn't a city council in the country that would give out a cable-franchise contract that didn't have access written into it."

But cable isn't necessarily the promised land. "Cable is simply a useful rehearsal ground," Stoney says. "We need public access to all electronic media."

In the summer of 1980, Congressman Van Deerlin, sometime opponent of the groups on media issues, urged the movement to come to grips with current realities before it was too late. Pointing out in *access* that the combining of the telephone with computer, satellite, and broadcast technologies would transform American lives, Van Deerlin wrote: "Technological change and industry reorganization raises a host of vexing policy problems. For example, what public interest responsibilities accrue to a direct satellite-to-home broadcaster? What First Amendment restrictions, if any, should be imposed on an electronic publisher? What common-carrier obligations should be assumed by a cable-television operator who offers data transmission or other information services?

"While the media-reform movement concentrates its effort on blocking radio deregulation and imposing new rules on children's television," Van Deerlin warned, "it is missing an excellent opportunity to shape the new telecommunications industry."

Many of those in and out of government pushing for deregulation believe that the proliferating new media are going to solve all the problems. But the new media will by no means assure diversity. All the electronic media are awesome tools of power. Whoever can dominate them can determine not only how people spend their money, but also what ideas people are exposed to, the decisions they make based on these ideas, and ultimately the political process.

Are the groups of the old media-reform movement capable of leading the fight to assure that all electronic communications truly serve a diverse public, and are not monopolized to serve narrow interests? Can they tackle such a monumental job in their present fragile condition? The corporations interested in shaping the new telecommunications industry are certainly not going to welcome them onto the field of battle. And these corporations seem to have momentum on their side.

The imbalance is tremendous, especially now, between the public interest groups in broadcasting and their opponents, the well-financed, politically influential companies who would gobble up the entire communications pie solely for profit. "It's David and Goliath," says George Stoney. The analogy sounds like an admission of defeat. Until you remember who won that one.

---

14 The Charge of the Right Brigade

by Robert Becker, Judy Kantrowitz, Conrad MacKerron, Nick Ravo, Susie Smith

Control of the mass media has become an important issue for nearly every institution in our society, particularly (but not limited to) those with a political mission. Right-wing political groups have been extremely active in pressuring the media, as this essay demonstrates. But they are by no means alone in their attempts to influence media decision

making. Robert Becker, Judy Kantrowitz, Conrad Mackerron, Nick Ravo, and Susie Smith were graduate students at
the American University School of Communications when
this article was written under the direction of Professor
Richard T. Stout. It is reprinted from the *Washington
Journalism Review*, November 1981.

For years, politicians and pundits of the right have bemoaned "liberal bias"
in the media. From the McCarthy era through Spiro Agnew's attacks on the
"nattering nabobs of negativism" to the rise of the Reverend Jerry Falwell,
staunch conservatives always felt maligned and under-represented in the
press.

In recent years, however, virtually unnoticed by political and media
analysts, the New Right has built its own alternative press, moving from
newsletters to newspapers, from mimeo to video, as a way of gaining
influence and respectability.

Today, the New Right press wields widespread influence in small
towns and in Washington. It even has its own tax-exempt school of journalism—the National Journalism Center—located just five blocks from
Capitol Hill.

Unseen and unpublicized for the most part, the New Right press
played a key role in conservative gains in the 1980 elections. The networks,
wire services, news magazines, and major newspapers focused on the
extensive fund-raising and virulent anti-Carter commercials of the New
Right and Moral Majority, while ignoring or giving short shrift to the
unifying thread of New Right publications that constantly reinforced the
messages of the more visible campaigns. "By use of their literature, they set
the public mind to the point that people will believe that the key issues are
those determined by the New Right, no matter what issues the candidate
wants to discuss," says George Cunningham, director of George McGovern's
Americans for Common Sense, created after the election to combat the
New Right.

Cunningham follows the New Right press assiduously, as do a growing
number of liberals. At least one major union, the International Association
of Machinists and Aerospace Workers, has a staffer who monitors organs of
the New Right and other anti-labor groups. Some Iowa liberals this year
began issuing a monthly newsletter, "Watch on the Right," to chart budding
strategies and developments that may guide future campaigns to unseat
moderates and liberals. Wesley McCune, who has monitored conservative
publications for the past 19 years as director of the Washington-based
Group Research, Inc., says today's proliferation of right-wing publications
has never been greater. Even some representatives of the New Right are
astounded. "Four years ago, I could count on one hand the newsletters that
dealt with social issues from a Christian viewpoint," says William Billings,
editor of "Alert," a well-established evangelical New Right newsletter.

"Now there are about 160 groups, and many have their own newsletters."

Indeed, the bedrock of the New Right press is the burgeoning number of single and multi-issue letters that unite their readers around social and moral issues in the fervent tones of pre-Revolution pamphleteers.

With names like "Point Blank," "Moral Majority Report," "Roundtable Report," "Family Protection Report," and the "New Right Report," the newsletters are spin-offs of pamphlets, handbills, and direct mail that right-wing zealots in the past typed on kitchen tables and mimeographed in church basements.

Individually, they are not impressive. But collectively, they constitute a potent political force. Their readership is mostly the already committed. "You don't create something out of a vacuum," observes McCune of Group Research. "You've got to have something for the troops to read."

What the troops read in the newsletters, magazines, and newspapers amounts to a steady drumbeat of opposition to certain issues the New Right deems detrimental to society—the decline of the family, women's rights, and gun control. Consider these examples:

• "Family Protection Report," published by Paul Weyrich, director of the Committee for the Survival of a Free Congress, alerts grassroots activists to "family issues" under consideration by Congress, the White House, or state legislatures. The 12-page monthly newsletter, circulating to 14,000 subscribers, blasts sex education and abortion while applauding prayer in the school and the catch-all bill for the pro-family movement, the Family Protection Act.

• "The Right Woman," published monthly by conservative pro-family activist JoAnn Gasper, reports on government's "intrusion" into family affairs, devoting most attention to the status of congressional legislation. Gasper, considered a prime mover in the pro-family coalition, links "equality" and "women's rights" with feminist attempts to change radically social values and family life.

• "New Right Report," published twice monthly by New Right paterfamilias Richard Viguerie, keeps political activists informed of legislative and political developments. Since the 1980 elections, the 4,000-circulation newsletter has harped on ways to "defund the left" by targeting groups for extinction, such as Legal Services Corp., and by trying to derail Thomas P. ("Tip") O'Neill's (D-Mass). reelection as House speaker.

• "Political Gun News," another Viguerie publication, boosts the repeal of all gun control laws. A recent "quote of the month" in the 4,000-circulation newsletter came from Senator Strom Thurmond (R-S.C.): "I've got my gun ready if anybody comes to get me in my house."

• *National Educator*, published by James H. Townsend in Fullerton, Calif., is in its thirteenth year of disseminating right-wing views. The 16-

page monthly has a worldwide circulation of 65,000, according to Townsend. Public schools and Israel are only two of the publication's frequent targets. Wesley McCune says Townsend is "far, radical right," and that the *Educator* "is a real mish mash of stuff—antiabortion, anti-pornography, and anti-communist, of course."

Publications of the new Christian Right are also plentiful. Consider these:

• *Moral Majority Report*, the Reverend Falwell's monthly tabloid, reaches 560,000 readers. The 20-plus-page newspaper covers timely political and social issues with more depth than most New Right publications, but also with a dose of extremism. The *Report* recently reprinted a U.S. Labor Party article linking *Playboy* magazine and the National Organization for the Reform of Marijuana Laws to a bizarre conspiracy to return society "to a new dark age."

Dr. Stan Hasty, information director of the Baptist Joint Committee for Public Affairs, calls Falwell's views a "gross distortion of the gospel" and his newspaper a mere "pep sheet" for Falwell's outbursts on the nation's moral agenda.

• "Alert," edited and published by William Billings of the National Christian Action Coalition in Washington, D.C., "protects, preserves, and promotes" the Christian home, school, and church in America. Billings has fashioned a New Right press network of sorts by channeling press releases, newspaper clippings, and other political information to New Right activists' groups across the country. "We are not ridiculed as much as we are ignored, so we have our own undergound press to get the word out," Billings says.

• "Roundtable Report," a four-page newsletter published monthly by Ed McAteer, president of the Religious Roundtable in Arlington, Va., reminds its 7,000 subscribers about the "moral" side of issues and teaches them rudimentary political skills, such as how to address letters to legislators or determine the status of bills. "Its purpose is to educate people, not convert them," McAteer contends. A biblical quote hanging on the wall behind his desk reflects that philosophy: "'My people are destroyed for a lack of knowledge'—Hosea Chapter 4:6."

• "Legislative Alert," a one-page newsletter published by the Christian Voice in California, is distributed to 40,000 ministers throughout the country. The ministers, in turn, are encouraged to crank out mimeographed reprints of the newsletter and distribute them to their flocks each Sunday. While claiming to have helped turn the evangelical vote for Reagan, Phil Sheldon, national field director for the Voice, admits his publication "is just a part of a larger effort to mobilize support for candidates deemed most representative of Christian moral values."

The political message to Christian followers is limited only by Internal Revenue Service restrictions. Since most enjoy a tax-exempt status, the religious wings of the New Right press can lobby only for issues, not specific candidates.

The *Moral Majority Report* typifies how New Right publications can sidestep that limitation. One article may tell what the "moral" side of an issue is, while a companion piece identifies the candidates on the moral side. The decision of whom to vote for is left to the reader, but the implication is obvious.

The flagship of the New Right press is the 70,000 circulation *Conservative Digest*. Edited by former Republican National Committee staffer John Lofton and published by Richard Viguerie, the *Digest* is a glossy, literate magazine that is beginning to compete with mainstream conservative publications such as *National Review* and *Human Events* for influence, prestige, and power. It has also become must-reading for reporters and congressional aides of all political persuasions eager to keep an eye on the New Right.

The *Digest*, a monthly, covers a wide range of national and international issues, and differs from most other New Right publications in its ability to attract commercial advertising. (Among its most faithful advertisers are a manufacturer of orthopedic shoes and a publishing house owned by the John Birch Society.)

The *Digest* also manages to attract the full constellation of New Right political leaders as contributing columnists. In addition to Lofton and Viguerie, the *Digest* regularly features Conservative Caucus director Howard Phillips, National Conservative Political Action Committee (NCPAC) chief John T. (Terry) Dolan, Phyllis Schlafly, Falwell, Gasper, and Weyrich.

What also sets *Conservative Digest* apart is its reach into the White House. Morton Blackwell, a Reagan liaison to special interest groups, and Lyn Nofziger, top presidential political adviser, are both former *Conservative Digest* contributing editors.

The *Digest* exemplifies the differences between the New Right and the William F. Buckley school of mainstream conservatism. The magazine and its New Right allies spearhead the drive for social conservatism, the family protection issues, and the opposition to gun control. *National Review* and *Human Events* more often emphasize foreign and economic issues, and usually shun the rhetoric of proselytizing and goading to action. Most issues of *Conservative Digest* carry a signed Viguerie editorial telling readers how to influence an election or promote a cause.

Though the New Right constantly fumes at the regular news media's "liberal-leftist" bias, the media's lavish coverage of the New Right during and since the presidential campaign has made the task of the New Right press easier.

"To some degree, the New Right was early given a size and influence greater than the facts warranted," admits Conservative Caucus director Howard Phillips.

Phillips's comments may be true about the New Right press as well. Some evidence suggests that these publications are nothing more than the bull horn of conservative political and religious movements. None is a money-making proposition. Some are financed through paid subscriptions, but subscription rates barely cover the cost of production. Interestingly, many New Right publications are wholly or partially subsidized by the fund-raising efforts of larger foundations and political organizations. For instance, despite *Conservative Digest's* $15-a-year subscription fee and substantial advertising revenues, Viguerie still subsidizes a third of the $900,000-a-year cost of producing his magazine by pumping in profits from his multi-million-dollar direct mail house, Viguerie Co. Other Viguerie publications, including the "New Right Report," also lose $40,000 to $50,000 a year and manage to stay in print only because of a hefty trans-fusion of Viguerie Co. money. Subscriptions to "Political Gun News," another Viguerie offspring, sell for $24. No figures are available on its financial status.

At least two New Right publications have ties, one close, one loose, to Richard Scaife, a prominent sugar daddy to New Right causes and publi-cations. Over the past eight years, both personally and through family foun-dations and trusts—including Carthage and Sarah Scaife Foundation and the Grandchildren of Sarah Mellon Scaife—Scaife has contributed millions to conservative groups.

Weyrich's Free Congress and Education Foundation is one benefactor of Scaife's generosity, receiving at least $700,000 since 1977. Interestingly, one of the Free Congress Foundation's endeavors is to publish the "Family Protection Report." According to Weyrich, in 1980 the Free Congress Foundation offset $46,000 in paper and printing costs for the "Family Protection Report."

Christian Voice, which publishes "Legislative Alert," also receives financial help from Scaife. According to Sandy Otsby, an executive director for the organization, Scaife's name is among 327,000 Christian Voice contri-butors who subsidize the cost of reproducing its one-page newsletter. "But he's not a major contributor," Mrs. Otsby points out, saying Scaife has donated no more than $100 or $500 "from time to time." The religious organization spent nearly $15,000 of its $750,000 budget reproducing "Legislative Alert" during the past year.

The "Moral Majority Report" also circulates free of charge. The parent corporation, Moral Majority, Inc., with its 1981 budget of $4 million, pays the full cost of production. Who actually pays is kept secret. Moral Majority, Inc., refuses to publish a list of contributors.

Several other New Right publishers charge a subscription fee that fully covers the cost of production. However, unlike other commercial publications like *Time* and *Newsweek*, they are not in business to turn a profit.

The "Roundtable Report" sells for $15 a year. But "Roundtable Report" editor Ed Rowe stresses. "This is not a money-making thing; the $15 subscription fee covers the cost of publishing it. We are not operating to make a profit. We are operating to inform people. It is information, motivation, and training for responsible citizenship."

William Billings' "Alert" is another publication in this category. "Alert"'s $10 subscription covers the cost of printing and first-class mailing, but little else.

Only one New Right publication, the "Right Woman," which is available for $28 a year, is self-supporting, receiving no financial support from a political or religious organization.

Nonetheless, the expansive credence given the New Right by the establishment press has been a boon especially for the growing number of conservative columnists. R. Emmett Tyrell, Jr., editor of the conservative *American Spectator*, now writes a weekly column for the *Washington Post* and is showing up in an ever-increasing number of other newspapers.

Conservative Digest editor John Lofton's feisty column sells well, as does cohort Patrick Buchanan's. Distributed by the Chicago Tribune-New York News Syndicate, Buchanan's column now appears in 120 newspapers, ten of which picked it up after the 1980 elections.

Phyllis Schlafly's column, which soared in popularity in the 1960s, is holding steady. Copley News Service distributes it as part of a package to about 700 papers. Kevin Phillips, another favorite among New Rightists, currently appears in 100 newspapers, and a column by National Journalism Center headmaster M. Stanton Evans runs in 40 papers, mostly in the Midwest, where he was once editor of the conservative *Indianapolis News*.

In fact, New Right and conservative columnists may now be in oversupply. "There is an absolute glut of conservative columnists out there," says Colman McCarthy, liberal columnist for the *Washington Post*.

In an effort to balance the more heavily conservative tone on many editorial pages, many editors say they are now looking high and low for new liberal commentators. McCarthy, for one, is benefiting; since Ronald Reagan's election the list of newspapers carrying his column has increased significantly.

Not satisfied with gains in taming the supposedly liberal regular media, the American Conservative Union's Education and Research Institute operates the National Journalism Center, headed by Evans. Over a 12-week course, young conservatives learn the "right" way to tell the news.

While the New Right press has yet to develop a television news arm, that medium is not being ignored. NCPAC's Terry Dolan now hosts a weekly *Today*-style program spouting New Right perspectives. He funds it with donations channeled through his National Conservative Foundation.

Pat Robertson's evangelical broadcasting network produces a daily Christian TV soap opera, *Another Life*, which made its debut last June in 37 markets. Paul Weyrich puts his pro-family stamp of approval on the show. "Instead of soap opera characters tripping out on drugs and incest, they find moral solutions to their problems."

But the heart of the New Right press remains its network of news-letters and a few magazines led by *Conservative Digest.* Many editors and publishers of the New Right seem to yearn for even broader respectability than election of a conservative president bequeathed them. Viguerie tried to buy several established, large-circulation, conservative publications, including Reagan-favorite *Human Events*, but failed. At the same time, he has urged a new "positive attitude" toward the rest of the media. Yet Falwell and *New Right Report* editor James Martin declined to be inter-viewed for this article. Lofton failed to return a dozen calls made to his office.

And Martin's March 13 *New Right Report* warned that the "left will try to choke us off by changing postal rates and tax laws. . . . We must develop our own for-profit publications."

Despite its Reagan-era respectability, the New Right still reflects its old style paranoia. That is a characteristic no amount of growth and success will easily erase from the New Right press.

15 Who's Watching the Watchdog?

by Neil D. Swan

Neil D. Swan describes a number of media reformers and pressure groups, including the National News Council (which has since gone out of business because it wasn't having much impact). Are they serving any purpose? In the 1980s, an increasing number of people think they are not and that the best watchdog of the press is the press itself. Swan is a staff writer for *presstime*, the monthly magazine of the American Newspaper Publishers Association. This article is reprinted from *presstime*, February 1984.

Americans have long had a love-hate relationship with their press but, at last look at the scoreboard, hate seemed to be inching up. And, as a result of recent events, more and more people are asking: Who watches the media?

Who even *tries* to keep tabs on the news media, the least regulated of all American institutions?

Recent events underscore the fact that virtually everyone who reads publications, listens to radio or watches TV monitors the performance of newspapers, magazines and broadcasters. But the fact that there is no co-ordination, no formalization and no enforcement powers in America's many media-monitoring efforts may lead to public frustrations that could prove troublesome for the press, some observers feel.

So who's watching the watchdog of the public interest?

Everyone. And no one.

Everyone's watching, yes, but no one—in or out of the media—appears satisfied with the process.

Many publishers and editors, wire service executives and broadcast journalists admit they were stunned at the anti-media sentiment expressed in the public's reaction to the Grenada news blackout. Countless Americans expressed outright glee at the frustrations of the media.

People in the press say they've heard it all before. The complaints against the media are, to many newspeople, hackneyed cliches. And many print journalists lay a large share of the blame on TV news, with its heavy emotional impact, its graphic view of sometimes-obnoxious reporters pestering people, and its dramatic intrusion into the viewer's home and family life. But to millions of Americans, these complaints are not trite cliches; they are the truth, as they gauge it as viewers, listeners and readers.

Grenada was simply the flashpoint.

And when the smoke had cleared, public opinion polls showed that a large number of Americans supported the blackout.

Although many people opposed the blackout, too, Grenada left a widespread perception that the rift between the press and the people it seeks to serve was very deep, with ominous and serious implications. And it proved that—whether or not the media are aware of it on a day-to-day basis—millions of Americans are watching them, with intense, emotional interest.

"I sometimes think half the American population considers themselves media experts," says Ben H. Bagdikian, writer on media issues and professor at the Graduate School of Journalism at the University of California at Berkeley. "But most of them just don't have the standards for valid criticism of the media."

"Everybody's watching the media, but there is no coordination of the efforts or the criticism," says Norman E. Isaacs, former editor of *The Courier-Journal* in Louisville. "It's scattered and kind of anarchic. But you wouldn't want it to be unified, anyway. That would be un-American. I do think the press is in trouble, though."

"The public is monitoring the press, and that is important," says Charles B. Seib, a retired editor who, like Bagdikian, once served as ombudsman for *The Washington Post*. "People really care about their newspaper. It becomes a part of their lives when it comes into their homes every day. And they become upset when they feel their newspaper is letting them down. But that's a healthy situation."

"Everybody watches us," says Jean H. Otto, editorial page editor of Denver's *Rocky Mountain News* and chairman of the First Amendment Congress, a media group dedicated to defending freedom of the press. "Everybody who watches TV and who reads the paper has views on our performance. But too often those views are not based on actual knowledge. They may be a gut reaction."

"Public opinion is the watchdog of the American media," says *New York Times* media reporter Jonathan Friendly. "The readers know us. Somehow the word gets around, (and) impressions are formed on our credibility.

"Of course, constitutionally, we are not supposed to have a media 'monitor' in this country," Friendly continues. "A monitor implies some sort of power that can be imposed, and it's hard to imagine any institution imposing powers on our media other than through intellectual or economic means."

Within the limitations of the First Amendment, however, there are groups and institutions that have assumed the role of trying, at least, to watch and critique the American media. They include ad-hoc groups, permanent organizations, professors, specialized publications and the media themselves.

Citizen's Choice

The latest entry among watchdog watchers is the Citizen's Choice National Commission on Free and Responsible Media, an imposing panel which is holding public hearings in a half-dozen cities and which will issue a report this summer on its findings concerning the relationship between the media and various aspects of society. . . .

"We have proven to people that this is not a sham job," says Thomas J. Donohue, president of Citizen's Choice, a 75,000-member taxpayers' lobby affiliated with the U.S. Chamber of Commerce. "We have had strong witnesses, and we are getting a body of information that can be the basis for, perhaps, a series of monographs that would include our witnesses' testimony and, separately, our observations on the testimony."

Donohue says the commission's observations on the media will receive extensive distribution through the vast resources of the Chamber of Commerce.

So far, however, the nation's media have not shown a great deal of interest in the commission or in covering its hearings, although prominent representatives of the press are participating in them.

According to staff members, the commission's "basic goal is to channel discussion on the media's role in American society in a constructive direction. The commission is not interested in laws or regulations governing the press, nor does it want to tell the media how to conduct their business. Rather, it intends to provide a forum on the state of the media for some of the best thinkers on the subject today."

The commission will terminate after making its report.

National News Council

The organization most frequently cited as an active, self-assigned watchdog of the media is the National News Council. It was created in 1973 to investigate complaints about controversial publishing or broadcasting decisions, and to determine and publicly report on whether those decisions were proper and responsible.

The council is voluntary, with no power of enforcement over the media it watches.

"The National News Council is victimized by the fact that most editors and news directors are so opposed to it that they don't see any news in its findings, and they fail to report those findings," says former Louisville editor Isaacs, who headed the council for six years.

"Most newspapers don't bother to publish News Council findings, and most people outside the profession—and a great many inside it—don't even know it exists," observes *Los Angeles Times* media reporter David Shaw.

"The council has minimal impact, I'm afraid," says Hodding Carter, host of the Public Broadcasting program "Inside Story" that focuses on media issues. Carter, who was a member of the commission that called for the council's creation, adds, "The council has [been] semi-strangulated because the press is not overwhelming in covering it. The first knife stuck in the council was the refusal of the *New York Times* to cooperate."

In an effort to win greater acceptance and cooperation from the media, the News Council is in the process of being restructured.

The 18-member panel, composed of eight news professionals and 10 non-journalists, is being supplanted by a two-level governing structure: a board of perhaps seven trustees, composed primarily of non-journalist "public" members; and a council, composed of 11 to 13 members, primarily journalists. The trustees will focus on management and fund-raising matters. The council will review complaints independent of the trustees.

Membership of the new board of trustees and council is not expected to be announced before April.

The News Council's president and chief executive officer, Richard S. Salant, sees this "significant" restructuring as the key to making the council work as it was conceived 10 years ago by the sponsoring Twentieth Century Fund. "It's a response to my own feeling that the press would cooperate much more willingly if it felt it was being reviewed by its peers" instead of outsiders, no matter how respected and independent-minded those outsiders might be, he says. "We'll never get support from news people unless they feel it's their peers judging them."

The council's annual budget, already expanded from $300,000 to $549,000, should be further increased to $750,000 "to get the job done," Salant believes. Plans call for a larger staff and the hiring of "academics and outside consultants" to assist in reviewing complaints in specific localities. Also planned is the preparation of "white papers" on common ethical questions, "but not an effort to set down rules," he says.

Yet even with these changes, the council may still find itself lacking widespread media support.

"Any outside organization that sets itself up as a watchdog of the media is immediately placed in a suspect status by those it is monitoring," explains Isaacs. "The National News Council is looked on with disfavor because it is seen by editors as too independent and because, if it works, its role could be taken over by the government."

In Canada, the news council concept is more firmly established, due largely to the specter of government action. The Trudeau government in 1983 proposed, but recently dropped, the idea of controlling mergers in the newspaper industry through legislation. However, there is still interest in a legislative approach to starting a national press council to deal with complaints about newspapers.

Meanwhile, Canada's voluntary, provincial press councils—which have proliferated in the last couple of years in an effort to head off the possibility of government action—are working to arrange a federation, either formally or informally.

At a meeting in October of representatives of the existing six press councils—including journalists, academics and politicians—it was charged that the voluntary councils are controlled by newspaper publishers and therefore may not fully serve the public's needs in responding to complaints. But supporters of the councils and of the effort to form a federation say voluntary press councils are nevertheless more desirable than a federally appointed and controlled council.

Special Interests

While news councils get some attention within the news business in North America, few self-appointed watchdogs of the media attract more attention from the public than Accuracy in Media, a politically conservative group. Many editors express hostility toward Washington, D.C.–based AIM and its outspoken chairman, Reed Irvine. But the group is sometimes cited as a media watchdog with at least some effectiveness, perhaps because AIM is unique in its status. AIM's conservative political leaning is no secret, and it differs from other interest groups in having a continuing, regularly scheduled voice in scrutinizing actions of the nation's print and broadcast media.

"I think AIM has some impact, and I think its activities are not a bad thing for the press," says Richard Reeves, syndicated columnist and author of the 1982 book *American Journey: Traveling with Toqueville in Search of Democracy in America.*

Some other observers disagree. "The AIM people take themselves so seriously," says Daniel Machalaba, until recently the media reporter of *The Wall Street Journal.* "They don't realize they lose credibility by nitpicking and harping on small points in their criticism."

Comments former *Washington Post* ombudsman Seib: "Reed Irvine is bright, and he works hard at what he does. Sometimes he's effective in spite of himself, but when he does latch onto a legitimate point in his criticism of the press, he tends to distort it."

AIM's criticisms are termed "pernicious" by author-professor Bagdikian, who adds that its "accusations are frequently not a good representation of the facts."

Organizations representing the interests of women, blacks, ethnic groups, Jews, the "Moral Majority" and others also critique the media. But they do so sporadically and largely on matters affecting their limited areas of special interest. Also, their criticism tends to be overwhelmingly focused on TV reporting, not published material.

"I guess we are pretty much alone out there," says AIM's Irvine. "There's room for a lot more of what we do because the media are too big. I don't feel we are doing all that much to keep up with the big media."

According to Irvine, AIM operates on an annual budget of $1.5 million, including donations of about $100,000 a year from the Scaife Family Charitable Trust and $75,000 a year from the Shelby Cullom Davis Foundation. Some 30,000 Americans pay $15 or more a year to subscribe to the *AIM Report,* a twice-monthly newsletter which recently stated that the "knock-American media seem not to understand what...hit them" after they "tried to stir up a little public hostility to the government by denouncing the military ban on reporters covering the troops" in Grenada.

AIM also produces a "Media Monitor" radio program that is carried as a public service message by about 65 stations, and a weekly column that is made available to and is published by about 100 newspapers, the largest of which is *The Detroit News.*

Also standing pretty much unique and alone but highly visible as a self-appointed media monitor is the Mobil Corp., which regularly critiques the media in newspaper ads and elsewhere.

"Herb Schmertz [Mobil's vice president for public affairs] is very talented, and he knows how to present an argument forcefully," says *New York Times* media reporter Friendly. "Does he convince people? No more so than an editorial. But he does focus public attention on the issues he selects.

"The Mobil ads certainly are timely, but I don't see anyone else [in the corporate world] joining Mobil in what they're trying to do," Friendly adds. "The [Mobil] ads may have the effect of making the press more careful in what it does," says Isaacs, "but I wish the thrust of the ads was not so antagonistic."

Academia, Reviews, Others

At perhaps the other end of the spectrum from skyscraper scrutiny of the media is the criticism emanating from the halls of ivy—journalism schools and their professors, candidates for advanced degrees and their research efforts, scholars, authors and others. The impact of this academic oversight is limited, however, according to most observers.

"There's so little traffic between academics and working journalists," says Seib. "Sometimes I see good material turned up in journalism reviews which gets very little attention in the real world."

"I wish I felt they [journalism reviews] had a more important role, but I just don't see it," says columnist Reeves.

"The journalism reviews tend to go to people in the journalism schools," notes media reporter Friendly. "The J-schools may take on a local TV station or newspaper for some valid, thoughtful criticism. But I have trouble finding academics who have good sources for criticizing the press in general, not just some limited local example."

A New York colleague has a different view. "I turn to academics and journalism reviews and find them helpful and insightful," says Machalaba of *The Wall Street Journal*, who has just moved to another beat on the paper.

Over the years, journalism reviews have come (*Washington Journalism Review*) and gone (*MORE*), but only a few have stayed for any length of time (*Columbia Journalism Review*).

Dr. Richard A. Schwarzlose, professor at the Medill School of Journalism at Northwestern University, feels J-schools and journalism reviews have lost influence in the last few years because "we seem to have crawled more comfortably into the industry's lap."

Journalism schools should be a major influence in media-watching, he says, but faculties—confronted with large enrollments, decreasing resources and increasing workloads—"get burned out in class." Many of the journalism reviews were established in the late 1960s and early '70s when "journalism education was not ready to rise to the occasion" and, as a result, many of the reviews "got a bad rap early on when they seemed to be the province of radicals," says Schwarzlose.

Although there may be little widespread reading of scholarly reviews, the public does avidly read and learn about the media from such best-selling books as David Halberstam's *The Powers That Be*, Gay Talese's *The Kingdom and the Glory*, Barbara Matusou's *The Evening Stars* and Ben Bagdikian's *The Media Monopoly*.

"The books show that people like to know how we in the media operate, as long as it's presented in an interesting fashion. But then, that often turns the spotlight away from more serious questions like ethics," notes Friendly.

Still another outlet for limited, largely locally focused media criticism is the non-establishment press—including some remnants of what was once called the "underground" press. Some of these, like the *Village Voice*, now plump with advertising, might not fit everyone's idea of non-establishment, but many obviously relish the opportunity to critique the news operations of the big dailies and the TV stations in their cities. "They're always jumping up and down and screaming about 'The Story You Didn't Read in the Daily Newspaper Because It Was Surpressed,'" notes Friendly.

There are those who cite the courts as another institution monitoring, or restraining to some extent, the activities of the media.

"Libel cases, or the threat of them, obviously have a monitoring effect on the press," says Friendly. "But most people in the media can live with the situation. It's only the really bad cases that get punished."

Of course, the First Amendment being what it is, courts, judges and juries do not actively seek a media-watchdog role. Except for occasional actions by prosecutors, courts enter the picture only in response to petitions from the public. But it's also instructive for the press to bear in mind that the public's representatives in the courtroom—the jurors—are the ones who are handing down the huge libel judgments against the press.

Self-Assessment

Most Americans' awareness of media monitoring probably comes from the media themselves. In various ways, from ombudsmen to "media" columns, some news organizations look critically at what they do.

There are many who feel, however, that the various elements of the press and their professional societies should do a great deal more in examining their activities and those of other publications, broadcast stations or networks.

Television, despite its pervasiveness in today's society and the amount of broadcast time it devotes to news and public affairs, is especially lacking in media reporting and criticism. Compared with the enormous amount of space the print media now devote to reporting on and criticizing television, TV coverage of any media is miniscule.

"I'm surprised that TV doesn't do more in this area," notes Carter of

PBS, a one-time Mississippi newspaper editor. "I guess it's partly a 'Why rock the boat?' attitude and partly a recognition that media criticism is not exactly a mass audience grabber compared to a lot of other things TV does. And local TV is simply not in a position to take on the print media. It doesn't have the space, and there is just not all that much substance to local TV news. Besides, they [local TV stations] depend on the print media for reviews."

Bagdikian agrees: "Local TV is rather simple-minded. It would be hard to argue its importance as an American institution."

Some of the greatest attention TV has focused on the media recently has been from six shows, two on CBS and four on PBS, produced by Stuart Sucherman, Columbia University communications professor, lawyer and writer, and Fred W. Friendly, also a Columbia professor and former president of CBS News.

The shows were videotapes of Media and Society Seminars produced by the Columbia University Graduate School of Journalism, with Columbia professors serving as moderators and guiding dialogue on hypothetical questions about the print and broadcast media. The seminars involve a large panel of press luminaries—network news anchors and producers, news executives, newspaper editors and publishers—plus First Amendment lawyers and judges.

AIM's Irvine finds the seminars' courtroom-like, cross-examination format an "interesting approach, but [they] deal with hypothetical situations rather than the real world."

Although CBS has broadcast two of the seminars, the biggest complaints have been the devastating scheduling of the shows in what were among the worst possible viewing times.

Irvine points to ABC's "Viewpoint" series as a notable exception in effective self-criticism by network television. "The network puts its stars out there subject to some serious criticism." For example, when the Kaiser Aluminum Co. was unhappy about coverage of it on an ABC "20/20" segment, ABC scheduled an appearance by the reporter involved, Geraldo Rivera. "'Nightline's' Ted Koppel did some serious questioning of Rivera, and as a result Kaiser was quite pleased it got its day in court," says Irvine.

George Watson, ABC News vice president in charge of the "Viewpoint" series, says he does not consider himself an "ombudsman" or "viewers' advocate," but it is his role to "ride herd on policies of good journalism" at ABC.

CBS News instituted a similar executive-review system after retired Army Gen. William Westmoreland filed a $120-million libel suit against the network. The suit is pending.

A few local TV news operations have tried media-monitoring activities, notably WHAS-TV in Louisville, where former newspaper ombudsman Bob Schulman began in 1981 to serve as media critic. But by and large, local TV avoids critiquing other local media, other than what PBS's Carter terms infrequent "nose-tweaking" by a TV station of the local newspaper for supposed errors or irregularities.

While it's true that ombudsmen are much more prevalent at newspapers than at TV news departments, it's equally true that only a small number of newspapers have such a "readers' advocate" to respond to complaints, look out for readers' rights, and monitor and critique the news operation.

The ombudsman concept is the news media's greatest commitment to self-examination. Its perception by readers as a genuine effort to provide quality news coverage while protecting average people from media abuse—intentional or accidental—is a tremendous source of credibility and respectability for those newspapers embracing the concept.

But the fact is, there just aren't very many papers willing to spend the time and effort to subject themselves to internally generated but publicly disseminated criticism.... A recent survey showed only 32 ombudsmen serving 39 North American newspapers, meaning only one daily newspaper in 50 has a readers' advocate.

Shaw of the *Los Angeles Times* says too many editors dismiss suggestions they hire a readers' advocate with this attitude: "Any editor who can't make value judgments on his own—and make them correctly—is in the wrong job."

Some newspapers with ombudsmen, and some without, have reporters who cover the media as a beat. Examples include Shaw, Friendly of the *New York Times*, Machalaba of *The Wall Street Journal* and Tom Collins of *Newsday*. They believe more are needed.

"I wish more newspapers would hire somebody to do what I do," says Shaw. "We [the media] are such a powerful institution. We need desperately to focus more upon ourselves—to explain how news-gathering works."

"Inside Story's" Carter puts it this way: "I would like to see the day when we [in the media] treat each other the way we treat any other institution. The [New York] *Times* and the [Washington] *Post* will not hesitate to go after any other institution. But you don't see them going after each other that way. There's just not an adequate job of public monitoring of the media by its own elements. It's a gentlemen's club."

Benjamin C. Bradlee, executive editor of the *Post*, denies the "gentlemen's club" notion—particularly that the *Post* and the *Times* decline to go after one another.

The *Post*, which has not had a reporter assigned specifically to cover the media, will remedy that situation early this year, says Bradlee. And that reporter will "damn sure" cover actions of the *New York Times*, he asserts.

At the *Times*, Friendly says that in his several years on the media beat, he has found that "people like to know how we operate." But he is somewhat bothered by the fact that a lot of his reportage "has economic roots rather than informational.... I'm amazed at how often I wind up quoting John Morton," a securities analyst specializing in newspaper properties.

The *Times* recently hired Greenville, Tenn., newspaper editor Alex S. Jones to cover the media for its business section.

Among the "must" reading for media reporters and ombudsmen alike are newspapers' letters-to-the-editor columns, where people disenchanted with media performance often vent their frustrations.

However, because of the heavy volume of letters and limited space in many metropolitan papers, not all letters make it into print. And those that do usually are edited. This can disappoint and further embitter readers.

At smaller newspapers, the problem is less severe. For example, the *Bluefield* (W. Va.) *Daily Telegraph* prints 95 percent of all signed letters it receives, according to Executive Editor Richard Wesley. "We run a full page of letters every Sunday, and it is very popular," he reports.

Also serving the function of providing readers' views, or reactions to them, are newspapers' corrections and apologies columns.

"People like to read corrections—they look for them—and they are a valuable means of maintaining credibility," comments Friendly.

Shaw of Los Angeles quotes research showing that about three-fourths of dailies over 100,000 circulation now run correction notices, up from only one-fourth 10 years ago. And he points out that papers are not just running more corrections, they are printing them in more prominent locations, often in a space regularly reserved for that purpose.

Owning up to mistakes is one way the media can help to overcome an image of arrogance and isolation. Taking additional steps to relate to readers, such as holding question-and-answer sessions with citizens and upholding standards of professional conduct, also can help.

"The media are not perceived by the public as 'friends' anymore," observes Shaw. "Most media people move in totally different circles than their readers or viewers. As a result, reporters and editors may not even be exposed to media criticism that is rampant right in their own backyard."

As for standards of conduct, a fair number of newspapers have adopted codes of ethics, as have professional organizations including the American Society of Newspaper Editors, the Associated Press Managing Editors Association and the Society of Professional Journalists, Sigma Delta Chi.

Most editors say they enforce their codes, but there is a reluctance to rely on them as hard-and-fast rules of the trade. It is feared that aggrieved parties could use written rules against the press in lawsuits or other action that could lead to government controls. Some editors have avoided codes because of this concern.

In another form of self-monitoring, industry groups like ASNE and APME are continually examining newspapers' editorial products.

"The main watchdog of the press, I suspect—and they don't get a great deal of attention—is the APME," says former editor Isaacs. The association conducts continuing studies and involves hundreds of editors in its committee work. "In the past 15 or 20 years, the APME has done a great deal to broaden and enhance the performance of the press," he says.

Bagdikian of Berkeley agrees and also notes that ASNE does an extensive but unheralded "periodic assessment" of the press that is "reliable and careful."

The *Times'* Friendly calls *The Bulletin* of ASNE one of the more laudable "internal things" being done to critique newspapers' performance by drawing attention of senior editors to common issues.

More Monitoring?

But is all of this monitoring by people both inside and outside the news business enough? Where is it leading?

Some journalists say that without adequate monitoring, the stage could be set for eventual governmental intervention. "There's a definite tendency around the world toward restricting the press," says media critic Collins of *Newsday*. "The movement here under Ronald Reagan is troublesome.

"I don't see a law being passed [limiting press freedoms], but it could start with an executive order," he said. "That's the way freedom in general is lost, little by little over a period of time."

Wesley of the 27,805-circulation *Bluefield Daily Telegraph* says that while future government intervention into media activities is a "possibility," of more pressing concern, he feels, is the "loss of credibility" in media grown remote from the public. "To a large extent, that loss of credibility has already happened to the networks," he says.

For this reason, some smaller news organizations like his believe it is prudent to distance themselves from the major media and their perceived evils.

"We're always editorializing about the left-wing, Eastern bias of the mass media," says Wesley. "Our readers certainly don't think of us in the same category as the network news."

Some other smaller dailies, while not editorializing against the major media, distinctly feel and cherish the hometown support granted them by their readers.

"They do see us in a different light than the national media," says James D. Ewing, publisher of the *Keene* (N.H.) *Sentinel* (evening, circulation 13,740). "It's a personal relationship, a feeling of intimacy."

And from one corner of academia, concern has even given rise to a challenge in the form of a "heresy." William R. Lindley, a one-time newspaper editor who is now professor of journalism at Idaho State University, says one way for the press to improve its standing with the public is to expand upon the concept of an ethical code—perhaps by adopting some form of certification for professional journalists.

"Professionalism means recognized standards and the disciplining of unethical conduct," he says. "Licensing is foreign to our tradition; its ready abuse by authoritarian governments makes it clearly unacceptable.

"But what about a national ANPA/ASNE exam, done by experts, leading to a certificate which optionally could be used as part of the hiring process, the certificate subject to suspension for unethical conduct?

"If the idea sounds heretical," he says, "let a [media] task force which can read public opinion as well as Ronald Reagan come up with something better...."

Something better, in the view of SPJ,SDX, is to concentrate its efforts on the public rather than on the press. Disturbed by opinion polls showing that many Americans do not see how a free press is important to them personally, SPJ,SDX is planning an ambitious advertising and education campaign to convince citizens that any effort to place outside controls or limitations on the press is a definite threat to their individual rights.

"The theme will be, 'The watchdog may bark at the burglar but occasionally bite the postman by mistake. But if you put too many restrictions on the watchdog, you don't have any watchdog at all," says R.T. Kingman, chairman of the society's Watchdog Project. The group is seeking the assistance of the influential and powerful Advertising Council in spreading its message, due to peak in 1987, the bicentennial of the Constitution.

So, who's watching the media?

Everyone...and no one.

But are the media being *adequately* monitored?

Yes, says Bradlee of *The Washington Post*: "I can't think of another institution that examines itself with anywhere near the thoroughness we do. Where's the ombudsman in medicine or in business?"

No, says Northwestern's Schwarzlose: "We have new-found power and we don't know yet how to handle it. We have not yet found the proper monitoring mechanism. I'd hate to see it be the courts...."

"In the last analysis, it comes down to the publishers, the owners and the directing editors," says Isaacs. "If we want a commitment to quality, that's where it'll come from."

Mass Media, Access, and Pressure Groups: For Further Reading

Lee Brown, *The Reluctant Reformation: On Criticizing the Press in America*. New York: McKay, 1974.

A. J. Liebling, *The Press*. New York: Pantheon Books, 1975.

National News Council, *In the Public Interest*. New York: National News Council, 1975.

Ithiel de Sola Pool, *Talking Back: Citizen Feedback and Cable Technology*. Cambridge, Mass.: MIT Press, 1973.

William L. Rivers, *Back Talk: Press Councils in America*. San Francisco: Harper & Row, Canfield Press, 1973.

Benno C. Schmidt, Jr., *Freedom of the Press vs. Public Access*. New York: Praeger, 1976.

Frederick Siebert, Theodore Peterson and Wilbur Schramm, *Four Theories of the Press*. Urbana, Ill.: University of Illinois Press, 1963.

V

Crime, Violence, and the Mass Media

The words *crime* and *violence* can quite easily prompt a variety of conjectures about what can be included in this chapter. Starting with *A*, arson is a crime that's covered by the mass media. So are robberies, murders and rapes, and so are terrorist activities. As you read the words, you are probably picturing some degree or kind of violence you attach to each of them. If there's been a particularly gruesome robbery or murder reported in the news or described in a TV drama, that's what robbery or murder means for you right now. If you've watched a rough football game, perhaps that's violence to you. Or if you were in that game, violence might be one particular tackle, done in sport but bruising nevertheless. Now that you have your own impression of crime and violence in mind, consider it as a possible issue involving the mass media.

Journalists know that people are interested in reports about crime. Sometimes news reports warn us to be more careful, sometimes they make us fearful or even frightened, sometimes they satisfy our streaks of morbid curiosity. Regardless, we pay attention to crime news; and it is often true that the more gruesome the story, the greater is our interest. So-called "white-collar crimes" don't seem to hold our interest as well. Editors have known this for centuries, so they often "play" crime news prominently—even crimes occurring great distances from our own communities. Screen writers, too, are aware of our interest in crime, and as a result, our television screens often portray gruesome activities in the guise of drama. In this section, authors discuss some of the ways the mass media are involved with crime and violence and why. The crime and violence described in the articles may not be exactly what you had in mind, but you can make the transition.

16 Crime Doesn't Pay Except on the Newsstands

by Mitchell Stephens

> Editors deny purposely giving greater coverage to crime, but violent crime has increased and readers stay interested in it, reports Mitchell Stephens, who teachers journalism at New York University and is the author of *Broadcast News*. This article was published in *Washington Journalism Review*, December 1981.

The words "torture" or "murder" in two-and-a-half inch bold type have helped make Rupert Murdoch's *New York Post* the fastest growing newspaper in the United States.

The *Post* is not the only paper that has been expanding its coverage of crime recently, and it certainly is not the first to fill its pages with reports of execrable behavior.

"Crime's been big news since Cain slew Abel," says Shana Alexander, one of a crowd of authors currently writing books on convicted murderess Jean Harris—whose trial was front-page crime news in newspapers all over the country earlier this year.

Crime has long obsessed journalists, and crime news has obsessed their critics. In 1883, the *New York Evening Post* lambasted Joseph Pulitzer for the *New York World*'s emphasis on the sordid and the sinful. Today, critics are still deploring what they argue is the inordinate press attention paid to shootings, stickups, and stabbings.

Despite centuries of scolding, crime news has flourished and today may even be enjoying a gentle boom.

"It may be that we're getting more crime news because the rest of the newspaper is so goddamn dull, filled with energy news, interest rates, and economic problems," suggests William F. Thomas, executive editor of the *Los Angeles Times*.

In Delaware County, Pa., H.L. Schwartz recently turned his *Daily Times* into a tabloid. Schwartz says, admiringly, that the *New York Post* seems to "oscillate" on a newsstand. Since the first modern American tabloid, the *New York Daily News*, was launched in 1919, tabloids have traditionally played up crime news, and Schwartz's *Daily Times* will not be an exception.

"In the past I anguished over having too much crime in the paper,"

Schwartz explains. "We tried to moderate crime coverage, but we don't do that now. We have taken steps to improve our relations with the police and to get crime news sooner and to get more excited about it."

The *Boston Herald American* was also revamped into a tabloid this year. Although *Herald American* executive editor James Toedtman denies his paper's new format will mean increased crime coverage, he says there had already been an increase in coverage before the switch: "We're running more stories in our display pages that involve crime. People are interested in it. There has been a substantial increase in people's perception that they're affected by crime."

William Giles, executive editor of the *Detroit News* runs a newspaper that, in his words, has been "very fulsome in its coverage of crime. As the economy has been getting worse, particularly in Michigan, there is more crime going on," Giles says. "And I think that's reflected in the paper, but I've made no deliberate decisions to cover more crime."

Most editors deny that they are purposely giving greater coverage to crime, yet most admit that their readers have grown more interested in the subject. If so, readers have good reason for their interest: there was a 60.3 percent jump in violent crime in the United States from 1971 to 1980, according to the FBI.

"There is an increase in public concern about crime," acknowledges *Los Angeles Herald Examiner* editor James G. Bellows. "The public is increasingly concerned about its own safety and security." Thomas of the *Herald American*'s more prosperous rival, the *Los Angeles Times*, agrees: "It's possible that we're covering more crime news simply because of the increased concern on the part of citizens, on the part of commissions, on the part of politicians."

A central issue in the controversy over crime and crime news has been that of race. Black Americans have been among the leading critics of crime coverage by the press, largely because, as one reporter says, "It seemed the only time blacks were getting into the paper was when somebody killed somebody else."

Black readers remain sensitive to newspaper discussions of crime. Hundreds showed up last summer at a demonstration organized by a black weekly, the *Los Angeles Sentinel*, to protest an article in the *Los Angeles Times* about crime. In the second of a two-part series on the "permanent underclass" in the cities, the *Times* had used its own statistical analysis to demonstrate how members of this underclass increasingly prey on other groups. Maps showed how the "marauders," using the freeways, leap-frogged from core urban areas into the affluent suburbs to commit their crimes.

"It made blacks seem like they were all animals!" charges James H. Cleaver, executive editor of the *Sentinel*. "All they showed was the bad side of the black community. It made it appear that all the bad people in the city are black or Hispanic."

Thomas says he is not surprised at the reaction to the article in his newspaper. "It was not a cheerful article for anyone with a black skin walking through a white suburb," he admits. "There isn't any question that the way the article came out it provides ammunition for bigots and it feeds stereotypes. But the question I have to ask is: What are we supposed to do about that? Nobody is disputing that the article was accurate."

Cleaver protests that there should have been more attempt at balance in the piece. Thomas answers that the first article in the series had provided balance by showing the hopelessness of the permanent underclass, and he adds that his newspaper revisits Watts every five years for a "huge" article on the problems of the community.

Robert Maynard, of the *Oakland Tribune,* is conspicuous among editors who admit their papers are paying more attention to crime. He is the first black to edit a major metropolitan daily. Maynard's decision to place more emphasis on crime reporting in the *Oakland Tribune* might seem surprising. He does not think it should be.

"We are printing more about the causes of crimes, more about the consequences of crimes, and more about the particular human circumstances surrounding individual crimes," Maynard explains. "I think it is a very bad idea to ignore a murder."

Blacks make up a disproportionate share of the victims of crimes. (Of the single-victim, single-offender murders in the United States last year, 47 percent of the victims were black, 50 percent of the offenders were black, according to the FBI.) Maynard is among those who believe the role of blacks as victims has been underemphasized as their role as offenders has been overemphasized.

"We have sensed that one of the problems in coverage of crime is a tendency to consider that some murders are 'quality' murders and some are 'ordinary' murders," Maynard says. "We find that one of the reasons for the misunderstanding of our crime rate is the mistaken belief that most of the victims of crime are upper middle-class whites, when in fact most of the victims are poor minorities."

A reporter for the old *Newark News* recalls being advised in the early 1950s that the newspaper was not interested in crimes committed by blacks against blacks, dismissed by some editors as "nigger cuttings." Such overt racism is rare in news rooms today, but some observers claim the murder of a white person is more likely to get into most papers than the murder of a black person.

The *Washington Post,* for instance, pays a significant amount of attention to the problem of crime in poorer areas, but its crime coverage raises some interesting questions.

Of the 52 black and Hispanic people murdered in Washington from

June 1 to August 31 this year, only one was considered significant enough to make the front page of the *Post*'s "Metro" section. Of three Washington murders with white victims during that period, one was considered newsworthy enough for the front of "Metro."

Although these statistics are far from conclusive—the sample is small and homicides in suburban areas are not considered—the imbalance is interesting—but not surprising.

Speaking of newspapers in general, Roger Wilkins, former associate editor of the *Washington Star*, says, "There is no question that there is more reporting of certain white murders than of certain black murders. And when you get to the issue of black murders in family fights, you don't get that at all. Absolutely nothing."

Washington Post "Metro" editor Bob Woodward defends *Post* crime coverage, saying, "I am not aware at all that we sit around and look at addresses, and if it's not in the Northwest district [where the largest percentage of Washington's white population lives] we decide not to cover a murder." Woodward admits that deciding what murders to cover is a "continual problem. If the president of the United States is shot, it's big news. If someone else is shot, it may not be. It's relative, and you're asking big questions about news judgment."

The *New York Times*, which gave heavy coverage to the murder of Dr. Herman Tarnower, a white, and the murder of Helen Hagnes, a musician at the Metropolitan Opera, a white—is not immune to charges of discrimination in its crime coverage.

"What I've noticed and what some other reporters here have noticed is that it becomes a matter of addresses," asserts one *Times* reporter. "If something comes over the police wire about a murder that has an address in a black neighborhood and it doesn't seem out of the ordinary, it doesn't get checked out, but if it has an address in a fashionable East Side neighborhood, it will be checked out."

Times metropolitan editor Peter Millones dismisses that charge and explains that his newspaper's decisions on what homicides to cover are based simply on news judgment. "Prominent people make more news than people who are not as prominent," Millones notes.

"The attitude may be that some deaths are more important than others," answers the *Times* reporter. "I can certainly understand that from a news judgment point of view, but from a moral perspective it does bother me."

Blacks are not the only critics of crime coverage in the nation's press.

Drew Humphries, a Rutgers University professor, believes news reports give a distorted picture of illegal behavior in our society. The incidence of violent crime is exaggerated, she says, while more subtle crimes—such as the violation of air pollution regulations—are slighted.

Boston communications researcher John Kochevar believes the problem is that crime reporting is usually "without context. There is very little in crime coverage that is of use, that tells why crime occurs, how it can be prevented or how real the danger actually is."

Humphries agrees: "Crime reporting divorces action from its context. It blinds you to both the causes and effects of crime. It's as if the crimes were occurring on an improvisational stage."

By covering one type of crime, a newspaper can give the impression that kind of crime is increasing. Philadelphia's news media are now reporting a wave of crime by "wolf packs"—teenage gangs—but there is no significant statistical increase in youth crime to support the increased coverage, says Humphries.

"Because of the tremendous emphasis on crime and violence in the news and entertainment media, children and adults tend to overestimate the extent to which crime exists in this society, and they tend to become overly cautious," warns Yale psychology professor Jerome L. Singer.

Whether crime coverage causes readers to be paranoid about the danger of crime or to perceive the danger accurately is a matter of debate. Executive editor Roger Wood of the *New York Post* maintains that it is healthy for newspapers to make people cautious: "We live in a very violent city here in New York."

Roger Wilkins has a different perspective. "There is no question that the city is substantially *less* dangerous than white people think it is," Wilkins says about Washington. He claims flawed crime reporting, along with dishonest politicians, create a public debate on crime that is "generally ignorant and ill-informed."

If crime coverage is increasing in today's newspapers, it is also changing. There is a growing realization by many editors that it is necessary to step back from reports of individual crimes to gain perspective on broader trends. Both the *New York Times* and the *Washington Post* have run sociological articles about crime—with information on its causes and effects that have focused on the problems of minorities.

"It's not as bad as it used to be when you sent some old rummy you didn't want around the news room down to the police shack," Wilkins concedes. "But it's still not the place eager young reporters want to go. With crime reporting of any kind you do not get the same consistent and sustained coverage that you get on, for example, economic news or the State Department."

Wilkins believes such a politically charged subject as crime deserves better treatment. "If crime is as important to this society as they say it is, first of all you upgrade the beat. Put your best reporters there. Send them off to study criminal law as the *Times* sends its Supreme Court reporter to Yale Law School."

With all its inadequacies, it is difficult to imagine newspapers without crime stories. The two grew up together, journalism attracted its mass audience in part through the blood, sex, and tears it was able to find in crime.

The last major boom in crime coverage by the press came in the 1920s when new tabloids were courting new readers among the urban poor. The most uninhibited of those tabloids was probably the *Daily Graphic* in New York, which had no peers in its ability to exploit a sexy trial, like the divorce trial in 1926 and 1927 of "Daddy" Browning and his 15-year-old child-wife, "Peaches." *Graphic's* headlines about the trial included these grabbers: "Peaches on Stand Tells How Daddy Made Love," "Peaches Admits Hiding Names of Boy Lovers," "When Peaches Refused to Parade Nude" and, "Daddy to Enter Cloister."

Joseph Pulitzer helped produce an earlier boom in crime coverage at the turn of the century. The circulation of the *New York World* went from 15,000 to over a million with headlines that would not be out of place in today's *New York Post*: "A Baptism of Blood," "In Prison for His Brother's Crime," "Maddened by Marriage," "'Let Me Die! Let Me Die!'"

It would be difficult to find any society—going as far back as Rome in 100 A.D.—that did not pass along tales of anti-social behavior.

Why?

"The traditional psychoanalytic explanation is that there is an instinctual tendency to harm and hurt, which we suppress and which tends to be expressed vicariously in reading about crime," Yale's Professor Singer explains.

Singer, however, subscribes to less Gothic explanations for the fascination with crime news: "There is an element of adventure and excitement about it," he says, "We've grown up with stories about crime; Robin Hood is basically a criminal. And there is an element of envy of people who can get away with crime."

The *New York Post's* Wood prefers to think that his readers identify and sympathize with the victims, not the criminals. Wood thinks crime coverage serves a civic purpose: "You make people more aware. You make them more careful. You make them more responsive."

Woodward of the *Washington Post* believes the fascination of crime is that it can strike anyone at any time—with an enormous impact.

Major crimes are shocking anomalies in otherwise ordinary lives.

"Horror, fear, curiosity, and sympathy are all involved," says Roger Lane, a history professor at Haverford College. "And these are all elemental emotions."

Giles, of the *Detroit News*, says the simplicity of crime stories makes them readable. "All the readership surveys we take find that crime news, per se, is very highly read," Giles reports. "It's simple. It says something to people about the community in which they are living or about a community in which they are glad they are not living."

Horse trainer Buddy Jacobson is arrested in New York for murder, and soon the newspapers are printing details of his steamy East Side life; during the murder trial of Madeira school headmistress Jean Harris, her love letters are printed on the front pages of the most serious-minded newspapers. Crime brings something special to a reader—a chance to peek at the most intimate details of another person's life.

Nothing is too private to reveal if it is relevant to the determination of guilt or innocence—that is the rule in court, and it becomes the rule when criminal trials are reported. Private lives are invaded with less restraint in crime stories than anywhere else in the news; that is what makes them so offensive to critics and so popular with readers.

"Crimes lead to all sorts of other interesting stories," say Bob Woodward. "My favorite example was a burglary some years back." He refers, of course, to Watergate. That burglary is a good example of how much more we can learn about men when they leave their protected roles as government officials and are caught committing a crime. Mitchell, Haldeman, Ehrlichman, and Dean became human only when looked at as potential crooks. Political stories are not peopled by vulnerable human beings; crime stories usually are.

Crime stories may increase racial tension, they may leave readers with a confused view of who is getting away with what in this country, but they provide rare chances to peer into the deepest recesses of other people's private lives.

Crime news is personal and intense—something Joseph Pulitzer undoubtedly realized when he put it on page one. Perhaps that is what H.L. Schwartz of the *Daily Times* means when he says crime news "is just good-reading stuff."

17 Go Get Some Milk and Cookies and Watch the Murders on Television

by Daniel Schorr

Whether the viewer is watching news or dramatic programs, the amount of violence shown on television and
what it can do to people are concerns of Daniel Schorr,
senior correspondent of Cable News Network. He explains
why in this article. Schorr is a former network correspondent for CBS News. This article is reprinted from *The
Washingtonian*, October 1981.

> *I believe television is going to be the test of the
> modern world, and that in this new oppor-
> tunity to see beyond the range of our vision we
> shall discover a new and unbearable distur-
> bance of the modern peace or a saving radiance
> in the sky. We shall stand or fall by television—
> of that I am quite sure.*
>
> E.B. White (1938)

John W. Hinckley Jr. causes me to reflect, having recently turned 65, on
what the media age has wrought. Hinckley's unhappy lifetime of some 26
years coincides roughly with my life in television. Whatever else made him
want to shoot a President, Hinckley epitomizes the perverse effects of our
violence-prone culture of entertainment.

Hinckley weaves together strands of media-stimulated fantasy, fan
frenzy, and the urge to proclaim identity by starring in a televised event.
His success is attested to by everything that has happened since March 30,
when he managed to disrupt the regular programs listed in his copy of *TV
Guide* to bring on command performances by Dan Rather, Frank Reynolds,
Roger Mudd, and the other news superstars. Since November 22, 1963,
these electronic special reports—the modern equivalent of the old newspaper extra—have been America's way of certifying a "historic event."

Much has been shown to Hinckley's generation to lower the threshold
of resistance to violent acts. When the time came for Hinckley to act—to
plug himself into this continuum of television and movie violence—the

screenplay was easily written, the roles nearly preassigned. The media-conscious "public" President, Ronald Reagan, attracted the cameras, which attracted the crowds, which provided both the arena and the cover for the assailant. The network cameras routinely assigned, since the Kennedy assassination, to "the presidential watch" recorded the "actuality" and showed it in hypnotic, incessant replays. The audience tingled to the all-too-familiar "special report" emblazoned across the screen.

To nobody's surprise, the celebration of violence stirred would-be imitators. The Secret Service recorded an astonishing number of subsequent threats on the President's life. One of them came from Edward Michael Robinson, 22, who had watched the TV coverage and later told police that Hinckley had appeared to him in a dream, telling him to "bring completion to Hinckley's reality."

Psychiatrist Walter Menninger examined Sara Jane Moore, who tried to kill President Ford in 1975, and found it no coincidence that two weeks earlier a well-publicized attempt on Ford's life had been made by Squeaky Fromme.

"There is no doubt," Dr. Menninger told me, "of the effect of the broad, rapid, and intense dissemination of such an event. The scene in front of the Washington Hilton must have been indelibly coded in everybody's mind with an immediacy that does not happen with the print media. We have learned from the studies of television that people do get influenced by what they experience on television."

The broadcasting industry says it can't help it if occasionally a disturbed person tries to act out depicted violence—fictional or actual. In 1975, a Vietnam veteran in Hyattsville, Maryland, who had told his wife, "I watch television too much," began sniping at passersby in a way he had noted during an episode of *S.W.A.T.*—and, like the fictional sniper, was killed by a police sharpshooter.

The American Medical Association reported in 1977 that physicians were telling of cases of injury from TV imitation showing up in their offices and hospitals. One doctor treated two children who, playing Batman, had jumped off a roof. Another said a child who had set fire to a house was copying an arson incident viewed on television.

No court has yet held television legally culpable for the violence it is accused of stimulating. In Florida in 1978, fifteen-year-old Ronny Zamora was convicted—after a televised trial—of killing his elderly neighbor despite the novel plea of "involuntary subliminal television intoxication." The parents of a California girl who had been sexually assaulted in 1974 in a manner depicted three days earlier in an NBC television drama lost their suit against the network.

That's as it should be. I support the constitutional right of the broadcasting industry to depict violence, just as I support *Hustler* magazine's right to depict pornography—with distaste. As Jules Feiffer, the cartoonist and civil libertarian, has noted, one sometimes finds oneself in the position of defending people one wouldn't dine with. What troubles me, as I reflect on the case of John Hinckley, is the reluctance of television to acknowledge its contribution to fostering an American culture of violence, not only by the way it presents fantasy but by the way it conveys reality—and by the way it blurs the line between the two.

> *Violence is one of the manifestations of the quest for identity. When you've lost your identity, you become a violent person looking for identity.*
>
> Marshall McLuhan (1977)

In 1974 Reg Murphy, then editor of the *Atlanta Constitution* (he is now publisher of the *Baltimore Sun*), was kidnapped. He says his abductors immediately sped to an apartment and turned on a TV set to see whether their act had made the evening news.

In 1971 prison rioters in Attica, New York, listed as a primary demand that their grievances be aired on TV.

In 1977 in Indianapolis, Anthony George Kiritsis wired a sawed-off shotgun to the neck of a mortgage company officer, led him out in front of the police and TV cameras, and yelled: "Get those goddamn cameras on! I'm a goddamn national hero!"

In 1974 in Sarasota, Florida, an anchorwoman on television station WXLT said on the air, "In keeping with Channel 40's policy of bringing you the latest in blood and guts in living color, you're going to see another first—an attempt at suicide." Whereupon she pulled a gun out of a shopping bag and shot herself fatally in the head.

These incidents—the list could go on and on—were all aspects of the phenomenon of the mass media as grand arbiter of identity, validator of existence. Descartes might say today, "I appear on television, therefore I am."

One becomes accustomed, after working a long time in the medium, to hearing strangers remark, without elaboration, "I saw you on television!" One even gets inured to being hauled over to meet somebody's relatives. It is as though the TV personality has an existence of its own. I experienced the other side of this phenomenon in 1976 when I stopped broadcasting for CBS. People asked, solicitously, if everything was all right—as though, being off the air, I had ceased to be in some existential sense.

"Getting on television" has become a preoccupation of people in government, politics, and industry, not to mention all manner of single-issue advocates. Candidates will fashion their campaigns around "photo opportunities." Senators will be drawn by the presence of cameras to legis-lative hearings they otherwise would skip.

Many people will do almost anything to get on TV. Some will even kill.

Anthony Quainton, former head of the State Department's Office for Combatting Terrorism, associates the increase in casualties during hijack-ings and hostage-takings with the desire of terrorists to insure news-media attention. Deliberate acts of horror—like the tossing out of slain victims—are planned as media events. On the other hand, the failure of the hijacking of a Turkish plane to Bulgaria in May was at least partly due to the fact that two of the terrorists had left the plane to give a press conference.

Sometimes the aim is to hijack television itself. When the radical Baader-Meinhof gang in West Germany kidnapped a politician in 1975 as hostage for the release of five imprisoned comrades, it forced German tele-vision to show each prisoner boarding a plane and to broadcast dictated propaganda statements. "For 72 hours we lost control of our medium," a German television executive later said.

When Arab terrorists seized the Vienna headquarters of OPEC in 1975, killing three persons and taking oil ministers hostage, the terrorists' plan called for them to occupy the building until TV cameras arrived.

A central feature of the plan of the San Francisco "Symbionese Libera-tion Army," which kidnapped Patricia Hearst, was the exploitation of the media—forcing radio and television to play its tapes and carry its messages.

The Hanafi Muslims' hostage-taking occupation of three locations in Washington in 1976 was a classic case of media-age terrorism. The leader, Hamaas Abdul Khaalis, spent much of his time giving interviews by tele-phone, while his wife checked on what was being broadcast.

"These crimes are highly contagious," warns Dr. Harold Visotsky, head of the department of psychiatry at Northwestern University. "De-ranged persons have a passion for keeping up with the news and imitating it."

It does not seem to matter much if they are keeping up with "the news" or with "entertainment," for more and more the distinction is thinly drawn. A real attempt on the President's life produces a rash of threats. A prime-time drama about a bomb on an airplane produces a rash of reports of bombs on airplanes.

In all of this, television claims to be innocent—a helpless eyewitness, sometimes even a hostage. It's not that simple.

To begin with, television has helped blur the lines between reality and fantasy in the general consciousness.

Television news itself—obliged to co-exist with its entertainment en-vironment, seeking to present facts with the tools of fantasy—ends up with a dramatized version of life. Everything that goes into making a well-paced, smoothly edited "package" subtly changes reality into a more exciting allegory of events. The confusion is compounded by the use of "cinéma réalité" techniques in fictional dramas, and the modern forms of fact-and-fiction "docudramas" and "reenactments" of events.

It began to come home to me that audiences were blurring the distinction between reality and entertainment when I received telephone calls from several persons, during the 1973 Senate Watergate hearings that preempted soap operas, asking that the networks "cancel" a boring witness and "put back John Dean and his nice wife." Moreover, some friends of mine praised a "documentary" shown by NBC, *The Raid at Entebbe*, and had to be reminded that it was a reenactment.

The gradual erosion of the line between fact and fantasy, between news and theater, can have serious consequences. People slow to react to accidents and muggings may be experiencing the existential question of whether these things are really happening. A woman wrote columnist Abigail van Buren of being bound and gagged by a robber who told the victim's four-year-old boy to watch television for a while before calling for help. The child looked at TV for the next three hours, ignoring his mother's desperate efforts to get his attention. Perhaps, to the child, the show was more real than his mother's muffled screams.

Having obscured the difference between fantasy and reality, television offers incentives to people who are seeking emphatic ways of getting recognition. Innocent hand-waving, as an attention-getting device, yields to demonstrations, which in turn yield to riots.

In my own experience, covering urban unrest for CBS in the 1960s, threatening rhetoric tended to overpower moderate rhetoric and be selected for the network's *Evening News* because it made "better television." I have no doubt that television helped to build up militant blacks like Stokely Carmichael and H. Rap Brown within the black community by giving them preferred exposure. Nonviolent leaders found themselves obliged to escalate the militancy of their own rhetoric. When Martin Luther King Jr. came to Washington to 1968 to discuss plans for the "poor people's march" that he did not live to lead, he told me he had to allude to possibilities for disruption as a way of getting media attention.

At a community meeting after the first night of rioting in the Watts area of Los Angeles in 1965, most of those who spoke appealed for calm. But a teenager who seized the microphone and called for "going after the whiteys" was featured on evening TV news programs. A moderate commented, "Look to me like he [the white man] want us to riot." Another said, "If that's the way they read it, that's the way we'll write the book."

In recent years, television news, compelled to come to terms with its own potency, has sought to enforce guidelines for coverage of group violence. Television tries to guard against being an immediate instigator of violence, but its reaction is too little and too late to overcome the cumulative consequences of a generation of depicted violence. It is like trying to control proliferation of nuclear weapons after distributing nuclear reactors over a prolonged period.

> *The most important thing is that a causal rela-*
> *tionship has been shown between violence*
> *viewing and aggression.*
>
> Dr. Jesse Steinfeld,
> Surgeon General of the United States (1972)

For three decades, since the time when there were 10 million TV sets in America, I have watched efforts to determine objectively the effects of televised violence while the TV industry strove to sweep the issue under the carpet.

What television hated most of all to acknowledge was that violence on TV was not incidental or accidental but a consciously fostered element in the ratings race. In 1976 David Rintels, president of the Writers Guild in Los Angeles, where most of the blood-and-guts scripts are spawned, told a congressional committee: "The networks not only approve violence on TV, they have been known to request and inspire it.

"There is so much violence on television," he said, "because the networks want it. They want it because they think they can attract viewers by it. It attracts sponsors. Affiliate stations welcome it."

A personal experience brought home to me the industry's sensitivity to the subject. In January 1969 my report for an *Evening News* telecast, summarizing the interim findings of the National Commission on the Causes and Prevention of Violence, was altered shortly before air time at the direction of Richard N. Salant, president of CBS News, to eliminate a comment about television. The passage cited the commission's view that while "most persons will not kill after seeing a single violent television program...it is possible that many learn some of their attitudes about violence from years of TV exposure and may be likely to engage in violence." For management to override the news judgment of the "Cronkite show" was extremely rare.

Riots and assassinations would bring the issue periodically to the fore, but the research had been going on for a long time. For more than a quarter of a century social scientists have studied the effects of violence-viewing— especially on children.

- At Stanford University, Professor Albert Bandura reported that children three to six years of age whose toys were taken away after they had seen films showing aggression would be more likely to pound an inflated doll in their frustration than children who had not seen such films.

- A Canadian study by R.S. Walters and E. Llewellyn Thomas found that high school students who had viewed aggressive films were more likely than others to administer strong electric shocks to students making errors on an exam.
- An experiment conducted in Maryland for the National Institute of Mental Health found serious fights in school more common among high school students who watched violent TV programs.
- Bradley Greenberg and Joseph Dominick, studying Michigan public-school pupils, found that "higher exposure to television violence in entertainment was associated with greater approval of violence and greater willingness to use it in real life."
- Drs. Dorothy and Jerome Singer of Yale University concluded from an exhaustive series of interviews that the children who watched the most television were likely to act most aggressively in family situations. Although they could not produce a "smoking gun" that would influence the TV industry, they argued that they had eliminated every other factor that could account for the high correlation between aggressive behavior and viewing of "action-oriented" shows.
- Dr. Leonard Berkowitz of the University of Wisconsin, in two experiments ten years apart, found that third-graders watching a great many violent programs were likely to be rated by other people as high in aggressive behavior and that, at nineteen, most of them were still described as "aggressive" by their peers. In fact, reported Dr. Berkowitz, the amount of television viewed at the age of nine is "one of the best predictors of whether a person will be found to be aggressive in later life."

Congress took an early interest in the question of violence in TV programs. In 1952 the House Commerce Committee held hearings on excessive sex and violence on television. Senate hearings on TV violence and juvenile deliquency, conducted by Senators Estes Kefauver of Tennessee and Thomas Dodd of Connecticut, stirred episodic public interest. The hearing transcripts make a tall stack, adding up to fifteen years of congressional alarm over television, and industry reassurance that it was addressing the problem.

The controversy over television assumed a new dimension of national concern in the wake of the urban riots and assassinations of the 1960s. In 1968, after the assassination of Robert Kennedy, President Johnson named a commission, headed by Dr. Milton Eisenhower, to inquire into the causes of violence and how it might be prevented.

Between October and December 1968, the Eisenhower Commission held hearings on television, questioning social scientists and industry executives about the extent to which the medium might be the instigator or abettor of violent acts. One commission member, Leon Jaworski, later to be the Watergate prosecutor, expressed the belief that television might have "a tremendous responsibility" for violence in America.

The television networks acknowledged no such responsibility. When Commissioner Albert E. Jenner asked whether "the depiction of violence has an effect upon the viewer," Dr. Frank Stanton, president of CBS, replied: "It may or may not have. That is the question we don't have the answer to."

Nevertheless, the commission decided to formulate an answer. After a long debate—from which Lloyd N. Cutler, the executive director, disqualified himself because of his law firm's TV-industry clients—the panel declared in its final report that it was "deeply troubled by television's constant portrayal of violence...pandering to a public preoccupation with violence that television itself has helped to generate."

The panel's report concluded: "A constant diet of violence on TV has an adverse effect on human character and attitudes. Violence on television encourages violent forms of behavior and fosters moral and social values in daily life which are unacceptable in a civilized society. We do not suggest that television is a principal cause of violence in our society. We do suggest that it is a contributing factor."

A two-volume report of the commission's "Task Force on Mass Media and Violence" concluded that, as a short-range effect, those who see violent acts portrayed learn to perform them and may imitate them in a similar situation, and that, as a long-term effect, exposure to media violence "socializes audiences into the norms, attitudes, and values for violence."

The Eisenhower Commission's report on television had little impact— it was overshadowed in the news media by its more headline-making findings about riots, civil disobedience, and police brutality. The networks acted to reduce the violence in animated cartoons for children and killings in adult programs, and the motion-picture industry quickly compensated by increasing the incidence and vividness of its bloodletting.

However, Congress, on the initiative of Rhode Island Senator John O. Pastore, a long-standing critic of television, moved to mandate a completely new investigation, calling on the US Surgeon General for a report on TV and violence that would, in effect, parallel the report associating cigarette smoking with cancer.

Worried about what might emerge from such a study, the television industry lobbied with President Nixon's Secretary of Health, Education, and Welfare, Robert Finch, to influence the organization and conduct of the investigation. It successfully opposed seven candidates for appointment to the committee, including the best-known researchers in the field. The Surgeon General's Committee on Television and Social Behavior, as constituted, comprised five experts affiliated with the broadcasting industry, and four behavioral scientists innocent of mass-media background.

Three years and $1.8 million later, the committee produced its report, "Television and Growing Up: The Impact of Televised Violence," supported by five volumes of technical studies. The full report, read by few, provided telling data on the role of TV violence as instigator of aggression in young people, but the nineteen-page summary that would determine the public perception emerged opaque and ambiguous, after an intense struggle within the committee.

"Under the circumstances," it said, watching violent fare on television could cause a young person to act aggressively, but "children imitate and learn from everything they see." The research studies, it said, indicated "a modest association between viewing of television and violence among at least some children," but "television is only one of the many factors which in time may precede aggressive behavior."

The summary danced around the crucial issue of causation: "Several findings of the survey studied can be cited to sustain the hypothesis that viewing of violent television has a causal relation to aggressive behavior, though neither individually nor collectively are the findings conclusive."

The ambiguity was mirrored in the pages of the *New York Times*. A front-page story on January 12, 1972, based on a leak, was headlined TV VIOLENCE HELD UNHARMFUL TO YOUTH. But when the report was officially released a week later, the *Times* story said, "The study shows for the first time a causal connection between violence shown on television and subsequent behavior by children."

"It is clear to me," said Surgeon General Jesse Steinfeld, presenting his report at a hearing conducted by Senator Pastore, "that the causal relationship between televised violence and antisocial behavior is sufficient to warrant appropriate and remedial action."

There was no significant remedial action. As the decade of urban violence and assassination ebbed, the issue of television violence faded, to come back another day. And another day would bring another report.

Even before the latest incidents of violence, a new inquiry had started. Dr. Eli A. Rubinstein had first come to the Surgeon General's committee as a vice chairman fresh from the National Institute of Mental Health. His experience with the investigation led him to make the study of the mass media his career.

In 1980, Dr. Rubinstein, now professor of psychology at the University of North Carolina, persuaded President Carter's Surgeon General. Dr. Julius Richmond, to assemble an ad hoc committee to prepare an updated version of the 1972 Surgeon General's report on its tenth anniversary. Two volumes of new technical studies have already been compiled. The conclusions are yet to be written, but there is no doubt that they will reinforce and expand the original timidly stated findings.

One thing the new report will do. Dr. Rubinstein said, is to lay to rest the theory that depicted violence can actually decrease aggression by serving as a "cathartic"—the cleansing and purging of an audience's emotions that Aristotle held to be the highest test of tragedy. Advanced by some behavioral scientists studying television, the theory was examined during the 1972 study for the Surgeon General, which concluded that there was "no evidence to support a catharsis interpretation." The updated report, citing new empirical studies, will make that point more strongly.

"A tremendous amount of work has been done over the past ten years, and the volume of literature has probably tripled," Dr. Rubinstein says. "If any mistake was made ten years ago, it was to be too qualified about the relationship between TV violence and aggressiveness. We have a lot of new evidence about causality, and about what constitutes causality. We know much more about how television produces aggressive behavior. We know more about how fantasy can crowd out reality, and the specific influences of television on disturbed minds.

"The fundamental scientific evidence indicates that television affects the viewer in more ways than we realized initially. You will recall that the original smoking-and-health study was limited to the lungs, and later it was learned how smoking affects the heart and other parts of the body. In the same way, we now know that the original emphasis on TV violence was too narrow. Television affects not only a predisposition towards violence, but the whole range of social and psychological development of the younger generation."

The new Surgeon General's report scheduled for release by the Reagan administration in 1982, is likely to be challenged by the TV industry with all the vigor displayed by the tobacco lobby when opposing the report on smoking and cancer. Inevitably, it will be read for clues to violent behavior of people like John Hinckley.

> In the absence of family, peer, and school relationships, television becomes the most compatible substitute for real-life experience.
>
> National Commission on the Causes and Prevention of Violence (1969)

What made Hinckley different, what made him shoot the President, are ultimately matters for psychiatry and the law to determine. But the "media factor" played a part.

As Hinckley withdrew from school and family life, he retreated progressively into a waiting world of violent fantasy, spending more and more time alone with television—an exciting companion that made no demands on him.

But television was not the only part of the media working to merge fact and fantasy for Hinckley. He was strongly influenced by *Taxi Driver*, a motion picture about a psychopath who found the answer to his anxieties through his obsession with violence. Like the taxi driver. Hinckley oscillated between wanting to kill a public figure to impress the object of his affections, and wanting to "rescue" her from "evil" surroundings. Paul Schrader, author of the screenplay, tells me that the moment he heard that President Reagan had been shot, his reaction was, "There goes another taxi driver!"

Hinckley was also affected by fan frenzy, a special manifestation of the media culture. It focused not only on Jodie Foster, the female lead in *Taxi Driver*, but also on former Beatle John Lennon, whose music he played on the guitar. Last New Year's Eve, after Lennon's murder, Hinckley taped a monologue, in his motel room near Denver, in which he mourned: "John and Jodie, and now one of 'em's dead.

"Sometimes," he said, "I think I'd rather just see her not. . .not on earth than being with other guys. I wouldn't wanna stay on earth without her on earth. It'd have to be some kind of pact between Jodie and me."

And the influences working on Hinckley extended beyond the visual media. The idea of a suicide pact was apparently drawn from *The Fan*, a novel by Bob Randall that Hinckley had borrowed—along with books about the Kennedy family and Gordon Liddy's *Will*—from a public library in Evergreen, Colorado. In the book, the paranoid fan of a Broadway star, feeling rejected in his advances by mail, kills the actress and himself as she opens in a theater production. Early last March, as Foster was preparing to open in a New Haven stock-company play, Hinckley slipped a letter under her door saying, "After tonight John Lennon and I will have a lot in common."

The plan that finally congealed this welter of media-drawn inspirations and impelled the young misfit to action was a presidential assassination. Before setting out, he—like the fictional fan—left behind a letter to be read posthumously. It was to tell Foster that he intended, through "this historical deed, to gain your respect and love."

As though to document his place in the media hall of fame, he dated and timed the letter and left behind, in his room in the Park Central Hotel, tapes of his guitar playing, his New Year's Eve soliloquy, and a telephone conversation with Foster.

A failure at most things, Hinckley was a spectacular media success who had survived to enjoy his celebrityhood—a lesson that won't be lost on other driven persons.

No one could doubt his importance or challenge his identity as the news cameras clustered around the federal courthouse when he arrived for his arraignment in a presidential-size limousine heralded by police sirens.

In the great made-for-TV drama, participants more "normal" than Hinckley seemed also to play assigned roles, as if caught up in some ineluctable screenplay. The TV anchors were reviewed for smoothness, composure, and factual accuracy under stress. Secretary of State Haig, making a gripping appearance in the White House press room, was panned for gasping and for misreading his lines. President Reagan, with considerable support from White House aides and from the smoothly reassuring Dr. Dennis O'Leary, himself an instant hit, won plaudits for a flawless performance as the wisecracking, death-defying leader of the Free World.

The effect was to reinforce the pervasive sense of unreality engendered by a generation of televison shoot-outs—the impression that being shot doesn't really hurt, that everything will turn out all right in time for the final commercial.

One can understand the desire to assure the world that the government is functioning. But Dr. David Hamburg, the psychiatrist and former president of the Institute of Medicine of the National Academy of Sciences, believes it harmful to imply that a shooting can be without apparent physical consequence.

"Getting shot is not like falling off a horse," Dr. Hamburg says. "To sanitize an act of violence is a disservice. It is unwise to minimize the fact that a President can get hurt and that he can bleed."

One more contribution had been made to obscuring the pain and reality of violence, to blurring the critical distinction between fiction and fact. The media President was, in his way, as much a product of the age of unreality as was John Hinckley, the media freak. In the media age, reality had been the first casualty.

18 Terrorism

by Margaret Genovese

Margaret Genovese concentrates on how newspapers have been forced to grapple with the challenges of covering worldwide terrorist incidents. Actually, *all* news media are facing those challenges. What can they do? This article is from *presstime*, August 1986.

Once again, talk about the relationship between terrorism and the news media is fashionable.

The topic has become standard fare at meetings of newspaper associations and in their publications. Dozens of academic researchers are engaged in a massive project probing the terrorism-news media connection.

A congressional subcommittee convened a hearing on the matter a year ago.

Six months ago, a cabinet-level, U.S. government task force on combating terrorism suggested that "journalistic guidelines," such as those developed for use during wartime, "in some circumstances should be considered appropriate during a terrorist situation."

Yet, among the nation's newspapers, that's just about all there's been so far. Talk. And, considering the options, that may be the best approach.

Neither the newspaper business as an entity nor individual U.S. newspapers have formalized procedures for covering terrorism, beyond those few papers that adopted standards in the late 1970s.

"I haven't seen any newspapers develop any formal guidelines or anything like that," says Michael Gartner, president of the American Society of Newspaper Editors and newly named editor of *The Courier-Journal* and *The Louisville Times*. "It's like almost everything else, you rely on reporters' judgments, on editors' judgments—the common sense and professionalism of newspaper people."

Gartner says it is up to individual newspapers to decide whether they want to adopt guidelines. However, he is among those who oppose industry-wide guidelines. Thomas Winship, president of the Center for Foreign Journalists, agrees. At the same time, Winship, former editor of *The Boston Globe*, brands terrorism as "possibly our number one communications problem today and probably will be for some time to come" because of the impact coverage can have on world politics and people's lives. "I don't think any of us feel comfortable about how we cover this story," he says.

Even those newspaper executives who believe individual newspaper guidelines are unworkable and industry-wide guidelines unwise say shop talk about terrorism is helpful, because it raises consciousness about the issue and its ramifications. "We do become more sensitive, and we are able to make better and more informed judgments about what we do," says Kent Bemhart, executive editor of the *Detroit Free Press*.

In contrast to newspapers, all three major broadcast TV networks have longstanding, written policies on covering terrorism incidents. For example, ABC, CBS and NBC prohibit live coverage except under special circumstances and only with the approval of top news officials.

Newspaper executives contend that television, because of its immediacy, has a distinctly different role and coverage needs and, consequently, must approach the subject from a different perspective.

The printed press and local television stations have "only a limited part to play in the drama of terrorism," observed Katharine Graham, chairman of The Washington Post Co., in a speech to the ANPA Government Affairs Committee last March. "Network television is the star."

"The problems of coverage are different," says Seymour Topping, managing editor of *The New York Times.*" Television feels a need to cover an event visually, while a newspaper, obviously, has more time for reflection in the way it handles a story and is able to deal with a problem in all of its complexities."

Says Nancy C. Monaghan, managing editor/news of *USA Today*: "We don't sit and think up hypotheticals and then talk about what we would do if that incident happened. It's just like any other big story, we do talk about it a lot when it happens. We are in a very different position, I think, than television. We are not the instant camera on the scene. I'm sure the television networks have a different set of criteria to consider."

Some observers consider terrorism a kind of warfare. Another reason newspapers have not adopted wartime-type coverage restraints is that the front lines in this war, at the present time, are overseas, and only about two dozen U.S. newspapers have their own foreign correspondents. "There are many, many local stories here that we are concerned about, other than terrorism," says Robert H. Giles, executive editor of *The Detroit News*. He places it "fairly far down the list of stories we are interested in, in Detroit, Michigan."

While the number of terrorist incidents around the world climbed 36 percent last year to 812 (177 of them involving U.S. targets), terrorism has been on the wane in the United States. Last year, the FBI counted only seven incidents of domestic terrorism, and it has recorded only one so far this year—a dramatic decrease from 112 in 1977. An FBI spokesman credits "effective law enforcement" for the decline, pointing out that many of the people responsible for prior incidents have been apprehended and that the FBI thwarted 23 incidents last year. Signs of U.S. efforts to counter terrorism are visible all around, from the sophisticated metal-detecting devices at airports to the crude garbage truck barricades at the entrances to the U.S. Capitol grounds.

Editors also say that because each terrorism incident is different, it is difficult to develop coverage guidelines in advance. The skyjacking of TWA Flight 847, the hijacking of the cruise ship Achille Lauro, and the assaults at airports in Rome and Vienna are just three of the major terrorism incidents that took place in 1985. "I would be hard-pressed to sit down and write a policy on this," says Tony Pederson, managing editor of the *Houston Chronicle*. "That is the nature of terrorism. It is unpredictable."

The experts find it difficult even to define terrorism. Attempting to do so is a "futile effort," says Robert H. Kupperman, a senior adviser at the Georgetown University Center for Strategic and International Studies in Washington, D.C.

However, like the late Supreme Court Justice Potter Stewart who, despairing of defining "obscenity," said "I know it when I see it," Kupperman knows terrorism when he sees it and lists these common characteristics:

- Normally, terrorism is the act of small groups, acting either independently or as a proxy for a large nation.
- Terrorists often attack innocent people with the intent to target a nation for political or ideological reasons.
- The act of terrorism is designed for high shock value. "It is intended to stimulate the media."

"I know some things it's not," Kupperman adds. "It's not the Tylenol killers." Although the cyanide contamination of the over-the-counter medicine can be said to have inflicted terror on the public, it apparently has no political or ideological motive, he notes.

Nor does the term encompass such things as the bungled burglary of a Beverly Hills boutique that turned into a hostage situation or, according to the FBI, abortion-clinic bombings. The FBI defines terrorism as: "The unlawful use of force or violence against persons or property to intimidate or coerce a government, the civilian population, or any segment thereof, in furtherance of political or social objectives." According to the State Department, terrorism is "premeditated, politically motivated violence perpetrated against noncombatant targets by subnational groups or clandestine state agents, usually intended to influence an audience."

Because the words "terrorism" and "terrorist" can be so politically loaded, some journalists avoid using them as much as possible.

Kupperman says that aside from occasional errors, such as the occasional labeling of would-be presidential assassin John W. Hinckley Jr. as a terrorist, the press has begun to understand terrorism "reasonably well."

Not a New Issue

Although the news media are still grappling with ways to deal with it, terrorism is nothing new.

"Terrorism goes back thousands of years," says Kupperman, "but you didn't have satellite television thousands of years ago, and you didn't have jet transportation." Without these, he says, terrorism would not have such a large, fundamental effect on society, simply because not as many people would know about an incident and, by the time they did, it would be of only "historical value."

Some date the beginning of modern-day terrorism from 1968, when an Israeli commercial airliner, en route from Rome to Tel Aviv, was hijacked by members of the Popular Front for the Liberation of Palestine. Another milestone was in 1972, when Arab terrorists stormed the quarters of Israeli athletes competing in the Munich Olympic Games. The ABC television network, on hand to televise the games via satellite, found itself providing instead what Newsweek magazine at the time called the "first, live, international coverage of a deadly terrorist raid."

The incident that prompts the current debate over the media's role in terrorism was last year's skyjacking of TWA Flight 847. Even some in the news media concede the coverage was marred by excesses and errors in judgment, particularly by television.

The incident provoked a long list of questions, among them: Should the hostages, obviously under duress, have been interviewed? Should the deployment of the U.S. Army's counter-terrorism unit Delta Force have been reported? Should so much time and space have been devoted to a single story? Should victims' families have been subjected to such heavy media attention? Should the media purchase pictures from terrorists? Should reporters act as surrogate negotiators?

(The American public has been somewhat less critical. Immediately after the conclusion of the Flight 847 crisis, an ABC News/Washington Post poll found that 67 percent of Americans approved of the way the television networks covered the hostage situation. Similarly, The Times Mirror Co.'s study on "the People and the Press" found that "despite the criticism of the media, public support for the press was actually higher during the crisis.")

The Canadian media, too, currently are engaged in soul searching, stemming from recent hostage-taking incidents in the capital of Ottawa. The *Ottawa Citizen* has directed its news staff not to make phone calls to hostage-takers or people involved in terrorist activities or any other violent criminal activities; the Canadian Press has asked the Ontario Press Council to look into possible guidelines.

The last time the issue was probed in a major way in the United States was in the late 1970s, sparked by a series of domestic incidents, including one in 1977 in Washington, D.C., in which Hanafi Muslims seized three buildings, killed a radio journalist and took more than 100 people hostage. There were several media blunders, including the broadcast by one TV station that persons who had eluded the terrorists were holed up in a room in one of the buildings, and repeated telephone calls to the terrorists from journalists, including one in which the terrorists were asked what their deadline was and what they proposed to do if their demands were not met.

Speaking at a recent American Bar Association symposium on terrorism, Benjamin C. Bradlee, executive editor of *The Washington Post*, says he learned a lesson on covering terrorism during that incident. After a *Post* reporter reached one of the terrorists by telephone, the District's police chief contacted Bradlee to say: "'Get off the blank phone.'" Bradlee says he agreed with the chief. "We had no business on that phone."

Following that incident, the National News Council (since disbanded) asked the media to "consider certain self-restraint"; specifically, to consider the dangers of providing live coverage and telephoning terrorists or hostages during the event.

Why Not Guidelines?

Believing their cities could be the location of incidents similar to the Hanafi Muslim siege, several newspapers subsequently developed written guidelines.

Among them were *The Courier-Journal* and *The Louisville Times*. According to the guidelines adopted in 1977, those newspapers will cover terrorist hostage takings "fully and accurately" but will exercise "care and restraint." To that end, the guidelines advise reporters and editors to: avoid sensationalism in writing and displaying the story; make every effort not to become participants; agree to publish terrorists' demands only if not to do so would endanger lives of hostages and only after consultation with the most senior editors and with proper law enforcement officials; be mindful of the danger of telephoning hostages or terrorists for interviews during the incident and avoid taking action that would interfere with duties of police or other officials.

The Louisville newspapers' guidelines never have been invoked but remain in effect. Newly named Editor Gartner has made no decision on whether to retain them. Paul C. Janensch, who until recently was the executive editor there, favors guidelines. "I think they should be available to help decision makers in a news organization do the right thing when they are faced with a crisis."

ANPA Executive Vice President Jerry W. Friedheim agrees. "Every editor and every publisher should know what their coverage and publication guidelines are for kidnapping, hostage or pure terrorist incidents and should think in advance about how they will relate to and work with law enforcement authorities," he says. "Almost certainly, basic policies and an emergency-action checklist should be written down, kept where they can be found, and periodically reviewed with both news staffs and government authorities."

The *Chicago Sun-Times* adopted a set of guidelines in 1977. . . . Although Don Kopriva, assistant to the editor, cannot say whether they have ever come into play, the guidelines remain valid. "All we are talking about here is good news judgment combined with good taste and good sense."

The *Sun-Times* is the only one of the 20 largest U.S. daily newspapers with written guidelines on terrorism, according to a presstime survey. The *Plain Dealer* in Cleveland is considering adopting some procedures on covering crises of all kinds, which would include everything from train derailments to nuclear accidents to terrorist incidents.

In addition to fundamental opposition to written guidelines, some editors doubt that any meaningful standard could be formulated. "I think any attempt at a guideline on local terrorism would either be so vague and general so as to be Pablum, or so restrictive that you would violate it more than you would honor it," says Tim McGuire, managing editor of the *Minneapolis Star and Tribune.*

Instead, these editors say they consider each incident on an individual basis and exercise their own news judgment—"being cognizant," as Thomas F. Mulvoy Jr., managing editor of *The Boston Globe*, puts it, "that it is not a baseball game."

"I think we all are sensitized to the need for discretion," says Heath J Meriwether, executive editor of *The Miami Herald.* If there is one rule that his newspaper follows, it is that "we've got to have top editor involvement in what our decision-making process is."

Similarly, Topping of *The New York Times* says "we have experienced editors who are capable of making sensible judgments, who can protect security interests of the United States and the safety of hostages or others who become victims of terrorism."

Topping recalls one incident during the 1979–81 Iranian hostage crisis in which he was called upon to make such a judgment. The *Times* was in touch with a person who had managed to escape from Iran but, before doing so, had taken refuge in the Canadian Embassy in Tehran. "Cyrus Vance, who was then the secretary of state, became aware that this information was in our possession. He telephoned me to ask us to withhold the information because it would endanger other Americans who had also taken refuge in the Canadian Embassy. I agreed to that, and when the hostages had left the Canadian Embassy and there was no more danger involved for them, Secretary Vance telephoned me and we published the story."

With correspondents all over the world, the wire services have more first-hand experience covering terrorism than most U.S. newspapers.

Neither the Associated Press nor United Press International has written guidelines, although UPI has had them in the past. "You have to deal with it [terrorism] on a case-by-case basis," says UPI Editor in Chief Maxwell McCrohon. Walter R. Mears, AP executive news editor, agrees. "The problem with this, as with so much else that we do, is that it almost defies simple rules," he says. "You can't say 'Always do this in this set of circumstances' any more than you can say 'Always write the story with this lead on it.'"

For instance, Mears says, AP would not seek to be a mediator in a terrorist incident. However, during a 1982 incident in Washington, D.C., in which a suspected terrorist threatened to blow up the Washington Monument, an AP reporter became a go-between between the man and police officials. "Given any options, I'd prefer not to have a reporter in that role, but there weren't any at that point," says Mears, who was Washington bureau chief at the time.

According to Mears, part of the way AP conducts itself, "I hope instinctively," is to avoid doing or writing things that could endanger people. The news cooperative is "particularly sensitive" to this, he says, because Middle East correspondent Terry Anderson is one of four Americans currently held hostage by terrorists in Lebanon. . . . "At the same time," Mears adds, "you don't stop doing what you do for a living, or the terrorists have won."

Cover or Cover Up?

When it comes to deciding how to play a story about a terrorist incident, each is "judged on its own merit," says George J. Cotliar, managing editor of the *Los Angeles Times*.

Two of the seven domestic terrorist incidents that took place last year occurred in suburbs of Los Angeles. Both were bombings, both have been attributed by the FBI to extremist Jewish elements, and both appeared on the front page of the *Los Angeles Times*. "What it is really is a news judgment, which we exercise with everything we do," says Cotliar.

But some government officials have suggested that newspapers and other media suspend normal news judgment when it comes to terrorism in the belief that withholding coverage will discourage such acts.

In a speech to the American Bar Association shortly after the TWA hijacking last year, British Prime Minister Margaret Thatcher said: "We must try to find ways to starve the terrorist and the hijacker of the oxygen of publicity on which they depend."

Some journalists subscribe to that view, including David S. Broder, national political correspondent and columnist for *The Washington Post*. "[T]he essential ingredient of any effective antiterrorist policy must be the denial to the terrorists of access to mass media outlets," he told a symposium on terrorism and the news media last fall. "The way by which this denial is achieved—whether by voluntary means of those of us in the press and television, self-restraint, or by government control—is a crucial question for journalists and for all other citizens who share our belief in civil liberties."

"If terrorists can gain leverage, influence and control in the battle for public opinion in free societies by their acts of terrorism, there is an enormous incentive for them to continue such acts," he reasoned.

But many other journalists are unconvinced, worrying that if the media ignore terrorist incidents, terrorists will escalate the volume of terror until the acts can no longer be ignored.

Others think it would be more terrifying not to publish information about terrorist incidents. "A news blackout might generate rumors, and perhaps wild rumors, that could create an even larger crisis," says William B. Ketter, chairman of ASNE's Press, Bar and Public Affairs Committee. Ketter, editor of *The Patriot Ledger* in Quincy, Mass., also says the press would face a potential loss of credibility if it did not report on terrorism, leading readers and viewers to ask: "What else is the press keeping from us?"

"The basic cause of terrorism is not news coverage," declares Ralph Langer, executive editor of *The Dallas Morning News.* "Terrorism comes from real or perceived disputes and problems that aren't resolved."

"We've certainly never been convinced that a lack of information about terrorism is going to be helpful," says Michael Blackman, foreign editor of *The Philadelphia Inquirer.* "Frankly, I think the more you expose these people to readers (and) to viewers, the more that the audience sees what they really are."

The accusation that the news media encourage terrorism by giving terrorists so much publicity is "really difficult to assess," says Brian M. Jenkins, a terrorism expert at the Rand Corp., a California think tank. "It is certainly true that publicity is one of the major objectives of terrorists. It is also true that where press coverage of terrorism has been prohibited, terrorism has tended to decline. But that decline is likely to be the result of other measures taken at the same time."

For example, Jenkins says, a decline in terrorism has been noted in some South American countries where press censorship of terrorist incidents has been accompanied by such things as arbitrary arrests and the use of torture and interrogation.

The question about terrorists' reliance upon publicity, and others, are being studied by academic researchers working under the auspices of the Association for Education in Journalism and Mass Communication. "This is going to be the biggest piece of research that has ever been done on the subject of the news media's relationship to terrorism," says Robert G. Picard, one of the project directors. Findings will be discussed at a conference, tentatively scheduled for winter 1987–88, says Picard, assistant professor at the Manship School of Journalism at Louisiana State University.

Whatever the evidence shows, newspaper editors clearly are concerned about being "used" as a platform for terrorist propaganda.

In September 1976, a group of Croatian nationalists hijacked a TWA jet bound from New York to Chicago and threatened to kill passengers unless a lengthy communique was published on the front page of several U.S. newspapers, including the *Chicago Tribune.* "From that point on, we have been struggling with policies regarding terrorism," says *Tribune* Editor James D. Squires.

Because of the variety of terrorist acts, the newspaper was unable to come up with specific guidelines. "Basically what we do is have a policy which balances out obligation to the reader against national security concerns and the loss of human life."

Adds Squires: "We don't want to be used and manipulated by anyone.

So we try to be as skeptical and as cautious about being compromised in the interest of some special cause or group of people as we are on a day-to-day basis when we deal with government."

The Washington Post is another of the newspapers that printed the terrorists' treatise. "I don't believe that we would do that now," says Executive Editor Bradlee. "I think that would be considered hopelessly wimpish, chicken. We pride ourselves that the president of the United States can't tell us what to put on Page One. Even some judges have difficulty telling us what to put on Page One."

Reuters, the London-based international news and information service, also recently took steps to guard against being used by terrorists. In March, Editor-in-Chief Michael Reupke directed reporters not to write stories about threats of terrorist actions, except on rare occasions and with the approval of top editors, and not to mention Reuters or any other news organization by name as having received statements of responsibility for terrorist actions. In most cases, he said in his directive, an unspecific term like "news organization" should be used. "We must discourage any idea that Reuters or other news organizations are suitable targets for terrorist activities or suitable channels for genuine or hoax threats or claims," he explained.

Seeking Solutions

So far, there has been no indication that U.S. government officials will seek to impose their own judgments over editors' news judgments.

After Prime Minister Thatcher's call for restraints on press coverage last summer, U.S. Attorney General Edwin Meese III said the Justice Department was considering asking the media to adopt written guidelines on covering terrorism. Subsequently, the cabinet-level task force, in which Meese was a participant, examined U.S. policy on combating terrorism, including problems caused by media coverage.

In its report, issued in February, the task force concluded that the solution to the problems "is not government-imposed restraint that conflicts with the First Amendment's protection of freedom of speech and the press." Rather, it said: "The media must serve as their own watchdog. Journalistic guidelines have been developed for use during wartime to protect lives and national security, and in some circumstances should be considered appropriate during a terrorist situation."

The only joint government-media action it recommended was "regular meetings" between media representatives and government officials on terrorism coverage, which, it said, "could contribute to more effective government-media relations."

That process has begun. On May 6, representatives from ANPA and

ASNE met with Parker W. Borg, deputy director of the State Department's office of the ambassador-at-large for counter-terrorism.

The most extreme call for government action appears to have come from a former general counsel of the Federal Communications Commission. Bruce E. Fein has said it should be against the law for the news media to disclose the citizenship, religious affiliation or nationality of any hostage, or to perform any role in transmitting demands of hostage takers. He sees little likelihood that such laws will be enacted, though. "The news media, of course, are very powerful on (Capitol) Hill and I think would oppose this with a ferocity that would perhaps make an atom bomb look mild in comparison."

To date, Congress has not made any move to legislate restrictions on press coverage of terrorist incidents. The House Foreign Affairs Committee's Subcommittee on Europe and the Middle East conducted a hearing last summer, following the TWA Flight 847 incident, on the news media and terrorism. The thrust of the hearing was not on the need for government regulation but rather on the need for media self-regulation and self-criticism. In addition, a dozen members of Congress have urged the television networks to convene a "summit" to consider coverage guidelines, a call that was renewed after NBC this year aired an interview with Abu Abbas, the terrorist wanted in connection with the Achille Lauro hijacking.

Thus far, however, there has been no movement toward formal, industry-wide, self-regulation.

Following the American Bar Association meeting last summer, two joint ABA-press committees were asked by ABA President William W. Falsgraf to discuss "the feasibility of the media developing voluntary guidelines." ANPA representatives sit on one of the committees. In a follow-up report to Falsgraf, the committees' co-chairmen reported "a consensus" that "terrorist incidents, because of their unpredictability and unique facts, are not susceptible to any kind of uniform approach, whether by the government or the news media."

In addition, some journalists say, guidelines are unenforceable and tend to wilt in the heat of a news event. "Industry guidelines are bad in almost every respect," says ASNE President Gartner. "Different segments of the industry have different missions, have different constituencies, have different philosophies. I think that almost as a rule, written guidelines of any sort are turned around and used against the press and have more of a negative effect than a positive effect."

But if newspapers have been lukewarm to suggestions that they consider adopting their own guidelines on covering terrorism and downright cold to the notion of industry-wide action, the idea of talking about the subject—with other media people, with experts in the field of terrorism and with government officials—has hit their hot button.

Within the past year, the topic of the news media and terrorism has been discussed at the annual conventions of ANPA, the Associated Press Managing Editors, and the Society of Professional Journalists, Sigma Delta Chi, and it was brought up in a question-and-answer session with President Reagan at ASNE's convention. It also has been the subject of numerous smaller meetings and seminars. In fact, some news executives on the terrorism speaking circuit joke about the "cottage industry" that has grown up around the topic.

And while from time to time there seems to be a lull in major terrorist activity, there is no letup in the press' preoccupation with the issue. At the APME meeting last October, the organization's president, Michael J. Davies, called for a conference at which representatives of broadcast and print media would "assess the complicated issues and...see if there are some general areas of restraint that could be agreed upon without compromising our standards."

The proposal by Davies, editor and publisher of *The Hartford Courant*, will become reality Sept. 27. A conference underwritten by Times Mirror, the *Courant's* parent company, will be conducted in Washington, D.C., by Media and Society Seminars, a program of the Graduate School of Journalism at Columbia University. The event will be videotaped for televising in three or four parts on Public Broadcasting Service stations later in the fall.

In congressional testimony last year, Fred W. Friendly, director of Media and Society Seminars, said that, to him, the "third worst outcome" of the controversy surrounding press coverage of the TWA Flight 847 incident would be if the U.S. government were to impose restrictions on reporting during a terrorist crisis. The second worst outcome, he said, would be if government and network officials were to come up with a list of agreed-upon guidelines. But, he said, "the most tragic course of action would be for American journalism—and I include the news magazines and the newspapers—to continue their defensive posture...and learn nothing and do nothing."

A year later, the former television executive is satisfied that at least half of what constitutes his worst fear has not come to pass.

"There has been much introspection and meaningful dialog," he reports. "The question is, when the roof falls...do those lessons that we seem to learn hold up, or do they just come crashing to the floor with the debris?"

19 What Did Mr. Dwyer Do, Daddy?

by David B. Dick

> When the treasurer of the state of Pennsylvania pulled a
> revolver out of his briefcase at a press conference and com-
> mitted suicide, the act of violence was news for the tele-
> vision and newspapers around the country. But reporters
> who witnessed the event had visceral reactions to it, and, as
> David Dick sums it up, many began to realize that they
> were human beings first, and journalists second. If such
> violence continues to be part of our evening news, suggests
> Dick, soon "there won't be anybody left to watch." Dick
> was a broadcast journalist for twenty-six-years, first in
> Louisville and then as a correspondent for CBS News. He is
> now a professor of journalism at the University of Ken-
> tucky. His article is reprinted from *The Quill*, March 1987.

"Well, as you could see,
he committed suicide, darling."

The medium has become the madness, and this just won't do if we are to
survive as anything resembling rational sensitive, caring human beings.

When R. Budd Dwyer, the treasurer of Pennsylvania, called a news
conference January 22 [1987] in Harrisburg, ostensibly to announce his
resignation before being sentenced for a fraud conviction, he talked for a
while, pulled out a .357 Magnum revolver, stuck it into his mouth and
pulled the trigger.

The subsequent news treatment of the incident became a terrifying
example of Professor Harold D. Lasswell's "silver bullet" theory of mass
communications.

The silver bullet zaps you before you have a chance to say, "Hell, no."

The question of what news people should do when a silver bullet
strikes is often described as a "dilemma." But it is a continuing problem,
and calling it a dilemma provides an unacceptable loophole through which
weak-willed, quick-and-dirty practitioners slip too easily and too piously.

"A tough one to call," I hear them saying darkly in their newsrooms
when a silver bullet strikes, meanwhile shouting to a colleague who has just
walked in from another assignment, and who has therefore missed the
really Big One: "Take a look at this!"

The fact is, in Pennsylvania a tormented human being blew his brains out, and for reasons known only to him did it not in the privacy of his garage but center stage before television cameras.

The matter should not have been ignored; but it should have been treated with a greater regard for TV viewers, the radio audience, and the readers of newspapers.

Before we rush to place the stamp of "insensitivity" on one news medium, TV, we should remember that radio and print journalists were also present at the news conference. *The Washington Post* and the *New York Daily News*, in fact, were among the papers that ran pictures of the final seconds of Dwyer's life.

There is no justification for naming television as the only bad guy in this bizarre Pennsylvania morality play. We journalists are all human beings first and journalists second. If journalists today are guilty, as some charge, of sometimes forgetting that maxim, then they have played a major role in the desensitizing of an entire generation with an unrelenting fusillade of silver bullets.

I've done my part in the desensitizing process. While a correspondent with CBS News, I was confronted with having to recommend whether or not to use footage of one human being killing another human being in the Baton Rouge airport. That was another silver bullet in the head. I now profoundly regret my recommendation to run the pictures.

It's time to recognize that we in the news media are part of the problem; it's time that men and women in the business had the moral courage to take a stand for a higher level of ethical conduct.

Forget the Dwyer suicide for a moment. I suggest that it's wrong as a general principle for one human being (an assignment editor, perhaps, or a news director) to say to another human being (a camera operator in the field): "You get the pictures, we'll decide whether to use them."

To be sure, the you-get-the-pictures business has been Standard Operating Procedure for many years. Perhaps media critic Ron Powers summed up the moral absurdity of it best when he quoted a photographer as having said: "I am a camera with the shutters open. . . . I am passive. . . . I don't think."

This handsomely paid passiveness serves the newsgathering process well—to a point. But every human being must have the option to turn the camera off and go to another human being's assistance when life itself has been placed in jeopardy.

Perhaps there was not time enough to help the state treasurer of Pennsylvania. Perhaps only in hindsight was there time enough to distract him and wrestle the gun from his hand.

But as one human being trying to be rational, sensitive and caring, I find no ethical justification for blindly broadcasting the tape of suicide, to surrendering to the mindlessness of, "If we've got it, we ought to use it." I think I hear some of my former professional colleagues saying something like, "Come off it, David. Now you're hiding behind your newfound academic gowns, preaching morality to us when in fact if *you* had staffed the Dwyer news conference, you would have expected your camera operator to have continued rolling, and you would have been disappointed if it had been any other way.

"After all, the Emmy sitting on your mantlepiece down on your retirement farm was won because cameraman Laurens Pierce kept rolling when George Wallace was gunned down in the Laurel, Maryland shopping center."

Partly true. The day Wallace was shot, I agonized with everybody else at CBS News while the film was in the processor, and I rejoiced with everybody else when it emerged with every frame in focus.

Nevertheless, there is a considerable difference between the attempted assassination of George Wallace and the suicide of R. Budd Dwyer.

And there certainly is a difference between the Dwyer pictures and the Abraham Zapruder footage of the assassination of President Kennedy, the CBS News footage of the murder of presidential candidate Robert F. Kennedy and the attempted assassination of President Reagan.

Jack Ruby's shot into the stomach of Lee Harvey Oswald, and the sight of more than 900 bloated bodies at Jonestown are exceptional and unavoidable situations. Jim Jones fired a silver bullet, too, but the story was not that he, as an individual, committed suicide. The story was the tragedy of more than 900 humans led astray.

Edward T. Adams won a Pulitzer Prize and a Sigma Delta Chi Distinguished Service Award for his photo series of the Saigon chief of police's point-blank firing of a pistol bullet into the head of a Vietcong prisoner. The prominence of those involved did not determine the news value of the photos; the brutality of the war did. Likewise, footage of the murder of ABC Correspondent Bill Stewart in Nicaragua was the turning point of that civil war. Whether we are talking about George Wallace or the brothers Kennedy or Lee Harvey Oswald or the Vietcong prisoner or Bill Stewart or the members of the Jonestown cult, we are talking about *victims* of violence. They were acted upon, and because of who they were, or because of the context of their times, what happened to them was indeed newsworthy. That news people were present at the time of the event, or shortly thereafter, was a matter of coincidence.

The death of Budd Dwyer was newsworthy, and should have been reported. But he was both victim and victimizer, a deranged man who chose to make us all victims of his madness. The news media cooperated, as planned—unwittingly before the shot, and mindlessly after the shot. Journalists were parties to the act.

R. Budd Dwyer was hardly a household name anywhere outside Pennsylvania. What made Dwyer "newsworthy" was not so much his prominence as it was his insertion of the .357 Magnum revolver into his mouth and the pulling of the trigger.

Representatives of the few television stations that aired the entire suicide gave a nobler explanation of why they did so. Said one: "It's a historic event. . . . It's a reflection of a very important man in Pennsylvania society and what he did." That's a peculiarly skewed definition of "historic," one that would fail any test of rigorous thought.

All right. Am I to understand that WPXI-TV in Pittsburgh and WPVI-TV in Philadelphia and other stations that carried it are comfortable with the knowledge that this gruesome, horrifying, brain-searing footage of one human being's death was seen in households where children, never mind "adults," were present?

"What did Mr. Dwyer do, Daddy?"

"Well, as you could see, he committed suicide, darling."

Duty supersedes comfortableness. I know that. But do professional and ethical journalists (which is not, I hope, a contradiction in terms) have a *duty* to show the public in complete or nearly complete detail the self-destruction of another human being?

I think not.

So, what to do?

Don't show the footage involving the gun. Simply tell the story with the following explanation: "We choose not to show the public pictures that exceed the bounds of our concept of what is decent and proper and above all, humane."

That course was not widely followed. And, predictably, other journalists (including at least one former professional turned academic) had a field day evaluating the sorry state of affairs. The Louisville *Courier-Journal* ran a headline: "Graphic suicide photos put news executives in a quandary."

Is there anyone out there who wonders why anyone should have been in a quandary about something so evident to a reasonably discerning person?

But then, what is to be said about R. Budd Dwyer's "use" of the media? Mr. Dwyer had the option to take his own life many ways, of course.

But if we journalists, broadcast and print, don't exercise our right of refusing to scatter Dwyer's brain fragments from one end of Pennsylvania to the other, and possibly from one end of the nation to the other, all in the name of "he did it, and we have pictures," then we've sold our souls to a devil who insists that the public has a right to see everything, no matter how macabre.

Media critic Powers longs for "guidelines for the human soul," but there is the possibility that for quite some time, in the rush to tell it like it is and show it like it was, some journalists have simply given up on the idea of guidelines.

They see guidelines as self-righteous intrusions into their lives, and R. Budd Dwyer will fade from memory—until the next time a silver bullet comes along.

We ought to meet this media devil head-on with language he just possibly may be able to understand. Putting the Dwyer footage on the air (or on paper) is very much like saying, "We've got a suicide, y'all come."

Let Hollywood dally with the grotesque: professional journalists have no business wallowing in that swamp. The silver bullets increasingly have become the shots heard around the living rooms of our nation. It's time to remember the simple guideline that we are human beings first, journalists second.

Anything less than that will lead eventually to destruction of the human soul, and at that point it won't matter if passive journalists are there to report it. There won't be anybody left to watch.

Crime, Violence, and the Mass Media: For Further Reading

Doris A. Graber, *Crime News and the Public*. New York: Praeger, 1980.

Philip Lesley, *Overcoming Opposition: A Survival Manual for Executives*. Englewood Cliffs, N.J.: Prentice-Hall, 1984.

Dan A. Lewis (ed.), *Reactions to Crime*. Beverly Hills, Calif.: Sage, 1981.

Abraham H. Miller, *Terrorism: The Media and the Law*. Dobbs Ferry, N.Y.: Transnational Publishers, 1982.

VI

Sex and Sensationalism in the Mass Media

Sex sells. That notion seems to have become axiomatic in modern American society. The mass media are business enterprises not supported by taxpayers or subsidized by government. They need to sell to make a profit to stay in business. Sex and sensationalism have therefore become staple ingredients in much mass communication in order to gain and hold an audience and earn a profit.

In truth, American newspapers on the whole are not nearly so sexually blatant or senationalistic as the tabloids of London's Fleet Street or so titillating as the photos of scantily clad young women that adorn nearly every page of South Africa's white and otherwise ultraconservative newspapers. But sex has often been used exploitatively in American media, and it will probably continue to be used so. The older, more journalistically conservative and econically well-established media have given up on sex and sensationalism. Look at early editions of the *New York Times*, the *Washington Post*, *Time*, *Harper's*, *The Atlantic Monthly*, etc., and you will see that in their youth these publications were not loath to tempt new audiences with promises of salacious content.

Younger, less well-established magazines and newspapers frequently use sex and sensationalism to build circulation and audience. Television continues to lure audiences with both sex and sensationalism. And it works, regardless of individuals and groups who try to prove otherwise. America is still turned on by sex. When *Time* magazine put a nearly nude Cheryl Tiegs on its cover, that issue sold far more copies than almost any other in its history. *Playboy* and *Penthouse* magazines are the most widely read magazines on American college campuses—probably more thoroughly read than college textbooks. Daytime and primetime television continue to treat sex and sex-related topics, with a manner sometimes shockingly candid and sometimes educational as it dramatizes formerly taboo subjects. Television and radio talk shows and news programs alike have begun to discuss topics previously only whispered about out of earshot of "polite" society.

What does all of this mean? How much should sex be discussed in the mass media? And how?

20 Censor Entertainment? Teens, Parents Speak Up

U.S. News & World Report

U.S. News & World Report asked adults and youths, in separate forums, to explore how sex and violence are portrayed in movies and on TV, in rock lyrics and in music videos—and their impact on child behavior. The report was published in the October 28, 1985, issue.

Nationwide, the youth-entertainment controversy shapes up as a home-front battle between the generations over standards of decency.

What outrages adults usually leaves their children unfazed. Yet sometimes it's the young who take a more critical stand.

The teenage daughter of Martha Davis, lead singer of a rock band, the Motels, was embarrassed by her mother's song "Hungry" in the newly released album "Shock." Davis, 35, says the lyrics are "pretty blatant" and she made a mistake singing them. She adds: "My daughter doesn't like the song. She makes fun of me constantly."

To gauge the differences between adults and youth, *U.S. News & World Report* conducted separate focus-group sessions with teenagers age 13 to 15 and their parents on October 2.

Here are samples of what each group said on topics such as movie and TV shows, rock lyrics, video images and their impact on child behavior—

Music

Teens

Stacie Meyers, ninth grade, Reston, Va.: My parents want to protect me from all the dirty lyrics. But they can't stop me. I was talking to my stepfather, and he said parents can only do so much. If you haven't learned right from wrong by age 10, then you're going to have to learn on your own. I believe that.

Maybe singers use the lyrics because they think teenagers think it's cool to talk about drugs and sex. They say it because they think they'll get a lot more publicity and fans.

Neal Miles, eighth grade, Springfield. Va.: Lots of parents, just because they don't like the music, think it's bad. They say, "That's garbage music; it's terrible." They don't think we should listen. Those are real protective parents. Mine aren't like that. I don't listen to songs like "Darling Nicki" around my parents. That would embarrass me. If there's a song on I think they would disapprove of, I just turn to another station.

Betsy Nord, ninth grade, Reston, Va.: I'll be listening to stuff like the Suicidal Tendencies down in my room, and my parents will hear it through the floor. They'll say: "That's trash. Why do you listen to that?" And I say: "I like it, it's not my problem if you don't like it. You're not the one listening." But it's not really a source of conflict. It's not like they won't let me listen.

My parents can't exactly handle the music I like. I came out of a Billy Idol concert, I could barely talk and barely hear. And my dad was like, "I am never going to a concert with you, *never!*" He just doesn't like the music; he thinks it's too loud.

Keith McAllister, 10th grade, Falls Church, Va.: We just went over rating of records in English class. It's nothing like the movies. You don't have to have your parents come with you to buy an R record. You just go in the store and buy it. I don't think parents really know that you already have most of the records they're going to rate.

Parents

Beth Nord: Having the words out in the open takes a lot of the charge out of them. But the image of women portrayed is very negative, and the kids can't help but absorb it. As long as women contitute to accept this and buy those records, it will continue. That is why there's need for record ratings. If we as women would not accept that, the problem would be considerably less.

Brenda Scruggs: I heard some lyrics on the car radio, and the kids were singing it. I tuned my ear in to make sure that's what I was hearing. I wanted to say something to them, but I didn't know what to say. It's as though I was invading their privacy because they were enjoying the song. It wasn't bothering them in the least; it was bothering me.

Helyn Davis: I don't like Prince. I don't like what he says in most of his songs, or the way he acts. He could make money by not being cheap, by not acting cheap. Michael Jackson doesn't act cheap, and he's making money.

Stephen Ansell: There are ghoulish death scenes, chains, the sadistic on MTV that just makes my blood crawl, and I just don't like even seeing it.

Pamela Miles: We have a flip side of this whole controversy. Our church is heavy into having programs about rock music right now, and my oldest son, who is in his 20s, is ready to go burn the place down. He feels that banning all rock music is censorship and that is wrong. I think the grading or the rating of songs is a good idea.

Movies and TV

Teens

Michael Ausell, the ninth grade, Fairfax, VA.: "Day of the Dead" and "Return of the Living Dead" are real popular now. They're R-rated and "Day of the Dead" is X rated, but I saw that, too. I know everybody who works at the movies. They card you, and I just walked right in. If you want to see a gross movie, they should let you. All it was, for about an hour straight, was killing. It was so stupid. It wasn't really violence; it was more gore.

Betsy Nord: My parents don't care if I see R-rated movies. They have this new thing, PG-13, which is pretty dumb because anybody who's not 13, they're like, "Well, why can't I get into this one? It used to be rated PG."

Neal Miles: I have my own card from the video store, and I just go to check out rated-R movies. My parents don't care. When I see a movie that's really weird or something. I don't like to have my parents sit with me. It's embarrassing to sit in front of your parents and watch these people smoke pot and stuff.

Crystal Scruggs, ninth grade, Alexandria, Va.: Bill Cosby is really a trip; he jokes, but he teaches you a lesson. He has a family, and they have problems that might be like you have in your own family. You can solve them through the Cosby show.

Parents

Stephen Ansell: Before we even had a VCR, Michael was already seeing R-rated movies at friends' houses. And then we got our Beta system, and we talked about movies to see, and he says: "I've already seen it at Joe Blow's house." And I go, "Oh!" There are a number of things I don't I want him to watch, but I really can't stop him at age 14. If he doesn't see it at my house, he's going to see it at someone else's.

Joana McCracken: My son's reaction to many of these movies is: "Oh, another teen exploitation movie." Its a big joke in our family: How bad can they exploit them this time? They sort of watch with a grain of salt. We need to give the children some credit for recognizing that a particular movie, song or group is not the real world or the world as we would like them to perceive it.

Pamela Miles: The worst thing they get out of watching television is they think everything can be solved in a half-hour segment.

As for movies, to start out we were not going to have R-rated movies in our house, but now we watch them. I'm concerned. Is it having a bad effect or not? We didn't sit there night after night watching this stuff when the older kids were teens. I hope that other influences in Neal's life are stronger than this kind of stuff.

Beth Nord: I'm real ambivalent about violence in movies like "Rambo." I feel that, on the one hand, it doesn't have an effect; on the other hand, maybe it does, maybe people who are kind of borderline might be affected.

Impact

Teens

Stacie Meyers: My brother, who is 12, is like hard-core. He wants to get a Mohawk [haircut]. My parents are totally against it. He listens to groups like the Dead Kennedys. He's just into all that. And my mom's like, "If you even get into that, you're out of the house."

Michael Ansell: Some of what you see influences you. If you see these guys doing great tricks on a skateboard in a movie, then you want to go and try it. And if you see these guys surfing, so you go to the beach and you surf.

You just watch "Miami Vice" and then go to the mall and buy those clothes. I know guys that wore spikes all over their body like that guy in Judas Priest did.

Crystal Scruggs: I know someone who dresses like Cyndi Lauper. She even shaved the side of her head and colored it. If you saw some of the things she wears, you'd think her mother would say something. My mother would never let me shave the side of my head and color it red and put light-yellow streaks in it.

Neal Miles: You don't come away with much from your average show or song. You come away with, "Oh, I like the music, it was exciting." But nothing like, "Oh, that kid has a 3-foot Mohawk dyed green and orange, and I think I'm going to do that, too."

Parents

Helyn Davis: The music isn't affecting my daughter Stacie, but the lyrics affect her 12-year-old brother. He keeps writing *anarchy* on my phone book, and I think he gets it from a group called the Dead Kennedys. He'll ask me a question like: "What do you think of the government?" I look at him and say: "I was a drill instructor of the U.S. Army; I was an officer in the Army, and you ask me what I think of the government?"

I also think some of this is making sex disgusting. A song came on the radio and my daughter Stacie said, "You know, I don't think I want to get married." From the way they're saying it on these songs and from what she sees on TV, she's getting the impression that sex is dirty.

Joana McCracken: My son has long hair and a pierced ear, and I feel that has something to do with the rock pictures he has plastered all over his bedroom. His room is wall-to-wall posters from the magazines he buys and concerts. I'm not thrilled. But he doesn't use alcohol and drugs or steal and lie. So I figure I'm not going to make a big scene about the hair and the earring.

Brenda Scruggs: I can't say too much for the rock concerts, but I know with Crystal viewing the videos, she wants to streak her hair, just one area in the front. She gets that from the different performers. They all either have purple, green, orange or yellow in their hair. I keep saying, "Well, as long as you don't make it in a point or shave one side." I really don't want her to dye her hair. She knows it, but I don't think that's going to stop her.

Michael McAllister: The real driving influence is peer pressure. If you take a kid, say, that is a ringleader, and he's influenced by this, then the kids who are followers will be.

Kids who have a problem are those not really making it in the real world, and their escape is in the fantasy land. But what we've been talking about here the kids see as entertainment.

21 Sex in the Media

by Jane D. Brown

There's plenty of sex and sexuality in the mass media, but it's unrealistic, according to research conducted by Jane D. Brown, who directs the Mass Media Research Center at the University of North Carolina School of Journalism. Her article focusing on what young people are watching and reading is from *Planned Parenthood Review*, Winter 1986.

Melissa, 12, came home from school, fixed a peanut butter and jelly sandwich, went to her room and turned on her TV set to the Music Television (MTV) station with the sound up loud. Billy Idol, dressed in black leather and riding a motorcycle, had just arrived at a church where his anxious bride awaits him. The "bridesmaids"—two temptresses similarly clad in black leather—gyrate on the altar. The sneering, provocative guests leer as the groom jams the wedding ring on the terrified bride's bleeding finger. A woman trying to get up from her hospital bed is pushed back down by a sinister doctor. A motorcycle crashes through the church's stained glass window, a coffin is nailed shut on the altar, and the bride becomes a cobwebbed skeleton.

Melissa turns the channel to her favorite soap opera, "General Hospital," in which Susan says to Allan, "My most vivid fantasy of all, to make love to you in the mansion, in this bed, the bed where you consummated your marriage . . . ."

Later, bored with television, Melissa picks up her mother's *Cosmopolitan* and reads an article called "How to Make a Guy Cry," and another called "25 Great Date Looks" while listening on her headphones to Madonna singing "Like a Virgin."

The media available to our children today are filled with information—or misinformation—about sex and sexuality. Academic studies of the content of the media have found, for example, that on:

Music videos

- Almost one-half of the songs are about sexual or romantic love.
- One-quarter to one-third of the characters on music videos are dressed provocatively.
- 60 percent of the videos include some portrayal of sexual feelings or impulses.
- The videos that portary sexually-related activity contain an average of five portrayals each.
- More than half of the videos contain violence, and more than three-fourths of these violent videos also include sexual imagery.

Soap operas

- On average, soap operas contain approximately 1.5 verbal mentions of intercourse in an hour, one act of erotic touching (touching with clear sexual overtones) every two hours, one visual implication of intercourse every 2.5 hours, and one reference to rape every 11 hours.
- Sexual activity among those not married to each other occurs at four of five times the rate found among married partners.
- In a six-month period on one soap opera, the show's characters went through eight divorces, two bigamous marriages, four separations, and the planning of six divorces. Twenty-one couples were living or sleeping together out of wedlock.

Other media

- More than one-third of the ads for network shows appearing in *TV Guide* contain sexual elements like, "She's the world's sexiest photographer," "Revenge-hungry model wants Jack dead!" or "These are the paper dolls and these are the people who control them. Racine uses her bed to build an empire."
- "Adult," sexually explicit videocassettes account for 15 to 25 percent

of total sales. Only one videocassette dealer in four does not carry X-rated selections.

- About 800,000 homes subscribe to the *Playboy* channel, which provides such "soft-core" pornographic moves as "Her Wicked Ways" and "Naked Sun" on cable television.

Effect on Children

Does this kind of media environment affect a child's own feelings about sexuality and subsequent behavior? Researchers are beginning to find out. Of course, it is extremely difficult to sort out the effect of media from all the other influences on a child's life, but some preliminary studies suggest that sexual content in the media can affect what an adolescent thinks of his or her own sexual experiences. For example, Stanley Baran, a communication researcher at Cleveland State University, in studies of adolescents and college students has found that when adolescents have positive perceptions of the sexual prowess and pleasure of television chaaracters, they are less satisfied with their own initial experiences with sexual intercourse. He found, too, that the more the older adolescent thinks sex on television is realistic and sees media characters as experiencing sexual satisfaction, the more he or she is dissatisfied with remaining a virgin.

Studies have shown that college students who watch soap operas believe that divorce, illegitimate births, and abortions occur more frequently in real life than non-viewers do. In one study of adolescents, I found that adolescents who view more "sexy" content on television are more likely to have had sexual intercourse.

We must keep in mind, of course, that these studies cannot assess which factor—the sexual activity or the media exposure—came first. We might easily conclude that television caused the adolescent to be less satisfied with her virginal state and thus stimulated her to set out to remedy that situation. However, the opposite sequence—in which sexual activity leads to increased interest in sexual content on television and a change in perception of that content—is equally plausible.

Direct Results Found

A recent series of experimental studies on the impact of erotic movies on attitudes toward women and on perceptions of sexual violence allows us to say with more certainty that this medium's sexual content does have direct results. Dolf Zillman and Jennings Bryant of Indiana University and the University of Evansville conducted a study that involved exposing college students to about five hours of explicitly sexual films over a six-week period. Subsequently these students were much more likely to recommend fewer months of incarceration for a convicted rapist than those who had less exposure or no exposure at all to the erotic films. Both males and females who had viewed the erotic content also were less likely to be supportive of the women's movement. And the males were more likely to respond affirmatively to such statements as, "Pickups should expect to put out." "A woman doesn't mean 'no' unless she slaps you," and "If they are old enough to bleed, they are old enough to butcher."

Studies such as these are especially frightening in the context of the increasing "eroticization" of much of mainstream media. Children today are much more likely to be exposed to what most would have considered erotic or pornographic content 10 years ago. We are only beginning to learn how this fact will affect their sexual views and behaviors now and in the future.

Citizens' Groups Active

What can be done in the meantime? A number of citizens' groups have begun to sound the alarm about the increasingly sexually violent content of the media. And, as a result, MTV, the 24-hour-a-day music video channel, has reduced the amount of air time for playing videos like Billy Idol's "White Wedding" described above. A number of congressional wives also have made some progress in their efforts to have the recording industry rate rock lyrics according to their sexual explicitness.

Unfortunately, the history of citizens' groups vs. the national media does not show many long-term victories. The frequency of violent portrayals on television did decrease to some extent as the result of public outcry in the late '60s and early '70s. But today we see that, to keep the audience "aroused," some of those previously violent portrayals have been linked with or replaced by sexual portrayals.

Citizens' groups most likely will have greatest success at the local level, especially in this era of deregulation at the federal level. Local television stations depend on the support of local advertisers and should be responsive to the communities they serve. Some communities have been able to get their local cable operators to take the *Playboy* channel off their systems, for example. Other groups have convinced local convenience stores to move the "sex" magazines out of children's eyesight or to stop selling them altogether.

Certainly, we also must encourage our local television stations to carry contraceptive advertising and public service announcements such as those recently developed by Planned Parenthood. It is clear that our sexually active children are interested in the sexual content of the media. Unfortunately, that sexual content almost never includes discussion of the potentially harmful consequences of sexual activity.

And finally, . . . we must be aware of the highly sexualized nature of the media our children are exposed to. We must talk with them about this content. We must help them sort out what is appropriate and fundamentally human from that which is cruel, inhumane, and unloving. While not an easy task, it is certainly a necessary task as long as we live in the current media environment.

22 Dirty Words and Blushing Editors

Warning: This Article Is Rated X

by Linda Lotridge Levin

When a news source uses dirty words or suggestive language, the news accounts should report what the person said—verbatim, in whole words, not hints and blank spaces, says Linda Lotridge Levin, a former reporter and now assistant professor of journalism at the University of Rhode Island. Levin's article is from *The Quill*. September 1986.

Journalism professors and city editors have been known to tell their neophyte reporters to "never lead with a quote unless the pope says 'shit.'"

I was reminded of that admonition in July as I groped my way through a puzzling wire story in my local paper, *The Journal* in Providence, Rhode Island.

The story was about a seven-to-two U.S. Supreme Court decision that upheld the right of a high school in the state of Washington to suspend a student for three days for using unsuitable language during a speech at a school assembly.

In nominating a friend for student government office, the student had used "sexual references but no obscene words," the story said.

Come on, I thought. If he had not uttered any dirty words, how bad could his language have been?

And if the student's non-obscene language got him into so much trouble that the Supreme Court had to resolve the case, shouldn't the paper have published his exact words so readers would know what was going on?

I'm a former reporter who now teaches journalism, and I have a longtime interest (which some of my friends probably find a bit peculiar) in how newspapers handle dirty words. So I decided to find out just how bad the student's language had been.

To find out, I consulted several out-of-town newspapers dated July 8, the day after the Supreme Court decision. It didn't take long to figure out that in reporting the court's decision, the press once again had pursed its collective lips and refused—with a few exceptions—to talk dirty. Even when, as in this case, no dirty words had been used.

The disputed speech consisted of just six sentences, according to press reports, which ought to have made the telling of the story relatively simple. However, what I found in the newspapers I looked at were out-of-context bits and pieces of the student's remarks—if even that.

The Boston Globe, which fancies itself a world-class paper, was no more useful than *The Journal* in helping me understand what had transpired at that school assembly. The student had made "sexual references" but had not used any obscene words, the *Globe* reported.

The Houston Post added a twist: Instead of using the phrase "sexual references," it described the speech as having contained "crude sexual innuendoes." The *Chicago Tribune* weighed in with "sexually suggestive." *The Detroit News* called the disputed words "crude sexual allusions" that caused a "brief uproar" among fellow students.

An uproar over what? Who knows? Surely the readers of these newspapers, and many others, hadn't a clue. And we weren't talking about a story that had been hidden away, either. The stories were generally on page one, or at least toward the front of the main news section.

The *Los Angeles Times* also ran the story on page one, saying that the student had made "several sexual allusions." But unlike the other papers, it also offered a sample of the speech: "Among other things," said the story, the student "referred to the candidate as 'a man who is firm—he's firm in his pants, he's firm in his shirt, and his character is firm.'"

The Plain Dealer in Cleveland reaffirmed the firmness bit, as did *The Washington Post* and the *St. Louis Post-Dispatch*. Pretty mild, I thought. The speech would produce snickers—but a three-day suspension?

The light dawned as I read *The Hartford Courant* in Connecticut and *The Courier-Journal* in Louisville, Kentucky. Both papers made it plain that the speechmaker had gone beyond "firm" and had created a sustained, locker-room metaphor, complete with talk about the candidate going to a "climax" for his constituency.

It was *The New York Times* that did the most thorough in-context job of describing what the student had said. According to the *Times*, the speech said the candidate was "firm in his pants," he was "a man who takes his point and pounds it in," and he was "a man who will go to the very end— even to the climax—for each and every one of you."

Finally, in this freedom-of-speech case, I knew what the offending speech had been. But it had taken a long time and a lot of research to find out.

Is this any way for newspaper editors to treat their readers? If the pope, heaven forbid, should ever utter the "S" word before a public audience, one wonders how many American papers would carry an accurate version of his remarks.

The let's-protect-our-readers-from-dirty-talk attitude is nothing new in the newspaper world. In 1976, then Secretary of Agriculture Earl Butz lost his job after he was caught with his foot in his mouth. He had said, in what he supposed was an off-the-record moment, "I'll tell you what coloreds want. It's three things: first, a tight pussy; second, loose shoes; and third, a warm place to shit."

Editors around the country grabbed their blue pencils and went to work on that quote. The results were embarrassing. *The Washington Post* offered this ludicrous account of the Butz quote: "I'll tell you what coloreds want. It's three things: first, a tight [woman's sexual organ]; second, loose shoes, and third, a warm place to [defecate]."

The Boston Globe came the closest to printing the quote in its entirety. However, it felt the need to protect its readers from seeing "pussy" in print; so it resorted to a favorite newspaper gimmick: hyphens replaced "pussy."

Both the Providence *Journal* and *The Hartford Courant* carried the Associated Press account, which avoided any direct quote. Instead, the AP reported that Butz used language that "referred to blacks' presumed sexual and bathroom predilections in a derogatory manner."

If that was not obscure enough, the story in *The New York Times* probably caused some readers to do a doubletake. The *Times*, reporting the "three things" that Butz said blacks want, wrote: "The things were listed, in order, in obscene, derogatory and scatological terms."

So, what the hell did any of that mean to a reader in search of The Truth?

(In Connecticut, *The Bridgeport Post* did not print the quote but informed its readers that if they were curious, they could telephone the newspaper and someone there would read the quote to them.)

What all this dancing around the complete quote probably signaled to most readers was that the secretary of agriculture had spoken some very dirty words, maybe even some or all of the FCC's seven "filthy" words that are generally not allowed over the airways (shit, fuck, tit, cocksucker, mother-fucker, piss and cunt).

Most children today know all or some of those words by the time they leave grammar school. Magazines print some of them, even the kind of magazine a junior high school student might read at home. Recently, *People* used one of the seven when it quoted Ted Turner as describing Atlanta's drinking water as tasting like it had piss in it. And what junior high student, with or without parental permission, has not seen the movie *Beverly Hills Cop* and heard its star, Eddie Murphy, utter some of the FCC Seven. Incessantly.

Nonetheless, the country's newspapers continue to "protect" the public from even the mildest expletives.

In 1985, I surveyed about 25 editors of daily newspapers in New England to find out how they handle quotations that include vulgar or obscene language when such language is uttered in a newsworthy context. What I learned was that in an effort to remain the guardian of the public's morals and to present, as several noted, "a family newspaper," most had written policies on the use of—or rather the avoidance of—"dirty" language.

The Providence *Journal*, for example, had a written policy that listed taboo words. They included "ass, unless it refers to a donkey"; "crap, unless it is used in the plural as a gambling term"; and "screw, only if it refers to a small metal object used by woodworkers."

The *Norwich Bulletin* in Connecticut had an unwritten policy; it was a simple one: "No vulgar language at all."

According to John J. Foley, then managing editor of *The Day* in New London, Connecticut, his newspaper had no written policy either. "We use good taste as our rule of thumb," he said.

The *Portland Press-Herald* in Maine had a written policy on obscenities. It said, "When the news involves obscenity, we skirt it with euphemisms, indirect quotation or blank spaces." The policy noted that even though other media are becoming more explicit in the use of vulgar and obscene language, newspapers are reluctant to do so. "One reason is that as locally based media, newspaper performance is judged and consequently conditioned by a local audience. The newspaper is close to that audience, as close as the homes to which it is delivered. As close as the families whose adults and children are exposed to it."

Perhaps the response I received from William B. Ketter, editor of *The Patriot Ledger* in Quincy, Massachusetts, best summed up the attitude of the press toward the use of "dirty" words in print. "Although profanity and obscenity have become more widely used in recent years," he said, "their use in a family newspaper can seldom be justified."

The Patriot Ledger had an in-house test for determining whether to print such words: "Why use it?" rather than "Why not use it?"

Why not, indeed? The pious press, in playing moral guardian—supernanny—to its readers, prints half quotes or doctored quotes or no quotes at all when confronted with "unacceptable" language. Such quotes leave readers wondering what the "real" story is.

Editors are concerned about establishing and preserving credibility with readers. To that end, being straight and candid with readers in all matters is very much in fashion.

Why, then, are so many editors willing to chip away at that hard-won credibility when confronted with dirty words or suggestive language? It's time to quit blushing, and to report the news as it happened.

Sex and Sensationalism in the Mass Media: For Further Reading

Stuart Ewen and Elizabeth Even, *Channels of Desire: Mass Images and the Shaping of American Consciousness.* New York: McGraw-Hill, 1982.

Wilson Bryan Key, *Media Sexploitation.* New York: New American Library, 1977.

VII

Mass Media and Politics

The newcomer to the American political scene can note the number and kinds of mass media available for informing the public and conclude that to get full coverage, to become known to the voters, all a candidate need do is send press releases to all the media, give them all statements, and be ready for the reporters and commentators who will call for interviews.

Of course, it doesn't work that way. Political candidates and political issues have to pass the test of newsworthiness and the idiosyncracies of the various media and the men and women who work for them in order to get space and time in the news. The candidates and their aides have to understand how the print and broadcast media differ in the ways that help the public decide what and who are important enough to support—even whether to vote. Most important in today's political climate, candidates must know how to entice the media to earn time and space, which leads to the accusation of "show biz."

The articles in this section concentrate on what television is doing to major political campaigns, because, barring revolution, candidates will continue to "dress" for television, to plan media events that make them look diplomatic or savvy or down-home or however their consultants tell them they should look. Print isn't to be forgotten, but the reporters and analysts have to wait until the bright lights and minicams are moved, or else watch from behind them.

Many local candidates, running "lesser races," follow the leaders, hoping—often against reality—that local stations and newspapers have staffs large enough and equipment mobile enough to follow them around their districts. Finding limits to both staffs and equipment, perhaps they will wisely turn from the proliferation of media events—pseudo-events in terms of news-worthiness—to discuss issues and their positions on them. Perhaps that's wishful thinking.

On the national scene, the 1980 presidential campaign marked the turning point. The predominantly male newspaper reporters who bused around the country with the candidates and the subjects of Timothy Crouse's popular book *The Boys on the Bus*, got moved because of television. "Packaging" and consultants have become newsworthy. What's next?

23 The Decline of the Boys on the Bus

by Joel Swerdlow

Television dominates political campaigns, but the candidates, not the journalists, call the shots, argues Joel
Swerdlow. It's a "campaign sham," he says, that reporters
resent and the public should, too. Swerdlow is coauthor
with Frank Mankiewicz of *Remote Control Television and
the Manipulation of American Life* and author of numerous
articles. This article is from the *Washington Journalism
Review*, January/February 1981.

In mid-October in Elizabeth, New Jersey, John B. Anderson stands waiting
in front of a microphone. His perfectly coiffed hair, sharply pressed suit,
and impeccably shined shoes are silhouetted against graffiti-covered buildings and rat-infested garbage. Winos wander into the edges of the tableau.
Beyond lies the decrepit waterfront. The air is foul.

On cue, cameras whir and Anderson opens a press conference. He
makes a lengthy statement that includes no new proposals or insights about
the urban blight around him. As cameramen maneuver carefully so that
none of the winos block their view of the presidential candidate, reporters
begin to shout questions—none of which acknowledge the stark evidence of
Elizabeth's decay. The press wants to know what Anderson thinks about the
coming Carter-Reagan debate. A few reporters drift off to a nearby bar. Ten
minutes later, the entourage of reporters and technicians scramble back to
their buses and head out for the next media event.

It is a typical campaign stop, 1980 style—cynically staged with little
substance, designed for television, and almost comically blatant in its disregard of the real issues.

The cold essence of presidential campaigning has become the television camera lens. Campaigns are organized for pictures, not words or
ideas. In fact, the Boys-on-the-Bus—the romantic truth-tellers licensed to
lurch from coast to coast with presidents and would-be presidents—have
become irrelevant. Reporters for newspapers and magazines have been
nudged, literally and figuratively, to the back of the bus by the steady, inexorable encroachment of television.

Television dominates the stage. TV reporters are the stars, but even
they are so controlled that some of the nation's highest paid journalistic

talent has become a virtual arm of the campaigns. Reporters covering the campaign have become members of a herd, physically as well as professionally, seduced—or at least tamed—with comfort and drugged with food and drink.

Presidential campaigning changed so much that veterans of the 1960s and early 1970s felt like antiques or vestigial remnants. Gone were the days when a candidate's chief goal was meeting people. Gone were pre-dawn handshaking at factory gates and the post-midnight meetings with campaign volunteers in storefront headquarters. Gone were the exhausted, bleary-eyed reporters, struggling to make just one more early morning baggage call before their flesh gave out.

The normal 1980 campaign day permitted plenty of sleep for candidate and reporter alike. "A synthetic campaign is just as successful at getting attention as the 16-event, bust-your-ass type of campaigning," explained a veteran reporter. Furthermore, when the schedule did pick up, as Jimmy Carter's did during the final weeks, it was simply to jam more "media markets" into a single day.

Police cars with flashing red lights rushed candidates from airports to campaign stops in serpentine motorcades made eerie by the absence of onlookers on sidewalks and street corners. Often candidates skipped the motorcade and simply landed at the airport, spoke to a crowd gathered by the runway, hopped back on the plane, and took off again.

At large rallies, the candidate's purpose was not to speak to live people, but to people watching television's evening news. In addition to national network coverage, every stop offered countless opportunities for local and regional exposure.

Beyond focusing on TV coverage, the campaign tried to control and shape the coverage, often in subtle and complicated ways. Reflecting and reinforcing the dissolution of traditional party coalitions, Jimmy Carter, Ronald Reagan, and John Anderson each carefully constructed his own personal coalition of images for the television camera. Each visited factories, truck stops, Chicano colleges, senior citizen centers, suburbs, and ethnic neighborhoods—not to meet people, but to have his picture taken with people of the "right" demographic characteristics.

NBC's Heidi Shulman said she was very conscious of how the campaign tries to manipulate the picture: "Most days it's all so obvious, everybody winds up with substantially the same thing."

"The Reagan staff knows that the picture carries an impact no matter what the correspondent says," Shulman explained, "so they give us a picture with a message, 'Reagan likes blue-collar voters.' And even if I say, 'Reagan is out to get the blue-collar vote,' people will remember the picture and not my words."

The networks did not heroically resist manipulation. Their principal problem, in fact, was which of the good footage to broadcast—a decision reached by a curious combination of news judgment and the outright triumph of appearance over substance. Often a shot was aired, not because of what the candidate said, but because of how he looked while he said it. "New York wanted me to lead with something about Iran," said a network correspondent, summarizing his day's work, "but I told them we couldn't because we have such good pictures."

Those TV pictures, however, depicted a different reality from what an onlooker witnessed. Raw footage of a typical Reagan campaign day, for example, revealed that the crowds always seemed much larger than they actually were. To a large degree, this resulted from clever advance work by the media-sophisticated Reagan staff. At almost every stop, it was the same: they positioned a raised camera platform close to the speaker's platform, and roped off a huge "press area," designated off-limits to the public. This forced the crowd to pack tightly into the space between the candidate and the camera, insuring that Reagan always spoke to an impressive-looking mass of humanity. Of course, the networks sometimes were able to get a wider panoramic shot, say, from the top floor of a nearby building. But the minute-by-minute schedules rarely permitted such innovation, and the risk of a camera crew being left behind was great. As a result, viewers back home got the incorrect impression that the candidate continually addressed massive crowds.

The campaign's virtually exclusive preoccupation with the TV audience made print reporters obsolete—and they knew it. "Where do you even find time set aside for us to file our stories?" rhetorically asked a *Los Angeles Times* veteran, holding up the neatly typed, multipage daily campaign schedule (or "bible"). The Associated Press and United Press International reporters reached tens of millions of readers daily, but they, too, felt like un-invited guests. "The campaign staff couldn't even care if we disappeared," noted one of the nation's leading wire reporters.

Self-pity flowed freely from ostensibly tough political reporters. "We're second class citizens," one muttered. "We shouldn't even be here," said another. Indeed, many of the trade's most famous names were not. Among the heavies canonized in Timothy Crouse's *Boys on the Bus* (1973) who spent less time on the 1980 campaign buses were David Broder and Haynes Johnson of the *Washington Post*, Jules Witcover, then with the *Los Angeles Times* and now with the *Washington Star*, and syndicated columnists Rowland Evans and Robert Novak.

Although frustrated, those who did show up accepted their lot docilely. In the not-too-distant past, print reporters complained—loudly and effec-tively—whenever a microphone or camera got in the way. But now, it is the other way around. Print reporters meekly stepped aside as camera crews pushed by with a barely polite "coming through." When their vision was obstructed by the camera stand, some of the nation's toughest reporters stood passively in the background taking notes.

Occasionally, the print people did assert themselves. For example, at a Reagan "press conference" heralding his endorsement by police and firemen's unions, Eleanor Randolph of the *Los Angeles Times* stood up and asked Reagan a question, pointing out that his position on handgun control differed from that taken by the police union.

"This is a photo opportunity," answered a top Reagan staff member.

Randolph repeated her question.

The aide repeated, "This is a photo opportunity."

Reagan continued to stand there quietly.

Once again, Randolph asked the question. This time, Reagan stepped forward and answered. (This incident provided one of the few insights into Reagan. His natural instinct seemed to be toward politeness and answering questions. "What you've got here is a nice old man with an overly ambitious wife and a good staff," old timers explained to the newly arrived. If you get the question within earshot, he'll answer it because he's a decent guy," said one experienced wire reporter. But this tendency seemed to scare his aides. At one stop, Reagan extemporaneously discussed the Equal Rights Amendment and his staff was visibly upset.)

The "programmed" candidacy, with its rare direct access to the candidate, was first noted by Joe McGinnis in *The Selling of the President*, when, in 1968, Richard Nixon essentially bypassed the press by appearing in public only under carefully controlled circumstances. Then came the Rose Garden campaigns—Nixon's in 1972, Jerry Ford's in 1976, and Carter's in the 1980 primaries. By the fall of 1980, campaign staffs had learned a valuable lesson—a non-traveling candidate gets as much attention as does an indefatigable hustler.

Whatever their personality and policy differences, Carter, Reagan, and Anderson used similar techniques. Ken Cummins of the *Florida Times Union* computed that during a week of travel to nine states, Ronald Reagan spent only 170 minutes speaking in public. Jimmy Carter was somewhat more active, but on a typical campaign day, running from 12 to 18 hours, the traveling press spent no more than 3 hours within 100 feet of him, and of those few hours, barely a second was made available for questions.

All three campaigns herded the press around. When the plane landed, buses were waiting to take them to the "event," where they generally had to walk through a roped-off gauntlet of sign-waving, campaigning partisans. As soon as the candidate finished his speech, reporters then lunged back toward the buses to begin the whole process all over again. The rules were brutally simple: buses waited for no one. So reporters had to forget about wandering off into the crowd for interviews, or seeking out local officials, or finding out how well organized the local Right-to-Life group was. If you indulged in such wanderlust, you might be left behind in Abilene, Texas, with no commercial flights scheduled to leave until the next day. (Once, ABC correspondent Ann Compton left the Anderson campaign in New York

City to stop at her office for a chat with her bosses. Catching up with Anderson's caravan in central New Jersey cost her a $70 cab ride.)

Reporters also had to endure the candidates studiously pretending they were not there. The candidates unabashedly played to the cameras, but in public comments, gestures, and eye contact they acted as though the herd of newspeople hanging on every word were invisible, uninvited voyeurs, unworthy of acknowledgement.

Despite the slights and snubs, however, just about every print reporter, just about all the time, dutifully followed along, scribbling down words he or she had heard dozens of times before, hoping against hope for something worth reporting to happen. "I don't know why I'm doing this," one muttered while writing the candidate's words. "No one wants to hear this stuff again." (Many reporters on the Carter plane carried their passports, hoping for a quick flight to West Germany to greet the released Iranian hostages.) The principal duty of reporters—and many regarded it as demeaning—was to be alert in case the candidate became a "textual deviate," one who strays from his prepared text.

Reporters engaged in a daily struggle to find a morsel, an unplanned quote, or a revealing statement. Whenever the candidate was available—generally while entering or leaving his limousine—camera crews and reporters zeroed in with the precision of heat-seeking missiles. This was called "door-stopping," and the press engaged in it as often as a dozen times a day. Shouting, sometimes on the run, reporters pinched and poked in the hope of eliciting a snappy comment to lead their story.

"What do you think of the polls showing you slipping?" one yelled in President Carter's direction.

"Oh, really?" came the response. "I don't think I'll quit."

Back on board the bus, wire service reporters already were writing their stories with tape recorders at their ears, playing back what the candidate had just said. Clusters of reporters sat listening to similar tape recordings. The candidate's latest evasions were played repetitiously, forming a discordant symphony to be carefully dissected in search of one clue, one nuance—*anything* newsworthy. After a while, the process became numbing, and some reporters simply stopped caring. "Do you think we'll ever find out what he just said?" a straggler asked while boarding the bus. "Who cares?" a colleague answered.

Such tight control suited the candidates perfectly and campaign staffs knew they held the traveling press hostage. Television people were content with pictures, but print reporters, whose employers paid up to a thousand dollars each day traveling with the candidates, were reluctant to tell their editors that nothing interesting had happened.

From the candidate's perspective, a major element in planning the day became control over the all-important lead. Campaign strategists determined the day's principal story—a Reagan statement on the economy, a

Carter attack on Reagan's judgment—and they constructed a vacuum around that story, forcing reporters to use it.

Most observers agreed that in 1980, the Reagan people were by far the most talented in controlling the day's lead. Carter, for all the technical and logistical sophistication in his traveling press operation, left too much room for reporters to do their own thinking. Rarely did he serve up the daily juicy tidbit around which an entire day's story could be based. On the Friday before the election, Carter finally did provide a morsel—material documenting Ronald Reagan's earlier opposition to socialized medicine. White House staff members played over the plane's PA system a recording of the offending 20-year-old Reagan speech. Sure enough, Carter's attack dominated the next day's newspaper stories.

Under the strict supervision of their media specialists, all three candidates remained cloistered, afraid that an offguard comment might ruin the day's plans. Even John Anderson, who used only one plane and rode all day just a few feet away from the press corps, did not walk back to say hello.

Instead, he, Carter, and Reagan used their isolation to, once again, manipulate the press. "Exclusive" interviews given to strategically selected journalists, bound by carefully agreed upon release times, helped to guarantee a steady flow of controlled news. Reporters who were not "in" gave candidates uncomplimentary nicknames. Reagan was "O 'n' W" ("Oldest and Wisest"), and Anderson was "the Sage from Rockford."

The campaign staffs were candid about their manipulation of the press. "Sure, reporters don't have much access to the president," acknowledged Jody Powell, his expression emphasizing that he considered the topic silly. "But he has stopped a half-dozen or more times during the campaign to discuss a particular issue when it was important."

Lyn Nofziger, Reagan's press secretary, was more explicit. "If we just let him [Reagan] go his own way, we'd have a perpetual press conference." When, by chance, a reporter got close enough to ask Reagan a question, Nofziger would wave his arms and shout. "No, no, no questions," and literally throw his body in the way. Sometimes, the fail-safe Nofziger system failed, and it was those times that Reagan made comments that seemed to threaten his campaign. His "trees cause pollution" remarks, for example, were made at an unguarded moment.

The public was surprisingly sophisticated about this game. At a rally in central Illinois, deep in the heart of Reagan country, a young truck driver held up a homemade sign that said: "Hey, Ron. Don't worry about a slip of the tongue. You won't let America slip."

Compounding the journalists' isolation from the candidate was their isolation from newscasts and newspapers. Campaign staffs encouraged this, presumably because it increased their control over what reporters wrote.

The Reagan campaign, for example, was so well organized that reporters often found name plates on their hotel room doors; but the campaign never managed to have newspapers, TV sets, or radios in the press room. And it did not arrange for hotel newsstands to order extra copies of the local morning paper. Reporters in need of a news fix after waking early often slipped into the hotel lobby and ripped open bundled newspapers stacked by the locked newsstand door. Even Tom Wicker of the *New York Times* sat on the bus reading a day-old *Times*. Later, he gave up and read Jane Austen.

Reporters, however, did have one crucial lifeline: their "desks." At each stop, they rushed to the telephones, not to file a story, but to "call my desk and find out the latest developments." They sounded like investors comparing stock brokers. "I'm trying to clarify this with my desk in New York," one said in hushed tones, "but you should know that [Iranian Prime Minister] Raji said the hostages might be released before election day." These calls cross-fertilized the individual campaigns—"Our guy on the Reagan plane says they're emphasizing the economy"—which, in turn, armed reporters with information needed to write the charge/counter-charge story that works so well on television.

The best source of information, however—in terms of actually witnessing what the candidate said and did—was the press pool. Generally comprised of a print reporter, a still photographer, the wire services, and at least one network crew, the press pool accompanied the candidate everywhere. They traveled on the candidate's plane, rode in every motorcade, and greeted him first thing in the morning. The other reporters traveled in the press plane, rode on the press bus, and often did not stay in the same hotel as the candidate.

Pools were called the "body watch," a public witness in case the candidate admitted he was a Nazi, or an assassin decided to strike (known in shorthand parlance as "the event"). But by real news standards, pools were a meaningless exercise. On the Anderson campaign, pool reports were virtually nonexistent. The Reagan campaign provided only sporadic, written pool reports, and once, when a Sioux Falls crowd was disappointingly small, Reagan's copying machine mysteriously broke and no pool report was prepared until the following day. For the most part, no one covering the Reagan campaign seemed to care: if you were interested, you could seek out one of the pool reporters and ask questions. "Did anyone get what's in the pool report?" someone asked. "It's just crap," came the reply.

Only the Carter campaign raised pooling to a science. Elaborate planning shuffled different pools for each event, and traveling typists and on-board mimeo machines guaranteed freshly minted pool reports within minutes of take-off. Carter pool members provided their colleagues with information reflecting their boredom and cynicism: "Before boarding Air Force One, Carter shook hands with every motorcycle cop in the state." "One large black woman began crying effusively when the president came into her line of sight. He didn't notice." "As he [Carter] bounded up the steps, Mr. [Sam] Donaldson [ABC News] asked him. 'How do you think you're doing?' 'We'll know next Tuesday,' the leader of the Free World replied."

It is no concidence that most of the stories coming out of the campaign trail—standings in the polls, the effect of the debates, the "mood" of the campaign, possible release of the hostages, Carter's attacks on Reagan—suited this process perfectly. The dominance of television images, lack of access to the candidates, door-stopping, and isolation bred a peculiar form of pack journalism. No pack existed in the sense of everyone copying CBS or the *New York Times*. The process was more insidious. It grew from using the same rules of objectivity and newsworthiness to piece together a story from the day's meager morsels. Joint efforts amounted to nothing more than reporters standing around tape recorders helping each other figure out what, if anything, was new. If the day was particularly slow, these groups congregated around the walking encyclopedias—people who had covered a candidate for so long they could say, "When Carter was here in 1976, there were 5,000 people standing in the areas that were empty today." ("When nothing jumps out at you and says. 'This is the story,' that's when you start to worry what the veterans will file," explained a younger reporter working his way toward one of the oracles.)

The pack was also quick to pick up certain feelings and attitudes about the candidates. During the final weeks, for example, Anderson was considered "dead and gone." (I've done the Anderson-is-dead story," said one network correspondent. "I put him in his coffin. Then I nailed him in. Then I lowered it. I don't have the imagination to think of anything else to report.") Carter was the object of scorn. ("Oh, Christ. Is he talking about his difficult and lonely decisions again?" one reporter whispered. Another reporter responded, "I almost got mugged by an old lady who thought I was a Carter supporter.")

More significantly, a full week before election day, the pack sensed that Carter was finished, but rules of objectivity prevented them from reporting it. They were too bound—and sometimes blinded—by the polls, by presumed truths emanating from their desks, and by the cynicism bred from isolation and daily repetition of self-serving exaggerations by the candidates. A desperate search for something newsworthy had worn away the fine edges of their political judgment. Many reporters knew they had big stories at their fingertips—Reagan campaigning against big government while promising vested interest groups at each stop that he would increase spending for them; Carter floundering, desperately pulling out quotes of past Democrats while rarely even mentioning his own record—and yet, most of these stories went unwritten.

Only those reporters who dropped off the campaign trail escaped this trap. Ronald Brownstein, a staff writer for *Ralph Nader Reports*, poked around Youngstown, Ohio, after Reagan's entourage left, and discovered

that the steel plant whose closing Reagan had blamed on government interference was, in truth, the victim of corporate mismanagement. Another
reporter went to a reception with Carter, asked everyone present for a
business card, and then stayed in his hotel room the next day, telephoning
them to find out the real extent of Carter's support in the community.

But such enterprising stories were rare. Leading reporters took to
joining the caravan for a few days and then going their own way. The 1980
campaign was noteworthy for the absence of permanent in-flight stars.
Frank Reynolds or Anthony Lewis would pop up and then disappear the
next day. Newcomers arrived armed with a tremendous fear that they
would miss a nuance that would appear in everyone else's story, or that they
would be excited about something which turned out to be old hat. So, instead of thinking—let alone asking—the tough questions, they tagged
along, emulating the pack and very quickly disappearing into it.

Campaign travel bred another kind of control: the tight, womb-like,
home-away-from-home environment in which television was head of the
household.

The first four or five rows of seats on the bus were always saved for
camera crews. It made sense: they had heavy equipment (tape recorders,
microphones, extra cameras, spare batteries, and cassettes) weighing up to
80 pounds and would have had difficulty fighting through the aisle. But woe
to anyone who broke apartheid. "You'd better not sit there," voices from
the back of the bus warned. If the crews found an intruder, "Hey, man. We
gotta have these seats" was only the beginning of their spirited reaction.

On the plane, chartered from commercial airlines, television crews
reserved the last dozen or so rows of seats, so they could enter and leave the
rear door more easily. Their area became known as the "zoo."

The "animals" were readily identifiable by their clothing—jeans, wild
hats, halloween masks—a sharp contrast to the jackets and ties and three-
piece business suits worn by reporters. Their behavior fit the zoo image. If
everyone on the plane had acted like the animals, then the presidential
campaign would have lived up to its romantic, devil-may-care reputation.

Animal games varied. The most noteworthy was blowing whistles. No
one has documented when whistles first joined the zoo, but myth has it that
in 1972, camera crews bought a whistle, and for some unremembered
reason, blew it at a top network correspondent as he was boarding the press
plane. The network star responded unfavorably so the animals bought more
whistles and blew them whenever he appeared.

Whistles then mostly disappeared until 1980 when, for reasons nobody
seems to know, they turned up again. The unquestioned king was an NBC
cameraman, Houston Hall, who covered Anderson. Hanging on Hall's
press credentials chain were two policeman's whistles, a siren whistle, a
crow call, a British Bobby's whistle, and a boat-swain's whistle. In his hand-
luggage he carried an 18-inch Clarabell whistle and a heavy train whistle.

"You gotta have a whistle nobody has," the champ explained. "Without at least a siren, you're nobody."

TV crews set up shops selling whistles "at cost." "Acme Whistle Company" a homemade sign proclaimed. Its proprietors came equipped with special tools to fix whistles that were literally blown out from overuse. For a while, the animals on the Carter plane blew loudly at every take-off and landing. Then, curiously, as Carter's imminent defeat became obvious, whistling virtually disappeared. On the other hand, as Anderson sank in the polls, his press entourage blew their whistles more and more wildly.

Whistles became a way of belonging, and many reporters wore unused whistles throughout the fall. "I don't know how I got it. It was just there one morning when I woke up," explained a network correspondent.

If the animals frayed the nerves of some of the others on board, flight attendants—the on-board mother and lover figures—were there to soothe them. "They're just like kids," a flight attendant muttered as the press trooped back after still another rally. Their warmth provided the traveling group with its cohesion. They greeted new arrivals by first name, and those so desiring got a hug or kiss on the cheek.

Whistles and flight attendants were harmless diversions in the press corps' constant struggle against boredom. Skyball proved to be something else.

In early October, newspapers showed pictures of Nancy Reagan bowling oranges down the aisle as her husband's plane was taking off. She was playing skyball, the object of which was to roll an orange, apple, or any other round object down the aisle during takeoff and try to hit the end of the plane. For the press corps, the obvious attraction, as with most activities aboard the plane, was that it flaunted the rules—skyball players actually stood in the aisle during take-off (that's about as naughty as press activity got during the campaign).

A few days after Nancy Reagan's picture appeared, however, a *Los Angeles Times* story called the press planes "a transnational Mardi Gras" in which "the general rules of commercial flights are ignored. . . ." The next day, UPI reporter Ira Allen filed a story that said: "Lustful innuendo between passengers and the three stewardesses fly faster than the plane itself, and safety regulations are unheard of." (It was one careless, exaggerated sentence in an otherwise accurate, interesting piece.)

For several days, nothing happened. Then through the curious chemistry that suddenly transforms a forgotten story into an earthshaker, disaster struck. Editors back home began to ask reporters about the lustful behavior, and an airline official yanked the female flight attendants off the charter plane and replaced them with men.

The press protested—"they helped us relax," one explained—and Reagan reportedly called United Airlines and officials of the flight attendants' union, pleading to get the women back.

At the same time, the plane's press corps turned against reporter Ira Allen. He returned to his seat one time to find a Secret Service man occupying it. Camera crew members issued childish threats. Prominent journalists made nasty, sarcastic comments. Over the PA system came jokes attacking him by name, and immediately after each take-off, a Reagan aide began to intone, "From the office of the press secretary, this flight is off the record." "It's just like they're back in a schoolyard," Allen said.

Then, only a few days after the departure of the much-missed flight attendants, they suddenly appeared back on board, not to work, but to sit among the passengers as "public relations representatives."

Ultimately, though, it was not romance or games that proved to be the main in-flight diversion. It was food. Not simply first-class fare, but meals specially catered by the best restaurants in each city. It was unbelievable. Fresh lobster, lamb chops, Chateaubriand, Eggs Benedict, fresh stone crab—all served on starched table cloths, with personal salt and pepper shakers, your choice of wines, and a hot towel to cleanse the fingers afterward. Between meals came endless snacks, trays of freshly cut vegetables, caviar, hors d'oeuvres, pastry, shish kebab, baskets of candy bars ("What, no Snickers?" cried a spoiled reporter), cookies and milk, and always from dusk to dawn, the beverage of your choice. "Oh no, not another meal!" was one of the campaign's most frequently heard remarks. Indeed, the hardest working person on board, putting in longer hours than the candidate himself, was the airline catering representative. Pan American's man in charge of the Carter people once checked into his hotel room after 2:00 A.M. "I'd like a three o'clock wake-up call," he told the clerk: "3:00 P.M.?" the clerk asked. "No," came the response, "in forty minutes."

Chided that food on the Carter plane was better than on Reagan's, press secretary Nofziger insisted that "anyone can have a bad day," and promised, with a straight face, that upcoming meals would certainly be top-rate.

It is unlikely that any story was ever slanted because the Chateaubriand was stringy. But the food subtly helped the press forget the basic senselessness that the traveling assignment had become.

Of course, it need not be that way. Nothing in American society, journalistic ethics, or communications technology *demands* that presidential candidates have extraordinary control over the news or that the most important thing left for the press to think about is the next meal.

However, nothing suggests that things are likely to change anytime soon. George McGovern in 1972 and Edward Kennedy in the early part of his 1980 campaign both operated free-wheeling operations filled with real access to the candidates and top staff. Both lost, a lesson that only seems to reaffirm what other presidential candidates want to believe anyway.

The Kennedy-McGovern approach is now widely regarded as antiquated and quaint. In fact, toward the end of the primary campaign, Kennedy's press operation had tightened considerably. To measure just how far things have gone, the control once held up to derision—Nixon's 1968 strategy—is now expected of so-called "smart" politicians. Not all of Nixon's media machinations are admired and emulated, but the practices he introduced have been refined and made respectable. The TV-oriented, tightly controlled, insulated political caravans of 1980 were noteworthy in that few members of the press or the public found them worthy of note.

The campaign sham, like all show business gimmickry, will change when the audience grows restless. Reporters know this, and deep inside, are eager for the public to react.

One day shortly before the end of the campaign, a reporter wanders aimlessly around the press room. He is tired of free coffee and donuts, tired of rereading the local newspaper, tired of calling his office for the latest political gossip, and tired of waiting for the candidate to leave his hotel room and do something.

"I resent this," he says, "Hell, I resent this. It's all show biz. And the public should resent it, too."

---

24 Presidential Timber: Grooming the Candidates

by Daniel Burstein

Along with the television campaign has come the candidates' television image—and a whole new set of advisers and consultants, says Daniel Burnstein, a New York freelancer. Political issues get attention well after the images of candidates do. This article is from *Advertising Age*, March 12, 1984.

Walter Mondale seemed to appear tired and even lifeless on occasion.

John Glenn lacked a theme for his campaign and was so uninspiring on the stump that "dullness" was becoming his image in the public mind.

Gary Hart had a tendency to be overly intellectual and too complex in answering questions posed to him.

Reubin Askew blinked too much when he was nervous and frequently shouted when giving speeches, a legacy of his early political days in West Florida when he campaigned without a microphone.

Thanks to the advice of media consultants, however, all four candidates have made progress overcoming these and other chinks in their personal armor. And while debate persists over how influential media consultants really are or ought to be, their importance is underscored by the fact that virtually every presidential candidate from Ronald Reagan to Jesse Jackson has one.

There is only a handful of media consultants capable of advising a presidential campaign—but then again, the client list is fairly short and only develops once every four years. Consultants come from diverse backgrounds in advertising, public relations, journalism, film making and even old fashioned organizational politics. Their role in a campaign can vary from simply producing TV spots or advising on time-buys to helping shape policy, write speeches and plan strategy.

For most consultants, working on a presidential campaign is a one-time experience. "Doing a presidential campaign costs any consulting company a fortune in lost business," says Raymond Strother. "Other people don't want you to represent them because they are afraid all your time will be taken up with the presidential campaign."

On the other hand, for top-flight mediamen and image-makers, the chance to have even a small hand in shaping the image of the next president—at least once—is usually too tempting to pass up.

For the most part, the consultants downplay their own role in "packaging" candidates. Says Mr. Mondale's Texas-based consultant Roy Spence (who spends his noncampaign time as a partner with Austin-based ad agency GSD&M, where he is senior vp-account services), "Walter Mondale has a keen sense of who he is and what he wants to do. Unlike some candidates, there is no need to try to turn him into something other than what he is."

Adds Eli Bleich, Beverly Hills-based consultant to the Askew campaign, "You can never create a whole new candidate. To try to do so would be a real disservice. The media consultant's job is more like that of an attorney trying to put his client's best possible argument in the best possible light. That's what we do—but it's still the candidate's argument, not ours."

Many consultants say that 1984 differs from past campaigns because the public is more aware and more skeptical than ever of "packaged candidates." Books like Joe McGinniss' classic *The Selling of the President 1968* and movies like *The Candidate* showing a vacuous Robert Redford being manipulated by his consultant have focused attention on the tricks used to project a candidate's image over his reality.

"Any time a political commercial goes on the air today, little red flags go up in people's minds, and they start to wonder if someone is trying to manipulate them," says Raymond Strother, a consultant who divides his time between Washington and New Orleans and who has handled 130 Democratic party candidates over the last 18 years. He enthusiastically believes in the cause of his current client, Sen. Hart.

Mr. Strother says that focus groups conducted by his organization revealed that voters today "want substance and specifics. They want more information than ever."

In Mr. Strother's recent efforts in behalf of victorious Kentucky gubernatorial candidate Martha Layne Collins, he found much more positive reaction to commercials in which her position papers were actually shown or quoted from on tv than those that stayed in the realm of political generalities.

Concludes Mr. Strother, "The days of cute, music-studded spots and glib answers are over. A new attention to detail and fact, suitable for the Information Age, is the order of the day in political advertising."

Mr. Strother claims to have been attracted to Sen. Hart's candidacy because of his "genuine intensity over the issues and impassioned, deeply caring personality."

If Sen. Hart's media convey that image, he insists, it's because it is real. Mr. Strother's imprint has come chiefly in the form of getting the camera in tighter on Sen. Hart to allow his intensity to come through more visibly and in showing the candidate how to be more concise and focused in his replies to questions.

"He knows too much about his subject, and his tendency is to answer a question so thoroughly that he may lose the questioner," observes Mr. Strother.

On the other hand, Sen. Hart also has a tendency to appear uninterested if a question asked of him indeed *doesn't* interest him. Mr. Strother has worked to even up Sen. Hart's tone so that he doesn't appear intense one moment and apathetic the next. On the whole, however, Mr. Strother has found that "Hart resists packaging. If he thinks he's being handled in any way, he'll fight back."

Like Sen. Hart, candidates Cranston and Hollings are thought of as coming across sincerely, without the filters of the image makers. Under the tutelage of the Campaign Group, a consultancy in Philadelphia, Sen. Alan Cranston reportedly gained some weight to appear less gaunt and haggard. But by and large, his advisers accept the fact that Sen. Cranston is not the handsomest candidate in the race and clearly is running on issues, not image.

Sen. Ernest Hollings is called "the unpackaged candidate" by one of his speechwriters, Mickey Kaus, who observes that Sen. Hollings may be the only candidate in the race whose public remarks are exclusively on subjects he deems important rather than ones designed to "correct some problem in perceptions of his positions."

Mr. Kaus acknowledges that the senator plays tennis regularly with one of Washington's top media experts and political consultants, Charles Guggenheim. But although Mr. Guggenheim has offered advice to Sen. Hollings, he is not working for the campaign on a paid basis, leaving Sen. Hollings and Sen. George McGovern the only candidates without paid media consultants.

Even the Rev. Jesse Jackson's campaign—by most estimates in the weakest position of the eight Democratic candidates financially—retained the New York advertising agency Mingo-Jones in February to produce commercials and advise on media issues.

Says David Garth, considered perhaps the shrewdest of all the consultants, "Packaged candidates just don't work since Watergate." He advised John Anderson in the 1980 election and has played a major role in victories of New York Mayor Ed Koch and Los Angeles Mayor Tom Bradley.

Mr. Garth is not working for a presidential candidate this year, preferring to stick to regional and local candidates, but he stresses that with the active, adversarial role of the press on the campaign trail, no presidential candidate can be significantly remade overnight.

"No candidate can stand up to all the tv debates, press conferences and public appearances involved in a modern campaign trying to act out drastic changes in his personality dictated by a media consultant," says Mr. Garth.

While some experts may see a trend away from the "packaged candidate," especially in the *au naturel* campaigns of Hollings, Hart, Cranston, McGovern and Jackson, they would get a strong argument from *New Republic* political correspondent Sidney Blumenthal, whose 1980 book, *The Permanent Campaign*, profiled more than a dozen top media consultants.

"Sincerity is the ultimate packaging," says Mr. Blumenthal, who will also serve as a roving commentator for the "Today Show" during the campaign.

"To talk about an unpackaged candidate is like talking about a virgin birth. All candidates use polls, all of them use media consultants, all of them advertise. There's this strange notion that somehow all these techniques are artificially grafted onto politics. But this *is* politics," asserts Mr. Blumenthal.

If there is a candidate more packaged than the others in this year's race, Mr. Blumenthal believes it is John Glenn. "Every other candidate has a real message and a real consistituency. Mondale really is very strong among labor. Jesse Jackson exists because there is an underclass. Gary Hart's talk of 'new ideas' is a direct appeal to people under 40. Glenn is the only one who lacks a specific social base and who represents no concrete force within the Democratic Party. The others are all packaged so as to more effectively reach their natural social and electoral base.

"But with Glenn the packaging itself is designed in the hopes of finding a base. This is the ultimate expression of the packaged campaign," he says.

David Sawyer, a New York media consultant working for the Glenn campaign, has been credited with doing a brilliant job of injecting vibrancy into an otherwise lackluster John Glenn. (A year ago, Mr. Sawyer received some unwanted publicity and in fact became a campaign issue himself while he was involved in the unsuccessful re-election campaign of former Chicago mayor Jane Byrne.) David Garth says Mr. Sawyer's commercials for Sen. Glenn are "the best I've seen in this campaign," and other experts agree that the emotional responses generated by commercials, with their outstanding production values and scenes recalling Sen. Glenn in a space capsule and Sen. Glenn with John Kennedy, have a powerful effect.

Mr. Sawyer's associate Mandy Grunwald denies reports that the consultants gave Glenn speech lessons and insists that "the John Glenn you see in commercials is the same John Glenn you would see in person on a campaign day."

But the impression held by correspondents who have watched Sen. Glenn closely is that the tv commercials—with their nostalgic references to the early '60s, the upbeat music and excited talk of "Believe in the Future Again,"—conflict sharply with the reality of Sen. Glenn and may actually hurt him because the candidate can't deliver on the image suggested by the advertising.

"The image-makers are moving in on John Glenn," said James Reston in a recent *New York Times* column entitled "The Wrong Stuff." "Nothing could be sillier than trying to make John Glenn anything but what he is. He's an intelligent, dead-honest character, a middle-of-the-roader, a bit of a 'square'. . . . Nothing could be worse. . .than to try, as his media advisers are suggesting, to be clever and fancy."

"The ads are dramatic but the candidate is prosaic," says *New Republic*'s Mr. Blumenthal. "In the long run, the ads will hurt because they are so good. At first it sounds very exciting to talk about the future, until you stop to think that the future doesn't exist, the present does, and John Glenn has nothing to say about the present."

Short of trying to recast a candidate in a whole new image, the consultants have put their imprimatur on the campaign in a variety of ways.

Eli Bleich, for example, suggested to the Askew campaign that given the candidate's lack of name recognition, early 30- and 60-second spots wouldn't accomplish much.

Instead, Mr. Bleich produced a more substantive 15-minute videotape on Mr. Askew. Rather than buy expensive media time, the tape was shown in small living room gatherings every night of the campaigns in Iowa and New Hampshire. The film was deliberately produced with close, tight shots of the candidate, and the presentation was right into the camera to accentuate the "personal" feel in the showings.

Roy Spence is credited with having helped turn a somewhat cold and aloof public image of Walter Mondale into a warmer and more friendly one by creating a five-minute piece that aired in December depicting a folksy, outdoorsy Mondale fishing, hiking in the woods in a pullover sweater, playing tennis hard and talking about growing up on a farm.

The latest Spence creation is a spot first shown in Iowa featuring small children with a dramatic narration accusing President Reagan of saddling the next generation with a trillion-dollar debt, cuts in educational spending and a nuclear arms race that is threatening the planet's survival.

Experts agree that because of Mondale's overwhelming lead over the other Democrats, he has a free hand to position himself against Reagan, while the other Democrats are left trying to position themselves against Mr. Mondale.

Perhaps the most innovative tv spots have evolved from Raymond Strother's collaboration with Gary Hart. Long thought of as an "Atari Democrat" espousing economic revival through investment in technology, Sen. Hart is supported in the spots with a variety of dazzling high-tech graphics. "These ads work well not only to galvanize Hart's base among the post–World War II generation," says Mr. Blumenthal, "but in juxtaposition to Mondale who appears as very much the candidate of the Old Guard by contrast."

If the consultants have a general public image of being all-powerful backroom kingmakers, the consultants themselves see more powerful influences.

David Garth evaluates the role of paid media in a campaign as fourth on a list of factors topped by that of the free media, the strength of the campaign organization and budget resources. He believes that the role of the political consultant has been "overestimated" in national campaigns and says that "the guy who runs the budget is probably much more important than the consultant." He adds that media consultants tend to have more influence in local elections—where they *can* tailor an image for a previously unknown candidate—that will withstand the scrutiny of the less inquiring local press.

Observes Mr. Garth, "The images being formed now in the minds of voters are far more the product of the network news than paid media time. Paid messages from Democratic candidates are reaching only a small number of people in and around the early primary states. In both the Carter and McGovern nominations, their successes came about to a large degree because the national media adopted them. If you are going to do Jesse Jackson's paid media how could you possibly get more results than what was gotten with the free media?"

The role of the consultant has itself become a hot topic in Campaign '84. The *New York Times, Wall Street Journal, USA Today* and numerous other publications have done stories on the strategies of the different consultants. Consultants now prescreen tv spots for the media and explain the strategy behind them, taking campaign coverage to the meta-level of covering what the consultants are trying to get voters to think.

David Garth, for one, thinks that approach is less than useful. "I prefer the mystery. Let the voter think what he wants about the commercial. I don't believe in re-screenings." David Sawyer complained in a recent *New York Times* interview about the news media's focus on internal issues of campaign strategy, saying that his polls showed that voters "know two things about John Glenn: He's an astronaut and he's got a disorganized campaign. They don't even know he is a senator."

Roy Spence attracted a good deal of attention—some would say notoriety—when he said in a recent interview that Walter Mondale had the "courage" to be "cautious."

Political analysts have been debating the remark ever since—did it help Mr. Mondale because it was a true characterization that resonates with voters in this chaotic political time—or did it hurt by portraying him as unimaginative and stodgy?

25 Trust Me: How TV Changed the Politics of America

by Charles McDowell

TV relentlessly shows the style of the candidate, and sometimes his character, writes Charles McDowell, columnist with the *Richmond Times-Leader* and a regular panelist on WETA-TV's "Washington Week in Review." This article is from *The Washingtonian*, May 1986, and is adapted from *Beyond Reagan: The Politics of Upheaval*, edited by Paul Duke.

In the summer of 1952, television dawned on American politics. The occasion was the Republican National Convention at Chicago, and, yes, there was one of those camera towers blocking the front of the hall, and the floodlights cutting through the traditional layers of cigar smoke seemed suddenly to be exposing a mystic rite. But the true dawning was the glow of 18 million little screens on which politicians walked and talked and looked citizens in the eye in their living rooms all over the United States.

Television had made a pass at the conventions in 1948, but only about

400,000 squinty sets were in use then. The coverage was a limited curiosity, not a national experience.

By 1952 television was ready to become a force. There would have been television interest in the convention as a folk festival, but the Republicans were offering more, a classic confrontation: the popular hero from World War II, General Dwight D. Eisenhower, taking on Senator Robert A. Taft of Ohio, who was not called Mr. Republican for nothing.

An austere and respected conservative, Taft had the support of the party bosses and nominal control of the convention machinery. He figured to hold off Eisenhower by using his insider's power in the ruthless custom of these things.

The first stage of Taft's nomination for President would take place in the convention's credentials committee, where his supporters expected to use their narrow majority to reject the Eisenhower side's challenge of fifteen Taft delegates from Louisiana. There was a case to be made that the delegates had been chosen unfairly in Louisiana, but Taft needed them.

I was in Chicago for my first national convention. When I showed up for the credentials committee hearings in the Gold Room of the Congress Hotel, no seats were available for junior reporters from the provinces. An official explained that television had to be accommodated in the press space. Alas, it was the beginning of that, too.

A kindly security guard let me slip into the serving kitchen adjoining the Gold Room, and from there I covered the credentials contest for a couple of days. The huge tiled kitchen, with its racks of glasses, stainless-steel sinks, and signs saying "Keep It Clean" became the caucus room for the members of the committee.

While witnesses testified and the committee argued before the television cameras in the Gold Room, the leaders of the Taft and Eisenhower factions came to the kitchen to talk tactics. I was taken for a hotel functionary of some sort and overheard a lot from both sides. By the morning of the second day, the Taft managers were talking about conceding the Louisiana delegates to Eisenhower.

What was happening was that people back home, following the debate on television, were telephoning and telegraphing their delegates to say that Taft's case was coming through as weak. Republicans of consequences were saying that a steamroller approach would look bad on television and hurt Taft more than yielding the delegates.

I particularly remember a Minnesota member of the committee, technically a backer of the dark horse, Harold Stassen, bringing Taft partisans from the Gold Room to the kitchen to persuade them of their public-relations problem. He rested an elbow on a dishwashing machine as he talked. He was earnest and deep-chested and had a big, hollow voice, and there was no trouble in hearing him tell the Taft people that they could ruin their candidate if they insisted on arrogantly running over Eisenhower in this little controversy. The Minnesota delegate was Warren Burger.

Taft's manager on the committee, Congressman Clarence Brown of Ohio, recommended to the candidate that he concede Louisiana as a public-relations gesture. He was talking to Taft headquarters by telephone from the kitchen. The candidate was instinctively against conceding Louisiana but told Brown to do what he thought best.

The concession would be on television in the Gold Room. Up to now in the debate, the Taft spokesmen had tended to be the crusty elders of the party. The Eisenhower spokesmen were somehow younger, trimmer, clearer of eye.

To make their motion to seat Eisenhower's Louisiana delegation, to claim acquaintance with fairness, the Taft side passed over the elders and chose a young, clean-cut, well-spoken committee member from Virginia: Eugene Worrell. Two days into the era of television politics, and everyone was beginning to catch on.

Worrell's talk of fairness in Louisiana only encouraged the Eisenhower supporters to press the same case in the Texas delegation and others. The Taft side became adamant and held the line in the committee. The Eisenhower managers announced they would appeal the decision and went before the cameras to explain their case again and to lecture on sportsmanship. The document of appeal was called the "Fair Play Amendment," and in retrospect that name will do for me as the first great artifact of the television era in politics.

So the crucial battle was fought amid the turbulence and drama on the floor of a national political convention, all on television. It became a morality play. Here was a national hero standing above politics and demanding simple justice from the cynical bosses of what had always been a closed process. By the rules of the Republican party and the customs of American politics, the merits of the proposition were at least doubtful, but there was no doubt about the public perception of the struggle. The telephone calls and telegrams poured into Chicago; public opinion was pro-Eisenhower.

The convention ended with the "I Like Ike" signs dancing in the almost blinding light. And there was the general on the platform with his arms thrown up in a V for victory and his smile beaming out to all those little screens. We could write like poets on the press stand or broadcast it faithfully on the radio, we could explain and analyze the event in the context of the great issues of the day, but now politics was acquiring a new reality and its medium was television.

Politics would never be the same again in a country where people in their living rooms could watch their politicians at work. Thirty years later, the *Economist* of London was still trying to help us get used to it: "Today's are the first politicians since the Athenian statesman Pericles, in the fifth century BC, to be seen by all their electors."

The people see the picture—moving, instantaneous, compelling. It is a personal experience, and the reaction is intuitive and emotional as well as logical. In this circumstance, the personal qualities of politicians matter very much. Television becomes a medium of personal trust—or mistrust or yawns.

In the time of Ronald Reagan, we have seen personal trust for a President at the core of an administration's viability. Over the long haul in politics, I would say, television's inherent function as a medium of personal trust is far more significant than all the passing sensations that often dominate discussions of the subject.

One way to trace the relentless rise of television in American politics is through the Presidents who used television most successfully.

John Kennedy, going for the Democratic nomination in 1960, hardly could have been a candidate without television. Besides being personable, he was running in a political landscape that had undergone tremendous change since television came on the scene in 1952. The nominating process was evolving into a whole new game.

In the selection of national-convention delegates, primaries were replacing the old state conventions and back-room appointments. Presidential candidates were not soliciting party leaders' support as much as before; they were campaigning more among the people. Television liked it: local color, crowds, hands to shake, competition out where you could see it.

There were only sixteen primaries in 1960, but we sensed watching television that somehow they had eclipsed the old system. Kennedy, campaigning in Wisconsin or West Virginia, was being seen and heard in all the states. An individual primary on television was a national event, and a sequence of strong showings in several primaries could become a national bandwagon.

When the Democrats gathered for their convention in Los Angeles, Kennedy had already done what had to be done. His first-ballot nomination was dramatic but a formality. In the first decade of TV politics, a young, Catholic, back-bench senator, and not one who had shown extraordinary promise in Congress, had knocked over Hubert Humphrey and Democratic elders in the primaries, then controlled the convention easily against Lyndon B. Johnson, the fabled inside operator and acknowledged leader of his party in Washington.

John Kennedy's successful campaign against Richard Nixon is remembered mainly for their four debates on television. More than 100 million adults watched. The issues, which both candidates discussed skillfully, are not much remembered.

At the time, people who heard the debates on radio were fairly evenly divided as to who had won. But on television, Vice President Nixon had problems. One was Kennedy. Not only was the upstart young senator more engaging, more relaxed, and cooler than Nixon, but he came through as more mature and thoughtful than the Kennedy many people expected. He turned out not to be a boy, somebody said. Other Nixon problems were pallor, five-o'clock shadow, and perspiration on his face.

Twenty-five years after Kennedy beat Nixon in an extremely close election, media experts still have difficulty assessing the relative effects of performance and substance on the public perception of a politician. Of course substance matters.

The crucial ability in the new era is to be heard and felt as an authentic person in a living room, one on one. The person, the performance, and the message merge. Television pulls the viewer past literal information into intuitive responses. It invites, almost demands, judgments on personal trust.

Tony Schwartz, the political consultant and disciple of Marshall McLuhan, says in his book *Media: The Second God:* "Radio, and then television, drew our attention away from issues and caused us to focus on the more personal qualities of the candidate, his ability to speak, and his style of presentation."

Voters watching candidates, Schwartz says, "look for what they consider to be good character: qualities such as conviction, compassion, steadiness, the willingness to work hard. That is why we have so large a party-crossover vote. This emphasis on people and feeling is the product of an instant-communication environment."

The good vibes received from a Kennedy or a Reagan do not convert droves of committed Republicans or Democrats. But 20 percent or more of the electorate have little or no commitment to party, and these are the people who decide most elections.

Long before television came along, many of these people were wary of politics in general. They voted for "the best man." Television gave them access to the personal evidence they wanted. And it increased their numbers, according to Edward J. Rollins Jr., director of the 1984 Reagan campaign. While some of his brothers talked about a realignment of the parties, Rollins insisted that the major political phenomenon of his time was a "de-alignment" attributable to television.

Isn't print journalism supposed to be in there somewhere, calling the voters' attention to the issues and away from personality? Yes, and the print press can seem gray and boring as it stakes out the important issues and summons television to the serious agenda.

But day by day in routine coverage, the print press is drawn into the same love of personality and performance that all those millions watching television are interested in. A combative exchange, a line misspoken, a sweaty brow—they become news if only because so many people are watching.

The press watches television and vice versa. A provocative sound bite from a campaign is validated for the television producers when the press writes about it, and it gets another round for reaction on the evening news, which makes it fodder for the weekend talk shows, which brings it back into the Monday-morning papers as something the syndicated heavyweights may want to write a column about, and on it goes.

Television on occasion conveys a truly important issue to the consciousness of the country, and with awesome effect. That has happened when television has been able to show the essence of the issue and not just politicians and commentators talking about it.

The Vietnam war is the classic example. When television gave the war reality night after night for American families at home, public opinion began to sour. At the same time, reporters in both print and television were becoming more aggressive in contrasting the government's claims and reassurances with other versions of reality. President Lyndon Johnson, one of the most accomplished politicians of the old school, decided in failure and frustration not to run for a second term in 1968.

In covering the civil-rights movement, television explored the historical background, the constitutional arguments, and the muffled themes of moderation in the South, but television's transforming power was simply in its pictures of events. The images defined the crisis in the starkest terms: There were the peaceful black protesters, the preachers of nonviolence, the marchers singing hymns, the children walking solemn and brave to school, and then there were the white hecklers and haters, the swaggering sheriffs, the Klan and the neo-Nazis, the violence. The impact was cumulative. The Reverend Martin Luther King's eloquent call to conscience went out from the Lincoln Memorial to tens of millions of television sets, where it was received amid the echoing images of the police dogs of Birmingham.

In its own time, Watergate was an event closed to cameras. It was uncovered by newspaper reporters and explored relentlessly in print as the third-rate burglary expanded into a constitutional scandal.

The television coverage had a secondhand quality; it could not seem to engage the issue on its own terms. But when television put Senator Sam Ervin and the Nixon staff conspirators on the screen for weeks at a time in 1973, and put the House impeachment inquiry on the screen in 1974, public opinion was mobilized to support the removal of the President from office.

Disillusionment with Watergate set the stage for Jimmy Carter, a presidential candidate who personified moralism and skepticism about politics. And he was as fascinating a television phenomenon as any we had seen before 1976.

Here was an obscure former governor of Georgia, distinctly from the boondocks, not a commanding presence personally, not a leader of any established movement, an outsider to the traditional political fraternity—and he came from nowhere to defeat a clutch of veteran liberal Democratic candidates for the nomination. Then he defeated the incumbent Republican President, Gerald Ford.

Carter understood how television had revolutionized the nominating system. He was willing to concentrate a couple of years' effort on the earliest tests, Iowa and New Hampshire, betting that a good showing would be a sensational payoff because expectations for his candidacy were so low. He was right, and he became a national figure within several weeks.

Carter believed that the delegate-selection process was subject to a sequential effect, state by state. He believed in momentum. With a front-runner's access to television and the conferred charisma of a miracle worker in Iowa and New Hampshire, he offered a vision that was essentially anti-political.

Carter knew people had long been skeptical of the whole pack of politicians and their big talk, big government, red tape, inside deals, and slickery. Well, he personified opposition to all that. The very look and manner of the man set him apart. He was slight, almost shy. He had a high voice and a drawl. He was a farmer and small-business man, trained as an engineer. For him problems had logical solutions. A plain, practical man without a politician's bombast and wheeler-dealer ways might impose some common sense and efficiency on Washington. He would stand up for morality, too, and was not too sophisticated to keep saying so. He was a religious man, a Sunday-school teacher in a fundamentalist church, and he called attention to his religion often. But he was not a hypocrite; he lived his commitment.

The crucial issue that blended into the image of Jimmy Carter was civil rights. It authenticated him as a southerner who could be President. In his long-shot bid for the nomination, his record in Georgia on behalf of civil rights brought him the support of southern black leaders, some of them associates of Martin Luther King. With black leaders seen around him from the beginning of the campaign—and going as his missionaries to the North and West—Carter overcame the suspicions that many liberals had of a white southerner and a relative conservative in the Democratic field. In the primaries, Carter ran strongly in predominantly black precincts, North and South, against famous liberals of his party.

Carter's defeat for a second term had a major television component, and it consisted of far more than Ronald Reagan, the Great Communicator. President Carter's fortunes had faltered at home and abroad.

The worst was the Iran hostage crisis, which obsessed television and the country for more than a year. In a regular ritual of humiliation, television counted off the days that the American hostages had been held by terrorists in a pitifully backward country while the United States engaged in futile diplomacy, empty threats, and, finally, failed military rescue.

Meanwhile, the terrorists demonstrated a keen sense of American television. By allowing crews from the West to televise images of the hostages and to interview their captors, Iran gained leverage over a superpower. As in the case of the TWA hostage crisis in Lebanon five years later, the American public's very personal concern for the safety of their fellow citizens soon began to dominate the policy options of the American government.

In the incident in Lebanon, the hostages on television—sometimes under threat of death as they spoke to us—tended to become our national authorities on the nature of the terrorists, their point of view, their demands, and the best American approach to the problem. Indeed, television became a medium of diplomacy. A representative of the terrorists was drawn out on possible settlement terms by network anchors and morning-show hosts. Officials in the State Department confessed that in some of the crucial moments of the crisis they had been watching television, trying to keep up. If that seems unsettling, that is because it is.

Carter's hostage crisis was not resolved quickly, as Reagan's was. For Carter, the preoccupying misery stretched out month after month and into a second year. What that did to Carter was to make him the living image of the country's humiliation, pain, and loss of confidence. And we had to watch that image on television. Understandably, there was not much inclination to reelect it.

Ronald Reagan came to office running against the hapless Carter but also against Washington and politicians generally, thus ironically doing what Carter had done. He was a Republican and a conservative, but he presented himself more as a citizen-reformer who would save us from politics. In saving us, he would reduce the cost, the size, and the meddlesome power of the federal government at home, strengthen it militarily in the world, and restore patriotism, religious values, adventurous free enterprise, and confidence. All this came to be called a conservative revolution.

But for many voters assessing Reagan in 1980, the big test was not whether he should have a mandate for his revolution. The text was whether he seemed safe enough to justify voting the incumbent out. He passed easily, although he was older and more ideological than many who voted for him would have wished. Reagan looked undeniably vigorous; the visible evidence minimized the age issue. As for the extremely conservative views he expressed, his temperate, amiable personality took the edge off. It was true, as the old Hollywood story had it, that Ronald Reagan just naturally fitted the role of best friend.

He had the qualities of a best friend on television, all right, and this level, likable man soon had the personal trust of much of the population. That Reagan had been an actor most of his life has been cited—beyond all previously known limits of redundancy—as the explanation for his success in communicating on television.

In my minority opinion, acting background is an all-too-convenient, point-missing rationale for Reagan's effectiveness on camera and microphone. Oh, experience might help him read lines and not squint into the lights and not trip over cables. But what makes Ronald Reagan effective on television is that he is authentic. He knows who he is; he is himself. He is comfortable with that, and he knows not to act.

This confident, consistent sense of self makes the compelling presence on television. A political scientist at the University of California at Berkeley picks up the argument that Reagan "knows who he is"—and carries it right back to Hollywood. Professor Michael Rogin says, "Ronald Reagan found out who he was by whom he played on film. Responding to typecasting that either attracted him or repelled him, making active efforts to obtain certain roles and to escape from others, Reagan merged his on-screen and off-screen identities."

Reagan seems especially effective because the television performance level of so many other politicians of the day is so low. They tend to strike attitudes. They project, or hold themselves in. They work at television and remember what the media consultant told them about posture and gesture and pace. They try to be natural while getting the effect they want. They act.

If Reagan himself is consistent and fairly uncomplicated, his presidency has been full of paradoxes. He is remote but somehow very much in charge. He has left an almost unprecedented proportion of his job to staff, yet he has to be ranked with the assertive, strong Presidents.

He is an ideologue who frustrates the Republican pragmatists in the Senate, and he is a pragmatist who disillusions the Republican right wing. He takes unyielding public positions on principle, and then allows them to be compromised—without apology, sometimes without conceding that they were compromised.

He holds relatively few news conferences, preferring set pieces to the risk of error in give-and-take, but he seems the most accessible President in the world as he walks from his helicopter on the White House grounds giving good-natured, noncommittal answers to the bumptious, shouted questions from Sam Donaldson of ABC—a ritual both Donaldson and the White House find useful for their own purposes.

Reagan is the natural man, just being himself, yet his staff spends more time than any in memory moving him around to appealing and symbolic settings, keeping him visible, contriving events to play to his credit and obscure his failings, and always promoting and briefing him for television appearances as if he were a forgetful old actor.

The paradoxes all are accommodated in the positive perception of

Ronald Reagan. It is not the people are fooled; many seem to be quite aware of both sides of each paradox. In crowds of Reagan supporters, reporters constantly encounter fans who will talk about his flaws. Public-opinion polls keep showing large blocs of voters who disagree with Reagan on this or that issue, or a whole swath of issues, but give him high ratings as President anyway.

Mary McGrory, the liberal columnist, has written in some despair: "Reagan has a lock on the affections of the American people. They are almost blindly fond of him. He is not exactly a father figure—he is rather too jaunty and nonchalant for that. He is more a jolly, reassuring uncle who comes to call amid much laughter and many stories. Never mind his views—wrong, but strong, they are generally considered, and they add to the fondness."

Christopher Matthews, who is on the staff of the Speaker of the House, says Reagan is "the nation's host." Matthews says Reagan has redefined the presidency: "He is not in government, but some place, previously uncharted, *between* us and government."

If we take that seriously, and we should, it carries us well beyond personality in explaining Reagan's success. His approach to the function of being President seems to be to reassure people that he has not given himself over to Washington. He shares the public prejudice about government and politics, and he keeps his distance. He would rather talk to the people.

Henry Fairlie, a journalist with a British background, made this observation in the time of Reagan: "The American presidency is being transformed into a radically popular institution—more and more dependent on, and at the same time able to exploit, a direct and uninterrupted relationship with the people.... For some years now almost every important development in the American political system has been encouraging the direct relationship between the President and the people. These include the weakness of the parties and disarray of the party system; the dissipation of power in the House and Senate; the reliance on direct mail and media consultants in election campaigns; and, of course, the new prominence of the media, dominated by television."

That assessment is not far out of line with the views of many American academics, politicians, and political reporters, although I would insist that television is not just one of the developments but the driving force behind all the others.

Politicans and consultants lavish creative energy and money on television commercials to make points already market-tested by pollsters. In buying their own airtime—the record shows Republicans can afford it more often than Democrats—candidates get at the viewers without intervening questioners or editors. For the television news shows, they contrive short, provocative statements that will intrigue producers and resist editing.

Former governor Jerry Brown of California is said to have been able to talk in twenty-second sound bites, stringing them together, each with a beginning, middle, and end.

For debates, an important strategy is to come up with one-liners catchy enough that they will become enduring images in a campaign—such as Walter Mondale's line to Gary Hart: "Where's the beef?" Spontaneity is rehearsed until it's right.

The political fraternity studies the personal quirks and presumed political biases of correspondents, morning-show hosts, news anchors. Conservatives take for granted a liberal bias in the networks; it is part of their ideology and has some public following. Liberals gripe less about philosophical bias; they complain about assorted slights and failures of judgment in the coverage of themselves.

The professionalism of network journalists is often admirable, but they are coping with burdensome logistics, ridiculous little time slots, and the need to shoot for the gist of a story on a visual medium whose impact is monstrous. So television news executives rarely get through a day without having to consider criticism of inconsistencies, sensationalism, superficiality, and perhaps plain irresponsibility in the snapshots they take of politics. When the networks really monkey with the minds of the electorate, as in broadcasting "exit polls" and "projections" while people are still voting, everyone from righteous print journalists to congressional committees comes down on them.

So television is subject to pressure and control from both outside and inside. Assignment editors, reporters, cameramen, producers, network management, and the Federal Communications Commission are forever making decisions that influence what is shown of politics. Politicians are forever devising strategies, ploys, and gimmicks to gain advantage on the tube.

Much of the apprehension about television politics arises from all this manipulation, and there is a notion that the effect is vast. This is exaggerated. For one thing, the television audience often knows when it is being used. It has lived with television and has some sense of illusion; what the audience will accept on a game show or a melodrama it will not necessarily treat the same way in true-life public affairs.

True, politics is trivialized when it is played for television. But that is only a part of the larger reality: Politics has been transformed by the very existence of television. Yes, the medium is the message. The medium itself has changed the way people connect to politicians and the way the political system works. As Reuven Frank, the former president of NBC News, has said, "The truly serious criticisms of television can be reduced ultimately to the proposition that it shouldn't have been invented in the first place."

It *was* invented, and in 1952 at the national conventions it became a part of the presidential nominating process. There has not been a contest that went past the first ballot at a convention since 1952.

The nominees since then have been designated before the conventions in a burgeoning series of televised primaries and caucuses. These contests in the states are open, competitive affairs for ordinary voters, not closed convocations of wrangling, deal-making factions and bosses. The old, closed process could not survive under television's eye.

Of course, television's eye did not really pick up the meaning of the old conventions: All that wheeling and dealing was a national political party negotiating among its constituencies, balancing its interests, compromising its differences. Such conventions were uniquely American, and political scientists gave them a lot of the credit for the stability of two-party government, for avoiding extreme swings to the right and left.

What is the purpose of the conventions now? Surely more than being a kind of electoral college to certify the results of the primaries and caucuses. Surely more than voting "aye" on the nominee's draft of a platform and choice for Vice President.

Besides those pro forma functions, recent conventions have settled for being reconciliation rallies to kick off the presidential campaign. But how long will the networks be willing to give away a week of prime time for that sort of enterprise? At the 1984 Democratic convention, even the rally was a charade because everyone in the hall knew Walter Mondale could not beat Ronald Reagan.

Aha! That became the unstated point of the convention, and prime time was devoted to showcasing likely Democratic candidates in 1988. Governor Mario Cuomo of New York was the big hit both as a television performer and as a prescriber for the party's future. Is the evolving role of the convention to present the candidates and themes not of the campaign at hand but of the next one after that?

The primaries are the nominating system now. In 1952 there were twelve primaries, and they bound only a small fraction of the national-convention delegates. By 1980 there were 30 primaries, and they elected more than 75 percent of the delegates. A slight reduction in the number of primaries in 1984 only increased the number of state caucuses, which usually were merely another format for popular voting to pledge the delegates to a candidate. The field was winnowed quickly in the first few contests, for they were crucial to a winning image and campaign contributions.

Over the years it evolved that the first caucus, in Iowa, in the winter before the late-summer national convention, would establish the contenders in rough order. Then the first primary, amid the frosty scenery and commercialism of New Hampshire, would narrow the race to two serious possibilities, or maybe one—such was the national impact of the television battle.

The primary schedule ran on, from February into June.

The candidates, not the constituencies of the party, controlled the delegates elected in their names by the voters in the primaries and caucuses. The presidential nominee in such circumstances was less a product of a party process than an independent operator with his own political base and organization, his own obligations and agenda.

When I think I overstate, I reread Professor David B. Truman, formerly of Columbia University, who said the primary system "tends to destroy accountability. It does so because it disintegrates and ultimately eliminates the political party as an organization which the voter once could hold accountable for the performance of a government. The single-issue groups, political-action committees, faceless image makers, and professional media manipulations that occupy the resulting vacuum cannot be held accountable for the results that they produce. They are basically irresponsible and ultimately subversive of the common good."

Most observers would agree anyway that political parties have undergone a drastic decline in the age of television. The party program can be a burden to a candidate appealing to voters essentially as an individual. Politicians are less dependent on the party as an organization that develops leaders and promotes them through the ranks. Now the sharp ones can promote themselves.

In the matter of campaign finance, where television advertising is a wildly escalating cost, the parties' role is far less important than it once was. Television candidates increasingly rely on contributions directly to themselves from individuals and from that booming new source, political-action committees.

PACs represent special interests—insurance companies, defense contractors, all kinds of corporations, labor unions, trade associations, a mind-boggling assortment of ideological groups—and often a PAC's concern is so narrow that it comes down to a single issue. The distinctive thing about most PACs is the sheer specificity of what they want in return for their contributions; they don't trouble the office holder for accountability on any issues but theirs.

Ten years ago there were 600 PACs. In 1984 there were 4,000 of them raising and distributing campaign money. Presidential elections, which are federally financed, are somewhat insulated from this influence, but Congress is up to its knees in PAC money.

Senate and House candidates, especially incumbents on key legislative committees, frequently get more financial help from PACs than from their own parties. For the last election, PACs raised $288 million. The total receipts of the Republican party were $300 million; of the Democratic party, $97 million.

The PACs delivered a much higher proportion of their receipts directly to individual candidates than the parties did. That was because each party spent so much to sustain itself as an organization and to promote itself and its entire team of candidates as representing a coherent political philosophy. Meanwhile, as the PACs grew, a candidate could pay less attention to parties and coherent political philosophy and rely more on his own conglomerate of assorted special interests.

If strong parties really matter in the American system, if accountability is a good thing, if compromise is the essence of viable politics, then some of the trends since the dawn of television are troublesome at best.

Maybe the political system will adapt without severe damage; it has adapted to new conditions before, though not to a universal, instantaneous communications technology that keeps throwing off secondary effects that nobody expected. Those secondary effects are organic changes in the system—the erosion of old institutions, including the conventions and the political parties themselves, the rise of the distorted sequence of primaries, the quantum leap in the cost of campaigning, and the emergence of the mighty swarm of disparate new special-interest lobbies to finance the new politics.

Meanwhile, the primary effect of television—to focus the attention of huge audiences on the visible personal qualities of politicians—will presumably endure. And there will be those compelling presences on the little screen reassuring us that they are not politicians at all but something more independent and righteous.

I, for one, lament the passing of politicians who are frankly politicians. For it is still the politicians who balance competing interests, negotiate coalitions, see a wisp of glory in the notion of consensus, and make our kind of government work.

We are a diverse people. We are a collection of factions, minorities, and ideologies. More than television is needed to hold us together.

What does hold us together, as from the beginning, is the practice of politics under a Constitution drawn up by politicians.

Mass Media and Politics: For Further Reading

James David Barber, *The Pulse of Politics: Electing Presidents in the Media Age.* Beverly Hills, Calif.: Sage, 1980.

Gerald Benjamin, *The Communications Revolution in Politics.* New York: Academy of Political Science, 1982.

Peter Clarke and Susan H. Evans, *Covering Campaigns: Journalism in Congressional Elections.* Stanford, Calif.: Stanford University Press, 1983.

Doris A. Graber, *Mass Media and American Politics.* Washington, D.C.: Congressional Quarterly Press, 1980.

Ray E. Hiebert, Robert F. Jones, John d'Arc Lorenz, and Ernest A. Lotito, *The Political Image Merchants: Strategies for the Seventies.* Washington, D.C.: Acropolis Books, 1971, 1976.

Gladys Engel Lang and Kurt Lang, *The Battle for Public Opinion: The President, the Press and the Polls during Watergate.* New York: Columbia University Press, 1983.

Martin Linsky, *Television and the Presidential Elections.* Lexington, Mass.: Lexington Books, 1983.

Myles Martel, *Political Campaign Debates: Images, Strategies, and Tactics.* White Plains, N.Y.: Longman, 1983.

Dan D. Nimmo and James E. Combs, *Mediated Political Realities.* White Plains, N.Y.: Longman, 1983.

David L. Paletz and Robert M. Entman, *Media Power Politics: A Timely Provocative Look at How the Media Affect Public Opinion and Political Power in the United States.* New York: Free Press, 1981.

Michael J. Robinson and Margaret A. Sheehan, *Over the Wire and on TV: CBS and UPI in Campaign '80.* New York: Russell Sage Foundation, 1983.

Austin Ranney, *Channels of Power: The Impact of Television on American Politics.* New York: Basic Books, 1983.

Larry J. Sabato, *The Rise of Political Consultants: New Ways of Winning Elections.* New York: Basic Books, 1981.

VIII

Mass Media
and Government

Although the U.S. government cannot legally censor the press, the press can and does censor the government. Reporters, editors, correspondents, producers, and directors are the people who decide what news about the government will be communicated in the mass media.

Our Founding Fathers gave the press a powerful role when they formed our country, and some of them even felt that the press should be more powerful than government. "That government is best which governs least," was the cry of the day. Thomas Jefferson took the point to the extreme when he wrote: "Were it left to me to decide whether we should have a government without newspapers or newspapers without government, I should not hesitate for a moment to prefer the latter."

In 1828, the English writer Thomas Macaulary wrote, "The gallery in which the reporters sit has become a fourth estate of the realm." Freedom of the press in England had made the newspapers as powerful as the House of Lords, the House of Commons, and the church.

In the late 1950s, an American writer, Douglass Cater, wrote a book describing the Washington press corps as the "fourth branch of government," as powerful and as important as the legislative, judicial, and executive branches. Yet the press is not government, it is private industry. Often, however, the three other branches of government cannot win the public support necessary to carry out their mandates without the cooperation of the mass media.

The press is not perfect, and it is not all-powerful. The individuals who make up the mass media are small in number compared to the legions in government. And they are only human, just as those who are the bureaucracy. Perhaps it is the continual adversarial struggle between the two that makes the world safe for democracy.

As government has come to take a larger and more complete role in our lives, the mass media too have faced increasing government manipulation. In the 1960s, talk began about "government management of the news," as politicians and bureaucrats learned how to use increasingly sophisticated methods of influencing and pressuring the mass media. Rulers have probably always known how to bend the press to their purposes, and few American presidents have not been involved in one way or another in trying to control the news to further their administration's interests.

Yet government can exercise few legal constraints over the mass media. The famous "Pentagon papers" case in the 1970s reaffirmed the notion, upheld by most court rulings over the years, that the government cannot exercise prior restraint or censor or block publication of any item, no matter how damaging, unless the government can prove that grave national security is involved. To date, few such cases have come to court.

While the government cannot use the law to control the press, it can use techniques of public relations and persuasion to influence the mass media. It can censor itself; it can withhold information from the press and the public. It can stage events, such as presidential press conferences and congressional hearings to capture the spotlight of news. It can shape the news by timing and orchestrating the staging of events. It can manipulate the flow of information by selectively releasing those facts and figures that give the government's slant to an issue. And it can influence news coverage by persuasive techniques, which might include intimidation as well as friendly persuasion. John F. Kennedy was a master at winning the friendship and good will of reporters; Richard Nixon often had to resort to bullying the press to try to get his way.

We have, in fact, come to think of the government and the press as adversaries, battling each other rather than cooperating with each other. The government has played that role just as often and just as well as the media. Such management of the mass media by government in our society will probably grow in the years ahead, as the media become more powerful and the issues, more complex.

26 The Media as Shadow Government

by William L. Rivers

> William L. Rivers feels that the press has become so powerful in influencing government that it might be going far beyond what the Founding Fathers originally had in mind. Rivers is a former Washington correspondent who has written widely about the press and government. He is now a professor of communication at Stanford University. This article is reprinted from *The Quill*, March 1982.

The capital city of the United States of America, like the federal government it houses, was constructed according to plan. The original city, most of which still stands, is the physical equivalent of Jefferson's Declaration of Independence, of Madison's Constitution, and, in general, of the whole assortment of utopian notions that Carl Becker has called "the heavenly city of the 18th-century philosophers." As London's Crystal Palace symbolized, for all the world, the progressivism, utilitarianism, and scientism of the 19th century, so the Washington of L'Enfant, at least in certain kinds of weather, is an artwork of the Enlightenment—a perfect emblem of the 18th century's spacious, optimistic, slightly naive view of man.

As with any good work of art, every feature of official Washington has a meaning. The various presidential monuments, the Supreme Court building, and the Capitol itself reflect, massively, the founding fathers' dream of resurrecting the Roman Republic (there even are fasci beside the speaker's platform in the House of Representatives). A tall, cigarstore Indian perched atop the Capitol's great dome can render the general effect, for the finicky observer, less classical than kitschy. But this touch of the frontier serves to remind us that the city of Washington was designed to be the set piece of a continental empire.

By contrast, the executive mansion, at 1600 Pennsylvania Avenue, is a structure so austere and virginal that posterity has named it, simply, the White House. Beside the White House, and housing its senior functionaries, is the EOB—the old Executive Office Building—a Victorian ostentation of *nouveau riche* power in which Walt Disney might have felt more at home than Queen Victoria.

Official Washington is majestic and orderly, erratic and tasteless. Its architecture represents the impossible simplicity and systematic character of the U.S. Constitution. It also reflects the labyrinthine complications and overelaboration that were the inevitable products of the Industrial Revolution, of Manifest Destiny, of one civil and two world wars, of bread-and-circus electioneering—the inevitable products, in other words, of two centuries of human foible.

But there is another side to Washington—another government. In a high-rise building on Pennsylvania Avenue, near the old Executive Office Building, is a floor of small offices whose windows overlook governmental Washington—the White House, the Capitol, the great monuments and museums along the mall, and the gargoyled mug of the EOB.

"Here. Look. This is the best view of Washington," says Mel Elfin, capital bureau chief of *Newsweek* magazine. If you can appreciate the incongruous, Elfin is doubly right. These windowed cubicles of one significant organ of that other government reflect not only a different organization from that of official Washington, but a distinct view of man.

Just outside Elfin's office window is a little balcony with a few chairs and a low-slung rail to keep one (barely) from becoming hamburger on the pavement below. The balcony is covered with screaming green Astroturf, which provides a startling emphasis in the foreground to the classical travertine and brownstone edifices beyond. Some old potted petunias and a couple of tomato plants struggle to cope with what appears to be constant neglect.

Somehow, the bedraggled pots fit the scene. Everywhere in the *Newsweek* offices are similar images of an eccentricity that is born of hard-nosed realism. Everywhere, there is also awesome disorder; for although the *Newsweek* offices are fairly plush by press standards, this week they are being renovated—new carpets, some rearranged partitions, and the addition of a kitchen and conference room.

Also being renovated is the National Press Building, some three blocks from the EOB and *Newsweek* offices, and fourteen blocks from the Capitol. Since 1908, this venerable structure has been the focal point for most Washington news operations. It was definitely showing its age. Its brickwork was crumbling, its hallways were yellowed and dingy. In the ornately plastered lobby, elevators chugged up and down like old mules about to give up the ghost, while reporters and editors muttered disagreeably about how long it took them to get up to their offices.

The National Press Building was in an advanced state of decay. It is certain that the Washington press headquarters is getting a face lift. The Other Government—the Washington news corps—has come to consciousness of its power and is gradually moving into larger, more official, less eccentric structures.

Richard Rovere once suggested that our attitudes toward national politics—and, indeed, our national politics—might have been profoundly different if the founding fathers, instead of creating the nation's capital on the mud flats of the Potomac, had set it down in the center of 18th-century

Manhattan. Our federal politicians and public servants would not now be jousting in the limiting and incestuous environment of a municipality given over entirely to government. With the national government as but one sector of a complex city, officials could not have avoided rubbing elbows and shaking hands with the nation's literati and its social critics. The condition that resulted might have rendered American politics less peripheral and vague in the national literature, and American social criticism less divorced from the political realities.

Rovere made this point most authoritatively. In order to write about national affairs for *The New Yorker*, Rovere himself commuted to Washington from his work in New York City. He often lamented that "very few reflective, literary intelligences deal with public affairs in this country," and he attributed this problem to the singularity of concerns and the cultural remoteness of Washington, D.C. For political man, no city is more exciting, more electric, than Washington. But for those with other or broader passions, no city is so stultifying. Among the intellectual and creative elite who have been honored in Washington, few have been willing to linger longer than it look them to finish their dinners at the White House.

The result of Washington's cultural estrangement from the nation has been the elevation of Washington's journalists to a kind of academy of national sages and prognosticators. In most other world capitals—which, usually, are also highly cosmopolitan cities—the journalist must vie with the novelist, with the playwright, with the artist, and with the critic in reporting, in analyzing, and in interpreting national public affairs. In Washington, news correspondents win by default. As a result, they have acquired the authority and sometimes even the power of a shadow government.

The Washington press corps has certainly acquired the trappings of power. Privileged as no other citizens are, the correspondents are listed in the *Congressional Directory*; they receive advance copies of governmental speeches and announcements; they are frequently shown documents forbidden even to high officials; and they meet and work in special quarters set aside for them in all major government buildings, including the White House. Fantastic quantities of government time and money are devoted to their needs, their desires, and their whims. Some White House correspondents talk with the president more often than his own party leaders in the House and in the Senate, and there are Capitol correspondents who see more of the congressional leaders than do most other congressmen.

No wonder, then, that Washington correspondents feel what one presidential assistant has termed an "acute sense of involvement in the churning process that is government in America." A close view of this involvement so impressed Patrick O'Donovan, a former Washington correspondent for the London *Observer*, that he said, "The American press fulfills almost a constitutional function."

Indeed, in Washington today, correspondents who report for the news media possess a power beyond even their own dreams and fears. They are only beginning to become aware that their work now shapes and colors the beliefs of nearly everyone, not only in the United States but throughout most of the world.

For the American public, full acceptance of the media's new authority and responsibility came at the end of the Watergate crisis, when the president of the United States posed his word against that of the press and lost. But Watergate was less coup d'état than it was climax. It was the end of a long evolution that was first observed by a newsman nearly fifty years ago, during the trial of the Lindbergh baby's kidnapper and killer. At that time, Walter Lippmann commented that in our democracy "there are two processes of justice, the one official, the other popular. They are carried on side by side, the one in the courts of law, the other in the press, over the radio, on the screen, at public meetings."

Lippmann's observation remains true today, yet those who would end this discussion on the question of the court verdict versus the popular verdict are missing a much greater issue. For the basic question is not just whether we have two parallel systems of justice in this country, but whether we have two governments. Do we have a second, adversarial government that acts as a check on the first and controls public access to it? Indeed we do—and this Other Government is made up primarily of the more than two thousand news correspondents stationed in Washington.

In our daily lives, we trace a path from home to work and back. Without the news media, we would know almost nothing beyond our own sphere of activity. The public's knowledge of national government depends not on direct experience and observation, but on the news media; and it is the media that set the agenda for public discussion and decision.

To a large degree, the employees of the government—including the president himself—must also depend on the reports of the news media for information about some of their most important concerns. In government, as elsewhere, each worker is circumscribed, and his sphere is small. A congressional assistant may spend much or all of one day absorbing details about the religious leaders of Iran and learning much more than is published or broadcast about the imminence of all-out war in the Middle East. But he hasn't the time to inform all of his colleagues about his new knowledge, and he is likely to know less about House debate that day than any tired tourist from North Carolina who wandered into the public gallery to give his feet a rest. Both the tired tourist and the congressional assistant must depend on the newspapers to find out what happened that day in the Senate.

In an article for a journal of political science, former Senator H. Alexander Smith of New Jersey made it clear that members of Congress are not Olympians who learn what they know in closed-door hearings and secret communiqués. They, too, must depend on the media. Senator Smith listed thirteen different sources of information for congressmen; but the news media, he wrote, "are basic and form the general groundwork upon which the congressman builds his knowledge of current events. The other sources...are all supplements to these media."

Even presidents, with their vast and powerful apparatus of information, often end up relying as much on the press as on their own informational systems. John Kennedy admitted that he acquired new information from *The New York Times* about his own secret sponsorship of the Bay of Pigs invasion. Eleven days before the invasion that the CIA had been shepherding so carefully, the editors of the *Times* informed Kennedy that their correspondent, Tad Szulc, had discovered the secret and that a detailed news report was imminent. Kennedy persuaded the publisher to postpone publication until after the landing in Cuba. But, during the discussions with the *Times* editors, the president picked up new information about the mounting of the invasion.

Afterward, in regret at the fiasco, Kennedy said to Turner Catledge, the executive editor of the *Times*, "If you had printed more about the operation, you would have saved us from a colossal mistake."

Even the strongest and most capable president requires such reporting; for he is *always* insulated from the realities of his administration by the fears and ambitions of his subordinates. He cannot possibly sort and absorb all of the vital information that is produced by governmental agencies and activities. Many believe that the fall of Richard Nixon was foreordained by his hatred of and isolation from the media.

The influence of the Washington press corps is also recognized in the third branch of the federal government. Justice Potter Stewart said in 1975, with something like wonder: "Only in the two short years that culminated last summer in the resignation of the president did we fully realize the enormous power that an investigative and adversary press can exert."

The courts have long been suspicious of that power, and over the years, they have waged a largely silent battle with trial reporters over the reporters' access to and publication of courtroom proceedings. Moving ponderously, the courts have attempted to close off much of the access of the news media. Moving quickly and sometimes deviously, the media have anticipated and occasionally foreclosed these efforts, very often using one judge against another.

The Other Government wins some, loses some. During the fifty years since Walter Lippmann's observation about public and private trials, legal maneuvers between the federal government and its courts and the national news media have resembled a very intricate and symmetrical minuet. The courts move to gag orders and to secret trials. The media, stalemated, take the issues to higher courts and begin to employ attorneys as reporters.

But the dance does not always include willing partners, and the Other Government is usually less effective than official Washington at some of the more subtle steps. Often the official government will make the news media an unwitting participant in the never-ceasing warfare among its various branches and agencies.

Twenty years ago, a young reporter was writing an article about the powerful Brooklyn congressman, John J. Rooney, who headed the House of Representatives subcommittee that controlled the State Department budget. Every year, Congressman Rooney savaged the State Department budget request by speaking against "booze money for those striped-pants cookie-pushers." He alarmed the young reporter by exclaiming angrily, "I want to keep an open mind and be fair, but if you people in the press keep harping on it, I'm afraid you'll make me whack the budget too much."

The reporter then interviewed the assistant secretary of state who had the task of arguing in Congress for whatever budget the department thought was reasonable. The reporter asked him how badly Rooney's attacks crippled the budget request. "Why, not at all," the assistant secretary answered. In fact, he explained, Congressman Rooney was "the best friend the Department of State ever had." By berating Old Foggy Bottom on the floor of the House, even as he was pushing a generous budget, Rooney persuaded the representatives who abhorred striped pants that he had the State Department's number. Rooney's strong words were a facade that enabled the congressman to sneak more into the budget than Congress would otherwise have granted.

That sounded to the reporter like doubletalk, but no matter how many people the reporter interviewed, they were almost evenly split on the question. In the end, the reporter decided that Congressman Rooney was not a friend of the State Department; that he was, in fact, an irresponsible budget slasher. But even as the reporter was typing his article, he worried: It *could be* that Rooney is a clever ally of the Department. Any Washington reporter can be convinced at times that Machiavelli is alive and advising congressmen.

A few months later, in 1961, the same young reporter was feeling the impact of the new Kennedy administration. Like other Washington correspondents, he was invited for the first time in history to share with a president both the crushing responsibility and the glittering aura of the greatest center of leadership in the Western world. Before 1961, the White House had been a closed preserve. Information was channeled through the president's press secretary, and some news correspondents never so much as met the White House advisers and chief assistants. A reporter who had arranged an interview with an Eisenhower assistant without going through Jim Hagerty, the press secretary, was so elated that he telephoned his editor in New York to say, "I broke around behind Hagerty!" The important news was not the substance of the interview but the fact that he got one.

When Kennedy took over, correspondents wandered through the White House offices in such numbers that they created a traffic problem. President Kennedy was his own most effective promoter. He practiced personal salesmanship with the élan of one accustomed to establishing the rules of the game. Kennedy made such a fetish of giving exclusive interviews that his press secretary, Pierre Salinger, once observed that he had to go to the Oval Office to find the White House correspondents.

The heady effect of this unaccustomed presidential attention is demonstrated by the behavior of our young reporter on the morning he received a call from the White House that the president wanted to talk to him. It was a snowy, miserable day. With a studied show of nonchalance, the reporter announced his coup to his colleagues, drew on his topcoat and one of his galoshes, and clumped out the door toward the elevator, leaving the other galosh on his desk.

The reporter who wrote the article about Congressman Rooney and who interviewed President Kennedy was me. I was then working for the now-defunct magazine *The Reporter*. Although I quit being a Washington correspondent near the end of 1961, I remained fascinated by the profession and by the sharpening power struggle between the Washington press corps and the federal government. Through secrecy, through the courts, through its press representatives, the government has awesome control over the public image of itself. Only the news media can exert an effective counterbalancing influence on the public's perception of government. Surely, if the government closes off freedom of access in any area, a balanced picture of government will give way to government propaganda.

Yet, there is another side to this issue. In 1978, philosopher-novelist Aleksandr Solzhenitsyn—an outsider, a Russian—observed, with considerable disapproval, that "The press has become the greatest power within Western countries, more powerful than the legislature, the executive, and the judiciary." How could he believe that? What of the overwhelming power of an attractive and canny president? What of the sheer size of the bureaucracy and its countless daily actions and decisions, which can vitally affect the course of society? Is it possible, despite the odds, that Solzhenitsyn is on to something?

We must remind ourselves periodically that the American republic's founders granted to the press, alone among private business institutions, the task of protecting the U.S. Constitution. Contemporary Washington correspondents are well aware of this responsibility and are proud of their independence from the official government and from the biases of their editors, publishers and station owners back home.

This independence marks the sharpest difference between Washington correspondents and their local brethren and between the Washington press corps today and that of previous generations. In 1936, Leo Rosten made this statement to a group of newspaper correspondents and asked whether it was true in their experience: "My orders are to be objective, but I *know* how my paper wants stories played." Slightly more than sixty percent of the correspondents replied yes, that they felt at least subtle pressure from their editors and publishers. In 1960, the mark came down dramatically; only 9.5 percent replied yes to the same question.

That difference is so dramatic that one may think there was a misunderstanding or a mistake. Another statement, which also tested freedom from home-office pressure, drew a similar response, however. Rosten asked the correspondents in 1936 whether this could be said of their work: "In my experience I've had stories played down, cut or killed for 'policy' reasons." Slightly more than fifty-five percent of the correspondents answered yes. In 1960, only 7.3 percent affirmed the same statement. During the twenty years since 1960, that downward trend has continued.

Yet, as my own experiences with President Kennedy and Congressman Rooney indicate, the independence of the contemporary Washington correspondents may be something of a mirage. In any event, what counts is not so much the independence of the reporters as it is their service of the public interest. How well do the news media serve our interests? How much do they show us of official Washington?

Learning about the national government from the news media is like watching a tightly-directed play. The director features the president at some length, the leading congressmen as secondary players, and the cabinet and justices of the Supreme Court as cameos and walk-ons. There are seldom any other entries in the dramatis personae, although there are *three million* employees of the national government. Any effort to move beyond the stage to see the undirected reality is useless. We must understand this: that the *reality* of government is often quite different from that reported by the two thousand news correspondents who help to create that image.

The public and the government are awash in a torrent of media reports. Yet, inquiring into how the news media actually serve the public yields a different perspective. Radio and television are mainly useful in signaling news events, providing the immediate—and sketchy—reports that announce happenings. More and more, we depend on television, despite the fact that our understanding is distorted by the brevity of the news reports. Broadcast journalists skim the top of the news, working with headlines, leads, and the bulletins that alert the public. Only occasionally does a documentary flesh out the news. Av Westin, a news executive of the American Broadcasting Company, has said: "I think television news is an illustrated service that can function best when it is regarded as an important yet fast adjunct to the newspapers. I know what we have to leave out; and if people do not read newspapers, news magazines, and books, they are desperately misinformed."

Newspapers cannot compete with radio and television for rapid transmission, and they cannot compete with television for the sheer impact of seeing and hearing news in the making. But a newspaper is available at any time, and it can provide a vast range of information on many subjects. The importance of the newspaper has been described best by a man who was interviewed during a newspaper strike: "I don't have the details now; I just have the result. It's almost like reading the headlines of the newspaper without following up the story. I miss the detail and the explanation of events leading up to the news."

Most magazines can treat their subject in greater depth than newspapers, but they generally cannot cover as many *different* subjects. Even the news magazines, which attempt to cover a wide range of subjects in some depth, do not publish as much information in their weekly issues as can be found in a single issue of a large daily newspaper. Like people who write books, those who write for magazines can seek out the unreported, flesh out the information that has been presented only in silhouette in broadcasts and newspapers, and report matters that the faster media have missed in the rush to meet deadlines.

It would seem that such a division of labor would help us to learn about *everything* that goes on in the government: radio and television rapidly reporting the action: newspapers putting most of the stories into context; and the magazine writers and book authors reporting the major stories more fully, and with more grace and flavor. But this range of public-affairs reports, however carefully some may be fashioned, often seems the reflection of a faulty mirror. The mirror is first held this way, then that way, but how narrowly it is focused! The presidency, the congressional leaders, the State Department, and the Department of Defense are in view. Only occasionally is mention made of such bureaus as the Departments of Energy, of Transportation, or Agriculture, or of such agencies as the Federal Communications Commission, the Food and Drug Administration, the Interstate Commerce Commission, and the many other-agencies that figure so importantly in our everyday lives. Only a few such agencies ever make it to the front page, to the television screen, to the radio interview.

Protesting the narrow focus of the Washington press corps, Derick Daniels, former executive editor of one of the Knight-Ridder newspapers, argued that journalists must recognize the reader's needs and desires:

> Yes, yes, we understand that the poor slob in the kitchen is interested in the price of soap when she *ought* to be interested in Congress. But I mean recognizing squarely, as a matter of intellectual honesty, that the

kitchen is really, *in fact*, just as important...the amount of knowledge and information collected, and the studies available through the U.S. government, are nearly limitless. A single document—the yearbook of the Department of Agriculture—contains more useful information in its pages than most newspapers report in a year.

The media are thus confronted with a dilemma. It is impossible for any news organization, no matter how large, to cover fully the entire federal government every day. And even if it were possible, no one would want to sift through such reports. So the real question is not whether the media are at fault for not covering the entire government all the time, or for printing only a small portion of what is knowable about the government. The more appropriate questions are: How good is the judgment of the Washington press corps as to what parts of the government to watch and which of its actions to record or investigate? And how good is the judgment of the Washington news bureaus and their outlets in deciding what information to print and to broadcast every day?

These are two important questions—as important as any questions we can ask about our official government in Washington: for, in a sense, the two governments—the official government and the national news media—increasingly form part of a single, symbiotic unit. The major difference between the real government and the media government begins with the conscious and deliberate action by most officials to insert the image they desire into the media process. The government nearly always attempts to create an image of itself. Whether this will be successful depends on the reporter. In some cases, the image of the officials vies with the reporter's own concept of those officials. In other cases, the images are a match.

Ben Bagdikian, one of the most powerful media critics in the United States, commented on the interrelationships between government image-making and press image-making when he made a study of newspaper columnists. He talked to many federal assistant secretaries for public affairs about how they briefed their bosses and how they preferred to break government news. Bagdikian found the secretaries were heavily influenced by what they saw in the news media, that they accepted this as what the media would respond to, and that, as a result, they fashioned their output to serve what they perceived to be the media interest. Thus, the work of the Washington columnists, Bagdikian speculated, "includes guessing what the government is doing." This produces a double-mirror effect, in which each side responds to what the other is doing, while at the same time adjusting itself to the other side's anticipated needs.

Thinking about the mirrors of politics, John Kenneth Galbraith commented wryly: "Nearly all of our political comment originates in Washington. Washington politicians, after talking things over with each other, relay misinformation to Washington journalists who, after further intramural discussion, print it where it is thoughtfully read by the same politicians. It is the only completely successful closed system for the recycling of garbage that has yet been devised."

Viewed in the rawness of this circus of political reporting, government news seems very complicated—and dangerous. It is true that since the Vietnam War and the Watergate crisis, Washington correspondents are much more suspicious of the announcements of government officials. More and more correspondents every year are asking sharp questions of officials.

The questions are important because there have been times in the past fifteen years when *no one* in the official government knew what was true. Phil Goulding, assistant secretary of defense for public affairs in the second Nixon administration, once said: "In our office, the secretary's office, or the White House, we never knew how much we did not know." Again, in reference to the Nixon years and the Watergate scandal, Senator Charles Mathias has said: "The more a president sits surrounded by his own views and those of his personal advisers, the more he lives in a house of mirrors in which all the views and ideas tend to reflect and reinforce his own."

When it became evident in 1973 that Nixon had been living in a world of mirrors—that he saw only the image that he had manipulated—Dr. Edward Teller, who had developed the hydrogen bomb in strict secrecy twenty years earlier, wrote ruefully, "Secrecy, once accepted, becomes an addiction." He might also have noted that secrecy, once the routine practice and defense of the official government, had, by 1973, finally given way to the angry probings of the Other Government.

By the time the Watergate case had brought an end to the presidency of Richard Nixon, the Other Government was firmly in control. Contemplating the Washington cityscapes from the barely contained chaos of the *Newsweek* offices, one wonders if this is what the founding fathers had in mind.

27 Dealing with the Media

by Griffin B. Bell with Ronald J. Ostrow

Public officials quickly learn how to deal with the press. That seems to go with the territory. When Griffin Bell was appointed attorney general by President Jimmy Carter, he was new to Washington and did not know how to manage "that Hydra-headed giant known as the Washington press corps." This article describes how he learned. Bell is now a managing partner in the Atlanta law firm of King and Spalding. Ronald Ostrow, Nieman Fellow '65, is a staff writer with *The Los Angeles Times* in Washington, D.C. This article is reprinted from the *Nieman Reports*, Summer 1982.

When President-elect Carter called on me to be his attorney general, I responded with considerable confidence. After all, as a member of the United States Court of Appeals for the Fifth Circuit, I had worked closely with the Department of Justice for fifteen years and had been immersed in the principal legal questions of the era—civil rights, labor disputes, consumerism, government regulation of business and the like. My earlier years in private practice and in Georgia state government had given me more than a nodding acquaintance with the national scene. In short, like most others in Jimmy Carter's circle of Georgians, I came to Washington with no great trepidation, despite my lack of experience there.

And like most of my Georgia brothers, I was to learn all too soon how much I did not know about operations in the nation's capital. Nowhere, however, was my lack of knowledge more acute than in my dealings with that Hydra-headed giant known as the Washington press corps. Fortunately, perhaps, my media baptism in Washington was in the born-again style— total immersion. I got in trouble with the press even before I arrived in Washington and stayed in trouble through my Senate confirmation hearings. And from my swearing-in to the day I left the Justice Department two and a half years later, there was hardly a day when I was not wrestling with a serious media problem of some sort. As a result, I had no choice but to concentrate a good deal of my time and attention on trying to understand the Washington press corps and figuring out how best to deal with it. On balance, I emerged reasonably satisfied with the results, but along the way I made some mistakes, not the least of which occurred in one major case when I forgot my own hard-earned lessons and got involved in a controversy that almost drove me to resigning as an embarrassment to the President.

As every schoolboy knows, the Founding Fathers attached so much importance to what we now call the news media that they made freedom of the press one of the handful of rights guaranteed in the Bill of Rights, along with freedom of religion, the right to assemble and petition for grievances and the right to be secure in our homes from unreasonable searches and seizures. Everyone in public life in America deals with the press—from selectmen in the smallest New England towns to governors of the largest, most populous states. Even judges do, including myself while I was on the bench in Atlanta, though in the comparative isolation of the federal judiciary I was rarely interviewed and never interrogated. Yet no amount of experience anywhere else is adequate preparation for doing business with the news media in Washington.

In large ways and small, the Washington press corps is unique. Politicians cannot escape it: they try to ignore it at their peril. Whether the newly arrived public official likes it or not, the press is, as Edmund Burke called it, "The Fourth Estate"—the fourth branch of government. Like the executive, the legislative and the judicial branches, the press does not possess absolute power: but it has enormous influence and can shape the issues government officials must deal with. It can color the public's perception of individual political leaders and their programs; and, most important of all, it affects the perceptions that officials in Washington have of one another. And the unique qualities—even idiosyncrasies—of the Washington press corps make it likely that, no matter how well intentioned a neophyte public official may be, he will often find the press hard to understand and sometimes impossible to handle successfully. As a starting point, though, I found that one of the most useful skills to develop was to be able to put myself in the place of a reporter and see how a particular set of facts or statements would look to one who was observing, not participating.

One thing that sets the Washington press corps apart is its sheer size. There are more reporters in Washington—thousands more—than in any other American city. This means the competition there is keener and the pressures greater. On the whole, the product is better, too. Most Washington reporters had to win their assignments by demonstrating that they had sharply honed the skills of inquiry, analysis and expression. But because of overreaching caused by competition, because of too little expertise in highly technical matters and because of the time pressures, errors are inevitable. Unfortunately, the errors are hard to catch up with. Once in print, they tend to be picked up by other publications as gospel. Despite their supposedly skeptical natures, reporters and editors apparently are the last of the vanishing breed who really think you can believe everything you read. For example, a profile of me done for *The Washington Star* shortly after I arrived was riddled with inaccuracies and distortions, some of which were adopted—without any attempt to check their accuracy—by Washington correspondents for publications that appeared all over the nation. Similarly, when *The Village Voice* reported, falsely, that I had discussed with the U.S. attorney in Atlanta the legal difficulties of Bert Lance, President Carter's budget director and longtime confidant, *The Washington Post* and others published the falsehood, attributing it to the *Voice* without checking with me. At least the *Post* had the grace to publish a correction when we complained.

The fondness of the press for dealing in drama, conflict and inconsistencies—a characteristic of news no matter where in the Free World it is published—is especially pronounced in Washington. This stress on what is wrong or could go wrong—virtually never what is right—reflects a "herd" instinct. Reporters cover events such as news conferences and congressional hearings in groups; and the group, as the late Senator Everett Dirksen of Illinois used to observe as he scanned the press gallery from the

Senate floor, too often operates like a pack of wolves or barracuda looking for mistakes on the part of potential prey. Also, Washington reporters are well aware that events in the nation's capital cast shadows across the country, as well as around the world. The result of this sense of being at the center of history's stage can be exaggeration and distortion, "hyping" the story, reporters call it.

The press corps' search for the negative was accentuated by the Watergate scandal. Previously reporters had generally believed that corruption was something politicians left behind when they reached the highest levels. After Watergate, with characteristic vigor, the Washington press corps set out to eliminate the cancer, with reporters seeking to scale ever-new heights of investigative journalism. The ensuing lack of restraint meant that public officials became suspect, virtually guilty, until proven innocent, and this attitude did not leave town with Richard Nixon. How routine the post-Watergate perspective became is illustrated by the fact that *U.S. News and World Report* reported that "not until recently was it disclosed that the attorney general and Senator Eastland reached a secret agreement in December 1976" on using commissions to help pick nominees for federal appellate courts. It is true that Senator James O. Eastland, chairman of the Senate Judiciary Committee, met with President-elect Carter and me in Atlanta a month before the inauguration and agreed to help get senators to accept the commission concept, a step that would reduce their patronage over the important judicial appointments. But there was nothing "secret" about the meeting or the subject matter. It was reported in *The Atlanta Constitution* the day after it happened.

However justified the media's attitude may have been during Watergate, it made things very difficult for officials who came later. And for the neophyte, the lack of previous dealing with the media was complicated by the difficulty of knowing what individual reporters were after from one moment to the next. I remember a day early in my confirmation hearings when the interrogation had grown tense. During a break, a reporter for one of the news magazines approached me as I sat at the witness table grinning and gritting my teeth.

"What did you have for breakfast , Judge, if you can remember?" she asked.

With some difficulty, I shifted my attention and recalled that I had consumed standard southern fare—grits. For a few seconds, as she jotted down my response in her notebook, I thought of telling her how to spell the delicacy and instructing her that the word always took the plural form, but I remained silent for fear of sounding condescending. Later, I learned that such details are the kind of information savored by reporters for a publication that appears only once a week. They use the extra bits of color to add drama and an "insider" aura to accounts of the basic news already published by their daily competitors.

Thus, one minute I was being questioned on a matter of profound legal policy, and the next a reporter wanted to know what I had had for breakfast. These shifts from the sublime to the ridiculous are so quick that it becomes difficult to keep your balance, and the unwary public official may make the mistake of regarding the exchanges with the press as a game rather than as a serious matter.

How serious a matter the Washington media really is I began to learn even before going to the capital. In Washington, the media not only deal in symbols, but have a lot to say about what those symbols will be. Not realizing this, I was taken unawares when, a few days after President-elect Carter announced that I was his nominee as attorney general, a reporter called my Atlanta home—I was still picking up my own phone in those days—to ask what I planned to do about my membership in private clubs. I belonged to several in Atlanta, including the Piedmont Driving Club and the Capital City Club, both of which had no black members. Without pausing for reflection, I told the reporter that I planned to retain my memberships. I viewed membership in private clubs as my private business, not realizing the media would use it as a symbolic clue to the ideology of the new administration. My attitudes were thought to be especially important both because I was viewed as a close friend of the President-elect and because my Cabinet post was responsible for protecting civil rights.

My nomination had already disturbed some traditional Democratic liberal constituencies who had candidates of their own and who were wary of Jimmy Carter and the Georgians around him. From the beginning, these liberals had doubted the new President's commitment to equal rights, even though blacks had given him strong support in the election. Now, in my too hasty defense of the clubs, they thought they saw the old southern bigotry they had feared all along. Using their ready access to the eastern press, they turned the glowing coal of my private club comment into a damaging fire. It did not matter that most federal judges in Atlanta belonged to the same clubs, including my friend Elbert Tuttle, whom the civil rights movement regarded as a hero, or that several of us sought to integrate other clubs such as the Atlanta Lawyers Club.

My wife, Mary, being more attuned to symbols than her husband, helped put out the fire. She recalled that a controversy over club membership had erupted during the Kennedy administration. The question then was how the President's brother and attorney general, Robert F. Kennedy, could maintain his membership in the Metropolitan Club, an English-style men's club in Washington that banned blacks and women. Many reminded me that Robert Kennedy had resigned his membership, saying it was important symbolically for an official who was responsible for enforcing civil rights laws. Realizing he had set an admirable precedent, I issued a statement that I, too, would resign from the clubs upon becoming attorney general. The statement dulled the club controversy but did not prevent my being scrutinized more closely during the pre-inaugural period than any other Carter appointee, except the President-elect's short-lived selection of Theodore C. Sorensen, the former aide to President John F. Kennedy, as CIA director. My senate hearing was televised live daily by Public Broadcasting, and my confirmation was delayed a week beyond Inauguration Day, when the other Cabinet members were sworn in. I survived the baptism and learned a thing or two about the media and symbolism in the process.

In some ways, the most worrisome characteristic of the Washington press corps to me is its northeastern bias. Former Vice-President Spiro T. Agnew's complaint that the influence of the Northeast dominates what is reported and how it is presented in print and on the air throughout the nation should not be dismissed just because a disgraced officeholder voiced it. I detected the slant immediately, referring to it as the bias of the Northeast Strip, the urban cluster running from Boston in the North through New York City to Washington at its southern end.

It is displayed in the values reporters and editors apply in defining what is important enough to qualify as news. Reflecting the Northeast, Washington Journalists are somewhat internationalistic, attaching more importance to events in Europe than in Kansas City; they place a high premium on formal education, preferably at an Ivy League school; they come down on the liberal or left side of civil rights and civil liberties issues; they regard federal programs as a solution for many of the nation's ills; and they see economic questions through the prism of Keynesian training rather than through that of some other theoretical analysis, monetarism, for example, or supply-side economics. They also suffer from a provincial tendency to attach very little importance to what happens west of the Hudson or south of Washington, D.C.

The impact of the prejudice is felt throughout the nation, reflecting the power of such major city dailies as *The New York Times* and *The Washington Post*. The headquarters of the news operations of the television networks are also in the Strip, as are the weekly news magazines and the press or wire associations. These media leaders feed upon each other in determining what is news and how it should be viewed. Their choices are adopted by news outlets throughout the country and, to a lesser extent, the world. *The New York Times* is particularly listened to. I've been told by a reporter for one of the news magazines that fresh, insightful observations of government activities have been rejected when he or a colleague proposed them as stories, because the *Times* had seen the event differently—or not at all.

If you run afoul of a Strip operation, the consequences are likely to be far greater than if your critic is from another sector. The pervasive role in news selection played by one region may partially explain the public distrust of the media that pollsters have been recording in recent years—a lack of faith I find disturbing. The power and population of the nation is heading west, but the news leaders and their values are still firmly implanted in a narrow, unrepresentative corridor of the country.

Despite experiences with newspapers and television that drove me to exasperation and threatened some of the most important work I was trying to accomplish as attorney general, I felt Washington convinced that the press is—however imperfectly—a surrogate for the public at large.

In addition to monitoring government for their readers and viewers, the news media have a voice in setting government's agenda. A President can propose programs and Congress can take them up, but if the news media don't pay attention, both the Congress and the President will find it difficult to make headway against special interests who are in opposition.

It has been written that we live under a government of men and women and morning newspapers, an observation that I found to be on the mark during my service as attorney general. On many days, an examination of the morning newspapers caused my agenda to be reset. A prime example of this took place during the administration's first year in office when *The New York Times Magazine* ran on its cover the photograph of a man wearing a loud suit that complemented the cocksure expression on his face. "Mr. Untouchable," the magazine's cover proclaimed. "This is Nicky Barnes. The police say he may be Harlem's biggest drug dealer. But can they prove it?"

President Carter saw the picture and read the article, and at the next Cabinet meeting asked me why the government couldn't do something about Nicky Barnes. I promised to look into the matter and called Bob Fiske, then the U.S. attorney for the Southern District of New York. Fiske, because of the call, decided to prosecute the case himself. Six months later, Leroy "Nicky" Barnes, Jr., "Mr. Untouchable," was convicted, along with ten codefendants, of conducting a criminal enterprise—what Fiske described as "the largest, most profitable, venal drug ring in the city." He was sentenced to a term of life in prison by U.S. District Court Judge Henry F. Werker on January 19, 1978. I cannot contend that the President's interest in the matter, which spurred my call and Fiske's decision to take charge himself, was solely responsible for the salutary result of taking Nicky Barnes off the streets of New York. But I do know that the prosecution received top priority once the President concluded from reading the newspaper article that Barnes was a national menace and, thanks to *The New York Times*, a widely recognized one.

In a way, the saga of Mr. Untouchable illustrates the power of the press of the Northeast Strip. The story had a visibility in the White House that it would not have if it had been carried only by the *Kansas City Star* or the *Des Moines Register and Tribune*, in part because such an article from Kansas City or Des Moines would probably not have been included in the news summaries of articles of interest that are compiled daily and circulated in the White House and Cabinet departments. The action against Mr. Untouchable was more than the government's responding to a particularly strong newspaper, of course. It also sprang from President Carter's intuitive response to a problem that millions of Americans worry about all over the country—the vulnerability of their children to drugs; but because the article had appeared in *The New York Times*, the case had a symbolic impact, even on the President, that it would not otherwise have enjoyed.

Along with resetting my agenda, the press indirectly helped me stay on top of my job by providing significant information, not just in what I read but also from what I gleaned from reporters' questions and comments in news conferences and interviews. The regularity of these confrontations proved useful in another way. When we traveled outside Washington for speeches and conferences, my practice was to meet with reporters in each area we visited—all part of the effort to rebuild confidence in the integrity and neutrality of the Department of Justice. To prepare for these encounters, Dean St. Dennis, a veteran member of the department's public information office, would compile a briefing book that spelled out in exhaustive detail what the Justice Department, including the FBI, the DEA, the Bureau of Prisons, and the LEAA was doing of interest in each spot we stopped. St. Dennis's briefing papers became a highly useful synopsis of substantive Justice Department activities.

Unfortunately, the press sometimes goes too far in being the public's monitor of the other three branches. It can get carried away by the sheer momentum of a breaking story and be influenced by values, priorities and even fads that prevail inside the corps. During my years in Washington, "Koreagate" was an example of that. Koreagate was the label attached by the press to the government's inquiry into attempts by the South Korean Central Intelligence Agency to buy influence on Capitol Hill. The label implied that the scandal approached or surpassed the scale of Watergate. Story after story speculated on the number and names of members of Congress involved in the Department of Justice's investigation. The numbers ran from seventy to ninety and even to more than a hundred.

The conjecture prompted me to state publicly several times that very few present and former members of Congress were seriously involved in the investigation. In the end, one ex-member, Richard T. Hanna, Democrat of California, was sent to prison on a guilty plea. Another, Otto E. Passman, Democrat of Louisiana, was indicted but acquitted. And three sitting members, Edward R. Roybal, Charles H. Wilson and John J. McFall, all Democrats from California, were reprimanded by the House of Representatives. Hardly worth comparing to Watergate.

Because of the importance of communicating to the public what you are seeking to accomplish as a public official, I never stopped trying to improve my skills in dealing with reporters. At the same time, I must acknowledge that part of presenting a credible case is doing what comes naturally.

Making yourself accessible and being open and candid are good starting points. I tried always to speak "on-the-record," a relatively rare way of communicating in Washington in which the reporter is able to attribute to you by name everything you say. Perhaps even rarer is the practice of admitting your mistakes rather than ignoring them or blaming them on subordinates or on the faceless bureaucracy. Above all, I found the use of one's sense of humor, particularly a self-deprecating one, went a long way.

My standard for candor was set even before the Senate confirmed me. At a hearing, Senator Mathias extracted a pledge from me to post publicly each day a log of my contacts with persons outside the Department of Justice. These included calls or meetings with members of Congress, judges, private attorneys, Cabinet officers and the White House staff—even the President. The log, which did not include people I saw at social receptions outside the office or calls to me at home at night or during the weekend, appeared daily in the Justice Department press room, down the hall from the attorney general's office. Early editions of the log included such significant data as my crossing Pennsylvania Avenue to use the FBI gymnasium, which promptly appeared in *The Washington Post*, and a visit to the barber in the Sheraton Carlton Hotel, which also was published. Occasionally, we would exercise some editing restraint. For example, when I was telephoning prospects to head the FBI, prospects whose names had not yet been made public, we would list on the log "conversation with a possibility for FBI director—name to be supplied later." I am convinced that the log helped persuade reporters who covered the department that we meant to carry out Jimmy Carter's pledge of an open administration. One of Attorney General William French Smith's first official acts during the Reagan administration was to do away with the logs. He contended that because they did not cover contacts over the weekend and away from the office they were not valuable in keeping track of the attorney general. Aides to the new attorney general said his decision reflected the fact that he "is a very private man." I must say that I gave Attorney General Smith my views on the value of the log system, stating that, while it helped me, the Republic would not fall if he discontinued it, especially since no other government official was following the practice.

As attorney general, I held frequent press conferences, gave scores of individual interviews and, particularly during my last year, invited reporters, columnists and television commentators to the attorney general's dining room for lengthy, informal conversations over quail, grits and rooster pepper sausage, a little-known South Georgia delicacy that Charlie Kirbo and I introduced to Washington. Reporters traveled with me on government planes and in commercial airliners, and I spent much of the time in flight responding to their questions.

Before I was confirmed, the Justice Department's Office of Public Information gave me a detailed explanation of the strange jargon that the media and the government use in communicating with one another. Ground rules under which the communication is conducted begin with "on-the-record" and range downward in terms of the official's willingness to be quoted and to be held publicly accountable for his statement through "on-background," to "deep-background" and, of course, "off-the-record." When a Justice Department official speaks "on-back-ground," his comments can be attributed to "a senior Justice Department official," or if the official feels that's too close to home—and the reporter agrees ahead of time—to "an administration source." When a reporter accepts information on "deep-background," he usually is agreeing to write it on his own, attributing it to no source, as if the information came to him from out of the blue. "Off-the-record" means that the reporter will not publish the information being given him and that he is accepting it only for the purpose of helping him to better understand the situation being discussed. Some reporters use off-the-record information as a lead to pry the same details from another official, under less restrictive rules of attribution. Others treat off-the-record the same way as they treat deep-background, reporting the details but giving no hint of their origin.

I found these tiered levels of decreasing responsibility offensive, believing that if something is important enough to be said, it is important enough for someone to say it publicly and take the responsibility for saying it. I must acknowledge, though, that my staff, particularly Terry Adamson, my special assistant and the department's chief spokesman, used all the guidelines of attribution in talking with the press. Adamson contended there were many times he needed to convey facts but that he couldn't do so if they were to be quoted as the official comments of an aide to the attorney general or those of the chief spokesman for the department. I can understand his argument, but I cannot be comfortable with it. When a government official backs away from standing behind what he tells the press, he injects deceit into his relationship with the public that he is supposed to serve.

Admitting mistakes seems so fundamental, especially when you want to convince people of your honesty, that it should not have to be mentioned. But it is apparently something extraordinary in the nation's capital. One of my initial ideas for reorganization was to merge the Drug Enforcement Administration into the FBI, a proposal that caused a stir, especially at DEA headquarters. When we sent a team of FBI experts to study the DEA, their report made clear that the merger would be a mistake. Reporters soon were asking what had happened. I told them it was one of those ideas that sounded good when you first heard it but that further study showed would be impractical. Not all notions for reorganization are good ones, I added, and it's better to consider a whole host of proposals than only advance those you are certain will work out. I gave this explanation several times, and each time reporters reacted as if the emperor were confessing that he had no clothes.

Another example of how unaccustomed the Washington press corps is to confession of error took place at the White House when I announced the President had selected Judge William H. Webster to be FBI director. Implicit in the announcement was the fact that we were not appointing any of the candidates proposed by the prestigious committee we had created to prepare a list of the best-qualified persons. Naturally, when I was making the announcement, a reporter asked about the committee:

Q: Does that mean that the previous system the President instituted is out the window? (Laughter)

Attorney General Bell: I will have to say that, number one, the President didn't institute it. I will have to take the blame for that. That was one of my brainstorms. (Laughter)

Q: He bought it though.

Attorney General Bell: He sometimes has too much confidence in his attorney general. (Laughter) I have seen some sign of that lately. (Laughter)... It looked like a good thing to do at the time.

My friend Reg Murphy, now publisher of the *Baltimore Sun*, has a sign behind his desk advising those who would take on the press that it is never wise to do battle with anyone who buys ink by the barrel. But there are times, particularly for the public official, when an erroneous account is so damaging that it must be challenged, and vigorously. For me, *The New York Times* published such a story on December 2, 1977, when its Pulitzer Prize–winning correspondent, Seymour M. Hersh, wrote in a front-page piece that I had delayed a "planned appointment" of a U.S. attorney in Pittsburgh "under pressure from investigators" in the Justice Department. The implication was that I had been about to appoint a man of questionable honesty. Hersh wrote that sources he identified only as "officials of the Federal Bureau of Investigation and the Justice Department" had charged that we "had improperly delayed a full-scale investigation" into payments from the candidate for U.S. Attorney, George E. Schumacher, to Representative Joseph M. Gaydos of Pennsylvania. There were many things in that story that were wrong, including several statements in the first paragraph. First, I was under no pressure. Second, the appointment was not planned but only under consideration. Third, our investigation of whether there had been payments and, if so, whether there was anything improper about them, had been proceeding for several weeks. Hersh had interviewed me and Associate Attorney General Michael J. Egan the previous day and reported correctly that both of us denied the accusations.

I called a press conference within hours after reading the story and denounced the article as "scurrilous, irresponsible and completely out of keeping with anything I thought *The New York Times* stood for." Hersh had reported that "one well-informed government official" told him that everyone in the investigation "is scared." That was too much for me. If there is anything the Justice Department and its investigative arm, the FBI, can do without, it is frightened investigators. I told the press conference I was sending for head of the Justice Department's Office of Professional Responsibility, the department's internal watchdog, Michael E. Shaheen, Jr., "to find out just what the trouble is there." Shaheen, whose reputation for independence later gained national attention through critical reports he issued concerning my successor, Ben Civiletti, and the President's brother, Billy Carter, had already demonstrated that he would report the facts as he found them, no matter how uncomfortable for anyone.

Shaheen's investigation unearthed FBI agents who readily acknowledged talking to Hersh but who insisted they had not told him they felt pressured. In the end, I decided not to recommend the nomination of Schumacher to the President—but not for any reasons Hersh had mentioned. Later, after I left office, Hersh told Terry Adamson that my reaction to the story had surprised him and that upon further investigation he had satisfied himself that I was telling the truth.

That departure from accurate reporting occurred because one of the nation's leading newspapers let its hunger for "investigative" journalism, a field in which it trailed during the Watergate era, overpower its good judgment. U.S. attorneys' posts are sought-after jobs, with rival factions supporting rival candidates. In the Schumacher case, I think *The New York Times* was used by one politically motivated side in the drive to obtain that appointment, which leads to the obvious conclusion that the reasons for providing a reporter with information should be a subject of that reporter's scrutiny before he runs the story.

Lack of restraint would be less of a problem if the press practiced more self-criticism. Our First Amendment's free press guarantee would not be harmed if the media began to hold itself accountable to the media. The increasing use of ombudsmen by newspapers to monitor their own performance is a step in the right direction.

28 The Fourth Branch of Government

by Walter H. Annenberg

Walter Annenberg feels that as the "fourth branch of government," the mass media have an obligation to be aware of their power and to use it with responsibility. He has been both a public official and a journalist, ambassador and confidant of presidents, and publisher of the most widely circulated periodical in America, *TV Guide*, where this article appeared in the May 15, 1982, issue.

Journalistic coverage of events in Washington during the past two or three decades removes any doubt that we now have, in effect, four branches of Government, not three, and that the fourth—the press—exercises at least as much power in determining the course of the republic as the executive, legislative and judicial branches set forth in the Constitution.

Sheltered by the First Amendment from accountability for what it reports, the press alone has the ability to reach the electorate directly and consistently. Its power lies in reporting and interpreting what the Administration does and how the opposition—and the public—react.

Throughout American history, newspapers have acted as gadfly and watchdog, sometimes defaming honest officials with false charges of misdeeds, sometimes courageously exposing corruption in high places. Some of our greatest Presidents—Washington, Jefferson, Lincoln, Theodore Roosevelt—were moved to anger when the press of the day accused them of everything from ignorance and incompetence to venality.

Lincoln, a mild-mannered man, complained, "If I were to try to read, much less answer, all the attacks made on me, this shop might as well be closed for any other business."

The Presidency survived the attacks and so did the Nation. And most Americans agree that despite its excesses, in the main the press has served us well through the years, has been a constructive factor in our growth and prosperity by keeping our citizenry informed.

In recent years the word "press" has come to include the electronic news media, radio and television, which have the advantage of immediate access to the public. Because television can show events as they happen and can present the words of public officials and their critics as they are spoken, that medium of communication has become by far our most important source of news information and the one Americans trust most.

Considering the press's immunity from the checks and balances that control the other branches of Government, it has tremendous power, power that should be exercised sensitively, especially by those engaged in the dissemination of television news. Certainly the majority of commentators and correspondents are dedicated to reporting the news as objectively as is humanly possible, and they strive to overcome the time limitations of television news that make it all but impossible to offer a well-balanced presentation of complex Governmental issues.

Unfortunately we also find some practicing adversary journalism, placing themselves in what seems to be reflex-action opposition to Government leaders, including the President himself. Although they cannot possibly have access to the same quantity or quality of background information as those in Government, these newspaper and television personalities frequently not only are skeptical—always healthy for a reporter—but question the officials' motives. Others scarcely conceal their advocacy, presenting arguments favoring or opposing Government policies, interviewing members of the public who support their ideas. They also bring before their cameras officials and others who either deliberately or because of lack of information distort the Administration's position and mislead viewers.

When the President makes a major speech or holds a press conference that is covered by the networks, it is usually followed by one or more commentators explaining which points made by the Chief Executive were important, what they really meant, what the opposing arguments are and whether the course he advocates might come to pass. All this in the interest of better informing the public and usually with an effort, not always successful, to be impartial.

As a result, as Theodore White observed some years ago, the President and the press have become the principal rivals in setting the national agenda. The difference is that the President has power with responsibility, the press has power without responsibility.

Far more important than the press's influence on the success or failure of one President's program is the matter of its effect on the Presidency itself. Is it possible for any President to govern effectively under the circumstances that prevail today: when secret international negotiations fast become public knowledge, when Presidential actions are relayed to the public along with uninformed or misleading conjecture as to their possible success, when Presidential efforts to bolster confidence in the economy (because public attitudes have a great deal to do with the strength of the economy) are immediately countered by gratuitously pessimistic reports?

Is it possible, any more, for a President to win a second term when every day in a majority of homes there is heard doubt about his wisdom and his motives? Indeed, is it possible for any President—in the face of the widely publicized criticism that is prompted by innovative programs—to change the course of our country? Can he do other than continue to increase welfare rather than emphasize private-sector job programs, continue to increase taxes, continue to permit the Soviets to maintain nuclear superiority in Europe and extend their influence in our hemisphere?

It certainly is not the place of the press to endorse or support, except in clearly identified editorial comment, the actions or policies of a President. Its job is to report the news, good and bad, fairly and impartially. Our argument is with adversary journalism and advocacy journalism, which are by their very nature biased. We believe there is no place on television news programs for such journalism, that it serves only to confuse the public and weaken the Nation.

More than ratings are at stake here; it is the effectiveness of the Presidency itself. Well-intentioned, patriotic men and women head network and station news operations. They must be more aware of their power and how they use it, of the responsibility that should accompany their influence and of their obligation as the fourth branch of Government to all the people of the Nation.

29 The Press and the President

There They Go Again

by George E. Reedy

George Reedy attempts to put the adversarial relationship between government and the press into a philosophical perspective. He shows that the president can and does manipulate the press but that such efforts can backfire, because the president cannot manipulate *all* the press *all* the time. Reedy has personal experience in the matter, since he served as White House press secretary during the early years of the Johnson administration. He is Nieman

professor of journalism at Marquette University and author
of *Twilight of the Presidency*. His article is reprinted from
the *Columbia Journalism Review*, May/June, 1983.

To the leisurely observer of the Washington scene, there is a distinct charm
in the startled air of discovery with which the press greets each step in the
entirely predictable course of its relationship with the president and the
White House staff.

Actually, the patterns are as well-established and as foreseeable as the
movements of a Javanese temple dance. The timing will vary as will the
alternating degrees of adoration and bitterness. But the sequence of events,
at least in modern times, appears to be inexorable. It is only the determination of the press to treat each new day as unprecedented that makes
the specific events seem to be news.

Seen from a little distance, cries of outrage from the press over the
discovery that Mr. Reagan seeks to "manage the news" have the flavor of an
Ed Sullivan rerun show on after-midnight television. They are reminiscent
of similar protests in the administrations of Presidents Carter, Nixon,
Johnson, Kennedy, Eisenhower, Truman, and Roosevelt. Presidents before
that do not offer much material for discussion simply because they served
prior to the FDR era, when press-White House relations were put on a
daily-contact basis for the first time in history.

The charge of management is a familiar one because it has a strong
element of truth. All presidents seek to manage the news and all are successful to a degree. What is not taken into account is that legitimate management of the news from the White House is inescapable and, human
nature being what it is, it is hardly surprising that presidents try to bend
this necessity for their own ends. Few men will decline an opportunity to
recommend themselves highly.

The press would not be happy with a White House that ended all
efforts at news management and either threw the mansion wide open for
coverage or closed it to outsiders altogether and told journalists to get facts
any way they could. Since the early days of the New Deal, reporters have
been relying on daily press briefings, prearranged press conferences, and
press pools when the president travels. There would be chaos should all this
come to an end.

The point is that the White House is covered by journalists through
highly developed and formal organizational structures. It is inherent in the
nature of such structures that they must be managed by somebody, and the
president's office is no exception. Management technique is employed
every time the president decides what stories will be released on Monday
and what stories will be released on Saturday; every time he decides that
some meetings will be open to press coverage and others will not; every
time he decides that some visitors will be fed to the press as they walk out of

the Oval Office and others will not. Anybody who believes that he will make decisions on the basis of what makes him look bad will believe a hundred impossible things before breakfast.

There are actually times when the press literally does not want news. This became very clear early in the administration of Lyndon Johnson when he inaugurated the custom of unexpected Saturday morning news conferences. This meant disruption of newspaper production schedules all over the United States. Printing pressmen had to be recalled from weekend holidays to work at exorbitant rates; front pages that had been planned in leisurely fashion in the morning had to be scrapped for new layouts; rewrite men who had looked forward to quiet afternoons with their families worked into the evening hours. It was a mess.

After two such conferences, I began getting calls from top bureau chiefs in Washington pleading with me to put an end to them. They made it clear they wanted stories timed so that they would fit conveniently into news slots. It took some doing on my part; Johnson would have enjoyed the discovery that he was putting newspaper publishers to so much expense and trouble. (I think he started these conferences simply because he became lonely on Saturday mornings when there was little to do.) I talked him into dropping the custom by producing figures which showed that the weekend audiences were not large enough to justify the effort.

While it was actually going on, the episode struck me as just another example of the Johnsonian inability to comprehend the press. It was not until later that I realized the deeper significance. The press had not only acquiesced in news management but had actually asked that it be instituted. The fact that nothing was involved except timing was irrelevant. The ability to control the timing of news is the most potent weapon that any would-be news manipulator can have. No absolute line can be drawn between the occasions when he should have it and those when he should not.

This may well account for the indifference of the public to the periodic campaigns against news management. Even to an unsophisticated audience it is apparent that journalists are not objecting to news management per se but only to the kind of news management that makes their professional lives more difficult. However it may look in Washington, at a distance the issue appears as a dispute over control of the news for the convenience of the president or for the convenience of the press. In such a situation, Americans tend to come down on the side of the president.

Of course, if the president is caught in an outright lie—a lie about something in which the public is really concerned—the public will mobilize against him swiftly. But many charges of news management are directed at statements that Americans do not regard as outright lies. Americans have become so accustomed to the kind of exaggeration and misleading facts that are used to sell products on nightly television that a little White House puffery seems quite natural.

There is, of course, another side to the coin. While presidents always try to manipulate the news—and all too often succeed—there is a very real doubt whether the manipulation performs any real service for them, even in the crassest image-building sense. The presidency is a strange institution. The occupant must accept never-ending responsibilities and must act on never-ending problems. It may well be that what a president does speaks so much more loudly than anything he can say that the normal techniques of public relations are completely futile.

In the first place, a president may be able to time his public appearances but he cannot time his acts. He *is* the United States and anything that affects the United States must have a presidential response. He must react to international crises, to domestic disasters, to unemployment, and to inflation; if he chooses to do nothing in any of these instances his inaction will be writ large in the public media.

In the second place, a president may be able to keep his thoughts to himself but he cannot act in any direction without causing waves that sweep through the Washington community. The federal bureaucracy is shot through with holdovers from previous administrations who do not like him; the Congress is loaded with political opponents with whom he must deal; the lobbying offices of the capital are staffed by skilled president-watchers who can interpret his every act and who have sympathetic journalistic listeners.

Finally, there is the overwhelming fact that the president has a direct impact on the lives of every citizen and there is a limit to his capacity to mislead. He cannot convince men and women that there is peace when their sons are dying in a war. He cannot hold up images of prosperity (although he will try) when men and women are out of work. He cannot persuade constituents that there is peace and harmony when there is rioting in the streets. There may be instances when he can escape the blame but only when his political opposition is not on its toes.

Against this background, the efficacy of manipulation is dubious at best. It may have a favorable impact on public opinion in the short run. But I know of no persuasive evidence that it helps to build the long-term support a politician needs. Every instance I have studied bears a close parallel to what happened when Lyndon Johnson held his meaningless meeting with the late Soviet premier Alexei Kosygin at Glassboro, New Jersey, in 1967. He was able to maneuver the press into treating it as a major summit conference for a few days, and his poll ratings rose accordingly. But it soon became clear that the meeting had produced nothing of substance and that there had been no reason to expect that it would. The poll ratings went right back down again.

On the other hand, efforts at manipulation invariably challenge the press to dig deeper than journalists ordinarily would. The stories they write about manipulation have little effect. But the stories they write as a result of the digging may have the kind of substance that does make an impact. The whole exercise can well be merely an invitation to trouble on the part of the president.

The bottom line can be simply stated. The president can, within limits, manipulate that part of the press which covers the White House. But he cannot manipulate the press as a whole, and it is probable that his efforts to do so will always backfire.

30 Always on Saturday?

by Ron Nessen

President Ronald Reagan's Saturday radio broadcasts might be newsworthy to the White House, but Ron Nessen, vice president for news and special programs of the Mutual Broadcasting System and former White House press officer, doesn't always agree. "It's not for the president to decide what we broadcast," Nessen says in this article from the *Washington Post*, August 20, 1986.

It's not uncommon in broadcasting to cancel a program or an on-air personality. But I recently had the unique experience of canceling the president of the United States.

For several years my company, the Mutual Broadcasting System, has broadcast live to its affiliate stations a five-minute statement by President Reagan every Saturday at 12:06 P.M. We also have transmitted one hour later a "reply" to the president from a prominent Democratic spokesman.

I had been troubled by this arrangement for some time, primarily because it surrendered to the politicians what is the basic responsibility of the media—deciding what is and what is not news. A.J. Liebling, the late media critic for *The New Yorker*, probably overstated the case a bit when he commented that freedom of the press belongs to the man who owns one. But, in fact, under our system of free media those who own the printing presses, the microphones and the cameras do have the responsibility for determining what is broadcast and printed. The president and the other politicians should not be allowed to encroach on that responsibility.

Having lived and worked in countries where government officials determine what the public hears and sees in the media, I am determined to resist that kind of encroachment here.

The surrender of air time every Saturday by Mutual and other networks to President Reagan and the Democrats has been justified on grounds that the statements are genuine "news" events. They rarely are. Often the president's statements are a rehash of his previously enunciated views on various topics. The so-called Democratic "reply" frequently isn't a reply at all. It's a statement on an unrelated issue or even a recorded message taped *before* the president's remarks to which it is supposed to be a reply.

My uneasiness about automatically giving up five minutes of air time to the president and five minutes to the Democrats every Saturday, regardless of the news value (or lack thereof), had nagged at me ever since I came to Mutual more than two years ago. But more pressing problems always seemed to demand my attention.

I finally decided to act on my concerns after Reagan taped his radio statement for Saturday, July 5, on Thursday, July 3. Even the most charitable interpretations could not support the contention that remarks made on Thursday were "news," justifying five minutes of network time, two days later. I notified Pat Buchanan, the White House communications director, that we were terminating the Saturday broadcasts because the taping was "in violation of an understanding that the statements would always be delivered live in order to be considered legitimate 'news.'" I also notified Linda Peek, press secretary for the Senate Democratic Policy Committee, that Mutual was canceling the Democratic reply.

From then on, Mutual would handle the president's and the Democrats' Saturday statements as it does any other event: we would listen to the statements and run any excerpts that contained real news as part of our regularly scheduled newscasts. (It's ironic, I suppose, that Mutual was the network to take this long-overdue step, since when I was the White House press secretary, it was a part of my duties to try to get President Ford as much free network time as possible.)

If I had any doubts about the decision, they were resolved on Friday, Aug. 15, when the president taped his Saturday statement for that week a day in advance. The tape arrived at Mutual about 4:20 P.M. that Friday, with strict instructions from the White House not to use it on the air until 12:06 P.M. the following day. But this time the statement contained real news, a harsh attack by the president on the House of Representatives for imposing a number of restrictions on his defense policies in the Pentagon budget bill. Reagan accused the House of a "reckless assault" on national defense in the budget bill, approved just minutes before he recorded the statement.

If I had followed the instructions of the White House public relations apparatus, Mutual would have kept those newsworthy comments secret for nearly 20 hours and then finally broadcast them on a timetable designed by the presidential media advisers to gain maximum space in the Sunday newspapers for Reagan's attack on the House. I wouldn't do it. Mutual broke the embargo and started running excerpts from the president's statement on the next available newscast. News is news when it's made, not when the White House says it may be released to the public.

Larry Speakes, the White House press secretary, was soon on the phone in high outrage over Mutual's refusal to follow the orders of the presidential PR flacks.

I explained to him that Mutual normally abides by embargoes on such releases as the annual federal budget or a complex presidential proposal, things that require time to absorb, analyze and write about. But the embargo on broadcasting Reagan's denunciation of the House defense vote had no other justification than the advancement of White House communications strategy.

Speakes wasn't having any of my viewpoint. "We're going to take punitive action against your reporter," Speakes threatened. "He's out of business. He'll have to figure out how to get his news some other way because he's not getting it from me as long as I'm here, and I'll be here 2½ more years."

Rising to new heights of petty arrogance, Speakes threatened the ultimate revenge: "Your White House correspondent will have to report from handouts. He can report on Chicken Week."

But, Larry, the Chicken Week press release is embargoed until Saturday.

Mass Media and Government: For Further Reading

Douglass Cater, *The Fourth Branch of Government*. Boston: Houghton Mifflin, 1959.

William O. Chittick, *State Department, Press, and Pressure Groups: A Role Analysis*. New York: Wiley, 1970.

Michael Barush Grossman and Martha Joynt Kumar, *Portraying the President: The White House and the News Media*. Baltimore, Md.: Johns Hopkins University Press, 1981.

Lewis M. Helm, Ray Eldon Hiebert, Michael R. Naver and Kenneth Rabin, *Informing the People: A Public Affairs Handbook*. New York: Longman, 1981.

Stephen Hess, *The Washington Reporters*. Washington, D.C.: Brookings Institute, 1981.

Ray Eldon Hiebert, *The Press in Washington: Sixteen Top Newsmen Tell How the News is Collected, Written and Communicated from the World's Most Important Capital*. New York: Dodd, Mead, 1966.

Ray Eldon Hiebert and Carlton E. Spitzer, *The Voice of Government*. New York: Wiley, 1968.

Michael Bruce MacKuen and Steven Lane Coombs, *More Than News: Media Power in Public Affairs*. Beverly Hills, Calif.: Sage, 1981.

Dan Nimmo and Michael W. Mansfield, *Government and the News Media: Comparative Dimensions*. Waco, TX: Baylor University Press, 1982.

James Reston, *The Artillery of the Press*. New York: Harper & Row, 1967.

William L. Rivers, *The Other Government: Power and the Washington Media*. New York: Universe, 1982.

Steve Weinberg, *Trade Secrets of Washington Journalists: How to Get the Facts about What's Going on in Washington*. Washington, D.C.: Acropolis Books, 1981.

IX

War, the Military, and the Media

In this age of mass media, war has become a media event. Sometimes, in fact, war seems to have become an event staged for mass media, to send a message rather than to conquer territory. That is certainly true of the wars waged by terrorists. Without a doubt, the nature of all warfare has been changed by the emergence of mass media.

The Civil War was the first war in U.S. history to be reported by correspondents on the battlefield. The Spanish-American War was supposedly "fanned into flames" by the headlines of the Hearst newspapers. World War I has been called the first real information war, where the battle was fought over people's minds as much as for their lands. During that war, the American government established the Committee on Public Information, to advise the government on how it should persuade the public to support the war effort. And since that time, government propaganda about wars has become almost as important as military preparation.

By the time World War II started, several new mass media had been developed, namely, radio and motion pictures with sound and color. They were enlisted for the government's war propaganda. Both the Allies and the Axis powers gave propaganda in the mass media a priority role. The Nazis were particularly good at using motion pictures to whip up fanatic patriotism in the German people so that they would willingly sacrifice all for the fatherland. And Hollywood rushed to put its technology and stars on the line for the American fatherland.

The war in Korea, in a media sense, was a minor repetition of

World War II. After all, television had not yet blossomed through the land. But the Vietnam War was an entirely new thing: Television was in place, ubiquitous, omnipotent. Indeed, starting with Vietnam, war has never been the same since the age of television began.

The war in Vietnam was the first war to be brought directly to the American people—into their living rooms, night after night, in full color. Prior to Vietnam, all dispatches from a war front passed through the hands of government officials, who cleaned them up for public consumption. Americans had never before been given body counts; had never been shown civilian villages being burned by American soldiers, or the cruelties and tortures of war.

Media coverage of the war in Vietnam taught governments everywhere lessons about how to deal with the mass media during war. We are now beginning to see the results of those lessons. The wars in the Middle East, particularly the Israeli invasion of Lebanon in 1982; Britain's war with Argentina over the Falkland Islands that same year; and America's invasion of the island of Grenada in 1983—these wars demonstrate how the media will be managed and manipulated as part of modern warfare. Media, in fact, have become a vital component of all wars.

31 War Isn't War without TV

by Amnon Rubinstein

> Israel was the first nation to suffer defeat at the hands of television even while it won its war. TV coverage of Israel's successful invasion of Lebanon in 1982 turned much of American public opinion against Israel, even though many Americans supported the general reasons for the invasion. Amnon Rubenstein, a member of the Israeli Knesset at the time, wrote this article for the *Washington Post* to put the problem into perspective. It is reprinted from the *Post*, July 18, 1982. Rubinstein is now Minister of Communication for Israel.

Jerusalem—The impact of television coverage on reactions to distant wars is being demonstrated again by the differences between Iran's invasion of Iraq, shrouded as it is by a TV blackout, and Israel's invasion of Lebanon, fully exposed by nightly TV coverage (albeit subject to Israeli military censorship).

War without television is an abstract affair, but war on the screen is a vivid experience literally brought home to millions of viewers.

This phenomenon also explains the striking discrepancy today between the self-image of Israel and outside criticism of its actions.

While outside Israel the war in Lebanon is denounced in unprecedented terms—Israel being accused of a Nazi-like action—within the country the army is praised even by the opposition for its humane conduct and consideration for life and property.

While Nicolas von Hoffman, in the *London Spectator*, writes that "incident by incident, atrocity by atrocity, Americans are coming to see the Israeli government as pounding the Star of David into a swastika," Israelis note that this is the first war in which refugees flee into the area occupied by the "enemy."

While the media abound—at least initially—with estimates of 10,000 dead and 600,000 refugees, Israelis regard these figures as preposterous and point out that precautions taken by the air force have practically emptied the bombed towns of civilians. Indeed, as any visitor to southern Lebanon can attest, Sidon and Tyre—allegedly flattened by the Israelis—have recuperated from the war with amazing sped. The unshuttered shop windows exhibiting expensive wares, as well as the friendly welcoming populace there—Christians and Moslems alike—contradict the image created by the mass media, and especially by television, of a World War II-type havoc.

The denunciation of Israel also stands in contrast to the almost total silence that greets other wars and acts of aggression whose barbarity and cruelty do not attract international reaction.

What is wrong? Many Israelis react to this discrepancy by falling back on the ever-present suspicion of lurking anti-Semitism and see the comparison with Nazi Germany as obscene proof that indeed the "whole world's against us." That some anti-Semitic elements—or, to use Conor Cruise O'Brien's phrase, "anti-Jewists"—have seized upon Israel's action as a respectable vehicle on which to hang their still unrespectable instincts cannot be doubted. But surely there's more to this story than bad old Jew-baiting.

A partial explanation lies in the very nature of the coverage of wars by news media in general and by television in particular. TV and satellite transmission may have reduced the world into a global village, but in this village some streets are inaccessible. Most wars raging at present are not seen on television simply because they cannot be covered. Indeed, because the impact of TV coverage on public consciousness and international opinion is so crucial, one may divide wars into televisable and non-televisable wars.

In the limbo of non-televisable nonevents is not only the Iran-Iraq war, which reportedly has flattened whole cities and whose cost in human lives is rarely even estimated. Ethiopia's two wars, with the Eritreans and the Somalians, the Afghan rebels' battle against the Soviets and the Afghan army, the continuing struggle in Cambodia and the Yemen wars have similarly become nonevents—not because shots are not exchanged but because shots are not taken.

There were two major wars in Southeast Asia. One, America's Indochina war, became synonymous with total exposure to TV coverage. The other, which continues to this day between Vietnam and Cambodians opposing Hanoi's invasion of their country, practically ceased to exist as far as western audiences are concerned with the withdrawal of camera crews from Vietnam and Cambodia. That struggle was brought back into public attention only because of the flow of refugees that could be seen on the small screen.

Indeed, one may say that in our day and age, war is war only if it is on the nightly news.

Non-televisable wars are generally associated with theaters in which nondemocratic states participate. But there are exceptions to the rule: Great Britain excluded regular TV coverage from its Falklands war and thus rendered its proceedings less real and less painful than the grisly scenes showing the bloody confrontations in El Salvador.

Moreover, not all televisable wars are given equal time. Visuals—to use TV jargon—are of major importance. The *polisario* war in the former Spanish Sahara is a non-visual war, consisting as it does of sporadic desert raids carried out at night, lacking the trappings of modern warfare.

Even in the same war, the actual coverage is often determined by visual considerations. Sidon—where only a small fraction of the city's buildings was hit—was depicted by TV news as a scene of total devastation, mainly because a number of high-rise buildings that collapsed like card houses under Israel's aerial bombing naturally attracted the focus of camera crews. At the same time, the refugee camps—some of them actually flattened by fierce house-to-house fighting—remained largely unnoticed because the damage to the one-story shacks was visually less impressive.

In addition, because of limited time slots, foreign wars make the evening news only if they maintain the public interest. Remote wars lose their interest as they become protracted and repetitive with their daily litany of clashing communiques. The Iran-Iraq war lost its ratings, so to speak, once it became a drawn-out affair, and, being anyway non-televisable, was quickly relegated, until recently, to the inner pages of the quality press.

The civil war in Lebanon—a televisable and occasionally televised event—suffered from a similar fate, although it ravaged the unhappy country since 1976 and has cost an estimated 70,000 lives. The regime of terror, rape and robbery imposed by the PLO on the Lebanese people similarly lacked visual angles.

Lightning wars—such as Israel's blitz in Lebanon—are the very stuff of which TV coverage is made. They also enable the networks to make an extra effort to send in a star-studded team to cover the war from start to finish. Because of this, and because Israel's wars concern a nation about which people have strong feelings one way or another, Israel's campaign in Lebanon was bound to fall victim to the arbitrariness of television coverage.

If the war in Cambodia and the Pol Pot regime—the worst human catastrophe since World War II—is on one end of the spectrum, being non-televisable and non-everything, Israel's wars are on the other end: televisable, visual, dramatic and highly visible.

Israel, which seeks the support of the free world, will have to face these facts of life. It cannot remove TV crews from the front line because of its nature as a democratic society. And even if it were to impose a TV blackout on war coverage, the Arab side would deliver the goods from its point of view. Israel, like other open societies, will have to take into account the adverse impact of TV war reporting when planning its moves or else pay the inevitable price it is now paying in Lebanon.

32 Beirut—and the Press— under Siege

by Roger Morris

Roger Morris takes a longer look at the Israel-Lebanon war in 1982 and concludes that the media covered it fairly and accurately, although with disastrous results for America's ally, Israel. Morris is the author of, among other books, *Haig: The General's Progress.* His research reported here was assisted by Vanderbilt University's television news archive and by *Columbia Journalism Review* interns Mark Silber and Claudia Weinstein. The article is reprinted from *Columbia Journalism Review*, November/December 1982.

For many American journalists, and much of their viewing or reading public, it was perhaps the most searing and controversial story in a generation. Israel's invasion of Lebanon in early June seemed to begin as one more round in a familiar cycle of violence and reprisal, one more almost routine combat assignment in covering thirty-five years of war in the Middle East. Yet as the fighting wore on, the Israeli attack not only overran the PLO; as never before, it soon engulfed the media as well, leaving newspapers and television under siege in West Beirut, both literally and figuratively.

As correspondents spoke into cameras or filed dispatches against the backdrop of the smoking city, partisans of both sides—and, increasingly, supporters of Israel—attacked the coverage for omission, distortion, or worse. Networks and newspapers were bombarded with letters and protests and besieged by angry delegations. In the heat of conflict at home and abroad, journalists lashed out at officials and at one another; there was a visible end to innocence and illusion among experienced newsmen who had prided themselves on having shed both long ago; and truth often became a casualty in the domestic war over the front-line reporting. When it was over, there was a sense that nothing scarred by the conflict—journalism, public trust, the Middle East, Israel's moral and political standing with Americans—would ever be the same again.

For sheer intensity and breadth, the controversy fueled by coverage of the Israeli invasion seems to have few parallels in recent journalistic history. After relatively brief and meager criticism of the reporting as anti-Arab, the storm centered on what *Boston Globe* editorial-page editor Martin Nolan called "general angst about the media's coverage of Israel." While criticism poured in on major papers such as the *Globe*, *The Philadelphia Inquirer*, *The New York Times*, and especially *The Washington Post*, the Anti-Defamation League of B'nai B'rith hired political consultant David Garth to review ABC, CBS, and NBC television news coverage of the entire conflict to document expected inaccuracies. To the *Jerusalem Post*, most American reporting on the invasion was simply "political pornography." Even *Variety* was troubled, in its own idiom, by the "serious short circuits...between reps of the international media" and Israeli authorities. Summoning Emile Zola and Colonel Dreyfus to the fray, Norman Podhoretz, editor of *Commentary*, eventually wrote his own "J'Accuse," an ardent defense of Israel's cause in which he strongly implied that a number of Israel's critics, notably *New York Times* columnist Anthony Lewis, were anti-Semitic.

Meanwhile, reporters lodged criticisms of their own. Writing in the *Washington Journalism Review*, for example, Israeli free-lance writer Pnina Ramati and *The Washington Post*'s Jerusalem correspondent, Edward Cody, deplored Israel's censorship and defended fellow writers on the Arab side whose dispatches "tended naturally to fill the vacuum left by Israeli silence." But the profession's varying frustration and concern with the coverage was turned inward as well. There was "some merit" to the charge of anti-Israeli bias in television reporting, NBC's Marvin Kalb was quoted as telling the August convention of the American Bar Association. On August 6 (in an incident discussed further below), Thomas L. Friedman, *The New York Times*'s bureau chief in Beirut, cabled his Manhattan editors in outrage when he awoke to discover that they had summarily cut the word "indiscriminate" from his lead on the previous day's Israeli bombing of Beirut. The bombing had "the apparent aim of terrorizing its [Beirut's] civilian population," said Friedman's telex. His editors had been "afraid to tell our readers," and the correspondent thought it "thoroughly unprofessional."

Even after the PLO departed and the siege of Beirut was lifted, questions about the quality of U.S. reporting continued to hang over the scene. Unproven by the critics, unanswered by the media, the charges seemed symbolized by an article that appeared in the August 2 *New Republic*, titled "Lebanon Eyewitness," written by the magazine's owner and editor, Martin Peretz. "Much of what you have read in the newspapers and news-magazines about the war in Lebanon—and even more of what you have seen and heard on television," Peretz wrote, "is simply not true." Railing against "journalists [who] think themselves chosen people" and a "peculiarly American mixture of ignorance, cynicism, and brashness," Peretz's travelogue through the Israeli occupation of southern Lebanon and its official rationalization did not constitute an intellectually serious critique. His attacks on *The Washington Post* and on the major networks were haphazardly documented; his praise for the *Times, The Wall Street Journal,* and other broadcast news was largely unsubstantiated.

But were the charges true? Had journalists, in fact, misrepresented the causes—and exaggerated the extent—of the carnage that dominated the news from Lebanon? Had they, in the process of reporting the invasion, somehow betrayed an American ally, as well as their own standards?

What follows is an effort to answer those questions by assessing not only the massive summer coverage of the invasion provided by *The New York Times* and *The Washington Post*, but also that provided by the nightly TV news broadcasts of the three major networks from June 4 through August 23, the day after the PLO started to pull out of Beirut and three weeks before the massacre in the Palestinian camps. The analysis concentrates, as did the critics, on four main elements of the coverage: Did the networks, the *Times*, the *Post*, and other major papers report fairly the historical context and justification of the Israeli invasion? Did they portray fully the political realities in a divided Lebanon in which many Lebanese welcomed the Israelis as liberators? Were they accurate in describing the human and physical cost of the Israeli attack? And, finally, were they balanced and factual in their nine-week accounts of the siege of West Beirut?

Beyond these issues, what were the crucial *unreported* stories of the invasion and siege? And what are some of the implications of the Lebanon coverage, and of the heated criticism it generated, for both journalists and the public?

The Reasons Why

The invasion broke onto the networks and into the headlines of the *Times* and the *Post* on the weekend of June 4–6. In swift succession there were the shooting of Ambassador Shlomo Argov in London, the Israeli bombing of Beirut, the PLO rocket attacks on northern Israel, and, finally, the massive movement of Israeli troops across the Lebanese border. From the beginning there was nearly uniform reporting of the reasons for the Israeli attack. "Terrorism has led to tragedy," said ABC's Frank Reynolds on June 4, in a broadcast that included Bill Seamans from Israel showing the damage PLO rockets had wreaked, together with segments depicting the Argov shooting and the raid on the Beirut sports stadium. The same day, CBS reported the bombing from Beirut as "retaliation," and from Israel, with scenes of the PLO shelling, as "reprisal," while NBC's Steve Mallory and Paul Miller, in segments that included file footage on guerrilla exercises in the Beirut sports stadium, emphasized that the stadium was a PLO ammunition dump and training site. *Times* and *Post* dispatches the next day likewise led with the "retaliatory" character of the Israeli attacks on PLO "training facilities" (*Post*) and "guerrilla camps" and "strongholds" (*Times*).

After another day's dispatches on how the attacks had been "triggered" by PLO provocation and were aimed at Palestinian "strongholds," both papers reported the Israeli invasion in similar terms. The *Post*'s William Claiborne, filing from Israel, wrote that the "declared objective" was to rid the border area of terrorists. The *Times*'s David K. Shipler told of PLO shelling and of how the guerrillas had become a menacing "army." Television news similarly emphasized that the Israeli aim was to "clear out" the terrorists (*NBC*) and "eliminate" their bases (*ABC*), with Seamans providing another vivid report on the PLO "rain of rockets" on Israel.

In those early days of the invasion, the networks repeatedly provided evidence that, in effect, documented Israel's case against the PLO and provided some historical context. On June 8, for example, there were reports by ABC's Seamans on how the fallen Beaufort Castle had been used to direct rocket fire into Israel; by CBS's Don Kladstrup on the Israeli assault on a PLO "stronghold" at Damur; and by NBC's Mallory and Art Kent on the "years of war" in Lebanon before the attack and on PLO artillery positions at the castle. On that same day, NBC's John Chancellor, later to become so controversial, traced the chronology of the outbreak, noting that Israel had been "ready for many months," that Jerusalem had tried before to subdue the PLO in 1978 when the Palestinians "got away ...only to start a serious buildup again," and that it was "probably useless today to say just who started the fighting." "What can be said," his commentary concluded, "is that Israel is trying to buy a few years of peace at a terrible human and political cost, and incidentally, making American policy in the Middle East a shambles."

As the Israelis swiftly struck against Syrian missiles in the Bekaa valley and drove to the heights around Beirut, on June 9 the *Times*'s Shipler from Jerusalem and Thomas Friedman from Beirut assessed Israel's war aims as twofold: to "destroy" the PLO and to bring about a "restructuring" of chaotic Lebanon. Meanwhile, the *Post*'s Claiborne described Israel's goal as being to free that nation of "the threat of terrorism," and Cody, on June 12, 14, and 15, provided readers of the *Post* with accounts of Galileans who had undergone PLO rocket attacks "rejoicing" as Israeli forces advanced through what had been "unchallenged guerrilla territory," and of the capture of Palestinian weapons caches said to be intended for "the final destruction of Israel." On June 15 Ike Pappas of CBS sent back through Israeli censors his own graphic report on PLO weapon stores, many of them "placed in schools and other public buildings."

Few if any of these early reports and commentaries on Israel's war aims provided a basis for later charges of omission or bias. In mid-June both the *Times* and the *Post* profiled Israeli Defense Minister Sharon in blunt terms. But if the *Post* reported an opinion that Sharon "skates at the edge of psychosis," he was also said to be regarded as "brilliant and inspiring." The *Times* noted that the minister was thought by many to be a "reckless bully" but had "armies of admirers." In short, both papers did no more than reflect faithfully the partisan debate over Sharon inside Israeli democracy.

Similarly, on June 16, Chancellor commented on "the growing feeling that Israel has turned into a warrior state," using "far more force than is necessary" and raising problems of "Israeli credibility." Yet he went on to say that "no one questions Israel's legitimate security problem in Lebanon." A different balance of justification and unease had been struck on CBS the day before. Bill Moyers in his June 15 commentary had told his audience that "more Palestinians are homeless than ever," and that they faced the prospect of a "fraudulent peace in an indifferent world." But Moyers also noted that "civilian casualties were sure to be high" because the PLO "had embedded itself in camps of innocent civilians," and that Israel was rescuing Lebanon from "murderous gangs."

The Lebanon Puzzle—Explained?

Moyers's editorial pointed to a second major area of controversy—whether the press was paying enough attention to the complex realities of Lebanese politics that could explain the Israeli invasion as something other than a simple attack on a neighboring state. Critics would allege that for many weeks the media largely ignored both the historical setting in Lebanon and the favorable Lebanese reaction to the Israelis. Yet a survey shows some twenty *Times* and *Post* stories on just those subjects from late May to the end of July, with nearly the same number on the major networks. In fact, Lebanon's prolonged era of civil strife before the invasion, its chafing under the PLO occupation, the welcome extended to Israeli troops in many areas —all these were major themes of the first weeks of war reporting.

Thus, in early June Cody reported in the *Post* on Lebanon's "impotence" before the PLO, and on the near anarchy of the "disintegrating" nation, while Claiborne on June 16 noted that Damur, the scene of much destruction blamed on Israel, had been "savaged by years of civil war" as well as by the "relentless" Israeli pounding. The *Post*'s Jonathan Randal, meanwhile, described a Lebanon "ever more cynical" about its Syrian and Palestinian "guests." At the same time, the *Times*'s William E. Farrell was filing on the "seven years of violence and killing" in Lebanon and on the "flowers and cold soda" given to Israeli soldiers being hailed as liberators by Lebanese Christians.

Much the same portrait of Lebanon was drawn on nightly television news. On June 7, co-anchor Peter Jennings led ABC's *World News Tonight* with scenes of Lebanese welcoming Israeli forces who had "flushed out. . . terrorists" and a report on the country's "opposition" to the PLO. Over the following four days, NBC's Art Kent reported from war-torn Nabatiye that the Lebanese were "glad" at the "peace" brought by the Israelis, and Bob

Faw, in a moving CBS report on refugees, observed by way of background that "what has been dirty and ugly and painful here will not change" simply because of the added violence of the invasion. For its part, ABC reported that the Lebanese were "simply glad the Syrians are gone" (Chris Harper, June 9), observed that Lebanon had "suffered a nervous breakdown long ago" (Peter Jennings, June 9), and showed one Lebanese civilian saying an emphatic "Never!" when asked if the PLO should return (Bill Seamans, June 10).

Later, as the siege of Beirut tightened, the papers continued their coverage of the Lebanese reaction. Writing in the *Post* June 28 and again July 5, William Branigin described the "terrible" destruction of the war, yet reported also that some Lebanese were "happy" to see the Israelis, and that in Damur the PLO had desecrated churches and used homes for stockpiling missiles. In the same vein, Shipler was reporting to the *Times* on June 21–22 on CHRISTIAN VILLAGERS' HAPPINESS AMID RUBBLE, on the humiliations inflicted on some Lebanese by the Palestinian forces, and on the "smiles and flowers" greeting Israeli troops as they took positions in the Christians' "lush suburbs" around Beirut.

Shipler and the *Times* returned to this theme in a major article on July 25 describing Lebanon's "anguish" under the PLO. Yet that lengthy dispatch, cited by critics as an exception, came not only in the wake of much other print and television reporting but three weeks after an equally impressive and similarly cast CBS feature by Tom Fenton. Illustrating his observations with colorful shots of the old Mediterranean playground, Fenton had noted that Lebanon had been torn apart by the "insertion of a state within a state" in the form of "hordes of armed Palestinians." The PLO, he added, had "destabilized Lebanon," and this had led to civil war, intervention by Syria, and, "eventually," Israel's invasion. Against film of PLO arms stashes, described as "an incredible quantity" of weapons, Fenton told his viewers that Lebanon was "never unified," but warned that the power of politicians like Bashir Gemayel, soon to be elected president of Lebanon, was based on "ruthlessly sectarian use" of the Israeli-armed Christian militia.

The Numbers War

Besides being attacked for scanting the politics and the bloody historical background of the invasion, the news media were soon being angrily criticized for their reporting on civilian casualties, refugees, and the destruction of nonmilitary targets. No single subject would more exercise the critics, who accused journalists of vast inflation, if not invention, in the war's war of numbers. "Arabs exaggerate," Peretz quoted "an Arab friend" as saying to him "coyly in Jerusalem." So, too, he and other critics concluded, did the media.

The allegation raised serious questions. Had journalists identified sources, checked independently where possible, attempted to place figures in perspective? With few exceptions, a thorough reading and watching from June through August showed that the *Times*, the *Post*, and the major networks had done just that.

While transmitting sometimes stark scenes of death and devastation, television news from the earliest moments of the invasion seemed almost self-consciously leery of the numbers game. Casualties were simply "unknown," said Steve Mallory in a June 5 NBC segment on the bombing of refugee camps and a school bus, as well as of "Palestinian strongholds." The next day Mallory reported Lebanese casualties "in the hundreds" from his own observation of the bombing and invasion, while anchor Jessica Savitch noted PLO claims of "six hundred" and "no word" from Israel. On June 7, CBS's Bob Faw, against smoking scenes of battle, reported only that "casualty lists climbed." From southern Lebanon the same day, Vic Aicken sent NBC battle scenes from the fight for Tyre, but offered "no figures" on casualties.

On June 8 ABC's Peter Jennings described "mounting casualties" on both sides, reporting that they were "particularly heavy among Palestinians and Lebanese"; again, he gave no numbers. Noting the same night the devastation in Tyre, Dan Rather on CBS reported that "guerrillas" had occupied a Palestinian school and had thus drawn fire. And completing NBC's extensive coverage of battlefield wreckage that Tuesday evening, Chancellor stressed in his commentary that while "civilians are suffering more heavily than units of the PLO...Israel is being as precise as it can be"—an assessment with which many Lebanese and Palestinians might reasonably have disagreed.

On June 9, ABC and CBS footage from Damur described the hard-hit town as a PLO "stronghold" where guerrillas were "entrenched," and NBC's Mallory, reporting a charge by Lebanon's president that the number of Lebanese killed or wounded "is in the thousands," emphasized that Israeli forces were concentrating on "Palestinian strongholds." The PLO "doesn't say how the figures were arrived at," said Jennings the following night in an ABC report on a PLO claim of 10,000 civilian casualties. Amid film of battle and bombs the same night, NBC's Roger Mudd, like his competitor at ABC, reported the figure of 10,000, attributing it to the "Lebanese Red Cross" but noting that it was also being "circulated by the PLO"; it was, he said, a number that "cannot be confirmed."

Twice the networks slipped noticeably. On June 11, Rather concluded the CBS invasion report by noting that unidentified "international relief officials" believed "thousands" of civilians were casualties in the fighting. A week later, Chancellor commented that Lebanese police estimates of 9,000 casualties and "Red Cross" figures of 300,000 homeless "may be high"—like

Rather's, a vague and lax reference even with the attributions. But on June 22, NBC's anchor Tom Brokaw led the news with the simpler, more accurate admission that "we don't know" how many civilians had perished in the invasion thus far.

While television news was scrupulously vague about the war statistics, the newspapers dealt much more specifically with the numbers, and occasionally suffered the consequences of their attempted precision. The *Times*'s Farrell, for instance, early in the war reported an estimate of 500,000 homeless—a figure attributed to the International Committee of the Red Cross but later denied by committee authorities in Lebanon. In the same June 12 dispatch, however, Farrell cabled from Beirut that "no one really knows" casualty figures, just as his colleague Friedman had earlier stressed that Beirut casualties were "not known." From Washington, the *Times*'s Bernard Weinraub on June 17 duly reported "no estimate" of casualties, pointing out, however, that U.S. relief officials were planning to provide aid to as many as 350,000.

It was *The Washington Post* that, by reporting extensively on civilian victims of the invasion, particularly refugees, drew most of the critics' fire. Their charges were lent some validity by a June 16 frontpage dispatch from Beirut by David B. Ottaway. Attributing the information to a combination of "Red Cross, U.N., Palestinian, and eyewitness accounts," Ottaway filed questionably high or at least unsubstantiated population and refugee numbers for the southern towns of Tyre, Sidon, and Jazzin. As a means of fleshing out a picture of the "devastating impact" on civilians, it was a dubious use of numbers. But higher in the same story, Ottaway had stressed that "figures seem guesses at best," acknowledged that other reports were only "fragmentary," and balanced his piece by quoting both Yasir Arafat's brother and an Israeli colonel who blamed the PLO for the civilian dead. In the end, Ottaway's slippery mid-June figures would be an exception in *Post* coverage, and he would go on to write another major article, on June 25, on the disagreement over casualty totals and the Red Cross denials of statistics printed by the *Times*.

Repeatedly, from June 6 through July, *Post* correspondents Ottaway, Randal, Claiborne, Cody, and Richard Homan told their influential readership that civilian casualties were "difficult" to measure (June 6), had "no independent confirmation" (June 8), and, in the case of one bombed apartment building, were far lower according to Beirut Radio than the PLO was claiming (June 12). They also took pains to make clear that, at a time when the Lebanese army was releasing estimates, "there was no independent confirmation of casualty totals" (June 14). In later dispatches, Claiborne noted the Israeli charge of "exaggerated" figures. Randal, for his part, referred to the "uncounted" dead of Sidon, adding that there was "little that can be confirmed" about alleged Israeli cruelty to local civilians, while Cody wrote about Israeli anger at and denials of the inflated numbers and went on to observe that it was "unclear" how Lebanese police or other authorities got their statistics.

Whatever the huge or shrunken figures ground out officially by the two sides, however ardent or effective the propaganda efforts of the belligerents and their partisans in the U.S., the major reporting from the battle zone itself was remarkably free of the ersatz authority of firm numbers. Even when the raw-nerve issue of civilian losses was hedged about by the plainest qualifications, the networks, the *Times*, and the *Post* also took visible pains to present Israeli doubts or rebuttals.

The Battle of Beirut

On June 11 a *Times* piece from Beirut described the city's "murdered sleep." Before the siege was over, the same term might have been applied to American viewers and readers of reporting from the scene. Day after day, with bombs and shells exploding along the skyline and sirens wailing through the rubble, television and print coverage of the siege shattered an otherwise relatively sleepy news summer. By almost any measure, it was one of the great sustained stories of the decade, and through more than nine weeks it would present nearly all the issues of accuracy and balance that stoked the controversy over alleged anti-Israeli bias in the media.

From the time the first Israeli bombs and shells fell inside the city, reporters and critics alike faced the question of whether a vast yet concentrated urban battleground was being portrayed fairly, and specifically whether journalists as well as Israeli gunners were distinguishing between the noncombatant city and the PLO forces lodged within it. Despite the medium's acknowledged weakness for wreckage and dazed, grieving innocents, despite its vivid reporting on civilian victims, television news for the most part struck the balance carefully. Characteristic of the early siege coverage was a Don Kladstrup report on CBS on June 10 that described the bombing of the city and nearby Palestinian settlements, but emphasized the destruction of PLO ammunition and supply depots, and noted that one of the buildings hit was near Arafat's headquarters. The following evening, NBC's Mallory sent out a somber report on the shelling of "nonmilitary" positions; it showed an old man weeping amid the destruction, and angry, unidentified Lebanese Moslems saying, "There are no military targets here," and "These are American weapons that are destroying our country." Mallory's images were admittedly sharp, but even here a conscientious attempt at balance was evident. Roger Mudd introduced the segment by saying that the Israelis had aimed their artillery at PLO headquarters and had scored a "direct hit," and minutes later, after Mallory, network correspondent Paul Miller reported from Israel on Defense Minister Ariel Sharon's justification for the continuing battle.

In the continual coverage by all three networks from June 4 throughout the month, there were very few questionable siege reports. One such report was aired on June 13. Chris Harper of ABC reported from Beirut on renewed Israeli bombing in which, "as usual, most of the victims were civilians." He then showed footage of the casings of U.S.-made cluster bombs, followed by a shot of a Lebanese woman who had lost her family in the "Israeli onslaught." Plainly an emotional portrayal, it left the then still-unsubstantiated impression, by juxtaposition, that the Israelis were dropping the brutal weapons on civilians. If noncombatants were now dying in the city, ABC at this early stage had an obligation to remind its viewers pointedly that the PLO had retreated into the heart of West Beirut, bringing the war with them like a plague. At the same time, the segment was a rare lapse in the month's network coverage, and in any case was followed on ABC by a Seamans report from Tel Aviv which explained that Israeli bombing was made necessary by the "organized and continuing" fighting by the PLO, and which showed still more captured weapons.

Far more typical was Mallory's graphic segment on NBC two days later showing a city "shelled to death from without and within." A powerful car bomb, its origins unknown, had destroyed a nearby Moslem building, and in the ensuing chaos of bloody victims, sirens, wild firing of guns, hospital confusion, and an old man pounding the rubble in rage, Mallory caught a West Beirut not besieged by partisan images but simply "overwhelmed by yet another disaster here."

Earlier in the month, as Mallory was reporting shelling of "nonmilitary" targets, the *Post's* Ottaway from another vantage point filed a June 11 dispatch about Israeli vessels firing "indiscriminately" into the city. Either the naval fire or land artillery had taken mainly civilian casualties, including children in a playground, Ottaway wrote. But his article also told of an attack on "Palestinian and Lebanese leftist positions," as well as on the PLO headquarters building, and there was no later dispute about the accuracy of his description of one of the city's bloodier days of investment. Ottaway's account would be typical of the *Post's* graphic and detailed coverage of the siege, and a mark as well of the growing contrast with the *Times*, whose Beirut reporting generally focused less on the battle in the streets than on the political and diplomatic aspects of the conflict.

Despite their differing thrusts, however, both papers provided admirably balanced reports throughout June. When the *Post's* Randal wrote (June 14) about cluster bombs hitting a hospital just outside Beirut, he reported "no evidence" that the Israelis had targeted the institution. Syrian troops had indeed been in the area, and the bombing seemed an "accident of war." Later, Ottaway described the encirclement of Beirut as a siege not of civilians but of "remaining Palestinian guerrilla strongholds," while Friedman of the *Times* reported similarly that Israel was after the PLO "nerve center." When a ceasefire was broken on June 23, Randal thought it "impossible" to say who had started shooting, while the *Times*'s Henry Kamm reported from Jerusalem that ISRAEL SAYS SYRIA BROKE CEASE FIRE. At month's end, both Friedman and his *Post* rivals were reporting on the PLO's cynical "waiting game" in the beleaguered city.

The Siege, the Bombings—and an Explosive Telex

In the second and third weeks of June, the lengthening siege of West Beirut and its undeniable human dimension would begin to dominate both print and television coverage. And while the carnage did not produce sudden sympathy for the PLO, it did impel journalists to write about the sheer horror of what was happening. Thus, on June 21 the *Post*'s William Branigin reported the bombing of a hospital said to be "well away from any military targets"—part of the "backlash" of the "dirty war." Eight days later, Randal filed a similar piece on how the Israelis had "mercilessly" bombed Palestinian refugee camps outside Beirut, and shelled a "clearly marked" hospital. Farrell of the *Times* filed a June 26 story on "fierce Israeli strikes" and on mass graves in a Beirut cemetery that included an interview about civilian casualties with Dr. Amal Shamma of Berbir Hospital, an articulate Lebanese doctor often interviewed by television reporters as well. In the same edition, Shipler told the painful story of a twelve-year-old "drafted" by the PLO, which perhaps technically provided textual balance but was no match for Farrell's images. (It was Farrell who, on June 30, brought the story home to New Yorkers, describing the "Gramercy Park" of Beirut as being now "a sunlit horror of dazed people.") However consciously weighed and tempered, reportage coming from inside Beirut took on gathering drama, and a gathering sense of the human cost, much of it inevitably reflecting on Israel's guns and policy.

Throughout July the siege was the daily staple of news coverage, but the overall balance was maintained. On July 5 Bob McNamara of CBS depicted the "war-weary" city, whose "innocent Lebanese civilians living among guerrillas are hostages trapped in the line of fire." Over the next two days Randal of the *Post* recorded, without assigning blame, the demise of the fifth ceasefire, and credited Israeli explanations for the blockade of water and other supplies. On July 10, Branigin's dispatch to the *Post* labeled the PLO and the Syrians as being responsible for the impasse in talks with Habib. Again, two days later, he wrote about Beirut's "mean streets" and concluded that the city "is suffering from the decay that years of civil war and lawlessness have brought at least as much as it is suffering from Israel's shelling." On July 15, ABC's Hal Walker gave a thoughtful report on the Palestinians trapped by the invasion—their homelessness, their support for the PLO, their fear of Lebanese reprisals when the PLO left, their children among whom "hardly a male over 12 [is] not armed." "Where am I to go?" a woman who had come to Beirut thirty-four years before from Galilee asked Walker. His report provided a relatively rare glimpse of the larger human anguish and history behind the battle, yet it concluded with no attack on Israel, but rather with sharp criticism of the refusal of other Arab nations to take in the Palestinians.

In a month of mounting death and destruction, and growing disillusionment with the siege, both in and out of Israel, coverage continued to be careful and fair. A rare exception was a report by NBC's James Compton. Although July 28 was what anchor Brokaw called "another wild day in Lebanon," Compton reported in obvious overstatement that "night and day Israeli bombs rain on this city," that "nowhere is it safe," and that "no neighborhood has been exempt"—this in a city that had yet to feel the far wider Israeli bombings of August 1 and 4. Compton showed the Canadian ambassador, whose official residence had been hit, talking about his "change of heart" and asking, "Where's the Israel that we know...where has it disappeared?" The segment, which was followed by an even-handed report from Martin Fletcher in Damur, took no note of a PLO that Friedman described a day later in the *Times* as burrowing into the city with relative impunity while ambassadors and others seemed to deplore Israel alone.

It was in early August, in the last bloody week of bombardment before an agreement on the PLO departure, that the siege coverage itself became most heated. During the first five days of the month, the papers recorded the "fiercest shelling" of the Israeli "onslaught" (*Times*, August 2) and "severe damage in practically every West Beirut neighborhood" in the "heaviest assault yet" (*Post*, August 5). "Where is the American administration?" asked one U.S. citizen trapped in a burning hotel and quoted in a UPI story by Julie Flint carried in the *Post*. "Either your country has changed or you are making the most appalling mistakes in your history," Randal's story on the fifth had a diplomat saying to an Israeli officer, who responded, "Maybe both."

No published comments, however, would be more telling than Friedman's impassioned telex to *Times* editors William Borders and Seymour Topping when the paper deleted the adjective "indiscriminate" from his August 5 lead on the Israeli bombing. He had always been careful, Friedman said (and his dispatches would document the claim), "to note in previous stories that the Israelis were hitting Palestinian positions and if they were hitting residential areas to at least raise the possibility that the Palestinians had a gun there at one time or another." He had used "a strong word" such as "indiscriminate" only after he had taken a hazardous tour of the city with Branigin of the *Post* and had concluded that "what happened yesterday was something fundamentally different from what has happened on the previous 63 days." The "newspaper of record should have told its readers and future historians" about the Israeli terror bombing, Friedman went on. It was the "very essence of what was new yesterday.... What can

I say?" he concluded. "I am filled with profound sadness by what I have learned in the past afternoon about my newspaper."

Sent over the Reuters open wire and widely read in the profession, Friedman's cable provided a remarkable inside look at the conscientiousness of reporters in Beirut and their awareness of the sensitivity at home of what they were reporting. In a sense, it would be a more eloquent rebuttal to critics of the war coverage than any dispatch from the front. But Friedman's were scarcely the only illusions destroyed that week in Beirut.

Chancellor and Editorial Pages: Unbalanced?

Over the first four days of August, with commentator John Chancellor now in Beirut, NBC aired some of the most provocative segments of the war. They began on August 1 with Rick Davis and James Compton reporting on the barrage. A bloody, bandaged baby, "innocent of any part of all the years of violence here," was shown; shells were described as falling in a "seemingly random way" on civilian targets; and Lebanese leader Saeb Salaam was shown asking Habib, "Will [the Israelis] be finishing us all before they finish?" The next day, Jim Bittermann depicted the bombardment of areas "long abandoned" by the PLO, with doctors saying that there were no military targets near the bombed neighborhoods, and Salaam touring the rubble and making such remarks as, "This was a school." The powerful segments mentioned Israeli claims that the PLO "fired first" that day, and that not only Israeli artillery but Palestinian mortars as well had hit an apartment building. But there was no explanation that Salaam was a prominent Moslem leader opposed to the Israelis (and a principal go-between with the PLO for Habib), and no independent confirmation of Salaam's description of the scenes.

Perhaps the most controversial moment in the coverage came at the end of the broadcast on August 2, when Chancellor, silhouetted against the Beirut skyline, reflected on "yesterday's savage Israeli attack...on one of the world's big cities." The area under bombardment was the "length of Manhattan below Central Park," he observed, and of the 500,000 who lived there, only "one in a hundred is a PLO fighter." The Israelis had claimed they were going after military targets with precision, but now "there was also the stench of terror all across the city." Nothing like it had ever happened in this part of the world, Chancellor went on. "I kept thinking yesterday of the bombing of Madrid during the Spanish Civil War. What in the world is going on?" he asked, shaking his head. Israel's security problem was "fifty miles to the south," so "what's an Israeli army doing here in Beirut?" He then concluded: "The answer is that we are now dealing with an imperial Israel which is solving its problems in someone else's country, world opinion be damned. . . . The Israel we saw here yesterday is not the Israel we have seen in the past."

Clearly introduced as editorial comment, Chancellor's words drew a torrent of protest, impelling the network to take the extraordinary step of showing three of the critical letters on the evening news two nights later, though with Brokaw repeating before and after the excerpts that the "very heavy" reaction had been "about evenly divided" between approval and disapproval.

Belatedly, perhaps, Chancellor's August 2 portrayal of Israeli-wrought devastation would be balanced by his remarks, on the next two nights, on the "resiliency" of the Lebanese and on the exploitation of the situation by the PLO as "civilians die and Yasir Arafat stays put." For that matter, the disputed editorial was scarcely fairer game for critics than Brokaw's ostensible news reference on August 4 to "what's left of West Beirut"—as if the entire city had been demolished, which even in the siege carnage was a definite exaggeration. In any case, Chancellor's comment was offset by August 4 and 9 reports on NBC showing the suffering of Israeli soldiers and their evident conviction that their cause was just. It was further offset by a thoughtful Chancellor commentary from a Palestinian refugee camp in which he observed that, although Israel bore "some of the blame" for the homeless people, it had been Arab countries that refused them refuge; the wretched Palestinians were "useful" because they "made Israel look bad."

Nor was Chancellor alone in his visible anguish. In one of the most moving television tapes of the siege, ABC, on August 10, broadcast Jack Smith's story from Beirut's neuropsychiatric hospital with its 500 patients "virtually abandoned," many of them wailing, retarded children without clothes or food. "They are dying," Smith reported of some of the children, because the PLO is "too busy fighting" and the Lebanese government "won't help"; meanwhile, Israeli shells "have killed or wounded nearly eighty patients." But the critics, revealing the same selective perception they charged with warping American journalism, seized on Chancellor's August 2 editorial as conclusive evidence of media bias.

At the same time, the editorial and op-ed pages of the *Times* and the *Post* also came under heavy fire. "According to one estimate of the first 19 pieces on the war in Lebanon to appear on *The New York Times* op-ed page, 17 were hostile to Israel...," Podhoretz wrote in his "J'Accuse." "I have not made a statistical survey of *The Washington Post* op-ed page, but my impression is that the balance there was roughly the same." With its unidentified "one estimate" and "impression," the claim was undercut by the same sloppiness that Podhoretz and other critics deplored in the media.

Even granting the legitimacy in media criticism of faulting a paper's editorial balance as apart from news accuracy, and leaving aside the tricky question of what constituted a view "hostile" to Israel, the reality of the *Times* and *Post* editorial battlegrounds was hardly what the critics reported. Both editorially accepted the invasion—"tragic inevitability," said the *Post*; part of a "tragic spiral," said the *Times*—and proceeded to offset sharp condemnations of Israel by columnists such as Anthony Lewis and Mary McGrory with pieces by the likes of William Safire, William F. Buckley, Jr., and Rowland Evans and Robert Novak, who described the PLO as "permeated by thugs and adventurers."

While the *Post*, on balance, deplored the invasion and ran conspicuous pieces implicitly critical of Israel—former Tel Aviv correspondent Alfred Friendly on how Israel had lost its "unique splendor" and Claiborne on Israel's "wounded soul," for example, and later editorials on the "unforgettably bloody" fighting in Beirut—its editorialists also thought that Israel was doing "a nasty job" which everyone else wanted done. Editorially, the *Times* did less hand-wringing about the invasion, emphasizing the postwar negotiating opportunities in the West Bank and elsewhere that would justify the carnage unfolding on the front page. On August 5, the day "indiscriminate" was cut from Friedman's dispatch, *Times* editors found the worst bombardment of the siege "lamentable" but an "unavoidable way to keep the heat on."

Other Papers, and Scanted Stories

A survey of other major newspapers reveals much the same news balance as evidenced by the *Times*, the *Post*, and the networks. While *The Philadelphia Inquirer*'s Richard Ben Cramer prompted protests with moving dispatches from Beirut on the plight of civilians, for example, the *Inquirer* also featured a syndicated piece by the *Los Angeles Times*'s Norman Kempster on how suspect all casualty figures were, as well as reporting from Robert J. Rosenthal on Israeli policy. Alex Efty of The Associated Press filed vivid stories on the siege, such as his June 25 dispatch on the Israeli shelling of a noncombatant area, but more often the AP wire was intent, as on July 30, on listing the PLO "targets" in the city, and on giving a paragraph-by-paragraph alternation of both sides' versions of the battle. *The Wall Street Journal* typically headlined the heavy Israeli shelling of August 1 as AIMED AT SPEEDING WITHDRAWAL OF GUERRILLAS.

Long respected for its Middle East coverage, *The Christian Science Monitor* duly reported "Israel's awesome pounding" of Beirut, yet editorially the paper made plain that "Yasir Arafat is stalling." The *Monitor* also carried an insightful three-part series by Trudy Rubin, beginning August 6, which emphasized the neglected reality that the Lebanese not only "hate the PLO" but feared the Israelis would "start to act the same" and simply install "new armed outsiders to replace the PLO." Meanwhile, the *Los Angeles Times*'s J. Michael Kennedy, Charles T. Powers, and Kempster filed graphic stories on both the siege and the "oppression" by the PLO in Lebanon, while, on the op-ed page, Kennedy wrote about how, with both the Israelis and the PLO locked in battle, a great city was "being destroyed by people who do not seem to care." Editorially, the *Times* observed during the early August bombardment: "Blame the PLO for the torment of West Beirut and blame Israel no less." (Letters printed on the same page accused the paper of both anti-Israeli and anti-Palestinian bias.)

In some cases, however, comparisons among the voluminous coverage only made more conspicuous certain unreported stories of the invasion. The *Inquirer*'s Robert Rosenthal and Ellen Cantarow for *The Village Voice*, for instance, wrote penetrating articles on the West Bank and the connection between the invasion and the stormy Israeli occupation of that area. In a sense, the West Bank was the gallery to which both warring sides played in Lebanon, its politics explaining the passion of the two armies and its territory likely to be the next symbolic if not literal battleground. But this story went largely ignored, especially by television.

So, too, their pens and cameras poised over the devastation of Moslem West Beirut and the PLO-held cities in the south, reporters barely glanced at what one *Times* writer called the "lush suburbs" of the Christians around Beirut, as well as farther south. The middle-class and wealthier Lebanese had survived the PLO occupation and the invasion by making their bargains with both sides. Telling that story would have provided a stark picture of the social and economic dimensions of the conflict.

With the exception of early reporting by Hedrick Smith in the *Times*, coverage was similarly absent on another front of the war—the U.S. Congress. The silence of Capitol Hill politicians on both sides, not to mention the impact of the invasion on close election campaigns starting up as the fighting and the media coverage grew most controversial was striking. But most home-front journalists tended to dive for cover on the issue along with the politicians.

Not least, there was little reporting on the fascinating "story of the story" in Lebanon—the burdens imposed by Israeli censorship, the conditions under which the doubly beleaguered journalists worked in Beirut, the sociology of their knowledge, the inner politics and reaction at papers and networks as the controversy exploded. It would have made vivid and unique firsthand war correspondence in a war in which the news media were a powerful force; but few in either print or television even brushed it, the networks' reporting on censorship being limited, by and large, to explanations of missing visuals.

But perhaps the most significant unreported story was how it all began. There were intriguing shards of the story here and there. In the *New States-man* of June 25, Amnon Kapeliuk from Jerusalem reported "hundreds" of articles in the Israeli press presaging the invasion and an interview with Sharon saying he had been planning it since the previous August, while Claudia Wright noted that U.S. arms deliveries to Israel for the first quarter of 1982 were almost ten times the amount during the same period in 1980, and almost half again higher than those in 1981. *The Wall Street Journal*, in an August 10 Gerald F. Sieb feature on the propaganda efforts in the U.S. by both sides, noted that Sharon had toured the U.S. earlier in the spring with a booklet that, in effect, justified invasion. On August 1, NBC's Bob Kur showed previously censored film brought out from Israel depicting Israeli troops and equipment poised along the border in May, well before the attempted assassination of Ambassador Argov or any PLO rocket attacks of early June. The *Post* ran fascinating excerpts of interviews with Begin and Secretary of State Alexander Haig, just before the latter's resignation, that suggested that Haig's views on Lebanon might be closer to Begin's than to Ronald Reagan's. Did the U.S.—or at least some officials—know about the invasion long in advance? What had been U.S. policy, or was there more than one policy? Was an American secretary of state one of the casualties of the siege, and was he really a noncombatant?

Lebanon—and the Vietnam Parallel

To Podhoretz and other critics, commentary on the Israeli invasion of Lebanon revealed the same "loss of nerve" that had afflicted the U.S. in Vietnam. Yet the legacy of the Vietnam conflict helped to produce quite the opposite effect on journalists: a plain determination not to be taken in, to question official claims on all sides. Again, while Podhoretz argued that the press should have celebrated the victory of a U.S.-armed conventional force over Soviet-supported guerrillas, the immediate Vietnam parallel for working journalists was the censorship in Jerusalem, which proved no more popular than slanted American press briefings in Saigon (where, ironically, one of the briefers was Philip Habib). Journalists appeared to resent in particular the transparent falsity of the original Israeli claim to be clearing out only a twenty-five-mile buffer zone.

On the other hand, there was also evident trauma for American reporters, many of whom seemed, for the first time, to be seeing the Palestinians in human terms, in the blood and tears of the street and crowded hospital wards, and not simply as "terrorists" and "guerrillas." As "the other side" took on human reality, reporters inevitably became sympathetic to the plight of civilians. Added to that was the shock of journalists like Chancellor and Farrell made evident by their allusions to Beirut in terms of Manhattan. For Americans watching a great urban center under attack, the first since World War II, the image was brutal and obviously close to home. This was no Asian village or Middle East desert vastness, but streets and apartment houses recalling lakefront Chicago or, as Farrell wrote, Gramercy Park. Moreover, the urban intensity gave what was television's war even more concentrated sights and sounds to compress into the medium's limited compass. In the smoldering streets of West Beirut, with its screaming sirens and people, television caught the story with rare fidelity. Altogether, the result was a story that showed genuine empathy for the suffering city, and dismay at the destruction wrought by the encircling army, however understandable its presence might have been.

But was that empathy somehow political? Would the press have been less sensitive to the story of the human suffering if it had been the PLO, not the Israelis, shelling a hostage city? Would John Chancellor have been less inclined to ask "What in the world is going on?" There was nothing in the coverage to suggest that double standard. Although journalists vividly depicted the suffering of civilians, they continued to credit the Israeli justification for the invasion—right up to the gates of Beirut. Indeed, they did so almost to the exclusion of that other history behind the invasion—the Palestinian exodus and suffering since 1947. When the focus of the siege journalism turned perforce in late June to the calamity of West Beirut, the story reflected sympathy not for the entrenched PLO but for the innocent people among whose demolished homes the two sides fought.

When the invasion and the siege story were over, much seemed buried in West Beirut—the old PLO, perhaps the old Israel, perhaps the innocence of the media, something almost certainly too of American foreign policy—but it was a graveyard as well of the critics' charges of unprofessional reporting. In June, American journalism came to a bloody new war in the Middle East, reported what it saw for the most part fairly and accurately and sometimes brilliantly, provided balanced comment, and provoked and absorbed controversy. For performance under fire, readers and viewers could have asked for little more.

33 How Britain Managed the News

by Leonard Downie, Jr.

When Great Britain went to war with Argentina over the Falkland Islands, the British brought with them the lessons learned from Vietnam and Lebanon. They thoroughly managed all the news about the event, much to their benefit, as Leonard Downie, Jr., explains. Downey was national editor of the *Washington Post* and completed a tour as London correspondent for that newspaper. This article is reprinted from the *Washington Post*, August 20, 1982.

Throughout Britain's war with Argentina over the Falkland Islands, the government and media in London reacted indignantly to wildly false claims emanating from Buenos Aires. With Argentine propagandists repeatedly sinking the British aircraft carriers Hermes and Invincible, even though neither was ever hit, frustrated foreign correspondents in Buenos Aires complained about the difficulty of separating fact from fiction in what they came to call "the Bozo zone."

But those of use trying to cover the Falklands war from 8,000 miles away in London felt nearly as far removed from reality, even though we had access to more verifiable information. We also were being denied significant facts and knew, though we could not then prove, that we were being purposely misled in many cases.

In a recent parliamentary inquiry, British officials for the first time acknowledged misleading the media about British intentions, strengths and weaknesses on numerous occasions during the war. They were, however, more subtle than their Argentine counterparts.

"We aimed throughout not to lie," testified Sir Frank Cooper, the civil servant who runs Britain's defense ministry. "But there were occasions when we did not tell the whole truth and did not correct things that were being misread."

Hours before 5,000 British troops were landed at San Carlos Bay on East Falkland Island in a massive amphibious operation, Sir Frank himself had confided to British newsmen in a restricted background briefing that there were "no plans" for a "D-Day–type invasion." This was not really a lie, he recently told the parliamentary inquiry, because the allies' World War II invasion on D-Day was "an opposed landing," while few Argentine defenders were expected or encountered in the British landing at San Carlos.

He and other officials also left uncorrected a number of news reports, based on speculative leaks from inside the British government, that made it appear the Royal Navy had significantly more ships, submarines and aircraft around the Falklands than it actually did at various times. A nuclear-powered hunter-killer submarine widely reported to be enforcing the original British naval blockade around the Falklands was later found in port in Scotland.

Good news was sometimes released prematurely, with the British recapture of Port Darwin and Goose Green announced a half-day before the Argentine defenders actually surrendered. Bad news, from accidental crashes of British warplanes and helicopters to the number of casualties inflicted by Argentine air strikes, often was held up for days.

Some facts, like the large number of British ships hit by Argentine bombs that failed to explode, have still not been officially released in Britain. In fact, the defense ministry in London has yet to provide reliable figures on either the equipment losses suffered by British forces or those inflicted on the Argentinians. Yet, just yesterday, officials of government-owned British Aerospace, Inc., here to promote the sophisticated British-made weapons that proved so efficient during the Falklands conflict, had no difficulty producing their own statistics on the number of Argentine planes downed by British Harrier jets and surface-fired anti-aircraft missiles.

Television networks were prevented from broadcasting live from the Royal Navy's Falklands task force, and their film of events in the South Atlantic took weeks to reach London by ship and plane. So the war was nearly over before Britons saw dramatic scenes of the destruction of some of their warships or heard emotional interviews with survivors. Still photographs of burning British warships, transmitted more quickly to London, were blocked from publication by military censors for days and sometimes weeks.

Among the strongest critics of British censorship and disinformation during the war are many of the British correspondents, photographers and technicians who were allowed to accompany the task force to the South Atlantic. The Royal Navy tried to keep all newsmen off the task force, but was overruled by Prime Minister Margaret Thatcher's press secretary, who interceded personally for most of the 28 successful applicants. Foreign newsmen were completely excluded.

The BBC correspondent with the task force, Brian Hanrahan, testified to the parliamentary inquiry that the British commander, Adm. John Woodward, told reporters he intended to use the media "to cause as much confusion to the enemy as possible." The newsmen reached an agreement with him, according to Hanrahan, "where he was entitled to stop us reporting things, but we were not prepared to report things that were incorrect."

For an American correspondent in London, none of this should be really surprising. In normal times, the British press accepts a far greater amount of government secrecy and news manipulation than American or foreign newsmen would put up with in Washington.

In place of any legal obligation on the government to make information public—such as the U.S. Freedom of Information Act—the pervasive secrecy of Britain's civil service, military and politicians is protected by an arsenal of powerful legal weapons. The sweeping Official Secrets Act, though only selectively enforced, threatens prosecution and imprisonment of anyone from bureaucrats to newsmen involved in making public any unauthorized government information. The "D notice" system, the provisions of which themselves were long an official secret, is used by the British military to routinely notify editors and broadcasters that they cannot report specific items of information that often have already been put on the public record elsewhere by the United States, other governments or international agencies. Wealthy, blue-blooded and prominent Britons, including politicians and government officials, have long used the country's strict, punitive libel laws to prevent publication of information they find uncomplimentary.

More insidious, however, is a practice that most British journalists agree to voluntarily and even help to protect. Most of their contacts with politicians and government officials are kept completely off the record through what is called the "lobby"—named for an area in the House of Commons where many of these contacts take place, although every government agency has its own lobby arrangement with newsmen covering it. Newsmen participating in "lobby" briefings and conversations are obligated to keep secret all their sources, all direct quotes, and even the times and locations of such contacts. They are sometimes forbidden by their sources to publish important information revealed in these contacts.

This system enables the British government to manage much of what is reported by the national newspapers and television and radio networks and to escape responsibility for planting information—true or false—that newsmen must report only on an "it is understood" basis. This was the system used by the British defense ministry to control through the lobby of defense correspondents most information about the Falklands war. Only these correspondents were allowed into secret briefings held throughout the war, while the rest of the large body of newsmen covering the conflict from London were told little in public statements and press conferences.

Few British newsmen sought to find out more from officials or senior politicians outside these government-controlled forums. The leading political correspondent for a respected British Sunday newspaper said he would not even try to contact members of Thatcher's inner "war cabinet" because he doubted they would talk to him and he wanted to avoid "doing anything that might endanger our boys." As a result of such self-censorship, it was left to an American newsman to report from sources in the war cabinet that it had unanimously made the decision to sink the Argentine cruiser General Belgrano, one of the most important military and political events of the war.

Much of this had shocked me when I first arrived in Britain as a correspondent more than three years ago. But by the time the Falklands war brought a large number of fresh American colleagues to London near the end of my tour, I was surprised by their outraged response to a system that I, too, had grown to live with.

Even after the Falklands war ended, only a few British journalists questioned whether such pervasive news management, in peace or war, was good for the country. One of them, Charles Wintour, writing in the Sunday *Observer*, emphasized that "the hidden attitudes of many people in authority toward the media have been exposed. They think the public should be told as little as possible. They don't object to deception on matters both large and small. They dislike reporters. And they prefer that ruling circles should be left to run the state without being bothered by troublesome disclosures and unpleasant truths.

"In fact," Wintour concluded, "some of them don't really care much for democracy either."

34 Too Bad for Our Side: War Is a Video Game

by Ben J. Wattenberg

The lesson we have learned from recent wars, says Ben J. Wattenberg, is that the most important new weapons of modern warfare are "light-weight television cameras and television satellites. They have unwittingly made it more difficult for free nations to operate in the real world." Wattenberg is an editor of *Public Opinion* and a longtime observer of American public attitudes and behavior. This article is reprinted from *Public Opinion*, August/September 1982.

Suppose you were a young military officer or a young diplomat. What would be the right lessons to learn from the recent wars?

It has been said that what's new about these wars has something to do with the devastating French missiles used by Argentina, or with the ingenious Israeli adaptation of American smartware, or with the deficiency of Soviet anti-aircraft technology used by Syria.

But I fear that the real lessons to be taught at West Point or the Fletcher School of Diplomacy will be very different. The most important new weapons are light-weight television cameras and television satellites. They have unwittingly made it more difficult for free nations to operate in the real world.

Consider the string of recent wars: Afghanistan, Iraq-Iran, El Salvador and, more recently, the Falklands and Lebanon. And consider some new rules of the road that every geopolitician and military tactician must now teach.

First Rule: Communist countries can wage long, brutal wars and pay very little for them. It is two and a half years since the Soviets rolled into Afghanistan. The Afghans continue to fight well, but the U.S. grain embargo has been lifted, sanctions were never imposed and the nightly news all over the world ignores the conflict. After all, if you can't get television cameras into a country to witness the poison gas, the dead civilians, the maimed children—then what can you show on television? No access; no horror.

Second Rule: Roughly the same guidelines hold for non-free, non-Communist countries. The Iran-Iraq war began almost two years ago; 100,000 people have been killed, including many civilians. The Iranians developed a new mine detector: young boys run across the battlefield to explode the mines. But there are no television cameras to record the battered bits of young life blown sky high. No cameras; no news. No news; no outrage. No outrage; no penalty. And so, Iraq still hoped to host the Conference of Non-aligned Nations; the United States buys oil from Iran.

Third Rule: A democracy can wage a quick war if it is on an isolated, faraway island—which enables it to control the news. There was plenty of television coverage of the ships leaving England to the tune of "Don't Cry for Me, Argentina." But there was no contemporaneous television film of the deaths of the British sailors in the icy sea or in melting aluminium ships. No foreign correspondents were allowed with the fleet; censorship was tight. In many ways, it now comes out, the British public was purposefully misled. Question: if English television had shown the gore of the war while it was happening, could Mrs. Thatcher have kept the political support necessary to finish the war?

Fourth Rule: Only at great cost can democracies get involved—even minimally—if the battlefield is an open country. America provided military aid and fifty advisers to the civil war in El Salvador. They were outnumbered by television folks; the coverage made us appear at times like conspiratorial, lying butchers. It sometimes seemed as if the war was about four dead nuns. Another big story revealed that an American adviser actually carried a rifle. Television coverage helped to turn the American public sour on a limited, moral enterprise; now U.S. political support for El Salvador is fraying.

Fifth Rule: On non-islands, democracies can wage only short wars, telling the whole truth, all at once and immediately. If the war goes on, if goals change as target of opportunity arise, if the government says something that is not so—beware of the wrath of the world. Because both Israel and Lebanon host plenty of television crews, because a television journalist can get to the front quickly in a Hertz rent-a-car, because the censorship is porous—every bit of the horror that any war produces is in everybody's living room the next day. In war, access equals horror.

The Israelis are complaining bitterly that Israel is unfairly held up to a double standard. Actually, it is more serious than that. The new rules of media warfare establish a double standard for all open societies. Television will show blood in El Salvador, in Lebanon—in any open country—and civilized people will be shocked and exert political pressure to make it stop.

This is important. The use of force and, more important, the threat of the use of force are still key parts of the global geopolitical equation. That is sad, but true.

The nature of television news demands that it show whatever horror is available. Our horror is available; our adversaries' horror is not. That process unwittingly presents our adversaries with a great gift. They can credibly use the threat of force in a harsh world; it is much more difficult for us. They know that; we know that; they know that we know that. Accordingly, they can be more adventuresome than they might ordinarily be. That is not the fault of television; it is the burden of the glory of a free press.

Of course, all this is not brand new. The same phenomenon was apparent in Vietnam, when only our half of a bloody war was shown in the living rooms of the world. Now it is apparent that it was no accident; it will keep on happening that way. That may be a tough lesson for would-be generals and diplomats to swallow, but it is a more important one than which side has the smarter missiles.

---

35 War Coverage in a TV Age
by Nick Thimmesch

> In response to Ben Wattenberg, Nick Thimmesch suggests that the answer is not less coverage of war by the media, but more. Television, he says, has been a force to reduce slaughter, "and perhaps has given many poor souls a chance to live a few more precious years." Thimmesch, a former Washington correspondent for the *Los Angeles Times*, is now a journalist in residence at the American Enterprise Institute. This article is reprinted from *Public Opinion*, October/November 1982.

Ben J. Wattenberg warns young military officers and diplomats in "Too Bad for Our Side: War Is a Video Game" that the television camera is the most important new weapon in modern war, and that TV technology "unwittingly" makes it "more difficult for free nations to operate in the real world."

Well, no question that television can bring war's gore into living rooms, and quickly affect, even change, public opinion about any nation, free or otherwise. The dramatic shift in American public opinion about Israel, following its invasion of Lebanon and the siege of Beirut, is the most recent case in point.

Wattenberg's lament that Communist and other non-"free" nations can escape such unfavorable exposure because they don't provide access when they wage war, also has some validity. Our sense of fairness is offended when the Soviets brutalize Afghanistan, *sans* camera, or when the Syrians kill their own people with artillery, with vengeance, in a television-free environment.

But Wattenberg's complaints push the reader toward the chore of trying to determine what the so-called good guys should do about the media when "our side" lets loose with bombs, shells, rockets, and other lethal devices. In citing El Salvador and Israel, Wattenberg implies that "our side" suffered because television captured the violence of these nations in unpleasant terms.

Does this mean that the U.S. government should follow General Westmoreland's advice, and impose censorship in any future military action involving U.S. forces? Or should nations presumed to be on "our side"—because they get huge amounts of foreign and military aid—restrict or even bar the cameras from witnessing the killing of war because that might reflect on the nobleness of our "cause"? Or should the media, after stern warning, practice self-censorship, turn cameras away, or perhaps not take them to the scene of carnage at all?

The presence of TV cameras is a risk to the reputation of a combatant, but the price a free nation pays for the presence is worth it. While Wattenberg remarks that television made the war in El Salvador sometimes seem as if it "was about four dead nuns," I want to know if the government we fund is responsible for the killing of those four nuns.

I also want to know about the My Lai massacre, the execution, by handgun, of a Viet Cong killer by a South Vietnamese police chief, and what Israel did in Lebanon, because I helped pay for it, and I am loyal to the U.S. government which had a hand in this violence.

It is to be hoped that the media are intelligent enough to put this sort of activity in perspective, and that we can make judgments on whether the American connection is worth it. Perhaps it is. But let us see it and then decide.

When a free nation's survival is at stake, as was the case in World War II, military censorship is justified on the grounds that the enemy can use freely dispensed information to hurt us. When the United States takes sides in El Salvador, ostensibly we are seeking to stabilize the region in our national interest, but the most hawkish advocate can't argue that our survival is at stake. There is a difference.

The loudest complaints about recent television coverage of military violence come from Israel and its supporters in the United States. Observers agree that since Israel was founded it enjoyed extraordinarily good treatment in the news and entertainment media, to the obvious disadvantage of the Arabs. In recent years, Arabs got better treatment, and the media turned away from showing Israel in romantic terms. Israel's high-technology military machine, superior to that of any Middle East nation, caused the media to cease portraying Israel as David vs. the Arab Goliath.

With all those TV crews in Beirut and Israel, it wasn't surprising that this invasion was seen on our TV screens for months. After all, an invasion is an invasion, and Israel's relentless bombing of Palestinian camps and Beirut neighborhoods, with the inevitable shots of wounded children and stunned elderly people staggering around—well, that's TV footage.

True, only a fraction of similar mayhem was shown a few years back when PLO and leftist forces fought Phalangists in a quite violent civil war which took upwards of 60,000 lives. Nor was there much television footage of the casualties and destruction resulting from Israel's bombing attacks on Palestinian camps and of Beirut itself, in the period of years before last June's invasion.

Television cameras had access to this earlier violence, but news editors in New York expressed only occasional interest in coverage. During this 1975–1982 period, the PLO learned how to cultivate the media, so when Israel invaded, the cameras were ready, Israel's censorship of the invasion in its early stages only heightened the interest of TV correspondents to get the story.

But Israel's press and public is fiercely protective of its freedom, and these tactics backfired, particularly when the massacre story broke. People in a free society expect their media to show what their government and military are up to. The media can't be stifled.

The American media correctly react to their news instincts about the deportment of nations using the lethal power of American-supplied weapons. Our media are right to show what both sides are doing in El Salvador. They should show more of the violence on the West Bank where rock-throwing Arab students have been killed—a score this year by last count—by Israeli soldiers.

Had there only been television cameras to penetrate and expose the persecution of Jews and other "enemies" of the state in the first years of Hitler's Nazi Germany, before he got a head start on the greatest human tragedy of this century, the cruelty may not have taken place. I am glad that TV cameras show the brutality of the Communist regime in Poland toward Solidarity.

We should televise more of the violence inflicted by nations and armies, not less. My hunch is that in a world loaded down with enormous quantities of conventional and highly sophisticated weapons—many supplied by the United States—television has been a force to reduce slaughter, and perhaps has given many poor souls a chance to live a few more precious years.

36 In Defense of Casualty Pictures on TV

by Ellen Goodman

> Ellen Goodman says there is some therapeutic value to the blood and gore of war on television. She agrees with Nick Thimmesch that war on television may be our greatest hope for ending war altogether. Goodman is a nationally syndicated columnist working in Boston. This article is reprinted from the *Boston Globe*, September 14, 1982.

Now that the heavy fighting in Beirut is over and the PLO has been shipped off to live in assorted nations, I am left with one lingering image of this war. No, for once, it's not an image I saw on television. It's an image I saw *of* television.

In my lifetime, I've watched a lot of wars in prime time. Usually there are good guys and bad guys. Usually, those wars are resolved before the commercial.

But in the news, it's different. In the news, wars go on and on. In the news, we see less glory and more gore. In the news, the sides are not divided into good guys and bad guys, but aggressors and victims.

It was true in Vietnam, it was true in Iran and Iraq, Afghanistan and El Salvador, and now in Lebanon. We beam home the pictures of the wounded, the innocent bystanders, the casualties. And the war lovers don't like that.

Ever since Vietnam, we've heard complaints that television news was somehow biased. There were angry accusations that the nightly news fomented the protest movement in the '70s. Now we hear that the camera, simply by filming the uprooted of Beirut, the refuse of war, made a statement against the Israeli artillery.

There were suggestions that it wasn't quite cricket to offer up "features" on the effects of the war on a family, a street, a building, a neighborhood. I even heard that there was something unfair about "human interest" stories on the wounded of the militarized zone, stories giving them names and faces and titles: aunt, son, father.

Well, I agree that television is biased. To the degree that TV does its job well, tells us the facts of life in a conflict, it is intrinsically anti-war.

It's anti-war because the average person sitting in the living room responds to another human being. However immunized by years of war movies, we know, as Eliot said in "E.T.": "This is reality." War may be impersonal. But introduce us to a single person, tell us what she thinks, tell us what he feels, tell us what happened to his or her life—and we will care. It is our saving grace.

In our war-sophisticated world, we have learned that before we can kill people, we have to dehumanize them. They are no longer human beings but gooks or kikes or animals. The Japanese who experimented on human guinea pigs in World War II called them "maruta": logs of wood.

It is even easier when we lob missiles from an invisible distance or drop bombs from 15,000 feet at "targets." It's more like an Atari game than a murder. Conversely, the more we humanize people, the more we personalize war, the harder it is to commit.

Our ability to make war impersonal is scariest when we think of nuclear war games. Some years ago, Roger Fisher, a Harvard Law School professor, made a radical proposal for bringing nuclear war home to the man who could actually wage it. We would implant the code needed to fire the first missiles in a capsule near the heart of a volunteer. The president would have to kill one human being before he could kill millions.

"I made the suggestion," says Fisher now, "to demonstrate the difference between the abstract question of saying that I am prepared to kill 20 million people in the defense of freedom and the personal human question saying I am prepared to kill somebody I know, in order to do this.

"There's a difference between saying, we'll exercise Plan A, Option 6B and saying, 'Uh, George, I'm afraid I have to kill you in order to exercise the nuclear option. Shall we do it right here on the White House carpet or in the bathroom?' It brings home what it's about."

In conventional warfare, television does the same sort of thing. It brings home what war is all about: killing, wounding, destroying. It doesn't film ideals, but realities. TV isn't in the war room or the computer room, but the hospital room.

This is not unabashed praise of TV. There are enormous risks in slanted war coverage. It's easy to make yesterday's villain into today's victim. It's easy to portray self-defense as aggression, and be manipulated into sympathy for terrorists.

But if we can't solve problems by confrontations that are resolved before the commercial, if war usually produces victims, not answers, then we have to see this in human terms and witness the personal edge of devastation.

There are people who worry that humanizing war will undermine our resolve to wage it. I say, that is our greatest hope.

War, the Military and the Media: For Further Reading

Michael J. Arlen, *Livingroom War*. New York: Viking Press and Tower Publications, 1969.

James Aronson, *The Press and the Cold War*. Boston: Beacon Press, 1970.

Peter Braestrup, *Big Story: How the American Press and Television Reported and Interpreted the Crisis of TET in 1968 in Vietnam and Washington*. Boulder, Colo.: Westview Press, 1977.

Gladys D. Ganley and Oswald H. Ganley, *Unexpected War in the Information Age: Communications and Information in the Falklands Conflict*. Cambridge, Mass.: Center for Information Policy, Harvard University, 1984.

David M. Johnson, *Korean Airlines Incident: U.S. Intelligence Disclosure*. Cambridge, Mass.: Center for Information Policy, Harvard University, 1984.

X

Mass Media and Nationalism

One of the most interesting new issues of mass media is also one of the oldest: the role of the media in furthering national causes. In many societies, of course, the media are part of the government's operations, so their obligation to spread the party line, support the government's policies, or inspire the patriotism and loyalty of its citizens goes without question.

In a growing number of societies where the press is supposed to be privately owned and (relatively) free, there are increased instances of the press being forced to knuckle under to the demands of government. This is true of most postcolonial Third World societies, which inherited notions of a free press from their colonial masters but have now found it necessary to shackle the press to preserve their powers from threats on all sides. It is true of societies such as South Africa's and Costa Rica's, for example, as well as other countries where the press has been either controlled or restricted to protect the status quo.

At the same time, other countries have discovered that they can manipulate American mass media to further their own ends. Many countries now employ American public relations firms to put their best face in front of American audiences through the media. Sometimes, as in the late Anwar as-Sadat's Egypt, the media are willing victims. In other cases, as in Mikhail S. Gorbachev's Soviet Union, the media seem to be easily used in spite of themselves.

There is also the problem of "media imperialism," wherein American mass media, eagerly sought by audiences worldwide, is regarded as cultural infiltration by American ideals and mores.

American TV shows such as "Dallas," "Dynasty," "Miami Vice," and "The Cosby Show" are popular throughout the world, but they carry along with them American materialism, violence, and obsession with affluence. Many countries have rebelled against the importation of such American values via American mass media.

And finally, we have the problem of the American media becoming involved in the politics of other countries. Reporting on the events in foreign countries is regarded as the right and privilege of the American media as much as reporting on events in their own country is. But in many countries, such reporting is regarded as interference. Good cases in point in the 1980s are media reports from the Philippines and Central America.

Indeed, the whole relationship between nationalism and international media communication is a subject that will be of increased interest to all serious students of the impact of mass media.

37 Eyeball-to-Eyeball with the Big Red PR Machine

by David M. Rubin

Other countries have learned that they can influence American foreign policy by using public relations techniques to get their point of view expressed in American media. The arms negotiations between the United States and the Soviet Union is a good example, and the Soviets have demonstrated in the 1980s that they understand how to manipulate American media in those discussions for their benefit. David M. Rubin is a professor of journalism at New York University and director of the university's Center for War, Peace and the New Media. This article was first printed in *The Quill*, February 1986.

> *Madison Avenue Comes to Moscow—*
> *Terence Smith, CBS News*

> *The slick public relations man...Georgi Arbatov...wise to American ways and American vernacular—*
> *Robert Healy, The Boston Globe*

> *Soviets Grab PR Advantage—*
> *The Dallas Morning News*

Who would have guessed that just as President Reagan was about to grasp the hand of Soviet leader Mikhail Gorbachev in Geneva last November, another "gap" would open wide to challenge renewed American strength? And in public relations, no less, the very battlefield beneath which the president has buried all domestic opponents for nearly two decades?

The Soviet PR offensive became one of the major stories of Summit I, and the American press corps was quick to outline the Soviet plan of attack. Platoons of articulate, English-speaking briefers, trained at some Moscow version of Hill and Knowlton, were popping up on every network and local news program to preach the Soviet gospel.

The Soviet spokesmen were available to print journalists at all hours, alone or in bunches. Armed with a megaton of position papers, they were poised to overrun European and American positions and sweep to victory in the skirmish for favorable Western public opinion.

No less an expert at media manipulation than David Gergen, the former White House communications director and now an editor for *U.S. News & World Report*, revealed to the *CBS Morning News* audience on November 20 that the United States was losing the war of words. "The Soviet propaganda effort is going to continue, and continue very skillfully," he said.

The London *Sun* was sufficiently alarmed by Gorbachev and the new strategy to warn its readers on November 18: "Don't Be Fooled By This Commie Smoothie."

Yet on this side of the Atlantic, something was clearly being lost in the translation; in truth, chief Soviet lobbyist Georgi Arbatov hardly resembled a Red-tinged Edward Bernays. How could Arbatov expect to profit, for example, by ridiculing at a press conference the acting ability and mental capacity of the popular American president?

What Soviet image-maker thought Gorbachev would be convincing if he said there was no problem for Jews in the Soviet Union (an issue he should have known was high on the agenda of American journalists)?

And how slick was it of Foreign Ministry spokesman Vladimir Lomeiko to answer a question about Soviet dissident Anatoly Shcharansky by lecturing reporters to "take care not to violate ethics and put questions of this kind"?

Did journalists actually think this Soviet Marx brothers act was capturing the *Dynasty* crowd back home? Did they believe images of the Soviet Union built up after five years of Evil Empire rhetoric and 40 years of nuclear confrontation would fade in a trice?

To ask the question is to answer it; American journalists are hardly naive about public relations campaigns. A more likely explanation is that by hyping the PR value of the novel Soviet information offensive, the American press corps was revealing its own discomfort in dealing with the Soviets as sources.

The rules of the game in reporting the views of a Schultz or a McFarlane are widely accepted. Everyone is on the same team. Anonymity is OK. A pattern of lying is not acceptable. There are rarely dangerous hidden agendas—only legitimate disputes over policy. If administration sources are quoted accurately, journalists don't expect to be burned.

But Soviet spokesmen are another matter. Leonid Zamyatin's International Information Department may be just the overt tip of a larger Soviet disinformation effort; Arbatov's research institute could be a KGB front. Some of what the Soviets say is undoubtedly true, some is false, but all of it is designed to befuddle the West. What's a reporter to do?

American journalists in Geneva responded to this tension in a variety of ways. The most popular tactic (the Dan Rather approach, although he was hardly alone) was to defuse the Soviet PR effort by labeling it as such.

As any public relations practitioner will testify, the successful PR campaign is one in which the public is not aware of an unseen source moving the reporter's pencil or lips. Once the audience has been taken behind the scenes to witness the mechanics of the manipulation, the game is over.

Reporters are usually content to let such manipulation take place because they recognize that journalism could not survive without PR people stoking the information furnace.

But public relations is still defined pejoratively in most journalists' lexicons. Thus the surest way to demolish an information campaign is to call attention to it. Journalists do this all the time to ham-handed politicians on the stump as well as to polluting companies.

This time they did it to the Soviets. The audience could hardly have missed the point: We *know* this is PR, and now you know it, too. We're passing their line along because it is unusual that the Soviets talk at all, and because we have a newshole to fill. But be warned.

A second approach was to present the Soviet spokesmen as props rather than as real sources. This served to communicate that the Soviets were talking to the Western press, without having to actually report much of what they said. A model for this sort of story aired on ABC the evening of November 11. Brief video clips of two Soviet spokesmen were shown. The viewer could see they were talking, but it was impossible to make sense of what they were saying. The story was only that the Soviets were in Geneva—talking.

The print equivalent of this was a *New York Daily News* story of November 18 by Barbara Rehm. Her lead set the tone: "The line of five old men looked for all the world like the dour row of Kremlin leaders that normally stands atop Lenin's Tomb at state ceremonies in Moscow—but this lineup marked an unprecedented break with the gray Soviet style."

Rehm provided not a word in the rest of the piece about what any of the men said. Fully half of the article was devoted to how their press conference was disrupted by the dissident "journalist" Irina Grivnina, a human rights activist who fought her own Cold War in Geneva.

A third approach was to limit the Soviet spokesmen to two subjects: Their reaction to President Reagan's Strategic Defense Initiative and their thoughts on human rights violations in the Soviet Union, particularly the fate of Soviet Jews.

To the credit of the press, Soviet positions on these two issues could not have been made clearer to the American audience. But given the news blackout on the main event, it was disappointing that the journalistic mob did not smoke out Soviet positions on more issues.

Former Reagan aide Michael Deaver, who now runs a public relations firm in Washington, said on the November 20 *CBS Morning News*, "It's refreshing to see the Soviets adopting a Western style approach. Maybe we'll learn a little more about them."

In their eagerness to show the Soviet PR effort for what it was, however, the press did not often fulfill Deaver's hope that the American audience "might learn something" about the Russians. The war in Afghanistan is a good example.

Over the last six years, the American press has been boxed about the ears for its sporadic coverage of that war. Critics compare the journalistic silence in which the Soviets operate with the blanket press coverage afforded the American war in Vietnam.

In Geneva various Soviet officials, including Arbatov, discussed Afghanistan with reporters and indicated a Soviet desire to find some way out. In hindsight it now seems possible that Afghanistan was one of the few areas of genuine diplomatic movement at the summit. (In his *New York Times Magazine* article of December 8 wrapping up the summit, for example, Hedrick Smith placed Afghanistan in the second paragraph.) The Soviets thus provided the perfect opportunity for the Western press to turn the spotlight on their behavior.

The Washington Post did present the Soviet position in some detail in an article by Gary Lee on November 18, and followed it four days later with American reaction as reported by Don Oberdorfer. *The Washington Times* provided another view in quoting Evgueny Primakov in a November 18 piece. Primakov charged that U.S. advisers were urging the Afghans to commit atrocities against Soviet soldiers.

This degree of attention to Afghanistan was unusual, however. Typically the press mentioned the possible Soviet military and diplomatic discomfort only fleetingly. *Time* gave it one paragraph in its lengthy summit roundup, less than a third the space devoted to the goldfish President Reagan was supposed to feed at his *Maison de Saussure* residence. *U.S. News & World Report* provided three paragraphs, *Newsweek* even less.

The New York Times did not catch up with the *Post* until after the summit. Then, on November 25, a story with no byline appeared on page 8 quoting unnamed Reagan administration officials as predicting that the Soviets might be on the verge of "offering a timetable for a phased withdrawal of its 100,000 troops," surely a story that would have merited front page attention had it been the American government making the offer in Vietnam.

The *Times*'s Flora Lewis contributed an eye-catching column on November 29 describing Soviet concern that their presence in Afghanistan was inflaming fundamentalist Moslems and Afghan refugees. This might pose a threat, the Soviets feared, to the stability of their own Moslem population.

In addition, wrote Lewis, the Soviet image in the Third World was being damaged by the war, and it was "an obstacle in Moscow's search for better relations with China." Might not this information have come out when the Soviets were on the griddle in Geneva, with public attention as focused as it is ever likely to be on this subject?

On the evening of November 20, ABC aired a canned report by Don Kladstrup, who had been on special assignment in Afghanistan, summarizing the Soviet military position in the war. But the network let slip the opportunity to flesh it out with diplomatic developments at the summit.

Similarly, CBS reported on the 19th that the Soviets had introduced napalm into the Afghanistan fighting, without providing at the same time special attention to the Soviet line in Geneva and the possibilities of a shift in policy.

The reluctance of the journalists to forget the Big Red PR Machine and just "learn something," as Deaver urged, permitted Soviet positions on Afghanistan (and intermediate-range missiles in Europe, to cite another subject) to go largely unexplored, despite the enormous newsholes to fill.

The press was committed to an agenda of "atmospherics" surrounding the Reagan-Gorbachev chat, SDI and human rights. Information being supplied by Soviet briefers on other subjects was dismissed as rehashes of the party line. This avoided, for the time being, the touchy problem of how to deal with Soviet sources across a range of issues.

(It is worth noting that the Right has already labeled the Soviet line on Afghanistan in Geneva as "disinformation." Robert Moss, the editor of an intelligence newsletter and a spy novelist, wrote in *The Wall Street Journal* on December 9 that Gorbachev's desire to withdraw Soviet troops from Afghanistan was "[A] recent example of the disinformation mill at work. . . .")

If the Soviets come to the projected Summit II in the United States with their open-mouths policy still in effect, American journalists will have a harder time dismissing it as the old Soviet PR game. If Georgi Arbatov is not George Shultz—then who or what is he?

Should Soviet sources routinely be accorded the convention of anonymity? How aggressively should they be questioned? Does the American audience deserve special cues that information from Soviets may be *dis*? Or are journalists better off trying to ignore the mirrors-within-mirrors theories of the disinformation professionals?

The core of the problem is the same for journalists as for the two leaders themselves: how can I really trust you?

Before the manipulation of the press begins in earnest as a buildup to Summit II, journalists might want to consider what the public needs to know to make sense of this next round—rather than what the Arbatovs and Weinbergers want them to know.

Three questions emerged from the torrent of summit coverage as significant and enduring; the answers to these questions will necessarily shape one's view of the arms control process.

The first is the alleged Soviet cheating on arms control agreements and the methods of verification available to both sides. Clearly the American public believes the Soviets cheat. A *Wall Street Journal*/NBC poll published just after the summit revealed that only 32 percent of those polled expect the Soviets to honor any arms control agreement. The leak of Caspar Weinberger's let's-take-a-hard-line letter to the president just before the summit was only a last-minute exclamation point to the record of Soviet cheating.

But is there more to be said? How certain are we that the Soviet measures complained of are examples of cheating, as opposed to actions based on differing interpretations of the governing treaties? Why would the Soviets cheat if they know we know they are doing it? How does that serve their interests (since they persumably act in their own best interests)? Does the United States cheat (at least in Soviet eyes)? What loopholes or ambiguities does the United States exploit? What is the overall record of the Soviets in adhering to signed agreements, in nuclear and non-nuclear settings?

Michael Gordon of *The New York Times* expanded the debate on this issue in a November 24 article headlined "U.S. Says Soviet Complies on Some Arms Issues." He described the possible removal of some Soviet missiles from a specific test site, and he provided various interpretations of the strategic significance of this activity.

Another article in the *Times* that day linked the verification issue with the sudden switch in strategy by the Reagan administration in its stance toward small, mobile missiles. The article traced the debate over the effectiveness of verification and the problems such mobile missiles create in detection, both for the United States and the Soviets.

Such pieces are a more valuable public service than the numbing repetitions of the simplicities and half-truths uttered by the secretary of defense (not that his views shouldn't be reported for the record).

A second issue worth more reporting is the extent of the Soviet space-based anti-missile effort. President Reagan first justified his Strategic Defense Initiative as the moral thing to do—switching from an offensive to a defensive strategy. But lately some of the old "missile gap" psychology has been creeping in. The United States, goes that line of reasoning, is working on an SDI system because the Soviets have been working on their own, and we can't risk falling behind. Therefore, what the Soviets are doing—and have done—has become important.

Various members of the Soviet road show in Geneva were pressed on this, but, from this news consumer's perspective, the question is still very much open.

Either the Soviets are or aren't doing this research. If they are, they've been at it for a short time or a long time. Their intention is to develop ground-based local defenses only, or they plan a system just as grandiose as the layered system Reagan envisions.

One of the best articles to come out of Geneva on the Star Wars business was by Robert Toth of the *Los Angeles Times* on November 18. Toth contrasted the statements of Soviet scientist Yevgeny Velikov (that the Soviets were not developing, deploying or testing space weapons) with the views of Gen. Nikolai Tchervov, a spokesman for the Soviet Defense Ministry, who said that the Soviets do indeed have lasers. But they are not, according to Techervov, space weapons, though they "are used for experiments and tests, to locate and detect [satellites] orbiting in our direction."

Toth noted for the reader that the difference seems to be in the stated intent of each country on the use to which the lasers will be put. Toth went a long way toward explaining why one might want to look skeptically at Velikov's denials, which were often allowed to stand unchallenged in brief TV interviews by journalists unfamiliar with the details.

Special praise is also due *Newsweek* for a three-page section in the summit roundup ("What's Next for Star Wars") that presented information on the European view of SDI and the accomplishments of the Soviets in this research. More, please.

Finally, as Summit II approaches, the press should focus on what the Reagan administration's arms control plan is. Leslie Gelb of *The New York Times*, Walter Pincus of *The Washington Post*, and a handful of other specialists noted the tensions in the administration before Geneva, but such information was overwhelmed by the relatively trivial question of whether Reagan or Gorbachev was winning the pre-summit PR war. Now that Robert McFarlane has been replaced by a new national security adviser, John Poindexter, who may have some ideas of his own to contribute, close attention from the press to the next game plan would be welcome.

A press corps 3,000 strong doesn't usually get the chance to cover the same event a second time. Thoughtfully, Reagan and Gorbachev have promised two more exercises in summit journalism. At Summit II, journalists as well as political leaders will be pressed to cut through the PR and get down to substance.

38 The Television Pharaoh

by Doreen Kays

American television made Egypt's late President Anwar as-Sadat a hero in America and a villain in his own land, says Doreen Kays. In this case, the media were caught in their own frozen patterns of what they considered news, and the Egyptian leader was a strange beneficiary/victim in the process. Kays was ABC News bureau chief in Cairo from 1977 to 1981. This article, printed in *The Quill*, May 1985, is excerpted from her book *Frogs and Scorpions: Egypt, Sadat, and the Media.*

Egypt's President Anwar Sadat, deciding he had had enough of war, announced he was flying to the "ends of the earth" in search of peace. The Arab leader's flight—a half-hour's journey away—would change the course of Middle Eastern history and nothing ever would be quite the same again.

Except, of course, the Middle East.

It was the classic Middle East story, and much more. It was Greek tragedy and American soap opera. And midway through it, I unashamedly longed for a good old-fashioned war; anything to end the agony of peace, and the media hysteria that seemed to have taken over everyone involved in this phenomenal piece of political theatre. The peace story whose beginning and end shook the world was also one—in this satellite age—which began and ended on America's nightly news. It was a prime-time "made for TV" drama, written and directed by its star performer and produced and sponsored by CBS, NBC, and ABC.

This drama had it all: war and peace; Arabs and Israelis; heroes and villains; power and politics; struggle and sacrifice; courage and cowardice; hope and despair; death and destruction. The audience, unfortunately, never got to see the whole show. It never does, given the nature of television news. Regular TV programming was interrupted four times during the story's four-year run: Sadat's peace mission to Israel in November 1977; the Camp David peace accords in September 1978; the signing of the peace treaty in March 1979; and the assassination and burial of President Sadat in October 1981. Between these historic events, the audience made do with dribs and drabs—highlights conveyed in one-minute, thirty-second spurts, "spots" or "pieces" as they're so aptly called in the TV trade.

From the feedback I was able to accumulate from both sides of the screen, on both sides of the Atlantic, ABC's news coverage of the peace story was exemplary, which translated means ABC acquitted itself rather well by more often than not cleanly beating its two chief competitors, CBS and NBC. Having been intimately involved with the story, I never had any doubt that what we did we did respectably well, by TV standards. It's what we did *not* do that disturbed me then, disturbs me now, and should disturb the majority of Americans who, according to polls of the past decade, get most if not all their news from television. This frightening statistic says as much about the power of television news in today's America as it does about the underinformed and/or uninterested masses. That TV news managers and producers traditionally complain about the difficulty of selling foreign news to the viewing public helps explain why so often it is sold in drag— dressed up in show-biz razzmatazz, sometimes beyond recognition or meaning.

The Sadat peace story, like so many events of international impact and consequence, fell victim to the paradox of TV news: media overkill on the one hand; one-dimensional images on the other.

In the version that ran for four years on American TV, the protagonist was Anwar Sadat, Egypt's magnanimous president for eleven years: a leader who did what no other Arab dared; a brave, courageous, charismatic, charming, handsome hero who won the Nobel Peace Prize and the attention of much of the world; a maverick who preached "no more war," single handedly demolished the stereotype of the Arab bad guy, and helped crack the psychological barriers between Arab and Jew. The man Henry Kissinger called "the greatest statesman since Bismarck" was assassinated by four young Egyptian Moslem fanatics. Millions mourned his death.

In the version never shown on American TV, the story's protagonist was also Anwar Sadat, Egypt's autocratic president for eleven years: an opportunist who signed a peace treaty with Israel in return for his beloved Sinai; a traitor who failed to end the Arab-Israeli conflict and did not bring peace to the Middle East; a megalomaniac who in his desire to forge a favorable imprint on history silenced his opponents and critics at home, alienated his country's finest intellects, isolated himself from his fellow Arabs, and neglected the economic and social welfare of his poverty-stricken people. A latter-day pharaoh in the mould of Ramses II, he sought peace at any price and died in a hail of bullets fired by four religious zealots from his own army. Few Egyptians and fewer Arabs wept at his death, for Sadat did not inspire the same love at home that he did abroad.

Both versions are accurate.

As 1977 ended and 1978 began, Anwar Sadat was an entrenched media celebrity, the darling of the Western world and America's newest hero, the first since Neil Armstrong went to the moon and back eight years earlier. When certain of his fans equated his "ends of the earth" journey to Israel with the first landing on the moon, Sadat did not disagree, such was the degree to which his ego was being massaged daily under a halo of fame and glory. A jestful Golda Meir aside, the Egyptian president was nominated for the Nobel Peace Prize, not the Oscar. In any event, Hollywood could not give him the exposure he was getting through the news media.

Time magazine cast Sadat as its "Man of the Year" for 1977, complete with a color cover portrait and a twenty-two page spread that included an article titled, "Actor with an Iron Will: An Intimate Look at the Villager Who Became a Ruler." But it was not this article or any other in the newsweekly's expansive tribute to an extraordinary man that provided an intimate look at Anwar Sadat. It was a picture, a photograph, that better captured, I felt, the essence of the man around whom my life now revolved. The color photograph was aesthetically stunning—and politically disturbing. There before the great pyramids of Giza, silhouetted against an azure-blue sky, stood a handsome, bronze-faced, pin-striped figure, black-booted feet firmly planted on the desert floor, gazing imperially into the unknown. This monumental figure totally overwhelmed those of ancient Egypt. It was a theatrically sublime image of a modern-day pharaoh played to perfection by Anwar Sadat. But this was not an actor playing the role of Pharaoh. It was a pharaoh playing the role of actor. That prophetic picture haunts me to this day.

I looked forward [after more than three years of being a virtual extension of Sadat's image] to meeting myself again. No more Cairo persona; no more bureau chief/correspondent; no more ugly mask. I dumped them overboard.

One month and $30,000 in moving expenses later, I was happily installed in the Paris bureau's sunny kitchen, a pleasant enough place to work except at lunch hour. Either the bureau had not anticipated my arrival, hoped I wouldn't show up, had no room for a third correspondent, or was flat out of funds. In any case I was without desk or typewriter, which given the beat designated to me by the bureau chief—fashion shows and Third World contacts—did not cause me to panic. My ambitions fell somewhat short of "*haute couture* correspondent"; as for the Third World, in this case Africa: It does not exist for American TV news except on days when the earth moves under it and the tremors are felt in New York or Washington— an event adequately covered by any "fireman" correspondent in the usual hit-and-run in-depth sixty-second backgrounder on the evening show.

Besides, I had other things on my mind, some unfinished business to attend to in the Middle East, and the individual best able to help just happened to be in town: ABC News executive Av Westin—the same Av Westin who more than three years earlier had sent me to Cairo and would subsequently proclaim that I "owned the story." No one was in a better position to buy or to reject my untold tale. Formerly executive producer of the evening news, Westin was now executive producer of the weekly magazine show *20/20* and ABC News's vice president for program development. That he was generally accessible and responsive to correspondents' ideas and proposals made him an especially attractive target of frustrated foreign correspondents whose isolation deprived them of the substantive give and take of the New York-based decision-making process.

Over a leisurely dinner, I exploited Westin's patience and interest by compressing a three-year experience into a four-hour, impassioned monologue on the current state of Egypt and its pharaoh-king and the threats facing both; a portrait clearly at variance with popular American perceptions as created, conveyed, and perpetuated by the media, especially television. I proposed an hour-long documentary exposing the paradox of Anwar Sadat, whose policies and style—foreign and domestic—had made him a hero in the West and a villain at home. In short, a candid, unvarnished, balanced look at Sadat and his Egypt; a multi-dimensional image of reality in which the voices of opposition and sources of discontent could be publicly aired through the medium most cherished by Sadat himself—American network television. How and why Egypt was smothering to death politically and economically; how and why despair had replaced the early hope and euphoria of peace; how and why Sadat had turned from benign dictator to dangerous despot; what this explosive situation meant for the future of Sadat, Egypt, peace, the Middle East, and U.S. interests in the region—this was my subject.

"Can you get the opposition to talk, on camera?" asked Westin.

"Yes, I think I can—a handful of his more vocal critics are ready to come out in the open, despite the repressive climate and inherent dangers."

"Can examples of corruption be documented?"

I confessed that this was more problematic, particularly with regard to the free-floating allegations against Mrs. Sadat, Sadat's inner circle, fringe family, and the ruling élite. People at the top tend to cover their tracks rather well, especially in a closed society.

Overall, though, I felt the corruption issue could be handled within the context of the story, which I felt was solid enough to stand on its own.

Westin, consummate television man that he is, was naturally looking for the sexiest exposé angle. Nonetheless, he agreed that the situation in Egypt merited our attention and wholeheartedly supported the idea that I return to Cairo on a feasibility mission. Having understood why I could not stay in Cairo, he wisely dismissed the irony of my need to return on special assignment. If such a probing documentary should prove possible, Westin —aware of the risks involved in airing it—was prepared to jeopardize ABC's Cairo operation; if Sadat chose to shut down the bureau, so be it.

He wanted to discuss the story with the rest of the ABC brass and get back to me. I thanked him for his support and courage and, while awaiting official approval, flew off to London to cover the Old Bailey trial of the Yorkshire Ripper. After two weeks of staring at a maniac and listening to the graphic details of how he mutilated and murdered thirteen women and how he failed to murder seven more, I was pulled off the story by New York: lack of interest. America apparently had killers every bit as perverse and sensational as Peter Sutcliffe; *Good Morning America* managed to serve up the Ripper for breakfast one morning—hardly enough to justify the cost of a court artist and me.

Back in Paris, authorization finally came through to proceed to Cairo on my mission; a mission—finally—with a purpose, one to which I could give my undivided attention without the distractions of stakeouts and satellite transmissions. It was May 1981 by the time I arrived, and there to greet me was a delighted Hassan [the bureau's factotum]. During the drive to the Nile Hilton, I briefed him and we arranged to meet the following morning. I did not see Hassan again for ten days.

Five minutes after unpacking my bags—shortly after midnight—the foreign desk woke me up with the order to repack my bags for an early morning flight to Istanbul. The Pope had been shot, and his alleged assailant was a young Turk by the name of Mehmet Ali Agça.

* * *

By mid-July [of 1981], Sadat's problems had expanded to cover the constituency that more than any other had given him the stature of international greatness: the foreign media, especially the American media. He should not have been so naïve; he should have known that those who build false gods tend to destroy them sooner or later. Chris Harper, my successor in Cairo, did a one-and-a-half-minute TV spot in which he hinted at possible similarities between Sadat and the Shah, and Egypt and Iran. The following day the government threatened to strip him of his presidential credentials with a warning to desist from such negative reportage. This was accompanied by an article in *Al Ahram*—the semi-official Cairo daily—stating that ABC News's *Nightline* program was planning an unflattering portrait of Sadat and Egypt on the eve of Sadat's Washington summit with President Reagan. Informally, ABC was charged with trying to sabotage Sadat's grassroots support in America and taint his image with the new U.S. administration. There were even suggestions of a conspiracy, an ABC News–State Department plot, to finish off Sadat in the same way Washington disposed of the Shah once he had become a liability. Sadat, after all, lived with that fear daily. And even though he abhorred the free-wheeling "American school of journalism," he and some of his officials still seemed to assume that the free press took its orders from Washington and—no doubt—that we were all CIA agents.

The honeymoon between Sadat and the American media was at long last officially over.

With his rule under increasing attack at home, Sadat finally resorted to his true instincts: He overreacted. By threatening to silence a powerful news organ, by trying to dictate what it could and could not report about him, he helped create the very impression and image he sought to avoid: a man and his régime on the verge of collapse; at the very least a dictator whose paranoia now stretched to New York and Washington and back.

When ABC executives telephoned me in Paris with news of the Sadat threat, we agreed that the Cairo bureau should neither lie low through intimidation nor launch a charge of the light brigade. Our reaction should be reflexive: business as usual. It might not, however, be business as usual for me and my September assignment. Clearly it was in jeopardy. With time and Sadat now working against it, I desperately suggested a preëmptive measure to Westin: devote a portion of that week's 20/20 program to a roundtable discussion of Sadat, his troubles, his opposition, and his fears—real and imagined. Westin rejected the proposal, preferring to take the risk and time of a studied documentary.

Daily pampered then by American television at home and abroad and regularly reminded of his virtues during forays into the power palaces of Washington and the West, it is little wonder that Anwar Sadat believed he might be God. There were days in fact when I thought I was hallucinating, so palpable was the halo circling somewhere between Sadat's brow and crown. Those first sixteen months of media and public adoration literally went to the man's head. That was the beginning of the end.

From then on—from the signing of the peace treaty in Washington on March 26, 1979 to the horrific end—it was hard to believe Sadat was not working from a master plan for self-destruction. The majority of Egyptians had stuck with him along the rocky road to peace. They were still with him. So were the political and religious dissidents—a minority albeit an irritating one—with legitimate and persuasive arguments against what clearly appeared to be a separate peace with Israel negotiated against a backdrop of Israeli intractability and American impotence. Shackled by a pseudo-democracy that Sadat had instituted as a good-will gesture to America during his seven-year prelude to peace, the opposition nonetheless was making itself heard and felt. Yet, the troublemakers in and out of government—the squawking intelligentsia that in most countries attempts to play the role of a nation's intellectual, moral, and social conscience—hardly constituted a unified or viable opposition in Egypt, let alone a threat to the régime. Furthermore, there was no broad-based, grass-roots anti-Sadat movement, no anti-peace demonstrations, the media were controlled by Sadat, the Parliament stacked with his party supporters. Where was the threat? Those thirteen misguided missiles in Parliament who voted "No" to the treaty? Those powerless Egyptian scribes like the Nasserist, Mohamed Heikal, voicing doubts and attacking Sadat's domestic and foreign policies in *The Sunday Times* and other Western publications? Those ex-foreign ministers living out their memoirs on the cocktail circuit? Hardly—Sadat's critics were simply an embarrassment, an affront to his glorified sense of self. Who were these mere Egyptians to criticize him when all the world sanctified him and his peace?

Interpreting criticism as threat, the egocentric Sadat set about dissolving the very Parliament that had overwhelmingly endorsed his peace treaty; rigging the national referendum on the treaty when it was in no need of his ritual tampering; banning all public debate on the treaty during the campaign to elect a new Parliament; rigging those elections to ensure that the thirteen MPs who voted "No" would never sit in his Parliament again (twelve never did); preventing other candidates opposed to him or his policies from running for office; and eliminating the small official opposition parties of the left and right, replacing them with his own official opposition party—of which he was also nominal head. In his little experiment with democracy, what he gave with one hand he took away with both.

Whatever political freedom of expression existed before the peace treaty was further curtailed. With one swift blow, Sadat emasculated Parliament—a move that amounted to a vote of no confidence in the Egyptian people. And the people didn't like it. The Pharaoh, it seemed, could not be criticized. Nor his family, his peace, his economy, nor the corruption and vested interests that made it run in circles. If you were not with the Pharaoh, you were agin'him, no ifs, ands, or buts. His worst enemies could not have done a better job of eroding Sadat's public support.

His new friends didn't help. The Israelis no longer bothered camouflaging their nefarious intentions concerning the Camp David Accord dealing with the Palestinians. The negotiations for "autonomy"—the only thing that might have allowed Sadat a modicum of face-saving with his Egyptian and Arab critics—were conducted against a background of regularly proscribed "facts on the ground" in the occupied West Bank: Jewish settlements built as fast as public land could be cleared and Arab land confiscated. That the minister responsible for these bouts of provocation, Ariel Sharon, was dubbed the "Bulldozer" by some of his own people was of little comfort to a cornered Sadat and Egypt. That the United States seemed neither willing nor able to force Israel to halt the *faits accomplis*; that the *de facto* annexation of the West Bank and East (Arab) Jerusalem, and Israel's first invasion of Lebanon, were carried out while the autonomy talks were under way, not only humiliated Sadat but made him look the fool and traitor his detractors were convinced he was. Yet he took it, took the humiliation lying down, which in turn rankled and humiliated the Egyptian people. It was one thing to have signed a treaty with Israel, quite another to have one's nose daily rubbed with what was not signed. Each time Sadat was reminded of Menachem Begin's fanatic ideology—a combination of Bible and bomb—he turned the other check (for the sake of Sinai) or, worse, responded with a double dose of Egyptian goodwill, like his offer to give away the precious waters of the Nile. Sadat's every ingratiating gesture infuriated many Egyptians, leading some to wonder, if only facetiously, whether their leader was prepared to go so far as to give away Egypt in return for the Sinai.

Summits such as the one in Haifa in the summer of 1979 exacerbated Sadat's image [problem]. More and more, Egyptians came to perceive their president as a hostage of the Americans and the Israelis, which might have been tolerable were they themselves not being held hostage by his imperial presidency, whose democratic pretensions had them playing a child's game of hide-and-seek. There was no escape for the escapist's subjects.

Another facet of Anwar Sadat's excessiveness that contributed to his waning popularity at home was his bear-hug embrace of America, Americana, and the West in general; his cultural as well as political pretensions. Here Sadat became a caricature of himself: the Abe Lincoln of the Nile on a binge in Disneyland. Ironically, I don't think he ever made it to California or Florida. He didn't have to. With his daily diet of American movies, he could indulge in the American dream factory in his own living room. Mit Abul Kum, his native village so often shown on American TV, never had a chance.

Of all Arab countries, Egypt, for reasons of history and geography, seems forever destined to juggle her cultural duality, her oriental and occidental souls. The brilliant American-Lebanese Arabist, Fouad Ajami, sees this historic dilemma as a cultural tug-of-war, what he calls "the push of the desert, the pull of the Mediterranean." Abdel Nasser pushed toward the Arab-Muslim desert; Anwar Sadat pulled back towards the cosmopolitan West. In the nineteenth century, Mohammed Ali (1805–42) and Ismael (1863–79) also pulled Egypt westwards. Although he is compared to both rulers, Sadat most resembled Ismael in that his vision rather exceeded his grasp. Poor Ismael tried turning Cairo into a Paris, and might have succeeded had not Egypt gone bankrupt in the process. His Paris-on-the-Nile, alas, became Egypt under British occupation. Sadat's pull—no less spectacular—helped push *him* over the brink.

In exploiting Egypt's occidental soul, Sadat unfortunately turned a dialogue into an orgy, his orgy with the West. Worse, he forgot to invite the folks back home.

As one of those American-television reporters who daily encouraged his Western ego trip, his pilgrimage in search of identity, his escape from reality, I watched oriental Egypt sitting on the sidelines wondering what in the name of Ismael was going on. Where would it all end? This eternally servile dependence, this blind faith in foreigners? Yesterday the Russians. Today, the Americans. Tomorrow. . . . Whoa! Hold it! Not so much as fast, Egyptians seemed to be saying. But Sadat was too far gone, too distant to hear or listen or care. He talked, behaved, and dressed as though his wretched country were beneath him and the new company he kept, as though it were an embarrassment to his new, superior identity. Sadat's mistake was not in exploiting Egypt's Western soul but in exceeding it, abusing it. Poor Sadat. Lost in a fantasy. Poor Egypt. Shoved aside. In the end, victim once more to a leader's delusions of grandeur.

The Egyptian ruler's final miscalculation came that September day in 1981 when he arrested those hundreds of religious and political foes. That was his death warrant. He realized it too late. That was part of his tragedy.

That ultimately he was guilty of his own death hardly exonerates those of us who served as his unwitting accomplices, those of us who were his partners in peace, notably the United States, Israel, Menachem Begin, and American television news. We all blew it. We failed. We missed our cues. We helped kill the "hero of peace."

Covering the peace story was an immensely intense, rich experience. Indeed, it was great fun for a while—full of novelty, excitement, anticipation, hope, and history—and for that I am grateful both to Anwar Sadat and to ABC News. My one personal regret perhaps is in having performed my job too well: Life in the Middle East is dramatic and perilous enough without the superimposed theatrics of a Sadat or TV's showbusiness-journalism. But since the Middle East story has become a permanent part of our satellite-age lives, war and peace will be decided in America's daily battle of the ratings.

By the time my episode ended, my feelings toward Sadat had gone all the way from admiration and respect through disappointment, frustration, anger, relief, and, finally, sadness. That is what I feel today when I think of the man who, in the words of one Egyptian writer, "lived like an American president and, sadly, he died like one." On American television, Anwar Sadat's drama ended as it had begun.

This made-for-TV tragedy did not end, at least, without a touch of poetic justice: As an accessory to the crime, I was not to be spared the bloody end; having fled Sadat, Egypt, and the "mission" once, circumstances would force me back to witness the brutal last act. As an accomplice, I would be positioned in the direct line of the assassins' fire.

Spared the bullets, my fate, nonetheless, seemed inextricably tied to Anwar Sadat's. In the end, the story I had once "owned" came to own me: Two months after Sadat and the story were dead and buried, ABC News informed me that my usefulness had expired, that my contract would be terminated after six months.

So, I packed my bags—one final time—and left Cairo and the debris behind me. I took Anwar Sadat with me. I had no choice.

39 Islands in the Swirl of the Storm

by Tom Shales

American media have been increasingly criticized by other countries for their reporting, which has often caused trouble for those countries' governments, In some cases, American media have been accused of bringing about the fall of foreign governments. Some people suggested that American TV played a key role in the downfall of Ferdinand Marcos from the presidency of the Philippines. Tom Shales examines that possibility in this article from the *Washington Post*, for which he is TV critic. The article was published in the *Post* February 24, 1986, during the climax of the drama of the Marcos fall.

Dictators of the world take note: Clean up your acts, or risk a U.S. media invasion. That may be one of the lessons to be gleaned from ongoing television coverage of the increasingly explosive situation in the Philippines. President Ferdinand Marcos thought he could go on television and defeat it. Instead he became the star of a continuing saga that played like a real-life version of "Sins." He played the sinner.

Americans are all too familiar with the role that television plays in U.S. politics. With its obsessive—arguably excessive—coverage of the Philippines, network television has reasserted itself on a global scale. Filipino political fates have been played out in interview after interview on U.S. newscasts and discussion programs. Revolution, it appears, can now take the form of serialized talk show.

Late yesterday, with rumors that Marcos had fled the country, revolution began to take on a more classic profile.

The media stampede to the Philippines continues. Tom Brokaw and Peter Jennings went over for fact-finding missions on Election Day. Now video statesman Ted Koppel has arrived in full panoply for a series of "Nightline" reports that starts tonight, proving by his very presence that the networks mean business. And while he's there, for good measure he'll coanchor "World News Tonight" with Peter Jennings, who will be in Moscow to cover the Communist Party Congress. The long arm of the media beams in by bird and dish.

Thus did "This Week With David Brinkley" devote yet another show to the Philippines yesterday, a look at the turbulent aftermath of the recent elections. They couldn't get cameras into the Defense Ministry, now controlled by opposition rebels, Brinkley apologetically told viewers, so Defense Minister Juan Ponce Enrile and Lt. Gen. Fidel Ramos, who'd seized the ministry on Saturday, talked to Brinkley and fellow inquisitors by telephone. All three Sunday morning network shows devoted themselves to the Philippines and Marcos himself appeared on NBC's "Meet the Press." Sen. Richard G. Lugar (R-Ind.), who had traveled there as an official election observer, made the rounds; he was on every network. He's been seen during the coverage almost as much as Marcos, who gambled that making himself wildly accessible to American TV would do wonders for his image, but who always came off looking guilty. It was a public relations battle. He lost. So it goes in Video Village.

Blas Ople, an envoy from the Philippines, was interviewed in Washington during the Brinkley show yesterday and was asked if he had made progress in securing support for Marcos from within the Reagan administration. He said he'd only just arrived. First things first. First you go to the Brinkley show, *then* you go to the White House and Capitol Hill.

The story has come almost full circle on "Brinkley," since it was there that ABC News commentator George Will actually baited Marcos into having elections in the first place.

Will grilled Marcos via satellite last November; it was one of those put-up-or-shut-up challenges. Marcos put up, and certainly did not shut up. What followed was perhaps the first foreign election in history to be called up by an American television network. Such power they have!

William Randolph Hearst, often blamed for starting the Spanish-American War with his newspapers, would surely be bemused by the role American media have played in the Philippines this year. It's not as if the networks barged in; Marcos and his opposition have resolutely been a-wooing. The election itself seemed secondary to the image war they have been fighting on American TV.

Marcos has been as convenient as he has been accessible. He makes a perfect new bad guy for a long-running network news story. Locked out temporarily from covering violence in South Africa, the networks needed a new trouble spot, a new Moldavia, and it came with a new villain. Viewers probably resented Marcos as much for his omnipresence on TV as for his alleged abuses of power. The more he asserted his innocence, the guiltier he looked.

Marcos even became a character in comedy routines, ridiculed and lampooned not only in Johnny Carson's monologues but also in satirical gibes on "Saturday Night Live." Marcos bridged the comedy generation gap. Maybe the administration began to abandon Marcos and rethink its allegiances when it heard not only the disapproving reports on network newscasts, but also the jeering laughter on "The Tonight Show."

In his interviews—and he's been on everything but "PM Magazine"—

Marcos has generally seemed cavalier and unrepentant, playing the dissolute despot in what became a terribly tidy TV scenario. Marcos let himself appear to be the 1986 ayatollah.

To watch the continuing coverage of the Philippines on TV has been to observe an Olympic-scale edition of the great media game Who's Using Whom? Such is life in a world that turns increasingly by the rules and rhythms of the almighty tube—*Realpolitik* à la "Fantasy Island."

Once the election wheels were set in motion, the campaign was played out on American TV as if Americans were going to be able to vote (perhaps via a 900 number phone-in poll?). Marcos and his opponent, Corazon Aquino, were roughly as available to the media as Democratic presidential hopefuls newly arrived in New Hampshire for a snowy primary.

Marcos looked bad, talked tough, conveyed corruption; Aquino maintained a relative dignity. U.S. policy began to turn. It didn't look good to be allied with this nasty little man on TV.

We certainly never got a huge bonanza of information on the fall of Somoza in Nicaragua, a country possibly of more importance to U.S. interests than the Philippines, but then Somoza never tried to turn himself into a TV personality. His war was fought the old-fashioned way—in the field, with guns.

On Friday night, there was an unforeseen wrinkle in the ongoing Philippine saga. Network newscasters had to eat a plate of crow l'orange. It evolved that the death of an anti-Marcos newspaper publisher in California, which everyone had earlier in the week attributed to some sort of roving Marcos hit squad, was, said the police, not a politically motivated death at all. The murderer instead was alleged to be the man's own son, who had always, the networks reported, "hated" his father. Ah, well. Meanwhile, back in the Philippines...

Yesterday, there came from that country a picture to help justify all the bushels and bushels of words network anchors and correspondents have lavished on this story: images of Filipino citizens lying down in the path of oncoming tanks, expressing their defiance in a stunningly visual way, so much so that even the implacable Brinkley was impressed. For a moment, too, the balance of power appeared to shift, and the fate of the Philippines seemed more in the hands of the people there than in the hands of the American television networks.

Network coverage of the Philippines story hasn't really been a triumph of reporting. It isn't reporting to get news sources to come into a studio and make news on the air. It's the art of booking. Maybe every ongoing news event becomes a talk show eventually. The suspicion lingers that television covers most eagerly those stories that most tailor themselves to television, and that the Philippines came along just when the networks needed something new in the crisis-of-the-week line.

Perhaps in their newscasts the networks have investigated nuances of the situation in the Philippines, but what they stress are the simplistics and the graphic contrasts, the cartoonish bold strokes. Suddenly we are all terribly aware of the Philippines, but we don't fully know why.

A tone of moralistic smugness has run through some of the coverage, as if the networks were the new "Mission: Impossible" force, a liberating army in Burberry coats and lapel microphones to be cheered on arrival by oppressed citizenries everywhere.

We're all terribly Philippines-conscious now. But we're very likely not to be a month from now, when the fickle eye of the networks, having looked, moves on.

40 Separating Fact from Fantasy
Letter from Managua
by June Carolyn Erlick

Some people have called Nicaragua America's Vietnam, or potential Vietnam, of the 1980s. The media covering the war in Nicaragua have become a part of the story, writes June Carolyn Erlick, leaving Americans wondering whether they know the truth about what is going on. Erlick is a freelance foreign correspondent who has lived in Latin American for a dozen years. This article is reprinted from the *Columbia Journalism Review*, January/February 1987.

Jan Howard, a freelance radio reporter and director of Nicaragua's 118-member International Press Club, planned to attend the U.S. Embassy's festivities in Managua last July 4th. Instead, she found herself, muddy and exhausted, spending that night in a warehouse with two dozen other journalists—17 rivers and several funerals after her departure from Managua at the crack of dawn.

A mine had exploded on July 2, killing 32 civilians on the dirt road between El Cua and San José de Bocay in war-torn northern Nicaragua. When the official Sandinista radio station broadcast the news on July 3, Managua's resident journalist corps—which includes correspondents from the three major U.S. television networks, numerous wire services, radio networks, magazines and newspapers, as well as a legion of photographers —immediately began angling for a way to get there. After incessant calls from journalists, the Nicaraguan Defense Ministry—one of the most sophisticated about public relations in the Sandinista government—organized an Army-escorted 14-vehicle caravan to Bocay.

"It's a small, muddy town, and it was raining, and the whole town was there. Outside, all these coffins were waiting," Howard recalls. "I remember the smell. You couldn't get rid of it. I have three children, and when you see tiny children, two months old, six-months-old babies dead, when you see one that's the age of your own child, well, it's like I feel obligated [not to] cry...if I show tears, that's not being objective, but yet these are human beings. These are children. Anyone, no matter what opinion they had of the revolution or the government, would cry to see tiny dead babies lying next to their dead mothers.

"There was a continuous wailing," Howard says. "Journalists came in and filmed and photographed and the radio people got sound and then quickly the people started to put the bodies in the coffins." Most assumed the contras had planted the mines (earlier, freelance radio reporter Joan Kruckewitt and former *Washington Post* stringer Nancy Nusser had reported on contra mining in the north).

The people at Bocay "couldn't really understand anything about our jobs or why we're here," says Kruckewitt, who covered Bocay for ABC Radio. "There were a lot of people, a lot of cameras, all these foreigners, a side-show. The people were involved in their own grief."

Most of the journalists at Bocay, however, were not thinking about their relationship to the villagers. After a day of stench and wailing, they wanted to get back to Managua to file and bathe. But a new element has entered reporting in Nicaragua, one that has been present in El Salvador for a number of years: land mines. Although no journalist has been killed in Nicaragua since the Sandinistas overthrew Anastasio Somoza in 1979, Lieutenant June Mulligan, the half-American Nicaraguan Army public-relations director who organized the Bocay trip, was determined the first casualty would not occur on her watch. She told the reporters they had to spend the night in Bocay. When NBC's crew slipped out to try to get film back to Managua, she radioed the next village to have them intercepted, but was told they probably already had passed through unnoticed. The next morning, the Army-escorted journalists found the NBC van stuck in a river and the crew waiting on the riverbank. The van had to be dragged out by oxen.

In leaving Lieutenant Mulligan's care, the NBC crew risked more than getting stuck. Over the last year, the counter-revolutionaries have riddled northern Nicaragua with mines.

On the trip back to Managua, Kruckewitt says, "Every puddle that we went through, I was looking at that puddle, thinking, is there a mine below it? Is this going to be the last puddle I ever run over in my life?"

The night before, while NBC was making its abortive escape from the caravan, the other reporters and photographers sat around a smoky bar-shack in Bocay, drinking rum and pineapple juice by kerosene lamp and arguing among themselves. Had the Sandinistas, who claimed the U.S.-based contras had planted the mine at Bocay, told the villagers to wait to bury the bodies until the journalists arrived? Most, including Howard and Kruckewitt, argued that the bodies had been stored two days simply because it took that long to make two dozen coffins. But at least one U.S. network employee insisted that he had seen the coffins earlier on a truck, and that the bodies had been on display as a "tragic show" for the journalists.

In Nicaragua, fear of manipulation is profound, for both journalists and their sources. Nicaragua's respected Catholic bishops, for example, have not publicly condemned incidents such as that at Bocay because they fear their statements will be used by the local—and some of the international—press as an endorsement of the Sandinista government.

For the same reason, journalists had worried about the implications of accepting an Army escort to Bocay, but it seemed the only way to go. They also argued about whether they had been used by the Sandinistas to make a dramatic propaganda point.

"You constantly either run the risk of feeding the Sandinista propaganda machine, or the Washington propaganda machine," says one wire-service reporter.

Nicaragua has few neutral sources for reporters to bounce their information off. In Nicaragua, most people are vehemently pro-Sandinista, vehemently anti-Sandinista or just too afraid to talk. And there is the constant fear of manipulation.

Later in July, when *New York Times* Latin America correspondent Stephen Kinzer returned to Managua from a trip to the United States, he decided to write about the Bocay incident. He talked to diplomats in Managua, some of whom cast doubt on the Sandinistas' claim that the mine had been planted by the contras. Kinzer alternated quotes from those who thought it could be a contra mine and those who suspected the Sandinistas.

His story, which ran in the *Times* on July 11, was carefully qualified: "Neither diplomats who believed the Sandinista version nor those who doubted it could offer concrete evidence for their theories. They said their conclusions were based solely on speculation and deduction, and they agreed that the truth would be almost impossible to determine."

Kinzer's qualifications did not please Lieutenant Mulligan. "I just don't understand what possessed him to write a story like that," she said as she looked for Kinzer futilely at a July 19 press party. (Parties for the press are a way of life in Managua, given the lack of normal gathering places in the geographically dispersed, earthquake-wrecked city.)

Reporters and photographers—especially those who had experienced the smells and sounds of Bocay—and non-journalists also bitterly complained about Kinzer's story. Ed Griffin-Nolan of Witness for Peace, a U.S. Christian group that keeps tabs on contra abuses in Nicaragua, went to see Kinzer to object. A Western diplomat says, "His story was probably well-received at the front office of the *New York Times* because it showed skepticism about the Sandinistas. I think his sources were stupid. His sources were not exercising dispassionate military analysis. They were venting spleen."

The diplomat's comment points up two dilemmas confronted by Kinzer and every member of the Managua press corps. First, any reporter is only as good as his sources, and sources in Nicaragua tend not to be objective. The truth is not necessarily reached—as in most routine reporting—by balancing one set of opinions against another, as Kinzer had done in his article.

The second issue is the U.S. role in reporting Nicaragua. Journalists who covered Bocay found their news organizations more interested in the Sandinistas' expulsion of Bishop Pablo Antonio Vega on July 4 than they were in the possible contra mining incident. The expulsion fit into Washington's political view of things; dead babies did not.

Kinzer traveled independently to the war zone a week later and wrote a second story attributing the mines almost certainly to the contras. That story also brought criticism, Kinzer says, from people who seemed to expect the mines to have "name tags or sign posts or some sort of definitive proof." His second story appeared on the front page in the *Times'* early editions on July 18.

Kinzer says he did not write the second story in response to pressure. He says he began to work on the original Managua-based story, thinking that diplomats would readily confirm the mines were contra-placed, and that he could write, "Contras Plant Mines, Diplomats Claim." Instead, he found a high level of skepticism in the diplomatic corps. "What am I going to do," asks Kinzer, "say they have no credibility because they don't say what conforms to my preconceived notions?"

Kinzer says he had planned his independent trip ever since the explosion, but did not see the sense of going on an Army junket. "I went in a one-car caravan, and when you talk about looking at every puddle, you certainly do," he says. "It became quite clear that the contras had put the mines there, but if I had gone on the official trip, I wouldn't have been able to fix responsibility in any way that would have been acceptable to my editors."

Yet Kinzer, who was a stringer in Latin America for years before he began writing for the *Boston Globe* in the mid-1970s and the *New York Times* in 1983, does not frown on government-sponsored trips. "I have the resources to take the trips on my own; many other reporters don't," he says.

Jeep rentals cost at least $100 a day; Kinzer also hired a driver and a mechanic for his independent trip to the north, and had to pay them healthily for the risky job.

Perhaps more than other reporters in Nicaragua, Kinzer—because of the power of the *New York Times*—is constantly under scrutiny. Because of his liberal reputation as author of *Bitter Fruit* (written with Stephen Schlesinger), a 1982 exposé of the CIA's role in Guatemala, people expect him to be what he calls "a morally outraged dragon slayer," but some say he is too anti-Sandinista. Others criticize him just as harshly for being pro-Sandinista, "humanizing these guys by making them into individuals," as he puts it.

Roy Gutman, *Newsday*'s diplomatic/defense correspondent who is currently working on a book about U.S. policy in Central America, agrees that Washington wishes to "dehumanize the enemy." After a several-hour interview with President Daniel Ortega in Managua on September 27, Gutman says, "Ortega is certainly more complex than Washington's characterization of him as a petty dictator. But Washington doesn't want to hear that."

"Reporters are crying out in the wilderness," says one ambassador in Managua. "Look, it isn't like Reagan says it is. He thinks he has to paint things as luridly red as he can. But the reporters are saying, 'Hey, I thought I was down here to tell the truth.'" He continues, "An interesting thing here is that the press has been saying—to one degree or another—the flavor, the texture of life, the revolution, the war and how people live their daily lives is not reflected in the pronouncements coming out of Washington. The administration and editors are interested in the political story. Sometimes it's hard to get into the paper with a human story. The editors say: it's a *news*paper, not a sociological journal."

Reporters covering Nicaragua for U.S. news organizations often are asked to come up quickly with reaction pieces: Can the Sandinistas confirm or deny they have received new Soviet helicopters? What is the reaction to U.S. Senate approval of contra aid? Even when U.S. flier Eugene Hasenfus was downed in Nicaragua, news dispatches focused on Washington and El Salvador more frequently than on Managua.

The demand for Managua-based reaction and high-level interviews sometimes keeps reporters from spending time in the countryside. Photographers are almost always the ones who go out to document the litany of burned cooperatives, funerals, ambushed trucks and destroyed homes as soon as incidents are broadcast or published.

"We go out into the countryside and risk our lives to take photos of death and destruction that are never used," says Lou Dematteis, a Reuters photographer. "It would help if reporters would go out more often. The editors are up in the States. They don't know what's going on. It's up to the reporter to tell them what's important."

But when reporters try to tell their editors what they see as important, they often are accused of being too pro-Sandinista. "I'm being judged by my editors," says Howard, the press-club director. "You are based in Nicaragua. You are almost in the position where you are giving the official word because you are here. I don't have access to the contras in Nicaragua," she says. (Some wire-service and newspaper reporters do routinely call contra sources in Miami or Honduras—others, particularly radio and television correspondents, must depend on their editors to balance stories with reports from other bureaus.)

Journalists are now part of the daily scene in Nicaragua, at funerals, press conferences or mass rallies. Although reporters have traveled frequently to Nicaragua since the 1978–79 insurrection against Somoza, until 1983 most journalists who covered the country were based in Miami or El Salvador, and forayed for only a few days or weeks to Managua's Inter-Continental Hotel before returning home.

In the early 1980s, however, when U.S. support for the contras picked up and local-currency devaluation and a flourishing black market made the cost of living cheap for foreigners, the country became attractive both to staffers of news organizations and to ambitious freelancers. NBC, CBS and ABC set up offices in local hotels. The *New York Times'* Kinzer, asked to set up an office in northern Latin America, considered Caracas, hedged on San José and finally decided with his editors on Managua, where in 1984 he opened the country's first full-fledged newspaper bureau in a residential house in Bolonia near "the hotel."

After the *New York Times'* arrival, press houses began springing up around Managua, some in large mansions with swimming pools, others in crumbling wood-frame houses. Most Managua taxi drivers can get to the "three arches house" without being given an address: it's the house shared by frequently visiting correspondents from the *Los Angeles Times, Newsweek*, the *Washington Post* and the *Miami Herald.*

Most of the journalists now covering the country do not remember the time when reporters were virtual heroes in Nicaragua. During the insurrection and the first two years of the Sandinista revolution, Nicaraguans would surround journalists on the streets and in the countryside, wanting to relate their version of what was going on. The Sandinista government erected a monument to ABC correspondent Bill Stewart, who was killed by Somoza's National Guard in 1979. "He did not die in a strange land," the inscription reads.

Many of the reporters who now live and work in Nicaragua do not feel it is a strange land, but journalists no longer are regarded as heroes or advocates—simply part of the scene.

It is not, however, an easy scene to cover. Journalists find that the two Sandinista newspapers, the two Sandinista television stations and the officially controlled radio give them clues to what is happening in the country. So do the Voice of America and the BBC. (Until recently, foreign newspapers and magazines did not enter Nicaragua; now, they are sold for hard currency to those who can afford them.)

"What makes it difficult here is the polarization," says UPI's Tracy Wilkinson. "One side says one thing. Another side says exactly the opposite, and somehow you have to find out the truth. It has made me much more cautious to take nothing at face value. I agonize over every word I write. I feel that everyone is evaluating."

Wilkinson, who set up the bureau last year, did her share of agonizing on the day her fellow journalists were slogging through the mud at Bocay. She had not gone with them because the trip involved time away from the capital, and UPI's Nicaraguan staffer was on vacation. Instead, she was busy filing stories based on information from the radio, newspapers and calls to the defense and foreign ministries when a bulletin came over the official radio. "Bishop Pablo Vega is in Honduras, and his right to remain on Nicaraguan soil has been revoked." The term used for "is" was the Spanish passive phrase "se encuentra"—which obscured the question of whether Vega had traveled to Honduras and would be refused reentry, or had been deported.

Wilkinson made a series of calls to church sources and other reporters. Finally, the bishop's secretary in Juigalpa told her Vega had been expelled. But reporters who called earlier had found the secretary as ambiguous as the government, afraid to talk until she was officially notified by the government of Vega's expulsion. Wilkinson had put out an earlier urgent bulletin, using the government's vague phraseology, but the first story she wrote for the English-language wire stated definitively that Vega had been expelled.

Local newspapers and radio stations, however, never clarified the government's wording. Weeks later, Colombian writer Hugo Niño, a government publishing-house consultant, declared to a reporter, "The government didn't let Vega back in when he went to Honduras because the political cost of expelling him would have been too high." The reporter looked at him with disbelief; here was someone who worked for the government, an intellectual and a sharp political analyst, and he was making an erroneous analysis based on the government's ambiguous wording.

A Nicaraguan government official told an NBC staffer earlier this year, "We want to fight Ronald Reagan's images with our own images." Reporters hope the propaganda campaign will gain them more access to war zones, which requires travel permission. If this is Sandinista manipulation, most reporters say, it also is a valid chance to see the reality of Nicaragua's five-year-old contra war first-hand.

Journalists can travel with BLIs—special counter-insurgency units—to report first-hand on the war. But even here, polarization enters in. *Time* magazine contract photographer Cindy Karp was called to task by another reporter for donning a Sandinista camouflague uniform for protection while out with a BLI last spring. "They can tell who will don a uniform, and who will not," snapped a more conservative colleague. Karp had to convince her editors that this was a standard safety measure to keep journalists from becoming individual targets in civilian clothing.

"It's the first time in history journalists have had so much access behind perceived enemy lines," says Wilkinson. "Reporters weren't traveling with the Vietcong."

Not only do journalists covering Nicaragua have to contend with their editors, their sources, their reporter colleagues and land mines, they also must deal with the tremendously convoluted Sandinista bureaucracy. Reporters must register with the government press center and fill out a multi-paged questionnaire about their education, marital status, prizes and religious beliefs. If one wants to interview a government official, an additional set of forms must be filled out. Many visiting journalists wait in Managua by the Inter-Continental swimming pool to get their interviews.

Resident journalists sometimes find ways around the bureaucratic ropes. Much of what makes Managua work for them is an intricate system of networking, whether for getting car parts brought from Panama or the States, for locating eggs or a good maid, or for finding who has what news-papers. Kinzer passes on his *New Yorkers*. Freelance reporter Larry Boyd can be counted on to monitor the radio. The TV networks help reporters get mail out.

Both local and visiting reporters find waiting for interviews an excru-ciating process, but resident correspondents have a better chance of button-holing a government official to ask for an interview or to toss a question on the spot. And if the government official himself is not available, residents can always talk to his secretary, aunt, cousin or dentist. Managua, although the capital, is a small town of less than a million people, where cows mingle on the city streets with East German trucks and battered Chevrolets.

But even the resident journalists cannot avoid institutions such as the "revision tecnica"—a security check that is imposed before many press con-ferences and interviews with government officials and that can take up to three hours and has been known to destroy camera equipment. Nor can residents avoid the requirement of getting permission to travel to special zones such as the Atlantic Coast.

"There are simply too many chiefs," says Reuters photographer Lou Dematteis. "One has to distinguish between the stated policy of access, bureaucracy and sheer incompetence."

One government official often tries to undo what another has already done. Thus, when resident journalist William Gasperini of *In These Times* was given permission in August to go out to the Atlantic Coast with a visiting freelance camera crew, the group was detained and their video-cassettes confiscated and possibly erased.

Several days of negotiations with the government followed. Finally, the government promised to send the crew back to the coast with all expenses paid and permission to reshoot. But even that did not work. The government took them to the coast in an Air Force plane. But after a week, they still had not received permission to travel to the small Miskito village of Yulu, which they had told the government authorities in Managua they wished to reshoot. They returned to Managua with nothing to show for their trouble but mosquito bites, and having paid not only for their expenses but for the return trip.

Because news is relatively closed in Nicaragua, reporters tend to collaborate more than in other Latin American countries. Women journalists have even organized an aerobics class at the international press club, located in the confiscated house of contra leader Adolfo Calero, and share information along with groans.

The press club often serves as a buffer between the government and reporters. Members come from many nations and political ideologies, and include stringers, staffers, photographers, camerapersons, reporters, writers, residents and visitors.

Calero's confiscated house was donated to the press club because UNESCO guidelines say the host country should provide a center for foreign journalists. The contra leader sometimes calls to make sure a statue in his garden is being cared for.

The club helps its members with many of the current headaches in Nicaragua: gasoline, tires, telephones, telex (the public telex office will not accept collect calls) and other facets of daily life in Managua. Many things that are taken for granted even in the most underdeveloped Latin country present problems here. No company, for example, will ship film to the United States, so photographers must rely on formal or informal couriers. The press club helps them find cooperative travelers.

Statellite service in Nicaragua is the most expensive in the world, the TV networks report, and the Sandinista government will accept only cash dollars. Even ordinary mail is highly unreliable. Envelopes, typewriters, ribbons and film are in short supply. Reporters do have access to a diplomatic store, where toilet paper, *Time* and tinfoil can be had for hard currency, but most journalists' needs can not.

Reporters often are told about "activities"—as press conferences are called here—depending on whether they are in the Sandinistas' current favor. At a recent celebration of the eighth anniversary of the National Palace takeover, an extremely limited group of journalists was taken from the sweltering public-relations office of the Defense Ministry—after the usual security check, but this time accompanied by crackers with salty cheese, orange juice and coffee—to a Mercedes-Benz bus festooned with balloons, white and yellow fresh chrysanthemums and colorful streamers— and from there to the ceremony at the National Palace.

Among the "specially honored" guests were *Washington Times* reporter Glenn Garvin and freelance photographer Sue Mullin, who had been deported from Nicaragua a month before on vague charges that they had collaborated with the CIA.

Garvin and Mullin are the only journalists ever to have been thrown out of Nicaragua, although at least two—a SIN television correspondent and a reporter for Britain's *Economist*—have not been let in. Although telexes are not censored and telephone lines are not cut, many suspect they are tapped. If anyone is favored here, it is the major U.S. media—Mike Wallace got more time with Eugene Hasenfus for "60 Minutes" than Hasenfus's wife did. Foreign Ministry press-conference spokesmen routinely answer questions in English and Spanish. The government recently has even tried to discourage the proliferation of pro-Sandinista "solidarity-type" journalists.

No matter how hard they try to avoid it, reporters in Nicaragua become part of the story. Some have been attacked for being "on the Sandinista payroll" by the contra radio station, rightist publications in the United States and even by the U.S. State Department. Gutman characterizes such attacks as a "smear campaign." Last June, the State Department even called a press conference to disparage an article by the *Washington Post's* Julia Preston, who had written about a hand-grenade massacre in the village of Comoapa. But the most painful attacks come from a reporter's friends and sources.

UPI's Managua bureau chief, Tracy Wilkinson, wrote a story last Christmas in which she tried hard to balance her holiday feature piece, first describing a Sandinista toy-collection program for war orphans and then telling that most Nicaraguans could not afford a turkey dinner in the country's disastrous economic situation.

Wilkinson's story was published in Spanish in *La Prensa*, the opposition newspaper that since has been shut down by the Sandinistas. Shortly thereafter, a little old lady came up to Wilkinson at a U.S. Embassy party and said, "Don't you know the Sandinistas are persecuting us, and everything is all their fault?" Then, a second little old Nicaraguan lady, a friend of the first, came up to Wilkinson and said, "I read that story. It was wonderful." The two women began to argue—not over their equally anti-Sandinista politics, but over their individual interpretations of Wilkinson's carefully balanced story.

"You know you're doing your job," says Wilkinson, "when both sides criticize it."

Mass Media and Nationalism: For Further Reading

Anne W. Branscomb, *Toward a Law of Global Communications Networks*. White Plains, N.Y.: Longman, 1986.

William A. Hachten, *The World News Prism: Changing Media, Clashing Ideologies*. Ames, Iowa: Iowa State University Press, 1981.

Cees J. Hamelink, *Cultural Autonomy in Global Communications*. White Plains, N.Y.: Longman, 1983.

Philip C. Horton, *The Third World and Press Freedom*. New York: Praeger, 1978.

Sean MacBride, et al., *Many Voices, One World: Communication and Society Today and Tomorrow*. New York: UNESCO, 1980.

Hamid Mowlana, *Global Information and World Communication: New Frontiers in International Relations*. White Plains, N.Y.: Longman, 1986.

William H. Read, *America's Mass Media Merchants*. Baltimore, Md.: Johns Hopkins University Press, 1976.

Alan Wells, *Mass Communications: A World View*. Palo Alto, Calif.: Mayfield Publishing Company, 1974.

XI

Mass Media
and Minorities

This collection of articles about the mass media and minorities represents a mix of viewpoints to prompt thinking and discussion and to challenge readers to go beyond thinking and discussing.

Two of the articles in this section quote from *The Report of the National Advisory Commission on Civil Disorders*, the Kerner Commission report that, for the first time, officially chastised the mass media for failing to warn the nation that festering inequities would result in rioting and burning in many U.S. cities. The report was published in 1968, though the conditions that prompted the violence had been seething for decades. It is worthy of consideration again, in the light of contemporary conditions of people in our cities and towns.

Moving from the premise that there are and will be minorities in a society, the bigger questions involve how minorities are included—even whether they are included—in the mass media that attempt to serve the society. Are there individuals from these ethnic and racial groups employed in the media and, if so, how? Are they decision makers? Are they seen and heard? Or are they hired and forgotten? Are there articles and programs about minorities in the media? Are they accurate and perceptive, or do they espouse stereotypes that are false and misleading? These are some basic questions for any consideration of the mass media and minorities. The articles in this section should prompt many more questions. Each should be followed with "Why?" and "What should be done now?"

41 American Indians and the Media: Neglect and Stereotype

by James E. Murphy, Sharon M. Murphy

> James and Sharon Murphy discuss the minority probably
> least portrayed in the mass media. The article should
> remind readers that neglect and stereotype are too often
> the media response to *all* minorities. Why? What can be
> done now?
>
> The authors trace the history of media treatment of
> American Indians. Their conclusion: Media neglect and
> stereotyping has been so thorough that Indians are
> forgotten people even in an era of civil rights accomplish-
> ments. The late James E. Murphy was associate professor of
> journalism at Southern Illinois University. Sharon M.
> Murphy is dean of the college of journalism at Marquette
> University. This article is from *Let My People Know:
> American Indian Journalism: 1828–1978*, published in
> 1981.

The mass media of the United States have historically followed a policy of
not-so-benign neglect of this country's native peoples. Media coverage
is also marked by a fair amount of cynicism about Indians, a prime
manifestation of which has been the portrayal of Indians as stereotypes.
This chapter traces nearly two centuries of such neglect and stereotyping.

When one thinks of such mistreatment, images of the Indian in Hollywood westerns come immediately to mind. Yet portrayals of the savage
Indian of the Old West are limited neither to film nor to the twentieth
century. Long before television and films, printed accounts did their part to
foster inaccurate images of Indians. In fact, much news reporting about
Indians was done in such a fashion that it encouraged or at least condoned
savage treatment of Indians. One scholar, Elmo Scott Watson, wrote:

> Depending mainly on volunteer correspondents more gifted in imagina-
> tion than in accurate reporting, [eastern newspapers] spread before their
> readers the kind of highly-colored accounts of Indian raids and "mas-
> sacres" that the most sensational yellow journalism of a latter period
> would have envied.[1]

Watson saw in the press performance of the 1860s a reflection of the strong, sometimes violent anti-Indian sentiment of the frontier. What the frontier readership wanted, the newspaper supplied, including hair-raising accounts of alleged Indian "uprisings."

According to historian William Blankenburg, before the Camp Grant (Arizona) massacre of 1871, for example, the three English-language newspapers in Tucson made every effort to arouse the white settlers, and the rest of the country, against the Indians of the region. Referring to the Apaches, the *Weekly Arizonan* recommended, as an appropriate Indian policy, "to receive them when they apply for peace, and have them grouped together and slaughtered as though they were as many nests of rattlesnakes."[2]

The papers continued to encourage white settlers to kill Apaches who raided livestock and who sometimes killed white persons in retaliation against white slaughter of Indians. They actively supported recruitment of volunteer whites and mercenary Papago Indians for the purpose of raiding the tiny Apache settlement at Camp Grant. The *Arizonan* urged: "Would it not be well for the citizens of Tucson to give the Camp Grant wards a slight entertainment to the music of about a hundred double-barrelled shotguns. We are positive that such a course would produce the best results."[3]

A week later, just before dawn, a hundred Apaches, mostly women and children, were slain in their wickiups.[4] Although the massacre might have occurred without encouragement from the press, it is hard to ignore the effect of unremittingly negative images of Indians. One would probably be justified in expecting something better of the journalists. Blankenburg, however, concludes his study with a commentary that is descriptive of much media treatment of Indians even today: "It's probably wishful thinking to suppose that those editors might have risked iconoclasm in those agonizing times."[5]

In 1876, as the United States prepared to celebrate its Centennial, the Oglala Sioux and the Northern Cheyennes successfully defended their women and children and old people against Colonel George A. Custer and his cavalry. The Sioux and Cheyennes fought with little advance warning and without the superior weapons available to the cavalry. But accounts in the eastern press called the Custer debacle at the Little Bighorn a slaughter of brave soldiers by the red devils. The *Bismark* (Dakota Territory) *Tribune* printed an extra edition on July 6, 1876, with such headlines as "Massacred," "General Custer and 261 Men the Victims," "Squaws Mutilate and Rob the Dead," and "Victims Captured Alive Tortured in a Most Fiendish Manner."

The report, pieced together from various accounts, spoke of the death of one soldier, Lieutenant McIntosh, who "though a half-breed, was a gentleman of culture and esteemed by all who knew him." McIntosh, the account reads, was pulled from his horse, tortured and finally murdered at the pleasure of the red devils. It was here that Fred Girard (another soldier) was separated from the command and lay all night with the screeching fiends dealing death and destruction to his comrades within a few feet of him, and, but time will not permit us to relate the story, through some means succeeded in saving his fine black stallion in which he took so much pride.[6]

Throughout the account, the Indians were pictured as marauding savages who were inhumanly cruel to the "gallant defendants" of the embankments thrown up by the cavalry. No acknowledgement was made that Custer's attack, unprovoked by the Indians, was part of a government compaign to steal the territory from its original inhabitants. Neither was there mention of the brilliant strategies employed by Crazy Horse and Sitting Bull at the Little Bighorn, leaders of its rightful defenders. Instead, the day was lost for Custer, and "of those brave men who followed Custer, all perished; no one lives to tell the story of the battle." The writer adds, however, that "we said of those who went into battle with Custer none are living. One Crow scout hid himself in the field and witnessed and survived the battle. His story is plausible, and is accepted, but we have not the room for it now."[7] It is curious that the journalist had no room for the only eyewitness account of the battle.

The tale of brave Custer and his band of heroes was carried in papers from east to west. It strengthened the whites' fears of the Indians. It also fed its readers' curiosity and sold newspapers.

Less than fifteen years later, fears were again fanned by reports of the dangers posed by the growth of the Ghost Dance religion, a messianic, pan-Indian religion of hope and peace. Its doctrine of nonviolence and brotherly love called only for dancing and singing. The Messiah, who had the appearance of an Indian, would bring about the resurrection of the land and of the many Indians slain by white soldiers. Newspaper coverage of the Ghost Dance movement and subsequent hostilities in 1890 and 1891 was inaccurate, sensational, and inflammatory. As one writer put it, the accounts "foreshadowed the 'yellow journalism' that was soon to stampede the nation into a real war. But that was not to happen until the seeds of journalistic jingoism, sowed on the bleak prairies of South Dakota, had borne their first bitter fruit in an 'Indian massacre' in which red men, instead of white, were the victims."[8]

One reason for this comparison to "yellow journalism" was the outright lying by reporters who were "space writers," free-lancers who sold gore by the column inch. They faked "reliable sources" and "eye-witness accounts" and wrote propaganda disguised as news that sent waves of alarm, preceded by vicious rumor, across Nebraska, the Dakotas, and Iowa. The stories, although repudiated by a few serious journalists near the scene, convinced the frontiersmen that Red Cloud's Oglala Sioux were preparing to go on the warpath. They also convinced the federal government that more troops must be sent to the South Dakota towns that were eager for the business that troops would bring to their merchants.

As soldiers began arriving, the Indians fled. The press interpreted and trumpeted their flight as an outbreak of hostilities. Big-city papers began preparing to cover the new Indian "war."[9] Correspondents on the scene were under pressure to send exciting stories. When Chief Big Foot's band was massacred at Wounded Knee as the Indians were being disarmed by the cavalry, the media again ignored the story of the Indians, outnumbered five to one and fighting for their existence. The story was rather one of the protection of innocent white settlers by soldiers who were finally putting an end to Indian treachery.

Only rarely did coverage of the Ghost Dance religion and the Wounded Knee massacre reflect a more accurate picture. One such better-informed account was that of reporter Teresa Howard Dean, who was sent by the *Chicago Herald* to Pine Ridge, South Dakota, in 1871. Before this assignment she had covered weddings, church and social events, and Indian affairs. Douglas C. Jones wrote: "Like a great many other writers who had never been near a Plains Indian, she wrote a number of items deploring the state of Sioux existence, brought on, she indicated, primarily through a native laziness and indolence."[10] She carried a gun and heeded a warning that reporters who were too friendly risked being asked to leave. She filed such tidbits as, "The only incentive to life is that fear of being scalped by red men."[11]

Yet because Teresa Dean boarded at the Indian school while she was in Pine Ridge, she got to know some young Indian students, and she soon became aware of the conditions under which the government forced them to live. Her copy soon reflected her impressions: hunger caused by lack of provisions, education far inferior to that offered by the nearby Catholic mission school for white children, the nonarable lands assigned by the Government, and the inability of the local Indian agent to deal with the Ghost Dance religion in any way other than to send for the army, which he had done (his response would be echoed in more contemporary reactions to "Indian problems").

Teresa Dean also met and talked with Indian adults (and brought what she called a "scalping knife," failing to note in her copy that such knives were used by Indians for skinning game and preparing food).[12] Other examples of her work show how even she, like her fellow reporters, failed to see Indians as people. One of her dispatches contained the statement that "the greatest crime for which the government must answer is sending the educated Indian girl back to her tribe where virtue is unknown." Again, after watching a Sioux policeman identify the bodies of his sister and her three children slain near the Wounded Knee battle site, she wrote: "He looked at me with an expression that was unmistakable agony and his lips quivered. For the first time, I realized that the soul of a Sioux might possibly in its primitive state have started out on the same road as did the soul of a white man."[13] The product of white schools and books and a reader of white newspapers written by reporters like herself, Teresa Dean's statements mirror the attitudes and viewpoints in the media of the time, as well as those of a political system that permitted and propagated the atrocities she was witnessing.

From the early years of the twentieth century through the 1960s, during that long period of Indian anguish and tribulation, little coverage of Indian affairs or events was provided by white newspapers.

Then in the 1970s a series of events in Indian country touched off the widespread media coverage that left some wondering if perhaps the earlier policy of media neglect of Indians was not somehow preferable. For the coverage was crisis-activated and did little to further the ongoing story of Indian life and needs in this country. The media gave heavy coverage to the 1973 occupation of Wounded Knee, South Dakota, by the American Indian Movement. One on-the-scene reporter at Pine Ridge said that correspondents "wrote good cowboy and Indian stories because they thought it was what the public wanted...the truth is buried in too many centuries of lies like fossils embedded in layers of shale."[14] The Associated Press, United Press International, *Newsweek, Time,* the *Washington Post* and the *New York Times* were there, as were the three major networks and many foreign press correspondents. The pattern this time was different, however, because the American Indian Movement was in control and was orchestrating the media's sudden curiosity. AIM leaders tried to use Wounded Knee as a stage on which to focus attention on government injustice to Indians. They had only limited success.

Wounded Knee and the events that followed gave birth to several Indian papers, because white-dominated media played the story as they had played the urban unrest in the late 1960s, and Native Americans continued to resent this misinterpretation and other plainly misinformed reporting. One collaborative account about Wounded Knee began:

> The people of the United States, by and large, would rule strongly in favor of native demands at Wounded Knee if they could only find out what happened there. But with the press and television personnel moving along to bigger and better and more violent headlines, with the U.S. Government managing the news emerging from the Pine Ridge Reservation, and with even the reports on the resulting trials of the participants absent from the media, the people of the United states will not have the information on which to base an intelligent judgment.[15]

One difficulty facing the establishment media was that Wounded Knee did not fit prevailing myths held and taught in the United States regarding

Indians. Wounded Knee did not coincide with the belief that America was a democratic country where the courts dispensed justice, government agencies dealt benevolently with Indians, and all people had opportunities to match their ambition and willingness to work hard. As the same source said, "Wounded Knee, people say, must be a bad dream—probably done by 'bad Indians,' influenced by 'outside agitators,' and unrepresentative of native people."[16]

Yet, for many Indians, Wounded Knee represented a last-ditch stand, a final plea in the court of public opinion and the arena of equal rights. Witness these comments by Russell Means, AIM leader, regarding media treatment of the life-and-death issues at stake at Wounded Knee:

> Now, this is our last gasp as a sovereign people. And if we don't get these treaty rights recognized, as equal to the Constitution of the United States—as by law they are—then you might as well kill me, because I have no reason for living. And that's why I'm here in Wounded Knee, because nobody is recognizing the Indian people as human beings.
>
> They're laughing it off in *Time* Magazine and *Newsweek*, and the editors in New York and what have you. They're treating this as a silly matter. We're tired of being treated that way. And we're not going to be treated like that any more.[17]

No matter how distorted the reporting, television coverage of Wounded Knee got "the whole world to watch what is happening to the Indian in America," as one Indian on the scene told the *Washington Post*.[18] Thus the takeover helped inform most Americans about things they had not known before: average per capita reservation income—$1,000; average unemployment rate among Indians—40 percent, with a higher percentage at Pine Ridge; a 900 percent greater incidence of tuberculosis on the reservation than in the white population; and a suicide rate twice that of nonreservation persons.[19] Except for a small number of Indian newspapers, the media had neglected to tell those facts to the American public.

They had also neglected, and continue to neglect, to inform the American public about other Indian grievances: that utility companies are being aided by the government in their attempt to take Indian lands that lie over rich mineral deposits;[20] that dams and waterway reroutings are threatening crop and rangelands upon which whole tribal economies depend;[21] that education available to tribal residents is substandard at best and criminal at worst.[22]

Nor surprisingly, Indian journalists have charged the white media with stereotyping. In May, 1973, the *Navajo Times* quoted Franklin Duchineaux, counsel to the United States Subcommittee on Indian Affairs, who said that the Native American often depicted in the press is a sophisticated and intellectual tribal leader. Yet, the counsel suggested, to call on one person and make him stand for or act as spokesman of all Indians is stereotyping at its worst, perhaps because it is at its least conscious level. *Wassaja*, one of two national Indian publications, frequently charges the establishment press with dishonest coverage of Indian affairs. In one article, the editor wrote:

> Information about Indian affairs is meager and largely inaccurate. People need a vast amount of information in order to make intelligent decisions. We need to know what legislation is being readied for action...what programs, educatonal and economic opportunities and experiences of one or another Indian tribe might help the others.[23]

In June, 1975, another incident at Wounded Knee showed that most journalists were unable or unwilling to probe beneath the surface with their questions. Three men, two of them FBI agents, were shot to death on the Oglala Sioux Reservation in South Dakota. Only hours after the shooting the wires were humming with deadline stories reporting that the shooting "stemmed from" the 1973 Wounded Knee disturbances. The shootings were called an "ambush" and the shots were said to have come from "sophisticated bunkers." The misinformation that emerged from these and other reports both developed from and led to more misinformation and stereotyping.

The exact cause of the FBI agents' deaths was never known. No "bunkers" were found. Trials and accusations failed to bring the incident into clear focus. The deaths of the FBI agents brought a massive siege on houses near the death site, and a search-and-destroy paramilitary occupation by hundreds of FBI agents that lasted for months.[24] Press releases by the FBI and other government agencies resulted in the newspaper headline: "FBI Agents Ambushed, Killed by Indians," although no evidence of "ambushing" had been established.

The Native American press has carried frequent accounts of what happened to Indian activists and "sympathizers" involved in the 1973 Wounded Knee occupation and to those suspected or accused of involvement in the 1975 incident. These stories usually were not picked up by the wire services and consequently did not find their way into the white press. Indian activists were beaten, their homes broken into, their families threatened, one of their spiritual leaders harassed and jailed—and the white press remained largely silent.

According to one source, six "Wounded Knee sympathizers" had been killed on the reservation by winter, 1973. In the winter of 1974 people talked of the "murder of the week" on the reservation. At least twenty killings occurred in the first seven months of 1975; it was "a reign of terror—bad before the occupation, but even worse now."[25] The established media gave scant attention to the deaths.

When the Menominee Warriors Society took over an abandoned abbey near Gresham, Wisconsin, in 1975, the media showed up in force and devoted much time and money to covering the incident. There too, however, Indians frequently protested that white journalists were supplying misinformation to their papers. Part of the problem may have come from the journalists' fear of missing good stories or disappointing their audiences. As one Milwaukee television editor put it:

> On several days, very little happened.... The question then became whether to report the fact that basically nothing was happening or ignore the story on those days. We decided nearly every day that we had to carry some work on the situation, for the sake of those viewers who were interested.[26]

But when all was quiet, reporters stayed around in the event that new developments occurred. Menominee leaders, however, claimed that the reporters could have used their time to obtain adequate background information from individuals whose views should have been heard.[27]

Fast on the heels of the Gresham incident came a series of Indian lawsuits aimed at keeping or regaining lands, mineral rights, and fishing rights promised to Indians in treaties but nullified or at least endangered by subsequent and current developments, legal and illegal. Montanans Opposed to Discrimination and the Interstate Congress for Equal Rights and Responsibilities (ICERR) were just two of the groups mounting massive lobbying efforts against Indian tribal interests. By early 1978, ICERR had chapters in twenty states, mainly in the West and Northeast, areas of the greatest activity in Indian rights. In the spring of 1978, Richard La Course, a prominent American Indian journalist, wrote:

> It's a new political epoch American Indian tribes are entering in the late 1970's. Some call it the "backlash period;" some call it a "state of siege." Others view it as the forced Era of Treaty Renegotiation. In any case, it's a new ballgame—with consequent new responsibilities for Indian journalists nationwide.[28]

Some of the responsibilities were directed toward Indian audiences and their education for survival. Others were directed toward the non-Indian public, which had to be reached with or without the cooperation of the white-majority media, either by the printed word or by broadcast. Again a good deal of educating had to be done to break through misunderstandings or biases. Said one director of a Native American studies program: "These people [news reporters and editors] really don't give a damn about Indians. We aren't dangerous enough. They think if they just move in on Indians, we'll be forced to give up. Maybe what we need is violence. That's all they seem to understand."[29]

In addition to newspapers, magazines, and the broadcast medium, the book-publishing industry has done its part to cast Indians in a false or negative light. Indian scholars frequently point to the misinformation and prejudice propagated by textbooks dealing with Indians and Indian affairs. *Wassaja* and the quarterly *Indian Historian* regularly publish reviews of current books about Indians. *Wassaja* editor Repert Costo published *Textbooks and the American Indian*, a carefully annotated study of books frequently used in Indian schools or as authoritative sources of information about Indians. The book, covering historical, sociological, anthropological, and religious studies, as well as basic materials used daily with young people, pointed to some reasons why journalists write about Indians as they do: One learns patterns of perception from teachers, parents, textbooks, and other environmental elements, and these patterns tend to persist beyond one's school days.[30]

As for film, that medium may have more responsibility for creating the current popular image of Indians in this country than all the print media combined. Writers and dramatists, either intentionally or inadvertently, have propagated the stereotypes: the filthy redskin, the noble savage tamed by white refinement and religion, the headdressed warrior who attacks a wagon train, or the swarming redskins attacking the isolated military outpost to the delight of rerun audiences everywhere.

Especially until about mid-century, films reflected largely hostile and negative attitudes in their representation of Indians, who appeared on the screen as bloodthirsty and treacherous. Since 1950 nostalgia or peaceful coexistence has been reflected in the demeanor of Indians in films. Still, today's screen Indian is often a sullen, broken spirit who drinks cheap wines and lives on the handouts of a sometimes benign, sometimes malicious tribal government, or he is the militant Red Power publicity seeker, burning buildings, taking hostages, stealing government documents, or desecrating church buildings.[31]

One writer points out other images, propagated through film reruns, that are still as convincing to a new generation of viewers. The men were lazy, shiftless, unable to conform to white values, not to be trusted. The women were unusually quiet, loyal, beautiful.[32]

That the Indians portrayed in most films about Indians have been inauthentic relates directly to the fact that in their creation and production American Indians have been largely excluded. Nor were Indians consulted by the film industry regarding authenticity of plots, settings, and characterizations. Consequently, Keshena writes:

> Movie makers focused on the tribes of the Sioux and the Apache, who thus became the white man's Indian, molded and cast in the white man's mind as he wanted them to be, but projected before the viewer's eye as convincingly authentic. Indians from all tribes were cast in the image of a prearranged reality.[33]

Some few genuine Indian actors surfaced, playing roles that quickly proved the dominance of white heroes: Jay Silverheels, of "Ugh, Kemo Sabe" fame, first appeared as Tonto in the Lone Ranger movies and series. A Mohawk, he also appeared in *Broken Arrow, Brave Warrior,* and other films. An earlier Tonto was played by Chief Thunder Cloud, an Ottawa Indian, who appeared in films in the 1920s and 1930s. He was also a radio Tonto.[34]

Only in very recent years, with the emergence of strong Indian actors like Will Sampson and Raymond Tracey, has the image of Indians in film begun to turn away from the degrading stereotypes that formed the material of a half century of filmmaking.

In his own powerfully sardonic way Edward R. Murrow commented in 1958 on the image of Indians in the media. Addressing a national convention of the Radio/Television News Directors Association, Murrow said:

> If Hollywood were to run out of Indians, the program schedules (for television) would be mangled beyond all recognition. Then, some courageous soul with a small budget might be able to do a documentary telling what, in fact, we have done—and still are doing—to the Indians in this country. But that would be unpleasant. And we must at all costs shield the sensitive citizens from anything that is unpleasant.[35]

Ten years later the National Advisory Commission on Civil Disorders, which published the respected Kerner Report, added its own commentary on the plight of America's minorities. It is interesting that the commission failed to mention American Indians explicitly. That failure is itself a comment on the problem. The call for improvement of media coverage of minorities seemed targeted at blacks and Chicanos. But the same criticism could have easily been applied to the media treatment of Indians.

Chapter 15 of the Kerner Report, supposedly well known to journalists and media critics, charged that the coverage of the 1967 civil disturbances contained "mistakes of fact, exaggeration of events, over-playing of particular stories, or prominent displays of speculation about unfounded rumors of potential trouble."[36]

Another criticism by the Kerner Commission was that white-dominated media have not communicated to the majority of their audience—which is white—a sense of the degradation, misery, and hopelessness of ghetto existence: "They have not communicated to whites a feeling for the difficulties of being a Negro in the United States. They have not shown understanding or appreciation of—and thus have not communicated—a sense of Negro culture, thought or history."[37] The Kerner Report also states that "it is the responsibility of the news media to tell the story of race relations in America, and, with notable exceptions, the media have not turned to the task with the wisdom, sensitivity, and expertise it demands."[38]

If this charge is true for black Americans, it is also true for American Indians. How many Americans know of the conditions on reservations or among urbanized Indians? How many are aware of the true story of how Indians came to be dispossessed of their land? How many have any more than a naïve, misleading vision of eighteenth- and nineteenth-century naked savages running through forests whooping and hollering and making off with the innocent children of equally innocent, brave, and honest white settlers? The story of America's birth and its early nationhood is laced with accounts of how white men tamed the wild land, educated the savages, and gradually assumed benign dictatorship over nomadic peoples unable to control their own destiny and unwilling to rear their children as God-fearing, civilized citizens.

Such are the images of Indians throughout nearly two centuries of media "coverage." The neglect and the stereotyping have served the needs of the majority and so perhaps have been inevitable.

NOTES

1. Elmo Scott Watson, "The Indian Wars and the Press, 1866–67," *Journalism Quarterly* 17 (1940):302.
2. William Blankenburg, "The Role of the Press in an Indian Massacre," *Journalism Quarterly* 45 (1968):64.
3. Ibid., p. 65.
4. Ibid., p. 61.
5. Ibid., p. 70.
6. *Bismarck Tribune*, extra edition, July 6, 1876, reprinted in *Wassaja*, August, 1975.
7. Ibid.
8. Elmo Scott Watson, "The Last Indian War, 1890–91: A Study of Newspaper Jingoism," *Journalism Quarterly* 20 (1943):205.
9. Ibid., p. 208.
10. Douglas C. Jones, "Teresa Dean: Lady Correspondents Among the Sioux Indians," *Journalism Quarterly* 49 (1972):656–62.
11. *Chicago Herald*, January 20, 1891, in Jones, "Teresa Dean," p. 658.
12. Jones, "Teresa Dean," p. 659.
13. Ibid., p. 662.
14. Terri Schultz, "Bamboozle Me Not at Wounded Knee," *Harper's*, June, 1973, p. 56.
15. Publisher's Introduction to *Voices from Wounded Knee*, p. 1.
16. Ibid.
17. Ibid., p. 136.
18. Neil Hickey, "Our Media Blitz Is Here to Stay," *TV Guide*, December 22, 1973, p. 22.
19. Ibid., pp. 22–23.
20. "An Empty Black Pit," *Akwesasne Notes*, Early Autumn, 1973, p. 4. Almost

every issue of *Akwesasne Notes, Wassaja,* and other publications carried further developments in the mineral-rights struggle.

21. "Yavapais' Historic Struggle to Keep Fort McDowell," *Wassaja,* October, 1976, p. 10; "Pima Hopes Dashed," *Indian Affairs,* no. 92 (July–November, 1976), p. 2.
22. Estelle Fuchs and Robert J. Havighurst, *To Live on This Earth.*
23. *Wassaja,* January, 1973.
24. *Voices from Wounded Knee,* p. 261; "SD Reservation Ambush: 2 FBI Agents 'Executed,'" *Akwesasne Notes,* Early Winter, 1975, pp. 5–9.
25. *Voices from Wounded Knee,* p. 260.
26. Rick Brown, "The High Cost of Gresham," *Once a Year* 79 (1975):6–8.
27. Ada Deer, head (at the time of the takeover) of the Menominee Restoration Committee, who opposed the action, in conversation with the authors.
28. Richard La Course, "'Backlash': Indian Media and the 'State of Siege,'" *Red Current,* Spring, 1978, p. 4.
29. Because of possible repercussions, the source remains unnamed. But it was thought appropriate to include this quote because it so effectively mirrors sentiments heard from many quarters.
30. Rupert Costo, ed., *Textbooks and the American Indian.*
31. Philip French, in "The Indian in the Western Movie," *Art in America* 60 (1972):32–39, begins to study this problem, as does Franklin Duchineaux in "The American Indian Today: Beyond the Stereotypes," *Today's Education* 62 (May, 1973):22–23. One is reminded also of Chief Bromden, an Indian character in Ken Kesey's *One Flew over the Cuckoo's Nest.*
32. Anna Lee Stensland, *Literature by and about the American Indian: An Annotated Bibliography,* p. 3.
33. Rita Keshena, "The Role of American Indians in Motion Pictures," *American Indian Culture and Research Journal* 1 (1974):26.
34. Richard La Course, "Image of the Indian," *Air Time,* January, 1975, p. 6.
35. Edward R. Murrow, in an address to the RTNDA convention, Chicago, Ill., October 15, 1958, quoted in Harry J. Skornia, *Television and Society* (New York: McGraw-Hill, 1965), pp. 228–29.
36. *Report of the National Advisory Commission on Civil Disorders* (New York: Bantam Books, 1968), p. 372.
37. Ibid., p. 383.
38. Ibid., p. 384.

42 The Navajos, the Hopis, and the U.S. Press

by Jerry Kammer

> The national press has ignored a massive conflict and
> relocation of two American Indian tribes. Why? asks Jerry
> Kammer, author of *The Second Walk: The Navajo-Hopi
> Land Dispute* and an occasional contributor to *The Navajo
> Times*, in this article from *Columbia Journalism Review*,
> July/August 1986.

About 100 miles to the east of the Grant Canyon, in the high desert
rangeland of northeastern Arizona, the federal government is carrying out
the largest program of forced relocation since the internment of the
Japanese-Americans in World War II. Thousands of Navajos are being
forced to leave nearly a million acres awarded to the neighboring Hopi tribe
in a congressionally mandated settlement of a century-old land dispute.

"Much of the blame for the dispute lies with the federal government,"
wrote *Arizona Republic* state editor Ted Williamson in an April 27 piece for
the paper's Sunday Perspective section. "For more than a century, it has
alternated between indifference and heavy-handedness in dealing with a
complex and delicate situation."

The same charge can be brought against the national press. "Every so
often they come up with an exotic story with nice pictures," says Sandra
Masetto, a member of the federal commission established to carry out
the relocation. "I would think they would look at it from a substantive
standpoint rather than a glamour standpoint. I mean, this is the biggest
Indian issue in the last fifty years."

At widely scattered intervals since 1979, when a federal court drew the
partition line Congress demanded, *The Washington Post*, the *Los Angeles
Times*, and *The New York Times* have splashed their front pages with
extensive pieces on the Navajo-Hopi turmoil, summarizing the dispute's
history and noting its simmering passions. In May 1985, for example, Iver
Peterson, *The New York Times's* Denver bureau chief, traveled to Big
Mountain, where he met Katherine Smith, one of the Navajo matriarchs
leading the resistance. Smith told him, "If they come to push me out, I will
just say, O.K., it is better if you just kill me now, and leave me here."

But while the dramatic stories from Arizona have implicitly recognized
the dispute as a fascinating and still-evolving issue of national significance,

national editors have refused to take it seriously. They have slighted or ignored completely recent initiatives to avert confrontation. Of the big three, only *The New York Times* paid attention last year when President Reagan took the extraordinary step of sending William Clark as his personal emissary to the two tribes. The *Times* account noted that the talks failed but it neglected to report on their substance: that Clark and his deputy, Richard Morris, called for land exchanges that would minimize forced relocation. Morris says that he was surprised at the press's indifference to the story, adding, "It could have helped bring about a better resolution if they had covered it."

In May of this year, when Congressman Morris Udall called representatives of both tribes to Washington for a hearing on his bill to enact land exchanges, the three big papers took a walk on the story. Shortly thereafter, a reporter at one of the big three acknowledged that his paper had slighted the issue. There was a sense, he said, that, having published a number of pieces on an Indian tribe two years before, "we had 'done Indians' for a while. It was as if to say, 'What more is there to say about Indians?'"

Generally speaking, the big three have hurried past the Navajos and the Hopis the way some tourists hurry across the reservations en route to the Grand Canyon. They have regarded the dispute and its people as little more than material for colorful features.

At least these stories have conveyed some sense of the drama of the dispute. The real failure of the big three has been their reluctance to follow up the field reports with coverage of less colorful but equally significant developments in Flagstaff, home of the relocation commission, and Washington. Four years ago, relocation commissioners Sandra Massetto and Roger Lewis called for land exchanges between the two tribes as a means of reducing the number of those who live on the "wrong side" of the partition line. Then Lewis resigned after saying—in an astonishing moment of candor—that in relocating elderly Navajos he sometimes felt "as bad as the people who ran the concentration camps in World War Two." At the request of Senator Barry Goldwater, the Reagan administration replaced Lewis with a man whose only qualification for the job was that he had run "Democrats for Goldwater" in the 1980 election. The big three ignored it all.

The few reporters who have lingered over the story have found it as intriguing as the desert itself. "It's so complex, so persistent in making you uncover layer after layer, that it's probably the most fascinating story I've ever worked on," said Bill Walker of *The Denver Post*, who was writing a series on the issue that was scheduled to be published in late June.

Those who would understand the story must probe its mysteries. Do the Hopis need their half of the partitioned lands for their economic and cultural survival, as the sponsors of the 1974 law insisted, or will the land be of benefit primarily to a handful of affluent Hopi ranchers, as the Navajos claim? Did the Navajos settle the land after driving the Hopis to mesa-top villages, or did the much smaller Hopi tribe use the land only for hunting, gathering, and visiting religious shrines? Is the battle for the land fundamentally a struggle between two competing tribal groups, or merely a divide-and-conquer stratagem devised by the federal government and energy companies to get the Navajos off the land so strip-mining can begin? And, finally, does relocation ensure justice for the long-suffering Hopis, or does it represent a racist double standard on the part of a government that normally settles Indian land disputes by compensating the Indians financially and allowing the settlers—who are usually whites—to remain?

The story is a logistical nightmare for reporters. Big Mountain, for example, is thirty miles from pavement and accessible only by roads like the ones that used to be featured in ads for radial tires. Many of the elderly speak no English, and the nearest phone is at Elijah Blair's trading post twenty miles away—two facts that make follow-up questions by phone an occasion for reporters' wise-cracks.

The two papers closest to the two tribes—*The Navajo Times* and the Gallup, New Mexico, *Independent*—have provided generally excellent coverage of the dispute. And the *Albuquerque Journal* has also covered it consistently. The most significant regional development, however, has been *The Arizona Republic*'s recognition of the inadequacy of coverage that for more than a decade had concentrated on spot reports of congressional hearings, meetings of the relocation commission, and press conferences organized by public relations experts employed by both tribes.

"We had given it a snapshot look, instead of helping people understand why it was important," says city editor Richard Robertson, who coordinates news coverage. "There we were, spending a lot of time with wire coverage of the West Bank, but missing a similar issue right here in our own backyard."

The *Republic* hired Paul Brinkley-Rogers to man its northern Arizona bureau, in part because of his interest in the Navajos and Hopis. Brinkley-Rogers, who covered the Vietnam War as a correspondent for *Newsweek*, calls the Navajo-Hopi story "overwhelming, almost to the same extent that living in Saigon was. In terms of its color, emotions, complexity, and consequences, I think it's without equal among national issues." His stories have provided *Republic* readers their first chance to enter the land and see the effects of government policy on its people.

In putting Brinkley-Rogers on the story, the *Republic* sought to position itself for a widely anticipated confrontation on July 6 of this year, which Congress had originally established as the deadline for relocation. (Nearly a thousand families—all but thirteen of them Navajo—have already been relocated. Another 1,500 Navajo families are scheduled to be relocated.) The defiance of Navajo grandmothers had been joined by rumblings from

Navajo veterans of the Vietnam War and pledges of solidarity from non-Navajo members of the militant American Indian Movement. Many observers expected July 6 to be an Indian D-day, and the regional and national press took note with big stories that focused on Navajo anguish under powerful headlines: U.S. DRIVING OFF 10,000 INDIANS in *The Sacramento Bee*; MOVING MEANS TRAIL OF TEARS FOR NAVAJO in the *Los Angeles Times*; WAR OF TWO WORLDS: NAVAJO ELDER IS EYE OF STORM in *The Arizona Republic*; "Two Tribes, One Land" in *Newsweek*.

Congress and the Bureau of Indian Affairs have since taken action that will extend the relocation deadline by about seventeen months. But in the meantime the stories had created a public relations problem for Hopi tribal council chairman Ivan Sidney, who called press conferences in Albuquerque and Phoenix to remind reporters that relocation, unpleasant though it was, represented the culmination of a string of Hopi victories in the courts and Congress. Wherever he went, Sidney carried a series of posterboard maps that drove home another key point: the Navajo Reservation has been gradually expanded to surround the Hopis. Sidney then began publishing a tabloid newspaper devoted to telling the Hopi side of the dispute and fighting "Navajo misinformation."

While both tribes have launched public relations efforts to bring national attention to the issue, the most provocative publicity has been generated by a group that calls itself the Big Mountain Legal Defense/Offense Committee. Comprising mostly youthful volunteers whose garb and idealism recall protesters against the Vietnam War, the committee has raised enough money to send Navajo elders and Hopi "traditionalists" (those who do not regard the tribal council as legitimate and who oppose the relocation program) on cross-country speaking engagements. The committee explains the government's relocation policy as the result of a conspiracy on the part of greedy coal interests, despite the lack of solid evidence to support the charge, and labels Sidney and his supporters "puppets" of the federal government. Sidney has responded furiously, denouncing the committee for disseminating "half-truths, innuendo, and outright falsehoods."

The countercultural ideals and rhetoric of committee members have inspired cynical reporters to call them members of the "Wanna-be Indian" tribe. No one can deny their effectiveness and commitment, however. They have generated a flood of letters to Capitol Hill. What is more, they have organized dozens of chapters across the United States, including one in Berkeley, California, that publishes *Big Mountain News*, a tabloid that calls the fight against relocation "a facet of the greater international struggles ... for indigenous self-determination, to end growing militarism and nuclear madness, and the day-to-day struggle in each of our lives for justice and equality." They have also gained a ready hearing abroad (see sidebar).

There is clearly a possibility of violent resistance to relocation. Given the size of the area awarded to the Hopis and the numbers of defiant Navajos and their supporters, the violence could easily be more widespread and intense than the confrontation at Wounded Knee in 1973. Already, American Indian Movement members have camped at Big Mountain under the banner "WK 1973," a reminder of their capacity for defiance of federal authorities. If there is a confrontation when a deadline is finally imposed, and if federal marshalls sent to evict Navajos do battle with an unlikely guerrilla force of AIM members, Navajo veterans of Vietnam, and grandmothers in calico skirts, the press will descend like Tom Wolfe's fruit flies, just as they did at Wounded Knee. They would feast on the violence of a tragedy that was spawned by competing tribes, compounded by the federal government, and neglected by the national press.

43 The Emergence of Blacks on Television

by Regina G. Sherard

In this article, Regina G. Sherard assesses the emergence of blacks on television. After reading it, compare her assessments with the current TV program schedules. Have there been changes since this article was written? Are the roles better or worse? What do viewers know as a result of these programs? Are other minorities "emerging" on television— and how? There's hope for new black involvement in television, but establishing independent black television networks will take the same pioneering spirit that gave birth to the black press, says Sherard—"We wish to plead our own cause." Sherard was a doctoral candidate at the University of Missouri school of journalism when this article was written. She teaches at the University of North Carolina school of journalism. This article is from the *St. Louis Journalism Review*, May 1982.

The political and economic development of blacks over the past two decades has been both dramatic and superficial. The pattern of the status of blacks in the media followed a similar motif. While the signs of progress show evidence of social change and a consistent, if not concerted, effort by the media to be responsive to the black community, they also reflect a growing black consensus and a progressing level of tolerance by a white-dominated field.

America's tendency toward supermarket journalism, where the consumer dictates what is or is not present in the media, has caused the media to place greater emphasis on the consumers with the largest amount of economic and social power. Historically, minorities have had neither the economic nor social power and, therefore, have not played a terribly important role in the media.

The involvement of blacks in the media has systematically focused on exposure, broad visibility, the creation of role models and the potential for effecting change in attitudes with respect to positive imaging. Although these priorities were fostered initially within the upper echelons of the media industry, they were dictated by the aggressive clamor of blacks for political and economic justice. While the crude reality bares such a quest to be nothing more than the adoption of an illusion of power, the black experience in the media derived its momentum from the "black power" movement of the sixties.

The ideology of black power, which found its support among the alienated masses of urban residents, has faded into the shadow of complacency. But during its zenith, the advocacy of black power embraced the bitter disaffection of the poor with a militant determination.

The powerlessness of blacks has been clearly identified as a lack of control over the institutions that affect and govern their lives, as well as the inaccessibility to the "channels of communication, influence and appeal," as the Kerner Commission reported. The struggle for power and control requires access to those institutions directly responsible for disseminating information to the masses and input into the depiction, whether real or symbolic, of the reformists to the mass audience.

The National Commission on Civil Disorders (the Kerner Commission) charged, "The absence of Negro faces and activities from the media has an effect on white audiences as well as black. If what the white American... sees on television conditions his expectation of what is ordinary and normal in the larger society, he will neither understand nor accept the black American.... But such attitudes, in an area as sensitive and inflammatory as this, feed Negro alienation and intensify white prejudices."

The report of the commission, which had been appointed by President Lyndon Johnson to discover the causes of the rioting, remains the definitive background piece on minority coverage in the media.

The commission stated: "By failing to portray the Negro as a matter of routine and in the context of the total society, the news media have, we believe, contributed to the black-white schism in this country."

The commission further emphasized this point by providing statistics concerning the small number of minorities employed in the media at that time.

As a result, the media reluctantly opened its doors to blacks. What has been described as a "running sore on the national body" by W.H. Ferry would have been allowed to fester had the issue of black representation in the media been left solely to the conscience of the industry.

Nevertheless, the response by the media found consolation in the fact that black people and their fight were big news, and the dictates of a black agenda for power created a fertile environment for the development of a righteously dichotomous relationship, which continues to this day.

Blacks are: inferior, lazy, dumb and dishonest; either clowns or crooks; professional quacks and thieves without adequate skill and ethics.

Such was the stereotyped portrayal of blacks perpetuated by network television in the CBS series, "Amos 'n' Andy." From 1951 until the network barred syndication and overseas sales of the program in 1966, the presentation of blacks was patently offensive. Although television had inherited "Amos 'n' Andy" from radio, the visual medium was explicit and glaring in its degradation and "black" humor.

The show's creators, Freeman Gosden and Charles Correll, expressed some concern over the visual adaption of the series. However, their concern did not reflect a sensitivity to blacks or the critical objections of the black community; instead the appeasement was in deference to the discomfort that white viewers may have experienced in seeing blacks on the television screen.

The U.S. Civil Rights Commission reports, "Gosden and Correll trained black actors to portray the characters in the nuances of the stereotype with which whites would be comfortable. Apparently, to avoid interaction between blacks and whites, Amos and Andy lived in an all-black world in which all the judges, policemen, shop owners, and city clerks were black."

To avoid affronting the sensibilities of a white audience and thereby risking the wrath of sponsors, network television focused its attention on blacks in roles that exploited the stereotype. As singers and tap dancers, blacks sustained the image of "having rhythm;" as maids, black women were doting "Aunt Jemimas" whose obeisant manner was met with condescension; as handymen, black men were basically slow-witted and recalcitrant misfits. To reinforce the idea of not taking blacks seriously, such "slice of life" programs portrayed them in contextual formats of comedy— situations in which they were ridiculed and laughed at under the guise of entertainment.

The 1950s was a period that saw a tremendous exertion of influence and control by advertisers in television programming.

Sponsors were also leery of having their products associated with blacks. An example is given of Nat King Cole, the first black to star in a network variety show, who experienced great difficulty in obtaining advertising support. When the show first aired on NBC in 1956, it was carried without commercial sponsorship. The popularity and performance in the ratings encouraged the co-sponsorship by Rheingold Beer, but it was not sufficient to sustain "The Nat King Cole Show" beyond a year.

When the networks began to assume control over program production, a ratings war ensued that pivoted around action-oriented entertainment shows. The "audience-flow" concept of television news imposes an entertainment function, which characterized news programming.

After the Supreme Court desegregation decision in 1954 and the acceleration of civil protests, the nation's attention was focused on the highly dramatic elements of the civil rights struggle. The vivid images of "...young Negroes dragged out of buildings, grim-jawed sit-ins surrounded by angry whites, hoodlums pouring mustard on the heads of blacks at a lunch counter, and police moving in with brutal swiftness" were brought into the homes of viewers during prime-time, reports William Small.

The television medium became very skilled at covering the "action" of the civil rights movement, with the "good guys and bad guys" clearly identified. Since the movement was for the most part a regional one in the South, the northern-based networks highlighted the atrocities with little recognition of the impending crisis at their own back door.

By 1964 a chain of events had been set in motion that did nothing less than shock an unprepared North and horrify an unsuspecting nation. Sixteen days after President Johnson signed the long-awaited Civil Rights Act, tension erupted in Harlem; after New York came Watts, Chicago, Cleveland, Detroit, Newark, Baltimore and Washington, D.C. As the black movement took a running leap in a direction that gave way to impatience and the assertion of power, the major issue became a question of control.

An idealistic goal at best, control of the community and control of institutions were interpreted as crucial in the decision-making that affects the black community. In the case of the media, the elements of control were realized through attempts to make news and programming relevant to the black community, reflective of the underlying cause of social unrest in the ghettos, a representative of a realistic as well as positive portrayal of blacks.

The dubiousness of some of these interests would cause some to wonder how relevancy is defined, for surely what is relevant to some may not be to all of the black community; and a realistic portrayal of blacks may not necessarily be a positive one. But as the formal news source relied upon in the black community, television was the main object of discontent.

In response to the charge that television coverage of the facts of black unrest had been magnificent in comparison to the underlying grievances, the networks hired a handful of black reporters to cover the riots and tell the story of the black experience. Some of the more noted reporters like Chuck Stone, Mal Goode, Robert Teague, Ted Coleman, William Matney and Wendell Smith achieved national acclaim.

A marriage of television and the black movement was imminent as

Molefi Kete Asante described: "For television, the black movement could produce a massive demonstration of singing, chanting blacks, frequently attacked by fierce-looking state troopers and policemen. For blacks, television could cover the grievances and abuses of the black masses and send them nationwide, perhaps world-wide...."

The vast coverage of developments on the civil rights scene served as a visual chronicler of black protest. Television newscasts presented blacks in a sympathetic light and familiarized the public with leaders who were recognized by the black community.

In news and public service programming that did not address the civil rights issue, blacks were conspicuously included to provide the "black perspective." On-the-scene reporters and field interviewers made sure that any representative group of Americans contained at least one black.

CBS broadcast a seven-part series, "Of Black America," in the "hot summer" of '68 that was hosted by black comedian Bill Cosby. But while the series was hailed as a first to address seriously the degradation of blacks by white America, it was severely criticized for employing few blacks in the planning and production of the series.

In the fall of that year, "Julia" made its debut on prime-time television with the recurring proclamation by NBC that it was being presented, "with pride." However what was labeled as pride over the air may have been a boardroom decision of sublime resignation.

The U.S. Commission on Civil Rights reports, "The previous January NBC had rejected the pilot for the series. In February when the network's programming executives were preparing the fall schedule, they were faced with a half-hour to fill opposite CBS' popular 'The Red Skelton Show.' Believing that any of their potential choices would fail to be a match against Skelton, Paul Klein of NBC's audience research department argued that selecting 'Julia' to fill the empty time slot would accomplish something of social value."

Klein further argued that while "Julia" might be saccharine, "...it had racial importance at a time when television was under heavy criticism as a lily-white medium. With Diahann Carroll in the lead it would be the first situation comedy since the opprobrious 'Amos 'n' Andy' to be built around a black person.... Although the show was a success by rating standards, the social value of 'Julia' as a response is somewhat ludicrous."

The 1960s also saw a sudden recognition of black consumerism. When in 1963 the American Federation of Television and Radio Artists issued a statement promising to "...take affirmative steps toward the end that minority group performers are cast in all types of roles so that the American scene may be portrayed realistically," it was met a month later with the NAACP's adopted resolution "...calling for selective buying campaigns against the products of those who sponsor offensive motion pictures, television and radio programs or whose programs ignore the presence and achievement of American Negroes, or who refuse to give equal employment opportunity to Negroes."

White-owned businesses discovered that the more than 20 million black consumers of products advertised on television constituted a visible market. Attractive, mulatto-complexioned models were the most frequently seen type in commercials that initially featured blacks. But advertising lagged far behind the news and entertainment areas in utilizing black performers.

A survey conducted in March 1966 by the American Civil Liberties Union showed that blacks had 3.36 percent of the speaking roles and 8.49 percent of the non-speaking roles in regular television programs; less than 1 percent of the roles in television commercials went to black performers.

According to a report issued in 1964 by the Committee on Integration of the New York Society for Ethical Culture, the comparative findings of its monitoring survey conducted in 1962 and 1964 showed an increase from 2 to 36 black appearances in commercials and public service announcements.

In 1965, a television audit by Schmidt for Los Angeles revealed 2 percent of the commercials had black models. By the end of 1969, one audit study showed an increase up to 8 percent of commercials containing blacks. While these figures do not reflect absolute numbers of blacks being used in television commercials and are not necessarily indicative of any particular sensitivity on the part of sponsors, they do reflect a growing trend in the '60s that signaled recognition of the black dollar, if not that of the black problem.

The "Swinging 70s" ushered in a more permissive, youth-oriented era that had been adversely affected by the war at home and the war abroad. In an effort to respond to some of the more salient issues permeating a troubled society, such programs as "Mod Squad," "Storefront Lawyers," "The Man and the City," "The Young Lawyers," and "The Young Rebels" attempted to offer solutions. One element of relevancy common to this new genre of shows was the inclusion of young blacks. With the exception of "Mod Squad," a show built around the premise that young, hip cops could be effective working outside the system and yet maintain the establishment's principle of law and order, all the other shows failed.

Les Brown attributes the failure to their having created a "false aura of relevance" that was unrealistic: ". . . militants were not angry revolutionaries but paranoiacs or agents of hostile countries; . . . bigots, not true haters but merely persons who lived too long in isolation from other races; drug users not the disenchanted but victims of ghoulish weirdos and organized crime. Television faced the gut issues with false characters and instead of shedding light on the ailments of the social system and the divisions within it, the playlets distorted the questions and fudged the answers."

Brown also pointed to the motives of these programs: "For all their genuflections toward social awareness, the networks' intent was not so much to involve themselves with the real issues of the day as patently to exploit them for purposes of delivering up to advertisers more of the young consumers than before without alienating the older habitues of the medium."

An obvious aspect of these and other programs that followed in the '70s was the depiction of blacks in the role of "good guys." To reinforce the down-to-earth quality of these shows, the dialogue was heavily weighted with such black colloquialisms as "right-on," "get down," "brother," "sister," "the man," and "honky." These shows were off-shoots of the black exploitation movies that had been so popular with an element of the black audiences.

The "super-black" period was followed by variety shows and situation comedies that featured blacks as stars in the primary roles. Flip Wilson, Redd Foxx and Bill Cosby capitalized on a style of black humor that forced blacks to laugh at themselves; ghetto jokes and similar travesties on black life were popularized by television. A paradoxical characteristic of such programs was that they projected a positive and negative image of blacks—the black star who exploited the nuances of deprivation and depicted the brutal realities of poverty. For all the subtle implications of the "super-black" stereotype in television, these shows did provide a cushion for the presentation of more serious dramas that explored provocative themes.

One of the most popular and humorous treatments of controversial issues on television may be attributed to Norman Lear, whose realistic approach to contemporary social problems gave us such hits as "Maude," and "All in the Family." The black series, "Good Times" and "The Jeffersons," which were the respective spinoffs from Lear's premier comedies, were a tremendous success during the early '70s. The black shows had antithetical themes: "Good Times" explored the lives of the Evans family whose futile efforts to escape a Chicago ghetto combined equal amounts of pathos and humor, while the Jefferson family was the all-American story of rags-to-riches. Lear's black characters brought bigotry, discrimination and racial inequality into the open.

The style of the new black comedies represented new ground in the TV medium. Viewers were presented with characters who could joke about their miseries and laugh at their ignorance despite a constant array of harassment and insulting innuendo. But the National Black Feminist Organization took opposition to the sophisticated demeaning of blacks in many of the shows during the 1974 television season. In a statement reminiscent of the NAACP's 1951 complaint against "Amos 'n Andy," the organization made the following observations:

1. Black shows are slanted toward the ridiculous with no redeeming counter images;

2. Third World peoples are consistently cast in extremes;
3. When blacks are cast as professional people, the characters they portray generally lack professionalism and give the impression that black people are incapable and inferior in such positions;
4. When older persons are featured, black people are usually cast as shiftless derelicts or nonproductive individuals;
5. Few black women in TV programs are cast as professionals, para-professionals or even working people;
6. Black children, by and large, have no worthy role models on television.

The seventies was an impressive decade for blacks on television as their visibility in commercials, comedies, news and other areas of programming increased significantly. However, the critics would question whether this visibility constitutes an improvement from a sociological perspective. Are programs with black performers and so-called black themes merely grafts of the white image of reality; or is the black experience being revealed in its own environment and on its own terms?

Is the "Amos 'n Andy" syndrome being subtly perpetuated to stereo-type blacks? Is television still stressing the "bad news" of the black community over its positive aspects? Has the television industry been as responsive in accelerating blacks behind the camera in management posi-tions as it has been in showcasing them in front of the camera?

The questions arise not from a dispute of whether improvements have been made, but from the extent to which progressive advancement of blacks in television has made a positive impact on the social inequities within the medium. These and other concerns have prompted the develop-ment in recent years of such groups as the National Black Media Coalition and Black Citizens for Fair Media to monitor programs for their authen-ticity and fair representation of blacks.

As of 1979, 11 years after the Kerner Commission blasted the media for being ". . . shockingly backward in hiring, training and promoting" blacks, statistics indicated that television had not risen to the challenge:

- While composing 17 percent of the population, only two percent of all media practitioners are black;
- Approximately 99 percent of all news editors and station managers are white. While Detroit had the first black VHF television station in 1975, WHEC-TV in Rochester, New York, became the first black-owned station in 1979;
- Blacks have not been able to control cable television franchises in urban areas with a majority black population;
- Black students in journalism schools comprise less than four percent of the total enrollment.

William Hines of the *Chicago Sun Times* remarks that in a city like Washington, D.C., where the population in the central city is 70 percent black, "...there is no real black TV presence (not counting the obligatory black anchorman on every white-controlled station's nightly news show)."

It was a relatively easy move to employ blacks in positions that afforded visibility during a time when the issues of civil rights lent themselves so well to the visual medium. But in the 1980s different issues have emerged, some of which may not be as clearly defined as those during the 1960s: "Today the struggle in journalism is over a second generation of issues; tokenism in employment (as intolerable today to minorities as was exclusion in the sixties), and inaccurate, inadequate portrayal of minority communities (even less excusable than was total neglect years ago)."

An examination of the two popular black shows, "The Jeffersons" and "Different Strokes," points to an exploitation of old stereotypes transposed to atypical environments. George Jefferson is an ignorant, loud-mouthed man who screams at his family, insults his friends and berates his interracial in-laws with one-liners that inevitably focus on the "honky."

Whereas at one time it was considered unthinkable to openly cast aspersions on blacks, it is acceptable for George to be openly hostile to every white character in the show. But George is rich, and he owns a chain of cleaning stores, thereby functioning ostensibly like any other white business executive.

Arnold is an apple-cheeked 8-year-old who lives with his rich white adoptive father and his interracial siblings in a posh apartment. Having come from a ghetto environment, little Arnold has adjusted remarkably to his new family, exhibiting none of the usual trauma that one would expect from a child who had lost his only parent, none of the anticipated identity problems that youngsters under similar circumstances might experience.

Instead, Arnold has made the transition into a predominately white world with humorous ease and precocity. Furthermore, no one seems to notice that Arnold and his brother are black. In fact, neither do they.

Within the past five years, black entrepreneurs have placed an increased emphasis on media ownership. Whereas black-owned and black-oriented radio stations have been relatively common for many years, blacks have traditionally been unsuccessful in making any significant headway in the television industry. The most obvious reason is that with limited frequencies, the three major networks have monopolized ownership and programming, and local markets have been unreceptive.

With the advent of "low power" television, market segmentation will provide opportunities for blacks. On a recent edition of the black news program, the discussion focused on one such service that is currently being developed. Known as the Community Television Network, this low-power television service will offer a variety of minority and children's programming plus a nightly news broadcast. The Community Television Network is coordinated through the efforts of three black lawyers, Dan Winston, Booker Wade and Sam Cooper, all of whom were previously with the Federal Communications Commission. The new television service is being backed financially with $60 million from the Golden West Corporation, an affiliate of Gene Autry Enterprises, Inc. The new service is described as an adaptation of an old technology known as "television translator service," wherein CTN will provide new programming outlets for the black community within a range of 12 to 15 miles, compared to a range of 40 to 60 miles for traditional frequencies. It will also incorporate a subscription television service for pay subscribers who will receive "premium programming," including movies, selected entertainment features and sports.

The new direction of black involvement in the television industry will undoubtedly be at a snail's pace, and without sufficient support and resources, it will remain a goal and not a realization. Although such efforts as those initiated on behalf of the Community Television Network are encouraging, the question of survival becomes paramount in consideration of competition, advertising revenues, and audience appeal. Nevertheless, independent black television networks suggest the same pioneering attitude that gave birth to the black press—an attitude that was built upon the founding words, "We wish to plead our own cause."

44 The Black Press: Down But Not Out

by Phyl Garland

An irony of civil rights and equal employment opportunities has been the increased strain on black newspapers to survive. They will survive, possibly as the urban newspapers of the future, predicts Phyl Garland, former New York editor of *Ebony* and now on the faculty at Columbia's graduate school of journalism. This article is from the *Columbia Journalism Review*, September/October 1982.

On a dismal midwinter morning earlier this year, managing editor Lou Ransom sat at the head of an oblong table in the cramped, windowless conference room of the *New Pittsburgh Courier*, its offices located on the blighted South Side of a city that once had been the very hub of northeastern industrial activity but now struggled to stave off the encroachments of economic decline. The sporadic clattering of manual typewriters, an obsolescent newsroom sound in this era of electronic VDTs, filtered into the room, which was adorned with trophies and plaques awarded to "America's Best Weekly" by the National Newspaper Publishers Association, an organization comprising most of those who own the nation's approximately 200 black newspapers.

Ransom, twenty-nine, summarized his analysis of the pressures that have plunged much of the black press into a state of crisis that has persisted for more than a decade and shows signs of escalating. "The way Reaganomics is hitting us, we're in a depression and it's *killing* us. Not only the *Courier*, but *all* black newspapers," he said. "The first place Reaganomics hits us is in advertising. Steel mills and other major businesses are closing down in this area, and firms that used to set aside a little bit of money to advertise in the *Courier* cut back on us before they touch the two local dailies [*The Pittsburgh Press* and the *Pittsburgh Post-Gazette*]. They're getting thinner too. It's not just us, but it's us first. And there has been an almost steady drop in circulation.

"If we're going to survive," Ransom went on to say, "we're going to have to re-evaluate the role we have to play because in the past the black press was everything for everybody. We can't afford to do that today. We must focus on who we want to reach. Most of our readers are older and buy the paper out of habit. But if we want to go for the money, we have to aim for the young professionals, the people advertisers want to reach. We have a lot of black college grads now and they're not being challenged by the *Courier* and other black papers. And they don't buy them either. They read the dailies, *Time*, and *Newsweek*, but they are *starving* for in-depth coverage of black affairs."

In his passion and profound concern for the future of the black press, Lou Ransom reminded me of myself so many years ago when I was an ardent reporter and editor for the old *Pittsburgh Courier*. (The word "New" was added to the name in 1966 when John H. Sengstacke, owner of the *Chicago Defender* chain, purchased the paper's assets in order to rescue it from impending bankruptcy.) One of two blacks to graduate from Northwestern University's School of Journalism in 1957, before student loans, ample scholarships, special programs, and affirmative action policies helped to boost the number of minority journalists, I had worked for the *Courier* during summers and joined the full-time staff in 1958.

Making Change Happen

Like most black journalists of my generation, I had not dreamt of seeing my by-line on the front page of *The New York Times*, *The Washington Post*, or the *Chicago Tribune*. This was not due to a lack of ambition but stemmed from an understanding of the realities that restricted our lives in those days of *de jure* segregation and overt racial hostility. Back then, blacks existed in a shadow world that was seldom, if ever, reflected in the pages of daily newspapers, which were staffed almost exclusively by whites and mirrored their mentality. If blacks were noticed at all, it was in a negative or condescending manner. *The Daily News* in my hometown of McKeesport, Pennsylvania, had carried a weekly back-page two- or three-inch column, headed "Afro-American," listing weddings, births, deaths, and club meetings, compiled from notes sent in by black readers. In white papers generally we were just as invisible as Ralph Ellison said we were.

But a far stronger element in the matter of career choice was the driving sense of commitment that impelled me, and others like me, to cast our lot with the black press. We considered it an effective, if sometimes strident, medium through which we might strike out at the forces that denied us opportunity and respect. This was in the years before the sit-ins, boycotts, freedom marches, mass protests, civil rights laws, and, quite significantly, the urban riots of the sixties had pried open the doors for black journalists, professionals, managers, educators, and skilled workers seeking a place in the mainstream of American life. For us, the black press *was* journalism. The best of our numbers considered ourselves warriors.

In my case, there was another decisive factor. Back in 1943, my mother, Hazel Garland, a housewife with bold aspirations, had liberated herself from the linoleum confines of her kitchen by becoming a stringer for the *Courier*, reporting on weekly events in the network of small towns surrounding Pittsburgh. Three years later when she joined the regular staff, receiving on-the-job training, she became a reporter and later women's and entertainment editor, eventually rising to the position of editor-in-chief in 1974—long after I had left the staff. So I had grown up with the *Courier*. She and her colleagues had been my role models. This was particularly important in a time and place where I had never seen a black sales clerk, bus driver, foreman, or school teacher. For me, journalists always had been special people who not only wrote about what happened but, as advocates of change, helped to make it happen.

The journalistic world that I had entered twenty-five years earlier differed dramatically from the one Lou Ransom was encountering. Though the *Courier*, founded in 1910, had begun its long decline by the fifties, some of the luster of its old glory days remained even then. My co-workers on the national and city desks could recall the boom of the World War II years that spilled over into 1947, when the paper had hit its peak of more than 350,000 copies distributed weekly through twenty-three editions covering all parts of the country. It had set an all-time audited circulation record for black newspapers, and the presses ran daily, from Sunday through Thursday. By contrast, Lou Ransom was presiding over the remains of an enterprise that had shrunk, almost unbelievably, to 10,000 local copies per week, with another 10,000 reached by a skimpy national edition. Even the handsome three-story structure that had housed the *Courier* of my day, set snugly at 2628 Centre Avenue in the heart of Pittsburgh's black Hill District, where folks from the neighborhood could bring their grievances with the guarantee of an immediate hearing, has been demolished. The current rented quarters on South Carson Street are at the edge of a white working-class neighborhood, far from the action.

No less severe had been the decline in prestige. "It was the kind of paper that commanded respect and was widely quoted. If you were running for office on any level, you stopped by the *Courier* to pay homage," recalls Harold L. Keith, who had worked there for eighteen years and was editor when he left in 1963. Now director of publications and information for the Department of Housing and Urban Development and a confirmed, high-level civil servant, Keith eagerly reminisces about the *Courier's* numerous crusades against Jim Crow, lynching ("seemed there was a lynching or two every week"), segregation in the armed forces, job discrimination, and rampant racial injustices. He remembers the time when Wendell Smith, the sports editor, helped negotiate Jackie Robinson's introduction into major league baseball, breaking that color barrier. "The galvanizing force that made it go was the institution of racism—we were Negroes then. All of us felt involved and it gave us the impetus to work for little money to do the best job we could to fight that institution. We had outstanding reporters in the South, some of them white, who risked their lives to do things like infiltrate the Ku Klux Klan to bring us the news."

And there was the camaraderie. "We had some of the best journalists in the country, trained and highly intelligent people," says Keith, who earned his master's degree in history from the University of Pittsburgh, where he also undertook pre-doctoral studies. "After we had finished our work, we would sit around the desk and discuss every conceivable thing. It was inspirational and informational. You looked forward to going to work because something was always happening. It was really a great place." He adds nostalgically, "I would have been at the *Courier* today if things were right."

But they weren't.

Out of Sync

Many have said that the *Pittsburgh Courier*, like other black newspapers and black institutions as a whole, was a victim of the integration it so doggedly fought for, that providence gave black people an ironic kick in the bottom when they were granted, at least ostensibly, what they had said they wanted. This is a simplistic view and Harold Keith maintains that poor management was a major factor, along with the impact of changing times.

"Advertisers pulled out when the paper began covering the movement, though it never had been that successful in getting ads," he notes. When advertising revenue was diminished, management responded "by cutting the staff, getting rid of the people who made it go, while the hangers-on stayed. Management was not willing to invest in newsgathering."

The mistakes of the fifties were considerable and consistent. In an attempt to modernize, the *Courier's* management invested heavily in a magazine section and color comics featuring black characters, a novelty that did not pay off. It reduced its size from that of a full-scale paper to a tabloid without preparing the public, which felt cheated by the smaller product. In the mid-fifties, when a young minister named Martin Luther King, Jr., led a boycott against segregated bus seating in Montgomery, Alabama, and a civil rights movement that was a alter American history had gotten under way, the *Courier* published a series of articles called "What's Good About the South" by George S. Schuyler, the house conservative and a literary holdover from the Harlem Renaissance. Readers were enraged and circulation dropped. During this critical period, a radical new columnist named Elijah Muhammad appeared in the *Courier's* pages, criticizing religious institutions, among other things, as he gained the national exposure necessary to build his Black Muslim organization. This enraged the ministers whose congregations had been the paper's mainstay, and circulation dropped even further. When the column, "Mr. Muhammad Speaks," was discontinued in 1959, followers of the Muslim leader took with them another 25,000 in circulation, for they had been selling the paper in the streets, a method they later used to boost their own publication, *Muhammad Speaks*, to a claimed half-million sales. And, as civil rights became news, mainstream dailies and television began covering stories that once had been the exclusive property of the black press, introducing an unprecedented element of competition.

In spite of these problems, the *Courier* might have continued to prosper had it not been for management's tendency to stand at political odds with its employees and its readership. In 1932, publisher Robert L. Vann had helped to swing the black vote from "The Party of Lincoln" to the Democrats. But Vann, like his successor, Ira F. Lewis, switched parties when he thought black support was being taken for granted, and when Vann died, in 1940, he died a Republican. In 1948 his widow, Jessie L. Vann, emerged from her Oakmont estate to assume leadership of the business. She decided that the paper should remain Republican in its endorsements at a time when blacks were almost solidly Democratic. As Keith recalls, "Their politics weren't right. They were totally out of sync with black aspirations in politics and other activities."

The situation was exacerbated in 1959 when S. B. Fuller, a conservative Chicago cosmetics manufacturer, assumed control. He decided that the *Courier* would no longer be a black paper but an integrated news organ emphasizing "positive" matters and avoiding all controversy, this at a time when blacks were becoming increasingly militant. For those of us who experienced these sieges of mismanagement, the sense of helplessness and frustration—it seemed ridiculous that, due to a lack of correspondents, we should be covering the civil rights movement largely by telephone—was all but unendurable.

Like many of my colleagues, I left the *Courier*, in 1965, moving on to *Ebony*, flagship magazine of the prosperous and soundly managed Johnson Publishing Company. Mainstream publications were beginning to hire blacks, but for some of us that still was not a choice we cared to make. As Harold Keith notes, "I never thought of the white press as a career. I saw no hope there, no future. The rule was that you might get in but you could not enter the boardroom. And it still is. Bob Maynard [editor and publisher of the *Oakland Tribune*] is the exception. The white press represents the same institutions that we used to fight. There was no way that I could do the kind of job I wanted to do there, and I would not be happy."

Of Dreams and Needs

Looking back over the years, those of us who were fortunate enough to pass through the world of the old *Pittsburgh Courier* realize that it was part of a dream that might never again be able to come true for the black press. Many others, throughout the country, shared that dream.

When Robert S. Abbott founded the *Chicago Defender* in 1905 with nothing but a card table, a few pencils, and a tablet as his assets, he foresaw the need for a black publication that would address not only the few educated blacks and their white sympathizers, as had been the case with the early black press, but that would appeal to and perhaps stir the masses. The *Defender*, which is credited with inspiring the great migration of blacks from the South to the North, a trend that has subsided only in recent years, attained a national circulation of more than 200,000 after World War I. Published on a daily basis since 1956, it now claims to reach 35,000 daily and 40,000 with its weekend edition.

A few of the old guard, especially the family-owned *Afro-American* chain of Baltimore, which dates from 1892, have retained a healthy level of respectability, but there are no real circulation giants among today's black newspapers. A 1981 marketing study undertaken for Amalgamated Publishers, Inc., which coordinates national advertising sales for eighty-eight of the largest black newspapers in sixty-eight cities, states that they have a combined readership of 2,537,000—a total arrived at on the basis of a telephone survey rather than circulation figures. This is pitifully small when one considers that a single "white" paper—the Sunday New York *Daily News*—has a circulation of more than 2,000,000. Increasingly, the question arises as to whether black newspapers will survive this period of integration, inflation, and recession.

"Black papers are a miracle in themselves because they have managed to survive on money so minimal that white publishers wouldn't even consider existing on that level," says Raymond H. Boone, who spent sixteen years with the nine-paper *Afro-American* chain and is now a visiting professor of journalism at Howard University. "Those black papers that have survived deserve a lot of credit, though they should be chided for not remaining committed to their basic purpose, which should be to provide leadership in attacking all the dangers that still confront blacks."

A firebrand who, as a Pulitzer juror, spearheaded the successful fight to have blacks and women represented on the Pulitzer board, Boone says that the objective of today's black papers should be to concentrate on "external and internal enemies." Of the "internal" type, he says, "Some of our problems are matters that only *we* can solve—getting out the vote, keeping our kids in school so that they'll be able to compete for jobs, learning how to use our money properly, doing something about black-on-black crime. Black papers need to offer leadership to the community and to encourage greater self-reliance." But he does not downplay the importance of "external" factors, noting, "We are involved in a war of ideas these days and the black community is so greatly underarmed. That's why we need a strong black press. Most owners of white papers are conservative and are concerned about maintaining white power in this country. Their papers are political weapons and *not* simply objective disseminators of the news."

When Boone, forty-four, left the *Afro* chain, he did not seek a job in the mainstream, although he had worked for dailies in Virginia and Massachusetts before earning his journalism degree from Boston University. "It is difficult to go to the so-called enemy when you have been critical of them, and that was the position I was in. But I never have considered the white press the ultimate. My position was, hey, they ought to take a look at what *I'm* doing. I think I did it *better* than they did when it came to covering race relations."

For younger black journalists, who tend to be as concerned about career-building as their white counterparts, there are too many competing lures to keep them long associated with publications that offer limited financial rewards, although they, too, retain a kind of loving loyalty.

"The only thing that distinguishes black newspapers from the others is their lack of resources. The best people are quickly stolen away," says Fletcher Roberts, thirty-five, who was stolen away from the *Baltimore Afro-American* on August 9, 1974. He recalls the date, for it was the day Richard Nixon resigned as president. Roberts and a friend had been drinking champagne in celebration of the event and of the *Afro*'s catchy headline: AMEN in two-inch caps. The phone rang and it was the executive editor of the Annapolis *Capital*, who knew of Roberts's work and offered him a job at the white daily for more money. He accepted. "At the *Afro* I was earning $135 a week, working sometimes fifteen hours a day. This was less than I had been earning as a school teacher, and then I had summers off." Now a staff writer for *The Boston Globe*, Roberts says he enjoyed his days in the black press. "I felt a sense of purpose because I thought that what I was doing was important. What went on there really *mattered* to me." During his eighteen months on the *Afro-American* staff, he shot pictures, worked in the dark room, did layouts, reporting, editing, and "learned the whole operation." But, he warns, the lack of resources is a serious handicap. "How many black papers use offset printing or have VDTs? How many can afford to hire specialists to cover the environment, the law, science, and other complex fields? At the *Afro* we had six reporters. Here at the *Globe* we have eighty-five to a hundred. If you don't have the resources, you can't even get people *to* the story."

Greener Pastures

Roberts is part of the shrinking group of black journalists who entered the field through the black press, once the common route. Far more of the students I meet in my classes these days at Columbia don't consider it a viable option. This translates into a problem for black publishers, who say they cannot upgrade their products because they have difficulty finding qualified people.

Linda Prout, twenty-nine, had worked in New York as a researcher at ABC-TV news, as a reporter-critic at WBAI radio, as an assistant editor at *Us* magazine, and as a general assignment reporter at the Newark *Star-Ledger* before earning her master's degree at Columbia and moving on to her current position as a reporter-researcher at *Newsweek*. Throughout her varied experience, she never considered working for a black publication because "those in the New York area weren't of a very good quality and also didn't pay that well. I didn't want to work for a publication that called itself black but didn't address important black issues or do it with any sense of quality. Besides, money would be a big factor because most of the people I know working in the black press have a hard time making it." She concedes that she would consider it a step backwards to move to a black publication even if the position were much higher than the beginner's spot she holds at *Newsweek*. "I don't even know that many people who, on a continuous basis, read black newspapers. Most of the people I know consider them pretty tacky." In spite of her reservations, Prout affirms there is a strong need for black newspapers, noting, "The white press doesn't address issues from a black perspective. If there were a really *good* paper, I know of a lot of people working in the white press who would contribute to it."

Those who have remained in the black press are not unaware of the criticisms that have been leveled against the papers they produce. And they are quite aware of the greener pastures out there. At the almost inaccessible editorial offices of New York's *Amsterdam News*, located at the top of four steep flights of stairs in the firm's building near Harlem's 125th Street, Melvin Tapley muses wistfully about his options. After more than twenty years on the staff as a cartoonist, writer, and entertainment editor, Tapley has not abandoned the thought of moving into the mainstream. "They used to say that the black press was made up of people who couldn't go anywhere else, and at one time there was no place else we *could* go. But that's not true of most of the people who are here now." Citing the names of some *Amsterdam News* alumni, notably C. Gerald Fraser of *The New York Times*, Tapley says of himself, "I figured that maybe if they thought I was doing something outstanding, they would tap me on the shoulder. But I'm still waiting." His main reason for moving would be "money, no doubt about it!"

Tapley does not flinch when the weekly's flaws are pinpointed, explaining, "I realize that we work under certain handicaps. We have a small staff—about a dozen, plus stringers—and there's a lot of pressure on us. People send in clippings to us circling the typos and grammatical errors, but that's not all bad because we know that at least they're reading the paper. But we don't have any copy editors. We have to proof our own stuff."

Although American life has changed much over the years, Tapley sees few major changes in the paper, the main one being a women's section that no longer focuses on society news. Says Tapley, "The change came in the late sixties when the attitude emerged that there was no black society to compare with white society, and that the demonstrators were protesting not only against whites but also against middle-class blacks who wanted to be white but couldn't quite make it." Social affairs and community events, he says, still get wide coverage because a void is being filled. "Even today, when it comes to matters like weddings, you don't rate the dailies unless you're Whitney Young's daughter or some executive known to the white world. For little black people, we're still the best chance they have. Little white people don't have anything at all."

The *Amsterdam News* has an audited circulation of 41,000, which is hardly impressive considering that New York City has a larger black population than any metropolitan center outside of Africa. Its managing editor, William Egyir, is perhaps even more critical of the paper than are some outsiders. A Ghanaian who studied journalism in his homeland and London before coming to this country ten years ago, Egyir spent four years as an editor at the *Baltimore Afro-American* and helped train young journalists at Brooklyn's minority-based Trans-Urban News Service between two stints as the *Amsterdam*'s m.e.

"The *Afro* is much better run, is a much more disciplined organization than this one," says Egyir with a sardonic grin. "It has been owned by the Murphy family for generations and they have trained their young to handle it, though relatives have been fired when it seemed that they were not doing their job properly. Here, there seems to be no sense of leadership, no direction. If this paper had the sort of direction the *Afro* had, it could be a tremendous success, for we are opeating in the largest market in the nation. We have two million blacks in this city. Think of what we could do if we could capture even *half* of them! But we haven't been able to address the issues as they affect black people. That is the most important thing. We need more investigative pieces and more well-written pieces."

Egyir joined the *Amsterdam* staff in the late seventies, after the paper had come under heavy attack for mixing private political concerns with editorial purpose. Founded in 1909, the newspaper had been primarily owned and operated by C.B. Powell, a Harlem physician, from 1936 until 1971, when it was sold, for $2 million, to a consortium of prominent blacks that included then-Manhattan borough president Percy Sutton. Under the editorship of Bryant Rollins, formerly a *Boston Globe* reporter and founding editor of the black-oriented *Bay State Banner*, the *Amsterdam News* abandoned its old sensational mold to emphasize in-depth treatment of pertinent issues and reflective social commentary. The new image was quickly tarnished when the paper increasingly began to reflect Sutton's personal views, its pages liberally sprinkled with encomiums to the politician, his relatives, and his friends. In 1972, worried about compromising his journalistic integrity, Rollins left the paper and it soon reverted to its old blood-and-guts format. But controversy continued to rage as to whose interests the paper was serving, Sutton's or the black community's. Sutton no longer has a financial interest in the paper, but the *Amsterdam News* has not recovered from the loss of stature it suffered during that period.

New Leaders

If the old war-horses of the black press are having such a difficult time merely going through their traditional paces, then where is there any hope of revitalization?

One beam of light seems to be flickering up from Philadelphia, where a new national black weekly newspaper began publication at the end of April. The promise it offers was strong enough to attract Lou Ransom, who left the *Courier* shortly after I interviewed him to join the staff of *The National Leader* as senior editor and production manager. The new paper is the brainchild of Ragan Henry, a Harvard-trained attorney who entered the media investment field in 1972. Two years later, he created Broadcast Enterprises National, Inc., now the largest black-owned radio-television company in the country. To launch the paper, which has an initial $600,000 capitalization, he formed a sister firm called Publishers Enterprises National, Inc., with seven other black investors.

A tabloid-sized publication that incorporates some aspects of both magazines and newspapers, *The National Leader* features long articles focusing on issues of national importance to blacks, such as the plight of the Haitian boat people; the hardships endured by migrant workers; the threat to Meharry, the nation's oldest black medical school; and the NAACP boycott of Hollywood. Separate sections cover topics in education, religion, business, culture, style, and sports, while the paper's editorials are sharply to the point. The columnists are leading black journalists long associated with the mainstream press: Dorothy Butler Gilliam and William Raspberry of *The Washington Post,* syndicated columnist Carl T. Rowan, and Claude Lewis, whose commentary appeared in the Philadelphia *Bulletin* for twelve years before he became publisher of *The National Leader.*

For Lewis, whose journalistic career encompasses ten years at *Newsweek* plus stints at the *New York Herald Tribune,* NBC, and Westinghouse Broadcasting as well as *The Bulletin,* this is an initial venture into the black press and he is starting at the top. It is a challenge he welcomes. When *The Bulletin* folded, Lewis had eleven job offers from the mainstream, but he willingly accepted Ragan Henry's invitation to head up the new enterprise because "this seemed to be the most fun and the most challenging. In any of the other places I would essentially have gone on doing what I already had done, but this was something black and national. We are writing for people who have common interests and we can address them. These are people with whom we can identify. It frees you up to be more open, honest, and direct."

He asserts that this publication, which, unlike the black national papers of the past, does not have a locally based market, is filling a void. "There's a need for a national publication of this sort because events in Boston have implications for people in Berkeley, as those in Selma have implications for people in Seattle. There is a need for black people across the nation to share information so that they might better understand their situation. We are establishing a network that will address problems and keep black Americans informed on major events." The need is pointed up, Lewis says, by a sharp decline in coverage of blacks by the dailies and television. "We are no longer chic. Meanwhile, other organizations and movements have stolen our thunder and our techniques—feminists, the gays, and other groups—and attention has turned toward these others. They do deserve notice and have legitimate claims, but this should not be at the expense of blacks."

The National Leader seems to be off to a healthy start. The operation is streamlined, with a core editorial staff of six in the Philadelphia office; correspondents or stringers file from twenty-eight cities throughout the country. Initial paid circulation was 30,000, but by late July it had grown to 63,000, the bulk of distribution being through subscriptions as efforts are made to develop newsstand sales.

While Claude Lewis is new to the black press, managing editor Pat Patterson brings to the venture a rare breadth of view. The second black to join the staff of *Newsday*—he was hired as a general reporter back in 1963—Patterson has reported for, edited, and published black newspapers and was the founding editor of *Black Enterprise* magazine, where he still holds the title of editor at large.

Evaluating the current conservative drift in society and comparing it with the liberalism of the sixties and early seventies, Patterson says, "In the sixties, we rather blindly fell for an integrationist philosophy without considering the consequences to ourselves. We had the mistaken assumption that there was this great pool of benevolence out there that had been untapped and that, as soon as it was, everything would be all right. There was an awful lot of naiveté. I think we've learned from our mistakes. I think we've learned not to forsake ourselves for something at the end of the rainbow. Enough of us have learned through experience that we must maintain our strong identity with things black, that we must strengthen our institutions, whether they be the press, the schools, the church, or black business. We may make some other mistakes, but I don't think we're going to make that *particular* mistake again."

If *The National Leader* is a promising beam, the virtual beacon of a promise fulfilled beckons from California, where William H. Lee's *Sacramento Observer* might well hold the key to a bright new future for black journalism. Lee, a successful real estate broker, founded the weekly in 1962, when he was only twenty-six. In 1968, he sold his real estate business to become a full-time newspaper publisher with his wife, Kathryn, as managing editor. That was the turning point for a publication that now is widely regarded as the best black newspaper in the United States. In 1973, the National Newspaper Publishers Association first presented it with the John B. Russwurm award. It has earned the award, which commemorates the founder of the first black newspaper, in five out of the last eight years. Based in Sacramento County, where the census says there are 59,000 blacks out of nearly 800,000 residents, the paper claims a circulation of 44,000. Its success has given rise to offshoots, including a San Francisco paper called *The Observer*, which claims a circulation of 48,000; a two-year-old paper in Stockton with 6,000 readers; and an entertainment magazine called *The Happenings*, published in Los Angeles.

A cursory examination of any issue of *The Sacramento Observer* yields ample evidence of the reasons why it is succeeding while so many others are floundering. Its graphics are boldly imaginative. While local stories are played aggressively, it includes neatly encapsulated portions of national news. Major issues are given thorough and thoughtful treatment and special sections provide extensive coverage of a single topic from a variety of perspectives, from black-Jewish relationships to the questions blacks should consider when sending their children to private schools.

Bill Lee approaches publishing with an ebullience that seems to be lacking elsewhere, and his aspirations as to what he might accomplish with his paper apparently know no bounds. In November, he is planning to celebrate the paper's twentieth anniversary by publishing a 500-page edition, to be distributed statewide, that will serve as a major source reference on black life in California.

But what makes Bill Lee go? What does he have to say to other black publishers who seem to be struggling to avoid extinction?

"Creativity in approach," Lee responds. "We don't pretend to have all the answers, but we know that we've got to be more competitive in trying to get readers. We must provide them with something they'll buy because they want it. We can't just give them civil rights news and black news; we've also got to show them how they can survive, how they can buy a house or live happily. In our communities we have acute health problems, acute crime problems, and we must provide some of the answers through our papers."

Good enough, but nothing that has not already been said by others. What distinguishes Lee from other publishers is his conception of a totally different role for black newspapers. "I honestly see us assuming a new role, becoming the urban newspapers of the future," he comments. "Our cities have become increasingly black, and white papers have been unable or unwilling to reach this audience. Some have brought blacks in and tried to incorporate them into the operation, but this still can't give them the kind of credibility we can have. Our papers can fulfill the function of providing urban news and showing people how to cope with the urban environment, a role that white newspapers ultimately may give up. That can be our future."

It is an idea well worth considering.

45 Minority Press

by Marcia Ruth

Hispanics, Blacks, Asians, and American Indians rely on specialty newspapers, *presstime* staff writer Marcia Ruth writes, but the influence of these publications wanes as assimilation increases and as general-circulation papers increase minority hiring. This article is from *presstime*, August 1986.

Newspapers geared to minority groups have been a part of U.S. journalism since Colonial times, and they continue to be part of community life in cities with high concentrations of minorities.

In general, the historic pattern for such newspapers is that they are strongest when groups are least assimilated into American life.

"As long as there is any vestige of segregation and discrimination, there will be a need for the black press," says John H. Sengstacke, president of Sengstacke Newspapers, the largest black newspaper group, with a combined circulation of about 100,000 from publications in Chicago, Detroit, Pittsburgh and Memphis. "When that (need) is eliminated," he says, "the black press will become a good community newspaper."

Nationally circulated black newspapers reached their zenith before World War II, before other strong institutions emerged to fight for equality and civil rights. But in the decades that followed, such papers were largely replaced by small community weeklies, now the most numerous black newspapers read by America's 26 million blacks.

Among minorities whose first language is not English, the ethnic press generally reaches a high point during waves of immigration, then fades as the second generation learns English.

The "peak year for foreign-language newspapers" was 1914, say newspaper historians Edwin and Michael Emery, with "approximately 1,000 papers, of which 140 were dailies." After the flood of immigration in the early part of the century subsided, the figures dropped. "By 1983 there were fewer than 40 dailies and perhaps 200 other papers in some two dozen languages," say the Emerys in the fifth edition of *The Press and America*.

Not surprisingly, Hispanics, the fastest-growing minority in the United States, have the nation's strongest foreign-language press. A 1985 survey by the National Association of Hispanic Publications shows that 56 percent of its readership is first-generation Hispanic, but most observers say the rate of immigration is high enough to keep the Hispanic press growing for decades.

Hispanics are expected to become the largest ethnic group in the country by the middle of the 21st century.

Because of the size of the group—14.6 million in the 1980 census—and its concentration in specific parts of the country, a major question is to what extent will the Hispanic press become a bilingual press. "Will it follow the audience (as it learns English), or will it continue to be identified as a Spanish-language press?" asks Felix Gutierrez, associate professor of journalism at the University of Southern California.

Since the Immigration Act of 1965 opened up the opportunity for more non-European immigration, Asians have become the second most numerous immigrant group in the United States, with 1980 population of 3.2 million.

In the past decade, the Asian press has grown rapidly in most U.S. cities with a high concentration of recent Asian immigrants. But unlike Hispanic communities, which rely more heavily on Spanish-language papers published in the United States, Asians read a greater mix of foreign-language papers published locally and those imported.

Also noteworthy are recent developments among newspapers read almost exclusively by the United States' indigenous minority—1.4 million American Indians. There is a move to upgrade existing publications and to establish new ones independent of tribal governments, which now own most of the Indian press.

In the sections that follow, presstime presents a brief status report on these four mainstays of the minority press in the United States.

Hispanic Movement

Among Hispanic papers, "what you're seeing right now is a 'movement,'" says Joseph Garcia, publisher of *El Heraldo*, 25,000-circulation weekly in Chicago.

"About 1979–80, things started to take off, and since '80–81, things really blossomed," says Kirk Whisler, executive director of the National Association of Hispanic Publishers.

According to a 1985 study for the Los Angeles–based NAHP, there are 10 Hispanic dailies, 140 weeklies, 76 "less than weeklies," 114 magazines (20–25 published regularly), 91 journals and assorted other publications.

Nonetheless, Whisler predicts that this burgeoning circulation of more than 6 million, which has more than tripled since 1977, will coalesce into a smaller number of publications by the end of the century.

Several strong dailies have already emerged in major Hispanic centers, with the five largest based in Los Angeles, New York and Miami.

Of these, two are owned by Hispanic families:

- *La Opinion*, circulation about 62,000, is the oldest continuously published Hispanic daily in the United States. Founded in Los Angeles in 1926, it is now run by the second and third generation of the Lozano family.
- *Diario las Americas*, circulation about 67,000, was founded in 1953 by Nicaraguan exile publisher Horatio Aguirre who, with his son, still operates the newspaper in Miami.

The other three members of the "big five" are owned by U.S. media companies:

- *El Miami Herald*, circulation about 85,000, founded in 1975 by Knight-Ridder Inc.'s Miami Herald.
- *El Diario–La Prensa*, circulation about 60,000, purchased in 1981 by Gannett Co. It is published in New York City.
- *Noticias del Mundo*, funded in 1980 by News World Communications, which launched *The Washington Times* in 1982. Circulation of the original New York edition is about 50,000, and that of a Los Angeles edition is about half as many.

News World Communications is the only publisher of these dailies with public aspirations to go national with locally focused editions. Earlier this year, the parent company added small operations in San Francisco and Chicago. It plans to test market this fall in Miami.

In varying amounts, Hispanic papers mix coverage of local Hispanics with news of their countries of origin. "The focus is to serve the local community," which also means "you must let them know what is going on in their (home) countries," says Carlos Ramirez, *El Diario*'s president and publisher.

Like general-circulation papers, Hispanic papers are in pursuit of national ad dollars, most of which go to Spanish-language television.

"Up to now, the broadcasters have done a job on Madison Avenue, which is convinced Latinos watch TV and listen to radio and don't read newspapers," says Gutierrez of USC. "Until the publishers can effectively make their case to national advertisers and make it (newspaper advertising) easier to buy, then print growth will be stifled."

Estimates vary on how much of Hispanic advertising generally is going to the print medium. Both Hispanic Business, a magazine published in Santa Barbara, Calif., and the NAHP agree that the amount for all media is about $333 million.

But Hispanic Business maintains only 10 percent, or $33.3 million, of that goes to print. NAHP contends, however, that the amount is closer to 20 percent, or $61.2 million.

Seeking an increased share of the Hispanic market, Hispanic newspapers are "finally getting our act together," says NAHP's Whisler.

Last year, NAHP formed Entrada, a New York City advertising-rep firm that now offers one-order-one-bill purchasing of 38 Hispanic publications with combined circulations of over one million.

Black Re-evaluation

Five years ago, John L. Procope, publisher of the New York *Amsterdam News*, proposed a "national editorial board" to spearhead stronger "advocacy" journalism on the part of the 100-plus members of the National Newspaper Publishers Association. . . .

That editorial unity did not occur, says long-time NNPA Executive Director Steve Davis. Instead, he says, concerted action has focused on the business side, where "black newspapers have to go out and fight like mad for advertising"—a struggle in which they have been only marginally successful thus far.

Following predictions in the early 1980s by a historian of the black press, Boston University Professor Henry G. La Brie III, that black newspapers were headed for hard times, Christopher H. Bennett, now in his second term as NNPA President, committed the organization to aggressive pursuit of national ad dollars.

Bennett, publisher of *The Seattle Medium,* says he was not selected as a priest or an undertaker. "I was not hired to do the last rites or the burial." He claims that since he took over as NNPA president, black publishers have obtained commitments for $100 million in advertising over the next few years.

Precise figures are hard to pin down, owing to lack of centralized data.

Circulation is also hard to determine. Audits are done by several different firms, and some papers do not have them. But in 1984, La Brie estimated circulation of black newspapers at 3.6 million, one million of which was free circulation, and only 538,000 of which was audited.

But publishers say that the black press is stronger than circulation figures would indicate because they have more readers per copy than mainstream newspapers.

On the national advertising scene, most black newspapers are represented by one of two New York City firms—Amalgamated Publishers Inc. and Black Media Inc.—but some, including Bennett's Seattle paper, market independently.

Those involved in advertising sales point to several signs of progress. In the past year, national advertising for the more than 80 papers represented by Amalgamated Publishers increased by $1.2 million over the $7 million obtained in fiscal year 1984–85, says General Sales Manager Karl D. Jackson.

This upward trend will continue, Jackson predicts, because of the general decline of "mass media" buys. "Fortune 500 advertisers are moving to a new stance, and it's called 'segmentation,'" he says. "They have now realized segmenting is the wave of the future."

Also growing is membership in NNPA. Executive Director Davis says that over the past five years, it has increased from 115 to 138. The only three black dailies in the country are members—the *Chicago Defender, Atlanta Daily World* and *New York Daily Challenge.*

Meanwhile, the black press is evolving to meet the changing needs of its readers. While acknowledging the historic function of the black press to serve as a "watchdog for the black community and principle advocate for social justice," NNPA First Vice President William H. Lee says, "We also serve as a publication for survival news, which is the type of news urban Americans need for everyday existence." With this emphasis, says Lee, publisher of The Observer Newspaper Group in Sacramento, "you begin to attract more than just blacks."

An attempt to launch a national black newspaper, the *National Leader,* failed in mid-1984 after almost two years of operation. The weekly failed to obtain the advertising needed to survive, but its 96,000 circulation shows there is a demand for such a product in the black community, says former editor Claude Lewis, now a columnist and editorial board member at *The Philadephia Inquirer.*

Ironically, one problem being experienced by black newspapers—that does not plague minorities with a foreign-language press—is that as general-circulation papers increase their efforts to hire and promote minorities, black publications have been losing talent. "Over the years, we have been training them (journalists) and they have been stealing them," says black publisher Sengstacke.

Asian Diverse

Wide variations exist among foreign-language newspapers read in the United States by people from various Asian countries. Unlike the black and Hispanic newspapers, those with an Asian connection have no overall trade association, and information is more difficult to come by.

But, generally, the Asian press follows the same growth pattern as that of other minorities. "What you find in Asian communities is that the newer group of immigrants have the more vibrant ethnic press," says Gil Roy Gorre, editor of the *Philippine American News*, a biweekly paper published in Los Angeles.

Among Americans of Japanese origin, Japanese-language newspapers published in the United States are on the wane, while there is a brisk importation of newspapers published in Japan.

"Virtually none of the American-born Japanese read Japanese, and most are so Americanized they really don't care about Japanese affairs," says William K. Hosokawa, former editorial page editor of *The Denver Post* and now ombudsman for the *Rocky Mountain News*.

On the other hand, the large numbers of Japanese businessmen temporarily in the United States have created a market for the importation of newspapers printed in Japan—10,000 a day, according to Nihon Shinbun Kyokai, the Japan Newspaper Publishers and Editors Association.

However, in U.S. cities with large Chinese-speaking populations, the picture is reversed. There, as many as a dozen dailies produced in the United States may compete.

In an article headlined "Newspaper Wars—the Battles Rage," the *Los Angeles Times* last year characterized the Chinese press in that city as a "free-for-all reminiscent of bygone days in American journalism when newspapers divided along fiercely partisan lines."

The major papers "have their political stand clearly designated," says Oscar Chiang, a reporter-researcher at *Time* magazine who has studied the Chinese press. This reflects the sharp political division in the U.S. Chinese community between loyalty to Taiwan or mainland China.

Fierce competition is also a function of increased professionalism, says Charles Lai, executive director of the New York Chinatown History Project. "In the last 10 years, there are more professional journalists that are entering Chinese newspapers," he says. "The stories are becoming more fine-tuned. There is more investigative work."

A few Chinese-language newspapers circulate nationally. The *World Journal* and the *Chinese Daily News* claim circulations of about 100,000, the *Centre Daily News* about 65,000, and the *International Daily News* about 58,000.

But sources consider the figures suspect: "I would not take anybody's numbers seriously because they (the papers) tend to exaggerate," says Chiang. "They always seem to inflate their numbers," agrees Lai.

In Korean-speaking communities, there is another pattern—localized editions of papers published in Korea.

"What happens is that in every major city where Korean-Americans live, people apply for a sort of franchise and operate out of a small office," says Choi Sung-il, executive director of the U.S.-based Council for Democracy in Korea. In general, when such papers are distributed on U.S. newstands, about 80 percent of their pages are printed in Korea, with the rest added locally, also in Korean.

Indians Unifying

In contrast to the free-for-all environment of the press of the most recent wave of immigrants, America's indigenous minority—American Indian—is presenting an increasingly unified front.

Since the formation of the Native American Press Association in 1984, many leaders of the Native American press have pushed for significant upgrading of the more than 350 publications read primarily by American Indians. As tangible evidence of this effort, more than 100 people, mostly publishers and editors, attended the NAPA's second annual convention in Scottsdale, Ariz., June 5–7 [1986], which included workshops on all phases of newspaper production.

But beyond technical development, many are also concerned about a problem not shared by other U.S. minorities—reservation living and government.

"There is a real difference in Indian country," says Tim A. Giago Jr., owner and publisher of *The Lakota* (S.D.) *Times*, one of the few privately owned Indian papers and the largest Indian weekly.... What most of these papers print is subject to approval by tribal boards, he says, and unless they become independent, "they are up against some very harsh censorship."

Of the approximately 350 Indian publications in the United States, only one is a daily, less than a quarter are weekly, and the rest are published monthly or less often, says Margaret A. Clark Price, NAPA's executive director.

Of these, "several are truly independent rather than published by a tribe," says Loren Tapahe, a founder of NAPA and former publisher of *The Navajo Times* in Window Rock, Ariz.—the only Indian daily. Others are owned by tribes but approach being editorially autonomous, and some are "house organs," he says.

Although such issues are prominent among American Indian publishers lately, most of the minority press weighs similar questions of independence.

And most would probably agree with the dual function of minority newspapers articulated by John H. Murphy III, publisher of the Afro-American group, whose papers in Baltimore, Richmond and Washington, D.C., have a combined circulation of about 50,000. "We serve the same general needs as any community paper," he says. "We let people know what's happening in the community."

At the same time, he observes, the minority press shares a goal with its readers: "We're doing the same things all other minority groups are doing—trying to get a piece of the action."

Mass Media and Minorities: For Further Reading

David Armstrong, *A Trumpet to Arms: Alternative Media in America.* Los Angeles, Calif.: Tarcher, 1981.

Gordon L. Berry and Claudia Mitchell-Kernan, *Television and the Socialization of the Minority Child.* New York: Academic Press, 1982.

James E. Murphy and Sharon M. Murphy, *Let My People Know: American Indian Journalism: 1828–1978.* Norman, Okla.: University of Oklahoma Press, 1981.

Report of the National Advisory Commission on Civil Disorders. Washington, D.C.: U.S. Government Printing Office, 1968.

Bernard Rubin, *Small Voices and Great Trumpets: Minorities and the Media.* New York: Praeger, 1980.

XII

Mass Media and Women

"The ladies, bless 'em, have to be protected. No general assignment reporting. No police beat—unless, of course, in disguise to help on an exposé. The desk? Let them read proof because they're good with details. Or let them be in charge of 'Society.'"

Those clichés from the newspaper business are dying out—thanks, in part, to the men and women who are proving them absurd. But across the mass media there are still problems to be solved; goals to be set and achieved. In her 1986 annual survey of women in newsroom management, Dorothy Jurney counted 421 women and 2,987 men in directing editorships at U.S. daily newspapers. In 1977 the numbers were 165 and 3,025. But, as in earlier years, there are more women policymakers—234—on the under-25,000 circulation papers than on all the others put together.

In terms of recognized leadership roles, women have made it at smaller papers. On magazines and in broadcasting, the situation is much the same, though there is no Dorothy Jurney in those media to keep track of the numbers.

Concern about women in the media is not limited to women in management. There are questions about equal pay for equal work, equal assignments and equal working conditions. And there are questions about the portrayal of women in news, features, entertainment programs, and advertising.

The variety and number of women's magazines, and the advertising that supports them, have changed in recent years, partly because of the changing roles of women in society and partly because of their changing interests. The new publications will continue as long as reader interest and advertising support for them do. The question is, What's next—in all the mass media? From a marketing viewpoint, how long will women be the conspicuous consumers at whom so much product promotion is aimed?

46 Getting There: Women in the Newsroom

by Terri Schultz-Brooks

Terri Schultz-Brooks, chair of journalism at New York University, recounts the changes in newsrooms since the late 1960s and challenges the media and women journalists to "scale the topmost peaks." This article is from *Columbia Journalism Review*, March/April 1984.

When I walked into the city room of the *Chicago Tribune* my first day on the job, I saw a sea of white male faces above white rumpled shirts; in true *Front Page* tradition, a few reporters puffed on cigars and a few editors wore green eyeshades. That was in 1968. When I left four years later, things hadn't changed much, and I filed a sex discrimination complaint against the paper. Now, twelve years later, 29 percent of the *Tribune*'s general assignment reporters are women. The associate editor is a woman and so is the head of the sports copydesk. "In the old days, women turned on each other; now we turn *to* each other," says Carol Kleiman, associate financial editor and columnist for the paper and a member of its women's network. "The only place I'm weak is getting women into the higher positions—running the foreign, national and local desks. But they'll get there," says James Squires, the *Tribune*'s editor.

Gone are the days when women in journalism who wanted to write hard news were condemned to the "soft-news ghettos" of the society, food, or gardening pages, the sections considered second-class journalism by the men who run the papers. Now they not only report on issues of significance to women—from day care to birth control—but also cover the White House and the locker room, the streets of Beirut and the villages of El Salvador. Thirty-six years ago, when Pauline Frederick was hired by ABC as the first woman network news correspondent, she was assigned not only to interview the wives of presidential contenders at a national political convention, but also to apply their on-camera makeup. Today, on most large papers, 30 to 40 percent of the hard-news reporters are women. In television, 97 percent of all local newsrooms had, by 1982, at least one woman on their staffs, as compared to 57 percent in 1972.

Some women have even worked their way into upper management: Mary Anne Dolan is editor of the *Los Angeles Herald Examiner*; Kay Fanning is managing editor of *The Christian Science Monitor*; Sue Ann

Wood is managing editor of the *St. Louis Globe-Democrat*; Gloria B. Anderson was managing editor of *The Miami News* until October 1981, when she co-founded the weekly she co-publishes and edits, *Miami Today*. "I remember when there was no such thing as a woman copy editor—the reasoning being that you can't give a woman authority over a man," says Eileen Shanahan, former *New York Times* reporter (one of seven who sued that paper for sex bias) and now senior assistant managing editor of the *Pittsburgh Post-Gazette*, the number-three spot on the paper.

One hundred and twenty newspapers now have women managing editors, according to Dorothy Jurney of Wayne, Pennsylvania, an independent researcher and veteran editor whose annual survey of women in newsroom management appeared in the January issue of the *Bulletin of the American Society of Newspaper Editors*. And about fifty of the country's 1,700 daily papers have women publishers, says Jean Gaddy Wilson, an assistant professor of mass communications at Missouri Valley College who, aided by grants from Gannett, Knight, and other foundations, will release in early summer the first results of what promises to be the most comprehensive study to date of women working in the news media.

The Limits of Change

But serious barriers do remain. "I've seen a lot of change, but it hasn't gone far enough," says Shanahan. Top management jobs in large media corporations are nearly as closed to women now as they were twenty years ago. The situation at *The Washington Post* is fairly typical. The *Post* has beefed up the number of women on its news staff considerably since it reached an out-of-court settlement in 1980 with more than one hundred women there who had filed a complaint of sex discrimination with the Equal Employment Opportunity Commission; it has even appointed a woman, Karen DeYoung, as editor of foreign news, and another, Margot Hornblower, as chief of its coveted New York bureau. "The number of qualified bright female candidates has never been higher," says executive editor Benjamin C. Bradlee. But there are currently no women staff foreign correspondents, and "there aren't many of us in power jobs," says Claudia Levy, editor of the *Post*'s Maryland Weekly section and head of the women's caucus that negotiated the settlement. While Bradlee says he "sure as hell" plans to move women into top editing jobs, they don't include his. "I've seen ten thousand stories on my possible successor, and none has mentioned a woman," he says.

More than half of the women managing editors are at newspapers of less than 25,000 circulation; at large papers, men still hold 90.4 percent of the managing editorships, Jurney has found. Indeed, only 10.6 percent of all jobs at or above the level of assistant managing editor at all daily and Sunday papers are filled by women. And most of those editing jobs are in feature departments, positions generally not considered "on line" for top management slots, which are usually filled from within the newsroom.

In broadcasting, progress is equally mixed. Ten years ago, there were almost no female news directors. Now, women are in charge of 8 percent of television newsrooms and 18 percent of radio newsrooms. More than one-third of all news anchors are women, but there has never been a solo woman anchor—nor, for that matter, a female co-anchor team—assigned permanently to any prime-time weeknight network news program. Nor is there likely to be in the near future.

On local stations, the news team is usually led by a man with a younger woman in a deferential role. Only 3 percent have survived on-camera past the age of forty; nearly half of all male anchors, on the other hand, are over forty. And only three women over age fifty appear regularly in any capacity before network cameras—Marlene Sanders, Barbara Walters, and Betty Furness. (One reason Christine Craft was pulled from her anchor slot at KMBC-TV in Kansas City, Missouri, was because she was "not deferential to men." She was also told that, at age thirty-eight, she was "too old" for the job.)

In top broadcast management jobs, many women feel they are moving backwards. A few years ago, NBC had one female vice-president in the news division: now it has none. CBS had four out of eleven; now it has one out of fourteen. "There are no women being coached for key positions." says a female former vice-president of the CBS news division, who requested anonymity. "There's no more pressure from Washington, so anything management does for women it views as makenice, as charity."

"Women feel fairly stuck," concurs CBS correspondent Marlene Sanders, who has broken a number of broadcast barriers—as the first woman TV correspondent in Vietnam, the first woman to anchor a network evening news show (she substituted temporarily for a man), and the first woman vice-president of news at any network. "We may have to wait for another generation—and hope those men in power have daughters whom they are educating, and whom they can learn from."

Resistance—and Revenge

What progress has been made has not come easily. Although Carole Ashkinaze, for example, wanted to be a political reporter, she accepted a position as a feature columnist with *The Atlanta Constitution* in 1976, bringing with her nearly a decade of experience as a hard-news reporter at *Newsday*, *The Denver Post*, and *Newsweek* (where about fifty women filed a sex-bias complaint in 1972). Her first column—about Jimmy Carter's 51.3 Percent Committee, formed to develop a pool of women for possible political appointment—sent ripples of disapproval through the *Constitution's* management ranks. "The editors' reaction was: 'We hope you're not going to do that kind of story as a steady diet,'" she recalls. "But women came out of the woodwork, saying 'Please keep writing about this kind of thing.'" Subsequent columns were about battered women, problems in collecting child-support payments, abortion. She wrote about inequality wherever she saw it, and even began a crusade to get a women's bathroom installed near the House and Senate chambers in the state capitol. While male legislators could run to their nearby private bathroom, listen to piped-in debates, and return to their seats in less than a minute, women legislators had to go to the far end of the capitol building and line up behind tourists in the public restroom. "They finally gave the women a restroom, and the women gave me a certificate of commendation," says Ashkinaze.

After about a year, management gave in to her request and she was moved to the city room as a political reporter, but kept her column, in which she now writes about everything from racism to feminism to the environment. In August 1982, she became the first woman ever appointed to the paper's editorial board. "I'm very proud of it, and very humble, because I realize it's a result not only of my talents, but of what women in the South have been fighting for for decades," she says. "It's wonderful for other women at the paper to see more women here in positions of authority. It's something we've never had before." Fifteen women now hold editing and management jobs at the paper. "When I came here," Ashkinaze recalls, "these positions truly weren't open to women. Now, even with the political backlash in Washington, there is a much larger awareness here that women are an extremely valuable resource."

Emily Weiner, a coordinator of the women's caucus at *The New York Times*, was hired by the *Times* as an editorial artist in the traditionally all-male map department in December 1978, shortly after the *Times* had settled its class-action sex discrimination suit. (The *Times* agreed out of court to pay $233,500 and to launch a four-year hiring and promotion program for women.) "I was in the right place at the right time," Weiner says. "There were gold stars out there for *Times* managers who hired women. I am damn good at what I do, but I'm sure there are other good women who wouldn't have gotten this job if they had applied for it earlier."

"The sad part," adds Weiner, "is that the benefits have gone mainly to us younger women, not to those who filed the suits and took the risks, who expended their emotional energy and time and got the wrath of management." As a friend in management told Betsy Wade Boylan, a copy editor on the paper's national news desk who was one of the plaintiffs in the *Time*'s discrimination suit, "The *Times* is not in the business of rewarding people who sue it."

Indeed, more than one woman who has laundered her company's dirty linen in public has found herself writing more obits, working more grave-yard shifts, subjected to lateral "promotions," and passed over in favor of women hired from outside. But the same kind of shoddy treatment has been too often dished out to women whether they sue or not.

The Butcher Treatment and Other Games

The story of Mary Lou Butcher is a case in point. A few months after graduating from the University of Michigan in 1965 with a political science degree, Butcher was hired by the *Detroit News* to write wedding announcements—the only kind of position then open to women with no prior reporting experience. (Men were trained in the city room.) Determined to move into hard news, she began writing stories on her own time for the city room and after a year and a half of "pushing and pleading," was transferred to a suburban bureau, a move that gave her a chance to cover local government.

Three years later, after volunteering to work nights as a general assignment reporter, she finally made it into the city room. But after about six years of covering a wide range of stories—for a while, she was assigned to the Wayne County Circuit Court—she was given a weekend shift, normally reserved for new reporters. Men with less seniority had weekends off, but when Butcher—by now a veteran of eleven years—finally asked for a better shift, she instead found a note on her typewriter saying she was being transferred back to the suburbs.

Other women at the *News* had been similarly exiled. In 1972 there were eight women reporters in the city room. When Butcher was "demoted" to suburbia in 1976, she was the last remaining woman reporter in the newsroom on the day shift; all the others had been moved to the life-style, reader-service, or suburban sections—or had left. When the *News* used its city room to film a TV commercial promoting the paper, it had to recruit women from other departments to pose as reporters.

"When I saw that note, a light finally went on," Butcher says. "I thought: 'Wait. There's something strange going on here.' I had proven myself to be a good hard-news reporter. I saw no reason for being treated like this. It took a long time for it to occur to me that there was something deliberate about what was happening here, that I was the victim of a pattern."

As has been the case with many women reporters, that pattern also appeared in her story assignments. When she volunteered to help report on Jimmy Hoffa's disappearance, she was turned down because, she believes, it was considered "basically a man's story." During United Auto Workers negotiations in the mid-1970s, she—getting much the same treatment as Pauline Frederick thirty years earlier—was assigned to interview the wives of the Ford management team negotiators; the talks themselves were covered by reporters who were male. And when an education official from

Washington came to Detroit to talk about how sex stereotyping in schools can lead to stereotyping in jobs, the editor assigned her to cover it because, she recalls, "he said he wanted a light story, and 'we figure we can get away with it by sending you.'" She argued with him and wrote the story straight; it was buried in the paper.

Butcher and three other *News* women eventually sued the paper, which agreed last November in an out-of-court settlement to pay $330,000, most of which will go to about ninety of its present and former women employees. Butcher decided to leave journalism because, she says, "My advancement opportunities were almost totally blocked at the *News*. And after filing a lawsuit, it wasn't realistic to think that other media in Detroit would be eager to hire me. Management doesn't like wave-makers." She is now account supervisor for the public relations firm of MG and Casey Inc. in Detroit. "Newspapering is my first love, but I think the sacrifice was well worth it," she says. "Now the *News* is recruiting women from around the country, putting them in the newsroom, and giving them highly visible assignments. I feel really pleased; that's what it was all about."

Not all women feel that their complaints against their employers harm their careers in the long run. "Sure, there may be adverse consequences to signing on to these suits. But there are adverse consequences to being a woman working in a man's world. Some managers may punish you for it, but others believe it shows a certain amount of gumption," says Peggy Simpson, one of seven female AP reporters who last September won a $2 million out-of-court settlement of a suit charging sex and race discrimination. (The AP, like other defendants cited in this article who have agreed to out-of-court settlements, has denied the charges of discrimination. "But when a company settles for two million dollars, it suggests they had good reason to want to avoid going to court," says New York attorney Janice Goodman, who represented not only the AP plaintiffs but also sixteen women employees of NBC, who won their own $2 million settlement in 1977. In such settlements, the money is usually divided among the women employees who have allegedly suffered from sex discrimination.)

Still, for various reasons, all the AP plaintiffs have left the wire service for other jobs. Simpson is now economic correspondent for Hearst and Washington political columnist for *The Boston Herald*. Another plaintiff, Shirley Christian, who was on the AP foreign desk in 1973, went to *The Miami Herald* and in 1981 won a Pulitzer for her work in Central America.

It is not only the plaintiffs who may find their jobs on the line. Vocal sympathizers within a company can suffer recriminations as well. When Kenneth Freed, who at the time was the AP's State Department correspondent, won a Nieman Fellowship at Harvard in 1977, he says he was told shortly before his departure that the wire service would not supplement his fellowship money with a portion of his AP salary—a practice it had generally followed up to then. He later learned from friends at AP "that the reason was to punish me for my union activism—especially my role in the suit pressing for women and minority rights. They felt I had betrayed them. After all, I had one of the best beats in Washington and was paid considerably over scale. When I supported the women's suit, it just angered them even more." Thomas F. Pendergast, vice president and director of personnel and labor relations for the AP, says Freed was a victim of circumstance rather than of deliberate ill will. He says AP president and general manager Keith Fuller decided for financial reasons to stop supplementing all fellowships after he took over in October 1976. But unfortunate coincidences did not stop there. When Freed was ready to resume his old job after his year at Harvard, he says he was told by his Washington bureau chief that "there was no longer anything for me at the State Department." He adds, "I told them the only thing I *didn't* want to do was cover foreign policy on the Hill and, after that, it was all they offered me." Freed quickly left AP, and is now Canadian bureau chief for the *Los Angeles Times*.

Newspapers and broadcast stations that have agreed to fill goals for women have often failed to meet them. They blame slow employee turnover, and the general doldrums that have hit the newspaper business, for those failures. *The New York Times*, for instance, agreed in its consent decree to give women 25 percent of its top editorial jobs; in fact, only 16 percent had been so filled by 1983. Out of sixteen job categories in which hiring goals were set for women, the *Times* had met those goals in only eight categories—mainly the less prestigious ones. "We feel it has lived up to neither the spirit nor the letter of the law," says Margaret Hayden, counsel for the *Times*'s women's caucus.

And numbers can be dressed up to look better than they are. Several women at *Newsday* report that, since the out-of-court settlement in 1982 of a suit filed by four women employees, lateral moves by women are sometimes listed as promotions in the house newsletter. And when attorney Janice Goodman inspected the AP's records in 1982, she found that the wire service was giving inflated experience ratings to the men it hired, so that many were starting with salaries higher than those of women with equal experience.

A few years after the Federal Communications Commission started monitoring broadcast stations for their employment practices, the United States Commission on Civil Rights noted in its report, *Window Dressing on the Set*, that the proportion of women listed by stations in the top four FCC categories had risen "a remarkable—and unbelievable" 96.4 percent. In fact, the commission found that, as a result of a shuffling of job descriptions, three-fourths of all broadcast employees at forty major television stations could be classified as "upper level" by 1977, an "artifically inflated job status" that the commission found again in a follow-up report it issued in 1979.

Setting the Pace—and Pushing Hard

Yet even after discounting for such creative manipulation of statistics, the figures do show solid gains for women. At Gannett, the largest newspaper chain in the country, chairman and president Allen H. Neuharth has been a pacesetter at moving women into jobs: its eighty-five dailies now have twelve women publishers, two women executive editors, five women editors, and fourteen women managing editors. Cathleen Black is president of *USA Today* and a member of the Gannett management committee. "For twenty years Neuharth has been working creatively to make it happen," says Christy Bulkeley, editor and publisher of Gannett's *Commercial-News* in Danville, Illinois, and, as vice-president of Gannett Central, in charge of overseeing six of the chain's papers in four states. Neuharth, for instance, sent Bulkeley and another woman to the 1972 Democratic convention, which they saw as an opportunity to "produce enough copy so the all-male staff of the Washington bureau couldn't say we weren't doing our share of the load," Bulkeley recalls. Shortly after, the first woman appeared as a full-time reporter in Gannett's Washington bureau.

The AP is now hiring women at a rate equal to men for its domestic news staff. In 1973, when the suit began, only 8 percent of its news staff was female; now it is up to 26 percent, and rising. In 1973, the AP had only two or three women on the foreign desk, a position that prepares reporters for assignments abroad; now six out of seventeen on the foreign desk are women.

At *Newsday*, 41 percent of reporters and writers hired for the newsroom over the past nine years have been women. "Before we filed our suit [in 1975] there were no women in the bureaus, no women on the masthead, no women in positions of importance in the composing room," says Sylvia Carter, a *Newsday* writer who was a plaintiff in the suit. "Now, a woman is Albany bureau chief, a woman is White House correspondent; there are lots of women editors, three women on the masthead, and a woman foreman in the composing room."

The most visible gains have been made in cities where women have pushed hardest for them. Take Pittsburgh, for instance. In general, the town "is far and away less than progressive towards women; if someone calls me 'sweetheart' I don't even notice anymore," says the *Post-Gazette*'s Shanahan. But a chapter of the National Organization for Women threatened for several years to challenge local broadcast licenses in FCC proceedings if the city's stations did not improve women's programming and employment. The result: media women are doing very well in Pittsburgh. Today, five women hold top administrative positions at CBS affiliate KDKA-TV, including those of vice-president and general manager. At WTAE-TV, Hearst's flagship station, four women hold top-level jobs. KDKA radio has three women in high executive news jobs, and three women co-anchors. And Madelyn Ross is managing editor of Shanahan's rival paper, the *Pittsburgh Press*.

"When one of the media is a target, it raises other people's consciousness," says ex–*Detroit News* reporter Butcher. "It has a ripple effect." At the *Detroit Free Press*, for example, the managing editor, city editor, business editor, graphics editor, and life-style editor are all female. (At Butcher's former paper the news editor is a woman and women hold about 30 percent of the editorial jobs.) In addition to Butcher's suit against the *News*, the Detroit chapter of NOW and the Office of Communication of the United Church of Christ also negotiated aggressively for women's and minority rights with local broadcasting stations. Today, two major network affiliates—WDIV-TV and WXYZ-TV—have women general managers.

Pressure on broadcasting stations in the form of FCC license challenges has subsided in recent years, in part because improvements have been made in the broadcast industry, and in part because "we don't have the votes anymore at the FCC, which is now controlled by right-wing Republicans," says Kathy Bonk, director of the NOW Legal Defense and Education Fund Media Project in Washington, D.C.

But in many broadcast news organizations a solid groundwork has been laid. "Those women created opportunities for the rest of us, and I will always be grateful for that," says Sharon Sopher, who was hired as a news writer and field producer for NBC in 1973, a few months after several NBC women employees filed a sex-discrimination complaint with the New York City Commission on Human Rights. Sopher became the first network producer to go into the field with an all-woman crew, and has been allowed to do stories previously off-limits to women—from a feature segment on street gangs to a special assignment to cover the Rhodesian war from the guerrilla perspective. Her first independent documentary, *Blood and Sand: War in the Sahara*, aired on WNET in 1982.

Will the Advance Be Halted?

Once at or near the top, women can have significant professional impact on the attitudes of their male colleagues. Richard Salant was president of CBS News in 1975 when Kay Wight was appointed director of administration and assistant to the president. "She made me realize what a rotten job we were doing about hiring and promoting women," Salant says. "She kept at me all the time, in a diplomatic but insistent way, about how few women we had in every department except steno and research." As a result, Salant, who has four granddaughters, began to insist on monthly reports from his subordinates on the numbers of women in each department. "I finally wouldn't approve any openings unless they put in writing what they had done to recruit women and minorities. The paperwork was a pain—but at least it made people conscious of the issues." During his time at the helm (he left CBS in 1979 and is now president and chief executive officer of the National News Council) the number of women in important positions rose dramatically, but not enough to satisfy Salant, who maintains that his greatest disappointment is that "I never got a woman on *60 Minutes*." (Salant was among the first members to resign from New York's all-male Century Club over its discriminatory policies. Similarly, Arthur Ochs Sulzberger, chairman of the board of *The New York Times*, warned his top executives last year that, as of January, they would no longer be reimbursed for expenses incurred at the club.)

When *Chicago Tribune* editor Squires was Washington bureau chief for the paper, Eileen Shanahan, then with *The New York Times*, and Marlene Cimmons of the *Los Angeles Times* convinced him to join them in a project to eliminate sexism from the AP and UPI stylebooks. They "raised my sensitivity about women's issues above what I ever thought it could be raised," he says. Now, many women at the *Tribune* feel they have an ally in Squires. "The pioneer women in journalism were friends of mine—Nancy Dickerson, Eleanor Randolph, Elizabeth Drew," he says. "A lot of them had a rough time just because they were women. And seeing what has happened to them makes me feel I have to take steps to overcome the problems of the past." But performance can lag far behind promise. Five major editing jobs opened last year at the *Tribune*—managing editor, copydesk chief, metro editor, assistant metro editor, and national editor— and none of them went to a woman.

"The battle isn't over for equal rights in any profession, including journalism," says Helen Thomas, UPI's veteran White House reporter, who has covered six presidents and toted up a number of firsts—first woman president of the White House Correspondents Association, first woman officer of the National Press Club, first woman member of the Gridiron Club. Yet she remains optimistic. "It is impossible for women to lose what we've gained," she says. "We're now secure in our role as journalists—we just have to expand that role."

"We're fighting against enormous odds," says Joan Cooke, metro reporter for *The New York Times*, chair of the *Times* unit of The Newspaper Guild of New York, and a plaintiff in the suit against the *Times*. "Look at the masthead. [Out of seventeen people listed, two are women.] That's where the power is, and they're not going to give up power easily. And most women don't want to devote all their extra energy to equal rights—they want to go home like everybody else, to be with their families or friends. But if the spirit is there, and the will is there, it can be done." Sylvia Carter, a *Newsday* writer who was a plaintiff in the sex discrimination case against her paper, advises women to "be tough, keep your sense of humor, and form a women's caucus—but don't do it on company time."

Slowly, discrimination is easing as men see that women can do the job.

The courage, persistence, and sheer hard work of women journalists have made these changes possible. But, at too many news organizations, women have yet to scale the topmost peaks; despite their increasing visibility, they do not have much more power than before. And the important question is: Will they ever? In the past, government pressure in the form of lawsuits and the threat of revoking broadcast licenses forced the news media to give women a chance. Now, in the hands of a conservative administration, the tools by which that pressure is exerted—the EEOC and the FCC—are being allowed to rust. It is up to the news media, then, to spur themselves on toward greater equality in the newsroom and resist the temptation to backslide into the patterns of discrimination that have limited and punished women because of their sex.

47 Mythogyny

by Caryl Rivers

The media continue to propagate distorted information about women, says Caryl Rivers, professor of journalism and director of the science communication program at Boston University, novelist, and essayist. This article, adapted from "Women, Myth and Media" in *When Information Counts: Grading the Media*, edited by Bernard Rubin, was published in *The Quill*, May 1985.

The image of women in the media is more often than not strangely contorted. Much of what the media present as "objective fact" about women is in truth a mishmash of myth and misinformation. This is little changed from the days before the women's movement. Behind the headlines on such contemporary staple stories as sex and the brain, premenstrual syndrome, math genes, and stress and "superwomen" boils a streaming cauldron of mythology, of which few of the journalists who write these stories are aware.

As Elizabeth Janeway points out so incisively in *Man's World, Woman's Place*, every society invents myths about itself and then proceeds to act on those myths as if they were fact. Mythmakers are usually small, powerful, élite goups—referendums are not held on popular mythology. In time, myth becomes indistinguishable from truth. Plato's cave-dwellers, inhabiting a world of darkness, saw their shadows dancing on the wall in the firelight and thought it was the shadows that were real.

The people who can learn to manipulate social mythology are powerful indeed. One of the great inventions of the twentieth century was the studied, methodical engineering of myth for political ends. Aryan supremacy is an absurdity, but it still managed to plunge the entire world into war and madness.

More often than not, the mythology that operates where women are concerned is of the unconscious rather than the programmed variety. One of these myths with roots deep in history is the myth of feminine weakness. Women are not as rational, as stable, as competent, as logical as men. (Thus, they are not to be trusted.)

In the nineteenth century, the conventional wisdom of the medical profession was that the brain and the reproductive organs could not develop at the same time. Women were to be kept away from rigorous intellectual activity to protect their ability to function as wives and mothers. Does this sound dated, old hat? Indeed. But its residue can be found in intriguing places.

For example, Theodore H. White, writing in 1984 in *The New York Times Magazine* about the election campaign, looks askance at the women's movement, fearing it will lead to the "Balkanization" of American politics. (Translation: When anybody other than white males gets power, it's Balkanization.) White says that laws are necessary to protect women against "the hazards visited upon them by nature."

Is he speaking, perchance, of the vapors? Men die, on the average, some eight years earlier than women; they are much more likely to drop dead in the prime of life with a heart attack, to die of lung cancer, to get ulcers, to drink themselves to death. But would any journalist *ever* write of "the hazards visited upon men by nature"? When it comes to hazards, both women and men have their share, though women come off a little better. But the only weakness that is perceived is the female one.

It intrigues me that any piece of "news" that seems to document female instability vaults right into the headlines. Pre-menstrual syndrome is a classic example. Here is a condition that, in its extreme form, affects only a tiny minority of women. Indeed, many women do experience physical symptoms before the onset of their periods, changes in mood among them. For most, it's a minor inconvenience. Most women do not go berserk, cause mayhem, or go after their lovers with butcher knives. Why, then, did this syndrome get headlines all over the globe and its own thirty minutes on *Nightline* while more devastating medical problems get barely a mention?

Because the story validates a long-cherished myth about women—they are unpredictable, crazy creatures who are prisoners of their hormones. Men, of course, never go berserk or hack up their families, pick off pedestrains from a twenty-second-story window with a rifle, abuse children, or beat up little old ladies. Will *Nightline* ever do a story on testosterone poisoning?

The myth of female weakness also lurks behind much of what passes for "objective" reporting on scientific theory. In recent years, theories of biological determinism have become chic, especially sociobiology and "genes-and-gender" science.

Sociobiologists, many of them, dismiss culture with a nod and insist that just about everything we do is programmed into our genetic structure. Harvard's E.O. Wilson suggests there may even be a gene for religion. (Different genes, one wonders, for Orthodox and Reform Jews, and for Baptists and Unitarians?)

Sociobiology's critics point out that much of this stuff is highly theoretical and simplistic; sociobiologists tend to take wild leaps in their search for a theory that wraps everything up in a neat little package. But it is not the least bit surprising, and not at all accidental, that sociobiology became so trendy.

In a time of diminishing resources, how comforting it is to have a theory that says things are the way they are because of inevitable genetic forces. Forget Head Start. Forget the ERA. Forget affirmative action. Social justice is expensive—and painful. Articles in the popular media in recent years have suggested that there are people with "criminal" genes. Don't waste money on rehabilitation. Rape and wife-beating and child abuse are natural genetic adaptations—so women and children just have to relax and enjoy it.

"Genes-and-gender" science and the game I call "musical hormones" are very much in vogue these days. Take, for example, the flap over "math genes."

Two scientists at Johns Hopkins University, looking at national math testing data, found that boys did very much better than girls. This was nothing new; such results have been popping up for years. What was new was the scientists' interpretation of the data. They said that the gap was so large that it had to be due to some genetic differences, not just to culture. Headlines all around the country trumpeted that boys have better "math genes" than girls.

Critics, of course, attacked this interpretation. They found little solid evidence for such a statement, given the intense social pressure on girls to avoid math and the sciences. The Hopkins researchers cited special programs set up to help girls in math. But is it not a bit naïve to expect that the existence of special programs over a relatively short time span would undo a deep cultural bias? The critics, of course, didn't get the same play in the press that the original story did. And the reference to "math genes"—as if they were fact, not disputed theory—keeps cropping up in the media. Its very persistence could mean that slowly and quietly programs to seek out and encourage talented young women in math and science will quietly choke and die, the victims of another bit of media mythology.

Sex differences sell. We are seeing a whole spate of stories about differences between male and female brains, about male and female hormones and behavior. This is new, very complex research, and there is great debate among scientists about the findings. But in the headlines, speculation becomes fact, theory becomes gee-whiz prose. As science writer Barbara Beckwith points out in her research on genes-and-gender science, this genre has been grist for the mill of a whole range of magazines, from *Science* to *Cosmopolitan*. (Pack journalism being what it is, one cover story begets another faster than two bunnies in heat.) Most of the stories give short shrift to critics who say that connections between hormones and genes and behavior are tentative, and much of the speculation may turn out to be eyewash—just like the "science" of measuring the brain to discover which ethnic and racial groups are smarter.

Oversimplification abounds in much of the coverage. One newspaper headline announced that brain differences were the reason there were few female geniuses. The article, about left-brain/right-brain differences, never gave the reader the notion that there might be some other historical reason for the dearth of female genius. The fact that in the first two centuries of the Republic women were not permitted through the doors of universities might have had some slight impact on their intellectual accomplishments.

Gee-whiz science stories tend to accept uncritically the latest—and most chic—authority the reporter has interviewed. An example comes from the *Playboy* series on sex differences by Jo Durden Smith and Diane de Simone. The writers detail and interview with a scientist who speculates that females, because of brain function, may be better than males in integrating verbal and nonverbal function. She says that this may be at the root of what we call female intuition.

The writers describe leaving the interview convinced that she is right:

"'Female intuition!' says one of us as we walk outside into a bustle of students.

"'Men's difficulty with emotions!' says another. 'In the brain!'"

If these writers had been a bit more critical, they might have examined other explanations of the same phenomenon. Let's take a look at one, from another scientific discipline. Psychiatrist Jean Baker Miller (*Towards a New Psychology of Women*) suggests that societies have two categories of people, the dominants and the subordinants, who behave in different ways. Dominants are powerful, and they assign to themselves the jobs that are high in status and material rewards. The less valued jobs are assigned to subordinants, who are encouraged to develop a certain cluster of traits —submissiveness, dependency, passivity. Subordinants quickly learn how to use this behavior for protective cover. Blacks often had to learn to shuffle and the "Yassuh, Boss" to survive. Women got very good at the Dumb Blonde and Clinging Vine routines. Subordinate groups, unable to make demands or reach openly for power, become experts at manipulation. They know much more about the dominants than vice-versa, because their survival depends on it. They become highly attuned to dominants, able to predict reactions of pleasure or displeasure.

Miller writes: "Here, I think, is where the long story of 'feminine intuition' and 'feminine wiles' begins. It seems clear that these mysterious gifts are in fact skills, developed through long practice, in reading many signals, both verbal and nonverbal."

Women, says Miller, are aware early on that they have a duty to nurture: "I must care for those who are not me." Female socialization is akin to a Ph.D. in caring. I have two teenagers—a son and a daughter. My daughter is deluged with teen magazines that tell her how to handle jealousy, friendships, her friend's feelings, her boyfriend's feelings, breaking up, making up—she is being schooled to manage emotions. My son gets absolutely no such advice from society. Boys grow up expecting women will manage emotions for them. No wonder they aren't very good at it.

So—is it hormones or training that accounts for behavior? The truth of the matter is that human behavior is a very complex affair, a tangle of biology and environment that is extremely difficult to sort out. To understand it, one must be able to examine elaborate sets of forces, acting in concert. The "reductionism" that often operates in the sciences makes this nearly impossible. It's like saying a car runs because of the spark plugs, and then looking very intently at the spark plugs. You wind up knowing a lot about plugs, but not a lot about the engine. And gee-whiz science writing often falls prey to this fallacy.

It's important for women to understand all this, because of the absolutely dismal history of the interaction between biological determinism and politics. It's a truism that biological theories of differences between the sexes and the races are inevitably used against the group that doesn't have political power. Harvard biologist Jon Beckwith sees a chilling parallel between today's "genes-and-gender" fad and the popularization of the "science" of eugenics early in the century. Popular science journals then ran such articles as "A Study of Jewish Psychopathy" and "The Racial Element in National Vitality," promoting the idea that social behavior was inherited. *The Saturday Evening Post* took up the cudgel as well, with the result that there developed popular support for sterilization and miscegenation laws, and immigration laws that discriminated against Slavs, Jews, Southern Europeans, and other groups.

The "genes-and-gender" stories of today often are very slick; the bias is buried in jargon and pseudo-science. But they can indeed build popular support for slowing the drive for equality between the races and the sexes. For example, an *Education Digest* article, citing brain research, proposes setting up different learning sequences for boys and girls to "allow for their separate predispositions." If that happens, guess who's going to get the good stuff and who's going to get the *drek*. Separate but equal? Ho, ho, ho!

Many of the genes-and-gender articles appear, on the surface, to be somewhat even-handed, since they seem to be saying that both boys and girls get a share of "good genes." Boys are good at math; girls are good at verbal skills and communication. This, they say, is the decree of nature, and will always remain so.

Well, then, shouldn't we expect some action? Certainly, women, with their marvelous intuition and their ability to communicate, will immediately be appointed to most ambassadorial posts. Surely they will get the lion's share of editing and writing jobs. They will be made tenured professors of literature. They will be made managers in major corporations, where their ability to communicate will doubtless boost productivity.

Don't hold your breath. Women will keep on getting the low-paid jobs in the day-care center, in the elementary school and the typing pool —unless the drive for equal opportunity is kept in high gear. Remember, this is a society that hasn't even been able to pass the ERA. Women had better be on guard; they could be talked out of the rights they've won the hard way by people who say they haven't got the right genes, or hormones, or the right structure in the brain.

One thing we do know is that social change *does* change behavior. It didn't take thousands of years of genetic change to end slavery. It took an act of law. The quantum leap in performance displayed by American women in the 1984 Olympics came not as a result of any change in hormones, but from Title IX of the Elementary and Secondary Education Act, which insisted that money and resources be allocated to women's athletic programs. In the early 1900s, the "criminal class" was overwhelmingly white, often Irish, Jewish, Slavic. Now it's largely black, Hispanic, or other minority. Was there a sudden genetic change among Jews, Irishmen, and Slavs? No. They just moved up and out of poverty, to be replaced by newer groups at the low end of the totem pole. Social justice doesn't have to wait for evolution.

The myth of female weakness, as we've seen, can be a powerful force in the distortion of reality. There's another, nearly as potent: the myth of female strength. (Illogical? Mythology doesn't operate by the rules of logic.)

Rooted deep in our culture is the notion that if women obtain political power, the world will go to hell in a handcart. Not only will the world go awry if women have power, says the myth, but women themselves will suffer. This bogeyman runs through the women-and-stress stories that are popping up in the media like mushrooms these days. The advice in them is seductive, because it seems so sympathetic: "You poor dear, we don't want to see you harmed!" The scent of crocodile tears is overwhelming.

The message being beamed to women is that if they set their sights too high they will start having heart attacks, develop ulcers, and hound themselves into early graves.

It's interesting to see that these warnings are almost always aimed at women heading for high-prestige jobs. How often do you see a headline that says. WATCH OUT FOR THE TYPING POOL! IT'S A KILLER! Not often. But it may be the truth.

The Framingham Heart Study shows that working women do not show increasing coronary symptoms, with one exception: women in low-level clerical and secretarial jobs. And a major study by Columbia University's Robert Karasek, an industrial engineer, shows that lack of decision-making power is a factor in coronary risk. The truly lethal combination, his study shows, is high psychological demand and little decision-making power.

Karasek and his colleagues indexed jobs according to the demand-control index. Many of the jobs in the high-demand/low-control quadrant were "female ghetto" jobs—sales clerk, telephone operator, waitress, mall worker, garment stitcher. Why aren't women being warned away from these jobs? Because society needs drones, that's why. Disturbing projections on the future of the work force show that it's not in the glamor fields of high tech that the greatest number of jobs will be created, but in the low-paid service sector of the economy.

Another bogeyman to emerge from the myth of female strength is the new darling of the feature pages: Superwoman. She's chairman of the board, a dazzling dresser and party-giver, but she always has time to dash home and read *Winnie the Pooh* to the kiddies and whip up a batch of nutritious, non-carcinogenic Toll House cookies. It's an image that, on the surface, seems flattering. In reality, it's designed to scare "ordinary" women right down to their toes. The message underlying Superwoman stories is that a woman has to be more than a mere mortal to manage having both a career and a family. If you can't scare women away from achievement by saying it's going to make them sick, try another tack: Imply that only exceptional women can do it. And Superwoman does scare women off. When a student newspaper at Boston University did an informal poll of women students, asking whether they could manage career and family, most expressed serious doubts. These young women were ignoring the experiences of millions of real women around them—women who manage job and family but are not Superwoman—and listening to the siren song of myth.

The media inadvertently foster the Superwoman myth in stories about women with good jobs, because the emphasis is always on what such women accomplish, but not the ways they manage or the tradeoffs they make. As an author, I am interviewed fairly often, and there are times when

I do not recognize the disciplined, dynamic, supercharged woman on the printed page. The stories do not mention that I never remember my dentist appointments, that my office looks like the town dump, or that my children say my home-cooked meals could inspire a TV show: "That's Inedible."

But the Superwoman image just seems too sexy for the media to let go of. Recently, I was interviewed by a reporter who did an excellent story about how working women aren't Superwoman and the image is harmful to women. But what headline was stuck on the story? This one: THOSE SUPERWOMEN ARE REAL—AND HAPPIEST!

The myth of female strength also means that when things go wrong, women will get blamed—mothers in particular. When a woman has a child, perhaps the best thing she can do is absolutely refuse to read any newspaper or magazine article with the word *mother* in it. You can bet she's going to catch hell for something.

In the fifties, when women stayed home dutifully and lavished their time on their children, they were blamed for destroying their kids' character. "Momism" became a national buzzword. Critics said that American POWs broke under torture in Korea because their mothers had spoiled them. (Maybe their mothers should have locked them in the closet for days on end, blindfolded, to prepare them for brainwashing.) When mothers went out to work, they were blamed for alienation, latchkey children, low SAT scores, drug abuse, teenage pregnancy, cavities, and the decline of American civilization. Mothers are the favorite scapegoats of the media. There is *no way* they can win.

We are going to see, I think, more and more in the media of biological determinism and myth-as-science. The economic picture does not seem rosy; already a mean-spiritedness seems to be rolling across the land. Many Americans want to believe that people go to soup kitchens to save money, or sleep on sidewalk grates for kicks. The time is ripe—perhaps overripe—for theories that buttress the status quo.

At the same time, information is increasingly becoming a commodity to be sold to the affluent. Magazines desperately try to purge their subscription lists of readers who are not the Yuppies advertisers adore. Bestbagel and boutique journalism spreads like a malevolent weed. Editors grow increasingly impatient with the notion of giving their upscale readers information that will make them uncomfortable. Stories about affirmative action, poverty, the mentally ill, the homeless are just not "sexy."

It's not only women, of course, who need to beware such trends—but also men who are committed to the idea of a society where social justice is not a hollow phrase. Blacks, Hispanics, gays, Orientals—all will be affected directly by social mythology. As our society becomes increasingly Hispanic and Oriental, I await the new scientific findings about these groups. Will Hispanics be found to be overly "right-brained"—perfect for playing guitars and doing the tango, but for God's sake keep them out of Harvard? Do Orientals lack "originality" genes? Maybe their SAT scores go off the scale, but everybody knows they're just great copiers.

The media are an enormously powerful force—for good or ill—in all of this. They can shift the rudder that steers us in one direction or another. But if neither the practitioners nor the consumers of journalism understand the forces to which they are subject, we are all in trouble. If they continue to believe in the illusion of "objective," value-free "news," if they can't detect the strong distorting current of mythology, we may sail our ship in directions that many of us do not wish to travel.

---

48 Women's Magazines

by Sheila J. Gibbons

Publications for women are changing, according to this article. Women's magazines, like the women they serve, have moved out of the home. Dozens are being published to meet the ever-changing interests of women—and these magazines advertise hundreds of products. Sheila J. Gibbons is manager of public affairs for Gannett Co., Inc., one of the nation's largest media companies. She is the former editor of LADYCOM/Military Lifestyle, a magazine edited for wives of U.S. servicemen and women in the armed forces. This article orginally appeared in *USA Today*, December 7, 1982, and is updated for the second edition of this book.

Women's magazines are alive and well, according to Madison Avenue. As a group, they're enjoying better prospects than they were in the early 1980s, when magazines edited for women comprised a mixed bag—for some, success; for others, uncertainty and decline.

Comparatively speaking, women's magazines as a publishing category have stabilized. Gloomy predictions of the demise of this one or that one, rampant earlier in the decade, are not heard much any more, even though several are not entirely without problems. Women's magazines continue to be popular and influential with an ever more sophisticated, more prosperous, more independent, and more demanding audience.

What has made the difference for women's magazines? The increasing affluence of their readers, and American women's loyalty to magazines as a medium.

The women's movement that exploded in the 1960s shook U.S. society to the rafters. Twenty years later, its effects are easy to see, though the process of change for women is by no means finished. Women now are recognized for their irreplaceable contributions to the family and to the workplace, and their commitment to the former is no longer regarded as rendering them ineffective in the latter. That women have flooded the U.S. labor force and, in more recent years, have become a presence in corporate boardrooms and at the highest levels of organizational management, is considered by many to be the single most significant change in this country's social structure in the last half of the twentieth century.

This dramatic change has affected family relationships, consumer buying behavior, levels of prosperity and aspiration—every ingredient of life. The huge numbers of women working outside the home, whose own mothers enjoyed reading well-established women's magazines that reflected a more traditional view of home and family, want magazines that can help them to live with the changes they see all around them and that suggest ways to enjoy the lifestyle that more independence gives them.

Also, these women have more media to choose from than their mothers did. They have television, cable TV, VCRs, tape decks, and professional publications. Because so many media are available to them but their personal time is limited, they are forced to be more selective in their choices. And so the media themselves have been forced to fight harder than ever for the consumer's time.

In response, the older and more traditional women's magazines, faced with a rapidly changing audience, gradually began experimenting with their content. While the "Seven Sisters"—*McCall's, Ladies' Home Journal, Woman's Day, Family Circle, Good Housekeeping, Better Homes & Gardens,* and *Redbook*—tinkered with their editorial direction, a new generation of magazines offered additional opportunities to advertisers as well as to readers: *New Woman (1976), Working Woman (1976), Working Mother (1979), Self (1979),* and *Savvy (1980).*

The combined circulation of these new magazines (4 million) compared to that of the "Seven Sisters" (34 million) seems miniscule. These smaller magazines, by themselves, will not put any of the larger ones out of business. But their impact has been felt by everyone in the publishing triangle: readers, editors, and advertisers. And the new generation of magazines has posted substantial circulation increases since 1981, when their combined circulation was 3.4 million. In contrast, the Seven Sisters have *lost* more than one-fifth of their combined circulation, which in 1981 was 43 million.

But numbers alone don't tell the whole story. Two of the Sisters, *Ladies' Home Journal* and *Redbook,* in failing health at the beginning of the decade, have turned around under new ownership. And the giants of the

Seven Sisters, the well-known "store books" *Family Circle* and *Woman's Day*, are seeing an erosion in their combined circulation of 12 million.

"No one can pinpoint why the store books are going down," says Irwin Srob, director of print operations at Saatchi & Saatchi Compton, New York. "Some people speculate that it's because working women make fewer trips to the store. Other say it's because they have alternative media, such as VCRs, which they can program to watch whenever it's convenient and which compete with magazine reading."

But circulation isn't the only measure of success (or lack of it). *Woman's Day* is a top advertising magnet, ranked No. 1 in page growth and No. 2 in revenue growth on Adweek's "Hottest Magazines" list for 1986. *Woman's Day* is an example of an older Sister still a strong contender on the U.S. magazine scene.

The unqualified success story of the contemporary women's magazine market is undoubtedly *Working Woman*. Its 1986 circulation approached 800,000—pretty good for a magazine that was celebrating only its tenth anniversary that year. Its ad revenues for 1986 were up 400% over revenues recorded five years earlier.

"The name says it all," Srob says. "A lot of our clients want to reach the working woman, and you don't have to do a whole lot of computer analysis to figure which book will do it."

Kate Rand Lloyd was the managing editor of *Vogue* when she left to become the editor of *Working Woman*. After thirty years at Conde Nast (publisher of *Vanity Fair, Glamour, Mademoiselle, Bride's,* and *Vogue*), she found herself at the helm of a magazine that had just survived a Chapter 11 bankruptcy proceeding and had only 90,000 subscribers.

"You know, when I first came to *Working Woman*, the editors of the older women's magazines had an attitude that was very sweet," Lloyd, now *Working Woman*'s editor-at-large, recalls. "They would say wonderful things about the magazine, how good it was that someone had finally done something like *Working Woman*. I think the happiest day of my life, though, was when I was on a panel with one of those editors, and she took off after me, throwing verbal knives. She kept insisting that 50% of *her* readers work, that *she* had the working woman's market." That editor's eagerness to claim Lloyd's readership conferred on *Working Woman* the status of a serious competitor—a moment Lloyd still savors.

"At about the same time, a big-time publisher said to me, about working women, 'Don't you think it's just a fad?' At that point there were 38 million women in the work force," Lloyd says. Today, 51.8 million women are employed.

Advertisers also had to be convinced that the new magazine was viable, a process Lloyd says took "quite a while, but which broke new ground in advertising directed toward women. One of the reasons that we're successful is that we've attracted advertising that never used to appear in women's magazines—office automation equipment, insurance, investments, executive recruiting, automobiles—things that aren't 'normal' for women's magazines." *Working Woman* has its share of traditional women's advertising, too.

It's a rags-to-riches tale. The upstart magazine that was rescued from bankruptcy became so successful so fast that it attracted the interest of Time Inc. In 1986 *Working Woman's* owner, Dale Lang, formed a joint venture with Time Inc. to purchase *McCall's* and other titles owned by McCall's Publishing. As part of the deal, Time Inc. purchased a half-interest in *Working Woman*. The joint venture, named The Working Woman/McCall's Group, gives Time what *Adweek* called "a hefty stake in the women's market" and gives Lang the clout behind Time Inc.'s vast resources.

The *Working Woman* story is an indicator of how attractive the women's market has become to advertisers and how broad its possibilities for innovative editorial content are. Other indicators are the emergence of regional women's magazines, such as *Boston Woman* and *New York Woman*, which is testing the magazine in Miami, Philadelphia, Los Angeles, and seven other cities where it believes there are substantial concentrations of expatriate New Yorkers.

At the same time that we look at the new directions for the women's magazine market, it's instructive to consider the reader loyalty and success of the magazine with the plain-Jane name and a sought-after seal of approval. *Good Housekeeping*, with a circulation of 5.2 million, has held its own in the competitive sorority of women's magazines. Its editor, John Mack Carter, attributes the magazine's success to its singularity of purpose: remembering who the GH reader is and never "graying" the editorial content with material out of *Good Housekeeping's* realm.

"I have had a very clear picture of the purpose of *Good Housekeeping*," says Carter, who also has been editor of *Better Homes & Gardens* and *Ladies' Home Journal*. "Our readers do all the same things other women's magazines readers do—they work outside the home to the same degree as average, they are married and they have families—but the purpose of *Good Housekeeping* is to serve that woman as she is responsible for her family. We have not been deflected from our purposes as a magazine by trying to serve the reader in her career. We serve her as a mother and a homemaker.

"Some of the other women's magazines, confused by the changes in women's roles, compromised their purposes by becoming far more general-interest in scope and less helpful specifically," Carter says. And that type of publication won't make the cut as women choose from an ever-widening array of information and entertainment sources, Carter predicts. Consequently, he believes there will be fewer of the same types of magazines in most homes: "The woman reader of today and tomorrow is not going to be as likely to have *McCall's*, *Ladies' Home Journal* and *Family Circle* in her living room as, perhaps, *Woman's Day*, *Ski*, *Business Week*, and *Glamour*."

Asked what women magazine readers will be like in the future, Kate Rand Lloyd says: "I don't believe women's basic impulses are going to change. I think they are going to go right on thinking about men and falling in love and worrying about kids.

"But I do believe, as everyone else does, that their numbers in the work force will continue to grow and because of that, there'll continue to be a shift in lifestyles," Lloyd says. "Segmentation will continue also: We'll have more women's magazines, more precisely focused on the type of woman they serve."

---

49 Bringing the Moving Picture into Focus

by Lori Kesler

Changing roles and interests of women are responsible for changing media. It's a marketing situation that can frustrate or enrich advertisers, manufacturers and media, writes Lori Kesler, a St. Louis freelance writer. This article is from *Advertising Age*, April 2, 1984.

> *"Despite my 30 years of research into the feminine soul, I have not yet been able to answer that great question: What does a woman want?"*
>
> Sigmund Freud

Freud, poor fellow, wasn't the first person to ask that question. A guy named Adam beat him to it. And ever since it was asked the first time, that question has been on the top 10 hit parade of puzzlers.

The advertiser who answers it correctly stands to reap generous rewards. Likewise, the one who guesses wrong suffers the consequences.

Such is the power of marketing to women.

Experts who watch the trends say advertisers and marketers have made considerable progress during the last few years.

They've learned, for example, that the women's market does not consist of legions of fretful females agonizing over dirty laundry and dirty floors (and probably it never did).

During the 1980s, they also learned that today's woman doesn't claim to be Superwoman. After a short flirtation, advertisers agreed to send that lady packing.

Superwoman, you remember, is that disgustingly perfect specimen who serves her family a bountiful hot breakfast, dashes off to run a corporation all day and then glides in at 6 p.m. to create a lavish gourmet meal while at the same time changing diapers, leading Cub Scouts and carrying on stimulating conversation with her husband. Thank goodness she's gone.

But if today's woman wants to be neither a drudge nor Superwoman, then—as Mr. Freud pondered—what does she want?

Advertisers today seem to be telling us she wants to show off different personalities at different times. In a Jergens commercial, she's soft and cuddly as a kitten. In a Buick commercial, she declares confidently that she bought a car. *Her* car.

Rena Bartos, senior vp-director of communications development at J. Walter Thompson USA in New York, believes advertisers these days are trying harder to understand what women want in products and services.

She works with clients to explore social changes, marriage patterns and trends in life styles "and then we get into the nitty gritty of how all this can be factored into their marketing and product opportunities," she says. "In the last couple of years, we've gone from cocktail conversation to action."

According to Ms. Bartos, the companies that sell big-ticket items—cars credit cards, financial products, life insurance and investment services— have demonstrated the greatest awareness of women's changed status.

"I think that's because until recently those folks assumed they were dealing only with men. When they began to recognize women as customers, they looked at women who were earning their own money and making their own decisions. Or if the women were married, they were part of an equal household," Ms. Bartos says.

Because the companies didn't have to overcome bad habits *vis-a-vis* their approach to women, "you don't see a condescending approach to women in those product categories."

Household products have made less progress, she says, "but even there we're beginning to see the husband in the kitchen and the family sharing duties."

Judith Langer, who heads her own marketing and social research company in New York, finds the working woman now ranks as an accepted figure in advertising and marketing, not an oddity.

"A few years ago, when the career woman was discovered, she got rather naive treatment," she says. "Advertisers wanted to show high-level achievers, women in nontraditional jobs. Unfortunately, they often did it in ways women couldn't relate to."

Now advertisers tend to take a more subtle approach. "They picture a woman who is out in the world, active and well dressed," she observes. "But we don't really know her job. It's intentionally ambiguous."

A commercial for comfort-stride pantyhose, for example, shows a woman getting on an elevator. "Is she a secretary or a company president?" asks Ms. Langer. "She could be anybody."

Fulltime homemakers also are demanding more respect, and this attitude, she notes, is beginning to have an impact on advertisers.

For example, many marketers who spent the last few years targeting working women now are broadening their focus to include the active nonworking female. And laundry detergent ads are beginning to show the homemaker pursuing her own interests and hobbies, not simply washing clothes.

Even the Wisk commercials have caught the spirit. Now a man worries about how to wash out his own ring around the collar.

Many women have waited a long time to see that.

With the baby boom generation well into its 30s, advertisers also are having to deal with another emerging trend: The graying of America.

The result? "We're definitely seeing more mature women in ads," Ms. Langer says. "And I think, too, advertisers have come to understand that women want a strong positive image of themselves."

Not too long ago, cosmetics marketers assumed a 40-year-old woman's fondest wish was to look 25. "Now there's the feeling that a woman of 40 just wants to look her best," she says.

"We're not kidding ourselves so much anymore. At one time the ad community played on our fears of getting older. Now they're showing a line now and then. There's more honesty.

"One nice commercial that would never have been done years ago is for Oil of Olay," Ms. Langer says. "It starts out with, 'The first time I saw your face. . . .' What's interesting is you know the woman's in her late 30s or 40s. They shoot it so you do see she's got lines.

"At one time, that would have been an anxiety campaign. Instead, this has been presented in a positive way."

Experts see romanticism and glamor returning to many women's product ads, but this time it's accompanied by a startling new kind of sensuality. "Sex is no longer a taboo subject," Ms. Bartos acknowledges.

She points out, however, that current ads showing women taking an "overt, frank approach to pleasure and sensuality" are different from those of the past which portrayed women as sex objects.

"These new ads show women in a pleasure relationship," she says, "not submitting to a power relationship."

Notes Ms. Langer, "What the new sensuality proves is that women feel comfortable having this as part of their lives. The achievement-oriented woman feels she can relax a little bit. She feels it's okay for her to look feminine on the job and to look sexy in her personal life. She's past the proving stage."

Meanwhile, some kinds of products and services that by-passed women in the past are being recruited in marketers' efforts to catch up. Take automobiles, for example.

Sandy Chumack, an account supervisor for the Ford division at J. Walter Thompson USA, says women represented more than a third of the new car market—fully 38%—in 1983.

That's up from 22% in 1973. And, she adds, "we expect this percentage to increase in the future."

Ms. Chumack is a member of a women's professional review committee, which analyzes and reviews all Ford advertising. She says the committee's research indicates that women want to see some technical information in auto advertising, but not too much.

"If an ad talks about rack-and-pinion steering, it should emphasize the benefits," she says. But above all, a woman wants a safe car, says Ms. Chumack, and that image of reliability should be projected in the advertising.

As examples, she points to two ads for the Thunderbird and the Mustang convertible, which appear in women's magazines.

The ads, headlined "Executive Air" and "Upward Mobility," were designed to appeal to the professional woman's sense of taste and style. But both also include technical details that reinforce the idea of safety and reliability.

Ms. Chumack reports both have received a good response from nonworking as well as working women.

Other industries promoting heavily to women include insurance, financial services and investment companies.

Merrill Lynch regularly conducts educational seminars for women because they make up the largest group of new investors, "and we've known all along they wanted to know more about investing," explains public relations spokeswoman Ellen Golden of Burson-Marsteller, New York.

It all started with fashion and finance seminars in the 1970s when "you still had to sugar coat financing," she says apologetically.

Through the years, though, the seminars have taken on more sophisticated subjects. One series explored investing for the two-income family, and last year Merrill Lynch joined *Working Woman* magazine and several other sponsors to conduct seminars for women entrepreneurs.

Ms. Langer recalls that a few years ago, most of her clients were small package goods companies. Today, it's the insurance companies, computer marketers and financial services companies who are interested in researching the women's market.

"Sometimes," she says, "we find the women's consumers want something different from men. For example, in hotels, they want skirt hangers and good lights. Those things are important to women.

"In many cases, though, we find women don't want different products or services," she says. "They just want to be treated as equals, and the marketers simply have to help them recognize that they need things like pensions, IRA plans and disability insurance—just as men do. There's a dawning awareness of this."

Mass Media and Women: For Further Reading

Helen Baehr (ed.), *Women and the Media*. New York: Pergamon Press, 1980.

Maurine Beasley and Sheila Silver, *Women in Media: A Documentary Source Book*. Washington, D.C.: Women's Institute for Freedom of the Press, 1977.

Matilda Butler and William Paisley, *Women and the Mass Media: Sourcebook for Research and Action*. New York: Human Sciences Press, 1980.

Laurily Keir Epstein, *Women and the News*. New York: Hastings House, 1978.

Judith S. Gelfman, *Women in Television News*. New York: Columbia University Press, 1976.

Anita Klever, *Women in Television*. Philadelphia: Westminster Press, 1975.

Marion Marzolf, *Up from the Footnote: A History of Women Journalists*. New York: Hastings House, 1977.

Betsy Covington Smith, *Breakthrough: Women in Television*. New York: Walker and Company, 1981.

Mass Media
and Religion

Traditionally, religion in the mass media was restricted to ceremonies and to controversies involving religious denominations.
Ceremonies could be reported as simply as a listing of local
services in Saturday editions, or as elaborately as broadcasting
services live from some distant city. The controversies could
involve covering a noisy new splinter group from an established
denomination, or reporting arguments about changes in the
structure of worship services.

Religious beliefs and matters of faith are so intangible and, so
private, the media seemed to say by their silence, that broader
media coverage would be intrusive, inappropriate. In reality,
religion and religious beliefs permeate the daily lives and activities
of millions of people in the United States and billions around the
globe. Religious leaders and denominations now take active roles
in U.S. politics, and they rally support for and against many social,
economic, and technological movements. They have not stayed
confined to theology and traditional pulpits and pews but have
reached out, often ecumenically and electronically. In reaching
out with messages of salvation, and in some instances, for membership and money, some have invited media and public scrutiny
as never before.

The articles in this section raise questions about how the news
media cover religion and how some religious groups use both
print and broadcast media to "spread the word."

50 Media View Religion in a News Light

by David Shaw

Religion is important to the average American. It is difficult to cover, to get beyond the superficial and the predictable stereotypes, but it is newsworthy, reports David Shaw, a staff writer for the *Los Angeles Times*. This article is from the December 28, 1983, issue of that paper.

Kenneth Briggs, religion editor of the *New York Times*, is an ordained Methodist minister. Russell Chandler, one of the religion writers at the *Los Angeles Times*, is an ordained Presbyterian minister. Louis Moore, religion editor of the *Houston Chronicle*, is an ordained Baptist minister—an evangelical Christian, in fact, who speaks periodically to church groups, refers colleagues for pastoral counseling when they have problems and, on occasion, officiates at their weddings and funerals.

But Joseph Berger, the religion writer for *Newsday* on New York's suburban Long Island, is a former junior high school English teacher and investigative reporter—and a Yeshiva-educated Jew—who says he attends synagogue only a few times a year and who never considered writing about religion until he failed to get his paper's job as a television reporter and found that religion writing was the next job available.

Virginia Culver, the religion writer for the *Denver Post*, is a self-proclaimed atheist, a woman who writes about religion not out of any personal spiritual conviction but simply because she considers religion the most interesting assignment on the paper, "the one subject that interests almost everyone and touches almost every issue."

Despite their disparate personal beliefs and professional backgrounds, these five journalists have one important common bond: They are among only 15 or 20 religion writers in the entire secular press in the United States who are widely respected in their field, according to a just-completed *Los Angeles Times* study that included almost 100 interviews with editors, religion writers, clergymen, church officials and theologians across the country.

The number of good religion writers on American daily newspapers has begun to grow in the last few years, these experts say, and religion coverage is vastly improved over what it was 20 years or even 10 years ago. Belatedly alerted to the dominant role religion often plays in most wars, civil unrest and social change throughout the world, some newspaper editors are gradually coming to recognize the importance of religion as a field for legitimate journalistic inquiry.

A 1982 survey of 30 newspapers by the Department of Mass Communications at Middle Tennessee State University showed that the percentage of papers devoting more than 100 column inches to religion news each week has more than doubled, from 27% to 59%, in the last decade.

But 100 column inches—less than a full page in most newspapers—is far less than the average paper devotes to sports every day, and it is clear that the newspapers that treat religion seriously and intelligently are still a tiny minority.

Fewer than 200 of the nation's more than 1,700 daily newspapers have religion writers, and only about a third of these 200 cover religion full time. Although some of these full-time religion writers do consistently excellent work, most religion stories that appear in the nation's newspapers are written by general assignment reporters, political reporters, feature writers or others with little understanding of—or interest in—religion.

Most of these reporters are lazy, unwilling to do their basic homework and display "an appalling ignorance" of the traditions and influence of religion, said Msgr. Francis J. Lally, who deals with the press frequently in his role as secretary of the Department of Social Development and World Peace for the United States Catholic Conference.

Thus, most people interviewed for this story said, the vast majority of newspapers—even many of those with full-time religion writers—still do a shamefully inadequate job of covering religion.

Jeanne Pugh, religion writer for the *St. Petersburg* (Fla.) *Times*, said she is "appalled by what I see in religion coverage around the country," and she is far from alone in this judgment.

William P. Thompson, co-stated clerk of the General Assembly of the Presbyterian Church (U.S.A.), said most newspaper stories about religion are "based on incorrect assumptions leading to incorrect conclusions."

"Most reporters just don't understand the subject they're trying to report," Thompson said.

It is widely agreed, for example, that the press was late in recognizing the growth of evangelical Christianity and that it then badly misunderstood and misreported the phenomenon, including its influence on former President Jimmy Carter.

The press was equally delinquent in assessing the role of religion in the social revolutions that have shaken Iran and Latin America and in explaining the relationship between what one editor called "the Muslim psyche" and the recent suicide missions that killed so many Americans, French and Israelis in Lebanon.

Black religious denominations are also widely ignored in most press coverage, as are most Asian denominations—despite the enormous increase in the Asian population in many sections of the United States (and especially in Southern California) since the end of the Vietnam War. In fact, there is little in the press to reflect the findings of a study last year by the National Council of Churches and the Glenmary Research Center in Atlanta showing that almost half the American population is outside the traditional Judeo-Christian denominations, either belonging to other denominations or having no religious affiliation.

In essence, many theologians and spiritual leaders say, the press too often misses (or misinterprets) substantive developments in religion while giving space to "religion" stories that are sensational, superficial, scandalous or stereotypical.

Most major newspapers gave prominent front-page play in October, for example, to stories on the publication by the National Council of Churches of a lectionary of non-sexist Bible readings, but few (if any) papers have written about the significant upsurge in female enrollment in the nation's seminaries.

The percentage of women in seminaries has more than doubled in the last 10 years, and this could have a major impact on those religious denominations that do not permit the ordination of women.

But in covering religion, the press often seems obsessed with conflict, controversy and the kinds of trivial personality stories—or offbeat but ultimately meaningless "religion" stories—that critics (including some religion writers) dismiss scornfully as "Geek of the Week" or "Jocks for Jesus" or "I was a clown for Christ" or what one religion writer called "the old 'nuns playing softball' story."

George Cornell, who has been writing about religion for Associated Press since 1951, said, "There's a tendency (for newspapers) to prefer the silly aspects. . .the circus aspects of religion to serious religion news."

Even when serious issues are covered, they tend to be formal and denominational—mergers, power struggles and policy statements—rather than personal; there is very little in the American press about how religion actually influences people's daily lives.

These same criticisms are often leveled against the press in its coverage of other subjects, of course. Indeed, charges of superficiality, sensationalism and impersonal, institutionally oriented coverage are leveled against the press in its treatment of virtually everything.

"You're basically dealing with a journalistic phenomenon. . .not just religion coverage," said James Wall, editor of *Christian Century* magazine.

Journalists themselves readily admit this.

"We're. . .good at fires, but ideas are a little harder to cover," said Louis D. Boccardi, executive vice president and chief operating officer of Associated Press.

Moreover, it would be impossible for the press to provide either the quality or the quantity of religion coverage most people deeply interested in religion would like to see, just as it would be impossible for the press to fully satisfy those who want comprehensive coverage of the law, science, literature or any other field.

A general-interest daily newspaper is not a journal of religion (or law or science or literature). There is neither the space nor the expertise nor the general reader interest to warrant such comprehensive, detailed treatment of any single subject.

But just as most newspaper editors admit they could do a better job on law, science, literature—and virtually everything else—so they could do a better job on religion. The gap between what they are doing and what they could and should do is perhaps greatest in religion coverage, however, because (1) most do so little, so poorly, (2) religion is so important to so many people and (3) the press could be the best vehicle for furthering religious understanding and tolerance in our society.

William C. Martin, chairman of the sociology department at Rice University in Houston, said he has often been surprised to find out how "biased or ignorant" most of his students are about religions other than their own when he assigns them to review various church services. Many otherwise intelligent adults also know little about other peoples' religions, Martin said, and he worries that the failure of the press to report on religion in a responsible fashion helps to maintain dangerous cultural barriers between people of different religious backgrounds.

Other critics say the failure of the press to cover religion comprehensively denies some believers the public reinforcement they need to sustain their spiritual commitments and thus could contribute to a decline in religious commitment and activity.

Is religion really all that important to the average American in our modern, cynical, technological age?

Yes.

A national survey conducted in 1981 for Connecticut Mutual Life Insurance Co. found that 74% of all Americans consider themselves religious. More recent surveys, conducted by the Gallup and Roper organizations, have found, variously, that 94% of all Americans believe in God or in some universal spirit (and that 67% are members of a church or synagogue); that 65% say they cannot live without religion; that 76% say they pray at least once a week (and 50% said they had prayed within the previous 24 hours); that 54% say they go to religious services at least once a month (and 40% had gone the previous week); that 54% say religion is the solution to today's world problems.

Most surveys show America to be the most religious society in the world today. In one recent study, 58% of Americans said they consider their religious beliefs "very important." In no other industrialized country was the percentage more than 36%. More than 50 million American adults are involved in Bible study, prayer groups or similar activities, and the number is growing.

But there has been little detailed press coverage of this increased religiosity. Nor has the press spent much time examining the seeming contradiction between this increase and the concomitant shift away from traditional denominations and, among some people, away from religion itself.

Many scholars and religious leaders say this neglect occurs because most journalists in America are not themselves religious and are unaware of—or even scornful of—their readers' religious beliefs and commitments.

"Most journalists are simply blind to religion," said Robert Bellah, a professor of sociology at the University of California, Berkeley. "They think it's somehow slightly embarrassing, a holdover from the Dark Ages... something only ignorant and backward people really believe in.

"This is not necessarily a conspicuous judgment on their part," Bellah said. "It's just part of their general world view... in which religion is seen as an aberrant phenomenon."

Because of this attitude, even newspapers with good religion writers often give the subject too little space.

Many journalists tend to be confirmed in their views of religion by the essentially secular and pluralistic nature of American society. There is no single dominant church in the United States; instead, there are more than 1,000 denominations, no one of which accounts for more than a quarter of the nation's population. Except in certain areas, religion is a fragmented—and to some, invisible—force in American society.

Moreover, because the separation of church and state is mandated by the Constitution, religion is essentially a private matter, largely devoid of political impact, and most American journalists seem ignorant of the enormous influence the church exerts in public policy matters in other countries, with different state-church traditions.

This ignorance, many critics say, helps explain why the American press—like the American government—was so late in assessing the religious aspects of strife in Vietnam and, more recently, in Iran.

"For vast numbers of the world's people, the symbols of religion sum up their highest aspirations," said Mary Catherine Bateson, former dean of social sciences and humanities at the University of Northern Iran. But Bateson said most Western journalists tend to dismiss religion as fanaticism or as a cloak for other political or economic interests.

Bateson is not alone in this judgment.

Peter Steinfels, editor of the liberal Catholic magazine *Commonweal*, said most journalists saw the uprising against Shah Mohammed Reza Pahlavi as "a 'human rights' story or a 'torture' story or a 'U.S.-supporting-dictators' story—all of which it was—but... they almost totally overlooked the role of traditional religion forces."

Religious leaders are equally critical of the press's failure to explain early on the role of the Catholic Church and liberation theology in the political unrest in Latin America.

A few newspapers did write about this in the 1970s—and some newspapers have begun publishing such stories recently—but critics say Americans would understand the sensitive, volatile problems of Latin America much better today if the press had provided more intelligent reportage on the church in Latin America a decade ago, or even five years ago.

Even in the United States, religion occasionally plays a public policy role—and that, too, is largely ignored by the press.

In a recent interview with the *Times*, former President Carter said that because the press had "exalted" the Rev. Jerry Falwell as "the spokesman for born-again Christians in the nation," Carter often worried that Falwell was having "an unwarranted impact on members of Congress."

Carter said Falwell was "preaching. . .rather effectively" that anyone who favored his foreign aid legislation or opposed the Panama Canal treaty, SALT II negotiations or the establishment of a Cabinet-level Department of Education "was not a Christian."

Carter said he retaliated by "bringing in Christian leaders by the hundreds to the White House" to solicit their support. Carter asked these clergymen to let Congress know that Falwell did not represent most Christians and to ask members of their congregations to do likewise.

The clergymen "played a very crucial role" in mustering congressional support for Carter on most of these issues, but the press reported virtually nothing of their activities on Carter's behalf, although it would have been a good and important story by any journalistic standards.

Rabbi Marc Tannenbaum, director of interreligious affairs for the American Jewish Committee and a participant in several meetings with Carter, attributes this neglect in part to a "deep-seated bias" in the press, a widespread sense that clergymen are "outsiders," incapable of dealing with serious questions of public policy.

The press assumed that Carter was meeting with clergymen as a public relations exercise, "to put a halo of morality" around his political efforts, Tannenbaum said.

All these criticisms and shortcomings notwithstanding, religion coverage is clearly improving in the American press, no matter how uneven and incomplete that improvement may be.

Until about 20 years ago, newspaper religion coverage was largely limited to Saturday "church pages"—a journalistic ghetto filled with listings of the next day's sermon topics, schedules of church-sponsored rummage sales and pot-luck dinners and press releases from local ministers. Some papers also published Bible verses on their editorial pages and "news" reports on the Sunday sermons in their Monday papers.

Most newspapers assigned their church page duties to their oldest over-the-hill reporters or to the staff alcoholic or, most often, to their youngest, least-experienced reporters. A.M. Rosenthal, executive editor of the *New York Times*, remembers being paid $3 a week to cover Sunday sermons when he was a college correspondent for the paper 40 years ago.

Newspapers had (and many still have) these weekly religion pages largely because the papers "get a lot of (church) ads, and they have to put something around it," said Benjamin C. Bradlee, executive editor of the *Washington Post*.

But the sweeping reforms in the Catholic Church that began with the Second Vatican Council from 1962 to 1965, combined with the active role many clergymen played in the civil rights and anti-war movements, suddenly awakened some editors to the news-making potential of religion and to the need for good, well-trained reporters to cover that news.

In quick succession, other events increased the editors' awareness— and their needs—in this field. The socio-political upheaval of the 1960s —most notably the sexual revolution and the resultant controversies over birth control, abortion, homosexuality and promiscuity—had a strong spiritual component. So, obviously, did the rise of various religious cults. And Carter's presidency. And the emergence of Falwell, the Moral Majority, the New Right and the evangelical movement. And a whole range of issues cutting across the domestic news making spectrum: capital punishment, arms control, genetic engineering, euthanasia.

Most newspapers still do not assign such stories to their religion writers—if they have religion writers—so coverage of these issues often remains inadequate. But some editors are at least aware of their spiritual aspects, and some mention of that aspect is sometimes made; when the best members of the new generation of religion writers—thoughtful, well-educated, many with degrees in theology—report on these subjects, they provide a much-needed extra dimension.

Thus, in several of the best daily newspapers—and, interestingly, in several daily newspapers not otherwise known for their editorial quality— religion has been taken from the church-page ghetto and put on the front page with growing frequency.

Some newspapers—the *New York Times* and the *Detroit Free Press*, for example—have no weekly religion pages. Their editors think religion news should compete with other news for space in the daily paper. Most papers still have weekly religion pages, but the best papers also carry religion news in the regular news pages when the stories warrant that play.

A few small- to medium-size papers—the *St. Petersburg Times*, *Tampa* (Fla.) *Tribune*, *Ogden* (Utah) *Standard-Examiner* and *Warren* (Ohio) *Tribune-Chronicle* among them—have weekly tabloid-size religion sections, in addition to daily religion coverage in their news pages.

Are religion stories well-read?

The *Warren Tribune-Chronicle* reported a 10% increase in Saturday circulation—and a quadrupling of its Saturday advertising linage—after it began publishing a community news-oriented tabloid, including eight pages of religion news, in that day's paper.

There are no definitive studies on the readership of religion stories, but because other studies show that the most religious people are also those most likely to vote and to feel a sense of community—both also characteristics of frequent newspaper readers—it seems probable that religion news is widely read, even in large, sophisticated metropolitan areas.

Thus, better religion reporting may be good business as well as good journalism. No wonder then that even the decidedly secular *Wall Street Journal* has been paying increasing attention to religion. In the last two months, the *Journal* has published front-page stories on seminaries, Islam fundamentalism, Chicago's Cardinal Joseph Bernardin, the Mormon Church (a two-part series) and young Mormons working as *au pair* girls for families throughout the United States. The *Journal* also published, on its editorial page, an excerpt from the statement on nuclear arms by the bishops of France.

Earlier this year, most American newspapers also gave thorough coverage to the more strongly worded American bishops' pastoral letter on nuclear arms. Many critics say that much of that coverage was deficient, though—significantly and characteristically so in that it too often failed to place the bishops' apparently unprecedented action in historical perspective. But the press generally did a much better job covering the bishops' pastoral letter than it does on most other religion stories. Indeed, it can be argued that the press routinely covers matters involving the Roman Catholic Church more thoroughly than it does issues involving any other denomination.

A careful examination of major newspapers and news magazines shows that although the best way for a religion story to get good play is, generally, for it to involve the colorful, the controversial, the charismatic, the crooked or the concupiscent, it also helps if the story involves Catholicism.

Over the last two years, for example, about half the religion stories in *Time* and *Newsweek* involved some aspect of Catholicism—the Pope, Jesuits, nuns, the bishops' letter, gays in the church, a new saint, a new cardinal.

Judaism receives far less coverage in the nation's press. It is noteworthy that the Religion Newswriters Assn., to which most of the nation's religion writers belong and which meets annually in conjunction with the meeting of one major religious group or another, has never met in conjunction with a Jewish group, according to several past and present association officers.

Association members select their annual meeting site based on the likelihood that the religious organization meeting there will produce enough news to warrant their editors paying their expenses to attend. Jewish organizations are not thought to be sufficiently productive of such news, they say.

Religion writers admit that their coverage of Judaism is weak, but they insist that is because the most interesting Jewish stories tend not to be "religion" stories per se. Jewish activity on behalf of Israel or various domestic social and civil liberties causes, for example, is generally covered as non-religion news by political or feature or general assignment reporters, not by religion writers.

"The American Jewish community is not sure whether...what it does is motivated out of any sense of religious convictions," said Bruce Buursma, religion writer for the *Chicago Tribune*. "It comes sometimes out of a sense of peoplehood...a sense of cultural heritage.... Religion gets bound up in that, but it's not necessarily the primary or even motivating force."

But that argument ignores the many strictly religious issues that do confront Judaism.

Rabbi Alexander Schindler, president of the Union of American Hebrew Congregations, and other Jewish leaders say that the press largely ignores such Jewish concerns as intermarriage, assimilation, conversion, proselytizing, differences among the Reform, Conservative and Orthodox branches of Judaism and the controversy over whether a child's religion should be determined by the religion of its mother or its father.

Jews make up only about 3% of the nation's population, though. The Roman Catholic Church accounts for almost 25%; its roughly 50 million members make it the single largest religious denomination in the country (it is also the largest in the world, with 606 million members, about 13% of the total population).

But the Catholic Church has more than size. After all, mainline Protestantism still accounts for the largest segment of the American population, and it, too, receives little press coverage.

But Protestantism is fragmented among many denominations. Besides, *Commonweal's* Steinfels said, "the press pays attention to dramatic events, sharp conflicts and interesting personalities, and...the Catholic Church has had a corner on all three of those categories for a while."

Or, as the outspoken priest and novelist, Father Andrew Greeley, put it: "We may not be much as a church just now, but we're splendid theater...great copy."

Why? In part because the Catholic Church always seems riven with conflict and controversy: disputes over birth control, abortion and divorce; debates over the church's role in liberation movements abroad; disagreement over the bishops' letter on nuclear arms; charges of financial misconduct in the archdiocese in Chicago. Moreover, the Catholic Church has a large, formal, recognizable hierarchy—headed by the Pope, the most identifiable religious leader in the world.

Michael Novak, a Catholic writer and resident scholar in religion and public policy at the American Enterprise Institute in Washington, D.C., said, only half in jest: "The Pope was invented for a mass communications age; that's what the Lord had in mind in the first place."

Many Catholics think the press spends too much time and space on the Pope, though, and not enough on the less clerical manifestations of daily church life.

When Pope John Paul II visited America in 1980, the press turned out en masse. More than 14,000 journalists were accredited, and most of their coverage was as worshipful as it was voluminous.

Such headlines as "We Loved Him" and "A City Nestles in the Hands of a Gentle Pilgrim" and "A Day of Love and Joy" filled the tops of front pages of major newspapers.

Author (and Catholic) Garry Wills wrote scathingly in the *Columbia Journalism Review* of this "embarrassingly...perfervid" journalistic reception and concluded that for the press to have covered the Pope properly "would take a historical consciousness that the press seems unwilling or unable to acquire."

Religion, as embodied for the press in the Pope's visit, is still too often seen by editors as "a big story but soft news," in Wills' words—a story calling for mass coverage, big headlines and big pictures but not necessarily the "hard discipline" that the best papers accord to politics, the economy, law and science.

Greeley, Novak and others say the press too often oversimplifies religion stories, turning every church-related issue into a battle of conservatives against liberals or young against old—writing in predictable stereotypes and "mythic terms," in Novak's words.

51 Not Ready for Prime-Time Prayers

by Cal Thomas

"There's a lot of joyful noise out there, but news people aren't tuned in," says Cal Thomas, former broadcast newsman and vice president for communications of Moral Majority, and currently syndicated columnist for the *Los Angeles Times* and commentator on National Public Radio's "All Things Considered." This article is from *The Quill*, October 1986.

Two ordained clergymen are likely to run for president in 1988, the reverends Pat Robertson and Jesse Jackson.

Meanwhile, scores of men and women with profound religious belief, be they ordained or not, will be candidates for a host of lesser offices.

Millions of people for whom religious faith is a daily reality will be voting in these elections. And these voters will be influenced, at least in part, by the religious views of the candidates, as interpreted through the prism of the voters' own religious experiences.

Unfortunately, most journalists are ill-equipped to adequately report on these candidates or on those who will vote for them because they are unable to identify with religious ideas, and they may be hostile or apathetic toward the people who hold them. Consequently, their judgment has been severely impaired.

The flip side of this impairment is that reporters also may be ill-prepared to ask the kinds of questions of religious leaders that would expose some of these leaders as frauds or, at best, as being duplicitous in their dealings with the public.

Because the press so often turns to opinion polls to chart trends and to predict the future, we ought to examine data contained in a speech given in Amsterdam last July by pollster George Gallup.

Gallup noted that "enormous effort has been placed on the exploration of outer space, but hardly any effort has been expended on exploring inner space." He described two dominant trends in our culture as we approach the end of the 20th Century: an intense search for depth and an equally intense search for relationships.

In making a case for the necessity of exploring inner space, Gallup said that surveys indicate spiritual belief often has more to do with behavior than do race, gender, economic conditions or educational background.

"The religious dimension of life is the final frontier of survey research," said Gallup. "We need to discover the extent to which belief is acted upon."

There is, says Gallup, "a rising tide of religion in the world and a return to faith. A majority of Americans are interested in spiritual things."

The Gallup data reveal that there has been a marked increase in Bible studies, prayer and fellowship groups in the United States, brought on, he says, by a disenchantment with modern lifestyles, a pervasive feeling of emptiness and a growing awareness of the nuclear threat. Also propelling this trend back to spirituality, says Gallup, is the "failure of the *isms* to provide answers: materialism, spiritualism, agnosticism and atheism."

Gallup estimates that up to 25 million Americans profess a high degree of spiritual commitment. As the feminist singer Helen Reddy once sang in *I am Woman* about another group, those are numbers too big to ignore.

The problem is that many of us in the news business have traded our natural skepticism for cynicism when it comes to spiritual things.

We have dealt in stereotypes, or with the excesses of those who profess religious commitment, or we have tried to ignore the subject altogether by dumping everything "religious" (except great controversies) into the ghetto of the religion page. Does anyone have "women's pages" anymore? How about "black news" sections?

As the religion editor of *The New York Times*, Kenneth Briggs, once observed, "Most editors are working off a negative Sunday school experience," and that is why they turn a blind eye in the direction of anything remotely resembling a story with a spiritual dimension.

Surveys have shown that most of us in the press do not attend a church or a synagogue or demonstrate much interest in anything "not of this world." That is tragic, because many of the men and women we cover do attend, and they do believe. Our inability to understand the nature of those beliefs compromises our ability to report fully on what makes these men and women who and what they are.

It is not necessary to believe what they believe to report well. But it is critical to understand *what* they believe and *why* they believe it.

Our profession could benefit from a little consciousness raising. We're up to that. We proved during the civil rights movement and later during the feminist movement that we were not irredeemably inflexible in our thinking. As of yet, there has been no similar commitment to consciousness raising since this latest political and spiritual phenomenon began to appear in the 1970s.

Many of our critics mistake blindness for bias. They believe that we conspire during editorial meetings to deliberately slant the news or trivialize a point of view with which we might personally disagree.

That sort of thing happens, I imagine. But not often. The few persons who do this ought to be out of the business, perhaps writing press releases for the political party that best reflects their ideology.

Nevertheless, the question needs to be asked: Why do so many people—conservative, religious, or both—feel this way about us? For that matter, in an age in which we over-cover everything (such as the latest royal wedding), why do we under-cover or ignore values and ideas that 25 million Americans consider central to their lives, and at least as many more consider to be very important?

Experts abound on virtually every subject, except spiritual ones. When the Soviet nuclear reactor at Chernobyl exploded last spring, nuclear experts were busier than at any time since the accident at Three Mile Island. Their advice and expertise were immediately sought and plastered over our front pages and on our television screens.

But when testimony before the Rogers Commission investigating the Challenger disaster revealed large scale cover-ups of equipment problems both at NASA and at Morton Thiokol, and there was subsequent testimony that the employee who blew the whistle at Morton Thiokol was demoted, no experts were interviewed who could explore the moral dimensions behind such human failings. Not one.

What makes some politicians tick? Do they possess the same character flaws that fueled the excesses of Ferdinand and Imelda Marcos? Why don't news people consider human frailties called greed or the lust for power in discussing these people and how they operate?

The chaplain of the United States Senate has written a book on the subject of power. As I write this, not a single talk show host or newspaper has interviewed him. Are there not people, religious and non-religious, who would like to hear what he thinks about power? Does anyone know his name (Richard C. Halverson) without looking it up? This man exerts a significant influence on the lives—and therefore the policies—of a large number of senators.

Why is the deadly sin of greed so deadly, and to what extent can it potentially affect us all, including those of us who criticize others for submitting to the siren call? Our coverage of sleazy politicians and bureaucrats, the Marcoses, and similar events and persons could benefit from such analyses.

An instance that demonstrates how blindness has affected our professional judgment occurred when evangelist Billy Graham held his first crusade in more than 25 years in Washington, D.C., last April. Press coverage, with the exception of *The Washington Times*, was pitifully meager.

The local television stations considered these stories more important than Graham and the tens of thousands who came to hear him each night: fires in an apartment house and in a shopping center, with no injuries in either incident; a car in the river; a terrorist killing; a local suicide; Reagan talking to Marcos by phone; a Christmas in April project; a bubble festival; weather; and, of course, a feast of sports events.

The vice president of the United States and the mayor of Washington attended the opening night of the crusade. One TV station did not mention their presence and spent only 10 seconds on the story, saying that Graham hoped to draw 140,000 people during the week and, in other news, . . .

I cite the Graham story as an example of our failure to go deeper, our failure to tap stories, legitimate stories, that are representative of and appeal to large numbers of people who feel left out of news coverage. These people have seen every weirdo imaginable given the attention of the press, including the Bagwhan Shree Rajneesh, who was followed to the ends of the earth. . . . But when someone representing their point of view comes to town, he is ignored.

Conflict between blacks and whites in South Africa is news, but harmony between blacks and whites in Washington at a Graham crusade is not. Is it any wonder that so many people do not trust the press? And do we care enough about their distrust to do what we can to win them back? We should. I am disturbed by the large numbers of people who have told me they gave up reading their local newspapers because they no longer saw their views reflected. Such feelings can become a threat to press freedoms and to a free society.

Why is it important that we become more sensitized to this moral-spiritual-religious strain that runs deep in our country? Don't we have religion pages for such stories?

That is precisely the problem. We are sometimes embarrassed to discuss these subjects, fearing our own inability to deal with them, so we relegate them to a "safe" section and assign one or two people to "deal with those stories." Out of sight, out of mind. Separate, but unequal.

With these stories removed from even our peripheral vision, we are free to deal with "legitimate news," which poses no threat to our ideas or ideology.

Confronting eternal and transcendent values makes us uncomfortable, for to do so in our professional lives means we might have to come to grips with such ideas in our personal lives, and too many of us would just as soon avoid starting down that road for fear of where it might lead.

Louis Moore is the editor of the *Star-Courier* in Plano, Texas. He is also a former award-winning religion editor of the *Houston Chronicle* who, over a 14-year period, managed to place many stories with a religious-moral-ethical dimension throughout the *Chronicle* in addition to overseeing what was probably the best religion page in the country.

Moore says one of the reasons he was successful in getting stories with a religious perspective off the religion page and into the rest of the *Chronicle* (including page one), was that he had several allies in management positions who believed as he did that religion was too important to be relegated to a single page once a week.

He sympathizes with the problems religion poses for the uninitiated editor or reporter by noting that there are about 260 denominations in the United States, each with its own vocabulary, or variations on a vocabulary, and all with their own incidents involving in-house fighting and rivalries.

He says, too, that more than any other subject, religion is simultaneously personal and public, emotional and intellectual and produces a strong response among those we serve. All the more reason to cover it.

But the diversity and size of the religious dimension is no excuse for ignoring it. At a minimum there ought to be journalists who understand the vocabulary of the major religious faiths in America. Unfortunately, even the largest body of believers, Christians, find few in the press who can define the terms associated with their faith.

During the 1984 Democratic National Convention in San Francisco, a reporter for *The Christian Science Monitor* approached me seeking some information. At the end of a brief interview, she asked me if I was born again.

"What do you mean by that?" I asked her.

"Well, you know," she said.

"Yes, I do know," I replied, "but do you?"

She admitted she did not know the definition of "born again," but she was prepared to use it in her story anyway. I quoted the third chapter of the Book of John in the Bible, in which Jesus, the author of the term, said, "You must be born again," and I went on to explain that the term refers to a spiritual conversion that occurs when people repent of their sins and invite Christ into their hearts and lives, which produces a spiritual rebirth.

How can we communicate truth if we can't define our terms?

And what about the incorrect, and often pejorative, use of the word "fundamentalist," which has come to mean anyone behaving in a fanatical manner. One never sees a story about a group of fundamentalists operating a soup kitchen in an inner city, though many do. The word is reserved for the most unacceptable and idiotic behavior that some fundamentalists occasionally participate in. But most fundamentalists are not like that and many who are cannot properly be labeled fundamentalists.

The classic story that focuses on the ignorance of journalists of religious subjects occurred during the 1976 presidential campaign. Shortly after Jimmy Carter told Bill Moyers in a PBS interview that he had been born again, NBC's John Chancellor said on the *Nightly News*: "We've looked up this 'born again' business and it's nothing new."

This almost flip reference was an affront to the millions of American Christians who regard being born again as the central fact defining their lives.

Quiz yourself: Do you know anything about Armageddon? Do you know it is an actual place in Israel? Do you know what the Bible says about it? Do you care? You should, because even Ronald Reagan has mentioned it in connection with U.S. relations with the Soviets and U.S. policy in the Middle East.

The *Star-Courier*'s Moore says that many journalists are cynical about religion, but display no similar disdain for certain religious leaders upon whom they have, in effect, conferred sainthood because of these leader's congenial political views. How often does one hear a journalist challenge any statement by South African Bishop Desmond Tutu, whose every word is treated as if it's a direct message from God?

The recent Times Mirror poll on attitudes toward the press indicated that the greatest consumers of news trust us the least. This is dangerous for a free society.

We ought to be reaching out to new constituencies, and we should be building our circulation and audience base. We ought to be including new groups of people in our sphere of interest, and we ought to be doing it not just to sell more ad space or to increase our broadcast rate card, though that can and should result. (Man may not live by bread alone, but we do live by bread a little bit.) We ought to be doing it for the same reason that we reached out to attract more blacks and other minorities and women: Because we can't report on the fullness of American life unless we include everyone in our coverage.

The blindness that causes many editors and reporters to pass by stories with religious dimensions is not congenital; neither has it been acquired by a freak accident or by disease. Rather, it is a consequence of a refusal by many to simply open their eyes. Instead of saying with the hymn writer, "I once was blind, but now I see," many in our business say that when it comes to religious stories, "I was blind and I intend to remain blind, so go away and leave me alone."

The next presidential campaign may include those who are supposed to represent the kingdom of the next world grasping for the earthly power in the here and now, as well as non-ordained candidates whose faith is a motivating force in their lives.

The campaign is likely to offer an exciting and, perhaps, unique opportunity for us to break out of the predictability of much of what we cover and to rise above the usual ignorance and stereotyping that has accompanied our coverage of this subject in the past. But we can do a good job only if we are properly equipped. And there is not much time left for that task.

Who among us truly understands what makes Pat Robertson run (and not just for office)? And does anyone know where Jack Kemp and his wife attend church or the story of how he invited Jeane Kirkpatrick (a possible running mate) to begin attending, too. And how Kemp's wife, Joanne, has been a Bible study leader among congressional and ambassadorial wives for more than a decade and what impact this might have on the political life of Washington and the country? Does it matter? You bet it does.

Reporters ought to start attending evangelical and fundamentalist church services as they did the black services during the civil rights movement—not just when someone they are covering is there, but for their own education on the values and beliefs of these people. Their failure to do so will render them unable to report fully on the candidates and the voters of 1988.

Technology and techniques change, but basic human needs and emotions never change. Those in our profession who grasp the significance and the depth of the social, cultural and spiritual changes now sweeping America will be far better equipped to serve the public than those who are blind to these trends and wish to remain so, largely for personal reasons.

52 The New Awakening: Getting Religion in the Video Age

by Margaret O'Brien Steinfels, Peter Steinfels

> Will the electronic church become so pervasive that it replaces traditional worship and established denominations? No, say Margaret O'Brien Steinfels and Peter Steinfels, as they describe the evolution of religious programs on television and radio. Margaret O'Brien Steinfels is an editor, writer, and business manager of *Christianity Crisis*. Peter Steinfels is executive editor of *Commonweal* and author of *The Neoconservatives*. This article is reprinted from *Channels of Communications*, January/February 1983.

For millions of Americans, Jerry Falwell is not a real person. He is the symbol of an explosive mixture of fundamentalist faith, right-wing politics, and modern technology. People who wouldn't know the difference between Rex Humbard and Mother Hubbard, people who might well assume that Oral Roberts was a toothbrush manufacturer, are nonetheless worried about the power of the "prime-time preachers." Not even when Bishop Fulton J. Sheen scored a hit with his prime-time series in 1952 was there such a furor over religion and television.

The resources—and resourcefulness—of the so-called electronic church are indeed impressive. Not only have the fundamentalist evangelists on television created a single but effective TV message, they have mastered the means of delivering it. They produced their own shows in their own studios with their own production facilities. They own TV cameras and transmitting equipment, and have begun to acquire transponder time for satellite transmission, enabling their programs to run on a growing number of cable systems across the country. They pay for their own broadcast time, and they've developed extensive support organizations to build their "congregations" and raise funds.

Religious networks are springing up. Pat Robertson, one of the most successful of the TV preachers, has organized the Christian Broadcast Network (CBN), headquartered in Virginia Beach, Virginia, which uses a twenty-four-hour-a-day transponder on Satcom IIIR and computerized production and transmitting facilities. CBN owns four UHF television stations and five FM radio stations, and keeps a staff of more than seven hundred busy. It operates seventy-one regional call-in centers, staffed mainly with volunteers who follow up on financial pledges and provide prayerful counseling. CBN University offers graduate training in communications and theology. Recently Robertson has spun off a secular counterpart, the Continental Broadcasting Network, which will transmit general programming suitable for family viewing.

It is the political potential of establishments like Robertson's that has stirred so much controversy—at least since 1979, when Jerry Falwell used his "Old-Time Gospel Hour" television program as a base for organizing the Moral Majority, and even more so since 1980, when the Religious New Right not only contributed to Ronald Reagan's victory but was widely regarded as a decisive factor in the defeat of several leading liberal Senators. At the same time, the media success of the fundamentalists has posed a direct challenge to the other churches, giving a new urgency to longstanding questions about organized religion's approach to television.

Not that the churches have ever lacked individuals aware of television's power—critics who worry about the medium's destructive or trivializing impact on personal values, enthusiasts who hope to exploit its hold on mass audiences for explicitly religious purposes. But the success of the prime-time preachers, linked as it is to the advent of new technologies, has added fuel to old debates. To some, the electronic church is further evidence of television's distorting effect on authentic religion. To others, it is an implicit call to "go and do likewise."

Swaggart in the Morning

Getting perspective on the electronic church itself is not easy, in view of the political passions it has stirred. In an effort to raise funds to combat TV evangelists, Norman Lear has claimed, "The ability of moral majoritarians to shape public attitudes and to influence the climate of public debate is unprecedented and poses an enormous danger. The leading 'television preachers' alone have an audience approaching 40 million." In sum, says Lear, "The moral majoritarians have overpowered America's airwaves with their messages of hostility, fear, and distrust."

The casual viewer of these programs might be hard pressed to see why Lear was so incensed. For a start, few prime-time preachers actually appear during prime time. In most major markets, they are still likely to be found early in the morning, late at night, or in the Sunday-morning "religious ghetto." Lear also fails to acknowledge the sheer variety of the programming—everything from fire-and-brimstone preaching pitched to stir fear in the backsliding Christian, to staid Bible-study programs sending all but the truly devoted into a stupor.

In the morning, Jimmy Swaggart pedantically explains God's views on first and second marriages; in the evening, he paces the platform, conjuring up pathetic scenes of the alcoholic so wretched that he stole the shoes from his own child's corpse to buy liquor.

Jim Bakker, one of the born-again, gesture-for-gesture imitations of network talk-show hosts, publicly shares the domestic dramas of his marriage to gospel singer Tammy Fay.

Ben Kinchlew, Pat Robertson's athletic-looking black co-host, presides over a slickly produced edition of "The 700 Club," featuring:

- the author of a book claiming that low liquidity among major corporations lies at the root of our economic troubles;
- a reformed workaholic who, but for seeing the light and being saved by Jesus, would have lost his wife and children;
- a clip of a conference on cable television and "narrowcasting," from which *Screw* magazine publisher Al Goldstein's remarks had to be deleted because of his language;
- a woman, once gay, who turned to Jesus and now offers a ministry to homosexuals.

Not to everyone's taste, certainly, and clearly laced with political conservatism. But have the TV evangelists truly "overpowered America's airwaves"?

If audience size is any measure, the evangelists have hardly been a resounding success. During the 1980 elections, normally skeptical journalists were reporting that Jerry Falwell reached anywhere from 18 million to 30 million people each week; by contrast, the Arbitron and Nielsen reports revealed that Falwell was actually reaching fewer than 1.5 million viewers. Contrary to Norman Lear's assertion that the "leading" preachers alone had an audience of 40 million, the 1980 Arbitron figures showed a combined audience of half that size for all sixty-six syndicated religious programs. Furthermore, as Jeffrey Hadden and Charles Swann reminded the readers of their book, *Prime Time Preachers*, not all the top syndicated religious programs were conservative, not all the conservative programs were political, and most of the religious and conservative programs, at least during the greatest public uproar, were losing rather than gaining audience. (More recently, the top programs have recouped their losses, although without any startling growth.)

None of these facts should lead one to underestimate the power of the Religious New Right, but they do suggest that the television component in that power is easily inflated. In this tendency to overrate the influence, critics like Lear mirror the attitude of the right-wingers themselves, who commonly attribute the successes of liberalism to the media power of a small number of established liberals—including Norman Lear. It is easier for all of us to believe that unpopular ideas prosper because their advocates hold some "unfair" technological advantage than it is to think they actually resonate with the experience of large numbers of people.

Quite apart from the appeal of their right-wing ideology, the evangelical programs have more going for them than their willingness to invoke the Lord's name. The talk, the accents, the clothes, the tragedies and comedies of God's people have a touchingly real quality about them—a quality they retain even amidst their studied imitations of "real" television. The electronic church is, if nothing else, one of the few places on television where you encounter genuinely homely people. Neither the stars nor the guests hold back: They exhort, they preach, they laugh, and they cry— oh, do they cry! Not for them the deep-chested authoritativeness of Dan Rather, the cool mien of Barbara Walters, or the impish savior-faire of Johnny Carson and Dick Cavett. These programs remind viewers that most of the country is not, after all, so slick, so professional, so well-dressed, and so damnably *in control.*

Despite the claims of Falwell and others to a truly national audience, the TV congregants are still predominantly female, Southern, small-town or rural, and getting on in years, according to Hadden and Swann. To see people like themselves, or at least like someone they know, confirms their sense of reality. If the guests on some of the shows—ex-alcoholics, former drug addicts, widows with young children, victims of unhappy marriages and miserable childhoods—routinely strike a maudlin note, the viewer can nonetheless identify with these all-too-familiar casualties of ordinary life; this is something every successful soap-opera writer understands. And the casualties are always repaired, with the help of friends, of the church, and above all of Jesus. Though the world's problems can seem insoluble, viewers may take some small comfort in the apparent capacity of individuals and small groups to deal with their own problems.

Obviously the electronic church trades in a kind of unreality of its own. Indeed, it is commonly accused of misleading people about the true nature of the human condition. According to the Reverend James M. Dunn, "The quick, certain, black-and-white theologies so made to order for television are inadequate for life in the real world."

Dunn's criticism is especially interesting because he is a leading staff member of the Baptist Joint Committee on Public Affairs—an agency sponsored in part by churches that many Americans might fail to differentiate from the electronic church itself. Even Carl F. H. Henry, elder statesman of evangelical Protestantism, has echoed this criticism. The strongest reproof, of course, has come from the mainline Protestant churches, generally those belonging to the National Council of Churches (NCC). Their leading complaint is that electronic churches twist the Gospel into a quick fix, promising a painless life, and aping, rather than questioning, the values of secular culture. If you accept Jesus, you will enjoy immediate relief from suffering. Success, prosperity, and earthly happiness will be yours. This presents an odd contrast to Jesus' message, but it bears more than a faint resemblance to the run of TV commercials.

A Far-flung "Congregation"

The religious critics' second objection is that Jesus called people into a church community—a fellowship of worship and service. The electronic church, however, substitutes for this a pseudo-community of isolated viewers. Finally, TV evangelism fosters the cult-like following of a single leader. In 1979, a habitually measured and good-humored commentator on American Protestantism, University of Chicago church historian (and Lutheran pastor) Martin E. Marty warned that "the electronic church threatens to replace the living congregation with a far-flung clientele of devotees to this or that evangelist. This invisible religion is—or ought to be—the most feared contemporary rival to church religion."

But isn't that rivalry only the latest chapter in an old story? Religious "awakenings" have frequently been tied to new forms of communication—like the printed book in the sixteenth century or the open-air revival in the eighteenth and nineteenth—and on each occasion the established churches have warned that the new techniques were altering the character of the faith. In a sense the established churches were right. Certainly the Protestant emphasis on "scripture alone" derived from both Renaissance humanism and the new power of the printing press. Likewise, the simplified theology and emotional fervor of American Protestantism sprang from the needs of the faithful in the camp meeting. And church structures could no more escape alteration than church doctrine. When so many more people could read and own their own Bibles, the need for a teaching hierarchy diminished. Revivalism put a premium on showmanship and platform oratory, rather than theological training, as a path to religious leadership. The electronic church is not terribly sophisticated about answering the establishment's criticism, seeing it mainly as a reflection of the mainliners' lack of fervor and enterprise. But paradoxically, if it wanted to, it could defend its innovations as nothing new.

To the Electronic Collection Plate

But the tension between independent evangelists and the mainline churches is also part of a larger story—that of broadcasting in America. The early days of radio saw all kinds of religious groups not only buying time but frequently owning stations—which were often used as weapons against one another. By 1934, however, when the Federal Communications Act established a "public interest" obligation for licensees, a less chaotic pattern began to develop. Led by NBC, most major stations—and eventually the other networks—provided free time to broad, ecumenical groups, which in turn produced religious programming of a nondivisive kind. (NBC, for example, worked in partnership with the Protestant Federal Council of Churches [now the NCC], with the National Council of Catholic Men, and with the Jewish Theological Seminary of America.) As they were providing free time to such mainline groups, NBC, CBS, and ABC actually refused to sell others any time for religious broadcasting, and many local stations followed suit. The Mutual Broadcasting System did sell time, but in 1944 it forbade soliciting funds on the air—a sharp blow to paid-time preachers. In short, the new arrangements left independent evangelicals to fend for themselves—buying time where they could, or owning and operating their own commercial stations.

With the advent of television, a consortium of Protestant, Catholic, and Jewish groups divided free network time on a 3,2,1 basis: Of every 6 hours the networks allotted, the Protestants would receive 3, the Catholics 2, and the Jews 1. The networks subsidized the programming, and local affiliates carried it free. This arrangement allowed the stations to meet their public-interest obligations and avoid sectarian strife, while the major religious groups controlled their allotted time (mostly on Sunday mornings, when audiences were small and advertisers few) and benefited from network expertise and technology.

Richard Walsh, former director of communications for the National Council of Catholic Men and producer of "The Catholic Hour" from 1953 to 1968, remembers the arrangement as highly practical and conducive to good relations between the churches and the networks, as well as among religious groups. "The purpose of network programming for the religious groups was not to convert, and they did little direct preaching *à la* today's electronic church," says Walsh. In his view, the point was to foster dialogue. "The Catholic Hour," though addressed to Catholics, was on subjects that might be of interest to others. While financial support varied with each network, Walsh recalls enjoying great independence from the networks in producing a variety of programs—talk shows, operas, plays, documentaries.

Though generally comfortable, the relationship between the networks and mainline religious groups did have its share of ups and downs even before the electronic church hove onto the scene. Some Protestant groups continued to complain that the NCC did not represent the totality of Protestant views—and NBC, for one, provided time to the Southern Baptists. By the end of the sixties, network funds began to shrink and affiliates to be more reluctant about providing free time. Some of this may have been due to a perception, perhaps exaggerated, that religion was no longer, in the cant term of the day, "relevant," a view that declining church attendance figures supported. Bill McClurkin, director of broadcast and film for the NCC, adds another factor: The increase in Sunday sports broadcasting narrowed the time boundaries of the Sunday-morning "religious ghetto." In any case, when enterprising evangelicals proposed to pay for air-time that affiliates had been giving away—why, that was an offer the affiliates could hardly refuse.

More than ideology, program content, or style, money may be the key to the electronic church's rise. As Hadden and Swann point out; 1970 to '75 were years when the costs of video production dropped. They were also the years when the evangelists' audiences doubled, often at the expense of the mainliners' programs. The fact is that mainline and evangelical programs have never gone head-to-head, on the same terms. Would the mainline shows have been dropped by so many stations if they, too, were paying their own way? The TV evangelists, having been forced to wander in the paid-time wilderness for so long, have simply played by the free-market rules and won.

Money may also prove to be the Achilles heel of the TV preachers. Secular critics dwell on the huge sums the electronic church rakes in: the "electronic collection plate," they call it. But the TV ministry not only draws in support; it has to pay it out as well. Television is an expensive habit to maintain, and the TV preachers are hooked. Also, large amounts of money flowing in and out of the coffers are a constant temptation, even to the righteous. With or without scandal, the moderately prosperous lifestyle of most TV evangelists sits uncomfortably with their constant solicitation of funds and the panoply of memberships, pins, study guides, and booklets that they dangle before their followers. Some preachers resolve the incongruity by emphasizing their own versions of Save the Children campaigns— relief and missionary work in impoverished areas of the globe. But that appeal has provoked further demands for accurate accounting of how much money really goes where.

Jerry Falwell has joined with Billy Graham and some other evangelical ministers in establishing an Evangelical Council for Financial Accountability to insure financial self-regulation. Most of the other TV preachers have kept their distance.

Television's Calling

The success of the electronic church has given the established denominations the "feeling of being outflanked, threatened," according to Stewart M. Hoover, TV producer, lecturer on mass communications, and author of *The Electronic Giant*, published by the Church of the Brethren. Why, then, don't they simply start paying their own way too?

The question ignores the important *organizational* consequences of church involvement in television. With the electronic church, what you see is pretty much what there is. Television is at the heart of these ministries. "My specific calling from God," Jim Bakker has written, "is to be a television talk-show host. I love TV. I eat it. I sleep it." Most other church organizations are complex and their activities highly decentralized. Most of their personnel serve local congregations; most of their financial resources are invested in church buildings, community centers, schools, hospitals, and so on. The major churches all have skilled, respected individuals dealing with television. But enlarging their activities would mean switching substantial funds and energies from other areas.

For reasons of theology, propriety, and concern for the effect on other church activities, most of these churches object to soliciting funds on the air. Accordingly, they're not ready to give up on the free-time tradition. In the face of FCC deregulation policies, many church groups have defended the practice of free air-time for public-interest programming, and not just that of a religious nature either.

The cause is not lost. Free air-time does continue to be available. "Insight", a drama program produced by the Paulists, a Catholic order of priests, is shown free by about a hundred stations. In 1980 it was among the top ten religious programs in the Arbitron ratings, and in 1981 it won three Daytime Emmy Awards. "Davey and Goliath", a cartoon series for children produced by the Lutheran Church in America, continues to be re-run in free time slots—and to gain quite respectable ratings.

The networks, however, no longer seem interested in supporting these kinds of shows, so without giving up entirely on free time, the mainline churches know they have to explore other alternatives. Basically there are three:

1. to follow the lead of the electronic church by building their own production and distribution apparatus for religious programming;
2. to concentrate on influencing the effects of non-religious television on public and personal morals;
3. to reject using television entirely.

The last, most radical course has been proposed by Harvey Cox, a noted Harvard theologian. Suppose, he argues, that "all the mass media of all the countries of the world could be turned over to the churches for one whole week, or one whole month, exclusively for making the Gospel known. At the end of the month, do you really think the world would be much better off, or the Kingdom of God be appreciably closer?"

The problem, says Cox, is that the mass media are one-way, hierarchical systems inherently incapable of eliciting the profound belief the Gospel demands. The media "are controlled by the rich and powerful," while "God comes in vulnerability, and powerlessness. The message of the Gospel is essentially incompatible with any coercive form of communication. All 'mass media' are one-way and therefore inherently coercive."

Cox derides Christian "communicators" who want to infuse the networks with "a new and spiritually significant content. The churches should not be wasting their efforts trying to pilfer a few minutes of time from the reigning Caesars of the 'communications industry.'" Instead, "the Christian strategy *vis à vis* mass media is not to try to use them but to try to dismantle them. We need a real revolution in which the control of the media is returned to the people and the technical development of media is turned toward accessibility, two-way communication, and genuine conversation."

Less radical than Cox's approach, but still having something in common with it, are the efforts of some individuals concentrating on influencing non-religious television. Dr. Everett Parker, for example, is director of the United Church of Christ's Office of Communication, a veteran of religious broadcasting, and a leader in struggles to widen access to the airwaves. Under his leadership, the United Church of Christ has tried to influence the values communicated on television by insuring that all community groups are represented on the air. Parker's Office of Communication is a leading critic of FCC deregulation plans, and a sponsor of educational efforts and consulting services. The church-launched Community Telecommunications Service, for instance, has developed a workshop curriculum to teach local churches how to produce cable programs, and another to teach community and church leaders how to negotiate cable contracts, assure public access to cable, and enforce fair employment practices.

Other church programs try to influence the impact of television on values by educating the viewers: The Media Action Research Center, a body sponsored by several denominations and headquartered in the National Council of Churches office in New York, developed television awareness training in the mid-seventies. Its *Viewer's Guide* shows "how we can take command, use TV intelligently and creatively, instead of mindlessly letting TV use us."

Finally there is the first option—getting into the TV business in a big way. There are three outstanding examples of this besides those of the electronic church.

The United States Catholic Conference (USCC) has taken two steps toward keeping its hand in the game. First, an annual Catholic Communications Campaign raises about $5 million a year, 50 percent of which remains in the local dioceses where it is collected; the other half is used to support the USCC Office of Communications and to award grants to a range of communications-related projects.

Second, the USCC has formed the independent, for-profit Catholic Telecommunications Network of America (CTNA) to provide local dioceses with a variety of satellite-transmitted services: news and photo services for diocesan newspapers, electronic mail, videoconferencing for church leaders, administrative and educational materials, and TV program redistribution. The network, which began transmitting last fall, is supported by voluntary affiliation and maintenance fees from local dioceses—and by the sale of its services to commercial users. As of November 1982, 33 out of 172 local dioceses had signed affiliation contracts. Wassyl Lew, head of CTNA, expects that a number of religious orders, Catholic colleges, universities, and hospitals may eventually affiliate with it. Lew emphasizes the word "telecommunications" rather than "television" in describing the network: Its primary purpose is to provide a communications service for the bishops, though TV programming provided by the network will be available for redistribution to local TV stations or cable systems.

The fifteen hours of programming per week that CTNA currently plans to redistribute include programs on marriage counseling and enrichment; an interview program called "Christopher Close-Ups"; several Bible and theology programs; two Spanish-language programs; a missionary program produced by the Maryknoll religious order, and a variety of magazine-format and entertainment shows. All of this will be produced not by CTNA but largely by religious orders and local dioceses. Lew anticipates that as the system becomes fully operational, some of its downlinks will also serve as uplinks, thus allowing dioceses to be senders as well as receivers of TV programming. In the meantime, programs will go out from CTNA's New York transmitter.

CTNA is an attempt to meet the diverse needs of a decentralized church organization with the capacities of the satellite for coast-to-coast transmission. As such, the network might become a model for other church groups. Yet it is unlikely to increase the number of Catholic TV shows available to a large television audience.

One reason that telecommunications will always play a less important role for the Catholic church than for TV evangelists is that it "just doesn't fit with what Catholics think of as a church," argues Richard Hirsch, head of the USCC's Office of Communications. "The electronic church is not a church; it is a pulpit." The point applies to a number of other churches as well—those that consider sacrament and ritual as important to their worship as preaching, in particular the Episcopalians and Lutherans. It is interesting to recall that Bishop Sheen's famous programs had nothing of a church service about them. The bishop was dressed in resplendent episcopal garb, but *not* in his vestments for celebrating mass. The format was one of teaching, not preaching or prayer; a blackboard was the chief prop. Sheen's example suggests the distance that the "ritual" churches are apt to see between effective television and the central acts of their faith.

The Eternal Word Network, another of the three noteworthy efforts by religious groups to build a television base, also depends on satellite technology. Mother Angelica, a Franciscan nun whose convent in Birmingham, Alabama specializes in preparing and printing religious pamphlets and other materials, made the leap from the printing press to a satellite transponder on Satcom IIIR with four hours of programming seven nights a week. From a converted garage, she produces her own show, "Mother Angelica Talks It Over", makes time available to other religious programs, re-runs old favorites, and subleases unused transponder time to the First United Methodist Church in Shreveport, Louisiana. She reports that forty-two cable systems, reaching up to 800,000 homes, carry her programming. The network is supported by direct-mail donations, unsolicited contributions, and foundation grants.

The United Methodists tried a different approach: In 1980, they launched a fund-raising drive to buy a TV station. The church group planned to produce its own religious programs with the projected $1 million profit from the station. But ownership of a commercial station posed conflicts between the values of Methodism and the values the station would be communicating much of the time. The sheer expense of the project has also deterred some church members, who have asked, "How many hungry people can you feed with that money?"

The pitfalls encountered by the United Methodists illustrate the dangers for mainline churches that might be tempted to emulate the fundamentalists. According to Stewart M. Hoover, writing in *The Electronic Giant*, "The mainline churches could probably not 'beat the electronic church at its own game'; they probably would not really want to."

But it should be remembered that the electronic church itself was not born yesterday—which is when it first began getting national attention. It was more than two decades ago that Pat Robertson managed to put back on the air the defunct UHF station he had bought. Jerry Falwell went on the air in Lynchburg, Virginia, six months after he started his church there—in 1956. Oral Roberts first appeared on television in 1954, and his current TV format dates from 1969. At that time, the other churches were comfortably ensconced on the networks; twenty-five years later, they are groping. The outcome of that groping may not be clear for another quarter-century.

53 Exploring the Role of the Ethnic Press
by Robert Israel

The editor of the *Rhode Island Jewish Herald* proposes that ethnic and religious newspapers should reach out and encourage a diverse range of opinions. This article is from *Editor & Publisher*, December 7, 1985.

Ethnic and religious newspapers should establish an active presence in their specialized communities and within their communities-at-large.

Journalistic options should be kept open without losing sight of the exclusive readership, but acknowledging that readership's interdependency with neighbors in all areas of the globe.

Editing a 58-year-old Jewish oriented weekly with a circulation of 18,000 in the Rhode Island and southeastern Massachusetts area, I have found it possible to produce dynamic results.

When I became managing editor three years ago, the paper had drifted into becoming a tired organ most people ignored and discarded. It featured canned news from the Jewish Telegraphic Agency, by-passing local stories. It was unorganized and had no clear format or focus. It provided loyal subscribers with announcements of births, deaths and weddings, as well as the going price for a corned-beef sandwich at Miller's, a local deli, but not much else.

I felt readers deserved a better deal and went around to meet with them, scheduling speaking engagements, getting to know them, asking for their ideas and participation. They had plenty to tell me. They were itching to get involved, to communicate.

Someone suggested the return of a Yiddish column, or rather, a Yiddish-English column. The Jewish press began in this country as the Yiddish press when the immigrants first arrived here at the turn of the century. I went out and found a writer who files a column bi-weekly.

The local board of rabbis wanted input. They also write a bi-weekly column on a rotating basis among their members.

The synagogues and agencies in the area regularly participate. The Jewish Family Service has a monthly column written by their staff. Community centers send news releases and photographs of activities. Religious schools are involved and are highlighted in a special education issue each year. A stringer that free-lances for the paper regularly makes the rounds and reports on social functions. People I meet while on speaking engagements routinely call me with story suggestions.

Balanced, unbiased reporting is my credo. When a labor strike occurred at the Jewish Home for the Aged, I interviewed strikers, management, elderly residents, union organizers and families. Volunteers that gave of their time to keep the Home running during the strike were profiled.

Yet the scope of the newspaper is not isolated to the Jewish community. The community-at-large is encouraged to exchange ideas and opinions. And I have sought a reciprocal agreement with other media outlets.

The *Providence Journal-Bulletin* has published several of my commentary pieces on their opposite-editorial page. When I traveled to Israel this summer, they published my report on Rhode Islanders who had made Israel their home in the *Sunday Journal Magazine*.

The local chapter of the National Conference of Christians and Jews asked me to join their panel of judges for the "Books for Brotherhood and Sisterhood" contest. Together with three other judges, we read several hundred essays by Rhode Island school children who discussed ways of combating prejudice in their communities. The winning essays have been published in their hometown newspapers.

Television station Channel 12 invited me to be on their questioning panel for the "Newsmakers" program, interviewing clergymen about the controversial creche in Pawtucket (where my newspaper is published), and about other religious and civic issues. Radio station WHJJ now features one of the newspaper's columnists every week for a talk show.

The newspaper regularly features announcements of interfaith services. My weekly editorials explore ways of establishing racial and religious harmony, especially in the light of recent anti-Semitic and inflammatory remarks by Louis Farrakhan and others.

One of the problems facing the ethnic and religious press today, particularly the Jewish press, is competition with house organs run by philanthropic organizations which publish public-relations newspapers. These newspapers present the "news" in a one-sided pro-agency format. This distorts the purpose of a newspaper which is to inform its readers in an unbiased manner.

If my newspaper publishes an editorial critical of Israel, lets's say, people get upset, but for the wrong reasons. They are so used to seeing positive reports from the philanthropic agency, the Jewish Federation, they get miffed when we don't follow the party line.

This distortion of the newspaper's function in the community has created what one writer referred to as "the Jewish press wars."

At a recent conference at Harvard's Widener Library, 100 Jewish journalists from around the world addressed this issue. An editor told me a horror story of how a Federation newspaper successfully put an independent newspaper out of business by starting a rival publication. This has prompted a professional organization, the American Jewish Press Association, to form a watchdog committee to mediate future disputes.

Ethnic and religious newspapers were founded to provide a vehicle of communication to newly arrived immigrants to this country. Now that these immigrants have been absorbed into American culture, many are searching for their roots and are turning to the newspapers to find them.

But it is important not to dwell in the past but to continually illuminate and educate readers, to seek their input, to encourage a diverse range of opinions.

We live in a society where we must openly exchange views with our neighbors. Why not guide a newspaper to provide open access to these views?

A healthy forum, initiated even by a small newspaper, can unify people by calling attention to the rich ethnic diversity within our society.

In other words, rather than publishing in the dark, an ethnic or religious newspaper, aware of its unique identity and heritage, should actively seek to be part of the mainstream.

Mass Media and Religion: For Further Reading

Gergor T. Goethals, *The TV Ritual: Worship at the Video Alter.* Boston: Beacon Press, 1981.

Peter G. Horsfield, *Religious Television: The American Experience.* White Plains, N.Y.: Longman, 1984.

XIV

Business
and Mass Media

When colleges and universities explain the tradition of academic
garb, there's often a chuckle when the person in charge describes
the color that designates graduates of business departments and
schools. "The academic hood is trimmed in a drab brownish
color," the speaker will say, and invariably someone in the
audience will comment, "Just like business."

That has not been the case with business and the mass media
in recent years, however. Business coverage has increased and
improved. Many, though not all, business pages and programs
have sparked controversy and are no longer simply repositories of
dull news releases and tables of stock quotations. Readers and
listeners and viewers have indicated interest in business, and
media management has begun to give staff support to business
coverage in print and on the air.

Lest it appear idyllic, healthy tensions remain; reporters and
editors worth their paychecks continue to question the motives
and activities of business. Some business leaders are beginning
to respect hard-hitting reporters who are fair and accurate in their
assessments of business. Others accuse reporters—sometimes
justifiably—of being ill prepared for the work and prejudiced
against business. The arguments will continue. The articles in this
section should indicate that business news should not be drab or
superficial.

54 Business and the Media: Stereotyping Each Other
by Jim Hoge

> The public wants information about the economy, so
> business and the media have to peel away stereotypes and
> find ways to present it. Jim Hoge, former publisher of the
> *Chicago Sun-Times* and now of the *New York Post,*
> succinctly tells how to do it. This article from *ASNE
> Bulletin,* February 1984, is based on Hoge's remarks during
> a workshop at Harvard University.

The public isn't particularly interested in the business vs. media imbroglio.
What the public wants is more information from business and the media
about changes occurring in the economy and society.

Both business and the media need to think more constructively about
the public's information needs and about each other.

Here are three major business perceptions of the media:

1. Business sees the media as essentially *getting it all wrong.* The
   media write about the bad and ignore the good; they are fascinated
   by corruption, unsafe products, lawsuits and bribery, and run
   toward sensationalism and conflict. To top it all off, the media are
   careless, cursory, inaccurate and, for the most part, underqualified.
2. The media are biased and anti-business, tending to depict business
   as greedy, antisocial and insensitive to social needs. Media favor
   public interest groups, are pro the government, pro almost anything which is anti-business.
3. The media are too powerful. They are capable of souring the body
   politic by encouraging irresponsible behavior by politicians. They
   hide behind First Amendment rights but are quick to trample on
   the rights of others, particularly their privacy. The media are rather
   lame in providing space for rebuttals and equal time.

And I see these media perceptions of business:

- Business constantly hides behind a stone wall, covers up its own
  wrongdoing. Business stalls needed reforms and fights not only
  unnecessary regulation but necessary regulation.

- Business is manipulative, at times even deceptive, with information about itself. Business uses its public relations arm as a defense mechanism to stall and mislead rather than to facilitate.
- Business has unrealistic expectations about how it should be treated. Business sees itself as different from government because it is primarily responsible to its shareholders; it sees itself as having the right to determine the timing and relevance of information about itself. Further, it ignores its own power and pervasiveness and its impact on society, while hiding behind the cloak of being a "private" institution.
- Business is arrogant and self-deluding. As an oil executive said to a *Los Angeles Times* reporter who inquired about a public relations release that was not all that clear, "Just print it the way I wrote it, Sonny." Business, in the eyes of the media, assumes unfavorable stories are based on deliberate distortion, and overlooks the large quantity of good or neutral coverage which is given to business and business-related stories. Business overemphasizes government restrictions and underestimates government supports, many of which have been sought by business. Business is too quick to show deference to experts and to experts' solutions, and to expect that the rest of us should have the same kind of confidence in the technocratic approach.

What are some of the remedies?

For the media, an effort must be made toward a balanced skepticism —of government as well as business, of critics of business as well as of business.

It always interests me, whether we are talking about business, media or anything else, how long mythologies of institutions and historical events linger to affect us all. An example is the depictions of business that derive from the days of the robber barons. We must all be released from the images of such outdated stereotypes.

We need more self-examination. In the last few years, print journalism's survival-of-the-fittest trend has led to fewer papers in major metropolitan areas. But the survivors are stronger than they were. That's affected the relative power of business vs. the metropolitan press.

In another age, business might have been able to threaten media by withdrawal of advertising. These days, the shoe is on the other foot. Most of our large newspapers can't be threatened by the withdrawal of an individual advertiser, or even of a whole product category. Today, perhaps, it is far more possible for the media to harm business. We ought to recognize this.

We need further education for our reporters. Some in the media— but not enough—have taken this seriously in recent years.

One analogy: A number of years back, when environmentalism was first breaking upon us, we sent one of our reporters to the University of Wisconsin to get a master's in environmental subjects. We need this same kind of attentiveness to business and the economy.

We should also pursue some internal reforms. One of these is the use of ombudsmen. Another is the expansion of access, particularly to our opinion columns, so they represent views and expertise beyond our own. A third is an alertness to the prominence of corrections and clarifications, clearly understanding that to act as if none are necessary is a sign of weakness, not of strength; that weakness undermines our credibility. Finally, we should meet far more frequently than has been the case with various interested parties, including the people we report about; that, of course, includes business.

Business can do some things, too.

There is still too little recognition, and certainly not enough follow-up action, that reflects an understanding of the need for openness. Business indeed lives in an open society, is powerful, and is held accountable by a public which is increasingly of a mind to hold us *all* accountable.

Business must get to know us better and how we work. People in business must drop some of their comfortable assumptions and their self-defeating biases about the media.

Business understands that media can affect it greatly, and yet business people bother very little to know much about us and how we operate. In no other area does business behave similarly. For example, it is a virtue in business to know the customers and their wants and needs. It is a virtue to know about the financial markets.

Business must improve the performance of the corporate communications functions. Timeliness and candor, active rather than reactive postures, must be honed in business to a finer degree than they have been.

Let me move to some very specific issues of process that I think will facilitate media perceptions of business and business perceptions of the media.

The first question is: *Do you talk to the media when we come calling? And to whom should you talk?* Common sense suggests you should make distinctions, reserving your fullest and highest level responses for reporters who are well prepared and have sound credentials.

Well, when to talk? One of our problems is deadlines. You know about them in business, but you have trouble understanding them in ours. News is perishable, particularly for television, so if you decide not to cooperate, it does not mean that we cannot report the story. It does mean that whatever you might have to say is going to be unrepresented.

Reporters will still talk to whomever they can—critics, government agencies, whomever. We will do the story...we have to. Our product is perishable.

You cannot satisfy every want we have, and understanding editors and broadcasters know this. They usually know when you are attempting to cooperate, and when you are just stonewalling and attempting to sabotage the story altogether.

What should you talk about? Obviously, you should talk about your own business and what affects it. Beyond that, however, business must be represented by leaders who can talk to the larger issues in the society— what business thinks about them, what business can or cannot do about them. Only a handful of current senior executives have been able to do this effectively. In business, as in other walks of life, real leaders will be speaking out. Consequently, they won't always make the institutions happy with the positions they take. That is part of being a leader.

What to say? Whatever is asked? Certainly not, at least rarely. In part, it seems to me you have to know what you want from an interview when one is scheduled, as well as what you think the reporter is going to want.

Should you lie? Since I am a practical fellow, I never say, "never," so I'll just say, "rarely." You must understand that lies linger on, and they color more deeply than you may know the attitudes of reporters, of newspapers, and of broadcasting stations. Remember how vulnerable *we* are because we go public every day. When misinformation is our fault, we are upset; when we have been deliberately misled, we are angry as hell!

One last piece of advice: Don't let one bad experience seal your lips. Steady engagement with the media is the way to foster better—if not always adoring—public understanding.

55 The Corporate Complaint against the Media

by Peter Dreier

Big business spends big dollars to get its messages across, and journalists need adequate resources to cover the economy and corporations. Business writer Peter Dreier asks if this is too much to expect when the major national media are themselves big business. This article is from *The Quill*, November 1983.

n a series of advertisements currently featured in newspapers op-ed pages and major magazines, Mobil Corporation takes on the bias of the news media. In one of them, titled "The myth of the crusading reporter," Mobil cites a study purporting to show that "leading reporters and editors of major newspapers and television networks have distinct hostilities toward businessmen." These journalists, utilizing "publicity-hungry critics of business" and anonymous sources, may then "use the press to 'crusade' on behalf of these [personal] beliefs." Worse yet, Mobil informs us, the next generation of journalists is even more hostile to business, if another survey, of Columbia University Graduate School of Journalism students, is any guide. Only one-quarter of them believe that the private-enterprise system is fair.

America's business community did not need Mobil's public-relations department to warn it that the media are hostile to business. Since the late 1960s, when public-opinion polls began to report a dramatic decline in public confidence in big business, corporate leaders have discovered a convenient scapegoat—the news media. In speech after speech, business spokespersons have accused reporters of being "economically illiterate," of sensationalizing stories to attract (and frighten) readers and viewers, and of wanting to put business out of business.

At every turn, they see the wrongdoings of big business—windfall oil profits, nuclear power-plant accidents, chemical waste-disposal hazards, bribery of public officials, death and injuries from unsafe automobiles—splashed across the front pages and the evening news.

Business leaders worried that in a hostile climate, elected officials would translate what they saw in the polls into anti-business legislation. They viewed the gains of progressive groups—embodied in the activities of such bureaucracies as the Environmental Protection Agency, the Equal Employment Opportunity Commission, the Occupational Safety and Health Administration, and the Federal Trade Commission (all but the latter products of 1960s activism)—as obstacles to corporate profits and a healthy economy.

Corporate captains genuinely felt maligned and misunderstood. And they were firmly convinced that the public's disapproval of their performance was based almost entirely on misunderstanding rather than on corporate behavior. If those responsible for shaping public opinion (particularly journalists) were accurately informed about the benefits of our economic system, they believed, business's standing in the polls and among elected officials would improve.

The study cited by Mobil—conducted by political science professors Stanley Rothman of Smith College and S. Robert Lichter of George Washington University—simply confirms what corporate leaders have long suspected.[1] Their findings—though not significantly different from those of a decade's worth of academic research on journalists' backgrounds and attitudes—are being widely circulated. Their research has appeared in magazines, been quoted in mainstream newspapers, and summarized in an op-ed page column syndicated by *The Washington Post*. This study should be seen not simply as a fact-filled academic report, but as ammunition in a full-scale propaganda war being waged by the business community to make the news media more sympathetic to corporate America.

Since the mid-1970s, big business has been on the ideological offensive to change the public's perceptions of the profit system, the role of government, and the dangers of alternative ideas and arrangements. *Business Week* sounded the battle cry in 1974:

"It will be a hard pill for many Americans to swallow—the idea of doing with less so that big business can have more. . . . Nothing that this nation, or any other nation, has done in modern economic history compares in difficulty with the selling job that must now be done to make people accept this new reality."

The business community began a five-part "selling job" that is still in process, but has already had a significant impact. The campaign has been only loosely coordinated. It is not headquartered in any one boardroom or among any one business clique. There has been, however, a common message and common targets.

The most obvious approach has been the emergence of "advocacy advertising" by large corporations, particularly the oil and energy companies that have been under the closest scrutiny by public-interest groups and government. Their expensive ads in major newspapers and magazines (Mobil's are the most visible) extol the virtues of free-enterprise capitalism and decry the dangers of regulation. To deflect their Robber Baron image, they promote themselves as socially responsible corporate citizens—selling the system rather than specific products. Or, they ask people to view them not as impersonal corporate giants but—as reflected in Bob Hope's TV ads for Texaco—as enterprises owned by folks like you and me. Growing corporate sponsorship of public television is designed both to reveal business's civic-mindedness and to divert public TV from controversial (and potentially anti-corporate) programming. Ads for the corporate-sponsored National Right-to-Work Committee, placed in major magazines, depict powerful trade unions trampling on the rights of beleaguered individual workers. Corporate PR departments place ads in major magazines that reach opinion-makers and journalists, urging them to call to get the facts on industry-related public issues.

Second, corporations and corporate-sponsored foundations organized a variety of forums at which corporate executives and media executives could discuss the media's "anti-business" bias. An early effort was a series of exclusive seminars, sponsored by the Ford Foundation in 1977, that brought together high-level corporate executives and lawyers (most of them from Fortune 500 firms), executives of the major national media, and a few reporters, to engage in frank, off-the-record discussion for two days. The results are summarized in *The Media and Business* edited by corporate lawyer Joseph Califano and *The Washington Post*'s Howard Simons. Similar seminars soon followed. Also, corporate executives and media executives increasingly were invited to speak to each other's organizations on the general topic of "détente" between business and the media. Gannett's Allen H. Neuharth addressed the Cincinnati Chamber of Commerce in 1979 on "Business and the press: Why we ought to understand each other." A few months later, Thomas J. Donohue, vice president of the U.S. Chamber of Commerce, told media executives and journalists at the First Amendment Congress that "Business and media must respect each other's First Amendment rights." The American Society of Newspaper Editors chose as its 1976 convention theme, "Is the press giving business the business?"

The corporate executives' message—that the media needed to become more sensitive to business and to improve their business coverage—obviously had an impact. Since 1978, almost every major newspaper in the country has expanded its business pages and added reporting staff to cover business. A few, such as *The New York Times, The Boston Globe, The Washington Post*, the *Chicago Tribune*, and others, have added special business sections. (In contrast, there are only about twenty-five full-time labor reporters on American newspapers). Although news executives justify this trend as a response to the public's demand for more in-depth news about the economy, the timing of the expanded business coverage appears to be more than coincidental. Much of it is simply boosterism—glowing stories of new investment plans, fawning profiles of corporate executives, summaries of quarterly and annual corporate reports. Stories about personal finance—how to start a new business, where to invest your savings, problems of finding a second home—take up much of the remaining space. There is almost no investigative reporting on these pages and little good to say about unions or consumer groups. Their focus is on "upscale" readers, not inflation-pinched working folks.

Third, big business began cultivating current and future journalists directly. Programs in business or economics journalism are among the fastest growing additions to journalism-school curricula. Corporations and their foundations have targeted journalism schools with endowments for undergraduate, graduate, and mid-career programs to improve journalists' understanding of business and economics. The National Association of Manufacturers joined with the American Newspaper Publishers Association and the Association of Education in Journalism to develop a program to "improve business reporting" through workshops at journalism schools. Because most economics departments and business schools communicate a narrow range of ideas, most journalists and students are exposed primarily to mainstream thoughts. They may improve their technical competence in economics, but the hidden curriculum is never identified in the course outlines.

Says Gar Alperovitz, director of the National Center for Economic Alternatives, "In the United States the economics profession is dominated by a debate between moderate conservatives and conservative conservatives. In the business schools and economics departments, they tend not to talk about the social consequences of economic decisions and economic arrangements, so they miss new intellectual ideas. The range of economic debate in the press in Western Europe and Japan is much broader and more sophisticated than in the U.S. There they talk about planning—not whether, but how—and about worker control, industrial strategy, and credit allocation."

Fourth, business realized that as a profession, journalism—highly individualistic and competitive, but with few agreed-upon standards to evaluate performance—equates prizes with excellence. As a result, the number of awards of excellence in some aspect of business reporting has spiraled upward in recent years. Not surprisingly, most of these contests are sponsored by corporations, industry groups, or business schools with a particular view of what constitutes high-level business reporting. The prestigious Loeb Awards—the "Pulitzer Prizes of financial journalism"—are administered by the Graduate School of Management of UCLA. The Media Awards for Economic Understanding program—which annually receives more than one thousand entries from eager journalists—is supported by Champion International Corporation and administered by the business school at Dartmouth College. Westinghouse offers an award for science reporting, Carnation for nutrition reporting, and the National Association of Home Builders for housing reporting. The list of similar prizes fills pages each year in *Editor & Publisher*. Almost all the prizes include cash awards.

The sponsors may claim that they do not meddle in the contest, that winners are chosen by impartial judges, but the invisible hand surely operates. These corporate-backed awards help, subtly, to shape the kinds of stories journalists pursue and the kinds of standards that editors recognize. This is less blatant than the more traditional means of seduction by which businesses finance luxury trips to various conferences revealing the wonders of corporate technology, new food products, new auto models, and so on. But it has the same intention and—to some degree, at least—the same effect.

Finally, big business, convinced that ideas have consequences, launched a massive effort to provide journalists with "research" and to make friendly "experts" more accessible. Best known are the recent activities of the American Enterprise Institute, a well-endowed right-wing think tank, that has a small army of neoconservative social scientists and economists grinding out studies that "prove" the harmful effects of government regulation, corporate taxes, and labor unions; the misguided or subversive motivations of consumer and labor advocates; and the weakness of the United States' current defense posture. Similar think tanks—the Hoover Institution at Stanford, the American Institute for Public Policy Research, the Institute for Contemporary Studies, the Heritage Foundation, among others—provide the same message and ammunition. Their reports, books, magazines, and pamphlets are sent to journalists on newspapers and magazines around the country. Their authors are promoted and made available for interviews and background briefings with reporters. For journalists—always hungry for "informed sources" with the stamp of scholarly legitimacy—these corporate-sponsored, conservative think tanks and intellectuals are a gold mine. Their ideas became the ideological underpinning and policy guidelines of the Reagan administration.

Enter Rothman and Lichter. The two political scientists had earlier conducted research on the New Left (leading to their book, *Roots of Radicalism*), concluding that students' activism was rooted in personality problems, not idealism. Previous studies had found that most sixties activists were bright, emotionally healthy, and dedicated to pragmatic change. Rothman in particular was well known in conservative academic circles for his efforts to discredit this view and thus lend comfort to those who viewed such challenges to the establishment as the work of misguided and selfish malcontents.

Rothman viewed journalists in a similar way. Two years before he began his interviews with reporters and editors, he wrote an essay for a book published by the right-wing Hoover Institution, blaming liberal journalists of the national media for "the decay of traditional political and social institutions." The essay then repeated the familiar litany of criticism against the so-called liberal media.

When the two professors proposed conducting a large-scale study of various leadership groups (including journalists, business executives, TV and film producers, corporate lawyers, clergy, federal judges, government officials, and Pentagon officials), they had little trouble finding support from right-wing foundations. They received grants totalling more than three hundred thousand dollars from several conservative sources, among them the Scaife Foundation, a major funder of New Right organizations. The research project was headquartered at Columbia University's Research Institute on International Change, a Cold War outpost.

Their initial findings, focusing on business-media comparisons, have already found a home in several conservative publications, including *Public Opinion* (sponsored by the American Enterprise Institute), *The Public Interest* (a leading organ of neoconservatism, edited by Irving Kristol), *Across the Board* (the magazine of the business-sponsored Conference Board), and *Business Forum* (a journal of the School of Business at California State University, Los Angeles). Obviously, their agenda went beyond earning academic credits by publishing in limited-circulation scholarly journals.

Rothman and Lichter's study is fairly straightforward. They interviewed 240 reporters and editors at major national media—*The New York*

imes, *The Washington Post, The Wall Street Journal, Time, Newsweek,*
.*S. News & World Report,* the three commercial TV networks, and public
·levision. They also interviewed 216 top- and middle-level executives at
:ven Fortune 500 companies. The gist of the study is a comparison of the
·cial backgrounds, personality characteristics, and opinions of these media
d business élites.

Their study is grounded in a theory formulated in the 1970s by conser-
.tive intellectuals to explain, and to discredit, the growing influence and
sibility of the environmental, consumer, women's, and peace movements.
ving Kristol, Daniel Bell, and others began to argue that postwar America
s produced a stratum of well-educated, upper-middle-class, cosmopolitan
ofessionals that they label the "new class." These professionals are pro-
·cts of urban, affluent families. They are based in the universities, govern-
ent regulatory agencies, legal services offices, public-interest movements,
d the media. It is this "new class," they argue, that is responsible for the
allenges to business power that emerged in the 1970s—the followers of
arry Commoner, Ralph Nader, Gloria Steinem, Tom Hayden, Helen
aldicott, Daniel Ellsberg, and their counterparts. Despite their claims of
truism, however, this group is actually out for itself; cleaner air, new
·xual morality, and expansion of government social programs (but not the
:ntagon) mean greater happiness and more jobs for the élite, according to
·e "new class" thesis.

[The "new class" theory has some merit as an explanation for expansion
a sector of professional employees in certain institutions. But to view this
oup as a rival "élite" is misleading. The American economy is dominated
ı a small upper class based in the largest banks and corporations; stock
vnership is highly concentrated and income distribution is heavily skewed
well. The capitalist class may be under attack, but it is in no danger of
·ing replaced by this "new class." See *Who Rules America Now?* by G.
'illiam Domhoff for a full discussion.]

Spiro Agnew foreshadowed this theory when he attacked the liberal
·edia as "nattering nabobs of negativism." Joseph Kraft lent it credibility in
ı article for *Commentary,* a neoconservative opinion journal, entitled,
'he Imperial Media." Rothman and Lichter have now translated Agnew's
·etoric, Kraft's self-confession, and the neoconservatives' "new class"
·eory, into social science.

Journalism's élite, they found, consists primarily of highly educated,
·ll-paid white males. They come from educated, high-status families; 40
·rcent of their fathers were professionals and an equal number were
·sinessmen; only 12 percent of their fathers were blue-collar workers.
·e business executives, too, are primarily educated, affluent white males.
ıt only 53 percent came from business or professional families while 28
·rcent had blue-collar fathers. More journalists than businessmen
·ended prestigious colleges and grad schools. More journalists come from

big cities. Business leaders were only slightly better off economically tha
the journalists. Fifty-seven percent of the businessmen, compared to 4
percent of the journalists, reported annual family incomes of $50,000 (
more. (Of course, since more male journalists than businessmen ar
married to professional women, *family* income may be misleading. Busine:
execs generally make more than even top reporters. And the inclusion (
leading network TV newspeople may skew the journalists' income towai
the higher end).

[All sociological evidence indicates that corporate directors and to
management come overwhelmingly from upper- and upper-middle-cla:
backgrounds. Domhoff's *Who Rules America Now?* is also instructive c
this point. Rothman and Lichter's businessman sample must be heavi.
skewed toward middle-management. Their claim that big business is ope
to upwardly-mobile blue-collarites is thus misleading.]

Not surprisingly, the journalists' social and political views are to the le
of the businessmen's. For example, 88 percent of journalists, compared {
65 percent of businessmen, believe that the U.S. legal system favors tl
wealthy; 48 percent of journalists, but only 29 percent of businessmei
believe that government should guarantee jobs; 68 percent of journalist
compared to 29 percent of business execs, think the government shou
substantially reduce the income gap between rich and poor. Journalis
were more likely to favor government regulation of business, to believe th
corporations put profits before the public interest, and to believe that tl
U.S. is responsible for Third World poverty and gobbles up too much of tl
world's resources. As Rothman and Lichter acknowledge, journalists ai
hardly socialists; only 13 percent think large corporations should be public
owned. (Seven percent of businessmen agreed—these guys should I
fired!) Instead, these élite journalists are "welfare state liberals."

In terms of their social orientations, journalists are clearly mo:
influenced by the post-1960s "new morality." Few attend church or sy
agogue. Ninety percent believe that a woman has a right to an abortion; {
percent of the business execs share this belief, only a slight difference. B:
47 percent of the journalists, compared to 76 percent of the businessme
think adultery is wrong; 25 percent of journalists, but 60 percent of busine
execs, believe homosexuality is wrong.

Their social orientations are consistent with the two groups' personali
characteristics. Rothman and Lichter administered Thematic Apperceptic
Tests to their respondents. The psychological profiles are fascinatin
briefly, the businessmen were straightlaced, achievement-oriented, ar
more self-controlled. Journalists were more "narcissistic," personal
insecure, and thus likely to build themselves up by devaluing other peopl
They also scored higher on a "fear of power" scale, which the researche
suggest reveals that they want power but are afraid to pursue it directly,
they attack those who already have it.

Rothman and Lichter interpret their findings in terms of a widenii conflict between the media and business in American society, and more broadly as part of the growing rift between the "new class" and the traditional establishment. The hostility, Rothman and Lichter report, is real:

"We asked all of them to rate the influence of various groups in our society and to express their preferences for the power that each group should have. Each group rates the other as the most influential group in America; moreover, each wants to reduce substantially the power of the other and to take its place as the most influential."

But what really worries Rothman and Lichter, and their corporate sponsors, is that the ascendancy of the "new class" has not only tainted the public's faith in business, but has also eroded businessmen's confidence in themselves and the system of which they are a part. In the ideology of capitalism, business pursuit of profits was not only compatible with, but helpful to, the public interest. Entrepreneurs had a sense of "calling," and the self-made businessman was a cultural hero. The rise of big business at the end of the Nineteenth Century—and with it the so-called Robber Barons like Rockefeller, Ford, and Carnegie—turned public opinion against corporate leaders, their brutal labor relations, and their giant holdings. The businessmen responded with a concerted public-relations effort to transform their public image. They set up philanthropic foundations, donated money for libraries and colleges, and established other "good works." The campaign was mostly successful, especially after the Depression. With the post–World War II economic expansion, most Americans agreed with Charles Wilson that "what's good for General Motors is good for America." Prosperity not only restored public faith in business, it also gave businessmen themselves a much-needed shot of self-esteem.

How, then, to explain the sharp drop in public confidence in big business since the late 1960s, which accelerated during the past decade? One answer would be to relate it to the sagging performance of the American economy. Simultaneous high inflation and rising unemployment—stagflation in economists' jargon—can certainly shake a family's belief in free enterprise. Business, of course, has a different answer. The "new class" assault not only on business, but on business-oriented values, has undermined public confidence in corporations as institutions and free enterprise as an economic system. The media, they claim, share much of the blame.

Conservatives worry that there is no longer the widespread sharing of key values that helps hold society together. Many divergent "interest groups" are pursuing their own political and economic agendas; the growing pluralism of lifestyles has replaced the mythic churchgoing/nuclear family. As the economic pie stops growing, people begin to compete for slices of what economist Lester Thurow has called a "zero-sum society." These competing values, lifestyles, and interest groups can have a contagious effect, even on top and middle corporate management. If leaders begin to doubt their own role in society, and society's commitment to their business values, the entire social fabric begins to unravel. As Richard Nixon told *The New York Times*'s C. L. Sulzberger in 1974, the trouble with the country is the weakness and division among "the leaders of industry, the bankers, the newspapers.... The people as a whole can be led back to some kind of consensus if only the leaders can take hold of themselves."

This, in part, explains why business has devoted so many resources to its ideological mobilization and schizophrenic efforts to both seduce and discredit journalists. The Mobil ad that cited the Rothman/Lichter study, as well as much of business's advocacy advertising, and self-promotion, is designed not only to influence journalists and, through them, the public, but also to reassure business people themselves that they are not to blame for the nation's economic tailspin. It's the fault of ill-informed or hostile journalists, a confused public, and opportunistic or misguided politicians. Without faith in themselves, corporate leaders and conservative intellectuals worry, businessmen and women will be ill-prepared for the challenges of the coming decades.

Still, Rothman and Lichter's survey begs an important question. We have known for a long time that journalists, in general, are more liberal than the general population. The ranks of journalism have always been filled with reformers and crusaders. Recent sociological studies, such as Gan's *Deciding What's News*, Epstein's *News from Nowhere*, and Johnstone, Slawski and Bowman's *The Newspeople* only confirm what Leo Rosten observed in his 1937 book, *The Washington Correspondents*. If journalists have *always* been reform-minded, then what explains the increase of investigative and muckraking reporting during the past fifteen years? Perhaps reporters and editors used to keep their political views to themselves, but recently have allowed more of their personal beliefs to spill onto the news pages. Some say that the emergence of "interpretative" journalism, replacing the "just the facts" school of reporting, gives journalists greater leeway to introduce their own biases in the selection, editing, and writing of news. The growing acceptance of "advocacy" journalism, since the 1960s, perhaps gave credence to a generation of reporters who wanted to be agents of social change, not simply chroniclers of the passing scene.

These explanations share a common thread: The national media's growing criticism of traditional centers of power, particularly big business, stems from changes within the profession of journalism and journalists themselves. This is clearly the message of the Rothman and Lichter study even though the authors themselves never explicitly make the leap of saying that the journalists' values influence their reporting and editing (They are, however, now completing a study of news coverage which Rothman indicated in an interview, is likely to discover a liberal bias in news coverage on such controversial issues as busing, abortion, human rights in Latin America, nuclear power, and the energy crisis).

A somewhat different explanation, however, emerges out of the past decade's sociological research on how "news" is created. This includes Herbert Gans's *Deciding What's News*, Michael Schudson's *Discovering the News*, Steven Hess's *The Washington Reporters*, Gaye Tuchman's *Making News*, Mark Fishman's *The Manufacture of News*, David Altheide's *Creating Reality*, Leon Sigal's *Reporters and Officials*, Todd Gitlin's *The Whole World is Watching*, and David Paletz and Robert Entman's *Media Power Politics*. Earlier studies, including Warren Breed's 1955 "Social Control in the Newsroom" and Bernard Cohen's *Press and Foreign Policy*, reached similar conclusions. According to these studies, "news" is a product of the daily organizational habits of journalists and their contact with sources. Most daily news stories originate from *routine* channels—press release, official proceedings (Congressional hearings, courtrooms, regulatory agencies), reports, staged media events such as press conferences, and background briefings. With limited staff, the media station reporters at "beats" where they expect "news" to happen. This, of course, becomes a self-fulfilling prophecy. Under deadline and competitive pressures, reporters file stories from these beats rather than venture off the beaten track. When reporters spent most of their time hanging around at precinct stations, crime stories dominated the news. Today news tends to flow from reporters positioned at city hall, the state house, the White House, Capitol Hill, the Pentagon, and other centers of power. In addition, as a result of their day-to-day routines, reporters develop cooperative relations with regular news sources. The reporter wants a story and the source wants his/her version of reality reported. This reinforces the tendency to promote an establishment-oriented flow of news. Finally, because high-level government, corporate, and foundation officials have greater resources to reach reporters, they are able to initiate and dominate the flow of what becomes "newsworthy." These powerful organizations have the resources not only to stage events and hire public-relations staffs, but also to fund and publish reports and books by "experts" who can become "reliable sources." In contrast, the poor, the powerless, and the unorganized lack the resources to command such routine access to reporters and the media. To make news, they must disrupt "business as usual." Labor relations becomes news only when strikes become violent or inconvenience the public. Ghetto conditions become news only when the poor or tenants riot or boycott. Nuclear power becomes an issue when demonstrators occupy a nuclear construction site. Otherwise, reporters rarely go to union halls, ghettos, or offices of social-movement organizations.

The accumulated findings of these studies indicate that, as Tom Wicker wrote in *On Press*, objective journalism is essentially "establishment" journalism. News tends to flow from powerful sources and reflects their version of reality. Whatever their personal values, journalists tend to adjust to these professional standards and daily routines.

There appears to be a conflict between the angry complaints by conservatives and business leaders that the press is hostile to the establishment and the overwhelming consensus among sociologists that the press serves as a transmission belt for establishment views. The paradox, however, is not difficult to resolve. The press, the sociologists agree, goes to where the power is. During the past fifteen years or so, the political and business establishment has been deeply divided over how best to cope with foreign policy, economic crisis, and social upheaval. In such a context, journalists' high-level sources are telling them different things.

Similarly, the past fifteen years have witnessed a growing upsurge of grassroots political activism. Although the student New Left disappeared, many of its adherents—as well as a new and more heterogeneous group of activists—have built a more sophisticated range of social movements than existed in the 1960s. These include the women's and senior citizens' movements, the consumer and public-interest groups like Common Cause, the nuclear-freeze and peace movements, the community and neighborhood organizing of such groups as Massachusetts Fair Share and ACORN, environmental groups, and even a growing militance among some segments of organized labor, especially among working women (like 9 to 5) and on issues of workplace health and safety. Some of it, for sure, fits the conservatives' stereotype of the "new class" adherents. But much more of the upsurge has been truly a grassroots phenomenon among what we once called "middle America." It has not gotten the headlines of its counterpart on the other end of the spectrum, the "New Right," but it has been a major influence in politicizing average citizens and shaping the political agenda.

In the light of these two trends—a widening split within the establishment and the upsurge of grassroots protest—the press has shown a greater tolerance for controversy and conflict. What some view as the national media's "anti-establishment" bias is, in fact, a reflection of the canons of objective journalism.

In the 1950s and early 1960s, when there was a national bi-partisan consensus around Cold War foreign policy and domestic welfare-state goals, the press mirrored this in a celebration of Pax Americana and Luce's "American Century." The Vietnam War produced a split within the establishment over the conduct of foreign affairs, a split that has not been mended. It is between a conservative wing pushing for greater military strength and tough talk with the Soviets, and a moderate wing, concerned about bloated defense budgets and the potential for global conflict. The conservative wing is best represented by such groups as the Committe on the Present Danger and the Hoover Insitution at Stanford, groups favored by the Reagan administration in filling State and Defense Department slots. The moderate wing is best represented by the Council on Foreign Relations and the Trilateral Commission, corporate-sponsored policy groups whose leaders have filled high-level places in every administration since Truman's.

In domestic economic and soical policy, there is a conflict between *laissez-faire* advocates like Milton Friedman and his ideological friends at the American Enterprise Institute and the U.S. Chamber of Commerce, and the moderate Keynesians at the Brookings Institution and the Business Roundtable.

These organizations are simply surrogates for ideas and perspectives. In the real world, the lines between competing establishment points of view are blurred and overlapping. But, if anything, the national media still report conflict within very narrow limits. In the entire spectrum of American political and economic thought, the distance between the Committee on the Present Danger and the Council on Foreign Relations on foreign policy, or between the American Enterprise Institute and the Brookings Institution on domestic policy, is relatively short. But it is the views of the experts at CFR or Brookings—and the politicians who take their advice—that the conservatives treat as the left end of the spectrum, and thus harass the press for its "liberal" bias. There is no denying that the major national media are more in tune with these groups. But, in the broad range of political views, these are hardly "anti-business," or even "anti-establishment." They reflect a struggle *within* the American power structure.

It is worth recalling that when currently fashionable conservative ideas were put forward by Barry Goldwater in 1964, they were considered extremist. The right-wing think tanks have benefited from a decade of heavy financial support from friendly business groups and respectful media coverage that have brought them off the fringe and into the mainstream.

The accompanying table indicates what a real spectrum might look like. Obviously the left side of the table is conspicuously absent from the daily flow of national journalism (except, perhaps, among guest contributors to the op-ed pages). Mary McGrory, perhaps the most progressive national columnist, is at most a McGovern-style liberal. Evans and Novak are Henry Jackson Democrats. There are plenty of right-wing opinion-shapers, such as George Will, William Buckley, and James Kilpatrick. But there is not *one* nationally syndicated columnist who is a socialist, or, in European parlance, a "social democrat," such as Michael Harrington or Barry Commoner. When journalists look for experts on foreign policy, they rarely go to the Institute for Policy Studies, a well-respected left-oriented think tank. When it's economic expertise they're looking for, few turn to the new generation of left-oriented academics (such as Samuel Bowles at the University of Massachusetts, David Gordon at the New School for Social Research, Bennett Harrison at MIT, Barry Bluestone at Boston College, or Gar Alperovitz at the National Center for Economic Alternatives.) The farthest to the left they travel is Harvard (to talk to Robert Reich) or MIT (to interview Lester Thurow).

Reporters doing stories about the nation's housing crisis, or issues like rent control, typically talk to groups like the National Association of Realtors, the National Association of Home Builders, or the Mortgage Bankers Association of America for statistics and analysis. The two most frequently quoted "experts" on the subject are George Sternlieb, a Rutgers University professor, and Anthony Downs of the Brookings Institution, both of whom have close ties to the real-estate industry. Grassroots groups like ACORN, Citizen Action, and National Peoples Action, left-oriented housing experts like Chester Hartman of the Insitute for Policy Studies and the Planners Network, Peter Marcuse of Columbia University, Cushing Dolbeare of the National Low Income Housing Coalition, and John Atlas of Shelterforce, are virtually invisible to the National news organs.

The same could be said for any number of issues—food policy, environment, labor relations, health care, welfare, and many others.

This isn't to say that the "left" is totally left out. There are occasional feature stories on "new trends" among intellectuals that note the growing influence of radicals and democratic socialists. And, when a social movement begins to pick up steam and can mount large demonstrations and rallies—such as the nuclear-freeze campaign—the press quotes its leaders and reports its ascendancy. But in the daily routines of journalism, these "left" oriented views don't come into journalists' line of vision, and journalists rarely go out looking for them.

In the past decade, journalists have covered the major issues and events that cast doubt on the wisdom or managerial skill of American business. The Santa Barbara oil spill, Hooker Chemical's Love Canal problems, and the Three Mile Island power plant incident were all technological accidents that became grist for journalists' mills. Questionable business practices may be hard to uncover, but corporations that break the law—J.P. Stevens' labor law violations, companies that knowingly manufacture and sell unsafe products (like the Dalkon Shield or Ford's Pinto) or business that violate trade embargoes or bribe foreign officials (like ITT)—find themselves subject to journalistic scrutiny.

What is interesting, however, is that most of the so-called "antibusiness" stories were not initially uncovered by the major media, but by either social-movement organizations or politically-oriented publications. Conditions in J.P. Stevens' textile plants were brought to public attention by the union and its national boycott, not a crusading reporter investigating workplace atrocities. The Love Canal episode—which triggered a national concern over toxic chemicals—came to public attention because of a grassroots effort by working-class neighbors (led by Lois Gibbs) concerned about their children's health.

Both the Ford Pinto story, and the exposé of the dumping of unsafe birth control devices (the Dalkon Shield) on Third World nations, were uncovered by the leftist *Mother Jones* magazine.

ACCORDING TO WHOM? ...

The spectrum of American politics: a sampling of sources

Topic	Left	Liberal	Moderate	Conservative
Foreign policy	Institute for Policy Studies Inst. for Food & Devel. Policy Coalition for a New Military and Foreign Policy	Ctr. for Defense Information Jobs with Peace Amnesty International Comm. for SANE Nucl. Policy	Council on Foreign Relations Trilateral Commission Club of Rome	Comm. on Present Danger Hoover Institution Georgetown Center for Strategic & Int'l. Studies
Domestic, Economic & Social Policy	Nat'l. Ctr. Econ. Alternatives Council on Econ. Priorities Conf. on Alternative State & Local Policy	Brookings Institution Urban Institute Ctr. for Social Policy	Nat'l. Bur. of Econ. Rsch. Comm. for Econ. Devel. Business Roundtable	U.S. Chamber of Commerce Amer. Enterprise Institute Heritage Foundation
Legal Institutions	Nat'l. Lawyers Guild	Amer. Civil Liberties Union	Amer. Bar Association	Mountain States Legal Fdtn.
Foundations	Stem Fund Field Foundation of N.Y. Haymarket People's Fund	Stewart R. Mott Ford Foundation Rockefeller Family Fund	Rockefeller Bros. Fund Chas. Stewart Mott Fdtn. Twentieth Century Fund	Scaife Foundation Smith Richardson Fdtn. Lilly Endowment
Opinion Journals	The Nation The Progressive In These Times	The New Republic Washington Monthly N.Y. Review of Books	Foreign Affairs Harper's The Atlantic	The Public Interest Commentary National Review

(continued)

ACCORDING TO WHOM?... (continued)

Topic	Left	Liberal	Moderate	Conservative
Major New Books	Rebuilding America (Alperovitz & Faux) Beyond the Wasteland (Bowles, Gordon, & Weiskopf) Deindustrialization of Amer. (Bluestone & Harrison) Economic Democracy (Carnoy & Shearer)	The Zero Sum Society (Thurow) The Next Amer. Frontier (Reich) Winning Back America (Green)	The Energy Future (Yergin & Storbaugh) Theory Z (Ouchi) Industrial Renaissance (Abernathy, Clark, Kantrow)	Wealth & Poverty (Gilder) Post-Conservative America (Phillips) The Way the World Works (Wanniski) Amer. Politics: Promise of Disharmony (Huntington)
Political Organizations	Dem. Socialists of America Citizens Party Citizen/Labor Energy Coalition	Democratic Party (liberal wing) Common Cause Americans for Democratic Action	Democratic Party (moderate wing) Republican Party (moderate wing) Ripon Society	Republican Party (conservative wing) Nat'l Conservative PAC Moral Majority

440

Most journalistic exposés focus on the public sector—primarily public officials' conflicts-of-interest and primarily with local entrepreneurs, real estate, insurance, and construction firms. This is relatively small-time, low-level corruption. The information is usually dug out of public documents. But unless government regulatory agencies have done the work already—they are frequently the source for investigative reports—documents about wrongdoing by major corporations and industries are hard to come by.

By fighting for legislation that opens up information on both government and corporate practices, reform movements have aided journalists. Common Cause, for example, helped win passage of laws requiring disclosure of campaign financing, enabling journalists to link wealthy individuals and corporations to elected officials and their voting patterns. The neighborhood movement won passage of the Home Mortgage Disclosure Act requiring banks to disclose lending patterns—permitting urban reporters to investigate "redlining" practices. The Freedom of Information Act has been extremely useful in gaining access to information about FBI infiltration of protest groups, government reports about exposure to nuclear radiation, and many other issues. Reporters interested in piercing the corporate veil, however, still face many legal obstacles. Our legal system protects private businesses from having to disclose very much about their inner workings, even though their decisions have significant public consequences.

For many reasons, journalists tend to avoid the hard work required to investigate corporate behavior. Their employing organizations provide few resources, or incentives, to do so. As Mark Dowie, who investigated and wrote the Pinto story for *Mother Jones*, explained, the story was available all along to anyone who knew how and where to look for it.

"Stories like this are very much like photography," Dowie said. "It's not enough to know how to use a camera. You have to know what you're looking for."

What conservatives view as the press's "anti-business" hostility is, in reality, a quite tame form of objective journalism. Journalists report different views *within* the establishment, and they report the views of protest groups when those groups are able to make a stink, but they rarely go beyond exposing what Herbert Gans has called violations of "responsible capitalism." The national press may criticize or expose *particular* corporate or government practices or *particular* corporations or elected officials who violate the public trust. Thus, the Watergate scandal (and its many counterparts at local and state levels), or the Pinto case (and its many parallels), or a Pentagon weapons boondoggle, lends credence to the view that these violations are *exceptions* to an otherwise smoothly-running system. The bad apples are purged, while the good ones remain. Even the so-called "liberal" media view such occurrences from the viewpoint of "situations needing to be managed," not basic flaws in an unjust or inefficient economic and political system.

Business leaders, obviously, have little patience for the "bad apple" theory. Any public exposure of corporate wrongdoing can taint the entire profits system. And when these stories appear in a context of economic hard times, the bad publicity can become contagious. As a result, what some may view as the media's occasional slaps on the wrist, business feels as a punch in the jaw.

If the national media have contributed to the public's distrust of big business, it is not because reformist reporters and editors have waged a war with corporate America. Whatever their personal beliefs (and, to my mind, Rothman and Lichter failed to capture the somewhat muddled, wishy-washy, non-ideological character of journalists' reformism), journalists are constrained by the routines of daily journalism and the conventions of objective reporting from a consistent assault on corporate America.

The United States has many conservative and right-wing newspapers and a host of moderate liberal papers that take their cue from *The New York Times* and *The Washington Post*. But there is no major daily today that is as far to the left as New York's *PM*, the York, Pennsylvania *Gazette*, the Madison, Wisconsin *Capital-Times*, or the Chicago *Sun* were in the 1940s. At that time these papers were hardly out on a political limb. The 1948 Progressive Party campaign of former Vice President Henry Wallace (more progressive, in context, than McGovern's 1972 platform), the stands of the leftist CIO, and even President Truman's call for national health insurance were opposed by most daily papers, but were popular with millions of American citizens. The Cold War consensus and McCarthyism soon set in, and the "left" voices in American life quieted down. Today, with both conservatives and moderate-liberals unable to find any solutions to gnawing political and economic problems, there's a resurgence of protest and intellectual ferment on both the left and right. But while the national news media find it easy to cover the right flank (if with little sympathy), they have all but ignored the left side of the debate.

Moreover, while the media may occasionally expose both government and corporate wrongdoing, they are even less interested in examining possible solutions to chronic social, economic, and political problems. For example, the U.S. is one of only two industrialized nations (the other is South Africa) without a system of national health insurance; but while Americans can read a great deal about the problems of Britain's national health program, they know very little about its effectiveness in reducing major health problems, and much less about the overwhelming success of Canada's, Sweden's, or Germany's health measures. Experiments with consumer cooperatives, worker-owned or publicly owned enterprises, and other "social democratic" reforms—in the U.S. and elsewhere—might help Americans see some possible light at the end of our narrowing economic tunnel, but if, as Rothman and Lichter report, thirteen percent of élite journalists believe that "large corporations should be publicy owned," they certainly aren't getting their ideas into the news. With few exceptions, the national media are blind to reforms that challenge basic economic arrangements.

The series of Mobil ads attacking the media is designed to intimidate journalists into greater caution in reporting the wrongdoings of big business and the flaws of private-enterprise capitalism. By portraying liberal journalists as motivated by irrational subconscious impulses, Rothman and Lichter's study contributes to three objectives on the corporate agenda: It discredits journalists as being politically and socially out of touch with the readers and viewers and advertisers; it shores up the confidence of the business community by identifying an "outside" source of its problems; and it helps make journalists doubt themselves by replacing credo ("Afflict the comfortable and comfort the afflicted") with ego and Rorschach-blots.

If there is room for improvement, and I think there is, the direction must be not toward making journalists more cautious in scrutinizing the workings of our economy and its central institutions, but in giving journalists the resources to do so better. Perhaps this is too much to expect when the major national media are themselves big business, as Ben Bagdikian notes in his recent *The Media Monopoly*. But it would certainly be worth the effort.

NOTES

1. The Mobil ad includes Linda Lichter as a third researcher, but the published articles are co-authored by the two males. She headed the study of the Columbia students.

56 Business and the Media: Sometimes Partners, Sometimes Adversaries

by Ward Smith

> The president and chief operating officer of White Consolidated Industries, Inc., polishes the two-edged sword of business-media relations in a speech delivered at the Third Annual Business and Media Luncheon of the Public Relations Society of America/Press Club of Cleveland, September 17, 1985.

I am not entirely comfortable speaking on the subject of business and the media. I am afraid I am either supposed to be the point man for one more "let's-pick-on-the-media" session—one of the longer-running top ten cocktail party topics in business circles—or a surrogate corporate whipping boy for the media—an equally-popular past-time, I would bet, among journalists.

As cathartic as one or the other of these roles may be, both have been beaten to death. And both are red herrings.

They miss the point of the inherently (if not invariably) adversarial relationship between two powerful institutions, each integral to our society, each at times as guilty of abuse as its victim.

We all know the litany: journalists are anti-business, economic illiterates with chips on their shoulders. They are smugly blind to the mechanics, styles, and necessities of business in a capitalist competitive society, either U.S. or global. They skip the complex meat of an event to grab at some sensational, irrelevant garnish, and they are indifferent to the real world survival requirements of business in a global fight to the death.

They compact immensely complicated transactions into screaming, slanted headlines which pander to readers' prejudices—etc., etc., etc. Republic Steel lays off 4000; White Motor slams the doors at 77th Street.

Sniping, superficial and simplistic.

And, business executives are arrogant, defensive, and antagonistic and self-aggrandizing. They stonewall and stall. They are secretive and inaccessible. They double-talk the media, refusing to acknowledge responsibilities to any constituencies besides themselves. "The CEO syndrome," etc.

Caligulas in Brooks Brothers suits.

Each of these briefs against the other carries some truth. At times. No doubt each of us here can cite examples of frustrating and egregious behavior by the other side. (Though, alas, what I consider irresponsible behavior, a reporter may consider the model of professionalsm—and vice versa.)

But the point is: business and the media are different institutions—with different objectives and differing perspectives.

Potential conflict is inherent in the nature of what the two are and must do.

Business must make products, deliver services and make a profit. The media must inform, play watchdog, entertain and sell papers or audiences to advertisers.

Against this background, let me suggest my "information" obligations —and constraints.

My company is in the business of making machine tools and home appliances. My job is to keep my company prosperous and do what I can to make it more so.

That's what I am paid for.

Consequently I have obligation and responsibilites to various constituencies—the company itself and its 55 plants in four countries, 17 states and 39 cities—its employees and their representatives, shareholders, the investment community, local, state and federal governments, the general public and, as a steward of a corporate citizen, the broader public interest.

I have some resulting news and information obligations, as well: Internally, to the management and employees of each of the entities which make up White Consolidated Industries; externally, to sharesholders, the investment community and to the general public.

Indeed, I want as well informed a public as possible. A well-informed, competent, savvy public understands and appreciates the way business works, will not be overly suspicious of its motives, and will be sympathetic to its problems.

While some of my information obligations are simply good management practices or good p.r., virtually everything I say publicly is legally controlled, as all of you know, by the securities laws and regulations of the United States and the individual states. The SEC requires that we report certain events—financial results, certain strikes, major divestitures or acquisitions and other information which may materially affect our company and stock.

Good business practices require that certain happenings or events not become the subject of premature public disclosure such as pending merger explorations short of negotiations, possible discoveries of products or processes where premature disclosure might be misleading, the results of internal forecasts where the forecasts themselves—while useful from a management standpoint—might be misleading to the public, and the like.

Some of these matters might nevertheless be newsworthy, and if you learn of them you will report them.

At the same time, the First Amendment—in which I deeply believe—largely protects you to say whatever you like and permits you to inform, educate, amuse and titillate, the public and proffer opinion with respect thereto. Good journalistic practice, I should think, should require that you clearly label such opinion. The label is normally "editorialize."

What I as a business executive may owe to the media—or, really, to the general public for whom you are the mediator—is thus only part of the obligation I bear.

In the same way, the obligations you owe to me and the business community are only part of the obligations you owe—you have obligations to the public, the community, your publisher, your profession, your colleagues, etc.; and because you are constitutionally protected, I put it to you that you have the heavier burden.

Because we work out of different obligations and perspectives, as well intentioned as I may be to be forthcoming and open—and I hope I always intend to be forthcoming and open—it is not always possible.

These are distinct and at times, antagonistic obligations. I can be the most open and honest of corporate executives. Nevertheless, there will still be times as I said earlier when I do not see it in the best interest of my company or even legally appropriate to release information or to fully discuss a proposed or contemplated sale, merger, reorganization, stock issue, etc.

Besides, the fact is that from the standpoint of me as a proprietor of a publicly-held corporation, in my concerns about the investment community, I theoretically should be indifferent to the popular press or television. The popular press is not where the investment community goes for information. I don't believe most stock is bought or sold based on what is read in the press or seen on television. These are only one (normally minor) factor in the decision-making process.

The good broker or analyst first goes to his primary sources then to his internal research department and gets the numbers—his trip there may have been triggered by a story in the *Times*, the *Wall Street Journal*, the *Plain Dealer* or wherever, but his informed judgment, if he is any good, is based on something that is far more complex than just one story in one newspaper. That is not to say that sensational extraordinary news such as Bhopal will no have an immediate, short term or not, impact upon share prices of the company involved.

No one, however, is immune from publicity—good or bad—and speaking more generally, if I deliberately or otherwise lie or cheat, mislead, or break the law then I deserve to get nailed—by the press, the government, whomever.

Short then of being derelict in some aspect of *my* duty, I'm not stone-walling. I'm not double-talking. I'm doing my job. In my considered opinion of what's best for my company, I will or will not want to give information out.

Faced with that situation, a reporter has different objectives: he or she wants information. The journalists' corporate and professional obligations conflict.

All any executive can ask for is that the journalist come to that story grounded in an understanding of the nature and dynamics of the business. That the reporter not have an ax to grind. That the reporter not be playing solely to the grandstand; e.g., painting management as unfeeling, non-communicative ogres with no thought for those who may be affected by a decision.

Granted, it's an imperfect world and nothing is going to be done perfectly. The free press we cannot do without. Neither can we do without American business people.

All we can do is try and persuade.

But I will no more jeopardize the stewardship of my company than you will jeopardize your professional and Constitutional duties.

And what that means is that some level of conflict is inevitable—not every day on every issue—indeed, very often we work together and share similar goals.

But even in some utopic [*sic*] best of all possible worlds, at times you will be as frustrated with me as I am with you. As Arthur Miller said of Willy Loman the salesman, it comes with the territory.

The best we can do I guess is to be aware of the possibilities of an adversarial position in our relationship with each other and recognize it for the control dynamic which it is. If we are not always comfortable at least we know it is serving some useful purpose, assuming reasonable people are dealing with each other. I as a corporate executive recognize my public disclosure obligations and responsibilities and honor them.

The peace of sylvan grove will not thereupon descend upon us all. But the media and the business community and the public interest, which we both exist to foster in different ways, will be better served.

The roots of our First Amendment, in our view of the role of the press, lie in an essay John Milton wrote in 1644, reaming the censorship laws of the Crown. Milton wrote that truth only emerges through a clash of voices and perspectives.

I may not be happy with what comes out of that clash all of the time—some times I'm going to be damned unhappy.

But if we both live up to the high standards of our two callings, then sometimes we'll be partners; sometimes we'll be adversaries, but we'll be worthy adversaries—and the public interest will be best served.

57 Media and Business Elites

by S. Robert Lichter and Stanley Rothman

One of the chief complaints made about the mass media by
the business community is that most of the leading reporters and editors for the influential media have socio-
economic, educational, and cultural backgrounds that predispose them to liberal politics and cynicism about big
business. The authors of this article are the leading
academic exponents of that point of view, and they maintain
that their conclusions are based on extensive social research. Both authors are professors of sociology. Their
study was completed under the auspices of the Research
Institute on International Change at Columbia University,
and the surveys of media and business leaders were super-
vised by Response Analysis, a survey research organization.
The article is reprinted from *Public Opinion*, October/
November 1981.

Yesteryear's ragtag muckrakers, who tirelessly championed the little guy
against powerful insiders, have become insiders themselves. Newsmen
have long cherished the vantage point of the outsiders who keep the
insiders straight. But now, leading journalists are courted by politicans,
studied by scholars and known to millions through their bylines and
televised images. In short, the needs of a society increasingly hungry for
information have contributed to the rise of a national news network—the
new media elite. Leading figures within this network are anything but the
low-lifes and ambulance chasers mythologized in *The Front Page*. Instead
they consistute a new leadership group that competes for influence alongside more traditional elites representing business, labor, government, and
other sectors of society.

As columnist Joseph Kraft writes, "in the past two decades, those of us
in the press have undergone a startling transformation. We are among the
principal beneficiaries of American life. We have enjoyed a huge rise in
income, in status, and in power. . . . We have moved from the sidelines to
the center of the action."[1]

Eric Sevareid, in his final CBS commentary, put it even more succinctly:
"We are no longer starvelings and we sit above the salt. We have affected
our times."[2]

The influence of the press is based not on money or political power but on the information and ideas they transmit to other social leaders, as well as to the general public. Even those who question the media's power to persuade grant their ability to help set the agenda for discussions about social policy. Bernard Cohen notes, "the mass media may not be successful in telling us what to think, but they are stunningly successful in telling us what to think *about*."[3]

As part of a larger study on elites, we surveyed members of the national media elite during 1979 and 1980. We wanted to discover their backgrounds, attitudes, and outlooks toward American society and their own profession. We conducted hour-long interviews with 240 journalists and broadcasters at the most influential media outlets, including the *New York Times*, the *Washington Post*, the *Wall Street Journal*, *Time* magazine, *Newsweek*, *U.S. News and World Report*, and the news departments at CBS, NBC, ABC and PBS, along with major public broadcasting stations.[4]

Within each organization, we selected individuals randomly from among those responsible for news content. In the print medium we interviewed reporters, columnists, department heads, bureau chiefs, editors and executives responsible for news content. In the broadcast medium we selected correspondents, anchormen, producers, film editors, and news executives. A very high proportion of those contacted, 76 percent, completed the interview. The response rate was high enough to insure that our findings provide insight into the composition and perspective of this new elite.

To provide comparisons with a more traditional leadership group, we also surveyed executives at several major corporations. We interviewed at seven *Fortune 500* companies, ranging from a multinational oil company and a major bank to a public utility and a nationwide retail chain. We chose randomly from upper and middle management at each company and completed 216 interviews, or 96 percent of those contacted. The focus of this article is, of course, the media elite. At appropriate points, however, we will compare their attitudes to those of the successful and influential leaders in the business world.

Who Are the Media Elite?

The social and personal backgrounds of the media elite are summarized in table 1. In some respects, the journalists we interviewed appear typical of leadership groups throughout society. The media elite is composed mainly of white males in their thirties and forties. Only one in twenty is nonwhite; one in five is female. They are highly educated, well-paid professionals. Ninety-three percent have college degrees, and a majority (55 percent) attended graduate school as well. These figures reveal them as one of the best educated groups in America. They are also one of the better paid groups, despite journalism's reputation as a low paying profession. In 1978,

TABLE 1. BACKGROUNDS OF THE MEDIA ELITE

White	95%
Male	79
From northeast or north central states	68
From metropolitan area	42
Father graduated college	40
Father occupation "professional"	40
College graduate	93
Postgraduate study	55
Income $30,000+	78
Family income $50,000+	46
Political liberal	54
Religion "none"	50

78 percent earned at least $30,000, and one in three had salaries that exceeded $50,000. Moreover, nearly half (46 percent) reported family incomes above $50,000.

Geographically, they are drawn primarily from northern industrial states, especially from the northeast corridor. Two-fifths come from three states: New York, New Jersey, and Pennsylvania. Another 10 percent hail from New England, and almost one in five was raised in the big industrial states just to the west—Illinois, Indiana, Michigan and Ohio. Thus, over two-thirds of the media elite come from these three clusters of states. By contrast, only 3 percent are drawn from the entire Pacific coast, including California, the nation's most populous state.

Journalism is a profession associated with rapid upward mobility, yet we found few Horatio Alger stories in the newsroom. On the contrary, many among the media elite enjoyed socially privileged upbringings. Most were raised in upper-middle-class homes. Almost half their fathers were college graduates, and one in four held a graduate degree. Two in five are the children of professionals—doctors, lawyers, teachers, and so on. In fact, one in twelve is following in his father's footsteps as a second generation journalists. Another 40 percent describe their fathers as businessmen. That leaves only one in five whose father was employed in a low status blue or white collar job. Given these upper status positions, it is not surprising that their families were relatively well off. Forty-five percent rate their family's income while they were growing up as above average, compared to 26 percent who view their early economic status as below average.

In sum, substantial numbers of the media elite grew up at some distance from the social and cultural traditions of small town "middle America." Instead, they were drawn from big cities in the northeast and north central states. Their parents tended to be well off, highly educated members of the upper middle class, especially the educated professions.

Social and Political Attitudes

All these characteristics might be expected to predispose people toward the social liberalism of the cosmopolitan outsider. And indeed, much of the media elite upholds the cosmopolitan or anti-bourgeois social perspective that Everett Ladd has termed the "new liberalism."[5]

A predominant characteristic of the media elite is its secular outlook. Exactly 50 percent eschew any religious affiliation. Another 14 percent are Jewish, and almost one in four (23 percent) was raised in a Jewish household.[6] Only one in five identifies himself as Protestant, and one in eight as Catholic. Very few are regular churchgoers. Only 8 percent go to church or synagogue weekly, and 86 percent seldom or never attend religious services.

Ideologically, a majority of leading journalists describe themselves as liberals. Fifty-four percent place themselves to the left of center, compared to only 19 percent who choose the right side of the spectrum. When they rate their fellow workers, even greater differences emerge. Fifty-six percent say the people they work with are mostly on the left, and only 8 percent on the right—a margin of seven-to-one.

These subjective ratings are borne out by their voting records in presidential elections since 1964, summarized in table 2. (The interviews were conducted before the 1980 elections, so our most recent data are for 1976.) Of those who say they voted, the proportion of leading journalists who supported the Democratic presidential candidate never dropped below 80 percent. In 1972, when 62 percent of the electorate chose Nixon, 81 percent of the media elite voted for McGovern. This does not appear to reflect

TABLE 2. PRESIDENTIAL VOTING RECORD OF MEDIA ELITE 1964–1976*

	Percent	Percent Voting
1964		
Goldwater	6	(62)
Johnson	94	
1968		
Nixon	13	(67)
Humphrey	87	
1972		
Nixon	19	(74)
McGovern	81	
1976		
Ford	19	(82)
Carter	81	

*Percentages based on those who voted for major party candidates. Third party vote never exceeded 2 percent.

any particular personal aversion to Nixon, despite the well-publicized tensions between the press and his administration. Four years later, leading journalists preferred Carter over Ford by exactly the same margin. In fact, in the Democratic landslide of 1964, media leaders picked Johnson over Goldwater by the staggering margin of sixteen-to-one, or 94 to 6 percent.

Most significant, though, is the long-term trend. Over the entire sixteen-year period, less than one-fifth of the media elite supported any Republican presidential candidate. In an era when presidential elections are often settled by a swing vote of 5 to 10 percent, the Democratic margin among elite journalists has been 30 to 50 percent greater than among the entire electorate.

These presidential choices are consistent with the media elite's liberal views on a wide range of social and political issues, as table 3 reveals. They show a strong preference for welfare capitalism, pressing for assistance to the poor in the form of income redistribution and guaranteed employment. Few are outright socialists. For example, they overwhelmingly reject the proposition that major corporations should be publicly owned. Only one in eight would agree to public ownership of corporations, and two-thirds declare themselves strongly opposed. Moreover, very few sympathize with Marx's doctrine, "from each according to his ability, to each according to his needs." Instead, they overwhelming support the idea that people with greater ability should earn higher wages than those with less ability. Eighty-six percent agree with this fundamental tenet of capitalism. Most also believe that free enterprise gives workers a fair shake, and that deregulation of business would be good for the country. Seventy percent agree that private enterprise is fair to working people, and almost as many, 63 percent, say that less regulation of business would serve the national interest.

Despite this basic support for private enterprise, we should not expect the media elite to lead the cheering section for Reagan's economic policies. Leading journalists may subscribe to a capitalist economic framework, but they are equally committed to the welfare state. Sixty-eight percent, about the same proportion that praise the fairness of private enterprise, also agree that the government should substantially reduce the income gap between the rich and the poor. They are almost evenly divided over the issue of guaranteed employment. Forty-eight percent believe the government should guarantee a job to anyone who wants one, while a slight majority of 52 percent oppose this principle of entitlement.

Of course, there is no necessary contradiction between praise for private enterprise and calls for government action to aid the poor and jobless. These attitudes mirror the traditional perspective of American liberals who—unlike many European social democrats—accept an essentially capitalistic economic framework, even as they press for expansion of the welfare state.

TABLE 3. MEDIA ELITE ATTITUDES ON SOCIAL ISSUES

	Strongly Agree	Agree	Disagree	Strongly Disagree
Economics				
Big corporations should be publicly owned	4%	9%	23%	65%
People with more ability should earn more	48	38	10	4
Private enterprise is fair to workers	17	53	20	10
Less regulation of business is good for USA	16	47	24	13
Government should reduce income gap	23	45	20	13
Government should guarantee jobs	13	35	33	19
Political Alienation				
Structure of society causes alienation	12	37	32	20
Institutions need overhaul	10	18	31	42
All political systems are repressive	4	24	26	46
Social-Cultural				
Environmental problems are not serious	1	18	27	54
Strong affirmative action for blacks	33	47	16	4
Government should not regulate sex	84	13	3	1
Woman has right to decide on abortion	79	11	5	5
Homosexuality is wrong	9	16	31	45
Homosexuals shouldn't teach in public schools	3	12	31	54
Adultery is wrong	15	32	34	20
Foreign Policy				
U.S. exploits Thrid World, causes poverty	16	40	25	20
U.S. use of resources immoral	19	38	27	16
West has helped Third World	6	19	50	25
Goal of foreign policy is to protect U.S. businesses	12	39	28	22
CIA should sometimes undermine hostile governments	26	19	36	19
	None	Democracies	Friends	Anyone
To what countries should we sell arms?	19	29	48	4

453

Despite their acceptance of the economic order, many leading journalists voice a general discontent with the social system. Virtually half, 49 percent, agree with the statement, "the very structure of our society causes people to feel alienated." A substantial minority would like to overhaul the entire system. Twenty-eight percent agree that America needs a "complete restructuring of its basic institutions." The same proportion generalize their criticism to include all modern states. They hold that *all* political systems are repressive, because they concentrate power and authority in a few hands.

It seems that a substantial portion of the media elite accept the current economic order, yet remain dissatisfied with the social system. Indeed, it is today's divisive "social issues" that bring their liberalism to the fore. Leading journalists emerge from our survey as strong supporters of environmental protection, affirmative action, women's rights, homosexual rights, and sexual freedom in general.

Fewer than one in five assents to the statement, "our environmental problems are not as serious as people have been led to believe." Only one percent strongly agree that environmental problems are overrated, while a majority of 54 percent strongly disagree. They are nearly as vehement in their support for affirmative action, an issue that has split the traditional liberal constituency which favored civil rights measures. Despite both the heated controversy over this issue and their own predominantly white racial composition, four out of five media leaders endorse the use of strong affirmative action measures to ensure black representation in the workplace.

In their attitudes toward sex and sex roles, members of the media elite are virtually unanimous in opposing the constraints of both government and tradition. Large majorities oppose government regulation of sexual activities, uphold a pro-choice position on abortion, and reject the notion that homosexuality is wrong. In fact, a majority would not characterize even adultery as wrong.

When asked whether the government should regulate sexual practices, only 4 percent agree, and 84 percent strongly oppose state control over sexual activities. Ninety percent agree that a woman has the right to decide for herself whether to have an abortion; 79 percent agree strongly with this pro-choice position. Three-quarters disagree that homosexuality is wrong, and an even larger proportion, 85 percent, uphold the right of homosexuals to teach in public schools. (A mere 9 percent feel strongly that homosexuality is wrong.) Finally, 54 percent do not regard adultery as wrong, and only 15 percent strongly agree that extramarital affairs are immoral. Thus, members of the media elite emerge as strong supporters of sexual freedom or permissiveness, and as natural opponents of groups like the Moral Majority, who seek to enlist the state in restricting sexual freedom.

In addition to these social and cultural issues, we inquired about international affairs, focusing on America's relations with Third World countries.

Third World representatives to UNESCO have argued that the American press serves the interests of capitalism by "presenting developing countries in a bad light and suppressing their authentic voices,"[7] as a recent *New York Times* article put it. Such charges are supported by media critics like Herbert Gans, who claims that "conservative dictators...are apt to be treated more kindly (by the press) than socialist ones."[8] We cannot address these questions of media coverage. But we can assess the sympathies of the elite press on several of the controversial issues raised by these critics. Among these are U.S. arms sales, C.I.A. activity, and alleged American exploitation of developing countries.

In most instances, majorities of the media elite voice the same criticisms that are raised in the Third World. Fifty-six percent agree that American economic exploitation has contributed to Third World poverty. About the same proportion, 57 percent, also find America's heavy use of natural resources to be "immoral." By a three-to-one margin, leading journalists soundly reject the counterargument that Third World nations would be even worse off without the assistance they've received from Western nations. Indeed, precisely half agree with the claim that the main goal of our foreign policy has been to protect American business interests.

Two issues dealing more directly with American foreign policy elicit a similar division of opinions. A majority of 55 percent would prohibit the C.I.A. from ever undermining hostile governments to protect U.S. interests. The question of arms shipments produces an even split of opinion. Forty-eight percent would ban foreign arms sales altogether or restrict them to democratic countries. Forty-seven percent would supply arms to any "friendly" country, regardless of the regime. Only 4 percent would be willing to sell arms to all comers.

Thus, in several controversial areas of U.S.-Third World relations, the media elite is deeply divided, with slight majorities endorsing some key Third World criticisms of America.[9] We noted earlier that many leading journalists criticize the American system from within, as "alienating" and in need of an overhaul. It appears that even larger numbers extend their criticisms to the international arena. About half charge America with economic exploitation and seek to limit C.I.A. activity and arms sales as instruments of our foreign policy.

Toward the Good Society

Thus far we have examined elite journalists' opinions on the great and small issues of the day. By charting their responses to numerous social issues, we try to gain an intuitive feel for their general perspectives on society and politics. The results can be deceptive. They create the impression of a broad ideological portrait of the media elite without ever asking journalists to deal with the "big picture." Their attitudes toward issues like abortion, affirmative action and arms sales provide us with benchmarks for understanding their outlook, since most of us have opinions on such pressing and hotly debated questions. But they do not address some of the most basic underlying issues of political life: What direction should American society take? What groups exert the most influence over social goals and political processes? How much influence *should* be wielded by such forces as business, labor, minorities, and the media?

These issues are as old as political philosophy. But it is not only philosophers who grapple with questions like "who should rule?" and "what is the good society?" Most people have answers to these questions, even if they haven't consciously arrived at them. Their answers express basic attitudes that underlie their transient opinions on current social issues.

In the interviews, we tried to tap these fundamental predispositions of political thought. First, we asked journalists about the goals America should pursue during the next decade. From a list of eight choices, we asked them to select the most important, second most important, and least important goal. The list, created by political scientist Ronald Inglehart, includes:

- Maintaining a high rate of economic growth
- Making sure that this country has strong defense forces
- Seeing that the people have more say in how things get decided at work and in their communities
- Trying to make our cities and countryside more beautiful
- Maintaining a stable economy
- Progressing toward a less impersonal, more humane society
- The fight against crime
- Progressing toward a society where ideas are more important than money

He classifies these choices as either "instrumental" and "acquisitive" values, on one hand, or "expressive" and "post-bourgeois" values, on the other.[10] In this list, the "post-bourgeois" choices are those dealing with participation, a humane society, beautiful cities, and placing ideas above money. On the basis for their other opinions, we would expect the media elite to be relatively supportive of these types of social goals. But relative to whom? Unlike standard polling items, these choices are not presented periodically to cross-sections of the American public. This is where our sample of business leaders comes in. As archetypal representatives of a bourgeois society, they should be oriented toward more conservative "acquisitive" values like a strong economy and national defense. Thus, they provide an appropriate comparison group for the media elite.

We found that substantial segments of the media elite endorse the "post-bourgeois" value orientation that Inglehart calls a "silent revolution" transforming the political culture of advanced industrial society. The results re shown in table 4. Only one in eight business leaders picks any of the expressive" values as America's most pressing concern. By contrast, one in hree journalists deems citizen participation, a humane society, or a society ?ss oriented toward money as our most important goal—more important han either economic well-being or national defense.

Even among the journalists, a slight majority favor economic stability s the most important value. However, almost half of the media elite (49 ercent) pick post-bourgeois values as their second choice, compared to 30 ercent of the business elite. Forty percent of these leading journalists elect a humane society as either their first or second priority, more than ouble the proportion among business leaders. Conversely, the business- 1en list national defense more than twice as often as do the newsmen. 'inally, the journalists are almost twice as likely as the executives to choose cquisitive values as the *least* important for America to pursue.

Overall, the media elite shows a clear preference for post-bourgeois oals, relative to the business elite. For many leading journalists, liberal iews on contemporary political issues apparently reflect a commitment to ubstantial social change in pursuit of the good society, as they visualize it. uch a commitment would align them with emerging forces of social beralism which are pitted against more established leadership groups. 'herefore, as the final focus of our inquiry, we shall examine the media lite's evaluation of its competitors for social influence.

Vho Should Rule?

3eyond inquiring about the direction our society should take, we asked a nore pointed question: Who should direct it? Specifically, we asked the ournalists to rate seven leadership groups in terms of the influence each vields over American life. Then we asked them to rate the same groups ccording to the amount of influence they *should* have. Each group was ssigned a rating from "1," meaning very little influence, to "7," repre- enting a great deal of influence.

The seven groups rated represent a cross-section of the major com- etitors for social power in contemporary America. They include black aders, feminists, consumer groups, labor unions, business leaders, and he news media. The journalists' perceptions of these groups' influences are ictured in figure 1. They see four of the groups as relatively disadvantaged 1 the competition for social power. Feminists are least powerful, followed losely by black leaders, intellectuals and consumer groups. All four are lustered tightly together, however, well below the big three of labor, usiness, and the media. The unions rank third, leaving the media close on he heels of business leaders, who are perceived as the most powerful social roup in America.

Thus, the media elite recognizes its own position of power, viewing

TABLE 4. MEDIA AND BUSINESS ELITES' CHOICES OF MOST IMPORTANT GOAL FOR AMERICA IN THE NEXT DECADE

	Acquisitive				Post-Bourgeois				Totals	
	Economic Growth	Stable Economy	National Defense	Fight Crime	Humane Society	Ideas, not Money	Community Participation	Beautiful Cities	Acquisitive	Post-Bourgeois
Most Important										
Media	10%	52%	6%	0%	17%	5%	11%	0%	67%	33%
Business	14	60	13	1	6	3	3	0	88	12
Second Most Important										
Media	9	18	14	8	23	15	8	3	51	49
Business	18	15	30	8	13	11	3	3	70	30
Least Important										
Media	15	2	12	10	10	9	22	17	39	61
Business	8	1	7	5	12	13	32	23	21	79

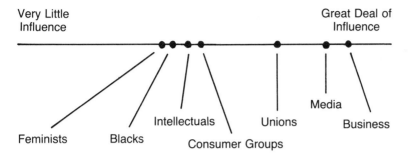

Figure 1. Media Elite's *Perceptions* of Influence among Leadership Groups

itself as more influential than any other leadership group except the business community. It places itself between business and labor, traditionally the leading contenders for influence, and pictures the emergent forces of consumers, intellectuals, blacks, and feminists as playing a decidedly subordinate role.

When members of this elite are asked their preferences, this picture changes drastically, as figure 2 illustrates. They would strip both business and labor of their current perceived power, while raising the status of all the other groups. In the media elite's preferred social hierarchy, business leaders fall from first to fifth position, and unions drop to the very bottom of the ladder. Feminists move up only slightly, but blacks, intellectuals and consumer groups would all have more influence than either business or labor. Emerging at the top of the heap, as the group most favored to direct American society, are the media.

There is a certain irony in the media elite's choice of itself as preeminent in the race for influence. The press is traditionally ambivalent about its power, and journalists often either deny or decry the growing

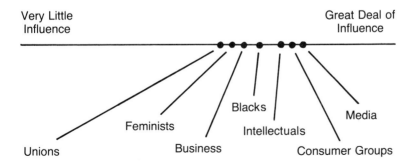

Figure 2. Media Elite's *Preferences* for Influence among Leadership Groups

reality of a powerful media elite. In a 1976 study of elites conducted by the *Washington Post* and Harvard University, the media leaders were the only group to claim they want less influence than they already have.[11] In fact, one could say the same of our subjects, but it would be a deceptive interpretation of our findings. In absolute terms, these journalists would assign themselves a lower influence rating than they now have. On the other hand, they would assign even *lower* ratings to all the other groups, thereby leapfrogging themselves from the second position, as they perceive it, to the top spot they would prefer.

The business leaders, by the way, return the compliment. They perceive the media as far and away the most powerful influence on American society, with labor a distant second and business only third, followed by the four emergent groups. Not surprisingly, they, too, would prefer to sit atop the influence hierarchy, while burying the media well back in the pack in fifth position, precisely where the media elite would place them. Indeed, the hostility these two elites seem to feel toward each other is rather striking. Business leaders regard the media as the most powerful group of those listed and would reduce the power of journalists more than any other group. Media leaders perceive business leaders as the most powerful group and would likewise strip away most of their influence. One might speculate that these elites view each other with such mistrust precisely because each attributes great power to the other. In the ongoing struggle over the direction of our society, each appears wary of the other as its strongest competitor.

* * *

The pointed views of the national media elite are not mere wishes and opinions of those aspiring to power, but the voice of a new leadership group that has arrived as a major force in American society. Cosmopolitan in their origins, liberal in their outlooks, they are aware and protective of their collective influence. The rise of this elite has hardly gone unnoticed. Some hail them as the public's tribunes against the powerful—indispensable champions of the underdog and the oppressed. Others decry them for allegiance to an adversary culture that is chiseling away at traditional values.

While we advocate exploring the attitudes of the national media elite, we side with neither their extollers nor critics in declaring what kind of role the media do or should play. The crucial task that remains is to discover what relationship, if any, exists between how these individuals view the world and how they present that world to the public. This is the next key step to understanding how the evolution of the media elite has transformed American society.

NOTES

1. Joseph Kraft, "The Imperial Media," *Commentary*, May 1981, p. 36.
2. Quoted in Gary Paul Gates, *Air Time* (New York: Harper and Row, 1978), p. 424.
3. Bernard Cohen, *The Press and Foreign Policy* (Princeton, N.J.: Princeton University Press, 1963).
4. Several studies have shown these media outlets to be the most influential in influencing other social leadership groups. See, for example, William Rivers, *The Opinion Makers* (Boston: Little, Brown and Co., 1965); Carol Weiss, "What America's Leaders Read," *Public Opinion Quarterly*, Spring 1974, pp. 1–22; J. W. Johnstone, Edward Slawski, and William Bowman, *The News People* (Bloomington, Ind.: University of Indiana Press, 1976). For an extensive discussion of the news media elite, see Stanley Rothman, "The Mass Media in Post-Industrial America," in S. M. Lipset, ed., *The Third Century* (Stanford, Cal.: Hoover Institution Press, 1979), pp. 346–388.
5. Everett Ladd, "The New Lines are Drawn," *Public Opinion*, July/August 1978, pp. 48–53.
6. For a discussion of the effect of Jewish ethnicity on elite journalists' attitudes toward Israel, see S. R. Lichter, "Media Support for Israel: A Survey of Leading Journalists," in William C. Adams, ed., *Television Coverage of the Middle East* (Norwood, N.J.: Ablex, 1981), pp. 40–53.
7. Paul Lewis, "Gloves Come Off in Struggle with UNESCO," *The New York Times*, May 24, 1981.
8. Herbert Gans, *Deciding What's News* (New York: Pantheon, 1979), p. 37.
9. For a more extensive dsicussion, see S. R. Lichter, "America and the Third World: A Survey of Media and Business Leaders," in William C. Adams, ed., *Television Coverage of International Affairs* (Norwood, N.J.: Ablex, 1982).
10. Ronald Inglehart, *The Silent Revolution* (Princeton, N.J.: Princeton University Press, 1977).
11. Barry Sussman, "Media Leaders Want Less Influence," *Washington Post*, September 29, 1976.

Business and Mass Media: For Further Reading

Benjamin M. Compaigne, *Who Owns the Media? Concentration of Ownership in the Mass Communications Industry.* New York: Harmony Books, 1979.

Louis M. Kohlmeier, Jr., Jon G. Udell, and Laird B. Anderson, *Reporting on Business and the Economy.* Englewood Clifts, N.J.: Prentice-Hall, 1981.

A. Kent MacDougall, *Ninety Seconds to Tell It All: Big Business and the News Media.* Homewood, Ill.: Dow Jones-Irwin, 1981.

Nelson Smith and Leonard J. Theberge (eds.), *Energy Coverage—Media Panic: An International Perspective.* White Plains, N.Y.: Longman, 1983.

Joseph Turow, *Media Industries: The Production of News and Entertainment.* White Plains, N.Y.: Longman, 1984.

XV
Mass Media
and Culture

Some critics of mass culture have, like Caesar, divided all of the new world into three parts: highbrows, milddlebrows, and lowbrows.

Highbrows are those who prefer Shakespeare plays, Beethoven string quartets, T.S. Eliot poetry, lithographs by Picasso, movies by Bergmann, chess and tennis, novels by Thomas Mann and Bernard Malamud, the *Christian Science Monitor, Commentary* magazine, and *Foreign Affairs.*

Middlebrows go for Hemingway and Steinbeck, waltzes by Johann Strauss and the Nutcracker Suite by Tchaikovsky, baseball, movies by Steven Spielberg, *Time* and *U.S. News & World Report*, the *Washington Post* or the *Baltimore Sun, Saturday Evening Post* covers by Norman Rockwell, middle-of-the-road radio and easy listening music.

Lowbrows are interested in soap operas, situation comedies, professional football, poker, Michael Jackson, comics in the newspapers, *Reader's Digest* and *TV Guide*, country-western music and detective novels, romance and movie stars.

Of course, critics say that the mass media are reducing us all to the lowest common denominator, degenerating culture into a wasteland of pop art and corn.

On the other side of the argument, however, are critics who note that high culture is flourishing as never before. America has more symphony orchestras than ever before, more museums and art galleries, more bookstores, and more students seeking a higher education.

In addition, they argue, out of the mass culture of the mass media have frequently come works of high merit that can stand the test of the most exacting criticism and live on in our culture as works of art.

There is probably no end to this argument, except to say that all sides can win.

58 The Guilt Edge
by Clark Whelton

One point of view is that we all suffer from guilt for liking
the mass culture of the mass media. It has become a status
thing to be highbrow, but secretly we sneak off and enjoy
our soap operas. We prefer "M*A*S*H" to Mendelssohn,
says Clark Whelton, but we don't want our neighbors to
find out. Whelton has been a speech writer for the mayor of
New York and is author of a book on television. This article
is reprinted from *Channels of Communications*, February/
March 1982.

Guilt: The small, insistent voice telling you that with a little more effort you
could be having a really miserable time.

Guilt. For me it began on May 9, 1961, in a remote and dusty corner of
Fort Bliss, Texas. I was watching television in the day room of Company D.
The rest of my platoon had trudged off to the mess hall after our evening
ritual of watching the cartoon adventures of Huckleberry Hound, but I had
stayed to catch the first few minutes of the evening news. The army was
buzzing with rumors about American involvement in a place called
Vietnam, and I wanted to see if anything was happening that might interfere with my imminent return to civilian life.

But the lead story that night was not about Vietnam, or even about
astronaut Alan Shepard, who had grazed the edge of outer space in a sub-
orbital rocket shot four days earlier. Instead, the announcer was talking
about someone named Newton Minow. Minow, recently appointed chairman of the Federal Communications Commission by President Kennedy,
had delivered a blistering speech to television broadcasters in which he
invited them to watch their own programming from sign-on to sign-off.

"You will see," Minow said, "a procession of game shows, violence,
audience-participation shows, formula comedies about totally unbelievable
families, blood and thunder, mayhem, violence, sadism, murder, western
badmen, western good men, private eyes, gangsters, more violence, and
cartoons. And, endlessly, commercials—many screaming, cajoling, and
offending. And most of all, boredom."

There was more. Minow acknowledged that a television western draws
a larger audience than a symphony, but scolded. "It is not enough to
cater to the nation's whims—you must also serve the nation's needs." The
thirty-five-year-old former law partner of Adlai Stevenson cut loose with

a condemnation that echoed throughout the country. Television, Minow asserted, is a "vast wasteland."

I cringed, besieged by feelings of shame. If television was a vast wasteland, then I, a founding member of the Fort Bliss Huckleberry Hound Society and television fan extraordinaire, was clearly a vast wastrel. I loved it all, the whole Newton Minow hit list. I loved the game shows, the formula comedies, the unbelievable families, the private eyes, gangsters and gunplay, cartoons, cajoling commercials, the works. I can still sing the Mott's applesauce jingle from 1950, and as far as I know I hold the record for continuous contemplation of a test pattern.

But ever since Newton Minow painted a "wasteland" label on my viewing habits, I have been dogged by doubt. Whenever I settle back for a Mary Tyler Moore rerun or another session with *Family Feud*, I hear that small voice telling me I am contributing to the decline of Western Civilization, and I feel guilty. I have spent more than a little time examining this curious exercise in self-condemnation, and I know there are millions of others who suffer from the same affliction.

How did a mechanical contrivance like television get cross-wired into the American conscience? Did it really start with Newton Minow? In fact, the origins of television guilt go back a long way, and are probably as old as the medium itself. *New York Times* critic Jack Gould had already taken a swipe at television as early as 1948, when sets had tubes instead of transistors. Gould wrote that children's shows appeared to be a "narcotic" administered by parents, who had learned that plunking junior down in front of the Philco would keep him out of their hair for an hour or two. By calling television a narcotic instead of something that kids enjoy watching, Gould helped to establish a pattern of overkill in television criticism that would largely be delivered via television's major competitor—newspapers.

Very early in the struggle for media domination, the newspaper business showed its fangs: It was the summer of 1950. At the editorial offices of the *New York Journal-American*, flagship paper of the Hearst publishing empire, a sudden meeting was called. Among the handpicked reporters attending that meeting was Atra Baer, daughter of the well-known humor columnist Bugs Baer.

"The editor came right to the point," Baer recalls. "A message had been received from William Randolph Hearst, the chief himself. It seems that Mr. Hearst was very worried about television, especially about the 'deleterious' effect that it might be having on the American public. So a team of *Journal-American* reporters was assigned to canvass the New York City area and come up with some quotes—particularly from mothers—that would focus on the 'bad effects' of television."

Orders in hand, the reporters fanned out. Atra Baer was sent to a nearby suburb, where she asked the requisite questions in the requisite way: "Madam, are you worried about the harmful effect television is having on your children's eyesight? Are you concerned about the harmful effect television has on your children's reading habits?" The sought-after answers were easily obtained, and a story on the "dangers of television" was easily written. At that time there were Hearst papers in every section of the country.

Merrill Panitt, the editor of *TV Guide*, remembers just how effective anti-television journalism was.

"In our early issues," Panitt says, "we constantly had to answer all the negative stories circulating about television. We ran articles reassuring our readers that no, television is not bad for your eyes; no, television is not bad for your back; no, television does not cause cancer, and it certainly doesn't cause constipation."

Given the newspapers' antipathy toward radio, their alarm at the arrival of television—radio with pictures—can be imagined. The antagonism even extended into press conferences, where newspaper reporters often salted their questions with expletives ("Senator, don't bullshit us, when the hell is Congress going to pass that goddamn tax bill?") so that broadcasters, whose vocabularies are sanitized by their license obligations, couldn't run the footage on the air. When naughty language didn't do the trick, light plugs were pulled, doors were slammed, and coughing epidemics broke out whenever a television reporter asked a question.

'It worked for a while," says a former newspaper reporter who admits to a minor career in sabotage. "But we could see who was winning the war. Politicians wouldn't even let a press conference begin until the cameras arrived."

Newspapers grudgingly accepted the inevitable. The immense popularity of television stars like Milton Berle and Ed Sullivan had helped to sell millions of sets, and the daily papers had to give their readers what they wanted. Bans against television listings were dropped, even though many papers quietly decided that television coverage deserved to be crammed in with the comics or buried deep inside. This snobbery toward television still exists today. A reporter who worked for *The New York Times* in the 1970s recalls an editor saying that the *Times* would not "debase" its culture section with television news. Television reporting was—and still is—relegated to the back pages.

However, it was in the area of television criticism that newspapers made their biggest dent in the competition. Syndicated columnists like John Crosby specialized in scathing reviews of television programs, reviews implying not only that certain shows were inferior, but that television itself was a medium only a lowbrow could love. Although theater critics were expected to love the theater, and dance and movie critics to revere those art forms, television critics were often people who disdained television.

At the center of this conflict between newspapers and television was a life-or-death struggle. Publishers were well aware that someone who gets his nightly news from the tube is less likely to buy an evening paper. Even before television went on the air, newspapers had been fighting for survival. Dozens of double-barreled logotypes (*Post-Dispatch, Herald Tribune*) revealed the many newspaper mergers inspired by the fear of bankruptcy. Fresh competition from television gave newspapers the shudders, especially in large cities where the new medium flourished.

On a national basis, however, there was little reason to fear that television would undermine American literacy. Official figures reveal that the United States had only nine fewer daily papers in 1980 than there were in 1950, and circulation had climbed by more than eight million.

Nevertheless, enemies of television were ever on the alert. In 1963, psychologists claimed to have discovered a "TV Syndrome," which supposedly made kids cranky if they were overexposed to the tube. In the seventies, reports indicated that by the time they reached first grade, television-watching children had spent an average of 5,000 hours in front of the set. A variety of social problems now began to be blamed on television. Low reading scores? College Board scores taking a tumble? Crime and vandalism on the rise? Blame television. And let's not forget the recent news from Tulsa Central Academy in Oklahoma. When English teacher John Zannini's seventh grade class heard that President Reagan had been shot, most of the class cheered. Mr. Zannini blamed it on television.

Television has been subjected to constant scorn and sniping by critics who would have you believe that unless you were watching a show introduced by Alistair Cooke, you had no taste at all. Writer Richard Schickel summed it up this way:

"Television criticism, especially that which aspires to the broad scale and the theoretical, has become, in recent years, little more than a branch of the ecology movement. The brightly glowing box in the corner of the living room is perceived by those who write sober books and Sunday newspaper articles about it as a sort of smoking chimney, spilling God knows what brain-damaging poisons not only into the immediate socio-political environment, but also, it is predicted, loosing agents whose damage may not become apparent to us for decades to come."

In the short run, however, the damage done by snobbish criticism of television is very apparent. America may be the only country in the world where people actually feel guilty about watching. Unfortunately, it is very easy to bully the average American on matters of culture and taste. This vulnerability probably dates back to our colonial past, when most settlers were too busy surviving to give much thought to gracious living. All that was refined and cultured arrived on packet boats from Europe—which to a considerable extent is still true today—and Americans became accustomed to taking orders on questions of taste, anxious to be accepted by the root of the world. Newton Minow betrayed this anxiety in his "wasteland" speech when he asked: "What will people of other countries think of us when they see our western badmen and good men punching each other in the jaw, in between the shooting?"

I can answer that question. American television is very popular through-out the world, where most people consider it a source of entertainment, not of guilt. I once stayed at a small hotel in Barcelona where the only regu-lation was: "Never interrupt the manager when he's watching *Sea Hunt* or *Have Gun Will Travel.*" When Americans assigned to a NATO air base in Iceland broadcast old *I Love Lucy* tapes, the show became the number-one hit in nearby Reykjavík. In England, where television is a popular pas-time, viewers watch anything and everything without apology. But here at home it's a different story. Americans are plagued by guilt for enjoying television.

There is, for example, the guilt parents impose on children. Michael J. Arlen, television critic for *The New Yorker*, compared this parental harrass-ment to the guilt-mongering and mythologizing frequently surrounding the subject of masturbation. "Authorities, for example, such as parents and educators, suggest that it may cause vague harm...though generally speaking there are rarely any visible signs of ill effects." Instead of en-couraging children to develop good judgment about their television habits, parents sometimes taint the whole topic with implications of moral failure by those who watch any television at all. The result is not less television viewing, but subterfuge and feelings of guilt when the set is on.

There is also the vague fear that the tube is wasting your time. You spent all day Saturday watching a *Gilligan's Island* festival, and when you're through you discover that the lawn still isn't mowed. And you feel guilty. Obviously, television offers extraordinary opportunities for wasting time. There is nothing easier than turning on a set, and if television is being used as an excuse for avoiding other duties, then guilt feelings are probably justified.

Then, of course, there is status guilt, the least logical variety of television angst. You prefer *M*A*S*H* to Mendelssohn, but you're afraid the neigh-bors will find out. You've read critic John Mason Brown's quip that tele-vision is "chewing gum for the eyes," and now you deny that you like to chew gum. Status guilt can be a serious problem; however, it will help to know that those who regularly demean television do so out of a need to feel unique. It's easy to be snobbish about the theater, restaurants, clothes, or literature, because status seekers can always claim to have been the first to discover a new play, bistro, fashion, or book. Television, which reaches everyone at the same time, offers little in the way of snob appeal. The viewer can only claim to have done what everyone else in the country could have done if he had turned on his set, and there is no distinction at all in such a boast. Now and then a "cult" show like *Mary Hartman, Mary Hart-man* will come along, but as soon as enough people tune in, the snobs tune out and turn up their noses at anyone who doesn't do the same.

The fact that most television guilt has no basis in reality does not mean that television is without flaws. However, it takes more than one generation to shape and refine an innovation so powerful and revolutionary, and we're learning all the time. As for those who agree that television is indeed a vast wasteland, and that those who watch it deserve to be burdened by guilt, I suggest that the world before television was not exactly paradise. Boredom, loneliness, ignorance—these and other social ills have been around for a long time.

From the window of the Company D day room where I watched *Huckleberry Hound*, I could see the distant summit of Guadalupe Peak, ninety miles away across the high plains desert. Ninety miles of sand and chaparral. Ninety miles of nothing. But the Company D television set brought the world a little bit closer. Anybody who has seen a real "vast wasteland" will tell you that television is a vast relief.

59 Archie Bunker and the Liberal Mind

by Christopher Lasch

Archie Bunker is perhaps the most archtypical lowbrow ever produced by the mass media. Has his popularity turned us all into Archie Bunkers, making us tolerant and accepting of his bigotry and ignorance? Christopher Lasch argues that there are other, more important aspects to Archie Bunker and the kinds of material sometimes developed by the mass media for mass audiences. Lasch is a professor of history at the University of Rochester and author of *The Culture of Narcissism*. This article is reprinted from *Channels of Communications*, October/ November 1981.

In the late sixties, advertisers discovered a new market. Surveys told them that the most voracious consumers were now affluent, urban, educated people under the age of thirty-five. In an attempt to reach this audience, the networks began to experiment with programs slightly more sophisticated than *The Beverly Hillbillies*, *The Ed Sullivan Show*, and *Marcus Welby*. After much hesitation, CBS—which had least to lose at the time—introduced Norman Lear's *All in the Family* in January 1971. For the first time, a network had dared to confront its audience with a middle-American antihero who vents the most outrageous opinions, tyrannizes over his wife, and bickers endlessly with his daughter and her husband, who struggle unsuccessfully to overcome his prejudices against blacks, Jews, women, and other "un-American" minorities. Archie Bunker proved so durable a character that he has been with us eleven years, now as the hero of *Archie Bunker's Place, All in the Family*'s successor.

From the start, Archie Bunker became the object of passionate controversy. Did the depiction of his bigotry have the therapeutic effect of dragging a sensitive issue into the open and forcing viewers to confront their own prejudices? Or did it reinforce bigotry by making it respectable? According to Robert Wood, former president of CBS, *All in the Family* helped to "ventilate some of the prejudices and misconceptions in American society today." Many reviewers agreed that *All in the Family* served an "important purpose," even if it offended liberals and other "up-tight viewers." A CBS survey of the show's audience indicated that most viewers took it as a satire, not a vindication, of prejudice. But a somewhat more extensive (though still flawed and simplistic) survey, by sociologists Neil Vidmar and Milton Rokeach, concluded that the program probably reinforced prejudice instead of combatting it.

Laura Z. Hobson, author of *Gentlemen's Agreement*, claimed in a 1971 *New York Times* article that *All in the Family* sanitized prejudice and made it socially acceptable. Her vigorous attack on Archie Bunker and his creators captured the indignation of an older generation of liberals appalled by what they saw as an attempt to make bigotry loveable, "to clean it up, deodorize it, make millions of people more comfy about indulging in it." In reply, Norman Lear accused Hobson of underestimating the intelligence of middle Americans, who could be trusted, he insisted, to recognize his work as satirical in its intention. Yet surveys showing that most viewers identified with Archie (even though many of them thought son-in-law Mike got the better of their arguments) strengthened the fear that the program elicited a "sadistic response," as one educator put it, and served "no constructive purpose." (These views and others were recently collected by Richard P. Adler in a volume entitled *All in the Family: A Critical Appraisal*, published by Praeger.)

Both Archie Bunker and the controversy he has generated tell us a great deal about the liberal mind today. *All in the Family* and *Archie Bunker's Place* implicitly take the position that resistance to social change, failure to "adjust" to change, and fear of change have pathological roots. Lear has argued that Archie Bunker's bigotry rests not on hatred but on the "fear of anything he doesn't understand." Because this fear is irrational, Archie's prejudices cannot be corrected by rational persuasion. Although Mike's arguments always "make sense," according to Lear, while Archie's rebuttals are "totally foolish," Archie can't be decisively defeated by Mike.

Liberals of Laura Hobson's type, convinced that bigotry can be combatted by propaganda depicting it in the most unattractive light, mistakenly see the Archie Bunker programs as a capitulation to popular prejudices. What the programs really seem to say, however, is that prejudice is a disease and that the only way to overcome it, as in psychotherapy, is to bring to light its irrational origins. *All in the Family* "simply airs [prejudice]," according to Lear, "brings it out in the open, has people talking about it."

The series seems to have been influenced, at least indirectly, by the theory of "working-class authoritarianism," which has played an important part in the thinking of social scientists and members of the helping professions ever since the late forties. According to this widely accepted interpretation, prejudice, ethnocentricity, and intolerance of ambiguity originate in the authoritarian child-rearing practices allegedly characteristic of working-class families. Archie Bunker has all the traits commonly attributed to the authoritarian husband and father. Lear's dramatization of Bunker's anti-Semitism, racism, male chauvinism, and xenophobia shares with the sociological literature on authoritarianism a tendency to reinterpret class issues in therapeutic terms and to reduce political conflicts to psychological ones. It ignores the possibility that "middle Americans" have legitimate grievances against society, legitimate misgivings about what is called social progress.

Yet the few gains that have been made in race relations, desegregation, and women's rights have usually been achieved at the expense of the white working-class male. His anger cannot be understood, therefore, as a purely psychological reaction; it has an important political basis. His dislike of liberals, moreover, springs not so much from "anti-intellectualism" or ethnocentricity as from the realistic perception that working-class values are the chief casualties of the "cultural revolution" with which liberalism has increasingly identified itself. With his unsentimental but firm commitment to marriage and family life, his respect for hard work and individual enterprise, and his admittedly old-fashioned belief that people should accept the consequences of their actions, the working-class male rightly regards himself as a forgotten man in a society increasingly dominated by the permissive, therapeutic morality of universal understanding. He sees himself, not without reason, as the victim of bureaucratic interference, welfarism, and sophisticated ridicule. Lacking any real political choices, he sometimes vents his anger in an ill-considered politics of right-wing moralism. But it is well known that many of the same voters who supported George Wallace also supported Robert Kennedy (and in any case the Wallace vote did not by any means come exclusively from the working class).

All in the Family and *Archie Bunker's Place* make no attempt to depict the political basis of working-class prejudice, or even to capture the complexity of the attitudes it dramatizes. The programs reduce a complex historical experience to the single issue of "bigotry," which they then approach as a form of pathology.

But what is true of Norman Lear's famous series is equally true of the commentary they have inspired. Both critics and defenders agree that the "disease" of bigotry is the important issue; they differ only on the question of whether Lear's talking-cure may be worse than the disease itself. Thus historian John Slawson (after stating flatly that "bigotry is sickness") argues that Archie Bunker brings out the worst in his fans. Quoting political sociologist Seymour Martin Lipset on working-class authoritarianism, Arthur Asa Berger (author of *The TV-Guided American*) congratulates *All in the Family* for demolishing the "myth of the common man." But whereas the myth upholds the working man as the salt of the earth, Lipset, and Norman Lear, suggest that he is actually a bigot, endowed with attitudes "to make you shudder." Like many critics, however, Berger would prefer a more straightforward and unambiguous condemnation of Archie Bunker and his kind. Lear's comedy, he thinks, embodies a kind of pornography of prejudice, ridiculing ethnocentric attitudes but at the same time inviting the viewer to find titillation in their frank expression.

There may be some justice in Berger's charge that *All in the Family* delivers a "double payoff": "We enjoy the ethnic humor yet feel superior to it." But instead of asking whether such ridicule serves a useful social purpose, commentators might better ask whether anything of artistic value is served by appealing so consistently to an audience's sense of superiority. Laura Hobson considered the program "elitist" because only well-educated liberal intellectuals would feel superior to Archie Bunker. Lear, noting that Hobson had unwittingly exposed her own elitism, replied in effect that liberal attitudes are now so widely diffused (at least among the younger viewers he was trying to reach) that almost anyone would feel superior to such an antiquated buffoon. When it nevertheless turned out that many viewers do identify with Archie, even though they do not necessarily endorse all his opinions, this fact—instead of prompting speculation about the complexity of the emotional response elicited by the series—simply reinforced the fear that it might have undesirable social effects.

Yet art of any merit to some extent transcends the immediate intentions of its creators. Although *All in the Family* and *Archie Bunker's Place* invite ridicule of their hero, as their defenders contend, the programs also seem to evoke a more complicated response. For one thing, these programs—especially the original series—deal with emotionally resonant themes of family life. In one survey of *All in the Family*'s audience, the children in a working-class family told an interviewer that their mother, like Edith Bunker, mediated generational arguments. Many middle-class mothers could doubtless say the same thing.

Part of the Bunker household's appeal to a more "sophisticated" audi-

ence, I suspect, lies in its power to evoke reminders of ethnic neighborhoods and ethnic cultures that the program's upwardly mobile young
viewers have left behind in their climb into the "new class." In the conflict
between Archie Bunker and his son-in-law, who rises during the course of
the series from a Polish working-class background to a university teaching
position, *All in the Family* dramatizes experiences central to the formation
of a new, liberal, managerial intelligentsia, which has turned its back on the
ethnic ghettos, developed a cosmopolitan outlook and cosmopolitan tastes
through higher education, and now looks back on its origins with a mixture
of superiority and sentimental regret. This experience, repeated now for
several generations, has played a formative part in the development of
the managerial and professional class. Its ideology of tolerance and anti-
authoritarianism puts great emphasis on the ability to outgrow early prejudices. Because the new class has defined itself in opposition to the values
of "middle America," it needs to repudiate its own roots, to exaggerate the
distance it has traveled, and also to exaggerate the racism and bigotry of
those lower down on the social scale. At the same time, it occasionally sheds
a sentimental tear over the simpler life it thinks it has left behind.

All this finds almost classic expression in Lear's comedy of popular
ignorance and parochialism. In one of the more perceptive commentaries
on Lear's work, Michael J. Arlen, television critic of *The New Yorker*, suggests that 'modern, psychiatrically inspired or induced ambivalence may
indeed be the key dramatic principle behind this new genre of popular
entertainment. A step is taken, then a step back. A gesture is made and
then withdrawn—blurred into distracting laughter, or somehow forgotten."

America's new managerial elite has not only adopted an official
ideology of tolerance, in which it does not yet feel completely secure, it has
also developed an "anti-authoritarian" style of personal relations that
forbids the expression of anger and violent emotion. *All in the Family* dis-
solves murderous impulses by foisting them on the father and by depicting
this father, moreover, as an opinionated but impotent autocrat crushed by
the wheel of historical progress. It helps the viewer not so much to come to
terms with anger as to displace it. Beyond that, it reinforces the collective
self-esteem of those whose ascendancy rests not on the secure command of
an intellectual and political tradition but on their imagined superiority to
the average unenlightened American bigot.

60 Showdown at Culture Gulch

by Brian Winston

With the introduction of cable to the mass media, a part of television can now go highbrow, catering to the needs and interests of a smaller group of people who want better programming than soap operas and sitcoms and Sunday afternoon football. But Brian Winston is somewhat cynical, following the premiere of a new cable service called ARTS. Winston is a contributing editor of *Channels* magazine and a professor of film and television at New York University. This article is reprinted from *Channels of Communications*, August/September 1981.

Limousines, champagne, searchlights, telegrams, and (if geographically possible) Sardi's—no industry celebrates new products with the verve, ballyhoo, and enthusiasm of the entertainment industry. But nothing of this disturbed the calm in the office of Herb Granath, head of ABC Video Enterprises, the day following the premiere of its first cable service, ARTS. The coming of this major endeavor, a "cultural" service specifically designed for cable distinction, was marked only by a huge bunch of flowers offered in congratulation by some Japanese television people Granath was entertaining that morning. How did the new service go? "The phone isn't ringing," said Granath. "I assume it's all right."

Narrowcasting culture might be a long way from the excitement of the 1976 Olympics, Granath's previous major programming task; the product might consist largely of esoteric material produced by others, mainly in Europe; the audience, a maximum universe of only four and a half million homes (most of which were tuned as usual to the networks) might be minuscule—but the seriousness of ABC's cable operation should not be doubted.

Cable, with only a quarter of the nation wired, is a long way from threatening the existence of broadcasting, but there have been some small yet ominous signs. In the summer of 1980, for instance, amid the usual reruns and without the promised Olympic delights from Moscow, pay feature-film services drew greater audiences in cabled homes than any network did during an entire "sweep" period. The cable industry might be somewhat optimistic in projecting an imminent doubling of cabled homes (to 46 million by 1990), but something is clearly going on out there and it would be corporate folly for broadcasters not to be part of it.

ABC, CBS, and NBC's parent, RCA, all intend to test the temperature of the cable water in much the same way—by offering upscale services that rely, albeit in differing proportions, on the arts (mainly in performance) and imported programming.

There is no question the networks are in earnest about cable. But whether or not they are serious about this cultural programming is a moot point. After fifty years of popular—not to say vulgar—programs, their new-found interest in the highbrow is so universal and so sudden as to provoke cynicism in the eye of the beholder. It is widely suggested that corporate strategies, rather than the elevation of the human spirit, lie behind these developments.

In some sense the networks are being forced into culture. Federal Communications Commission rules virtually prohibit them from owning cable systems. And other entrees into the cable business are ancillary. RCA, for example, owns as a common carrier the Satcom I satellite, which transmits some twenty services, among them the most successful of pay channels, Time Inc.'s Home Box Office. But since satellite operations remain too limited a field to be appealing, ABC, CBS, and NBC/RCA have realized that the proliferation of programming services demonstrates a more easily exploited opportunity. With their vast experience as program-makers, they too ought to be able to offer specialized material that can join the galaxy of feature films, sports, fundamentalist preaching, twenty-four-hour news, dirty movies, children's shows, and ethnic services already up on the satellites.

But even here limitations exist. The networks cannot offend their affiliates by offering cable operators any popular forms of programming that would compete with their regular broadcast service. Between the Scylla of FCC regulations and the Charybdis of affiliate relations, very few routes are actually available. Culture is the best network solution. Nothing so clearly fulfills a demonstrated need, looks so good in public relations terms, and costs so little.

The need is clear. ABC's research reveals that 16 percent of the population, core culture-aficionados, do not watch television very much at all. These elusive folk—"light watchers"—are also better educated and richer than the population generally. A further 24 percent are described as "culturally receptive"—active PTA members and the like, who watch *60 Minutes* and network news but give television a low priority. Together these make a sizable, largely untapped universe. The Public Broadcasting Service currently has some 2.5 million subscribers, each paying an average of about $35 a year. The audience for live ballet, opera, and concerts is increasing by 8 percent a year, non-degree night-school enrollment in arts-related courses is up 23 percent a year, and the success of public television's *Live from Lincoln Center* demonstrates how attractive is television's ability to deliver performances beyond the confines of the great metropolitan houses.

But it is the cheapness of culture as it is currently defined that fosters cynicism. For ABC's ARTS, culture is either performance or documentaries about artists, both of which can be bought from foreign networks or produced by driving remote units into opera houses and concert halls. Each method results in minimal programming costs (by network standards), and these costs can be cut further by running repeats. HBO has demonstrated that a full-scale service can be maintained with only twenty-five or so new programs a month. Its audience views the six or seven repeats as a convenience, and all indicators suggest that potential light watchers of culture will do the same. So the basic cheapness of such a service can be yet further reduced by operating with only a few hundred hours of material a year.

So elegant is ABC's ploy with its new service that many are puzzled by CBS's contrasting response. CBS seems to be spending more money than necessary. "We are not packagers but producers, and we will do more than just performance," claims Jack Willis, the seven-time Emmy Award winner who is CBS Cable's programming chief. "*Live from Lincoln Center* is too narrow." Willis is heading the most distinguished broadcasting team in cable. Relying heavily on small-scale technology, he is promising a daily three hours of programming, repeated three times, beginning October 12. Willis says that despite his expenditure, "the project will be profitable within three years. We'll probably just do it smarter and better, given the talent."

Willis's boss, Dick Cox, the president of CBS Cable, seems to have slightly less ambitious plans. "The economics of cable at this stage require we act as prudently as we can." But Cox explains that original material can be resold, and already an announced jazz series has attracted European inquiries. "It is not as loony as it seems," he says. "Since everybody is running off to Europe, exporting programs to Europe is a good way to be distinctive."

ABC's ARTS and CBS Cable will rely on advertising revenue; cable viewers will receive the services as part of their basic subscription. NBC, via RCA's partnership with Rockefeller Center Inc., will offer RCTV, a pay service (one paid for by an extra subscription, as HBO is). The heart of RCTV's strategy is an exclusive deal engineered by its president, Arthur Taylor, with the British Broadcasting Corporation. Arnold Huberman, RCTV's programming consultant, claims a subscription strategy will help sell the service to cable operators, who could receive as much as 50 percent of each extra subscription. RCTV will not rely on ads, because Huberman does not believe "the ads are there going in."

RCTV's BBC raid is the most flamboyant of the acquisition strategies so far revealed. PBS, which stands to lose an important supplier of its prime-time fare, maintains that RCTV will find the full range of BBC programming simply unappealing to American taste, certainly after the backlog of suitable shows has been used. Public television, says PBS, has been importing all that is appropriate for this market. Huberman disagrees, although he has not tested his conviction scientifically. An ex-movie scheduler for ABC, he has been using showman's intuition rather than audience research to determine whether or not there is enough BBC fare to make up an American schedule. "I sat in London looking at stuff, thinking this is okay. And when I looked at it here, it was still okay. I showed it to the secretaries, and they, with their Bronx accents, confirmed it. It will be entertaining to the U.S. audience." In fact, so far from "culture" is RCTV's material that the service, which will premiere early next year, has been christened "The Entertainment Channel."

In competitor Marc Lustgarten's opinion, "Culture is a defensive term." As the programming executive of Rainbow Programming Services, Lustgarten represents the new breed, his whole career having been in cable. Rainbow's cultural offering, Bravo, began life in tandem with a dirty-movie service, about which Lustgarten is not at all defensive. From December 1980 until July 1981, Bravo (a subscription service) occupied two nights of a schedule that otherwise carried such delights as *Lickerish Quartet*, *Cheerleaders Beach Party*, and *Part-time Wife* under the generic title of Escapade. (The trade likes to think of these offerings as adult/ action.) "We are good smart businessmen," says Lustgarten. "Escapade will help defray Bravo's cost, and there is nothing to be ashamed about." As of mid-1981, a second transponder has allowed both services to operate as separate entities seven nights a week.

Bravo has benefited from what Lustgarten knows about the cable industry's subscribers: "They're almost like your best friends after awhile." But Bravo reveals an equally proper understanding of broadcasting. It's a much better-produced service than ABC Video's ARTS. Like ARTS, it consists basically of performance, but it also offers a television magazine of reasonable quality. Acquisitions are heavily reedited—"Bravo-ized" is Lustgarten's word. This might displease the original producers, but it certainly gives the service a coherence ARTS lacks, despite the latter's attempt to achieve the same effect with thematic "wrap-around" (i.e., Alistair Cooke-type) material. Bravo is more adventurous and entertaining—and, unlike ARTS, not even occasionally embarrassing.

Rainbow's rationale for giving Bravo its frisky bedfellow was that each needed time to get into its stride and develop a seven-day service. But one can be permitted to offer other explanations of this strategy. Escapade is an obvious moneymaker, although cable operators, pressured by the local nature of franchising, might find it difficult to offer. A recent survey shows that 33 percent of cable subscribers would not buy pay cable at all because they would not want their children to see some of the programs. And in some cable communities, voices are being raised against Escapade. Hence Bravo, cynics might suggest, sugars the pill. (The National Christian Network, whose transponder is used for Escapade, keeps its opinions of the service a secret.)

PBS clearly shares the perception that this burst of culture on cable is in some way fueled as much by its own comparative success over the past decade as it is by cable's coming of age. PBS has proposed (somewhat belatedly, in the opinion of many observers) a further service, the Public Subscriber Network (PSN), which would be supported both by subscription and advertiser underwriting. It would involve, in the PBS phrase, "a grand alliance" between itself, the public, and the cultural institutions. Doc Jarden, PBS's director of development, suggests that these cultural institutions would do well to ask whether or not the new competing cable services will still be around in five years. PBS's current 2.5 million subscribers would be the heart of PSN. Persuaded to pay $135 or so a year—almost four times their 1980 average annual donation—they would form a more promising universe of proven loyalty and dedication than the competition could claim.

To PBS's own stations, for whom the scheme looks much like harakiri, Jarden makes this central point: The audience for PBS is now a curious amalgam of minorities and the cultural elite. It would do little harm to give PSN a single—essentially performance—element of prime-time PBS programming on a first-run basis, because the stations would carry it afterwards. And, he says, "Sesame Street would still be on PBS. So would *Black Journal*." The stations would be involved in selling PSN, and its profits could be plowed back into PBS programming. Finally, the stations have been promised a veto. "It won't happen without 51 percent of them." It won't happen anyway until 1983, as PBS is mounting an elaborate audience survey and viability study. In the meantime, at least two major PBS stations have established profit-making subsidiaries for the exploitation of cable and other commercial markets. Most observers agree that the whole situation bodes ill for public television.

But how does it bode for the new services? This proliferation of effort should not indicate that the area of cultural programming on television has magically ceased to be problematic. For ABC and CBS, it is likely to be as long a haul finding cable advertisers as it is finding the audience. Madison Avenue has been slow to explore cable as a national advertising medium, spending on cable advertisements less than 1 percent of the amount spent on television. The chances of this changing for culture seem uncertain. Furthermore, there is the strong possibility that the targeted audience might not want commercials. The growth of pay cable, fueled by HBO, is eloquent testimony that a significant number of viewers will spend money to avoid advertisements. The public has shown a startling willingness to pay millions for something it used to get for nothing, but there is resistance to paying yet more for cable services. Nearly half of those who already pay for basic cable said in a recent survey that price was the real reason they were not taking a tier service. Of those who do not have cable, the same survey reported that 49 percent said they did not want to pay for television at all, and 48 percent said it was too expensive. So although major urban areas remain to be wired, it is likely that there are some limits to cable's growth, certainly if the economy in general is not buoyant.

At the moment, most subscribers seem unwilling to contemplate giving the cable company more than about $30 a month. Nearly double the current average national payment, $30 might be stretched to cover all the proffered tier services—two movie channels, sports, dirty movies, and culture. But due to its small potential audience, culture is the most threatened option. It is the cable operator who makes the decisions about tiers of pay services, because a majority of them own systems with very few available channels. In this situation, the operator might sooner satisfy aficionados of the local ice hockey team and lovers of blue movies than the elite of culture buffs.

Cable operators create only one bottleneck in the market. Satellite distribution is crucial in building a universe, but not all satellites are equally efficient at this. Operators wanting the most profitable service but having only one small receiving dish, tend to point it in the direction of HBO, carried on Satcom 1. But satellites have limited capacity and there are fewer spaces (transponders) on Satcom 1 than there are services wanting them. Therefore spare transponders, even on the other two less favored domestic satellites, are worth somewhere around $5 million on the open market. For each of the new culture services, finding a transponder from which to reach a maximum number of cable systems is the single most important factor in getting started.

Bravo was sharing its transponder before Escapade gained its own. ABC Video, jointly with Warner Amex, puts out ARTS at night, on a transponder leased by the latter for its daytime children's service, Nickelodeon.

RCTV, still without a transponder for The Entertainment Channel, claims with admirable insouciance that its relationship with Satcom 1 owner RCA means less than nothing. RCA's allocation of transponders on the satellite in the past has not been without criticism. Now it must rent a transponder from itself or from one of its competitors.

CBS has been forced onto Western Union's Westar III, although the ground dishes of many cable operators are aimed elsewhere. CBS, therefore, goes into operation with a universe markedly smaller than ABC's; that's why it will offer some key cable operators a free dish—so they can receive Westar's signal.

Beyond the questions of audience, operators, and satellites lies the basic problem of production costs. With network prime-time television costing $500,000 or so an hour, and with a cable universe that is as yet very small, all these services must be produced inexpensively. Producting programs at about one fifth of prime-time cost by using the latest light-weight equipment and paying talent at scale, importing programming even more cheaply, and repeating material at an unheard-of rate, are among the techniques being deployed.

Still, the days of buying hours of La Scala opera for pennies will not last long. For one thing, the networks have already begun their competition. (ARTS's Granath scooped CBS by getting on the air first—a deal he initially arranged following an accidental meeting, crossing Sixth Avenue, with Warner Amex's Jack Schneider, an ex-CBS executive.) And for another thing, the Europeans are getting smarter.

Professional opinion in Britain, for instance, is that the BBC has perhaps not shown the greatest acumen at this stage in making an exclusive deal, especially one that ties it down while leaving RCTV free to trade with its British competitors. One leading British commercial-program exporter said, "I think the BBC is nuts, because this is a very flexible market. It is rather potty to be making such a deal, especially when you have no agreement with the artists." (British commercial television is in the middle of negotiations with the unions.)

Theodora Sklover, adviser to a number of American cultural institutions, warns them not to expect "big money up front" from the new culture services, but also advises, "at this stage, don't do exclusive deals."

Even at this experimental stage, the feeling that all is not as it seems—especially with the networks—is unavoidable. Culture programming might be part of the networks' larger strategy to stake out cable territory before it all gets claimed. Some of their major communications-industry competitors are currently having a field day. Warner Amex and Time Inc., for example, are "vertically integrated operations"—that is, they are both major operators *and* providers of programming. They are also among the six users about to control a majority of the available transponders. There are a number of such vertically integrated operations in the industry, but the latest authoritative judicial opinion is that "the extent of vertical integration in the market does not appear to constitute an insurmountable barrier to entry into the market."

But in the cable market, the major urban areas still to be wired require an infusion of capital that only those vertically integrated companies will be able to provide. As their dominance over cable programming threatens the networks ever more seriously, it is difficult to believe that ABC, CBS, and NBC will not put up a fight.

CBS, in a significant move, has petitioned the FCC for a waiver so that it might operate cable systems with a total of up to 90,000 subscribers (the FCC's limit) as a testing ground for programming and technical experiments. The cable industry is not at the moment opposing this. But the

Justice Department has made it clear that it regards CBS's entering cable ownership, on however limited a scale, as a threat that would "undercut the cross-ownership rule's goal of promoting economic competition and diversification of control of the channels of mass communication."

With such an uncertain future, and in an already difficult present, culture begins to look like nothing so much as a means of commandeering terrain. The cultural elite is given to sniggers whenever television tries to heighten its brow. And rather than winning that elite over, all the current cavortings are likely to turn the sniggers to guffaws.

There is good reason for the cynicism. These corporations are using the term "culture" as it refers to those court arts taken over in the early nineteenth century by the European haute bourgeoisie. Television as a popular form has never really developed meaningful versions of those arts. And no television service—not PBS here or the BBC in Britain or ZDF in Germany—has created satisfying television from their theatrical incarnations. More television imagination is displayed in covering baseball than is seen in *Live from Lincoln Center*.

It is difficult not to be skeptical about any of the networks' forays into culture. How seriously can ABC be taken as a purveyor of the arts when Granath contends that culture is like the Olympics because the folks doing it are "(a) foreign and (b) largely unknown"? This comment makes sense only in a corporate strategy, one more concerned with dominance and survival than it is with art.

RCTV's attempt at buying American middle-class loyalty to a British middle-class product makes some sense, especially if it can tailor-make some BBC-American co-productions. But Huberman's program choices seem to be avoiding the radical, difficult, and challenging stuff that gives British television its piquant taste. He is certainly avoiding a contentious kids' series because he says the accents are too difficult.

At CBS, Willis seems to understand full well the scope of the task of bringing these refined entertainments to the vulgar little screen. But so far, some of CBS Cable's announced programs look like reruns of the ideas that have already earned the CBS team its many broadcasting awards. The question remains: Will the elusive 16 percent buy this stuff on cable from producers they have already in large part rejected, as it were, over the air?

Huberman says upscale television service "is a baby—but it's going to grow up and go to college." One can only ask—what college? And what grades will it get? Two or three years down the road, all these companies might well have decided to give up and go back to attending the University of Life, just as they always have.

Mass Media and Culture: For Further Reading

Daniel J. Czitrom, *Media and the American Mind: From Morse to McLuhan.* Chapel Hill, N.C.: University of North Carolina Press, 1982.

Thomas M. Inge (ed.), *Concise Histories of American Popular Culture.* Westport, Conn.: Greenwood Press, 1982.

David Marc, *Demographic Vistas: Television in American Culture.* Philadelphia, Pa.: University of Pennsylvania Press, 1984.

John M. Phelen, *Media-World: Programming the Public.* New York: Seabury Press, 1977.

Jean-Francois Revel, *Without Marx or Jesus: The New American Revolution Has Begun.* Garden City, N.J.: Doubleday, 1970.

Bernard Rosenberg and David Manning White, *Mass Culture Revisited.* New York: Van Nostrand Reinhold, 1971.

Robert Sobel, *The Manipulators: America in the Media Age.* Garden City, N.Y.: Doubleday, 1976.

XVI

Mass Media, the New Technology, and the Future

Where will the mass media go from here? If the new technologies dictate the future, we will have more specialized media, more choices, and less mass communication in the years ahead.

The new technologies have made it possible to mass produce personalized messages and media. They have reduced the cost and complexities of mass communication, bringing about an exploding proliferation of publications and productions and broadcasts—at a price to both senders and receivers.

For the first decades of the television age, many of us worried about the leveling influence of the mass media: the blandness, the conformity, the uniformity; the control by big media corporations. The world of the specialized media of the future might pose more serious problems in the opposite direction. Instead of being acculturated into one nation, we may become polarized into thousands of separate enclaves—each using its own specialized media and developing its own specialized languages—accentuating our differences and flaunting our distinctions, until we confront a Tower of Babel.

The new mass media brought to use by the new technologies pose a new kind of danger. Now is the time to worry about the public policies we must develop to protect ourselves from the potential anarchy the new media could well bring.

61 Pass the Sugar and the Video Tube, Dear

by Jerome Aumente

Broadcasting is in search of an identity, says this newspaper journalist turned professor, and it needs trained journalists, "people who know how to write and how to put information together in an electronic format." The author directs the Journalism Resources Institute at Rutgers University. This article is from *The Quill*, February 1986.

At the *Los Angles Times*, management deliberately puts its electronic publishing operations in a high-visibility area of the busy newsroom. Unlike some electronic publishing operations, the Viewdata editors are not poor relations to the print journalists.

In fact, the Viewdata editors are seasoned print journalists. Working at their Coyote terminals, the same kind used by staffers on the nearby business and metro desks, they are indistinguishable from their newspaper colleagues. They attend the daily editorial meeting with section editors from the newspaper, and they receive the same front-page dummy to plan their budget of up to 175 stories a day.

What makes these editors different is that they call to their computer screens the full array of news and feature stories being readied for the next morning's paper and then edit the stories, along with summaries and headlines, for transmission to videotex systems in Southern California.

These systems, in turn, are able to electronically deliver large chunks of the paper's editorial content to homes and offices that subscribe to the news service—and to do it hours before the first edition of the newspaper is printed, let alone bundled and loaded onto delivery trucks.

The Times Mirror Corp., which owns the *Times* as well as broadcast stations and other publications nationwide, is intent on developing the newer media. It is very much in the information business with Gateway, its videotex service for California; Videotex America, its partnership in a transcontinental venture, and Grassroots, a videotex service for farm families and people in the business of agriculture.

But in blending the old and the new, it wants to acclimate its traditional print journalists to the newer technologies, and also see that its electronic journalists who have left the mother ship to explore new territories do not feel isolated from their colleagues.

Nevertheless, some professional and student journalists around the country are wondering if the new technologies constitute "journalism." They view the new technologies with skepticism—much the way print journalists warily observed the advent of radio and later television and debated how these media would affect the newspaper business.

Are videotex and teletext "legitimate" news media? Or are they little more than a curious stew of news, information, interactive banking, shopping services and games cooked up by a new breed of "information specialists"?

People who already have made the transition into the field insist that they are practicing the classical elements of journalism—the gathering, editing and timely dissemination of news and information, which require all of the editorial judgment, news sense, objectivity, balance and ethical standards associated with the more traditional print and broadcast media.

"I don't consider that I have left the newspaper business at all," says Larry Fuller, a former reporter, editor and publisher who now heads the Gannett New Media Services. "I am...working in the information business, and I am doing it a little bit differently, with a little different distribution. The communication lines are no more than our newspaper trucks; the personal computer no more than our printing press."

Yet, videotex and teletext operations are still evolving—videotex and teletext companies are still trying to figure out the right mix of text and graphics for their services; and they are still trying to find the markets they need to sustain the enterprises.

One thing about these media is certain: journalistic opportunities are widely varied in this developing industry. At the low end are some operations that take the Viewdata feed from newspapers or wire services and then do a cosmetic touchup for the screen.

Journalists in such operations advise their colleagues to avoid signing on with such companies. Instead, they say, journalists should seek out those electronic publishing ventures where true journalistic skills are more highly valued.

Similarly, those who want to be reporters doing long, analytical pieces should avoid working in *any* segment of the new media.

The electronic-publishing journalists who express the most satisfaction are the ones who have a clearly defined, central role in designing the editorial product, in making daily editorial judgments on news play, and who find a challenge in writing well-crafted, condensed material for the screen. They also relish the role of playing a part in the pioneering of new media.

But pathfinders also can end up with arrows in their backs. The technological battlefield is strewn with remarkable successes *and* smoking hulks of failed efforts. Journalists considering career changes should examine the nature of the organization, its financial staying power and its commitment to the editorial product over an extended period of time. Some electronic publishers are already engaged in cost cutting, throwing whole segments of their service overboard.

Top managers, such as Gannett's Fuller, Richard Levine, editorial director for Dow Jones News/Retrieval, and Larry Pryor, managing editor of Times Mirror's Gateway videotex service, advise college students to get solid newspaper experience. It will make them more attractive as job candidates, and it also will cushion their fall if a videotex or teletext venture fails.

"A lot of young people got burned," Pryor says, "because they went into it and suddenly the jobs evaporated."

It seems that advice would be well taken considering that Time Inc. abandoned its effort to get into teletext after investing $40 million in the project.

In addition, Keycom Publishing Co. of Chicago has dumped its videotex operation, as well as many editorial personnel, in favor of its teletext cable operation.

And Knight-Ridder also has made editorial cutbacks at its Viewtron videotex operation, based in Miami.

However, journalists in the field see the long-range prognosis for electronic publishing as good. They point to plans for nationwide systems such as Trintex, a joint venture of CBS, IBM, and Sears that will spend a reported $250 million on development.

Covidea, started last year, brings together Time Inc. (which wants a go at videotex instead of teletext), AT&T and two major banks with videotex experience, Chemical Bank and Bank of America.

And journalists point happily to Dow Jones News/Retrieval, which provides a solid news and information service without the gee-whiz bells and whistles featured by some less successful efforts.

Dow-Jones has found success with a combination of timely news, stored material from the *Wall Street Journal*, and a mountain of business/financial data made accessible through telephone lines and personal computers.

Richard Levine, editorial director of database publishing at the Dow-Jones operation, established the service after a career as a national correspondent for the *Journal*. He presides over two newsrooms near Princeton, New Jersey, with a staff of 40 editorial employees for News/Retrieval and another 17 for Dowphone, an interactive audiotext service.

Nationwide, more than 220,000 people subscribe to Dow Jones News/Retrieval, and the database publishing efforts are growing, with more than 215 employees in editorial, marketing, technical services and software operations.

Dow Jones has brought in veteran point journalists to operate its newer media ventures and to assemble the editorial product. It has integrated the operations into the journalistic mainstream of the company, something that Gannett's USA Today Update also is doing quite well.

At Gannett, an editorial staff of 36, headed by Nancy J. Woodhull, vice president for news, designed a videotex product aimed at corporate professionals in management, marketing, planning and communications. Subscribers use their phones and personal computers to tap into nationwide videotex systems such as CompuServe.

In this instance, Gannet acts as an information provider just as others like the Associated Press, *The New York Times*, Reuters, *Consumer Reports* or the *Los Angeles Times*—preparing Viewdata packages from their existing material for marketing by the videotex operators.

According to Fuller, the Gannett videotex editors cull through 200 sources each day, including the wires, *USA Today*, the Gannett News Service, newspapers in the chain and general interest and trade publications. They write a daily file—which is updated hourly—of national and international news with a business and financial focus.

They do capsule reports on selected topics and special reports on major events aimed at highly focused target audiences. This attempt to develop "niche" markets with highly specialized material reflects a trend that is increasingly evident in the field.

Half of the videotex staff members at Gannett come—on rotation— from newspapers in the company. Some bring skepticism, fearful that they will be assigned to do only news briefs, the bane of reporters in newsrooms across the country.

Fuller says that he has received letters from many who, after they return to their papers, find the videotex experience useful. They like the conciseness, he says, and they are less patient with loose writing and formula writing, and they have honed desk skills that they use on their newspapers.

"People find what we are doing is really an appreciation for writing and the word and language," Fuller said.

"When you condense a 30-paragraph story into one paragraph, you realize that every single word counts. You start to dissect people's stories and wire stories," Fuller said. "You start to find out very quickly there is a single nut of news around which is built a whole lot of background and quotes."

In the *Los Angeles Times* newsroom, a clear enthusiasm is evident among the electronic-publishing editors hired away from more traditional print careers by Jim White, head of the Times Mirror videotex operation.

The videotex editors select stories for their electronic publishing package, write tight summaries to precede the full text, write headlines and index the stories into computerized categories.

A news editor then goes over the stories before they are transmitted to Gateway, in Santa Ana, California, which might further edit and rewrite them before the stories are made available to subscribers.

When Pryor joined Gateway as managing editor in 1982, he found that news was considered just another customer service that could not be considered as important as videotex services such as banking or shopping.

However, early trials revealed that subscribers thought news services were important and made much use of them. Consequently, Pryor got an OK to increase the number of editors to seven, to start an intern program, and to hire people to gather "micro-news" at police stations and other neighborhood sources.

Now, Gateway is expanding into Los Angeles County, aggressively courting personal computer owners as new subscribers and fighting gamely to create a new market.

Pryor wants to see the news product further tightened to make it even more distinctly different from newspaper style, which is too wordy for videotex.

News managers at other videotex and teletext services share that feeling, noting, however, that a full text of a story should be available to readers who want to go from summaries to entire stories.

Pryor thinks that by providing capsulized stories specifically tailored for videotex, Gateway can attract subscribers from business, financial, and hotel concerns—the niche markets. Once these subscribers create a financial base for Gateway, he expects operating and equipment costs to drop enough to make the videotex service attractive to individuals.

American companies involved in videotex and teletext ventures look to Great Britain—the birthplace of teletext in the 1970s—for evidence that a market of individual consumers can be found. Approximately 2.5 million British households have television sets that can receive teletext. And 5.5 million other TV sets worldwide can receive the British standard.

Until a new generation of TV sets equipped to receive teletext makes its way to American shores, companies will concentrate on finding niche markets—and on attracting talented journalists to work in the new media.

"There is no way that someone can say this is not journalism," said Craig Udit acting manager of the CBS teletext operation in Los Angeles. "It requires someone with journalistic knowledge to write these stories, and it definitely meets the needs of people to acquire news quickly and easily."

Udit said that candidates for editorial positions at the company are carefully tested to see whether they can write quickly under stringent deadlines, spot errors, exhibit news judgment on a wide range of national and international topics, and condense material without damaging the editorial quality of a story.

Job candidates also must be familiar with computers and must have a self-discipline bordering on Zen self-mastery—a necessity for people writing for an audience that, they believe, will be there. . .someday.

"He's sitting down to type it for a technology that he *thinks* is really going to work," Udit said. "He brings in new ideas every day and puts them on the wall. He is trying to make it work."

At Udit's operation, staffers literally put new ideas on the wall. Udit's office wall is covered with notes tacked or pasted up by staffers who come up with new ideas for the database.

Udit is looking for staffers who can become part of a team. Design Director Gregory Thomas noted that editorial, graphics and production personnel have to work closely in the new media to produce a final product that is easy on the eye, interesting and informative. This interaction among staffers is much more evident than at most newspapers.

Peter Winter, president of Digital Applications International, thinks electronic publishing provides excellent job opportunities for journalists. Formerly a top editor at the BBC teletext service and executive editor of Keycom Publishing, Winter says the new media is facing a shortage of personnel capable of preparing databases, messaging and using interactive services. He estimates that about 5,000 people now work with databases in the videotex industry, and he says he is constantly asked for help in finding new qualified people.

"Journalists will find a pivotal role in delivering financial and business information," Winter said. "It requires skilled understanding of finance, of writing, of experience in design, layout and [database] navigation."

Richard Baker, director of communications at CompuServe, a national videotex service with 225,000 subscribers, says that electronic publishing ventures are "desperately looking for people who know how to write and how to to put information together in an electronic format."

He points out that his own company provides subscribers with access to more than 900 informational services, including the AP state wires. Baker encourages students at Ohio State University, where he is an adviser, to seriously think about pursuing a career in the new media.

In summary, electronic publishing offers a great deal of promise—as well as uncertainty. More and more colleges and universities are conducting research on the new media, and several—such as Rutgers University, the University of Florida, Michigan State University, and New York University—have courses designed to teach students about videotex and teletext.

The Association for Education in Journalism and Mass Communication teamed with the American Newspaper Publishers Association in 1984 to conduct a survey of 324 journalism programs, and the study revealed that 38 percent of those programs now include some material on electronic publishing in their curriculum.

"The field is too important to be ignored by any group concerned with the newspaper business," the report on the survey concluded.

College students interested in pursuing careers in the field would be well-advised to develop computer and database skills and to learn to write in the condensed formats required of videotex and teletext media. Students also should understand the importance of having a balance of graphics and text on the screen.

The new media also require job applicants to know the fundamentals of reporting and editing. In addition, they should keep abreast of regional, national and international events that may lead to stories they will have to work on.

"The ability to write and edit well, and use the mother language well—the same professional kind of skepticism and attention to detail, and care about 'getting it right'—all these apply to the new media," says Levine of Dow Jones/News Retrieval.

And they should understand the interaction of graphics and text on the screen, and how to move personal computer users through complicated pathways to get to news and information. The traditional approach to main news stories and sidebars can be infinitely expanded with the power of the computer as readers also access background files, diagrams, charts and even moving illustrations.

Aside from all the technology, the market strategies and the day-to-day developments in electronic publishing, the question of whether these new media offer job opportunities to people trained as journalists seems clear—they do.

62 Condominiums in the Global Village

by Richard A. Blake

Marshall McLuhan's vision of a world more closely united through communications technologies has been confounded by the new technologies that have made listening and viewing insulated experiences. As media audiences become more fragmented, writes Richard A. Blake, communicators spend more time talking to like-minded people. Blake is the managing editor of *America*. This article is reprinted from the June 5, 1982, issue of that publication.

Two full decades have passed since *The Gutenberg Galaxy* was published in 1962 and H. Marshall McLuhan became an academic cult figure whose writings many thought at the time would create the Copernican revolution of our age. As a professor of literature—and several other things as well—at the University of Toronto, he published a book on advertising techniques,

The Mechanical Bride, as early as 1951 and had edited with the anthropologist Edmund Carpenter a short-lived periodical entitled *Explorations*, some of whose essays appeared as an anthology, *Explorations in Communication*, in 1961.

There is no doubt, even now, that Marshall McLuhan was on to something important. As a man of many interests, he was able to send out "probes"—unmanned space probes were the miracles of technology at the time—in many directions at once. He was aware that the human environment, even our thought and sense patterns, had been undergoing enormous changes because of the development of communications technologies, and he had the temerity to ask what these shifts were. If, he reasoned, historians and anthropologists could chart the change when a society moves from an oral culture to one with a written language and then moves from a manuscript tradition to mechanized printing, then he believed they should be able to discover the changes taking place as contemporary society moves from a print-dominated society to the age of radio, television and film. In the 1960's this notion of a generation gap between old breed and new breed was a hot topic, and McLuhan believed it had something to do with the way we communicate to one another.

Despite the importance of his search, Marshall McLuhan was sadly an unwitting assassin of his own ideas. His prose poured out like water from a firehose with knots in it. He had an irrepressible lust for the catch-phrase, which he later mauled into puns that mocked the original concept. From the vantage point of the 1980's these phrases are quaint and oh-so 1960ish, hula hoops for the mind, Mickey Mouse ears for the intellect. For example, in *Understanding Media* (1964), the book that brought McLuhan celebrity and the rest of us headaches trying to understand what he meant by "hot" and "cool" media, he gave one chapter the catch title "The Medium Is the Message." By 1967, the phrase became the title of a book, *The Medium Is the Massage*, which dealt with the importance of tactility in communication—along with many other topics. By 1969, in *Counterblast*, it became an inset heading, "The Medium is The Mess Age," highlighting the proposition that one medium absorbs another, and both become changed or messed up." People who read, for instance, have speech patterns different from those who do not; people who watch television write differently from those who do not. Our own media-loaded culture is going through the media mixmaster: It is the mess age.

What is regrettable is that some of these ideas, torpedoed by the cleverness of their creator, deserve a better fate. Some of these key concepts should have remained alive so that they could be seriously tested and refined in the light of new data and new trends. After all, McLuhan was dealing with man in confrontation with his rapidly changing technological environment. Even the mustiest, library-bound scholar should be able to admit that technology continues to change and that its ongoing impact on the race should continue to be monitored. What would Marshall McLuhan be able to tell us, if he were still alive, of the meaning of the videogame, the desk-top home computer, the digital alarm wristwatch, or even that computer in Japan that last year stabbed a worker to death on the assembly line? When he was writing, space probes, those unmanned ventures into outer space, were exotic projects. He called his own essays "probes" because he fired them off into space with no idea what they would turn up. The data he uncovered always invited further exploration and refinement; they were rarely the final chapter.

One such probe, still intriguing but clearly in need of revision, is his concept of "the global village." Unlike some of his other aphorisms, like "The medium is the message," the global village keeps a certain ring of currency about it. It is will used by many organizations, especially religious ones, to describe a growing sense of awareness and responsibility for global problems, such as hunger, violence or the need for evangelization. It is a convenient term but a dangerous one, since injecting an old term into a contemporary situation can be misleading. On a practical level such a miscalculational can lead to a misreading of the signs of the times, to oversimplifications, to misdirected strategies and to a great deal of frustration.

The global village, an optimistic projection of the McLuhan era, probably never did exist in fact, and if it was the logical goal of a trend apparent at the time, that trend has long ago hit a detour. Technology, which McLuhan was ever sensitive to, has moved in like a greedy landlord and broken the global village into condominiums. Since the time of McLuhan's initial insight, the world has become less a tribal village and more an urban apartment building, where people in adjacent flats cannot recognize one another.

What kind of change took place? For Marshall McLuhan the notion of the modern postliterate world as a global village was a long time coming. It grew out of his major thesis that people raised in an age of print see reality as segmented and ordered, like letters of the alphabet on a line of type. Preliterate people, coming from an oral tradition, tend to apprehend the whole without awareness of individual components. Literate people rely on vision, and try to see connections between parts as though they were letters in a word; they feel secure in their understanding only when they can objectify something "out-there," even at times reducing reality to an outline or diagram, like a road map. Preliterate people make no sense out of maps and diagrams. They are involved with the topography and prefer to think of their environment in terms of hills, stars, ocean currents or dead trees.

Modern man, McLuhan observed, is in the process of returning to the sight and sound world of the preliterate. Even in academia, the clear, precise and diagrammatic answers of scholastic philosophy have become less interesting and less satisfying than the tentative answers based on the empirical data of the sociologist, novelist or psychologist. The age of the electronic media has retribalized us.

By 1967, in *The Medium Is the Massage*, McLuhan pointed out the effects of this new tribalization on a world scale. He announced: "We now live in a global village.... We have begun to structure this primordial feeling, these tribal emotions from which a few centuries of literacy have divorced us.... Electronic circuitry profoundly involves us with one another." He felt that it is no longer possible for pockets of humanity to remain isolated from one another; electronics was binding the race together. What seemed particularly attractive to religious people was the implication he drew from his observation: "Our new involvement compels commitment and participation." In another place in the same book, he returned to the theme: "Electric circuitry has overthrown the regime of 'time' and 'space' and pours upon us continuously the concerns of other men." Like it or not, electronics has made us, in the words of the Gospel, our "brother's keeper." The signs of the time, another catch phrase of the era, pointed to the social Gospel. Off to the inner city, the picket lines and the demonstrations!

Two of McLuhan's concepts must be distinguished. First, technology was providing more information about remote peoples and places, and, second, our postliterate sensibilities have conditioned us to respond differently. The first is self-evident. There is more news available, and it comes to us more quickly than ever before. As for the second, according to McLuhan, we are more involved with the hungry or the politically repressed because we cannot reduce them to discrete units of reality, separate from our own world, out there, objective and at a distance. When, for example—and this is not an example McLuhan gives, since he rarely gives examples—we see on television a black demonstrator at Selma attacked by guard dogs, we are personally involved and there is a visceral response because our own world is being subjected to the violence and oppression. Thus, the passionate radicalization of thousands of comfortable middle-class students during the civil rights movement was a result of both television information and television sensitivities.

For the religious person reading McLuhan, the one world of peace and harmony was becoming a reality through the miracles of modern technology, God's gift to His creature of intellect. The world of the future would be the ideal forum for extending the world of the Gospel.

Although Marshall McLuhan was a serious Catholic, he did not deal with these religious questions himself. He left such reflections to those who read his essays while they were reading the works of Pierre Teilhard de Chardin, S.J. Between Teilhard's "noösphere" and McLuhan's "global village" there are many congruent notions, but McLuhan chose not to explore in depth the theological implications of his ideas. It is doubtful that he ever thought that the global village, drawn into a tighter and tighter unity by the power of modern communications, would ever lead to the "recapitulation of all things in Christ."

As an interesting parenthesis, McLuhan did, however, include a brief chapter on liturgy in *The Gutenberg Galaxy*. This was 1962, when liturgical reformers were already stirring in their cocoons, but before Vatican II loosed a stampede of butterflies upon the church. Even then, McLuhan knew that the Tridentine Mass, with its emphasis on the literate person's reliance on the visual, on detachment, fragmentation and solitude would not serve the postliterate generation. After skipping through the works of Louis Bouyer, Thomas Merton and several other liturgical writers, he concludes: "The 'simultaneous field' of electronic information structures today reconstitutes the condition and need for dialogue and participation rather than specialism and private initiative in all levels of social experience." Thus this secular prophet warned us about the coming of the dialogue homily and the ever on-going effort to increase participation, even by down-grading the role of the remote, "visual" celebrant if necessary.

McLuhan's rather rosy picture of the dawning age of the global village should not be surprising. He was, as each of us is, a product of his times. (Even his relentless use of the word "men" and masculine pronouns dates his work as pre-women's movement.) His was an optimistic time for media analysis. As he looked to the future, communications satellites were just beginning to tie the world together with instantaneous relays. Television and telephone transmissions could reach any point on the globe. The paradigmatic event, of course, was the funeral of John F. Kennedy in 1963, when the world seemed bound together in mourning through television. By then virtually every household in the United States "had television," and instructional television had invaded many of the classrooms, promising an end to the drudgery of learning and perennial shortages of teachers. Families viewed television together. The set was called the "electronic hearth," and magazine writers praised the new "togetherness." The evening news was making civil rights an American issue, as a few years later it would make Vietnam the world's first television war. It was believed that the nightly newscast was turning the American people against not only that war but against all wars. It was a cheery time for media futurologists.

Things did not turn out as predicted, however. In a very few years the happy promise of the global village fell apart. Mass communication, as it penetrated the inner cities of the United States in the 1960's and the Third World in the next decade brought a sense not of participation but of exclusion. The image of the good life, available so readily to middle-class Americans on the gray-blue screen, was not accessible to everyone, and the result was outrage and violence. Murder on the streets became as insignificant as murder on the screen; heavy viewers became sociopaths. Instead of a new generation searching for "participation and dialogue" the 1970's brought the "me-decade," with the solitary jogger monitoring his heartbeat and fiber intake in private rather than sharing feelings in "small-group discussions."

Clearly, something went wrong with the prophecy, but what or how? Why are the media apparently desensitizing us to the needs of the rest of the world when we had expected them to heighten our sensitivities? If Marshall McLuhan were alive today, he would have to revise his projections on the basis of new data and new trends, and for him that always meant beginning with the technology of communication. In fact, he can be faulted for focusing too narrowly on this area to the exclusion of other social and historical factors. However, since the "global village" is his creation, it is only fair to retain his methodology.

In McLuhan's time, every development in communications technology pointed toward greater unification, but in the last 10 years every development has led to greater fragmentation of the world-audience. Equipment is an obvious example. First the transistor made radios cheap, portable and accessible to everyone in every environment. Stereo radios and cassette decks increased the volume, thereby ending conversation. Radio listening has become an essentially private experience. No longer do people gather around the radio, but each person creates a private acoustical shell. Finally, the new lightweight headphones isolate the individual from his surrounding environment completely. Watch a group of the new wired listeners standing elbow-to-elbow on the corner waiting for the light to change, each following the beat of his own drummer, with street noise and fellow listeners effectively filtered out.

The Ayatollah Ruhollah Khomeini understood this during the worst days of the Iranian revolution. He did not have to block out information from communication satellites, rather he supplied his followers with tape decks and cassettes of his speeches. He may have been the first prophet to realize that mass communication, even from a satellite, is becoming obsolete. The future belongs to the tiny tape deck, with its private, personal message enhancing the importance of the individual listener.

When McLuhan was formulating his theories, the networks were at their peaks. One might complain about the types of programs American audiences were watching, but there is little doubt that "I Love Lucy" or "Laugh In" did provide a source of common, shared and unifying experience. Everyone knew Fred and Ethel, Ricky and Lucy and what it meant when someone received a "fickle finger of fate" award at the office.

In the last few years, the trend toward unifying television experience has been reversed. On both networks and on local nonaffiliated stations, advertisers pinpoint their target audiences for age, sex, earning power and geography. This segmenting of the audiences has developed even more drastically with the arrival of the cable with its capacity for 40, 80 or even

120 different channels. As of March 1982, 23.7 million households in the United States, that is 29 percent of all television homes, now have cable, and the industry is adding a quarter of a million new subscribers each month. There are separate channels for sports, music, drama, movies, public affairs, and even pornography. Every language group in the community has its own programming.

The cable, however, is still a medium for more affluent neighborhoods, where enough subscribers can pay the fees immediately and thus make the installation of the system profitable in the near future. For the present, at any rate, the poorer and less educated will remain with the networks, a fact that can be expected to influence programming decisions. In other words, network television will become even more vapid, and the quality material that is available will be on the cable, where the viewers can afford to pay for it.

Developments in over-the-air broadcast technology are also in the process of fragmenting the audience. The Federal Communications Commission is currently sifting through 6,500 applications—the number is expected to reach 12,000—for new low-power stations that can be received on a non-cable set. These will have a very limited broadcast range, and thus will serve a specific local community. The industry now speaks casually of a "narrow-cast" concept rather than broadcast, to indicate its desire to pinpoint particular target audiences for its advertisers.

The cassette and videodisc business is booming, and as the prices tumble further, the growth rate will accelerate. Rental libraries of videotapes are springing up in shopping malls around the country. Combining videotape and cable technologies, ABC has even devised a system for transmitting films and other specials over the cable at night to a cassette recorder with an automatic timer. For a fee, the owner can play the tape back through a special decoder. For people using these services, viewing television has become as private and idiosyncratic a pastime as reading a book. In fact, by year's end Sony will begin marketing a pocket-sized television set no bigger than a paperback romance novel. Its two-inch screen is mounted on a case an inch and a half deep, and it will have the same lightweight headphones Sony made famous on its Walkman portable radio/tape deck components. The private acoustical shell will become visual as well.

A similar trend has been going on in radio. With the opening of the FM spectrum, radio, too, has been segmenting its audience. Of the 8,000 stations now operating in the United States, nearly half are associated with some kind of network, if only for news, but even the networks—and there are now 30 of them operating in the country—have become directed at specific target audiences. Some have nothing but talk, and the music networks are directed to a particular type of listener.

There is more news on television, but the happy-talk format that most of the stations have adopted means that there is less time for information on most broadcasts. With deregulation, limits for news broadcasting on radio have been dropped, so many people will no longer have even the five minutes of headlines and weather that used to break up music schedules.

As a result of these developments, it follows that there is more information around, but fewer informed people. As the media audiences become more fragmented, communicators spend more time talking to like-minded people, or at least those with similar interests. A church professional, for example, is likely to be inundated by information about the third world, while the congregation he or she deals with is likely to remain disinterested or apathetic simply because of a lack of effective information. The exchange of news release among interested parties has become not only overwhelming but incestuous.

The growth of neoconservative groups, even within religious congregations whose leaders are vocally liberal, is not a product of hardening of hearts or callousness or perversity but a lack of effective communication. Religious elites are talking to one another, and their congregations hear little of the conversation. If these elites issue a call for mobilization on behalf of a specific social program, they cannot presume that their congregations are informed or interested, even though the topic might be belabored to the point of cliché in the communications networks the church professionals are tuned into.

If the media are now leading us to greater fragmentation rather than unity, the liturgical renewal might have to stop to reassess its assumptions and goals. Many of the current reforms were put in during the 1960s with the presumption that worshiping congregations actually wanted, as McLuhan said, "participation and dialogue"—or at least would want it once they became accustomed to it. Perhaps now that the global village has been fragmented into condominiums of privacy, worshippers now want their own sense of the sacred. Congregational singing and the kiss of peace may be as alien to the sensitivities of the 1980s as benediction of the Blessed Sacrament was to the sensitivities of the 1960s.

The churches then might be faced with a problem in trying to transfer the wisdom of the 1960s into strategies of the 1980s. Should we then give up the goals of social involvement and worshiping community? Of course not. The Gospel has clearly mandated a mission "to all nations" and "to feed the hungry." We would, however, be wise to admit that the concept of the global village, which appeared so clear in the 1960s, never did materialize. Any strategies that take it for granted then run the risk of serious frustration. Steps to inform, to raise the consciousness or to build community cannot be omitted. If they are, the gap between church professionals and their congregations will widen, as the church people overload one another with information and the people they serve drift further away, into other concerns and other information networks.

Three centuries before Marshall McLuhan, John Donne wrote: "No man is an island." If he could see youngsters standing mesmerized in front of a videogame screen, he just might want to give that sentence a second thought. Despite the information explosion, people are becoming more and more "islands." The global village may soon become the global archipelago, with isolated tribesmen speaking in peculiar languages only to one another. If, on the other hand, people realize that they are living on a tiny island, they should have enough sense to build canoes to reach those other islands. Without that awareness, the world's loftiest projects, even evangelization itself, will remain a collection of photocopied notes, duplicated by the hundreds and written in a peculiar language understood only by the like-minded.

63 The Second American Revolution

by Benjamin Barber

The deregulation of broadcasting and the rise of cable television will change broadcasting from a national to a specialized medium, writes Benjamin Barber. Unless we plan policies to change the direction, he writes, "the electronic road to a national democratic neighborhood may be detoured down back alleys that terminate suddenly in the anarchic privatism of Babel, or in a world of Big Brothers ...." Barber is professor of political science at Rutgers University and author of novels as well as scholarly works. This article is reprinted from *Channels of Communications*, February/March 1982.

Democracy was conceived in an unwired world, one without telephones, computers, or television. When Alexis de Tocqueville visited America in the 1830s, he marveled at its "spirit of liberty," which, he concluded, arose directly out of vigorous civic activity, municipal self-government, and face-to-face interaction. Then, as now, democracy meant government by consent, and consent depended upon consensus and thus upon effective communication. In a society innocent of electronics, communications meant reading local newspapers, forming voluntary associations, developng public schools, and exploiting the American propensity for endless talk. Democracy survives, but de Tocqueville's simpler world of self-governing townships has vanished. The community of citizens governing themselves face to face has given way to the mass society, and live talk has been replaced by telecommunications. Once a nation of talkers, we have turned into a nation of watchers—once doers, we have become viewers—and the effect on our democracy has been profound. The average American watches television between six and seven hours a day; he votes just once a year, if that. Indeed, only one of every two Americans votes in Presidential elections.

Although every schoolchild knows that television is the national pastime and politics is only one feature of its coverage, not even university professors have thought very much about the medium's long-term impact on democracy. Yet we have already passed through one major age of telecommunications technology, and we now stand on the threshold of a second. This may be our last opportunity to turn the technology of the new age into a servant of an old political idea: democracy. Democracy will have a difficult time surviving under the best of circumstances; with television as its adversary, it seems almost sure to perish.

The first age of television—from its pre-war inception through the 1970s—was characterized by the scarcity of air-waves available for television transmission. This so-called spectrum scarcity gave us a system in which three mammoth national networks monopolized public communication, the government regulated in the name of the public interest, and viewers came to perceive themselves as passive spectators willing to leave programming decisions to network executives and their corporate sponsors.

The effects of this first age of television on America's political culture were mixed. But in one clear sense, network television's homogenized programming benefited democracy: By offering the country the semblance of a national culture and national political norms, it provided a consensus indispensable to national unity. Occasionally this was a direct result of network attitudes—as in the fifties with integration, the sixties with Vietnam, or the seventies with Watergate. But more often, the television consensus was informal and indirect. National debates such as the Kennedy-Nixon exchanges, national media personalities such as Ed Sullivan, Johnny Carson, and Walter Cronkite, and such national rituals as the Kennedy funeral, the moon walk, and the mourning for Martin Luther King—all these bestowed upon the country a legacy of national symbols and myths that cut across our divisive regions, sects, interest groups, parties, races, ethnic communities, and political constituencies.

In a nation as fragmented and pluralistic as ours, where from the very beginning—in the Federalist Papers—the "specter of faction" loomed as the greatest peril, television has offered perhaps the only truly common vision we can have. If there is an American melting pot, it is fired nowadays primarily by electronic means. How else than in front of the communal fires of television could Americans have mourned together their fallen leaders? If *Roots* had not been screened in prime time on eight consecutive evenings, would the meaning of being black in America ever have touched so many non-black Americans? *Roots* is a celebration not only of being black but of ·being American. Network television, both at its best and its worst—*Roots* and *Holocaust* as much as *General Hospital* and *Family Feud*—has helped us to subscribe to common values and to identify with a single national community. It is difficult to imagine the "Kennedy Generation," the "Sixties," Watergate, the Woodstock Generation, or even the Moral Majority, in the absence of national television. Who we are in common is what we see in common.

One aspect of this television consensus has been corrosive both to democracy and liberty, however. The dominion of a few media giants over scarce public airwaves has centralized control over information and entertainment. Democracy thrives on dissent, deviance, political heterogeneity, and individuality; network television catalyzes uniformity and homogeneity. Move a program too far off center as measured by the mass audience, and plummeting Nielsen ratings will chase sponsors away. Whether the media's middling vision is seen as the victory of bad taste (as the intellectuals claim), or of an Eastern liberal elite (as Spiro Agnew used to insist), or of crass secular materialism (as the Moral Majority asserts), or of the corporate establishment (as the Left believes), there can be little doubt that it is a safe and complacent vision that offers little hospitality to alternative perspectives. A common vision may also be a homogenized, plasticized, and intolerant vision, one that distorts America's defining pluralism by imposing uniform stereotypes on a heterogeneous people.

To the extent the networks succeed in making Americans think in common, they may destroy in us the capacity to think independently. The great American television consensus of the last thirty years dismissed the aspirations of both religion and socialism (thus the hostility fundamentalists and leftists show the media today). In place of genuine American archetypes, it gave us watery stereotypes: Archie Bunker, your friendly neighborhood racist, who wouldn't do any man real harm; Sanford and Son, who proved that black folks, aside from being a bit more hip, are just like every one else: Mary Tyler Moore, who could gently mock the patriarchal world without ever truly challenging it. There were tough-but-generous cops, misguided revolutionaries, reformed junkies, urbane preachers, and decent bigots— but no vicious detectives or legitimate terrorists or victorious punks or unbending Christians or despicable hypocrites. From the safety of the center, all differences were reduced to matters of style, while the difficult choices and grim polarities of real moral and political life were ignored. The first age of television gave us unity but exacted the price of uniformity.

Disturbing as these dilemmas are, they now belong to history. For we tand, prepared or not, on the threshold of a second television age. This ew age, with its own innovative technologies, promises to revolutionize ur habits as viewers, as consumers, and ultimately, as citizens.

Although cable television itself relies on a technology as old as comunication by wire, the convergence of a group of new technologies has nade possible an entirely new system of telecommunications, one that ffers us two-way and multiple-channel cable television, satellite distriution, video discs, video cameras and recorders, and access to remote omputers and data banks. These technologies will bring into our homes vastly expanded range of news and entertainment programming, diverse nformation services, consumer and financial transaction services, publicccess programming, security systems, and television referenda. Twentyight percent of American homes now receive some kind of cable service; hat number will double by the end of the decade. Already in some places eople are using interactive television to relax, look, talk, vote, play, shop, nform themselves, express opinions, secure their homes, and go to school. tate-of-the-art systems like Columbus, Ohio's QUBE will be installed in ll the major cities now being franchised. The prospect of a "wired society" s quite real.

What will be the likely effects of this new era of telecommunications on merican democracy? How will it compare to the first, now seemingly primive era? What sort of questions ought to be put to the new industry by he federal government, the municipal franchisers, and the public at large?

At present, the government seems disposed to put the new technoloies into the hands of an unencumbered private sector. The Federal Comunications Commission has consistently argued that cable's multiple hannels make spectrum scarcity—and the regulations that issue from it—bsolete. The Supreme Court in 1979 ruled that the FCC is not justified in equiring cable companies to provide public access. And Congress seems nclined to let "market forces" shape the development of modern telecomunications. Consequently, America is crossing the threshold of the new elevision age without reflection or planning; few seem aware, or conerned, that the new technologies may profoundly affect the nature of our ublic life and thus the character of our democracy. Yet present tendencies uggest the emergence of one of three distinct scenarios, each with fareaching political consequences. We might call these scenarios "The New ower of Babel," "The Corporate Big Brother," and "The Electronic Town Meeting."

The New Tower of Babel

'rom the perspective of the viewer, at least, the new technologies would ppear to decentralize television. In a cable system with fifty or a hundred hannels, the responsibility for selecting services and programming shifts from the supplier to to the consumer. The passive spectator of homogenized network fare is replaced by the active viewer, who creates his own information and entertainment programming by choosing among the hundreds of local and national program services, pre-recorded discs and tapes, and the various services two-way cable makes available.

But a political price is paid for this new activism among viewers and the apparent decentralization of television: Where television once united the nation, it will now fragment it. Those it once brought together it will now keep apart. In place of broadcasting comes the new ideal of "narrowcasting," in which each special audience is systematically typed, located, and supplied with its own special programming. Each group, each class, each race, and each religious sect can have its own programs, and even its own mini-network, specially tailored to its distinct characteristics, views, and needs. The critical communication *between* groups that is essential to the forging of a national culture and public vision will vanish; in its place will come a new form of communication *within* groups, where people need talk only to themselves and their clones.

This fragmentation is already well underway. Among the proliferating new program services available today are a Hispanic network, several Christian fundamentalist networks, a black network, and a number of highbrow culture networks. The U.S. Chamber of Commerce recently announced plans for the American Business Network, a private satellite television system. "BizNet" will enable the business community to organize and to communicate more effectively—with itself.

In the New Tower of Babel, all this programming diversity and special-interest narrowcasting replaces communication with group narcissism. The tube now becomes a mirror showing us only ourselves, relentlessly screening out any images that do not suit our own special prejudices and group norms. Fundamentalists no longer have to confront Carl Sagan in the course of a day's television viewing. No longer do special-interest groups have to filter their particular concerns through a national medium and adjust their message to a pluralistic nation. Faction—the scourge of democracy feared by its critics from James Madison to Walter Lippmann—is given the support of technology; compromise, mutualism, and empathy—indispensable to effective democratic consensus—are robbed of their national medium. Every parochial voice gets a hearing (though only before the already converted), and the public as a whole is left with no voice. No global village, but a Tower of Babel: a hundred chattering mouths bereft of any common language.

The Corporate Big Brother

The Tower of Babel may be a suitable metaphor for the heterogeneity and pluralism of the new media as they appear to the consumer; but the viewer's perspective is partial, and probably illusory. To examine modern telecommunications at the supplier end is to wonder whether Big Brother may prove to be the more apt metaphor for television's second age.

As abundant in number as these new channels and program services seem, they are rapidly falling under conglomerate control. The potential for leviathan profits from the new industries is drawing the attention of the communications giants. A few entrepreneurial upstarts—such as Ted Turner—may remain on the scene for a while, but they almost certainly will be absorbed or conquered. Diversity at one end of the cable may mask monopoly at the other.

If this picture of a few corporate elites playing the role of Big Brother under the camouflage of pluralistic special-interest programming seems exaggerated, it should be recalled that cable is a capital-intensive industry. The extraordinary costs of wiring America for cable or leasing transponder space on satellites suggest that only the most powerful corporations are in a position to sustain long-term interests in the cable industry.

Among these powerful corporations will be the networks, which are already actively moving into cable programming. ABC, in partnership with Westinghouse, will launch two cable news services to compete with Ted Turner's Cable News Network, a property in which CBS has expressed interest. Westinghouse's own position in cable is formidable: Not only does the company have several other program services on its drawing boards, but it will have enough transponders (fourteen) and cable subscribers (1.6 million, through its subsidiary, Teleprompter) to guarantee some success. And now that the government has lifted restrictions on AT&T, that company will also be in a commanding position. Even without its local subsidiaries, AT&T has research and development capabilities that could allow it to dominate videotex services.

Westinghouse, AT&T, Warner Communications, Time Inc., CBS, RCA, ABC: If all the new media are controlled by these few corporate interests, we cannot expect genuine political diversity or a truly free flow of information. Behind all those channels may eventually stand a single, prudent censor. Even if Big Brother is not watching us, we may find ourselves watching Big Brother.

And it does seem likely that if we are watching Big Brother, he will eventually begin to keep an eye on us. The very features of the new technology that make it versatile and exciting also make it frighteningly vulnerable to abuse. Warner Amex's QUBE system scans subscribers' homes every six seconds, recording what subscribers watch, their answers to poll questions, the temperature in their houses (for those who have signed up for energy management systems), and even (for subscribers who buy home security services) their comings and goings. Cable systems offering transaction services such as banking and shopping will accumulate detailed computer files on all subscribers. At present, there are no safeguards to

prevent the abuse of such records, other than the good will of cable operators. (Responding to these concerns, Warner Amex issued in December a
"Code of Privacy" under which the company promises to keep confidential
all information it gathers on individual subscribers. The legal force of such
promises remains to be tested.)

John Wicklein has elaborated on the dangers this new technology poses
to privacy and liberty in *Electronic Nightmare: The New Communications
and Freedom*. He argues that the new communications technology will give
a few powerful corporations dangerous instruments of social and political
control and, should democracy fail, of repression. Total television spells
total control, and total control in the wrong hands spells totalitarianism.
Indeed, can it be wise to place such information and power even in the
"right" hands? Either way, the specter of Big Brother skulks in the shadows, just beyond the glowing tube. The scenario of the corporate Big
Brother makes us pawns of a technology that controls us even as its versatil-
ity and diversity let us think we have mastered it.

Both this and the Tower of Babel scenario, for all their differences, are
equally inimical to democracy. Babel and Big Brother alike subvert citizenship by denying the significance of viewers as public persons with national
identities and public obligations.

The Tower of Babel subordinates commonality and public vision to
personal choice, private preference, and individual interests. It transforms
the most potent medium of public communication the world has known
into an instrument of exclusively private concerns. Ironically, it *privatizes*
us even as it imperils our privacy. It takes us seriously as consumers,
spectators, clients, and buyers and sellers, but it ignores us as citizens. It
services lust, religious zealotry, special interests, and individual needs
efficiently and pluralistically: It helps us relax or play games, exercise or
buy goods, pray or learn French; but it does not help us communicate or
seek social justice or formulate common decisions.

Corporate Big Brothers are no less privatistic in their methods: They
control by manipulating private wants and master by guiding private tastes.
Their world, like Babel, is inhabited by atomized and alienated individuals
seeking personal gratification in a society in which only individual wants
and corporate profits count.

The Electronic Town Meeting

Ten years ago, when he was an FCC commissioner, Nicholas Johnson said:
"As never before, Americans need to talk to each other. We hunger to be in
touch, to reaffirm our commitment to each other, to our humanity, to the
continuity of hope and meaning in our lives. . . . The ultimate promise of
cable is the rebuilding of a sense of community." The new television technology has at least the potential of becoming a remarkable new instrument

of public communication and collective deliberation. From the ancient world to the American founding, the great enemy of democracy has been scale: the repressive effect of mass society on the communication and participation necessary to self-government. Television in its second age *can* be to the problem of scale what drugs were to disease: a miracle remedy. People can be brought together across time and place and be permitted to confront one another in a continuing process of mutual exploration, deliberation, debate, and decision-making.

What I have in mind has nothing to do with the instant polls and uninformed votes that have characterized the QUBE system's dalliance with politics and that politicians rightly fear. Voting without prior debate, polling without full-scale presentation of positions and facts, expressions of preference without a sense of the public context of choice, all do more to undermine democracy than to reinforce it.

But the true promise of interactive-systems, public-access channels, and computer information-banks is that they can enhance knowledge as they enlarge participation. They can equalize by informing the poor as well as the rich and, by providing access to the powerless as well as the powerful, they can help to realize the ideal of an active and informed citizenry. But only if they are offered as a basic public utility at minimal cost to all Americans: otherwise, they will only increase the gap between rich and poor by dividing a single national constituency into two nations: one information-rich and able to participate and influence the national destiny more effectively than ever before, the other information-poor, relegated to still greater powerlessness.

Edwin Parker and Donald Dunn of Stanford University wrote in *Science* in 1972 that "the social goal of [cable television organized as a 'national information utility'] could be to provide all persons with equal opportunity of access to all available public information about society, government, opportunities, products, entertainment, knowledge and educational services." Today, equal opportunity may depend as much on equal information and equal access to communication as on economic equality; with cable television, this becomes a far more realistic aspiration.

In some places, the democratic capabilities of the new telecommunications technology have already been proven. In Reading, Pennsylvania, an experimental project sponsored by the National Science Foundation in 1976 (and developed by New York University) used the local cable system to establish an interactive communications network for the city's senior citizens. The elderly in Reading were able to create programming for themselves, and to hold their elected officials more accountable through a series of public meetings held on interactive cable television. Though this particular experiment has ended, cable's role in Reading's political system has not: Today all budget and community development hearings are conducted by two-way cable. Citizens can participate on-camera by visiting neighborhood centers equipped with television equipment; or they can ask questions from home by telephone. As a result, political participation increased dramatically. Reading's experience demonstrates the new technology's potential to create a more informed and active citizenry.

Perhaps the greatest promise lies with interactive systems like QUBE, which can link up thousands of citizens in an electronic town meeting where information and opinions can be exchanged, expert counsel called upon and formal votes taken. In Columbus, Warner Amex hasn't seen fit to exploit this capability except as a toy: In amateur talent shows, citizens there can use their two-way cable "vote" to yank acts they don't like. Still, the potential exists.

The promise of the second age of television for democracy remains largely unexplored. Among the thousands of cable companies now serving more than twenty million homes, only a handful offer local political-access channels or services, and none have made service to public citizenship their principal product. Cable television is servicing every conceivable constituency in America save one: America's citizenry, the sovereign governing body responsible for the survival of our democratic republic.

Yet if in this conservative era of deregulation it is too much to hope for a national telecommunications service devoted to democratic and public uses of the new technology, it is surely not too much to call for a public debate on the future of American telecommunications. A number of years ago, former CBS News president Fred Friendly suggested America needed an "electronic bill of rights" to protect it from its pervasive new technology. Even more than a bill of rights, today we need an "electronic constitution"—a positive plan for the public use of a precious national resource on behalf of our nation's faltering democracy. Without such a plan, the electronic road to a national democratic neighborhood may be detoured down back alleys that terminate suddenly in the anarchic privatism of Babel, or in a world of corporate Big Brothers willing to share with us the profits won from destroying once and for all democracy's proud, public "spirit of liberty."

Mass Media, the New Technology, and the Future: For Further Reading

Edward Cornish, *Communications Tomorrow: The Coming of the Information Society.* Bethesda, Md.: World Future Society, 1982.

Stuart M. DeLuca, *Television's Transformation: The Next 25 Years.* San Diego, Calif.: Barnes, 1980.

Howard F. Didsbury, Jr., *Communications and the Future: Prospects, Promises, and Problems.* Bethesda, Md.: World Future Society, 1982.

Wilson P. Dizard, Jr., *The Coming Information Age: An Overview of Technology, Economics, and Politics,* 2nd ed. White Plains, N.Y.: Longman, 1985.

Robert W. Haigh, George Gerbner and Richard B. Byrne, *Communications in the Twenty-First Century.* New York: Wiley, 1981.

Brenda Mattox, *Beyond Babel: New Directions in Communications.* Boston: Beacon Press, 1972.

Vincent Mosco, *Pushbutton Fantasies: Critical Perspectives on Videotext and Information Technology.* Norwood, N.J.: Ablex, 1982.

Anthony Smith, *Goodbye Gutenberg: The Newspaper Revolution in the 1980s.* New York: Oxford University Press, 1980.

Index

Abbott, Robert S., 342
Abrams, Floyd, 47, 53
Access to the media, 91–122
Adams, Edward T., 157
Adler, Richard P., 471
AIDS, 78–83, 87–88
Alexander, Shana, 125
Allen, Ira, 188–189
Alperovitz, Gar, 428–429
American Indians, 312–328, 355–356
Anderson, Jack, 81, 84, 88
Annenberg, Walter H., article by, 235–237
Arlen, Michael J., 469, 474
Ashkinaze, Carole, 363
Asians and the media, 354–355
Aumente, Jerome, article by, 486–492

Baer, Atra, 466
Bagdikian, Ben H., 110, 120, 222, 443
Bailey, Charles, 74, 77
Baker, Richard, 491
Bandura, Albert, 137
Banks, Louis, article by, 20–28
Barber, Benjamin, article by, 500–508
Bartos, Rena, 384
Bateson, Mary Catherine, 394
Bauer, Raymond, 43
Becker, Robert, article by, 102–109
Beckwith, Barbara, 374
Beckwith, Jon, 375

Behrman, Lori, 83
Bell, Griffin B., article by, 223–234
Bellah, Robert, 394
Bellows, James G., 126
Bemhart, Kent, 144
Bennett, Christopher J., 352-353
Benson, Steve, 64
Berger, Arthur Asa, 473
Berger, Joseph, 390
Berkowitz, Leonard, 138
Bernhard, Kent D., 80
Bertrand, Claude-Jean, article by, 66–72
Billings, William, 103–104, 105, 108
Blacks and the media, 15–16, 126–127, 328–350, 352–354, 457, 458
Blake, Richard A., article by 492–500
Blankenburg, William, 313
Bleich, Eli, 191
Blumenthal, Sidney, 193–195
Boccardi, Louis D., 392
Bogart, Leo, article by, 9–20
Bonk, Kathy, 94, 99–100, 101, 369
Boone, Raymond H., 343
Borg, Parker W., 153
Bradlee, Benjamin, 118–121, 147, 152, 362, 396
Branch, Bill, 75
Branigin, William, 260
Briggs, Kenneth, 401
Brinkley-Rogers, Paul, 326

Broder, David S., 150
Brokaw, Tom, 30, 257
Brown, Jane D., article by, 167–171
Brown, Les, 333–334
Brown, Tyrone, 99
Bryan, J. Steward, III, 54
Bryant, Jennings, 169–170
Bulkeley, Christy, 368
Burger, Warren E., 28, 87
Bursma, Bruce, 398
Burstein, Daniel, article by, 190–196
Business and the media, 9–28
Butcher, Mary Lou, 365–366, 369

Cantarow, Ellen, 265
Carpenter, Edmund, 493
Carter, Hodding, 112, 116–117, 118
Carter, John Mack, 382
Carter, Sylvia, 368
Catledge, Turner, 217
Chaing, Oscar, 354
Chancellor, John, 253, 254, 262–263, 267
Chandler, Russell, 390
Charren, Peggy, 95, 96, 100
Christian, Shirley, 366
Chumack, Sandy, 386
Claiborne, William, 253
Cleaver, James H., 126–127
Cody, Edward, 251
Cody, June, 254
Cohen, Bernard, 449
Compton, Ann, 182–183
Compton, James, 261
Cooke, Janet, 69, 71
Cooke, Joan, 370
Cornell, George, 392
Corry, John, 76
Cosford, Bill, 88
Costo, Repert, 320
Cotliar, George J., 150
Cox, Dick, 477
Cox, Harvey, 413–414
Cox, William, 81–82
Crime, violence, and the media, 42
Cronkite, Walter, 23, 24, 25, 29, 30, 31, 33, 51

Crouse, Timothy, 181
Culture and the media, 463–483
Culver, Virginia, 390
Cummings, Ken, 182
Cunningham, George, 103
Cutler, Lloyd N., 139

Daniels, Derick, 221–222
Davies, Michael J., 154
Deaver, Michael, 284–285
De Simone, Diane, 374
DeTocqueville, Alexis, 500–501
Dick, David B., article by, 155–159
D'Oench, Russell G., Jr., 77
Dominick, Joseph, 138
Donohue, Thomas J., 111, 428
Dowie, Mark, 23, 441
Downie, Leonard, Jr., 84–85
    article by, 267–270
Dreier, Peter, article by, 425–443
Duchineaux, Franklin, 317–318
Dunn, Donald, 507
Dwyer, R. Budd, 155–159

Egyir, William, 345–346
Elfin, Mel, 214
Engsberg, Janice, 94
Epstein, Edwin, 82
Erlick, June Carolyn, article by, 300–309
Ethics, including codes, 47–56, 59–89
Ewing, James E., 120

Fairlie, Henry, 205
Falsgraf, William W., 153
Faw, Peter, 255
Fein, Bruce E., 153
Finnegan, John R., 85
Flint, Julie, 261
Friedheim, Jerry W., 148
Friedman, Thomas, 253, 259, 261–262, 264
Friendly, Fred W., 154, 508
Friendly, Jonathan, 111
Fuller, Larry, 487
Fuller, S. B., 341

Galbraith, John Kenneth, 222–223
Galloway, Carl, 65
Gallup, George, 400
Gans, Herbert, 441–442, 455
Garcia, Joseph, 351
Garland, Hazel, 339
Garland, Phyl, article by, 337–349
Garth, David, 193–195, 251
Gartner, Michael, 39, 144, 148, 153
Garvin, Glenn, 309
Gasper, JoAnn, 104
Gelb, Leslie H., 76
Geller, Henry, 96, 98
Genovese, Margaret, articles by, 78–83, 143–154
Gergen, David, 282
Giago, Tim A., Jr., 355
Gibbons, Sheila J., article by, 379–383
Giles, Robert H., 145
Giles, William, 126, 130
Glasser, Theodore, article by, 44–51
Golden, Ellen, 386
Goldin, Marion, 86, 88
Gollin, Albert E., article by, 41–44
Goodman, Ellen, article by, 276–277
Gordon, Michael, 286
Gorre, Gil Roy, 354
Graham, Katherine, 144–145
Granath, Herb, 475, 481, 482
Greeley, Andrew, 398
Greenberg, Bradley, 138
Gregory, Bettina, 77
Gunther, Marc, article by, 73–78
Gutierrez, Felix, 350
Gutman, Roy, 304

Haight, Timothy, 95
Hamburg, David, 143
Hargrove, Mary, 84, 87
Harper, Chris, 292
Harwood, Richard, 80
Hasty, Stan, 105
Hayden, Margaret, 367
Henry, Ragan, 346
Hersh, Seymour M., 233–234
Hess, Stephen 49–50

Hinckley, John W., Jr., 132–133, 134, 141–143
Hines, William, 336
Hinterberger, John, 74
Hispanics and the media, 351–352
Hobson, Laura Z., 471–473
Hogan, Paul, 85
Hoge, Jim, article by, 422–425
Hosokawa, William K., 354
Howard, Jan, 300–301
Huberman, Arnold, 477–478, 482
Humphries, Drew, 128–129
Hunt, Albert, 86–87

Irvine, Reed, 96, 114
Isaacs, Norman E., 110–111, 112, 115, 119–120, 121
Israel, Robert, article by, 416–419
Izard, Ralph, 73

Jackson, Brooks, 86
Jackson, Karl D., 353
Jaffe, Sandy, 96
Janensch, Paul C., 148
Janeway, Elizabeth, 371
Jefferson, Thomas, 63
Jenkins, Brian M., 151
Jenner, Albert E., 139
Jennings, Peter, 31, 32, 33, 254–255, 256, 297
Johnson, Nicholas, 100–101
Jurney, Dorothy, 362

Kamm, Henry, 260
Kammer, Jerry, article by, 324–328
Kantrowitz, Judy, article by, 102–109
Karasek, Robert, 377
Karl, Peter, 85, 87
Kaus, Mickey, 192–193
Kays, Doreen, article by, 288–296
Keith, Harold L., 340
Kennedy, J. Michael, 264–265
Kent, Art, 253–254
Keshena, Rita, 320
Kesler, Lori, article by, 383–387
Ketter, William B., 150–151
King, James B., 75

Kinzer, Stephen, 302–304, 307
Cladstrup, Don, 253, 258, 285
Cleiman, Carol, 361
Knoll, Erwin, 54–55
Kochevar, John, 128–129
Kopriva, Don, 148
Kraft, Joseph, 448
Kruckewitt, Joan, 301
Kupperman, Robert, 145–146
Kurtz, Howard, 86

LaBrie, Henry, G., III, 352
Ladd, Everett Carll, Jr., 24, 451
Lai, Charles, 354
Lally, Francis J., 391
Lane, Roger, 130
Lang, Dale, 382
Langer, Judith, 384–387
Langer, Ralph, 151
Lasch, Christopher, article by, 470–474
Lasswell, Harold D., 155
Lear, Norman, 471–474
Lee, William H., 348–349, 353
Levin, Linda Lotridge, article by, 171–175
Levings, Darryl W., 92
Levy, Claudia, 362
Levy, Mark, 31, 32–34
Lewis, Anthony, 251
Lewis, Claude, 347, 353
Lewis, Flora, 22, 284–285
Lewis, Ira F., 341
Lichter, S. Robert, 426–427, 430–433, 434, 442–443
  article by, 448–461
Liebling, A. J., 241
Lindley, William R., 120–121
Lippman, Walter, 216
Lipset, Seymour Martin, 24, 473
Loyd, Frank, 98, 100
Loyd, Kate Rand, 381–382, 383
Lustgarten, Marc, 478
Lyons, Louis, 47

McAteer, Ed, 105
McClurkin, Bill, 411–412
McCrohon, Maxwell, 149

McCune, Wesley, 103, 104
McCutchen, Glenn, 82
McDowell, Charles, article by, 196–209
McGinnis, Joe, 182, 191
McGrory, Mary, 205
McGuire, Tim J., 85, 149
Machalaba, Daniel, 114, 115, 118
MacKerron, Conrad, article by, 102–109
McLuhan, H. Marshall, 492–500
McNamara, Bob, 260
Mallory, Steve, 256
Marro, Anthony, 81
Marshall, Pluria, 99
Martin, William C., 303
Marty, Martin E., 410
Matthews, Christopher, 205
Maynard, Robert, 127, 342
Means, Russell, 317
Mears, Walter R., 75, 149–150
Meese, Edwin, III, 152
Meriwether, Heath, 85
Micciche, S. J., 76
Miller, Jean Baker, 374-375
Millones, Peter, 128
Minorities and the media, 15–16, 126–127, 457, 459
Minow, Newton, 465–466
Moes, Garry, 75–76
Mollenhoff, Clark R., article by, 61–65
Monaghan, Nancy C., 145
Mong, Bob, 79–80
Montoya, Mauro A., Jr., 83
Moore, Louis, 390, 403
Moral Majority, 103, 104, 105, 106, 107–108
Morris, Roger, article by, 250–267
Moss, Robert, 285
Moyers, Bill, 254
MTV, 163–171
Mudd, Roger, 256
Mullin, Sue, 309
Mulvoy, Thomas F., Jr., 149
Murphy, James E., article by, 312–323
Murphy, John H., III, 356
Murphy, Reg, 134
Murphy, Sharon M., article by, 312–323
Murrow, Edward R., 321

National Advisory Commission on the
Causes and Prevention of Violence
(Kerner Commission), 15, 137, 321,
329, 335
National News Council, 26, 67, 112–113,
147
Nessen, Ron, article by, 241–243
Neuharth, Allen H., 368, 428
New Right. *See* Moral Majority
Nixon, Richard, 434
Nofziger, Lyn, 184, 189
Nolan, Martin, 250–251
Novak, Michael, 398–399
Nusser, Nancy, 301

Oberdorfer, Don, 284
O'Brien, Frank, 76
O'Donovan, Patrick, 215
Ostrow, Ronald J., article by, 223–234
Otsby, Sandy, 107
Ottaway, David B., 257, 259
Otto, Jean H., 111

Panitt, Merrill, 467
Parker, Edwin, 507
Parker, Everett, 95–96, 98, 414
Pastore, John O., 139–140
Patterson, Eugene C., 77
Patterson, Pat, 347–348
Paul, Dan, 52
Pederson, Tony, 145
Pendergast, Thomas F., 367
Peretz, Martin, 251
Perlman, David, 23, 25–26
Phillips, Howard, 107
Picard, Robert G., 151
article by, 52–56
Pierce, Laurens, 157
Poderetz, Norman, 251, 263–264
Powell, Lewis, Jr., 28
Powers, Ron, 156
Presidential campaigns, consultants,
179–209
Procope, John L., 353
Prout, Linda, 344
Pryor, Larry, 488, 490
Pugh, Jeanne, 391

Ramati, Pnina, 251
Ramirez, Carlos, 352
Randal, Jonathan, 254
Randolph, Eleanor, 182
Ransom, Lou, 337–338
Rather, Dan, 32, 33, 65, 132, 256
Ravo, Nick, article by, 102–109
Reedy, George E., article by, 237–241
Reeves, Richard, 114
Rehm, Barbara, 283
Reubens, Don, 55–56
Reupke, Michael, 152
Reynolds, Frank, 252
Rintels, David, 137
Rivers, Caryl, article by, 371–379
Rivers, William L., article by, 213–223
Roberts, Fletcher, 343–344
Robertson, Richard, 326
Rokeach, Milton, 471
Rollins, Edward J., Jr., 200
Rosenthan, Robert, 265
Rosten, Leo, 49, 220
Rothman, Stanley, 426–427, 430–433,
434, 442–443
article by, 448–461
Rovere, Richard, 214–215
Rowe, Ed, 108
Rubin, David M., article by, 281–287
Rubinstein, Amnon, article by, 247–249
Rubinstein, Eli A., 140–141
Russell, Cristine, 23
Ruth, Marcia, article by, 349–356

Salant, Richard S., 113, 137, 369–370
Sanders, Marlene, 363
Sanford, Bruce, 52
Sanford, Janet, 87–88
Sawyer, David, 193–194
Scharfenberg, Kirk, 79
Schickel, Richard, 468
Schmertz, Herbert, 26, 114
Schmidt, Richard, 55
Schmitt, Harrison, article by, 39–41
Schneider, Karen, article by, 73–78
Schorr, Daniel, article by, 132–143
Schultz–Brooks, Terri, article by,
361–371

Schuyler, George S., 341
Schwartz, H. L., 125–126, 131
Schwartz, Tony, 200
Schwartzman, Andrew, 97
Schwarzlose, Richard A., 115, 121
Seamans, Bill, 252
Seib, Charles B., 111, 114, 115
Sengstacke, John H., 338, 350
Seplow, Stephen, 84
Sevareid, Eric, 448
Sex and the media, 161–176
Shales, Tom, article by, 297–300
Sharon, Ariel, 64–65
Shaw, David, 112, 118, 119
    article by, 390–399
Sheldon, Phil, 105
Sherard, Regina G., article by, 328–337
Shindler, Alexander, 398
Shipler, David K., 253
Shulman, Heidi, 180–181
Simon, Samuel, 97
Simpson, Peggy, 366
Singer, Dorothy, 138
Singer, Jerome L., 129, 138
Sklover, Theodora, 481
Smith, H. Alexander, 216
Smith, Hedrick, 265, 284
Smith, Jo Durden, 374
Smith, Joe, 82
Smith, Susie, article by, 102–109
Smith, Ward, article by, 444–447
Sopher, Sharon, 369
Spence, Roy, 194–195
Squires, James D., 73, 77, 151–152, 361,
    370
Strob, Irwin, 381
Stawson, John, 473
Steinfels, Margaret O'Brien, article by,
    406–416
Steinfels, Peter, 394
    article by, 406–416
Stephens, Mitchell, article by, 125–131
Stepp, Carl Sessions, article by, 83–88
Stewart, Bill, 157
Stewart, Potter, 146, 217
Stoney, George, 101
Strother, Raymond, 191–192, 195

Sung-il, Choi, 355
Surgeon General's Committee on
    Television and Social Violence,
    139–141
Swan, Neil D., article by, 109–121
Swerdlow, Joel, article by, 179–190

Tapahe, Loren, 355
Tapley, Melvin, 345
Tarleton, Larry W., 80
Technology and the media, 9–20, 22–23,
    39–41, 43–44
Tennenbaum, Marc, 395
Thimmesch, Nick, article by, 273–275
Thomas, Cal, article by, 399–405
Thomas, E. Llewellyn, 138
Thomas, Gregory, 491
Thomas, Helen, 370
Thomas, William F., 73, 125, 126, 127
Thompson, William R., 391
Toedtman, James, 126
Topping, Seymour, 145
Toth, Robert, 287
Tuchman, Gaye, 47

Udit, Craig, 490–491
Ullman, John 88
U.S. News & World Report, article by,
    163–167

Van Atta, Burr, 83
Van Atta, Dale, 81, 88
Van Deerlin, Lionel, 93–94, 101–102
Vann, Robert L., 341
Venardos, Lane, 31, 32, 33
Vidmar, Neil, 471
Viguerie, Richard, 104, 106, 107
Visotsky, Harold, 135
Von Hoffman, Nicholas, 247

Walker, Bill, 325
Wall, James, 392
Walsh, Richard, 411
Walters, R. S., 138
Watson, Elmo Scott, 312–313
Watson, George, 76, 117
Wattenberg, Ben J., article by, 271–273

Weiner, Emily, 364
Weinraub, Bernard, 257
Weisman, John, article by, 28–34
Weitzel, Pete, 74
Wesley, Richard, 119–120
Westin, Av, 220, 290–291
Westmoreland, William, 64, 117
Weyrich, Paul, 104, 106, 107, 109
Whelton, Clark, article by, 465–470
Whisler, Kirk, 351
White, Byron, 28
White, Theodore H., 372
Wicker, Tom, 49, 435
Wicklein, John, 506
Wilkins, Roger, 128–129
Wilkinson, Tracy, 306, 309

Will, George, 298
Williamson, Ted, 324
Willis, Jack, 477, 482
Wills, Garry, 399
Wilson, E. O., 373
Winship, Thomas, 144
Winston, Brian, article by, 475–482
Wintour, Charles, 270
Witty, Susan, article by, 93–102
Women and the media, 18, 457, 459
Wood, Roger, 129
Woodward, Robert, 22, 39, 128, 130, 13
Wright, Claudia, 265

Zillman, Dolf, 169–170
Zollinger, John, 53